GENERALS IN BLUE AND GRAY

VOLUME TWO

DAVIS'S GENERALS

WILMER L. JONES

STACKPOLE
BOOKS

Published in paperback in 2006 by
STACKPOLE BOOKS
5067 Ritter Road
Mechanicsburg, PA 17055
www.stackpolebooks.com

GENERALS IN BLUE AND GRAY: DAVIS'S GENERALS, VOL. 2, by Wilmer L.
Jones, was originally published in hard cover by Praeger, an imprint of Greenwood
Publishing Group, Inc., Westport, CT. Copyright © 2004 by Wilmer L. Jones.
Paperback edition by arrangement with Greenwood Publishing Group, Inc. All
rights reserved.

Printed in the United States of America

10 9 8 7 6 5 4 3 2 1

FIRST EDITION

ISBN 0-8117-3288-6 (Stackpole paperback)
ISBN 978-0-8117-3288-8 (Stackpole paperback)

The Library of Congress has cataloged the hardcover edition as follows:

Jones, Wilmer L., 1931–
    Generals in Blue and Gray / Wilmer L. Jones
        p. cm.
    Includes bibliographical references and index.
    Contents: v. 1. Lincoln's generals—v. 2. Davis's generals.
    ISBN 0-275-98322-6 (set: alk. paper)—ISBN 0-275-98323-4 (v. 1)—
ISBN 0-275-98324-2 (v. 2)
        1. Generals—United States—Biography. 2. Generals—Confederate States of
America—Biography. 3. United States. Army—Biography. 4. Confederate States
of America. Army—Biography. 5. United States—History—Civil War,
1861–1865—Campaigns. 6. Lincoln, Abraham, 1809–1865—Military leadership.
7. Davis, Jefferson, 1808–1889—Military leadership. 8. Strategy—Case studies. 9.
Command of troops—Case studies. I. Title
E467.J795 2004
973.7'3'092—dc22   2004052153

To My Loving Family

Carol, Scott, Jolanta, Christa,
J.P., Ashleigh, Thomas, and Jordan

"You will see many errors to forgive, many deficiencies to tolerate, but you shall not find in me either a want of zeal or fidelity to the cause."

DAVIS at the time of being sworn in as president of the Confederate states

"When he fell, I realized that our strongest pillar had been broken."

DAVIS when he learned of Albert S. Johnston's death at Shiloh

"I fear it will be disastrous to our people, and I regret it deeply."

DAVIS when he learned of Lincoln's death

"It is well that war is so terrible. We should grow too fond of it."

LEE to Longstreet during the Battle of Fredericksburg

"He has lost his left arm, but I have lost my right arm."

LEE when he learned of Jackson's wound

"All this has been my fault—it is I who have lost this fight."

LEE to Pickett after his fatal charge

"He is at rest now, and we who are left are the ones to suffer."

LEE when he learned of A. P. Hill's death

Contents

Introduction

The famous Civil War historian, James M. McPherson, stated: "America prepares for war after the war has begun." Such was the case during the American Civil War. This preparation proved to be a monumental task for the two men destined to lead their countries during the war. One, Abraham Lincoln, had no prior military service and had been elected without a majority of the popular vote. He, at least, had a government structure and remnants of an army in place. The other, Jefferson Davis, a key character in this book, was a graduate of West Point and had served during the Mexican War and as secretary of war under the Pierce administration. Davis had to start from scratch to build both a governmental structure and an army.

Volume II: Davis's Generals is not a military history of the Civil War or a detailed description of the battles themselves. It is about Jefferson Davis's actions as commander-in-chief and the key Confederate generals who served under him. To this end, the book contains twenty-one biographies of the Confederate generals responsible for carrying out Davis's strategies. Obviously, the better-known generals such as Robert E. Lee, Thomas J. Jackson, James Longstreet, and Joseph E. Johnston appear in the book, but other, less well-known figures such as John C. Breckinridge, Richard Taylor, Daniel H. Hill, and John B. Gordon are included as well.

The format for *Volume II: Davis's Generals* is unique. This work is not a history book in the traditional sense; rather, it tells the story of the Civil War through the actions of the major participants. Though I have not neglected important events that occurred during the war, battles are discussed only to the extent necessary to understand the main course of events. In telling the story, each actor comes to life in incisive sketches. The main emphasis in each portrait is on the general's character, ability to command, personality, and family background, and on how these factors influenced his actions. The role politics, friendships, and competence played in the general's performance is also examined. Since the generals studied in this book served in various theaters of the war, insight can be gained on the entire war.

Each of the biographies stands on its own and can be read individually and in any order. They provide an excellent introduction to the lives of these important men. The extensive bibliography in the back of the book contains additional reading resources for those interested.

The Civil War was a long and deadly war. It lasted four years and resulted in over a million casualties. It was fought primarily to reunite the Union, secondarily to free the slaves. Repercussions from the war are still being felt today. Many heroic persons participated in this war; this book hopes to introduce a few of them to the reader.

Volume II: Davis's Generals is the result of my forty-five years of interest in the Civil War. It was written with the general reader and Civil War buff in mind and should appeal to a broad and general readership.

I would like to thank my two good friends, Shirley and Don Johnson, who read my manuscript and offered both encouragement and valuable suggestions and comments.

I hope you enjoy reading this book as much as I enjoyed writing it.

1   *The Making of a Rebel*

Shortly after noon on January 21, 1861, Jefferson Davis rose from his seat to make his final speech as a U.S. senator. Just a month earlier, South Carolina had left the Union followed by Mississippi, Florida, Alabama, and Georgia. Louisiana and Texas were expected to be the next to go. A convention was scheduled for February at Montgomery, Alabama, for the purpose of forming a Confederacy of seceded states. During the twelve days since Mississippi's secession, Davis had remained in Washington, distressed by the current events. Now he rose to say good-bye; his voice was low, more in sadness than in defiance.[1]

To those seated in the Senate chamber, Davis appeared proud and strong; but those close to him could see his pallid complexion. He had been sick the past month, and his face showed it; he looked like a man who had just recovered from a bout with fever. His personal physician insisted that he was still too weak to go back to work, but this occasion was important. Duty required him to speak.[2]

"I rise, Mr. President," Davis began, "for the purpose of announcing to the Senate that I have satisfactory evidence that the State of Mississippi, by solemn ordinance of her people, in convention assembled, has declared her separation from the United States." Davis continued, saying that he believed in the right of a state to leave the Union and that Mississippi was justified in doing so.[3]

"We have tread in the paths of our fathers," Davis continued, "when we proclaim our independence and take the hazard . . . not in hostility to others, not to injure any section of the country, not even for our own pecuniary benefit, but from the high and solemn motive of defending and protecting the rights we inherited, and which is our duty to transmit unshorn to our children."[4]

After a long silence, Davis concluded his remarks: "I see now around me some with whom I served long. There have been points of collision; but whatever of offense there has been to me, I leave here. I carry with me no hostile remembrance of any injury received, and having discharged the duty of making the only reparation in my power for any injury received. Mr. President and Senators, having made the announcement which the occasion seemed to me to require, it remains only for me to bid you a final adieu."[5] The genuineness of his sorrow and his appeal for peace held the chamber spellbound. There were wet eyes among those on the Senate floor, as well as in the galleries. For a moment there was silence; then came the ovation. For the first time, many of those present understood the catastrophe that faced the country.[6]

The man who left the Senate after years of service to his country was Jefferson Davis. He was born on June 3, 1808, in a small log cabin in Kentucky, although his family moved to Mississippi when he was still a child. Davis was named after Thomas Jefferson, the author of the Declaration of Independence. Jefferson's mother, Jane Davis, was forty-six when he was born and had already given birth to nine children. Jefferson's father, Samuel, had served in the Revolutionary War and had been given government land to start a farm. Fifteen years before Jefferson was born, Samuel moved his family, livestock, and a few slaves up through Tennessee and into Kentucky, where he worked side by side with his slaves, dawn to dusk, in his tobacco fields. After one more move to Louisiana, Samuel finally settled in Mississippi. As Davis put it, he wanted "higher and healthier" land where he could grow cotton. He found it in the southwest corner of the Mississippi Territory. Here, Samuel grew cotton and built a large house with a veranda, which Jane named "Rosemont."[7]

Young Jef began his education when he was six years old; it was varied, yet adequate. After two years at a Catholic boarding school, he returned to his father's farm and attended a succession of local schools. Davis did not like school, and on one fall day, he rebelled, refusing to go. His father was determined to teach him a lesson. Jefferson would not sit idly by; he would work in the field with the work gang, his father ordered. Two days later, Jef was back at school. "The heat of the sun and the physical labor, in conjunction with the implied equality with the other cotton pickers convinced me that school was the lesser evil," he later reported.[8]

In the spring of 1823, Davis entered Transylvania University in Kentucky, then considered the best school west of the Appalachians. It was there that Davis learned the art of public speaking, and at the spring graduation, he was selected to speak. He titled his address "Friendship." The local newspaper reported that "Davis on Friendship made friends of his hearers."[9]

Jefferson's older brother, Joseph, had a profound influence on him. Twenty-three years his senior, Joseph was a prosperous lawyer and planter who helped write Mississippi's state constitution. It was with his help that

Jefferson was able to receive an appointment to the U.S. Military Academy. The appointment was secured without first consulting Jefferson, but when presented with the opportunity, he accepted it, apparently because his father and brother seemed to want it. At the time, Jefferson was not interested in a military career but had expected to become a lawyer like his successful brother.[10]

In 1824, at the age of sixteen, Davis entered West Point. He was an undistinguished student and received numerous demerits for a variety of petty offenses. During his freshman year, he was arrested, tried, and nearly expelled for visiting Benny Haven's, a tavern off-limits to the young cadets. Brought before a court-martial board for out-of-bounds drinking of "spirituous liquors," he defended himself on the grounds that visiting Benny Haven's was not officially prohibited in the regulations and malt liquors were not "spirituous." Davis was successful with his defense and was not expelled. The following year, he was arrested and confined to quarters for six weeks after attending an illegal Christmas party.[11]

Although Davis never achieved academic or military distinction while at West Point, he was very popular with the other cadets and made friends. Among them were Albert Sidney Johnston and his roommate, Leonidas Polk, both of whom he admired. He also knew Robert E. Lee and Joseph E. Johnston, though he was not close to either. Davis and Joseph Johnston were both smitten with the local tavern keeper's pretty daughter; they tried to settle their differences by use of their fists. Johnston was the heavier of the two and won the fight. As a result of the encounter, from that day onward the two men were at odds with each other. Davis never forgot his old West Point friends and, even in the later years of his life, continued to correspond with some of them.[12]

In 1828, Davis graduated twenty-third out of a class of thirty-two, a decidedly mediocre performance. His undistinguished showing was partly due to his passion for extracurricular reading on a variety of subjects not related to his studies and to his undisciplined conduct. Although Davis's checkered West Point career made his future look uncertain, his years at the Academy positively affected his character and instilled in him a high sense of honor and duty. The friendships and memories he acquired at West Point never faded.[13]

Davis began his military career as a second lieutenant, serving dreary garrison duty in the old Northwest. Like his future counterpart, Abraham Lincoln, Davis was involved in the Black Hawk War in 1832. Davis was stationed at Fort Crawford, Wisconsin, and later at Fort Winnebago; he was anything but stimulated at the assignments. Army life at an isolated post in the wilderness was both tedious and dangerous. On one occasion while on woodcutting detail, Davis became separated from his men during an attack by hostile Indians but managed to escape by hiding in the thick brush.[14]

Wisconsin's weather was unhealthy for Davis. During one winter of unusually heavy snow and cold temperatures, Davis suffered from a severe case of pneumonia and nearly died. Even after recovering, he remained very susceptible to colds, which often led to bronchitis and attacks of acute neuralgia, leaving him incapacitated for weeks at a time.[15]

During his time in the army, Davis met Sarah Knox Taylor, the eighteen-year-old daughter of Colonel (and future president) Zachary Taylor. Sarah was a bright, delightful young lady, well educated for her time. Colonel Taylor approved of Davis as a soldier but, as a future son-in-law, wanted no part of him. Taylor disapproved of the match, having vowed that none of his daughters should ever have to endure the hardships of an army life. In 1835, Davis resigned his commission to marry Sarah. Colonel Taylor grudgingly consented to the marriage, but neither he nor his wife attended the wedding.[16]

The young couple did not attempt to reconcile with the bride's father. Rather, they took a steamboat south to Davis Bend, Mississippi, below Vicksburg where Davis's brother Joseph gave them an eight hundred-acre farm and fourteen slaves on credit. The marriage was tragically brief. Davis planted a cotton crop, but before harvest time, they both contracted malaria. Davis was in serious danger for over a month but survived; Sarah did not. Davis was too sick to attend the funeral; his doctor believed he was not far behind her but was proven wrong.[17]

Jefferson took the loss of his young wife very hard and would feel responsible for her death throughout the rest of his life. Although he recovered from this attack, he was not rid of malaria. Like many other victims of the disease, he would experience repeated episodes of chills and fever. He spent the next couple of years in relative seclusion on his plantation, immersed in reading books: law books, literature, political tracts, and, above all, the U.S. Constitution, which he is said to have memorized.[18]

Davis ran his plantation with the help of slaves. He was convinced of the fundamental inferiority of African Americans and considered himself responsible for the well-being of all his slaves. By the standards of the time, Davis treated his slaves leniently. They were educated, well fed, and rarely beaten. No slave was ever punished except after a formal trial. Davis did not discipline his slaves himself; rather, it was handled by courts made up of slaves from his plantation. Rules governing their punishment allowed Davis to intercede only when he thought the punishment was too harsh. Under the guidelines, Davis could not increase the punishment. Unfortunately for him, he never fully understood what slavery was like elsewhere. His plantation's success, along with the relative contentment of his slaves, reinforced this outlook. He therefore had a false notion of what slavery was and never fully understood its evil.[19]

From 1835 through 1843, Davis rarely left "Brierfield," his plantation. The area of cleared land steadily increased, and his cotton crop grew larger year by year. Within five years, Davis owned forty slaves, and by 1860, the number had grown to one hundred. Davis ran Brierfield with the conscientious paternalism of an enlightened despot. He did not view slavery as a permanent condition for blacks but thought their freedom would require several generations and should be allowed to occur naturally. "The slave," he said, "must be made fit for freedom by education and discipline." Years later, upon Davis's death, one of his former slaves was asked how he felt about his old master. "I loved him," he said, "and I can say that every colored man he ever owned loved him."[20]

In the years following Sarah's death, Davis paid little attention to politics. His brother finally convinced him to run for elected office. In 1844, he ran for Congress but lost the election. While Davis was becoming involved in politics, his personal life was also moving in a new direction. It was during this time that he was introduced to Varina Howell, whom he married in 1845.

Like Sarah, Varina was young (just seventeen years old); Davis was thirty-five. Like Sarah's parents, Varina's were at first reluctant to give their approval—this time because of the age difference. Varina was well educated for a Southern girl. Although her family was not wealthy, they had acquired the aristocratic manners of the Natchez, Mississippi, society. Varina was a fascinating person: emotional, puritanical, proud, and generous, with strong opinions and a powerful personality. She was loyal but jealously possessive. Although not by nature unkind, she sometimes hurt people with her sharp wit. Varina had a lively sense of humor and loved a good laugh. Davis understood both her strengths and shortcomings. As she matured, Varina exerted a strong and steady influence on her husband, not only at home but also in his political decisions.[21]

Jefferson and Varina Davis had a strong, sometimes volatile union that was frequently interrupted by tragedy. Their marriage produced six children, only two daughters of which survived into adulthood. Three of the boys died during childhood; the fourth, at age nineteen.[22]

Even before Davis married, his political aspirations extended beyond those of his county. In January 1844, he was named an elector to the state Democratic convention for the upcoming presidential race. The convention endorsed Martin Van Buren for president and James K. Polk for vice president. Davis, however, preferred John C. Calhoun, the strong states' rights advocate from South Carolina. Although the convention rejected Davis's candidate, they did not reject him; he was elected one of the delegates from Mississippi to the national convention.[23]

During the political campaign of 1844, Davis continued to make a name for himself. The Democratic win in Mississippi was part of a national Democratic victory that made James K. Polk the eleventh president of the United States and helped Davis when he ran for office in 1846.

A few months after his second marriage, Davis won the election to the House of Representatives. He and Varina left Brierfield and traveled to

Washington, D.C., where they would spend most of the next fifteen years. From the very beginning, Davis argued against the federal government's power to restrict slavery. As a freshman congressman, he warned, "The Union is a creature of the states. It has no inherent power. All it possesses was delegated by the state."[24]

When the Mexican War erupted in May 1846, Davis resigned from Congress to take an active role in the conflict. He was elected a colonel of the First Mississippi Rifles and served in northern Mexico in the army of his former father-in-law, Zachary Taylor. Colonel Davis proved himself an able commander. Under his leadership, the Mississippi Rifles fought bravely at Monterrey. At Buena Vista, Davis displayed courage and was wounded in the foot. He returned to Mississippi on crutches, where he was proclaimed a military genius and the hero of the South.[25]

Davis responded to the acclaim with modesty. When Polk sent him a commission as brigadier general of volunteers, Davis returned it saying that the president had no authority to make such an appointment; that power was the right of the states only. All of these honors were secondary to the compliment expressed by his former father-in-law, General Taylor, at Buena Vista: "My daughter, sir, was a better judge of men than I was."[26]

In August 1847, the governor of Mississippi appointed Davis to fill a vacancy in the U.S. Senate. Davis continued to suffer from time to time with malarial fever, but when he took his Senate seat, he was a vigorous person. A reporter who saw him in 1848 described him as "handsome, possessing a symmetrical figure, well up to medium size, a piercing, but kindly eye, and a gamy chivalric bearing." The observer continued, expressing his admiration for Davis because of his "genial personal kindness," that he was "a fluent and sometimes eloquent speaker."[27]

Davis was proud of his accomplishments and those of the Mississippi Rifles in the Mexican War and did not accept criticism well when directed at either. Any casting of aspersions on his regiment was likely to elicit from him a ferocious reply or even a challenge. One such occasion occurred on Christmas Day 1847. Davis was eating breakfast with Mississippi Senator Henry S. Foote at the boardinghouse where they both lived. Words were exchanged, and then blows. Davis, who was still on his crutches from his wound at Buena Vista, was not too ill to use his crutch in his defense. In the battle, Foote swung his fists, while Davis used his crutch. Although neither was hurt, Davis was able to knock Foote's wig from his head. An enraged Foote demanded satisfaction, but cooler heads intervened to prevent bloodshed.[28]

As a senator, Davis was unbending in his opinions and standards. Throughout his tenure in the Senate, he championed the position that the Constitution both recognized and protected the right of a citizen to hold property in slaves. The federal government, he believed, had no right to interfere or to pass laws that would prevent this right. As the battles over slavery continued in Congress, the feelings of national unity that followed the Mexican War quickly faded in the face of growing conflict between the North and South. Davis's loyalty to the Union began to fade as well.

In 1851, Davis resigned from the Senate to run for the governorship of Mississippi, a campaign that he lost. When Franklin Pierce was elected president, he appointed Davis to the position of secretary of war in his new cabinet. Davis was soon busy improving the army's weapons and equipment and doubling the army, all in the short period of two years. Davis has since been considered by many to be the finest secretary of war in the nation's history.[29]

As the issues of slavery and states' rights consumed the nation, Davis returned to the Senate in 1857, where he remained until his state seceded from the Union. As a senator from Mississippi, Davis followed the pattern of South Carolina Senator John Calhoun in championing states' rights, slavery, and free trade. He believed that the measures he supported were necessary for the security of his region and in accordance with the founding principles of the nation. In spite of his strong stance, Davis retained the respect and friendship of many Northerners who opposed his views.[30]

When the Supreme Court became involved with the slavery issue, all past laws were ruled unconstitutional. The Dred Scott decision of 1857 ruled that no African American could be a citizen of the United States. The South was overjoyed, but the new Republican Party stood firmly against any expansion of slavery into the federal territories. Republicans like William Seward of New York and Abraham Lincoln of Illinois were part of the protest against the higher court's decision.[31]

In 1860, Davis introduced several resolutions that took an uncompromising position on slavery. He insisted that the interference by Northerners in the "domestic institution" of the South subverted the Constitution and threatened the Union. He also believed that Congress did not have the power to prevent a citizen from emigrating into federal territory with his slave property and that Congress should ensure that this property be protected within the territory. Although Davis did not expect the resolution to be adopted, he hoped to influence the Democratic Party's platform in the upcoming presidential election.[32]

Davis's tactic worked well, but not in the way he had hoped it would. It played a major role in creating a split in the Democratic Party. The Northern wing nominated Stephen Douglas, while the Southern wing selected John Breckinridge. A third faction nominated John Bell of Tennessee as its candidate. Recognizing the problem this split created for the party, Davis tried to get all three to withdraw in favor of a compromise candidate. Breckinridge and Bell agreed, but Douglas refused. Douglas believed that, by withdrawing, his supporters would simply vote for Abraham Lincoln, the Republican nominee.[33]

Lincoln won anyway. His election sent fear throughout the Deep South.

While "Fire-eaters," radical Southern rights' advocates, urged that the South secede from the Union, Davis's viewpoint was much more moderate. Although he did not believe in the theories associated with slavery, he strongly defended the institution. Opposed to secession, he worked tirelessly to find a common ground for radicals in both the North and South. Because of the humanitarian way he treated his slaves, Davis was still very naive about the evils associated with the "institution."[34]

On December 20, before Lincoln took office, a specially elected South Carolina convention voted unanimously to leave the Union. On January 9, 1861, Davis's own state of Mississippi seceded. By February 1, the entire Deep South had left the Union. For all his protests and strong opinions, Davis did not really want to see the South leave the Union, viewing this development with regret and sadness. It was too late to do anything about it; Davis was ordered by Mississippi to resign from the Senate.[35]

Now fifty-four years old, Davis returned to his plantation. He was tired of politics and did not want to participate in the leadership of the new Confederacy. If war was to come, he hoped to serve in the military, but given his choice, he preferred to avoid war and simply stay at home and tend his plantation. This was not to be; his new country would soon call on him to serve again.[36]

2 *Jefferson Davis*

Confederate Chief

After resigning from the Senate, Jefferson Davis returned home to await a position in the new government. He was not interested in a political post but rather desired to be made a general in the war he believed would inevitably follow disunion. Davis was happy when the governor of Mississippi appointed him major general, commanding all the state's militia; he soon began to make preparations for the coming struggle.[1]

On February 10, 1861, as Davis and his wife were engaged in one of his favorite hobbies, working in their rose garden, a message arrived from the Confederate Congress meeting in Montgomery, Alabama. Just one month earlier, Mississippi had passed an ordinance of secession. By February, Florida, Alabama, Georgia, Louisiana, and Texas had left the Union to form a confederation. When Davis read the telegram, his face, Varina later reported, was that of a man reading his death sentence. "Oh God, spare me this responsibility," he groaned when he learned that the convention delegates had selected him to be president of the new confederation. After a few seconds of painful silence, Davis shared the news with his wife. Then he added, "I would love to head the army," but such was not the choice of the delegates. Once again, duty had called, and Jefferson Davis would not shirk his duty.[2]

Davis was a well-respected leader and a moderate. He was a war hero, a former secretary of war, and had served in the U.S. Senate. Above all, he was a passionate defender of slavery. For those in the South, Jefferson Davis seemed to be just the man to lead the Confederacy.

As a politician, Davis was able, experienced, and incorruptible. Privately, he could be warm and cordial; socially, he was pleasant and at times even charming. But when dealing with others on the Senate floor or in committee,

Davis was often aloof and obstinate. Once when asked by a Senate colleague if he would vote for an appropriations bill, Davis replied, "Sir, I make no terms. I accept no compromise." Whereas Lincoln had a common touch in dealing with people, Davis was stubborn and appeared to be self-righteous. For this reason, he was probably better suited to a military career than that of a chief executive—a view with which he agreed.[3]

Varina did not like the idea of her husband becoming president. "I thought his genius was military," she later wrote, "but that as a party manager, he would not succeed. He did not know the arts of the politician and would not practice them if understood, and he did know those of war." In the long run, her assessment would prove to be accurate.[4]

Although Davis was an honest, moral man with a firm belief in God, he showed little interest in religion until he became a member of the Episcopal Church in 1862. A person of strong convictions, Davis believed in the legitimacy of the Southern position almost to the point of obsession. Despite his many strengths, Davis was weak in other areas not apparent to those who selected him to lead the Confederacy. His shortcomings only surfaced with this crisis and the increased burdens of the war. Unable to delegate authority, he lacked the essentials of efficient administration. Rather than surrounding himself with a cadre of capable assistants and entrusting administrative routines to them, he spent precious time and energy on minutiae. Although Davis had many attributes in his favor—a good education, strong intellect, an excellent background in military and government affairs—he had serious flaws in personality and temperament. He had trouble getting along with people, was impatient with those who disagreed with him, and had little time for small talk. His lack of tact did incalculable harm to the Confederate cause.[5]

Davis's dealings with the Confederate Congress, the military, and the press left much to be desired. He did not prepare the South for the sacrifices it would be required to make during the war. Conscription and the suspension of the writ of habeas corpus, two controversial measures, were implemented without consulting the people. These actions provided grist for the mill for his enemies, who charged that he was trying to establish a dictatorship.[6]

On February 18, 1861, Davis was sworn in as president of the Confederate states. At 1:00 p.m., Howard Cobb introduced Davis, who rose "amid a storm of applause." In his inaugural address, he forcefully defined the Confederate cause. He proclaimed that the Confederacy "illustrates the American idea that governments rest upon the consent of the governed, and that it is the right of the people to alter or abolish governments whenever they become destructive of the ends for which they were established." The Southern people, he said, "had merely asserted a right which the Declaration of Independence of 1776 had defined to be inalienable." In his speech, Davis sounded no call to war; "Our true policy is peace," he said. He closed by assuring the audience that he would do his best: "You will see many

Before the Civil War, Jefferson Davis attended West Point, served in the U.S. Army, and was a congressman, senator, and secretary of war.

COURTESY OF THE LIBRARY OF CONGRESS

errors to forgive, many deficiencies to tolerate, but you shall not find in me either a want of zeal or fidelity to the cause that is to me the highest in hope and of most enduring affection."[7]

The new president of the Confederacy faced an overwhelming task. Whereas Lincoln had a government and an army chain of command in place, Davis had to start from scratch. Every office and position had to be filled. After completing the initial round of appointments, Davis spent the first six weeks of his presidency trying to deal diplomatically with the Northern officials in Washington. He hoped the whole problem could be resolved peacefully.

While Davis awaited developments in Washington, most of his attention was centered on South Carolina. Fort Sumter became the prize of the first conflict between the Union and the Confederacy. Throughout the South,

Federal troops had withdrawn from arsenals, army posts, and forts; however, the North still held Fort Sumter, an armed island in Charleston Harbor. Davis offered to negotiate with Lincoln over Fort Sumter, even offering to pay for it, but Lincoln had no interest in doing so. The situation was extremely volatile in South Carolina, with the local officials discussing attacking Fort Sumter. Davis cautioned the governor against taking action and sent Brigadier General P. G. T. Beauregard to assume command of all forces in the area. His orders were to get all in readiness but not to attack the fort unless in self-defense.[8]

When Davis learned that Lincoln was sending ships to resupply Fort Sumter, he ordered Beauregard to give Major Robert Anderson, commander at the fort, one last chance to surrender; if Anderson failed to do so, Beauregard was to take the fort forcibly. Just before daybreak on April 12, 1861, the first shot of the Civil War was fired at Fort Sumter. Thirty-four hours later, Anderson surrendered.[9] After the fall of Fort Sumter, Lincoln ordered loyal states to provide 75,000 militia to put down the rebellion. At Virginia's invitation, the Confederate capital moved from Montgomery to Richmond.[10]

The Confederacy's aim at the beginning of the war was simply to hold on to the de facto independence already obtained. It would be a passive defense, or what Davis preferred to call an "offensive–defense." Confederate forces would allow Union troops to advance, wait for an advantage, and then concentrate their troops for a counterattack at a point of their choosing. This strategy would mean surrendering a portion of the Confederacy to the Union army, but Davis believed it could be recaptured.[11]

The task of defending the Confederacy was a staggering one; the land area was the size of western Europe, with a coastline of several thousand miles. The Appalachian Mountains divided the Confederacy into two main theaters of operation—Eastern and Western. Of the two, the East received most of Davis's attention. It was more heavily populated, closer to the centers of power, and easier to defend. By contrast, defending the Western theater was a nightmare. Davis and his generals never did come up with a strategy for defending this vast territory.[12]

Davis believed there was no need to invade the North or dictate a peace treaty on the steps of the White House. The South merely had to continue the struggle long enough for the North to tire of the war and accept the fact of secession. In many respects, he believed, this strategy was little different than that of the American colonies during the Revolution.[13]

Davis ordered the first military draft in the history of the nation, a conscription act that required all males from eighteen to thirty-five to serve three years in the military. In addition to raising an army, he had to create a whole new breed of generals almost overnight. In doing so, he revealed one of the weakest facets of his leadership, a dependence upon old friends and cronies. Two of his poorest selections were old friends of his, Leonidas Polk and Braxton Bragg.[14]

Leonidas Polk was given command of the entire northern Mississippi area, one of the most vulnerable areas of the Confederacy. Polk and Davis had been friends at West Point, but immediately after graduation, Polk resigned his commission and never served a day in uniform. Instead, he became an Episcopal minister and later a bishop. The loss of the Mississippi River in 1862–1863 can be traced to mistakes made by the inexperienced Polk at the beginning of the war.[15]

Braxton Bragg had impressed Davis during the Mexican War. Although he had left the army in 1857 to become a planter in Louisiana, Bragg was among the first West Point graduates around whom Davis organized the Confederate army. He was given command of the Army of Tennessee, and before long, the total army was in disarray, with its generals arguing amongst themselves. Davis went to Tennessee to try to settle the differences between the feuding generals, but was unsuccessful. Despite observing the confusion and low morale of the army, Davis failed to replace Bragg.[16]

Davis was always loyal to his friends and supporters, while he would punish those who were critical of him. One such example was his treatment of P. G. T. Beauregard. Despite General Beauregard's victories at Fort Sumter and First Manassas, Davis went out of his way to avoid assigning him to any significant command after April 1862. Both men had similar personalities, their disagreements exaggerated by a strong sense of honor. Caught up in the pettiness of their personal quarrels, Beauregard said of Davis: "He is either demented or a traitor, a living specimen of gall and hatred." To rid himself of Beauregard, Davis transferred him to the Western theater, a move that actually harmed the Confederate effort. Even at the end of the war when experienced generals were in short supply, Davis avoided giving a command to Beauregard.[17]

Davis's problems were not unique. President Lincoln was also plagued with incompetent and self-serving generals, but he had a different way of dealing with the problem. Lincoln, unlike Davis, allowed himself to be embarrassed, slighted, and snubbed if it would help him win the war. Once, Lincoln said he would be willing to hold McClellan's horse if he would only give him a victory.[18]

Davis did make some good appointments. It was he who promoted and supported Robert E. Lee, with whom he would form one of the greatest military partnerships of the war. Lee deserves most of the credit for their close relationship; he understood Davis very well and knew how to get along with him. Lee had a strong self-image and could afford to defer to Davis's need to be in control. Davis gave Lee his full support, and Lee, in turn, gave Davis a string of victories.[19]

In picking his cabinet, Davis tried to include representatives from each state of the Confederacy. Although he had good intentions, he sacrificed talent and ability for geographical location. During the four-year history of the Confederacy, only two men—John Reagan and Stephen Mallory—held onto their appointments. There were four secretaries of state, four attorneys general, five secretaries of war, and two secretaries of treasury.[20]

Of all Davis's advisors, Judah Benjamin, the secretary of state, came to occupy a special place among his cabinet. Davis had not been close to Benjamin before the war, but shortly after Benjamin's appointment in March 1862, Davis began to value his brilliance and absolute loyalty. Besides having great intellectual ability, Benjamin brought an optimism to the cabinet that countered Davis's heavy sense of responsibility and constant anxiety.[21]

Benjamin was not the only cabinet member on whom Davis counted for sound advice. He spent hours each day with his war ministers, George Randolph and James Seddon, discussing all aspects of the war with them, including strategy, conscription, and the assignment of generals. Although Davis made all of the important decisions, he welcomed the advice of his cabinet before doing so.[22]

In the beginning, the Confederate Congress performed very well. The radical secessionists had played their part in launching the government, but as the war progressed, they were replaced by more moderate representatives. The Congress endorsed Davis's emergency war measures and appropriation requests as well as confirmed his cabinet. By late 1861, however, the good rapport between Davis and Congress began to deteriorate and continued to do so until the end of the war. Davis's insistence on having his own way and his inability to compromise contributed greatly to this break. A confirmed states' rights advocate, Davis as a wartime president found it necessary to increase the power of the central government to conduct the war. This caused dissension among the individual states that did not want to relinquish their powers to the president.[23]

The first major battle of the war occurred near Manassas Junction, Virginia, about twenty-five miles southwest of Washington, D.C. There, 20,000 Confederates under the command of Beauregard blocked the route to Richmond. On July 16, a Federal army of 35,000 under Brigadier General Irvin McDowell advanced on the Confederate capital. Davis ordered General Joseph Johnston to rush his 11,000 troops to join Beauregard. On July 21, the Federals attacked, and it appeared they would take the day, but the Confederate line held. It was here that General Thomas Jackson held his position like a stone wall, thus forever afterward to be known as "Stonewall" Jackson.[24]

As Union troops fell back, they came in contact with a frightened group of civilians who had come out in their Sunday best to watch the battle. Before the observers could get away in their carriages, the soldiers, wagons, and ambulances came down the road, creating a gigantic traffic jam. Seeing their escape route blocked, the Union retreat turned into a complete rout.[25]

When Davis learned of the battle, he hurried to the site. Only as he approached did he learn that the battle had been a Confederate victory.

Elated, Davis sent a telegram to Richmond: "We have won a glorious but dearbought victory: the night closed with the enemy in full flight, pursued by our troops." Davis met with Johnston and Beauregard, and the three agreed not to pursue the enemy. The inexperienced troops had been exhausted by the stress of the battle, and the supplies seemed inadequate for the task. Davis thus missed the chance for an early end to the war.[26]

The South rejoiced at the victory, but in the months that followed, their elation began to falter. While the war did not go away in Virginia, the situation in the West was a true nightmare. Davis seldom met personally with his generals in the Western theater, rather he dispatched orders to them. In Virginia, however, he would visit the troops, an activity he always found pleasing, and hold face-to-face conferences with his generals. In the West, Davis relied heavily on Albert Sidney Johnston to command virtually the entire army. Davis, who had served with Johnston in Mexico, admired him almost to the point of hero worship. Johnston did his best in the West; however, he was not the military genius Davis believed him to be. Davis's great confidence in the general sometimes proved a handicap for him. When Johnston requested more troops and supplies, Davis did not always fully comply, believing Johnston could get by with less.[27]

In the fall of 1861, Davis ignited a firestorm of resentment when he sent to Congress his ranking of five full generals. Earlier in March, Congress had passed a law that named full general as the highest rank in the army; an individual's previously held rank in the U.S. Army was to be used as the criterion for placement in the Confederate army. Davis had already appointed four full generals, but there had been no official seniority list until Davis's August list. His list named Samuel Cooper as senior, followed by Albert S. Johnston, Robert E. Lee, Joseph E. Johnston, and P. G. T. Beauregard. In assigning the ranking, Davis ignored the guidelines set by Congress.[28]

As a result of Davis's ranking, Joseph Johnston was enraged; he felt he had been insulted and his honor questioned. He was the only man to have held a permanent brigadier's rank in the U.S. Army, and he had no doubt that his name should have been at the top of Davis's list. Despite Johnston's protest, Davis did not change his ranking. The incident altered the relationship between the two, and neither man ever trusted the other again.[29]

During the winter of 1861–1862, the rapid and unexpected collapse of Albert S. Johnston's front in the West caused a great public outcry. The fall of Nashville and the surrender of Fort Donelson fueled the criticism. Letters poured into the president's office, including some that suggested he take command in the field to salvage the situation. Although he had no intention of doing so, Davis realized he would have to exert every effort to "retrieve our waning fortunes in the West."[30]

On April 2, Johnston attacked a Union army under Ulysses Grant encamped on the western side of the Tennessee River. Shiloh, a country church nearby, became the designation for the greatest and bloodiest battle of the war to that date. The casualties on both sides reached 24,000. On the first day of the battle, the Confederates were victorious. Although the encouraging news of the great victory reached Richmond, there was also bad news for Davis: Johnston had died on the battlefield while rallying his troops. Beauregard took command in the late afternoon and stopped the assault. Of Johnston's loss, Davis lamented, "When he fell, I realized that our strongest pillar had been broken."[31]

During the early stages of the war, Davis worked closely with Robert E. Lee. Their collaboration began in March 1862 when the Confederate Congress passed a bill authorizing the appointment of a general-in-chief. Davis, who considered such an appointment an encroachment on his position as commander-in-chief, vetoed the measure. Instead, Davis appointed Lee as his military advisor, a position with which Lee was not happy. Despite the fact that Lee preferred a field command, he nevertheless worked amicably with the president, something few men were able to do. Davis continued to call on Lee for advice even after his assignment to command the Army of Northern Virginia.[32]

During the spring of 1862, the Confederate capital faced a new Union threat, this time from Major General George McClellan's army of 100,000 moving up the Virginia peninsula toward Richmond. Confederate General Joseph Johnston, now in charge of the Confederate army in Virginia, retreated slowly as McClellan advanced up the peninsula. When the guns could be heard in Richmond, Davis could no longer sit at his desk. He arrived on the battlefield during the Battle of Fair Oaks on May 31, in time to see Johnston carried from the field, badly wounded in the shoulder. The next day Davis replaced Johnston with General Robert E. Lee.

When Lee took command of the Army of Northern Virginia in June 1862, Federal forces were within a few miles of Richmond. The Union army was close enough to see the spires of Richmond and hear the bells in the church towers as they chimed the time. What Lee was able to accomplish was remarkable; in just a few weeks, he drove the enemy from the outskirts of Richmond and back to the Potomac River. By August, Lee and his army were positioned to do battle at Manassas, where he defeated the Union army for a second time.[33]

Between April and June of 1861, tens of thousands of Southerners had rushed to join the Confederate army, signing up for one year. Now, one year later, a serious loss of manpower could affect the South's military strength. On March 28, Davis sent a message to Congress complaining of its patchwork method of raising armies and requesting that "some plain and simple method be adopted for their prompt enrollment." In less than three weeks, Congress passed the first conscription law in American history. Every white man between the ages of eighteen and thirty-five would go into the Confederate service unless exempted; those already serving would remain in the army for three years, dating from their original enlistment.

Although conscription solved the manpower problem, it hardened opposition to Davis from his political foes.[34]

Davis ran the war effort and the Confederacy from his wartime home, known as the Confederate White House, at Clay and 12th Streets in Richmond. Three-stories high and well furnished, it served as the president's home from July 1861 until April 1865. There, Davis poured over an unending stream of paperwork, finding it difficult to delegate work and responsibilities. Despite his heavy workload, Davis made an effort to spend at least an hour with his family every day and rarely missed attending worship services at St. Paul's Episcopal Church. When his responsibilities became so great that he could hardly bear them, he would collapse on the sofa in his study, often refusing to eat. As his wife later recalled, "I remained by his side, anxious and afraid to ask what was the trouble which so oppressed him." On these occasions, Varina would read to him; his favorite books were poetry and light fiction.[35]

The conduct of military operations took more of Davis's attention than did anything else. The president had an affinity for military strategy, and he felt that, if the Confederacy was defeated, nothing else mattered anyway. When he traveled to the fighting front, he seldom interfered.[36]

While Davis was busy directing the war, Varina was making the executive mansion a home for him and their children. As the first lady, she was an active hostess, holding numerous receptions at the White House, which became a lively place because of her. As the war progressed, the food served changed from sumptuous to only the "plainest and scantest" available. One of her friends remembered Varina as "very clever and brilliant in society," while another described her as a woman of warm heart as well as witty. As a presidential wife during wartime, Varina not only took care of her family and entertained Confederate officials and generals but did all she could to help out with the war effort. She provided food for officers who visited the White House and distributed provisions collected for families in need.[37]

In late summer 1862, Davis replaced Beauregard with Major General Braxton Bragg. On August 27, Bragg, along with General Edmund Kirby Smith, embarked on an audacious invasion of Kentucky. Davis hoped that the presence of the Confederate army in the state would provide the opportunity for Kentucky to join the Confederacy. At the same time, Lee and the Army of Northern Virginia slipped across the Potomac into Maryland.[38]

Lee did not receive the warm response in Maryland that Davis had expected. Davis had declared that "Maryland had been reduced to a conquered land by a ruthless enemy." The Confederate army, he declared, had come to enable the Marylanders to throw off the "foreign yoke." On September 16 and 17, General McClellan engaged Lee at Antietam Creek near Sharpsburg. The Battle of Antietam was one of the decisive battles of the Civil War with 23,000 casualties. Although Lee held his own tactically despite being heavily outnumbered, he was forced to return to Virginia.[39]

After the Union success at Antietam, President Lincoln issued his preliminary Emancipation Proclamation. The proclamation provided for the freeing of all slaves residing in the rebellious states if the South did not abandon the war. The proclamation enraged the South to the extent that some Confederates urged "the raising of the black flag, asking and giving no quarter thereafter." Davis considered the proclamation unconstitutional, calling it the "most execrable measure recorded in the history of guilty man." Most Southerners agreed with Davis, and it was one of the few times that he enjoyed the full support of the Confederate nation.[40]

Although both offensives in Maryland and Kentucky failed, the reactions to the failures varied in each case. Despite the fact that the Maryland campaign had not been successful, Lee enjoyed the overwhelming support of his officers and men. Braxton Bragg, commander of the Army of Tennessee, had Davis's support, but he did not have the trust of his officers. Many of Bragg's officers believed it was his ineptness that resulted in the failed Kentucky campaign and said so. General Smith dispatched a message to Davis requesting that he never have to serve under Bragg again. General Polk initiated a campaign to rally his fellow officers to call for Bragg's removal.[41]

Davis responded to General Smith by appealing to his sense of patriotism. "Bragg has never denigrated you," Davis said. Again, the president allowed friendship to influence his judgment. The Kentucky campaign was a clear indication of the disharmony that existed in the West, but Davis made no effort to correct it. Bragg remained in command.[42]

As the war progressed, other problems surfaced for Davis. His earlier view of states' rights and limited federal government had to be modified. As a U.S. congressman and senator, he had insisted on a strict constructionist interpretation of the Constitution. Because the war required a complete mobilization of all Southern resources, a degree of centralization was necessary. As soon as the war began, Davis ordered all forts, ammunition, and machinery for making weapons in the South transferred to the central government. Although troops were raised by the states, they became an integral part of the Confederate army, and by the spring of 1861, Congress authorized Davis to accept volunteers directly. Davis insisted on full control of the troops and rejected any military plans that allowed the defense of specific states by state forces. Davis's new position on states' rights provided fodder for his enemies, some referring to him as "King Jeff the First."[43]

After Antietam, a lot of fight remained in Lee's Army of Northern Virginia. Late in 1862, a number of events gave Davis and the Confederacy cause for hope. On December 13, Lee and Jackson smashed another "On to Richmond" drive under Major General Ambrose Burnside at Fredericksburg, Virginia. On December 27, Confederate Lieutenant General John Pemberton repulsed an attack by Major General William Sherman at Vicksburg. On New Year's Eve, a Union army under Major General William

Rosecrans attacked Bragg's army. In a savage three-day battle, both armies suffered heavy casualties. Bragg withdrew to Tullahoma, Tennessee, but the shattered Union army did not follow.[44]

In April 1863, the Union army, now under the command of Major General Joseph Hooker, marched South with a force of 130,000 troops. At Chancellorsville, Lee defeated Hooker with an army only half that size. The victories at Fredericksburg and Chancellorsville sent Davis's spirits soaring.[45] The victory at Chancellorsville, however, was dearly purchased. Confederate losses numbered more than 13,000, including Stonewall Jackson, Lee's subordinate general. Davis viewed Jackson's body as it lay in state in Richmond. When he was approached by a visitor, he said, "You must excuse me. I am still staggering from a dreadful blow. I cannot think."[46]

Civilian morale was also low, particularly because of Jackson's death and the food shortages and inflation on the home front. During a bread riot in Richmond in 1862, a crowd of several hundred women and children gathered in the business district, demanding bread from the bakeries. When the crowd quickly became a mob, Davis rushed to the scene and appealed to the rioters to disperse. When they refused, he took all the money from his pockets and threw it to the crowd, telling them they had to bear their share of the privations and that he would do what he could for them. Then he told the crowd that he would order arriving troops to fire upon them if they did not return to their homes; the crowd dispersed.[47]

While Davis was willing to take action in public, those who knew him best believed him to be compassionate. He pardoned nearly every soldier who was sentenced to death for desertion. His generals hated it when appeals for clemency reached his desk, because he usually granted them. The terrible slaughter of young men weighed heavily upon him.[48]

The Confederate victory at Chancellorsville was encouraging but incomplete. The Army of the Potomac had not been destroyed. It had retired to regroup and lick its wounds and would probably renew the offensive within a few months. After meeting with Davis and his cabinet, Lee proposed an invasion of Pennsylvania. This move, he hoped, would remove the threat to Richmond and open the way for a decisive victory over a disorganized Union army on enemy soil. An invasion of the North would also help relieve the pressure on Vicksburg in the West.[49]

At the end of June, Lee led the Army of Northern Virginia toward Pennsylvania, extremely confident of its invincibility. But the army had a serious weakness. After Jackson's death, Lee had reorganized his army. Only one of the three corps into which he divided his army was led by an experienced commander, James Longstreet, and even he had developed a habit of questioning Lee's plans. The other two corps commanders, A. P. Hill and Richard Ewell, had been able in subordinate positions but were unproven in their new responsibility.[50]

By the end of June, Lee's army had fanned out across southern Pennsylvania. On July 1, Lee engaged the Union army, now under the command of Major General George Meade, at Gettysburg. For three days, the two armies battled it out; initially successful, Lee's army was plagued with a series of setbacks. On July 4, Lee ordered a retreat. His army had suffered 20,000 casualties, a third of his forces, ending all possibility for a decisive Southern victory on Union soil. On the same day, Grant captured Vicksburg and 30,000 Confederate troops.[51]

The double defeat jolted the Confederacy. "The clouds are truly dark over us," Davis admitted. It became apparent that the war would not be a short one. When the South's casualties increased and supplies decreased, Davis was hard pressed to find ways of financing the war and keeping the ranks of the Confederate army filled. He called the twin Confederate defeats "the darkest hour of our political existence," which provoked another torrent of abuse from his critics.[52]

Despite the huge losses suffered by the Confederates in 1863, Davis refused to call a halt to the war. For two years, Confederate armies had fought well. He believed the South had already survived the worst of the fighting and that the courage of his people would eventually carry them through to victory. The loss of life, however, continued to increase as the war progressed. By mid-1863, the South had lost Mississippi, and Yankee soldiers had vandalized Davis's house at Brierfield, writing THE HOUSE JEFF BUILT in big letters across the front of the building. It made a nice background for those who sent photographs home.[53]

News from abroad was equally bad. By now it was clear that Great Britain would not help the Confederacy. Davis hoped the demand for cotton would force Great Britain to break the Northern blockade of Southern ports. Foreseeing the crisis, however, British merchants had purchased two years' supply of cotton before the war began. Davis failed to understand the strength of antislavery feelings in Great Britain. The British had abolished slavery years earlier, and Lincoln's Emancipation Proclamation helped convince their policymakers not to interfere with the war.[54]

By September, the Union Army of the Cumberland had entered Chattanooga. Bragg had the opportunity to deal Rosecrans's troops a crushing blow while they were scattered, but failure on the part of some subordinates prevented this move. On September 19 and 20, the Army of Tennessee defeated Rosecrans in the Battle of Chickamauga, forcing them to fall back to Chattanooga. Only Major General George Thomas, who thereafter was called the "Rock of Chickamauga," saved Rosecrans from complete disaster. Bragg took up a position on the heights above the city and subjected the Federals to a siege.[55]

When Bragg failed to follow up his victory, he blamed his generals. He suspended Lieutenant General Leonidas Polk and pressed charges against several other officers. Twelve generals signed a petition to the president asking that Bragg be removed from command. Davis came from Richmond to investigate the situation and to smooth things over. He convinced Bragg to drop charges against General Polk and decided to retain Bragg in command.[56] Before leaving this mishandled army, Davis praised the officers and men for their "gallantry and patriotic devotion" and told them "the hopes of our cause greatly depend upon you."[57]

Bragg still had a chance to capture Rosecrans's army penned up in Chattanooga, but he foolishly weakened his force by sending 20,000 of his troops on an unsuccessful attack on a Union army at Knoxville. In the meantime, General Grant replaced Rosecrans with General Thomas. On November 23, the Union army attacked Bragg on the heights outside of Chattanooga in what became known as the "Battle Above the Clouds." Two days later, Bragg's troops were routed at the Battle of Missionary Ridge.[58] In a message to Congress on December 7, Davis spoke of this humiliating defeat: "It is believed that if the troops who yielded to the assault had fought with the valor which they displayed on previous occasions, . . . the enemy would have been repulsed with great slaughter, and our country would have escaped the misfortune and the army the mortification of the first defeat that has resulted from misconduct of the troops."[59]

After the disaster, it was clear to Davis that changes had to be made in the leadership of the Army of Tennessee. Although not happy with having to remove Bragg, he nevertheless replaced him with General Joseph Johnston. At the outset, Johnston and Davis disagreed over the military operations of the Army of Tennessee. Johnston believed he had to rebuild the morale and confidence of the army before doing anything else, and he worked effectively to do so. Davis urged Johnston to go on the offensive; Johnston did not think the army was ready for an offensive, preferring to wait for the right time to attack.[60]

Davis bore much of the blame for the failed campaigns, and the strain showed on him. He worked harder for longer hours, pushing his poor health beyond its limits and becoming more estranged from Congress and the public. A virus blinded one of his eyes and badly inflamed the other. He also suffered from a digestive ailment called dyspepsia. Davis went into a protective shell, becoming obsessed with the details of troop movements and supply reports. He slept and ate very little and stubbornly battled through his recurring bouts of pain and exhaustion.[61]

In early 1864, President Lincoln gave his approval to Major General Hugh J. Kilpatrick for a plan the latter had developed for a raid on Richmond involving 4,000 mounted horsemen. Once in Richmond, the raiders would capture Jefferson Davis and free Union soldiers being held captive there.[62] For Kilpatrick's plan to be successful, he would need to surprise the Confederates. Under his personal command were 3,500 troopers who were to strike Richmond from the north, while a detachment of 500, led by Colonel Ulric Dahlgren, was to attack from the south. The raid began smoothly enough but soon ran into difficulty. Kilpatrick's force was turned back by Confederate cavalry under Major General Wade Hampton. In the meantime, Colonel Dahlgren attempted to enter Richmond, but his efforts were thwarted. In an ambush fight, Dahlgren's detachment was cut to pieces, and he was killed. Papers found on Dahlgren's body described plans to burn Richmond and kill President Davis and his cabinet.[63]

When the papers were taken to Davis, he found them amusing. "This means you, Mr. Benjamin," he said to his secretary of state. Others in Richmond, however, were not amused. General Bragg wanted the men who had accompanied Dahlgren on the raid to be executed. Robert E. Lee, however, was opposed to killing the captives: "Acts in addition to intentions," he said, "are necessary to constitute crime." The captives were not executed.[64]

In the spring of 1864, tragedy visited Davis even more directly when his young son Joseph was killed in a fall from the balcony of the Confederate White House. Overwhelmed with grief, Davis suffered from temporary shock. When messengers brought him news of the war, he said, "I cannot do it. I cannot. I cannot." He went upstairs and spent all night with his son. The next day, he was back on the job, doing what he had to do as the Confederate president. His public front never changed; he always remained stern and was often called "the Sphinx of the Confederacy."[65]

As the war continued, Davis's problems mounted; now the outcry came from the common people. Southerners resented the loss of manpower, particularly among nonslaveholders who had no one to work the land since all of the ablebodied men had gone off to fight. Class resentment also surfaced. Wealthy families did not suffer as much as those less fortunate. As late as 1864, men of means were able to pay substitutes to take their places in the army. Poor men who enlisted were required to serve three years, while sons of rich men were only required to serve twelve months.[66]

As the supply of labor diminished, Major General Patrick Cleburne, a division commander in the Army of Tennessee, proposed training slaves to fill the gaps in the armies' ranks. As a reward for their service, he said, they should be guaranteed their freedom within a reasonable time. It was an incredible proposal for a Southern officer to make. As an Irish immigrant, Cleburne did not take into account the native Southern feelings about blacks. General Johnston, who received the proposal, immediately rejected it.[67]

When Davis learned of the proposal, he wanted to keep it quiet. Arming the slaves was an explosive idea, and it would be "injurious to the public service," he said. The people of the Confederacy were not ready for such a concept. In a recent address to Congress, Davis had proposed using slaves in noncombatant roles, freeing white men to serve in the ranks, but for the time being, he deferred arming them. Within a year, he would be advocating Cleburne's idea before the Confederate Congress.[68]

In March 1864, the challenge to the Confederacy became more critical when Lieutenant General Grant took command of all Union armies. Grant's plan for winning the war was to advance all Union forces simultaneously. In that way, the Confederates could not shift their limited forces to protect each threatened point. Once Grant seized the initiative, he would not relinquish it.[69]

Developments in the West alarmed Davis as General Johnston continued to retreat. On July 9, Davis sent Braxton Bragg, now his military advisor, to confer with Johnston about whether he intended to fight to hold Atlanta. When Johnston's reply was evasive, Davis considered replacing him. Before doing so, he conferred with Lee about replacing him with Hood. "It is a bad time to release the commander of an army situated as that of Tennessee," Lee said. "We may lose Atlanta and the army too. Hood is a bold fighter. I am doubtful as to other qualities necessary." Despite Lee's caution, Davis appointed Lieutenant General John Bell Hood as commander of the Army of Tennessee.[70]

Hood had established a reputation as a bold, aggressive fighter. He had been severely wounded earlier, losing a leg and the use of an arm while leading his troops. Union General William Sherman was pleased with the change in command, for he had a low opinion of Hood as a general. Davis's removal of Johnston and the appointment of Hood became one of the most controversial military decisions of the war. Johnston's cautious approach and skillful maneuvering of his army had conserved his limited supply of manpower. Hood did exactly as the president wanted—he fought, but in the process destroyed his army.[71] Sherman took Atlanta anyway and continued his "March to the Sea," leaving a path of destruction sixty-miles wide behind him. Finally, Davis realized the folly of his appointment and removed Hood, replacing him with Johnston.

By the fall of 1864, the Confederacy had been split into three parts. Davis refused to make more than a halfhearted attempt to negotiate a peace settlement as long as Lincoln insisted on the abolition of slavery and reunification with the North as the conditions of a truce. There was a strong public demand for peace at any price, but Davis was determined to preserve the honor of the South.[72]

The fall of Atlanta sealed the fate of the Confederacy. Davis had been holding out hope that Lincoln would lose his bid for reelection in the fall of 1864. He believed that the North had grown increasingly frustrated with the war that seemed to have no end. With new leadership, the North might be willing to negotiate some sort of peace. With the fall of Atlanta, however, Union morale received an enormous boost. This, in conjunction with Major General Philip Sheridan's victory in the Shenandoah Valley, assured Lincoln's reelection. It was clear that the North was winning the war; it was just a matter of time before the Confederacy would collapse.[73]

In the East, Grant came in person to supervise the Army of the Potomac. After crossing the Rapidan River, he engaged Lee in the "Wilderness of Virginia." Both sides fought hard, with Lee inflicting heavy losses on the

Union army, but Grant did not turn back as other Union commanders had done in the past. He simply moved to the southeast and forced another major battle at Spotsylvania Court House. Both sides lost heavily, but a war of attrition favored Grant. As Lee fell back, Grant began the siege of Petersburg. Despite setbacks, Davis remained indomitable; he did not lose confidence.[74]

Davis's wife was more accepting of the Confederate defeat than was her husband. Throughout the war, Varina was aware of her heavy responsibilities. Still, she remained sensitive to her husband and her children's needs. Davis frequently discussed the state of the Confederacy with her, and she helped him make important decisions. In later years, Davis was heavily criticized for engaging in political conversations with her. Despite all the bad news in 1864, the first lady still found time to bring the spirit of Christmas into her house. For a time, Varina orchestrated a brief moment of joy for both her family and some of the less fortunate in Richmond. When she learned that the orphans in the Episcopal Home had been promised a Christmas tree, she saw to it that they got one. Determined that none of the orphans would be disappointed at Christmas, she oversaw the collection and the refurbishing of old toys. On Christmas Eve, she invited young people to the White House to prepare the presents and to decorate the tree. During the night, Davis had cake sent out to the White House guards. The day after Christmas, however, reality returned.[75]

Davis was willing to do anything that would keep his nation alive. In an effort to do so, he returned to Cleburne's earlier proposal of using slaves in the army. His decision shocked the South, but Davis pressed the issue until many agreed with him, including Robert E. Lee. By March 1865, Congress passed a law authorizing the recruitment of black soldiers, but the decision came too late.[76]

During the past year, living conditions in Richmond had deteriorated to the point where its residents were on the verge of starvation. Flour sold for $1,500 per barrel, live chickens for $50 each, butter for $20 a pound, and beef for $15. One woman described the nature of the inflation: "You can carry your money in a market basket and bring home your provisions in your purse." Some suffered more than others. One wounded soldier serving as a hospital guard was so weak from hunger that he could hardly stand watch, but he could not eat what his companions did: "The surgeons and matrons ate rats and some said they were as good as squirrels, but having seen the rats running over the bodies of dead soldiers, I had no relish for them," he said.[77]

In January 1865, Davis made one last effort to discuss peace with the United States when he met with Francis P. Blair Sr., a prewar friend of his from Kentucky. Davis tried to keep Blair's visit to Richmond a secret, but news of it leaked out anyway. Blair maintained that, with the war nearly over, the Union's goal was to reunify the country as quickly as possible. Davis was receptive to the idea of ending the war, offering to send a delegation to Washington or to receive a Union one in Richmond to discuss terms of peace.[78]

Blair returned to Washington with a letter to Lincoln from Davis declaring his interest in securing peace. Lincoln, however, would not consider any peace agreement that involved two separate countries. Lincoln responded that he would receive any person Davis might "informally send me, with a view of securing peace to the people of our common country." Although disappointed at the notion of "our common country," Davis decided to send a delegation anyway to discuss the possibility. The proposed conference, Davis believed, provided the opportunity to quiet his critics, who believed he had not pursued peace vigorously enough. If Lincoln's terms for peace were unconditional surrender, Davis hoped his detractors would be silenced.[79]

On February 3, a Confederate delegation met with Lincoln and Secretary of State William Seward on Lincoln's steamer to discuss terms of peace in what became known as the Hampton Roads Conference. Lincoln's terms were simple—end the rebellion and return to the Union. In addition, all executive decisions regarding slavery must remain intact. Davis's attempt for peace had been a complete failure; there had been no meeting of the minds.[80] The public reacted as Davis had anticipated, denouncing the terms proposed by Lincoln. One newspaper stormed: "Forbid it, Almighty God! Now, let us cease all bickering, and strike for life and liberty." The war would continue.[81]

By the end of March, Grant was ready to break the Confederate line at Petersburg. If Petersburg fell, Richmond would follow shortly thereafter. On March 31, Varina and her family left Richmond, taking with them nothing but their clothes. They were to go to Charlotte, North Carolina, first, and if necessary to Abbeville, South Carolina. From there, Davis wanted her to go to the Florida coast and then to sail to Cuba or even Europe. It was a tearful farewell. To Varina he said, "If I live, you can come to me when the struggle is ended, but I do not expect to survive." Varina believed this was probably the last time they would see each other.[82]

On April 2, defenses at Petersburg collapsed, opening the way for the Union army to capture Richmond. As Southern officials, troops, and civilians evacuated the city, Davis and his cabinet fled, leaving behind a city in near riot. The next day a fire began in the early hours and raged out of control with no one to fight it. Shortly after sunrise, Federal troops occupied the smoldering city.[83]

Davis had expected Richmond to fall eventually, but not as soon as it did. He and his cabinet and aides escaped to Danville, Virginia, a town selected because it could be defended by both Lee and Johnston and had good rail connections. Davis remained in Danville for a week until he learned that Lee had surrendered at Appomattox Court House on April 9. The news, Secretary of the Navy Stephen Mallory wrote, "fell upon the ears of all like a fireball in the night." Later that evening, Davis and his cabinet left by train for Greensboro, North Carolina.[84]

Davis was now a wanted man. His first thoughts were of his family, from whom he had become separated in the chaos. As he traveled south, Davis received a cool welcome. In Greensboro, all doors were closed to him for fear of reprisals by Federal troops if they found out residents had sheltered him.[85]

Davis was still not ready to surrender, convinced that the Confederacy could win the war. To everyone else, however, it was evident that the Southern cause was lost. Still determined, Davis met with Beauregard and Johnston and indicated that he still wanted them to fight. Both men were surprised and believed Davis had lost all sense of reality. In a second meeting the next day, Johnston bluntly informed Davis that it would be a crime to continue to fight the war. Beauregard agreed with Johnston, and so did most of those present.[86]

When Davis met with his cabinet, the response was the same; everyone agreed that the fight was over. The hopelessness of the situation became apparent when a dispatch from Lee arrived officially announcing his surrender. Davis read the dispatch, then passed it along as he "silently wept bitter tears." R. E. Lee Jr. was present and later wrote, "He seemed quite broken . . . by this tangible evidence of the loss of his army and the misfortune of its generals. All of us, respecting his great grief, silently withdrew."[87]

Davis left the meeting depressed; in the morning his depression had not passed, but he took time to write Varina a short letter: "Everything is dark. I have lingered on the road and labored to little purpose." He said he would try to join her if possible, but in the meantime he would prepare for the worst. Davis and his entourage left for Charlotte on April 15.[88]

On April 19, when Davis learned of Lincoln's assassination, he said, "I certainly have no regard for Mr. Lincoln, but there are a great many men whose end I would rather have heard than his. I fear it will be disastrous to our people, and I regret it deeply." Davis spoke of Lincoln in kind terms, not so much because he had mellowed but because of the new president. Upon assuming power, Andrew Johnson had proclaimed Jefferson Davis an outlaw, accusing him of being involved in Lincoln's murder and offering a reward of $100,000 for his capture. In addition, Johnson had told a crowd in Washington that he would hang Jefferson Davis and all the "diabolical" crew at Richmond if he ever got the chance.[89]

When Davis reached Charlotte, he found that his family had left for Abbeville; on April 26, Davis left Charlotte, hoping to catch up with Varina. When he arrived in Abbeville on May 2, Davis was greeted warmly, but his wife had left two days earlier. After the warm reception, Davis showed renewed enthusiasm for continuing to fight. That afternoon, Davis called a meeting of his generals, the men who were commanding the remnants of the cavalry escorting him on the trip. The cause is not lost, he said: "Energy, courage, and constancy might yet save all. . . . Even if the troops now with me be all that I can for the present rely on, three thousand brave men are enough for a nucleus around which the whole people will rally." Davis then asked for their suggestions for continuing the war. None could believe that Davis still held out hope for victory. There was a silence, then those present told him that the war was over and that a guerrilla war, such as Davis proposed, would lead to greater problems for the South than it could justify. Emphatically, they all said they "would not fire another shot to continue hostilities." Without adjourning the meeting, Davis stood and started to leave. When he did, he moved so feebly that he might have fallen had General Breckinridge not jumped up to assist him.[90]

On May 5, Davis was reunited with his family, but Varina begged him to continue on ahead of them. Davis took her advice, but his progress was slowed by a heavy rain, allowing Varina's party to catch up. Davis decided to stay in camp for the night with Varina.

On the morning of May 10, the Davises were awakened by a rifle shot from Yankee cavalrymen who had surrounded the camp. In the darkness inside the tent, Davis reached for his overcoat, grabbing instead Varina's cloak. As he stepped outside, Varina threw her shawl over his head and shoulder. Thus the story was born that Davis tried to elude capture by dressing as a woman. In time, the story was embellished to embarrass him, proclaiming that Davis was trying to escape in his wife's hoopskirt. Davis was disturbed by the challenge to his honor and deeply resented that anyone believed him capable of an act so "unbecoming a soldier and a gentleman."[91]

Already, the taunting and teasing had begun. The jubilant captors sang the favorite lyric of the time, "We'll hang Jeff Davis from a sour apple tree," and spoke profanely in front of Varina and her children. When the Union soldiers learned about the reward, they became even more insulting.[92]

Few men in American history had to face greater odds and discouragement than Jefferson Davis. Despite his shortcomings, it is doubtful anyone could have held the Confederacy together as long as he did; under crushing defeats, his indomitable will held firm. The war was over, but the postwar battles were about to begin for Jefferson Davis.[93]

3   Martyr of the Lost Cause

Once Davis was taken prisoner, his tribulations began in earnest. He was searched, and his currency was taken. Federal troops swarmed through the camp, plundering the tents and wagons, breaking into trunks, and throwing clothing onto the ground; gold and jewelry were taken from Varina. Davis complained to the commanding officer, Lieutenant Colonel Benjamin Pritchard, that his men were robbing his family of their personal belongings. Pritchard promised that he would see to it that all stolen items would be returned, but they never were. Despite the harassment and looting by the Union troops, the president maintained his dignity.[1]

Davis and his family were taken in an ambulance to Macon, Georgia. En route, the procession encountered numerous Confederate soldiers on their way home from the war. Jubilant Federal officers were quick to inform them of their captive and were both surprised and delighted by their response: "Hang him! Shoot him! . . . We've got no use for him. The damned Mississippi Mule got us into this scrape. Hope you'll hang every man in Mississippi and South Carolina."[2]

Davis was shocked and disheartened by their catcalls. For all that he had done and gone through for the past four years, he did not expect this type of treatment. With the Confederacy reeling, the economic system in ruins, and the South defeated, the white survivors were overcome with disappointment and despair. As Davis was the visible symbol of the Confederacy's failure, it is not surprising that some disillusioned Southerners would blame him for their plight.[3]

As news of Davis's capture spread, the public attitude toward the president changed. Crowds of civilians greeted him and his family at each station, some being permitted to board the train to talk to him. They begged

Davis to allow them to overpower the guards and rescue him, but he refused. In another situation, a Federal soldier shouted to a Confederate in the crowd, "Hey, Johnny, we've got your President!" The Rebel responded, "And the Devil's got yours!"[4]

Weary and ill, Davis expected to be immediately hanged. Instead, he was taken to Fort Monroe in Virginia, where he was imprisoned under conditions that outraged the Southern people and forever made him a martyr of the "Lost Cause." He was placed in solitary confinement under heavy guard to await his destiny. It turned out to be a long wait. The Federal government was in a highly vindictive mood after an actor, John Wilkes Booth, had assassinated President Lincoln, and there were some in the federal government who believed Davis was complicit in the murder plot.[5]

At Fort Monroe, Davis was placed under the supervision of Brigadier General Nelson Miles. With Washington's blessing, Davis was placed in irons and not permitted to leave his cell. Even when he exercised, he had to do so in his cell. When he stripped to bathe, or when it was necessary for him to use the portable commode, he was not allowed any privacy. General Miles even decided when Davis would be permitted to change his underwear. Fearful that he might attempt suicide, Miles did not allow the prisoner to use a knife and fork for eating. A light was kept burning inside his cell twenty-four hours a day. Guards were ordered not to speak to him, and his cell was inspected at fifteen-minute intervals. Davis's health suffered greatly as a result of his treatment. The endless glare from the light aggravated his neuralgia and chronic insomnia. It was a year before Davis was able to see his wife.[6]

Secretary of War Edwin Stanton tried by whatever means he could to implicate Davis in the Lincoln assassination plot. He seemed to see conspiracies everywhere and believed that Southern sympathizers might attempt to free Davis; he was resolved to make such a rescue impossible. Eventually the charges related to the assassination plot were dropped, but Davis still faced prosecution for treason against the United States.[7]

Other indignities befell the Confederate president. He received letters from newly freed slaves congratulating him on his confinement and their newly acquired freedom and sending him worthless Confederate currency. The Northern press took great delight in spreading the rumor that Davis had been captured wearing a petticoat and that he tried to escape in women's clothing. One paper expressed it this way: "A peal of laughter goes ringing around the globe. Davis, with the blood of thousands of noble victims upon his soul, will go down to posterity cowering under a petticoat."[8]

Davis received the first sign of humane treatment since his capture from an unusually kind medical officer, Lieutenant Colonel John B. Craven, who worked to foil the efforts to hold Davis in solitary confinement and forced a major change in the government's policy toward prisoners. Craven was startled to find Davis in irons and in such poor physical condition. In his report, he stated, "Mr. Davis presented a very miserable and affecting aspect, his eyes restless and fevered, his head shifting from side to side for a cool spot on the pillow. His pulse was full and at ninety, tongue thickly coated, his extremities cold and his head troubled with a long-established neuralgic disorder."[9]

It was clear to Craven that Davis was in need of immediate attention. That evening he took tobacco to the prisoner. Davis lit his pipe, the only object other than his Bible he was allowed to keep. "This is a noble medicine," he said. "With this I hope to become tranquil."[10]

Craven saw to it that Davis received a more comfortable mattress, but Miles refused to have the shackles removed. Only after the public outcry could not be ignored were the shackles removed.[11] Dr. Craven continued to assist Davis, insisting that it was vital he be permitted to leave his cell for short walks. Miles continued to refuse to allow him to do so, claiming that Davis would try to escape. "If all the doors and gates of the fort were thrown open, he would not leave," Craven said. "The only duty left to him—his only remaining object—is to vindicate the action of his people, and his own actions as their representative, by a fair and public trial." Soon afterward, Davis was permitted an hour of exercise outside his cell.[12]

Davis's suffering, however, made him a hero in the South. He was more popular now than he had been as president. Southerners began to view Davis as representing the embodiment of the Lost Cause. The poet Sidney Lanier, a Confederate veteran, wrote: "If there was guilt in any, there was guilt in nigh all of us. . . . The hearts of the Southern people bleed to see how their own act has resulted in the chaining of Mr. Davis, who was as innocent as they."[13] Davis became a martyr, almost a Christlike figure, paying for the sins of the South. The impression of martyrdom was further strengthened by a gift from the Pope, a crown of thorns, which he made himself to express Davis's suffering.

In the meantime, Varina and her children were taken to a hotel in Savannah and placed under house arrest. She was forbidden to leave the area or communicate with her husband or friends. Varina could endure her own confinement and impoverished lifestyle, but she could not bear to see her husband suffering in prison. She spent months petitioning government officials to allow her to communicate with her husband. Finally in September, her efforts were rewarded, and the two were allowed to communicate with each other on the condition that only family matters were discussed.[14]

Gradually, the terms of Davis's confinement were relaxed. The light was removed, and Davis was permitted to walk to the courtyard and receive books and newspapers. Not until April 1866 was Varina allowed to visit him, however. By the spring of 1866, Davis was the only Confederate prisoner behind bars, still being held on the original charges of complicity in the assassination of Lincoln and treason. After studying thousands of Confederate documents, Federal prosecutors decided to drop the charges related to Lincoln's assassination, believing that a trial in court would find him not guilty. They began to shift their focus to treason alone.[15]

As the months dragged on, Washington was not sure what to do with Davis. Many high-ranking Confederates had been granted pardons, but Davis refused to ask for one. He wanted to go to trial to prove that secession had been legal, for the legality of secession had not yet been settled in court. The federal government did not want to risk a trial in Virginia to answer this question, fearing that a jury might find for Davis.[16]

In the meantime, Varina was working hard to secure her husband's release from prison. Pressure for his release was also growing from a group of wealthy Northerners, including Cornelius Vanderbilt, who offered to pay Davis's bail. In May 1867, President Andrew Johnson authorized the transfer of Davis from Fort Monroe to the civil authorities to answer charges of treason. When Davis returned to Richmond, he later recalled, "I felt like an unhappy ghost visiting this much beloved city."[17]

As Davis's carriage moved through the streets of Richmond, a cry went up: "Hats off, Virginians!" together with the refrain, "God bless you." The crowd was so large that mounted police had to make room for the carriage. Windows were crowded, and people had climbed on the roofs to see Davis. Every head was bared, and ladies expressed their emotions by shedding tears.[18]

A newspaper reported Davis's appearance upon his return to Richmond: "A full beard and mustache concealed the ravages made by sorrow and suffering." Although his hair was now silvered, his face was bright, and he appeared to be "every inch a king." The man who had fled Richmond two years earlier in disgrace and defeat now returned a hero.[19]

Davis's cause was championed by a group of supporters, none of whom had been secessionists. They were led by newspaperman Horace Greeley, businessman Cornelius Vanderbilt, and a well-known lawyer, Charles O'Conor. With their support, Judge C. Underwood agreed to release the prisoner on $100,000 bail. The bond was signed by Greeley, Vanderbilt, and eight other prominent Northerners and Southerners.[20]

At the judge's order to release Davis, the audience broke forth with applause, the stamping of feet, and shouts from hundreds of throats "making the hall resound." After two years, Jefferson Davis was at last a free man. That evening, he and Varina departed for New York and then Montreal. Davis never again appeared as a prisoner in a court of law, nor would the bond ever be demanded. The case of *United States v. Jefferson Davis* had been, in effect, thrown out of court.[21]

After being released, Davis was taken to the Spotswood Hotel. All along the way, he was saluted with the rebel yell. When his carriage reached the hotel, a silence fell upon the crowd; they seemed too moved to shout. As he left the carriage, a voice from the crowd shouted, "Hats off, Virginians!" "Five thousand uncovered men," wrote an eyewitness, "did homage to him who had suffered for them." In tears, Davis descended the carriage and entered the hotel.[22]

Davis was free now, but he was a man without a country. President

Johnson had denied rights of citizenship to high-ranking Confederates. Neither Davis nor Lee regained his citizenship in his own lifetime; more than a hundred years passed before their civil rights were restored—to Lee in 1976 and to Davis in 1977. After the war, both men had done their part to persuade the South to accept defeat and to support the new Union.[23]

After his release from prison, Davis's personal life was seldom happy. He was almost penniless and with no prospects of employment. His Mississippi plantation had been confiscated by the Freedman's Bureau and given to his ex-slaves; it would be years before it was returned to him.[24]

Disappointment and tragedy followed Davis most of the twenty-two years that remained to him. In poor health, he first traveled to Canada and then to Europe. In the fall of 1870, when Robert E. Lee died, Davis was invited to speak at a memorial service for him in Richmond. The Richmond audience responded to its first glimpse of Davis with a roar of approval, a warm feeling for him that he had never experienced while he was president. The *Richmond Dispatch* reported the occurrence: "As Mr. Davis walked to the stand, every person in the house rose to his feet, and there followed a storm of applause as seemed to shake the very foundation of the building, while cheer upon cheer was echoed from throats of veterans as they saluted one whom they delighted to honor."[25]

Davis spoke of his friendship with Lee and praised his modesty: "I never in my life saw in him the slightest tendency to self-seeking." After a pause, Davis added, "Of the man, how shall I speak. . . . His moral qualities rose to the height of genius." Not even the most fervent members of the Lee Memorial Association could have hoped for a more favorable opening for this movement to honor Lee.[26]

For a while, Davis served as president of the Carolina Life Insurance Company in Memphis, Tennessee. He held the job there until the company went bankrupt during the Panic of 1873. Shortly thereafter, Davis returned to Mississippi and his plantation; it was now overgrown, and his house vandalized by Federal troops. Although his brother Joseph had never transferred the property title to him, the plantation was generally acknowledged as his. Eventually, Davis received ownership of the property, but he soon discovered that the shifting river and chronic flooding had made the plantation unprofitable.[27]

Pride prevented Davis from searching for employment; in a letter to Varina, he wrote: "We can fast, we can toil in secret, but we cannot crawl in public." At this time, Davis was asked to write his memoirs by Appleton & Company, a New York publisher. He viewed this opportunity as a way not only to earn a living but to respond to critics. While writing his memoirs, Davis hoped to find a secluded spot on the Mississippi Gulf Coast.[28]

An opportunity presented itself for just such a location when Sarah Dorsey, an admirer, invited Davis to live at Beauvoir, her estate near Biloxi. She rented a cottage to him at a very nominal sum and served as his secretary as he began to write his memoirs, *The Rise and Fall of the Confederate Government.* In his writings, he attempted to defend the South's right to secede and apologized to no one. Varina was very jealous of Mrs. Dorsey's close association with her husband and, for a long time, refused to set foot on the property. It was not sexual jealousy that upset Varina but rather an intense resentment that another woman had taken her place as his confidante. Mrs. Dorsey eventually sold Davis's residence to him for a modest price and, when she died in 1879, willed him Beauvoir and her entire estate.[29]

The last dozen years of Jefferson Davis's life may have been his happiest. He had always liked Mississippi's Gulf Coast. His home at Beauvoir enabled him to enjoy his remaining years where he found a sense of serenity and peace. Davis proved to be a genial host when old friends, including some Yankees, came to visit him. When he was not writing or entertaining, Davis would sit on the verandah and enjoy the sea breezes. The work on his history of the Confederacy gave him the opportunity to talk to old friends and recall memories. As he continued to write, his book got longer and longer, until it was finally published in two volumes. Initially, *The Rise and Fall of the Confederate Government* did not sell well. Northerners did not care, and Southerners could not afford the high price.[30]

In the spring of 1886, Davis was invited to make a tour of the South. The Davises reached Montgomery at 8:00 p.m. A drizzling rain did not dampen the spirited greetings of the 15,000 people standing in the muddy streets. Cannon, fireworks, and cheers boomed through the night, and a band played "Dixie." Huge banners welcomed "Our Hero."[31] At ceremonies honoring him, Davis spoke briefly, exalting the Confederate dead, "the spirit of Southern liberty," and Southern womanhood. The only expression of discord came when he spoke of the Civil War as "that war which Christianity alone approved—a holy war for defense."[32]

On the morning of April 30, the Davis party left Montgomery for Atlanta. In Atlanta, Davis was cheered by a crowd estimated at 50,000 in number. The *Atlanta Constitution* reported that visitors from Southern and Northern states had arrived for the festivities. Just before Davis spoke, ex-Confederate General James Longstreet suddenly rode up to the speaker's stand. Because Longstreet had suffered charges of deserting the South after the war, he had earned Davis's enmity as well as that of many other Southerners. Longstreet mounted the platform, approached Davis, and the two embraced emotionally.[33]

Davis lived well into his eighty-first year. He continued to make speeches on numerous public occasions. Sometimes conciliatory, he was more often defiant. "Nothing fills me with deeper sadness," he said, "than to see a Southern man apologizing for the defense we made of our inheritance." Long after most prominent ex-Confederates had regained their citizenship, Davis refused even to apply.[34]

On December 6, 1889, Davis died of bronchitis in New Orleans; he had caught a cold when he made his last visit to his beloved Brierfield. His body was laid in state in the city hall, while mourners came from all over the South to pay their final respects. It was believed that at least 50,000 people filed past his flag-draped casket. In May 1893, his body was moved from the grave in New Orleans to Hollywood Cemetery in Richmond.[35]

Despite Davis's unpardonable position on slavery, he possessed some admirable qualities. He was generous to the needy, loyal to his friends, and devoted to his family. His letters to his wife and children are marked by exceptional warmth and tenderness. Unfortunately for him, few people outside his family were aware of these fine features. People were, however, greatly impressed by his appearance, demeanor, and military bearing; Davis never failed to demonstrate dignity, courtesy, poise, and self-assurance. What set him apart from others was the exaggerated degree to which he possessed these characteristics. Where others might be dedicated, he was committed. Where others were enthusiastic, Davis was passionate. Where others were determined, he was resolute.[36]

Few men suffered more than Davis. One of the greatest sorrows of his life was the loss of all four of his sons. He often showed compassion for others, hesitating to inflict pain on them even when the life of the Confederacy depended on it. Few Southerners treated their slaves in such a humane way as Davis, yet he continued to believe that blacks were inferior to whites. Davis was generous in granting accolades to others but more insistent than most men on having the last word in an argument. The man who was selected to lead the Confederacy brought with him the accumulated traits and attitudes of fifty-three years of living in the South. In hindsight, Davis was probably not the right man for the job.[37]

Immediately after the Civil War, Jefferson Davis became the scapegoat for the entire country. In the North, he was blamed for helping to start the war; in the South, for losing it. Unable to blame the brave soldiers or generals like Lee, Southerners pointed their fingers at Davis. By 1880, however, the tide had turned. Southerners closed ranks behind Davis. His imprisonment at Fort Monroe contributed greatly to this change in attitude and helped ensure that he would be remembered as a martyr of what some Southerners referred to as the Lost Cause.[38]

Jefferson Davis remained a diehard Confederate to the end. Although finally accepting the reality of the Union, he never apologized for either secession or slavery. Just before his death he said, "Were the thing to be done over again, I would do as I then did. Disappointments have not changed my conviction."[39]

4   P. G. T. Beauregard

"Napoleon in Gray"

When Beauregard learned his state of Louisiana had seceded from the Union, he returned home, resigned his commission from the Federal army, and offered his service to the Confederacy. Recently elected President Davis quickly summoned him to Montgomery, Alabama, the Confederate provisional capital, and appointed him brigadier general.[1]

Little did he realize that his military career would be unique in the Confederate army. It was not limited to one theater of the war as was Robert E. Lee's or interrupted by periods of inactivity due to wounds as Joseph Johnston's; nor was his career cut short as with "Stonewall" Jackson. Beauregard was present in every important phase of the war. He fired the opening shot of the war at Fort Sumter, commanded forces at the first major battle of the war at Manassas, and served in the West, planning and fighting the Battle of Shiloh. Later he was assigned to Charleston to construct a defense against an attack from the sea. In 1864, he returned to Virginia to direct the defense of Richmond and, in the closing months of the war, joined Joseph Johnston in Georgia and the Carolinas to fight Sherman.[2]

Beauregard's first assignment was to the Charleston, South Carolina, harbor where the presence of Federal troops at Fort Sumter threatened the delicate peace. The Confederates held all points in and around the harbor except Sumter. Beauregard's job was to prevent the federal government from reinforcing and supplying the fort by sea. On March 6, when he assumed command, Beauregard immediately, but tactfully, began to rearrange the batteries set up by the Carolinians. As he performed this task, the Charlestonians, who were not accustomed to taking orders from outsiders, carefully scrutinized his efforts. Beauregard's appearance and military bearing quickly won the citizens of Charleston over to him.[3]

Now approaching forty-three years of age, Beauregard was quickly accepted into Charleston's aristocracy, and as one member put it, "Beauregard is a demigod here to most of the natives." Beauregard's good looks and physical characteristics made him stand out. Although a small man, only five feet, seven inches in height, he was quite muscular and proud of his physical strength. His olive complexion, carefully groomed mustache, and protruding chin made his face, in one officer's view, "that of a French marshal of the empire." In his new, tailored gray uniform, Beauregard stood out among other Southerners in Charleston.[4]

On March 11, Beauregard sent three of his aides to Sumter with a written demand to surrender the fort. After consulting with his officers, Major Anderson rejected the demand. With Anderson's refusal to abandon the fort, President Davis ordered Beauregard forcibly to take it. Although he had no qualms about carrying out the order, there was just one aspect of the assignment that troubled him—the fact that his adversary was Major Robert Anderson, his former artillery instructor, a friend, and a man he respected.[5]

When Anderson refused the last demand to surrender, Beauregard ordered a bombardment of the fort. On April 12, 1861, the first round landed on the parade ground of the brick fortification. For thirty-four hours, the shelling continued; finally, Anderson realized that he would not be relieved and was forced to strike the colors. Miraculously, only one Union soldier was killed in the brief affair—a victim of the accidental explosion of a gun during the firing of a salute after the surrender.[6] Beauregard's capture of Fort Sumter made him an instant Confederate hero. The press described him as one of the greatest soldiers in the world. President Davis praised Beauregard, saying that he "has reduced Sumter with skill to be expected of one with his reputation."[7]

The man lauded by the South was born on May 28, 1818, the third child of five children, into the Creole aristocracy of Louisiana. His father, Jacques, married a de Reggio; both sides proudly traced their family tree to French nobility. They named their son Pierre Gustave Toutant in honor of their heritage.[8]

Young Pierre grew up speaking French in an environment that was a combination of the Old South, with its plantations, and the European style of France. Because Pierre's parents intended him to be a Frenchman, he could not speak English until he was twelve years old. Young Beauregard attended a French-speaking private school until he was eleven years old. Then he was shipped off to New York City to attend a college preparatory school operated by two of Napoleon's former officers. It was under their influence that Pierre developed a desire to pursue a military career.[9] His parents were surprised and shocked when they learned of their son's desire to enter West Point. They objected loudly, but Pierre stood his ground, a trait he would demonstrate throughout his life, never yielding on an issue

General P. G. T. Beauregard had the most unique military career in the Confederate army. He was present at every important phase of the war. He fired the opening shot of the war at Fort Sumter, commanded forces at the first major battle at Manassas, and served in the West, planning and fighting the Battle of Shiloh. Later, he defended Charleston and, in the closing months of the war, joined Joseph Johnston to fight Sherman.

COURTESY OF THE LIBRARY OF CONGRESS

of judgment. In the end, the family gave in to his stubbornness and used their influence to secure an appointment for him.[10]

In March 1834, Beauregard was appointed to West Point. At the age of sixteen, he was one of the youngest to be admitted. Quickly he made friends, including a number of cadets who would gain fame during the Civil War. Among those were Jubal Early, Richard Ewell, Braxton Bragg, and Union generals Irvin McDowell, Joseph Hooker, and William T. Sherman. While at West Point, he decided that his name sounded too Gallic, and for a while he simply called himself Gustave. Later, he decided to use just his initials, P. G. T., a form he insisted upon for the rest of his life.[11]

Although friendly as a cadet, Beauregard was reserved and withdrawn by nature. Very few at the Academy really got to know him well. In later years, when his classmates tried to recall what he was like, they could only remember that he excelled in sports and horsemanship and did well academically. It was rumored that he had a tragic love affair with the daughter of Winfield Scott, one of the senior generals of the army. As the story goes, he and Virginia Scott became engaged, but her parents insisted they were too young to marry. The two separated but continued to write each other, but neither received the other's letters. Years later, Beauregard learned that Virginia's mother had intercepted his letters. Beauregard, embittered when he did not hear from his love, soon married another woman.[12]

Graduating second in his class, Beauregard's class rank entitled him to choose the branch of service he desired. The most ambitious young officers picked the Corps of Engineers, as did Beauregard; he was sent to Newport, Rhode Island, to work on the completion of the construction of Fort Adams, the second largest fort in the country. The fact that a newly commissioned second lieutenant would receive such an important assignment is an indication of the confidence his superiors had in his ability.[13]

In 1839, Beauregard, now a first lieutenant, was transferred to Pensacola, Florida, to construct coastal defenses. By the late summer of 1844, he was ordered to Fort McHenry at Baltimore. His experience there was a pleasant one, providing him with ample opportunities to be a part of the social scene in Baltimore. For many officers, the parties and balls were the high point of their army careers.[14]

In February 1845, Beauregard was back in Louisiana working on the forts around the Mississippi. It was here that he displayed a side of his personality that would emerge throughout his life. When another lieutenant, John Henshaw, and he became engaged in a war of words, the angry Beauregard challenged Henshaw to a duel. In April, friends of the two officers arranged for them to meet; the duel was to be with shotguns. Just before they were ready to blast away at each other, the event was broken up by a sheriff who arrested them both. The affair revealed Beauregard's preoccupation with his honor, considering criticism or opposition a negative reflection on him. He was always ready to defend his honor and challenge the offender to make good on his words.[15]

When the war with Mexico erupted in 1846, Beauregard found himself a member of an outstanding company of engineers serving under Major General Winfield Scott. Working under Captain Robert E. Lee and with Lieutenant George B. McClellan, he helped clear the way to Mexico City. He was given credit for developing the plan successfully adopted by Scott to reach the Mexican capital. A grateful Scott acknowledged Beauregard's help: "Young man if I were not on horseback I would embrace you."[16]

Twice wounded in Mexico, Beauregard was awarded two brevet promotions in rank, honors given as reward for gallantry or outstanding leadership.

But Beauregard thought he deserved even greater recognition for his efforts and began a campaign to see that he got them. For years afterward, he spent time campaigning for the honor he believed he deserved.[17]

With the end of the war, Beauregard returned to Louisiana and his career in engineering. In 1850, his wife of nine years died following the birth of their third child. He remarried another member of Louisiana's social elite, Caroline Deslonde, but the match was more a matter of political advantage than passion.[18] Beauregard's wife was related to U.S. Senator John Slidell. With the senator's help, Beauregard briefly entered politics, supporting Democratic candidate Franklin Pierce in the 1852 presidential election. In 1858, he himself ran for mayor of New Orleans but was defeated.[19]

Although Beauregard did not take an active part in the 1860 election, he made no secret of his sympathies with the South. In January 1861, despite his political views, Beauregard was appointed superintendent of the Academy at West Point. It seemed incredible, with the political situation being as it was, that he even considered going to West Point or that the government would let him hold the office. Beauregard, now a major, knew that Louisiana was close to seceding, and when it did, he would go with it. Nevertheless, he reported to West Point on January 23, 1861, to assume the new post. When Southern cadets asked him for advice about when to drop out of school to return home for the coming fight, his response was, "Watch me, and when I jump, you jump. What's the use of jumping too soon?"[20]

Beauregard never got the chance to jump. After five days, the appointment was rescinded, setting a record for the briefest tenure on record for a superintendent at West Point. Because of the "secession crisis," all Southerners in government service were suspected of turning men or materials over to the Confederacy. Beauregard was greatly offended that he would be suspected of disloyalty while still wearing the uniform of the U.S. Army. Again, his sense of honor came to the foreground, and he wrote, "so long as I remain in the service . . . I shall be most scrupulous in the performance of all my obligations to the Government."[21]

Although distressed at the aspersions cast on his integrity, Beauregard turned the command over to his replacement. When he attempted to claim a mileage payment of $165 from the government for his return trip from West Point to New Orleans, it was refused. Beauregard persisted in his request. Even after resigning from the army to accept a position in the Confederate army, he pressed Washington for his claim.[22]

Several weeks after returning to Louisiana, Beauregard resigned his commission and offered his service to the Confederacy. Jefferson Davis quickly invited him to Montgomery and appointed him a brigadier general, an extraordinary increase in rank for an officer who had only been a major in the U.S. Army.[23] Beauregard's first assignment was to Charleston, South Carolina. He arrived to a tumultuous welcome; Charleston was the center of secession, and its citizens were eagerly awaiting the war. Beauregard was charmed by the city and its people, finding it much like New Orleans. He felt right at home.

Beauregard's first responsibility as a Confederate was to capture Fort Sumter in the Charleston Harbor. When Union commander Major Anderson refused to give up, Beauregard began his bombardment of the fort. When no reinforcements came, Anderson surrendered. The news of Fort Sumter's fall inflamed the North but made Beauregard an instant hero in the South. Fort Sumter became a rallying cry for the North. Lincoln immediately called for 75,000 volunteers to join the Union cause. His call for volunteers drove four more Southern states from the Union, bringing the Confederacy to a total of eleven states.[24]

Proclaimed the "hero of Sumter," Beauregard was summoned to Richmond, the new Confederate capital, and placed in charge of one of the two forces preparing to repel an expected invasion of northern Virginia. After inspecting the 6,000 troops gathered at the rail junction at Manassas, he realized this was not enough to stop a Federal invasion. He tried to alert Virginians of the impending crisis. "A restless and unprincipled tyrant has invaded your soil," his warning began. "Abraham Lincoln, regardless of all moral, legal, and constitutional restraints, has thrown his abolition hosts among you, who are murdering and imprisoning your citizens, confiscating, and destroying your property and committing other acts of violence and outrage too shocking and revolting to humanity to be enumerated. All rules of civilized warfare are abandoned, and they proclaim by their acts, if not on their banners, that their war cry is 'Beauty and booty'."[25]

By early July 1861, the Confederate force had grown to 23,000 men. In the meantime, a Federal army, greatly outnumbering Beauregard's army, was gathering in Washington in preparation for an attack on Richmond. The Union army—all recruits—was under the command of Major General Irvin McDowell.[26]

On the morning of July 21, McDowell's army of 37,000 attacked the Confederate left flank across Bull Run, five miles northwest of Manassas Junction. General Joseph E. Johnston, who slipped away from the Shenandoah Valley, joined Beauregard at Manassas. Johnston was actually the senior officer, but when the two armies combined, Johnston deferred to Beauregard on the grounds that he was unfamiliar with the area and that Beauregard already had a plan in place.[27]

With the arrival of Johnston, Confederate forces had grown to 35,000. The battle was small compared to later Civil War standards and confusing for both sides. It involved two undisciplined, inexperienced armies, with units operating virtually out of control of their commanding officers.[28] All morning long, the Confederate left flank bore the brunt of the Union assault and, by midday, was giving ground to superior numbers. McDowell, feeling that victory was now his, ordered a general advance on Henry Hill.

At a critical time in the battle, General Barnard Bee pointed to General Thomas Jackson's brigade and cried out to his men, "There stands Jackson like a stonewall." Bee's comment rallied his men and gave Jackson and his brigade the war's most famous name. The Confederate line held and soon took the offensive.

The Union army began a retreat that quickly turned into a rout. Parties of civilians who had traveled out of Washington to watch the Union victory were caught in the stampede of fleeing troops. By late afternoon, Beauregard and Johnston had the enemy on the run, but they elected not to pursue them. When Jefferson Davis reached the field, he concurred with their decision not to press their advantage.

Although the battle had been chaotic, the result was what mattered. Beauregard, who had had a horse killed under him while leading his wing of the army, was again singled out as the hero. Exuberant over the victory, President Davis promoted Beauregard to the rank of full general. Beauregard was now the most popular general in the South, proclaimed even a greater hero than he had been after Fort Sumter.[29]

Soon after the battle, Beauregard's name was mentioned as a rival for the presidency in the November 1861 election. Although Beauregard disavowed these statements, they continued to find their way into the newspapers. As a result, Davis became suspicious of him, believing he was out to get his job. This was the beginning of a feud between the two.[30] Beauregard reported that he was not getting the supplies he needed, blaming it on Davis's jealousy. In turn, Davis complained that Beauregard had missed the opportunity to follow up his victory at Manassas. To the embarrassment of the Confederate government, Beauregard responded by blaming it for his inaction. He was quoted as saying that "the want of food and transportation has made us lose the fruits of victory."[31]

The damage was done. The unforgiving Davis terminated Beauregard's command in January 1862 and sent him to the West to serve under General Albert Sidney Johnston. In just six months, Beauregard's star had taken a sudden descent, but to his credit, he took up his new assignment in Tennessee with enthusiasm.[32] Johnston was glad to see Beauregard when he arrived. In February, Union Major General Ulysses S. Grant captured Forts Henry and Donelson, forcing Johnston to retreat into Alabama. Beauregard made his headquarters at Corinth, Mississippi, and encouraged Johnston to concentrate his army there too. When he did, he offered Beauregard command of the 40,000-man army to move against Grant. Beauregard declined the honor, claiming the troops would have more confidence in Johnston since he had been their original leader.[33]

With Johnston's approval, Beauregard drew up plans to reorganize the army. In the new organization, Johnston was designated commander, Beauregard as second in command, and Braxton Bragg, chief-of-staff. Just as Joseph Johnston had deferred to Beauregard to draw up the plans for

Manassas, Albert S. Johnston did the same, allowing him to plan for the Battle of Shiloh.

On April 3, Johnston's army left Corinth, intending to make a one-day march and quickly strike Grant before Major General Buell's troops could reinforce him. But poor organization and management and heavy rains delayed his movement. Beauregard believed that all hope for surprising Grant had been lost and urged Johnston to return to Corinth. Nevertheless, Johnston insisted that the attack must be made, saying, "I would fight them if they were a million."[34]

On Sunday morning, April 6, Confederate troops attacked the Union right flank near a small log church named Shiloh. Methodically, they pushed the enemy back until they struck the Union center; there they encountered stiff resistance. Finally, the Union line stabilized their position at what came to be called the "Hornets' Nest." Confederate assault after assault failed as they continued to storm this seemingly impregnable stronghold.[35] In the afternoon, General Johnston was fatally wounded during the attack. A stray bullet struck his leg, severing the popliteal artery, and he quickly bled to death. Beauregard assumed command and continued the attack on the "Hornet's Nest." The prolonged Union defense gave Grant the time he needed to move up reinforcements. At dusk, Beauregard suspended the attack to allow his men to rest, hoping to renew it in the morning.[36]

During the night, Grant's forces were bolstered by Major General Lew Wallace's division and Major General Don Carlos Buell's army. In the morning, Grant assumed the offensive, and by late afternoon, Beauregard was forced to order a full retreat to Corinth. Grant elected to rest his troops rather than pursue the enemy. The Battle of Shiloh had been a costly one for both sides. It was the first of the great bloody battles of the war; Union losses were in excess of 13,000, whereas Beauregard's army suffered nearly 11,000 casualties.[37]

After the battle, Major General Henry Halleck, commander of the Western forces, took control of the Union army, reorganizing it with Grant as his second in command. By the end of April, Halleck had assembled an army of 120,000 men. Beauregard realized the importance of holding Corinth, but with a force only half that of Halleck, he knew he could not withstand a prolonged siege. To withdraw from Corinth without alerting the enemy, he sent out "deserters" who were to get themselves captured and, by the use of misinformation, fool Halleck into thinking Beauregard was going to attack. In the meantime, Beauregard fooled Halleck into believing he was being reinforced, when in reality he was withdrawing his troops to the safety of Tupelo. By the time Halleck discovered what had happened, Beauregard had left the Union forces to occupy a deserted town.[38]

Beauregard's withdrawal from Corinth brought criticism and ridicule from the Southern press and the Confederate government. They lashed out at him for not capitalizing on the early gains he had made at Shiloh and for not engaging the timid Henry Halleck at Corinth. President Davis had emphasized the importance of holding Corinth, but now Beauregard had abandoned the city without a fight. At first Beauregard made no ex-cuse at all. When the president placed pressure on him, he responded in a letter, saying the retreat had been "most brilliant and successful." In a letter to a newspaper in Mobile, Alabama, Beauregard stated, "The retreat must be looked upon, in every respect, by the country as equivalent to a brilliant victory."[39]

President Davis did not see it that way and was beginning to doubt his decision to send Beauregard west. In a letter to his wife, Davis confided, "I fear he has been placed too high for his mental strength, as he does not exhibit the ability manifested on smaller fields. . . . We must make a desper-ate effort to regain what Beauregard had abandoned in the West."[40]

The opportunity for Davis to remove Beauregard came sooner than he had anticipated. The arduous campaign had weakened Beauregard's body. Never a man with a strong constitution, Beauregard had suffered for months with laryngitis and respiratory problems. Temporarily turning the army over to Braxton Bragg in mid-June and without requesting permis-sion, Beauregard took leave to attend the popular resort of Blanndon Springs north of Mobile.[41]

When Davis learned of Beauregard's absence, he was beside himself; he looked upon Beauregard as having "abandoned" his post. The president immediately removed him from command, replacing him with General Bragg. When Bragg learned of Davis's decision, he telegraphed Beaure-gard: "I have a dispatch from the President direct to relieve you perma-nently of command of this department. I envy you and am almost in de-spair." Bragg expressed his sympathy over what had happened and later stated that Beauregard had only sought "relief from the toils which have made him an old man in the short space of one year."[42] Beauregard was furious about being replaced. In a letter to a friend, he referred to Davis as "demented or a traitor to his high trust." He was angry with himself, as well, for having given Davis an excuse for relieving him from command.[43]

Beauregard spent the rest of the summer in Mobile, where he was wined and dined by the residents and where he answered letters from sympathiz-ers. In one letter denouncing Davis, he wrote: "My consolation is, that the difference between 'that individual' [Davis] and myself is—that, if he were to die today, the whole country would rejoice at it, whereas, I believe, if the same thing were to happen to me, they would regret it."[44]

When Beauregard was well enough to return to duty, he was assigned as head of the Department of South Carolina, with headquarters at Charles-ton. Beauregard hoped to use his political connections to regain his position as commander in the West. His brother-in-law, Congressman C. J. Villere, cir-culated a petition calling for Beauregard's restoration to Western command

and was able to garner the signatures of fifty-nine congressmen. Davis's reaction to the petition was not what Beauregard had hoped for: "If the whole world were to ask me to restore General Beauregard to the command which I have already given to General Bragg, I would refuse it."[45]

Beauregard would remain in Charleston for eighteen months; it was the most effective tour of duty of his career. By using his engineering skill and ability to maneuver troops into position, he was able successfully to resist Union assaults by both land and sea. For his efforts, he received more credit in the Northern press than he did at home. An editorial on April 24, 1863, proclaimed Beauregard's talent: "Truly he is boastful, egotistical, untruthful, and wanting in tact, but he is certainly the most marvelous engineer of modern times. By his genius and professional skill, he has erected batteries in Charleston Harbor that would sink all the wooden fleets of the world did they come under fire, and he has succeeded, moreover, in driving back in disgrace the most impenetrable ironclad fleet afloat. There is no denying what the man has done, unpalatable though it may be to the Northern people."[46]

For his efforts in defending the Southern coast, Beauregard was given a commendation by Congress. When Davis visited Charleston in October, he barely mentioned Beauregard and completely ignored his presence. Although Beauregard's efforts had been recognized by the Confederate Congress and admired by the people of Charleston, he was not happy there. He longed for an assignment with more action. Given to dark moods, his energy waned, and he suffered from melancholia. Placing the blame for his mental condition on the president, Beauregard told a friend that Davis had "done more than if he had thrust a fratricidal dagger into my heart! He has killed my enthusiasm in our holy cause."[47]

On March 2, 1864, when his second wife died in Federal-occupied New Orleans, Beauregard fell further into depression. "My poor Carolyn must have often asked herself on her bed of pain if she would ever see me again," Beauregard said. General Nathaniel Banks, the Federal commander in New Orleans, provided a steamer to carry her body upriver for burial in her home parish of St. John the Baptist.[48]

As the spring of 1864 began, Beauregard's star was once again on the rise. A Richmond paper pointed out that Beauregard was the only Confederate general to come out of 1863 with a winning record and implored the president to restore him to command in the West. Even Vice President Alexander Stephens spoke out against Davis's treatment of the able defender of Charleston.[49] As early as the fall of 1863, after the Confederate defeat at Chattanooga, Tennessee, when Bragg asked to be relieved, Bragg had recommended Beauregard as his successor. Still later, when General John Bell Hood lost Atlanta, it was rumored that Beauregard would be appointed to replace him. The *Richmond Whig* wrote, "Would that this were true! . . . His appointment would be worth 10,000 men. We entreat that Davis show his magnanimity by placing him in command."[50]

Finally in April 1864, Beauregard received a telegram from the War Department asking if he would be willing to join General Robert E. Lee in his defense of Petersburg and Richmond. He jumped at the chance, replying that he was "ready to obey any order for the good of the service." He then received orders to proceed to Weldon, North Carolina, near the Virginia border.[51] Beauregard was immediately thrust into the crisis. Lee was engaged with Lieutenant General Ulysses Grant in front of Petersburg, and a new Federal force under Major General Benjamin Butler was threatening Richmond. Butler, with an army of 40,000 men, was moving up the Bermuda Hundred, the neck of land between the James and Appomattox rivers. Beauregard's assignment was to block Butler's path and prevent him from cutting off the railroad to Richmond.[52] Instead of advancing with his superior numbers, Butler cautiously chose to entrench his army before moving forward. After carefully examining the terrain, Beauregard was able to bottle up Butler by setting up a line at the narrow neck. When Butler finally did attack Beauregard, he was repulsed by heavy losses. Grant sarcastically referred to Butler's situation as being "bottled up" on the peninsula.[53]

In June, when Grant slipped away from Lee and threatened Petersburg, Beauregard came to the rescue. Moving some of his troops from the Bermuda Hundred line, he was able to block Grant's advance until Lee could arrive and take over the defense. A grateful Lee complimented Beauregard for his placement of troops and thanked him for his initiative.[54]

In October, Beauregard's divisions were combined with Lee's Army of Northern Virginia, and he was placed in charge of the Military Division of the West, a position he had lost to Bragg two years earlier. Although Bragg was given the title, Davis placed certain limitations on his control. Seemingly in charge of General Hood and Lieutenant General Richard Taylor, Beauregard was given to understand that he was not to interfere with the operations except in a crisis; he was to act as an advisor and not a real commander. A similar arrangement had been tried earlier when Joseph Johnston held a comparable position, but it had proven to be an ineffective method of command. It was a position designed for failure.[55]

The new assignment took Beauregard to Georgia, where Major General Sherman was engaged in his famous "March to the Sea." Beauregard supported Hood's strategy of taking the fight to the enemy, hoping to strike him while his army was scattered and slow his advance in Georgia. But Beauregard was not the field commander and could not control Hood's tactics, nor did he employ the rash, suicidal assaults that followed. The Confederate disasters at Franklin and Nashville left a dazed and demoralized army. Beauregard described the army as "a disorganized mob."[56]

Although Beauregard had not carried out the plan, he was not entirely guiltless; he had approved it, failing to recognize that neither Hood nor his army would be able to carry out the plan. In February, when Hood resigned, Beauregard recommended that Joseph Johnston be recalled to take control of the scattered army. Before accepting the position, Johnston went to see Beauregard to ask him if he would be willing to serve under him. In defense of the cause, Beauregard said, he would be happy to work with Johnston, but below the surface, he was hurt. It seemed that he was destined to be second in command.[57]

The change in command did not change the military situation. By April 2, 1865, Richmond and Petersburg fell. While Lee's army retreated toward the west, Davis and his cabinet headed south to join what was left of Johnston's army. On April 11, Davis reached Greensboro, North Carolina, where Beauregard joined him. Beauregard was surprised to learn that the president still believed the war could continue, even though Lee's army had surrendered and Johnston's army was on the verge of doing the same.[58]

Johnston arrived the next morning. Shortly afterward, Beauregard and Johnston met with Davis and several cabinet members. The president proposed raising a large army by rounding up deserters and conscription enrolled men on draft lists. Both generals agreed that men who had deserted or avoided the army when the situation had been less critical would not fight now. Davis said he would delay his decision until Secretary of War Breckinridge arrived from Virginia.[59]

When Breckinridge arrived, the three generals talked together, agreeing that the "Cause" was lost and that the only recourse was to make peace. When the generals met with Davis again, he had not changed his mind, still believing they could whip the enemy. But Johnston strongly disagreed: "My views are, sir, that our people are tired of the war, feel themselves whipped and will not fight. . . . We cannot place another army in the field." After a long silence, Davis asked Beauregard what he thought. "I concur in all that General Johnston has said," he replied. On April 26, 1865, Johnston formally surrendered his army to Major General Sherman.[60]

After the surrender, Beauregard prepared to leave for home. In a farewell note to his staff, he said: "The day was, when I was confident that this parting would be under far different and the most auspicious circumstances—at a moment when a happy and independent people would be ready . . . to welcome you to your respective communities—but circumstances, which neither the courage, the endurance, nor the patriotism of our armies could overcome, have turned my brightest anticipations, my highest hopes, into bitter disappointment, in which you must all share."[61]

Beauregard returned to an empty house in New Orleans with only one silver dollar to his name, the mustering-out pay he received from the Confederate treasury. When he was offered a position with the Brazilian government, he declined, saying, "I prefer to live here, poor and forgotten, than to be endowed with honor and riches in a foreign country."[62]

Later, Beauregard took a position as president of the New Orleans, Jackson & Mississippi Railroad, which he held for five years. He was then named president of the Louisiana Lottery, a position that brought him criticism for the abuses and corruption that were uncovered in its operation.[63]

Beauregard participated in Confederate veteran affairs. When General Hood and his wife died in 1879, leaving ten surviving children, he arranged to have the general's memoirs published and the proceeds from its sale given to the support of his children. When Beauregard decided to have his own story told, he employed his former aide and inspector general, Alfred Roman. The result was a large, two-volume work that was highly complimentary to his military service.[64]

Beauregard died on February 20, 1893, in New Orleans at the age of seventy-five. Condolences and resolutions came from all over the South. His body lay in state at the city hall so his many friends and admirers could pay their last respects. On the afternoon of the twenty-third, his body was moved to the tomb of the Army of Tennessee in Metairie Cemetery.[65]

Beauregard was one of the most colorful of all the Confederate generals. His military career was marked by controversy, conflict, and fame. "As a military leader," Civil War historian R. M. Johnston wrote, Beauregard was "strong in fortifications and of unquestionable courage, but weak in strategy and wanting in coolness, insight, and method on the battlefield. His dispatches lack clearness and at times candor, while rhetoric is a pitfall he rarely resists."[66] Yet, Southerners idolized him, making him into a popular hero.

5   Joseph E. Johnston

"Retreatin' Johnston"

When the Civil War began in 1861, Joseph E. Johnston was a brigadier general in the U.S. Army, serving as quartermaster general. Johnston sadly resigned and offered his services to the Confederacy. When President Davis learned of his availability, he made him a brigadier general in the Confederate army (the highest rank possible by law at the time). As it turned out, Johnston was the only general in the United States to resign his commission and go South. Even his friend and West Point classmate, Robert E. Lee, was still a colonel.[1]

Johnston's first assignment was the command of troops gathering at Harper's Ferry, Virginia. Later, he moved his men east by rail to join General Beauregard at Manassas Junction, arriving in time to swing the battle in favor of the Confederates. By then, the Confederate Congress had created the rank of full general, and Davis quickly elevated Johnston to that position. After the Confederate victory at Manassas, the rest of the summer passed quietly. Johnston refused to go on the offensive until his army was ready for the task, but Davis did not press him to move, and the correspondence between the two remained cordial, even friendly.[2]

Then in the fall of 1861, Davis announced the names of the five men in order of rank who were to be confirmed as full generals in the Confederate army. Johnston was listed fourth behind Samuel Cooper, Albert Sidney Johnston, and Robert E. Lee. Davis had ranked the officers by their seniority within the branch of service in which they were presently serving. Although Johnston had held the rank of brigadier general in the U.S. Army, he was serving as the army's quartermaster and had never held that rank as an infantry officer. In that capacity, he was outranked by Cooper, A. S. Johnston, and Lee. Nevertheless, Johnston believed that method of ranking to be unfair. Since Johnston outranked the three in the regular army, he believed he should outrank them in the Confederate army.[3]

When Johnston complained to the president, Davis was angry with his impertinence. Johnston's letter of complaint marked the beginning of the breakdown in their working relationship. There was never again the kind of rapport between the two necessary for the commander-in-chief and a field commander. Other controversies between the two would develop as the war progressed.[4]

Johnston was the first graduate in the history of West Point to be promoted to the rank of general in the regular army. He was the only general to command both of the Confederacy's principal field armies—the Army of Northern Virginia in 1861–1862 and the Army of Tennessee in 1864. He was the ranking officer at the South's first victory at Manassas in July 1861, and its last, at Bentonville, North Carolina, in April 1865. Many of his contemporaries considered him to be the greatest Southern field commander of the war; others ranked him second only to Robert E. Lee. Both Ulysses S. Grant and William T. Sherman considered him the most skillful opponent they faced during the war. Yet, of all the generals who commanded major Confederate armies, Joseph E. Johnston remains one of the most ambiguous and controversial.[5]

Johnston's military career aroused debate even before the war was over. His supporters contended that he possessed the strategic and tactical ability necessary to be a successful field commander. His critics argued that he was more like a Confederate George McClellan—excellent at organizing, supplying, and raising the morale of an army but unwilling to fight on the offensive.[6]

Joseph Johnston was "Old Virginia," with a family tree of which he could be proud. His father, Peter, had fought in the Revolutionary War under the command of General Richard Henry "Light-Horse Harry" Lee. In the early 1800s, he became a judge, settling at Abingdon in southwest Virginia. Joseph's mother was Mary Valentine Wood, the niece of Patrick Henry. The couple's first child died in infancy, but then they were blessed with a succession of healthy children, all of them boys. Their seventh child, born on February 3, 1807, was christened Joseph Eggleston in honor of the man who had been Peter's squad commander during the war.

Young Joseph enjoyed playing typical games around the countryside like other boys his age. His father was an ardent hunter, and his sons naturally followed his interest. A number of veterans of the Revolution lived in the area, and their stories of adventure excited the Johnston boys. They organized themselves into armies, emulating their heroes, and Joseph was one of the leaders. Joseph became a fine horseman and a good marksman. These outdoor experiences contributed to a hardy constitution that helped him withstand the rigors of military campaigns and recover from a number of wounds he would receive as a soldier.[7]

After the Civil War, Joseph E. Johnston sought to
clear his reputation, trying to build a case against
Hood and Davis. Although advised not to pursue
his feud with Davis, Johnston persisted.

Joseph's parents were interested in seeing that their children were well
educated. Mrs. Johnston was a cultured woman, capable of instructing her
children in the classics and inspiring them with a love of reading and learning. On cold nights, the family would gather around the fire and listen to
one of the older boys read. It was then that Joseph was first introduced
to the novels of Sir Walter Scott; he would retain an affection for Scott's
writing throughout his life.[8]

Joseph's first formal education was at the Abingdon Academy founded
by his father. Although he showed an interest in the classics, his inclination
continued to be toward the military. Noticing this, his father gave him
the sword he had carried through the Revolution. Joseph would cherish the
sword as one of his prized possessions. Through a political friend, Joseph's
father was able to secure an appointment to West Point for him in 1825.

Among the new cadets from Virginia, along with Joseph, was Robert E. Lee, the son of Judge Johnston's Revolutionary War leader.[9]

Johnston and Lee quickly became good friends. Years later, Johnston wrote of Lee: "We had the same intimate associates, who thought, as I did, that no other youth or man so united the qualities that win warm friendship and command high respect. For he was full of sympathy and kindness, genial and fond of gay conversation, and even of fun, that made him the most agreeable of companions."[10]

Although Cadet Johnston was eager to be successful at West Point, he had to overcome one major handicap to maintain his scholastic average. For a time, he suffered from retinitis pigmentosa, a hereditary and degenerative disease that causes night blindness, which made it difficult to study in the evening. He did not, however, allow this ailment to hinder his early interest in books. Johnston was a good student, better than average, and his steady improvement over four years indicated that he was serious about his studies. Johnston received his highest grade at West Point in conduct, a category that included military bearing and behavior and was achieved by avoiding the kind of violations that earned demerits.[11]

Johnston's four years at West Point were a success. He earned few demerits, passed all his exams comfortably, and had the opportunity to exercise leadership. Graduating in 1829 and finishing thirteenth out of a class of forty-six, he was commissioned a second lieutenant in the artillery.

In 1830, the regular army had only four regiments of artillery, whose principal job was to man the guns of the coastal defense forts. As a second lieutenant in Company C of the Fourth U.S. Artillery, Johnston's duty was to serve as part of the garrison of Fort Columbus on Governor's Island in New York Harbor. In late 1831, his two-year stay there ended when his company was transferred to Fort Monroe in southeastern Virginia. In August, a slave named Nat Turner led a revolt that spread from plantation to plantation across the county, resulting in sixty whites and scores of blacks dead; it was every slaveholder's nightmare. When a request for military protection came, Johnston's company was sent to reinforce Fort Monroe.[12] By the time Johnston arrived in Virginia, the crisis had ended. Turner had been captured and executed, but the planters still feared other insurrections. Like most well-to-do plantation owners, his family owned slaves, but Johnston claimed that he had regarded slavery as a moral and political evil since boyhood.[13]

Johnston found his assignment at Fort Monroe one of the most pleasant he experienced in the military. There he met up with his old friend Robert E. Lee. Although the two were unusual in their temperance in both sex and drink, they thoroughly enjoyed the friendship of fellow officers who were not as inhibited.[14]

In May 1832, Chief Black Hawk of the Sac Indians violated what he viewed as an unfair treaty by returning across the Mississippi River to his tribe's ancestral hunting ground in Illinois. The local militia forces were unable to locate and capture the renegade chief and his followers. President Andrew Jackson ordered General Winfield Scott to raise an army of regulars to go to Illinois, capture him, and send him back across the Mississippi.[15]

Johnston participated in the Black Hawk War and quickly learned that war was not all heroics and glamour. After four-and-a-half months in the field, he returned to Fort Monroe. Although Johnston had traveled 2,000 miles and half his command had died from cholera, he had never faced or fired a shot at the enemy. Before Scott's army could catch up with Black Hawk's band, it had been annihilated in the Battle of Bad Axe. Johnston's experience during the Black Hawk War could hardly have appealed to his sense of glory.[16]

Johnston had to wait four years before he saw action under hostile fire. This time he had been sent to Florida to serve on General Scott's staff as he battled the Seminole Indians. Johnston welcomed the assignment as an opportunity to see action and to gain advancement. Given his unsuccessful campaign against the Seminoles, Scott failed to satisfy his civilian superiors and was forced to face a court of inquiry. Although Johnston's career was not damaged, the experience taught him that military service was not free from politics. Scott was replaced, and his successor accomplished what he had not. During the campaign, Johnston had a close call while on a surveying party. When his party came under fire, a bullet creased his scalp. The wound left its mark and was clearly evident in later years when his hair began to recede.[17]

With the signing of a peace treaty in 1837, Johnston resigned from the army with the intention of becoming an engineer. The low pay of an army officer played a major role in Johnston's leaving the army. In the 1830s, a second lieutenant earned less than $800 a year, while an engineer could command as much as five times that amount in the civilian world. Only five months later, war resumed again with the Seminoles, and Johnston volunteered to serve in a civilian capacity. In January 1838, he was caught in an ambush and took command when all the military leaders were wounded. "The coolness, courage, and judgment he displayed at the most critical and trying emergency was the theme of praise with everyone who beheld him," a companion later reported.[18]

The war in Florida continued for several more years until, one by one, small bands of Seminoles surrendered and were moved to the trans-Mississippi West. In April 1838, Johnston left the war behind and returned to the army as a first lieutenant in the newly formed Corps of Topographical Engineers. In the same month, he was breveted to captain for his gallantry during the recent Everglades expedition. Johnston's brief civilian career had convinced him that his proper destiny was in the military after all.[19]

When Johnston returned to the army, he was thirty-one years old and still single. When his brother Charles died in 1832, his two children were left without parents. Johnston adopted his twelve-year-old nephew, Preston.

He asked Preston "to regard [him] not as a formal old uncle, but as a brother." Their association became close, Johnston writing that his feelings were both "fatherly and brotherly." He took a father's pride in Preston's achievements and later encouraged him to enter West Point.[20]

Although Johnston had a rewarding relationship with his nephew, he was a prime candidate for marriage. While involved in a coastal survey, Joseph lost his heart to Lydia McLane of Baltimore. She was fifteen years younger than he and known for her quiet wit and intelligence. Johnston was immediately attracted to her, and after a lengthy courtship, the two were married. He had known her brother, Robert, also a West Point graduate in the Seminole War, and the two served together as engineers along the Canadian border. The McLanes were one of the prominent families of Delaware. Lydia's father had served in both houses of Congress, as minister to England, and in Jackson's cabinet. Joseph and Lydia were married on July 10, 1845.[21]

Johnston's greatest disappointment of his long marriage was that he had no children. The void was somewhat filled by Joseph's nephew, Preston, who had recently graduated from West Point. Lydia's frequent illness was also a constant concern for him; she made regular trips to hot springs and spas, hoping to improve her health. Twenty years later, when Lydia's illness began to age her beyond her years, she worried that her husband would no longer find her attractive. To assure her that such was not the case, he wrote: "Do you really think that what you describe would affect your appearance to me? Do you know that I see your face with my heart, and that is as lovely to me now—that it gives me as much happiness to look at it—as it did when you were eighteen?"[22]

In 1846, with the outbreak of the war with Mexico, Johnston requested to be assigned to that theater immediately. He was ordered to join the invasion force commanded by General Winfield Scott as it prepared to advance on Mexico City. His first assignment was as an engineer along with Robert E. Lee, Pierre G. T. Beauregard, George McClellan, and other promising officers he would meet again during the Civil War. Once Scott had assembled his army, Johnston was placed in command of a regiment known as the "voltigeurs."[23]

The voltigeurs were a specially trained outfit of expert skirmishers and, in Scott's army, wore gray uniforms instead of the traditional blue. Johnston led his regiment on a reconnaissance in advance of the army, hoping to hold the position until Scott could bring his main body into action. When the voltigeurs encountered the Mexican Army under General Santa Anna, Johnston was wounded twice.[24]

Although Johnston was badly hurt, his wounds were not life threatening. In recognition of his bravery, he was breveted to lieutenant colonel. Johnston was able to recover from his wounds in time to lead his voltigeurs in the battles of Padierna, Contreras, Churubusco, Molino del Rey, and Chapultepec.

Despite being hit three times while advancing up the slopes of Chapulte-pec, Johnston continued to lead his men forward. His bravery under fire was recognized with a citation from General Scott: "Johnston is a great soldier, but has the unfortunate knack of getting himself shot in nearly every engagement."[25]

During the war, Johnston's nephew Preston was killed in action. Johnston never fully recovered from the loss. More than forty years later, he reminded a friend how clever and winning Preston had been. "When Lee came to tell me of Preston's death," Johnston recalled, "he wept as he took my hand." Although Johnston ended his war in Mexico in military glory, the loss of Preston plunged him into a deep depression.[26]

In 1848, Johnston returned to the dull routines of an engineer; but the thrill of combat remained fresh in his mind. In 1855, he transferred to the cavalry, and two years later, when his friend McClellan left the army, he considered resigning himself. In a letter to McClellan he wrote: "There is no one left in the regiment or army to take your place. I wish I was young enough to resign too."[27]

One year later, Johnston was transferred to Washington. In 1860, Johnston was promoted to the rank of brigadier general and appointed quartermaster general. He now outranked his contemporaries Albert S. Johnston, Robert E. Lee, and Charles F. Smith, and in time, he hoped to become the army's senior officer. As quartermaster general, Johnston's principal responsibility was to manage the supplies and accounts for the army, administering a budget of over $7 million. Despite the controversy over secession that swept the country, Johnston carried out his assignment in good order.[28]

The crisis over secession caused Johnston a great deal of personal anguish. Johnston was not a proponent of slavery, and he doubted that secession was a Constitutional right, but he did believe in the right of revolution as a natural principle of a free government as expressed in the Declaration of Independence. His strongest loyalty was to Virginia. If Virginia remained in the Union, so would he; if she left, Johnston would go with her.[29]

Winfield Scott tried to convince Johnston to remain at his post. He even tried to get Johnston's wife, who had been born in Baltimore, to keep her husband from resigning. "[He] cannot stay in an army that is about to invade his native land," Lydia told Scott. Scott replied, "Then let him leave our army, but do not let him join theirs." Lydia Johnston had doubts of her own about the wisdom of her husband joining the Confederacy. She knew that Jefferson Davis, who had since become president of the Confederacy, disliked her husband. "[Davis] has power," she told her husband. "He will ruin you."[30] When friends urged Lydia to convince her husband to stay with the Union, she said sadly, "But how is Joe Johnston to live? He has no private fortune or no profession but that of arms."[31] Johnston, however, felt obligated to defend his native Virginia, and he submitted his resignation to

General Scott. He left everything but his father's Revolutionary War sword behind him in Washington and headed for Richmond.[32]

When Johnston arrived in Richmond on April 25, he went to see Governor John Letcher to offer his services. Lee had arrived four days earlier, and Letcher had appointed him commander of all Virginia's troops. On Lee's advice, Letcher appointed Johnston commander of the state forces in and around Richmond.[33] Johnston set to work to bring military order out of the chaos of arriving volunteers. His magnetic personality and military bearing made a strong impression on recruits and officers. By keeping busy with the endless demands of his work, he distracted himself from the sadness of the situation.

Two weeks later, when the Virginia Convention met, it decided that the state should have only one major general, and that it would be Lee. Letcher offered Johnston a brigadier general's commission, but he turned it down. Instead, he accepted the same rank in the Confederate army. Knowing that the Confederate Congress planned to elevate brigadiers to full generals in the near future, Johnston expected the automatic promotion to general as soon as the policy became effective.[34]

In May, President Davis appointed Johnston commander of the Confederate forces at Harper's Ferry. In this moment of crisis, Jefferson Davis anticipated great things from Johnston. Like his good friend McClellan, Johnston had a presence about him that impressed onlookers, appearing every bit a soldier, even in civilian clothing. Johnston, now fifty-four, had a grayish white Van Dyke beard and was slight of frame. He was graceful, elegant, and had a gentlemanly manner, exuding a magnetism that drew people to him. Because Johnston cared for his men and tried to fulfill their needs whenever possible, his soldiers loved him.[35] This charisma extended to the officer corps as well. Some of the best known leaders of the Confederacy expressed their friendship and esteem for Johnston. J. E. B. Stuart called him his best friend, and James Longstreet longed to return to service under him. Those who treated Johnston with dignity and respect found him to be warm and became his lifelong friend.[36]

Johnston, however, had less visible problems that inhibited his success with the president and other important government officials. These problems appeared during his first assignment. After two days at Harper's Ferry, Johnston's appraisal of the situation was that it could not be defended with the small force he had, stating that the town was "untenable by us at present against a strong enemy." It was his best judgment, he said, that the men under his command could be better used in defending the Shenandoah Valley. To stand and fight at Harper's Ferry might be a gallant act, but at best his unit would be removed from the war, which would do no one any good.[37]

Finally, after an exchange of correspondence with the War Department in Richmond, he was allowed to pull back to Winchester. In the first of many such maneuvers in the war, Johnston slipped away behind a cavalry screen, confusing his opponents who had no idea where he had gone. He occupied a position that would allow him to move with ease to prevent an invasion of the valley. Johnston's realistic evaluation of the situation at Harper's Ferry should have marked him as a commander with a good grasp of strategy; instead, he was considered by those in Richmond as a general who was reluctant to fight.[38]

From the outset of the war, Davis and Johnston disagreed on the conduct of the war. Johnston was a consummate realist, recommending actions only when he considered it prudent for the safety of his command, a military policy he believed should be adopted by the Confederacy for conducting the war. President Davis and the War Department held the opposite view, believing that every point of the Confederacy ought to be held despite the cost in manpower. Davis's problems were complex, and Johnston was not in a position to understand them fully. It was not an easy task to organize a nation into a unit capable of fighting a war. Davis was forced to consider the rights of the states within the Confederacy. Each state wanted its territory protected and not occupied by enemy troops. Johnston, however, had little concern for such political matters. His main concern was for the welfare of his men. Given the wide difference in their positions and their ideas on how the war should be fought, it was inevitable that the two men would clash.[39]

Johnston hurried his command from the Shenandoah Valley to Manassas when he heard that Union forces were moving into Virginia. Although arriving on the field after the enemy was engaged, he directed his men toward the Federal attack in time to halt their advance at Henry House Hill. His counterattack drove the Union forces from the field. Confederate reinforcements later in the day gave the South its first major victory. Just after nightfall, Davis met with Johnston and Beauregard for a briefing on the day's events. Davis urged a vigorous pursuit, but Johnston convinced him that prudence demanded a delay. Not long after the battle at Manassas, the relationship between Davis and Johnston began to show signs of strain. When Lee assigned an officer to Johnston's staff, he refused to accept the man. Davis endorsed Johnston's written reply with a single word, "Insubordinate." A few days later, Johnston challenged another order from Lee. Since he outranked Lee, he said, "such orders I cannot regard, because they are illegal." Davis again noted on Johnston's reply, "Insubordinate." The feud was on.[40]

In addition to his conflict with Johnston, Davis also had clashes with Beauregard. It was less a disagreement over strategy than a conflict in personalities. Unlike Lincoln, who could shrug off a snub by McClellan, Davis was "ready for any quarrel with any and everybody, at any time and all times."[41] Davis settled his disputes with Beauregard by sending him west where he would not have to deal directly with him. But Davis's problem with

Johnston ran deeper, dating back, it was rumored, to a dispute over a woman when they were cadets at West Point.[42] Although Johnston was genial and easygoing with subordinates, he was just as touchy as Davis when challenged. Because Johnston was so highly regarded by his fellow officers, Davis felt obligated to deal with him more cautiously than he had with Beauregard. Their differences were exacerbated when the president tried to settle the issue of rank. When Davis nominated five soldiers for the rank of full general, he placed Johnston fourth on the seniority list, despite the fact he had outranked all others in the prewar U.S. Army. Davis tried to explain his action on the grounds that Johnston had been a staff, not a line, officer. It was a poor excuse, for Davis had placed General Cooper, who had also been a staff officer, at the top of the list.[43]

Johnston was disappointed, and his pride was hurt. He wrote a nine-page letter to the president, protesting the attempt "to tarnish his fair name as a soldier and a man." Davis's reply was brief and insulting: "I have just received and read your letter of the 12th instant. Its language is, as you say, unusual; its arguments and statements utterly one-sided, and its insinuations as unfounded as they are unbecoming."[44] The two men never had cordial relations again. Their personalities were too much alike, each too anxious to find and take offense. Their dislike for each other only deepened as the war went on, with harmful results for the Confederacy.[45]

For a while, Davis and Johnston maintained a polite working relationship with each other, but in the spring of 1862 another feud erupted. This time Johnston had acted against Davis's policy of defending Confederate territory whenever possible. Davis was shocked when he learned that Johnston had retreated from Manassas and, in the process, abandoned or destroyed quantities of equipment, food, and personal baggage; all this had been without Davis's authority. Now Davis ordered him to select a new position "as far in advance as consistent with your safety."[46]

Johnston repeatedly advocated a strategy of concentration of forces. He urged that troops be moved from the coastal positions and secondary theaters to concentrate the necessary force needed to achieve a decisive victory. To Johnston, territory was just space that could be abandoned and traded for time and massing of troops until the enemy could be engaged in an all-out battle. For Davis, such a strategy was politically untenable. Congress would block any move that would leave areas of the Confederacy undefended, fearing it would demoralize its residents. Davis also realized that once Southern territory had been abandoned, it would be impossible to force freed slaves back into the system.[47]

When Davis insisted that the army be reorganized so that troops from the same state serve in the same unit, Johnston objected. Davis believed this would raise the morale of the army, but Johnston felt it was dangerous to reorganize his army at the time he faced an enemy force that was increasing in strength and now outnumbered his by three to one.[48]

In the spring of 1862, Major General George McClellan began his advance on Richmond from the southeast after landing troops on the Virginia peninsula. Davis wanted Johnston to engage McClellan as soon and as far from Richmond as possible. Johnston had no problem with engaging the enemy, but only on his terms, even if that meant giving up ground.[49]

During the Peninsula Campaign, Johnston retreated up the peninsula until Federal troops approached to within sight of Richmond, all without engaging in a single major battle. When Davis asked Johnston what his plans were to stop the Union advance, his only response was vague generalities. Despite Johnston's strategy for fighting the enemy, Davis was reluctant to relieve him. He believed Johnston had won the confidence of his men and that removing him now would be bad for morale, particularly in the midst of an important campaign.[50]

As the retreating Confederates reached the outskirts of Richmond, Davis placed pressure on Johnston to engage the enemy: "If you will not give battle, I will appoint someone to command who will." Under this threat, Johnston launched the attacks that resulted in the Battles of Fair Oaks and Seven Pines.[51]

Near the end of the Battle of Seven Pines, Johnston rode out to Fair Oaks to check on the condition of the battle. It did not take him long to determine that his men would have to spend the night there, hoping to complete their victory in the morning. Giving his staff officer the necessary orders, he left.[52] Suddenly, a bullet tore into Johnston's right shoulder. A moment later, he was hit by a shell fragment that knocked him from his horse. An aide picked him up and carried him back to a safer spot. Johnston was unconscious, and it seemed that he was dying. A few minutes later, Jefferson Davis arrived on the scene to check on the fallen general. When Johnston opened his eyes, he was surprised to see Davis. Despite their earlier disagreements, Johnston held up his hand for the president. Davis was gracious and took Johnston's hand. Johnston said he did not know the extent of his wound, but he thought the fragment had injured his back.[53]

Within a few minutes, Johnston realized that he did not have his sword and pistols. "The sword was the one worn by my father in the Revolutionary War," he exclaimed, "and I would not lose it for $10,000; will someone please go back and get it and the pistols for me?" Ignoring the enemy fire, his aide retrieved both sword and pistols. He hurried back to Johnston, who presented one of the pistols to him.[54]

Although Johnston's wounds were serious, he was determined to recover to fight again. He was a professional soldier. He had been wounded in battle before, and he had every reason to expect that he would receive other wounds. Wounds were of little consequence to him—the important thing to him was to serve.[55]

When Lee was appointed to take Johnston's place, the fame of the Army of Northern Virginia began. Shortly after his appointment, Lee wrote a message to Mrs. Johnston: "The President has thought it necessary that I take his place. I wish I was able, or that his mantle had fallen on an abler man." When Johnston learned that Davis was sending reinforcements to Lee, he said: "Then, my wound was fortunate; it is concentration which I earnestly recommended, but had not the influence to effect. Lee had made them do for him what they would not do for me."[56] Johnston's wounds were severe, and he was unable to return to action for six months. During that time, Robert E. Lee was able to organize the army into one of the finest fighting machines ever commanded by an American.

While recovering from his wounds, Johnston became friends with Confederate Senator Louis T. Wigfall, the leader in the anti-Davis faction in Congress. As a result, Johnston became not only a factor in Confederate politics but also a participant. Davis, who viewed all attacks on him as treasonous, now thought of Johnston as a political enemy whose motives were suspect. As a result, Johnston was doomed to be out of favor in Richmond for the rest of the war.[57]

Davis's political opponents were eager to see Johnston back in service and were convinced that his appointment to the Western theater would be the answer to their problems there. "Gentlemen," said Senator William Yancey of Alabama in a toast intended for Johnston, "let us drink to the only man who can save the Confederacy, General Joseph E. Johnston." Johnston rose from his chair, nodded to Yancey, and said, "The man described is already in the field—in the person of General Robert E. Lee. I will drink it to his health."[58]

Although Davis's confidence in Johnston had been shaken by his apparent willingness to retreat right up to Richmond without a fight, he still believed Johnston could be of value to the Confederacy. A month after Johnston was wounded, Davis wrote to his wife: "General J. E. Johnston is steadily and rapidly improving. I wish he was able to take the field. Despite the critics, who know military affairs by instinct, he is a good soldier . . . and could at this time render most valuable service." During Johnston's recuperation, Davis was bombarded by politicians and generals with requests that Johnston be given overall command in the Western theater.[59]

On November 12, 1862, Johnston reported for duty. It would take nearly a year for him to heal completely, and for some months to come he lacked the stamina for active campaigning. Nevertheless, in November, he was given overall theater command of Confederate forces between the Appalachian Mountains and the Mississippi River. From the beginning, Confederate forces in the West had taken one beating after another. The naming of Johnston was not the answer to the problems in the West, but the appointment was good politics and an excellent morale booster. Johnston was admired and respected by the citizens of the western states.[60]

Johnston had doubts about his new assignment, and he questioned that an arrangement in which he would be in command of two armies so widely separated was workable. In addition, Confederate forces would be at a severe numerical disadvantage. Johnston arrived in Chattanooga on December 4, 1862, to take up his command; almost immediately, he became involved in a quarrel with Davis over the disposition of troops along the Mississippi. Johnston recognized that the river port of Vicksburg was strategically important to the Confederacy and tried to get Davis to authorize the transfer of more troops to that area to join Pemberton's force. Davis refused. In the meantime, when Grant committed his forces to the capture of Vicksburg, Johnston differed with the field commander in the strategy to be employed. Against his advice, Pemberton withdrew his troops into Vicksburg.[61]

When Grant attacked Vicksburg, Johnston, fearing Pemberton would be trapped, ordered him to evacuate the city and join him, but Pemberton resisted. Because his force was small, Johnston elected not to attack Grant. When Pemberton surrendered his army and the city, Davis blamed Johnston, insisting that he had not done enough to break Grant's siege. The two continued their feud in a series of public letters. Johnston's wife advised her husband to resign, but the general replied that he was not serving Davis but a people who had never been anything but kind to him.[62]

The fall of Vicksburg had momentous consequences, bringing the tension between Davis and Johnston to open hostility. The Confederacy had lost what Davis would call "the nailhead that held the South's two halves together." In addition to being a tremendous blow to Southern morale, it freed Grant's army for use elsewhere. The focus of the war in the West now turned to Tennessee.[63]

By the end of November, Grant had defeated Bragg at Chattanooga and had driven the Army of Tennessee back into Georgia. When Bragg asked Davis to be relieved, his request was granted. Davis offered the command to Lee, who declined. Political pressure, especially by Senator Wigfall, was placed on Davis to replace Bragg with Johnston. Finally, after the president realized there was no one else to whom he could turn, he appointed Johnston as commander of the Army of Tennessee. Johnston was pleased with the appointment, but he delayed making the announcement of the change because Mrs. Bragg was very ill at the same time, and he wanted to spare Bragg's feelings.[64]

Johnston spent the winter of 1863–1864 preparing for the coming campaign against William T. Sherman. Because of his inferior numbers, Johnston's basic strategy was to use part of his army as a shield and then counterattack when the opportunity presented itself. Davis disagreed with Johnston's strategy, wanting him to be more aggressive. To convey his feelings, Davis sent Braxton Bragg, now his military adviser, to inform Johnston that he expected him to recapture Tennessee. Johnston felt his army was too weak to undertake such a venture, and he said so. As the weeks went by, Davis continued to place pressure on Johnston to take the offensive.[65]

Johnston was not, as his critics maintained, afraid to fight; rather, he saw no positive reason to expose his smaller Army of Tennessee to a senseless slaughter. Sooner or later, he believed, Sherman would make a mistake. When that happened, a Confederate offensive might be possible. For the time being and until he received reinforcements, he would stay where he was.[66] Davis was greatly distressed as Johnston continued to retreat, taking few losses but surrendering territory as he fell back. To Johnston's dismay, Sherman did not attack him directly as he had hoped for; instead, he flanked Johnston, forcing him to retreat further.[67]

As the campaign continued, Johnston was able to keep his smaller army together against overwhelming odds while remaining a barrier between Sherman and Atlanta. Davis continued to send aid and support but was growing increasingly impatient with Johnston's lack of aggression. Behind the scenes, Lieutenant General John Bell Hood, an ambitious corps commander in Johnston's army, had begun sending letters to the president stating that the army was in top shape "and eager for the fray." Davis did not inform Johnston of Hood's betrayal, nor did he question the truth of the reports. They merely reinforced what Davis suspected all along. To investigate the situation, Davis sent Braxton Bragg, a man beholden to Davis for his current position; it was unlikely he would be objective. Bragg informed Davis that Johnston had no future plans for attacking the enemy. Davis had to act. He did not want to lose Atlanta, a major industrial center and a critical railroad junction vital to the Confederate war effort.[68]

Despite his personal feelings about Johnston, Davis was reluctant to remove him. Yet, Davis knew the vital importance of holding Atlanta. Had he been able to foresee that Johnston would give up mountainous northern Georgia and retreat to the gates of Atlanta without a major battle, Davis would have removed him earlier. Davis kept hoping that Johnston would find an appropriate place to stand and fight.[69] Davis gave Johnston one last opportunity to attack the enemy. When he did not, Davis notified Johnston that he was being relieved: "Since you have failed to arrest the advance of the enemy to the vicinity of Atlanta . . . [and] express no confidence that you can defeat or repel him, you are hereby relieved from command of the Army and Department of Tennessee." John Bell Hood was appointed to take his place.[70]

When Sherman learned that Johnston was being replaced with Hood, he was elated. "At this critical moment," he said, "the Confederate Government rendered us a most valuable service."[71] Johnston's removal was not received well by the army. "An universal gloom seemed cast over the army," wrote Halsey Wigfall to his family. This gloom did not result because the men lacked confidence in Hood's ability but rather came from their "love for and confidence in Johnston." As some of the units passed Johnston's headquarters, they lifted their hats. "There was no cheering! We simply passed silently, with heads uncovered," wrote Colonel J. C. Nisbet of the

Sixty-sixth Georgia. "Some of the officers broke ranks and grasped his hand, as the tears poured down their cheeks."[72]

Before Johnston departed, he received a note from a brigade commander who told him that his officers and men "in silence and deep sorrow" had received news of his removal. "We feel that in parting with you as our commanding general our loss is irreparable, and that this army and our country loses one of its ablest, most zealous and patriotic defenders." In their opinion, it was Johnston's leadership that had enabled them to hold off an enemy superior in every respect but spirit. There was also discontent in the general ranks about Johnston's removal. Generals Hardee and Mackall asked to be relieved. Mackall, Johnston's chief-of-staff, received permission to leave the army within a week after Johnston's departure.[73]

Johnston returned to Macon and then to Columbia, South Carolina, to await further orders. The fall of Atlanta and the destruction of the Army of Tennessee under Hood in the Franklin–Nashville Campaign forced Davis to relieve Hood of command. With Sherman preparing to move into the Carolinas, Davis once again called on Johnston and appointed him commander of the Army of Tennessee. Still without adequate troops, Johnston faced overwhelming odds in trying to stop Sherman. He was able to launch one last attack at Bentonville, North Carolina. The attack slowed part of Sherman's army and held his old adversary in check for two days until Johnston was once again flanked. To the end of his life, Johnston always contended that he had won both the first and last Confederate victories.[74]

Johnston's only hope now rested with Lee; he hoped, somehow, that the two armies would be able to link up and deal first with Sherman, and then with Grant. The unification, however, never happened; Lee surrendered at Appomattox on April 9.

After Lee's surrender, Johnston realized that the war was irrevocably lost. He met with Davis one final time during Davis's flight south, hoping to explain his intention to surrender to Sherman. The meeting was held on the second-floor bedroom of a private home in Greensboro, North Carolina, with Davis's cabinet and General Beauregard also in attendance. The president began by saying: "I have requested you and General Beauregard, General Johnston, to join us this evening, that we may have the benefit of your views." Davis's opinion was that the situation was "terrible" but "not fatal." "I think we can whip the enemy if our people turn out." Johnston remained silent and had to be prompted by Davis: "We would like to have your views, General Johnston."[75]

"My views, sir," he said, "are that our people are tired of war, feel themselves whipped, and will not fight. Our country is overrun, its military resources greatly diminished, while the enemy's military power and resources were never greater and may be increased to any extent desired. . . . My men are daily deserting in large numbers and are stealing my artillery teams to aid their escapes to their homes. Since Lee's surrender they regard the war as at an end. If I march out of North Carolina, her people will all leave my ranks. . . . My small force is melting away like snow before the sun, and I am hopeless of recruiting it." Davis did not look up while Johnston spoke, but sat quietly, "with his eyes fixed on a scrap of paper, which he was folding and unfolding abstractly."[76]

After Johnston had finished, there was absolute silence for what seemed like several minutes. Finally, President Davis asked General Beauregard what his feelings were. "I concur in all General Johnston has said," he replied. Davis asked the cabinet members their opinion. Only Judah Benjamin, loyal to the end, believed they should continue to fight. "Well, General Johnston," Davis said at last, "what do you propose?"[77] Johnston suggested that he be allowed to negotiate peace with Sherman. After a pause, Davis said, "Well sir, you can adopt this course, though I confess I am not sanguine as to the ultimate results." Davis dictated a letter, Johnston signed it, and the letter was delivered to Sherman.[78]

Johnston met with Sherman on April 17 in the home of James Bennett near Raleigh, North Carolina. Sherman told Johnston of the assassination of President Lincoln two days earlier. Johnston said, "It was the greatest possible calamity" that could befall the South, and he hoped that Sherman did not think it was the result of a Southern plot. Sherman assured him he did not think the Confederate army had anything to do with it, but he would not say the same for Jefferson Davis. Johnston did not respond.[79]

Sherman offered Johnston the same terms that Grant had offered Lee at Appomattox: The men would surrender their arms and go home on parole. The next day, when Secretary of War John Breckinridge met with the two generals, Sherman brought with him a memorandum proposing the dissolution of all Southern armies and the restoration and recognition of state governments. Johnston rode away from the Bennett house thinking he had signed the document that ended the war. He found out later that it was not so.[80]

A few days later, the offer was rescinded when the Federal officials and press learned of the generous offer made by Sherman. Johnston, however, was not willing to ask his men to shed any more of their blood and accepted the revised terms. Finally on April 26, Johnston formally surrendered his army. For the rest of his life, Davis would consider Johnston's decision to surrender his army, when he was neither surrounded nor defeated, an act of treachery.[81]

On May 2, 1865, Johnston said good-bye to the Army of Tennessee in a general order:

> Comrades: In terminating our official relations I most earnestly exhort you to observe faithfully the terms of pacification agreed upon, and to discharge the obligations of good and peaceful citizens at your home as well as you have performed the duties of thorough

soldiers in the field. . . . You will return to your homes with the admiration of people, won by the courage and noble devotion you have displayed in the long war. . . . I now part with you with deep regret, and bid you farewell with feelings of cordial friendship and with earnest wishes that you may have hereafter all the prosperity and happiness to be found in the world.[82]

Although the war was over, for Joseph Johnston another one was just beginning. For the rest of his life, he would fight to defend his reputation. He became obsessed with setting the record straight, and he could think of no better way to do that than to discredit Jefferson Davis. Johnston's excuses for the defeat of his army and his public attack of Davis, a man the South now considered a martyr, tarnished his own reputation. It brought him no satisfaction and embittered his remaining years. After his death, one of his friends wrote sadly of his behavior: "If General Johnston had never written anything . . . how much better it would have been."[83]

For more than thirty-five years Johnston had made his way as a soldier. He prided himself on his ability as an engineer and had pioneered railroad construction in Texas in the 1850s. When a position as president of the Mobile & Ohio Railroad became available, he sought the job. When the position went to someone else, he was despondent, saying, "I have had another defeat." As his wife's health continued to deteriorate, it became important to find work.[84]

Johnston was employed with the National Express and Transportation Company until the company failed. He then took another position as president of the Selma, Rome & Dalton Railroad. He finally found permanent employment in the insurance business. A London insurance company invited him to become a manager of its southern department, which he established as Joseph E. Johnston & Company. With headquarters in Savannah, Johnston offered former Confederate officers positions with the firm. Within four years, he was in charge of 120 agents in Georgia, Alabama, and Mississippi. With this new security, Johnston had time to work on his memoirs.[85]

Johnston wrote to former corps and division commanders, requesting them to send him any papers and information they might have about the war. In some cases he wrote his recollections of particular events, requesting that they be confirmed or corrected. It soon became clear that Johnston was trying to build a case against Hood. He had not forgotten Hood's unprofessional behavior or role in having him replaced as commander of the Army of Tennessee. Johnston was also interested in gathering information that would show that Jefferson Davis contributed heavily to the defeat of the Confederacy. After having spent two years in the Fort Monroe prison, Davis proved to be a better martyr than he had a president. During his incarceration, his strongest critics came to forgive him; even his jailers developed a respect for his courage. Aware of this, Wade Hampton wrote to Johnston, advising him not to pursue his feud with Davis. It would affect the unity necessary for the South to survive, he said. "I feel sure no good could come in any way by any publication by you raising an issue on the point. Any controversy between Mr. Davis and yourself would jar upon the feelings of thousands who are friendly to both of you and would tend to throw discredit on our cause. . . . Do not allow yourself to be drawn into any personal altercation." It was good advice, but Johnston did not heed it.[86]

Johnston's lengthy volume titled *Narrative of Military Operations Directed During the Late War Between the States* appeared in 1874. Because Johnston was not a gifted writer and relied heavily on official correspondence and legalistic arguments, his book was very boring. The book not only failed financially but also in its purpose. His argumentative tone betrayed his continuing resentment and bitterness. Davis wrote to his wife that "Johnston has more effectively than another could have shown his selfishness and his malignity." Unfortunately for Johnston, the book not only angered his targets—Davis, Bragg, and Hood—but also some of his friends.[87]

Johnston continued to write articles to defend his actions during the war. "Mr. Davis condemned me for not fighting. General Sherman's testimony and that of the Military Cemetery at Marietta refute the charge," he wrote. It is ironic that Johnston's comrades in arms, Beauregard, Hood, Bragg, and Davis, were all offended by his writing, while his former adversaries, especially Grant and Sherman, strongly supported him. Johnston was pleased to read in both Sherman's and Grant's memoirs that they respected him as a dangerous opponent and were critical of both Hood and Davis.[88]

Like most professional army officers, Johnston showed little interest in politics. Johnston's prominence, however, caused his Richmond friends to consider him a good candidate to run for Congress. They maneuvered other aspirants out of the contest until Johnston was the only Democratic candidate.[89] During the spirited race, Johnston's supporters came up short in their financing of the campaign. They did not want to discuss the matter with him, knowing that he believed a large expenditure of money was paramount to purchasing the seat and would resign his candidacy if this became an issue. A close friend called upon Mrs. Johnston and advised her of the financial situation. Not wanting to see her husband disappointed if he lost the election, she offered to cash some of her bonds to provide the needed money. "If he's beat, it will be simply disgraceful and shameful! It will kill him. He shan't be beat; you must not allow it. I will not permit it," she said. They quickly raised additional funds and did not need her bonds, so they were returned to her.[90]

Johnston was elected, and when he took his seat in the 46th Congress in 1879, he found among its members a number of old Confederates. As a member of the House, Johnston served on the Military Affairs Committee and the Committee on Levees and Improvement of the Mississippi River. His chief interest seems to have been in improving the efficiency of the army and in those matters affecting local Virginia problems. After his two-year term was up, Johnston did not consider running for reelection.[91]

The Democratic Party's candidate, Grover Cleveland, was elected president in 1884. Johnston was seriously considered for a cabinet post in the position of secretary of war, even though he was a former Confederate general and now seventy-six years old. Although Johnston did not get the position, he was appointed U.S. railroad commissioner.[92]

By the beginning of 1887, Lydia's health was poorer than ever. Despite her numerous trips to spas, there was no improvement. On February 22, 1887, at the age of sixty-five, she died. Her death devastated Johnston, and for the rest of his life he could not bring himself to write or speak her name. He compensated by working even harder.

When President Cleveland left office in 1884, Johnston lost his federal position. Retiring to his home in Washington, Johnston still had time to attend Confederate memorial ceremonies. At one ceremony in Georgia, Johnston was assigned to share an open carriage with Edmund Kirby Smith. The parade had just begun when a voice from the crowd shouted out: "That's Johnston! That's Joe Johnston!" With that, hundreds of men burst from the crowd and surrounded his carriage, stretching out their hands to their old commander. Someone unhitched the horses, and members of the crowd pulled the carriage the length of the parade route, cheering wildly. The fact that his former troops continued to show their devotion for him brought tears to his eyes.[93]

Funerals were a regular part of Johnston's life now. In 1885, he served as a pallbearer at Grant's funeral. Later in the year, he did the same for his old friend and wartime adversary, George McClellan. In the winter of 1891, Johnston traveled to New York to attend Sherman's funeral. Johnston's duty as a pallbearer was strictly honorary, but he stood bareheaded in the cold rain as the coffin was carried from Sherman's house to the caisson. "General," someone said, "please put on your hat. You might get sick." Johnston refused saying, "If I were in his place and he were standing here in mine, he would not put on his hat."[94]

This was typical of Joseph Johnston's insistence on doing what he believed was right rather than what was expedient. All his life, he had behaved in this manner, and although he was eighty-four and tired, he would not let his own concern for his health prevent him from paying his last respects to Sherman. Earlier, his strict adherence to the professional principles of a soldier had cost him glory, the support of superiors, and the command of the Army of Tennessee. Now his belief in custom would cost him his life; he caught cold that day, and five weeks later he died. Tradition and honor were important to him, no matter what the cost. With Johnston, there could be no compromise.[95]

Johnston's funeral was held the day after he died. All day long there was a stream of callers at his residence on Connecticut Avenue. William Rosecrans and John Schofield, each of whom had fought against him in the field, were among the first to call. After the funeral, Johnston's body was moved to the Greenmount Cemetery in Baltimore, where his wife was buried. Newspapers across the South and throughout the North paid tribute to his memory. The best tribute of all came from the men who served in the ranks of his armies. It was a private from the First Tennessee Regiment who expressed it best: "Farewell, old fellow! We privates loved you because you made us love ourselves."[96]

6 Robert E. Lee

Man of Honor

In the spring of 1863, General Robert E. Lee's victory at Chancellorsville cleared the way for another Confederate invasion of the North. Confusion within the Union army, combined with its losses in other battles, gave Lee the opportunity he had been waiting for—a chance to crush the Union Army of the Potomac once and for all. Within weeks after his victory at Chancellorsville, he was on the move again, this time advancing into Pennsylvania.

On July 1, 1863, Lee's advanced troops strayed into the town of Gettysburg searching for supplies. There they encountered Union cavalry, a part of General George Meade's command. Lee had not planned to fight here, but as he passed through Cashtown Pass, he heard cannon fire and musketry to the east. Leaving Longstreet, Lee and his aides spurred ahead. When he arrived in Gettysburg, the fighting had begun; two great armies were about to collide.[1] The three-day battle that followed would be one of the bloodiest and most decisive in American history. Little did Lee know that the outcome would lead to his surrender at Appomattox less than two years later.

For Lee, the road to Appomattox began in Arlington, Virginia, on the night of April 19, 1861, when he resigned from the U.S. Army. The decision, like every decision in his life, was deeply rooted in the history of his family and his state. Lee was born on January 19, 1807, into Virginia aristocracy, the combination of two of the state's most honored families—the Lees and the Carters. Two of his uncles had signed the Declaration of Independence. Lee's father, Henry "Light Horse Harry" Lee, served in the Revolution, in the Continental Congress, for three terms as governor of Virginia, and for one term in Congress. He was a close friend and confidant of George Washington, eulogizing him as "first in war, first in peace and first in the hearts of his countrymen." Robert's mother was Anne Hill Carter, Henry Lee's second wife.[2]

Henry Lee had shown great promise, perhaps even an opportunity to become president. His later years, however, were darkened by land speculation and often bad investments that left him penniless. In 1810, Henry Lee was sent to debtor's prison in financial ruin, and the family was forced to leave Stratford Hall and move into a small house on Cameron Street in Alexandria. Robert was three at the time. During the midst of the Civil War, Lee recalled his happier days at Stratford Hall in a letter to his wife: "In the absence of a home, I wish I could purchase Stratford. This is the only place I could go to . . . that would inspire me with feelings of pleasure and local love."[3]

In 1813, Lee's father abandoned his family and went to the British West Indies. Although Harry had made a muddle of his life, Mrs. Lee always spoke of him in terms of love and respect and taught her children to do the same. In Robert's eyes, his father was always a hero of the Revolutionary War, the companion of Washington.[4]

Without a husband to care for her five children, Anne took on the full responsibility of raising them. Self-denial, self-control, and the strictest economy in all financial matters were attributes she taught her children. Throughout his childhood, Lee accepted responsibility, caring for his invalid mother in the absence of his father. She also taught her children the tenets of duty, honor, and country. In 1825, Lee's belief in these teachings played a large role in his decision to enter the U.S. Military Academy at West Point.[5]

At West Point, Lee completed the four-year program without a single demerit, attaining the coveted cadet rank of adjutant and graduating second in his class. He quickly made friends with fellow Virginian Joseph Johnston and was inspired by the magnificent adjutant of the cadet corps, Albert Sidney Johnston. Although having contrasting personalities, Lee also admired the tall, thin cadet from Mississippi, Jefferson Davis. Whereas Davis was carefree, often flaunting the rules of the Academy, Lee was a model cadet, exhibiting great self-control.

Lee seemed to feel the need to restore the family's name. This desire compelled him to do his best in all that he did; his record at West Point and during the Civil War and afterward illustrated his belief in duty and honor. Success often brings with it the jealousy of others, but not with Lee. "I doubt if he ever excited envy in any man," wrote a fellow cadet. "All of his accomplishments and alluring virtues appeared natural to him, and he was free from anxiety, distrust and awkwardness that attend a sense of inferiority."[6]

Lee's excellent West Point record enabled him to enter the Engineer Corps, an elite branch of the army that attracted the brightest officers. Lee loved the corps, but his duties were frequently grueling and unglamorous.

This photo is the first known of Lee after the war began. In June 1862 he assumed command of the Army of Northern Virginia after Joseph Johnston was severely wounded at the Battle of Seven Pines.

COURTESY OF THE LIBRARY OF CONGRESS

His first assignment took him to Cookspur, Georgia, to prepare the foundation for a coastal fort. Later he would work on constructing another coastal fort at Monroe, Virginia.[7]

Lee soon began to court Mary Anna Randolph Custis, the daughter of George Washington Parke Custis, the adopted son of the first president. Although her parents were fond of the young lieutenant, her father was reluctant to have her marry a soldier. George Custis, however, was finally convinced to give his approval. The young couple was married at Arlington on June 30, 1831. The Lees had seven children, four daughters and three sons. Over the next thirty-nine years, Lee was a devoted husband and father.[8]

Lee's duties as a soldier often took him away from his family while serving in a variety of engineering tasks. Among his assignments was one at

St. Louis where the Mississippi River threatened to move away from the levee, creating a real economic hardship for the city. Lee's creative plan redirected the water flow and eliminated the sediment deposits that had menaced the harbor. Lee learned from his service as an engineer the importance of terrain and topography. These insights served him well during the Civil War.

In the spring of 1846, Lee welcomed the chance to see active service during the Mexican War, his first chance to experience war. He had been in the army for twenty-one years and never faced an enemy or heard a hostile shot. Serving on the staff of General Winfield Scott, Lee distinguished himself during the war. As a captain, he was responsible for several courageous personal reconnaissance missions, which produced intelligence leading to American victories. At Cerro Gordo and the struggle at Chapultepec Castle, Lee found a route around the enemy's flank. During this time, the military had no medals for bravery, but officers were given "brevet promotions" for brave acts during the war. Captain Lee received three brevets, being promoted to major, lieutenant colonel, and finally to colonel. Lee also won the confidence of his brother officers and their superiors and, above all, General Scott, in whose eyes he was a paragon of military virtue. Scott described Lee as the "very best soldier I ever saw in the field." The Mexican War brought Lee more than promotion and glory—it gave him the training he would need for the far greater trials that lay in the future.[9]

Lee's Mexican War experience was helpful in many ways but may have given him an erroneous impression of what could be accomplished by daring frontal assaults. He participated in successful frontal attacks, but they were against poorly trained infantry armed with muzzle-loading muskets and were accomplished with a small number of casualties. There was to be very little resemblance between these victorious charges and the deadly, disastrous frontal assaults of the Civil War.[10]

After the excitement of the Mexican War, Lee returned to his former job of constructing coastal forts. He welcomed the opportunity to settle down with his family and friends. In 1852, he was assigned to West Point as the new superintendent. Although this assignment was considered an ideal one and most soldiers would have been pleased at the opportunity, Lee was not. He preferred active service or service near enough to Arlington to take care of his family and their estate. Nevertheless, he approached the assignment as he did all others, with his best effort. He oversaw the extension of the Academy's program of study from four to five years, encouraged the study of military strategy, and improved the quality of the cadets by weeding out the lazy and incompetent. His tenure at the Academy gave Lee the opportunity to get to know many young officers who would serve with him during the Civil War. Among those was J. E. B. Stuart, his future cavalry leader.[11]

While at West Point, Lee underwent a religious change, developing a deeper relationship with God. As a child he had been baptized in the Episcopal

Church but was never confirmed. Now that he was in charge of some of the nation's finest young men, Lee felt he should confess his faith and ally himself with the church. Side by side with two of his daughters, he was confirmed on July 17, 1853. Lee's alliance with his God would remain first in his heart his entire life. Lee's faith continued to grow, and he sincerely believed that Providence ordered everything and that man had only to do what was right and leave the rest to God.[12]

In March 1855, Congress authorized the formation of four new regiments. Jefferson Davis, now secretary of war, appointed Lee second in command and brevet lieutenant colonel in the Second Cavalry Regiment. This regiment was one of the army's most elite units, assigned to the Western frontier. Out of its ranks would come several leading officers during the war, including Albert Sidney Johnston, its commander.

In October 1857, Lee's father-in-law died, leaving his family in debt, a complicated will to handle, and a run-down estate. Lee took a leave from his army duties to return to Arlington to settle the estate. The family was "land poor," owning a great deal of property but no money for its upkeep. What was more depressing, Lee found that, in his absence, Mary had become physically impaired with painful arthritis and had great difficulty walking. Most of the children were away in the army or at boarding school. It was a difficult time for Lee, and he began to reconsider his life, seriously thinking about resigning from the army. His thoughts about the army were common in a profession that offered little more than routine service and low pay. Promotions were slow in coming or not at all, and many officers were forced to resign to pursue more lucrative civilian careers. Lee eventually decided to remain in the army, but it took him thirty years of service to reach the permanent rank of colonel.[13]

In 1861, people looked to Lee for his opinion on the matters threatening the nation—slavery and secession. Lee was opposed to slavery, strongly pro-Union, and against civil war, but above all, he remained loyal to Virginia. Lee acknowledged that "slavery, as an institution, was a moral and political evil," but he had owned at least four women slaves, part of his mother's bequest to him, and as late as 1852, he had owned a manservant. His wife also owned slaves that she had inherited from her father.[14]

Lee was in step with most Southerners of the time on this issue and did not accept any responsibility to act on his belief that slavery was "a moral and political evil." On December 29, 1863, in accordance with his father-in-law's will, Lee set free all the slaves owned by him. To be sure, Lee was only a limited emancipator, since he was only following the Custis will.[15]

After Lincoln's election, Lee denounced secession, stating that "secession is nothing but revolution." "Still," he concluded sadly, "a Union that can only be maintained by swords and bayonets, and in which strife and civil war are to take the place of brotherly love and kindness, has no charm for me."[16] In April 1861, Lee was offered the field command of the armies of the United States with the rank of major general, but he did not accept the position. One day after Virginia seceded, Lee resigned his commission. In a letter to General Scott he wrote: "Save in defense of my native state, I never again will draw my sword." Mrs. Lee understood and approved of her husband's resignation: "My husband has wept tears of blood over the war, but as a man of honor and a Virginian, he must follow the destiny of his state."[17]

Now fifty-two years old and still a handsome man, Lee had dark hair and a mustache; he had not yet grown the beard that would become his distinguishing feature during the war. Standing almost six feet tall with a burly upper torso, he exhibited a commanding appearance.[18] Two days after his resignation, Lee left for Richmond where he was offered command of Virginia's troops and a rank of brigadier general in the Confederate army. He never returned to his home at Arlington but elected to "share the misery of the people of his native state." It would be more than thirteen months before he assumed command of an army in the field. For the time being, Lee bided his time as military advisor to President Davis.[19]

During the early days of the conflict, Lee realized that the South would fight a defensive war and that Virginia would become the major battlefield of the war. He remained in a relatively obscure position during the first year of the war until his West Point classmate, Joseph E. Johnston, was severely wounded at the Battle of Seven Pines. In June 1862, Lee was placed in command of what was soon to become the legendary Army of Northern Virginia.

Lee had never held a field command before. As commander of the Army of Northern Virginia, he always faced a numerically superior enemy that was better supplied than his. Yet, during the next thirteen months, Lee engaged the enemy in a series of battles that have become legendary, and he enjoyed a reputation for invincibility.[20] On June 25, 1862, Lee initiated the Seven Days campaign. In a short time, he had pushed the Union army from the outskirts of Richmond. Lee's skillful use of defensive works south of the Chickahominy River allowed him to use his best troops on the offensive and, in some instances, to achieve numerical superiority. As a result, Lee was able to take the initiative away from his opponent. By acting boldly, he gave General McClellan the impression that he had a larger force than he actually did. Just hours after the Confederate victory at Mechanicsville, McClellan was planning to retreat.[21]

Although Lee had suffered heavy losses in his first campaign, he was acclaimed a hero in Richmond. "No captain that ever lived," wrote the *Richmond Dispatch*, "could have planned or executed a better plan."[22] In just a short time, Lee had completely changed the military situation for the South. In June, the entire Union army had been poised to attack Richmond; by September, Lee was in a position to threaten Washington, D.C.

Despite the prestige Lee achieved as the result of his Seven Days campaign, the strategy for the war was being determined in Richmond. In Lee's opinion, a defensive strategy would only delay their defeat. Lee was eager to seize the initiative whenever possible; he was convinced that time was not on their side and that the Federals must be brought to the negotiation table as quickly as possible. Even though Lee commanded the largest army he could ever expect to have, he was outnumbered and could expect the odds to worsen as the war progressed.[23] Numerical superiority for the enemy held no fear for Lee. He knew of Napoleon's success against larger armies in Europe and had seen General Scott's triumph over a numerically superior Mexican army. Although superior numbers were important, initiative, concentration of forces, surprise, determination, and good intelligence could enable a smaller army to be victorious over a larger one.[24]

No sooner had the Army of Northern Virginia disposed of one threat to Richmond than a new one appeared. In June, the Lincoln administration formed a new Army of Virginia composed of three corps under Major Generals McDowell, Banks, and Fremont and led by Major General John Pope. Pope's mission was to protect Washington and to draw Confederate strength from Richmond. Pope had earned Lee's contempt by publishing a series of punitive orders against Virginia's civilians, which violated Lee's chivalrous concept of war. In a letter to his wife, Lee had labeled Pope the "miscreant general."[25]

Lee was so incensed by Pope's actions that he wrote a letter to Henry Halleck, general-in-chief of the Union forces, regarding Pope's pronouncements. If the Federals began killing civilians, the Confederates would retaliate in kind. He would have no option but to fight the war in the same manner "until the voice of an outraged humanity shall compel a respect for the recognized usages of war." Lee made his point.[26]

Although McClellan still lay within striking distance of Richmond, Lee did not believe he posed any immediate threat. A campaign against Pope's army that threatened Washington, Lee believed, might force McClellan to withdraw his army from the Virginia peninsula. In a meeting with Davis on July 13, Lee acquired Davis's consent for an offensive against Pope. The campaign would be known as Second Manassas.[27]

In a series of brilliant strategic moves, Lee sent Stonewall Jackson with 23,000 troops to cut Pope's line of communication, while he, with only 32,000 men, blocked the upper Rappahannock crossing. Splitting his army in such a manner defied conventional military procedure, but the disparity in the size of the opposing forces made the risk unavoidable. Jackson marched his men sixty miles in two days and was successful in cutting Pope's communication line and destroying a large Union supply depot at Manassas Junction.[28] Pope attacked Jackson's forces but was unaware that Longstreet was marching to his aid. On the morning of August 30, while Pope was engaging Jackson, Longstreet struck the Union flank, driving the Federals from the field. Lee was not content for just a victory; he wanted to destroy Pope's entire army, but rain and fatigue deterred his efforts to do so.[29]

Casualties were heavy on both sides. At a cost of 9,500 men, Lee had inflicted 14,500 casualties upon the Union army. The Confederate triumph was complete. The Federals, who just weeks earlier were on the outskirts of Richmond, were now fleeing back to Washington. Lee's victory at Manassas was celebrated in the South and by the Army of Northern Virginia. Longstreet described the campaign as "brilliant," giving the entire credit to Lee. Brigadier General Dorsey Pender believed "there was never such a campaign, not even by Napoleon," and Jackson said "he would follow Lee blindfolded." It would be another two years before Richmond would be threatened again.[30]

With Pope defeated and McClellan's army withdrawing behind the Washington fortifications, Lee believed it was time to carry the war into enemy territory. Hoping to take advantage of a weakened and demoralized Union army and to permit his army to forage, Lee launched his campaign into Maryland. Spirits were high on September 4, 1862, as the Army of Northern Virginia splashed across the Potomac River into Maryland. Supplies provide strength to an army just as much as numbers and ammunition; if Lee could not feed his army, he could not fight with it. For most of the past year, Virginia had absorbed the brunt of the war as both Union and Confederate armies depleted agricultural and livestock supplies. Lee hoped to relieve Virginia by moving the scene of action into the North.[31]

Lee was determined to do more than feed and supply his troops at the enemy's expense. He hoped that an invasion of the North would encourage Maryland, a border state, to secede and that it would lead Britain and France to grant diplomatic recognition to the Confederacy. While regimental bands played "Maryland, My Maryland," Lee concentrated his army at Frederick, Maryland, just thirty miles upriver from Washington, where sympathetic Marylanders were expected to flock to the Confederate cause. Unfortunately for Lee, the Confederate supporters were concentrated in the southern and eastern parts of the state, and few came to Lee's support.[32]

The news of Lee's invasion threw Washington into a panic. Lee's objective was the Pennsylvania state capital, Harrisburg, where he planned to cut railroad connections with Baltimore and Philadelphia. To protect his rear, Lee split his army, sending Stonewall Jackson to capture Harper's Ferry and General Longstreet north to Hagerstown to gather supplies. Lee left Major General Daniel Harvey Hill's division of 5,000 men at Boonsboro to guard the rear of the army. Lee's plan to divide his army was risky, but he knew that command of the Union Army of the Potomac had been transferred to General McClellan. Although McClellan was an excellent organizer and popular with his men, Lee knew he was cautious and slow to move. Lee believed he had time to capture the Federal garrison at Harper's Ferry and reunite his army before McClellan could react.[33]

Unknown to Lee, a copy of his orders were found wrapped around a cigar packet at an abandoned Confederate camp at Frederick. They described in detail Lee's dispersal of his forces. The information was passed to McClellan, who quickly realized he had the opportunity to take advantage of Lee while he was vulnerable; he could destroy Lee's army piece by piece. McClellan was ecstatic. "Here is a paper with which if I cannot whip Bobbie Lee, I will be willing to go home," he said. But, despite his good fortune, McClellan was not spurred into speedy action; he did not have the killer instinct to capitalize on the situation.[34]

McClellan set his troops in action, but with his customary slowness. The critical battle began at dawn on September 14 when Union forces struck D. H. Hill's division at Turner's and Fox's Gaps. Hill's command suffered heavy losses, and only the timely arrival of Longstreet's corps prevented a total rout. The Battle of South Mountain, as the action became known, ended Lee's hopes for a Northern invasion. As evening fell, Lee ordered his army to regroup at Sharpsburg, a town west of South Mountain.[35]

Not until the evening of September 16 could McClellan move his 70,000 troops into position to attack the Confederates. By that time, Jackson had captured Harper's Ferry, and Lee had regrouped all his force except A. P. Hill's division, which was still at Harper's Ferry. Lee took up a position behind Antietam Creek.[36] With fewer than 40,000 men in position when the battle began, Lee's command of the situation was virtually flawless. His men performed magnificently, despite being outnumbered almost two to one. Although outwardly calm, Lee was under great strain. When he saw a straggler making off with a pig while his comrades were engaged in a life-and-death struggle, Lee's temper exploded. He ordered the man to be sent to Jackson to be shot. Exercising a calmer head, Jackson, who needed every man, placed the man in the thickest of the fighting.[37]

By late afternoon, it appeared that the outnumbered Confederates would be overrun. At the last moment, however, A. P. Hill arrived on the battlefield. Left behind by Jackson to complete the paroles of Union prisoners captured at Harper's Ferry, Hill had marched his division to Sharpsburg in time to repulse the final Union assault—the day was saved. By early evening, the battle ended. Longstreet later said that had McClellan committed his two reserve corps into the attack, he could have "taken Lee's army and everything in it."[38]

The Army of Northern Virginia had held its ground, but at a tremendous cost: 13,700 casualties against Union losses of 12,350, making September 17, 1862, the bloodiest one-day battle in American history. The Confederate army remained in place through September 18, but McClellan did not resume his attack. Lee correctly sensed that McClellan would not press his advantage but would allow him to withdraw his army to Virginia.

The fall of 1862 was personally difficult for Lee. His hand, injured in a fall from his horse, did not heal until mid-October, and later in the month, he learned that his twenty-three-year-old daughter, Annie, had died. In a letter to his oldest daughter, Mary, he wrote of his grief: "In the quiet hours of the night, when there is nothing to lighten the full weight of my grief, I feel as if I should be overwhelmed. I have always counted, if God could spare me, a few days after this Civil War was ended that I should have her [Annie] with me, but year after year my hopes go out, and I must be resigned." Just weeks later, Lee received the news of the death of his son Rooney's infant daughter.[39]

When McClellan was slow in pursuing Lee, Lincoln replaced him with Major General Ambrose Burnside. Lee expressed his regret at the loss of his opponent: "We always understood each other so well. I fear they may continue to make these changes till they find someone whom I don't understand." Within a week of assuming command, Burnside prepared his army for a new "On to Richmond" campaign.[40] In November, Lee divided his army into two corps; the first was placed under Longstreet, and the second under Jackson. All the cavalry remained under Stuart. Within just a few weeks after the new organization, Lee's army would face a new test. After taking command of the Army of the Potomac, Burnside moved eastward, placing his army on the northern bank of the Rappahannock River, opposite Fredericksburg. Lee followed him there, gaining the high ground on Marye's Heights behind Fredericksburg.[41]

Burnside put down pontoon bridges and was successful in crossing the Rappahannock and getting into the town of Fredericksburg. Lee made no serious effort to impede Burnside's movements; he wanted the Federals to attack him on Marye's Heights. On December 13, Union troops made six major assaults against the Confederate forces on the high ground; all failed—the result was a massacre. Lee watched the enemy rush forward and then, after leaving hundreds of dead on the slopes of Marye's Heights, fall back again. Turning to Longstreet, he said, "It is well that war is so terrible. We should grow too fond of it."[42]

The Battle of Fredericksburg ended in a Confederate victory. Federal losses were over 12,000 compared to fewer than 5,500 for the Confederates. The logistics of the battlefield at Fredericksburg limited Lee's opportunity for a counterattack. "We have really accomplished nothing," he later commented. "We have not gained a foot of ground, and I knew the enemy could easily replace the men he had lost."[43] Although Lee was not completely satisfied with his victory at Fredericksburg, Jefferson Davis was. For him it was a time to rejoice. In response to an enthusiastic crowd in Richmond, Davis said, "Our cause has had the brightest sunshine fall upon it. . . . Our glorious Lee, the valued son, emulating the virtues of the heroic Light-Horse Harry, his father, has achieved a victory at Fredericksburg . . . and driven the enemy back from his last and greatest effort to get 'On to Richmond.'"[44]

To climax Lee's six months of command, his army of 75,000 had blocked the advance of 130,000 Federals, causing heavy Union casualties and great jubilation in the South. General Johnston himself conceded that Lee was more fit to command, adding, "The shot that struck me down is the very best that has been fired for the Southern cause yet." Realizing that he did not have Jefferson Davis's confidence—but that Lee did—Johnston believed that his removal was for the good of the army.[45]

After the Fredericksburg debacle, Burnside hoped to try one final attack on Lee's flank on Marye's Heights, but his troops became bogged down in deep mud. After two frustrating days in January, Burnside called a halt to his offensive and withdrew to his winter quarters. Later that month, he was replaced as Commander of the Army of the Potomac by Major General "Fighting Joe" Hooker.

On January 26, 1863, Hooker assumed command and quickly proved himself a capable administrator. His first step was to raise the morale of his army. He improved living conditions, increased rations, and addressed the dysentery and scurvy that were taking a heavy toll. Discipline, which had become loose, was tightened. Hooker also reorganized his army into new corps, which were given distinctive badges of identification to boost esprit de corps. In the meantime, Hooker's army had grown to nearly 120,000—almost twice the size of Lee's force.[46] In April, Lincoln visited Hooker's army in the field. Hooker told Lincoln he had the "finest Army on the planet," boasting that it was not a question of whether he would take Richmond, but only when.[47]

After reconnoitering a number of undefended fords upstream from Fredericksburg, Hooker began his offensive on April 27. He was confident he could beat Lee. "If the enemy does not run," he said, "God help them." To officers in his tent, he reported: "My plans are perfect, and when I start to carry them out, may God have mercy on General Lee, for I will have none."[48]

Hooker detached a third of his army and sent them on a wide flanking movement to meet up with Major General Darius Couch's corps. Together there would be 70,000 men ready to attack Lee's exposed left flank. To conceal this movement, Hooker ordered Major General John Sedgwick and his Fourth Corps to attack Stonewall Jackson's troops on the Confederate right. At the same time, Major General Daniel Sickles's Third Corps would remain in its position across the Rappahannock River, ready to move if necessary.[49]

At first, Lee did not see the danger facing his army, but soon it became clear what Hooker was planning to do. When he saw Sedgwick's corps crossing the Rappahannock, Lee sent Major General Jubal Early to engage them. For some reason, Hooker lost his self-confidence and aggressiveness and allowed Lee to take the offensive.[50] Union General James McPherson described the scene: "Like a rabbit mesmerized by the gray fox, Hooker was frozen into immobility."[51]

Hooker would feel Lee's terrible swift sword and that of his subordinate, Stonewall Jackson. With astonishing boldness, Lee split his already outnumbered army. Leaving a small force of 14,000 to contain the 70,000 Federals at Chancellorsville, Lee sent Jackson on a fourteen-mile march around Hooker's right flank. The rapid flanking movement by Jackson caught the Union soldiers by surprise, and a rout developed when Jackson attacked. But the victory was a costly one. Jackson was wounded by friendly fire while conducting a reconnaissance of the enemy lines. In an attempt to save Jackson's life, doctors removed his shattered left arm. Lee was hopeful that Jackson would recover and be back at his side soon. On May 6, he sent Jackson his "affectionate regards" and urged him to "come back as soon as he could." Lee said of Jackson's wound: "He has lost his left arm, but I have lost my right arm."[52] On May 10, Jackson died of surgical complications. Lee was not prepared for Jackson's sudden death. "God will not take him from us," he said, "now that we need him so much." But God did take Jackson. His last words were of battles and victories, and then he said, "Let us cross over the river, and rest under the shade of the trees."[53]

Lee knew well the extent of his loss and that Jackson could not be replaced. The bond between the two was an unusual one. They had not known each other before the war, and it was not until the Battle of Seven Days that their paths crossed. Both men had a strong Christian faith in God. When speaking of the Union forces, Lee rarely referred to them as the enemy. To him, they were simply "those people" who had no business in Virginia. For Jackson, the Federals were the enemy, once exhorting his generals to "Kill them all! Kill them all!" Jackson once said that the only problem he had with Lee was that "he did not hate Yankees enough."[54]

During the fighting, Lee showed little fire or dash, but his mere presence on a battlefield could set off thunderous demonstrations when he rode among the men. With the strains of combat and death constantly tearing at him, Lee occasionally lost his temper. After such an outburst, he seemed ashamed and had a tendency to soften the blow, almost to the point of apologizing for it. For the most part, however, Lee was able to master his temper and displayed a friendly and generous attitude toward his staff.[55]

With Jackson's death, Lee organized his 75,000-man army from two infantry corps of four divisions each to three corps, each having three divisions. The First Corps was commanded by Lieutenant General James Longstreet, the Second Corps by Lieutenant General Richard Ewell, and the Third Corps by General A. P. Hill. Neither Ewell nor Hill had worked directly under Lee's command, and neither had Stonewall Jackson's ability to lead in combat. Lee and Jackson had been a team. Lee had come to rely very heavily on Jackson's ability to act on his own without very explicit instructions from him. Lee's failure to adjust his style in dealing with his two new corps commanders would prove to be troublesome and even disastrous at Gettysburg.[56]

After reorganizing his army, Lee did not have time to train his new leaders. Events made it desirable for him immediately to advance the Army of Northern Virginia into the Shenandoah Valley. Lee believed that Hooker would follow quickly, giving him a chance to defeat the Army of the Potomac once and for all. As Lee moved from Maryland into Pennsylvania, he issued General Order No. 73 proclaiming his lack of aggressive intent against the citizens: "The commanding general considers that no greater disgrace could befall the army, and through it our whole people, than the perpetration of the barbarous outrages upon the unarmed and defenseless, and the wanton destruction of private property that has marked the course of the enemy in our own country. . . . It must be remembered that we made war only upon armed men, and that we cannot take vengeance for the wrongs our people have suffered without . . . offending against Him to whom vengeance belongeth, without whose favor and support our efforts must all prove in vain."[57]

As Lee moved into Pennsylvania, his advance was almost unmolested, but his army was strung out over a wide area. In the meantime, Lincoln replaced Hooker with Major General George Meade who took command of the Army of the Potomac on June 28. Three days later, Meade would be involved in the most decisive battle of the war. When Lee learned of Meade's accession to command and his whereabouts, he immediately ordered his army to concentrate. On June 29, Lee remarked, "Tomorrow, gentlemen, we will not move to Harrisburg, as we expected, but will go over to Gettysburg and see what General Meade is after." Lee respected Meade's ability to lead, saying "General Meade will commit no blunder in my front, and if I make one, he will make haste to take advantage of it."[58]

When Lee encountered the enemy at Gettysburg, he did not have the benefit of Stuart's cavalry. Utilizing the confusing and discretionary orders Lee had given him, Stuart was engaged in a meaningless frolic behind enemy lines and did not rejoin the army until the end of the second day of the battle. By that time, Stuart was of little use to Lee. Without Stuart's "eyes" to tell him the location and size of the Union force, Lee was forced to operate in the dark. This reason alone was enough not to engage the enemy at this time, but events happened so quickly that Lee was drawn into a battle he did not wish to fight. Lee arrived on the field shortly after noon and consulted with Longstreet, who advised him not to engage the enemy at that location. However, after gaining the upper hand on the first day, Lee decided to stay and fight.[59]

Lee ordered Ewell to take the high ground "if he found it practicable, but to avoid a general engagement until the arrival of the other divisions of the army." Ewell did not consider the move practicable, with the result that Union forces used Cemetery Hill as the foundation upon which they constructed their defensive line. Ewell's hesitancy proved disastrous. Lee's failure to take full advantage of his temporary superiority and to issue definitive attack orders to Ewell allowed the Federals to gain the high ground for the battle.[60]

On the evening of the first day, Longstreet proposed a change in strategy. "All we have to do," he told Lee, "is to throw our army around their left, and we shall interpose between the Federal army and Washington. We can get a strong position and wait, and if they fail to attack, . . . we can move in the direction of Washington." Given this move, Longstreet believed, the Federals would have no choice but to attack, and the Confederates could set up a situation similar to what they had enjoyed at Fredericksburg. To Lee, Longstreet's proposal seemed like wishful thinking. "If the enemy is there, we must attack him," he said. "If he is there," Longstreet pressed, "it will be because he is anxious that we should attack—a good reason, in my judgment for not doing so." At the end of their discussion, Lee had not changed his mind. He would fight a full-scale battle at Gettysburg by going on the offensive.[61]

On the second day, July 2, Lee ordered Longstreet to attack the left flank of the Union army. Nothing seemed to work as planned. Longstreet took nearly all day to get his troops into position, and when he did, they were repulsed. At the other end of the battlefield, Ewell failed to begin his attack until dusk. It, too, did little but gain casualties for the Confederates. Despite the failed attempts on July 2, Lee remained determined to continue to attack the Union line.[62]

After two days of fighting, the Yankees still held a commanding position on Cemetery Ridge and Little and Big Round Tops. Again ignoring Longstreet's advice and pleas, Lee made a final effort to drive the Federals from the ridge. He believed if he barraged the Union front with a strong artillery attack, followed by a charge at the center, he could break the line. Pickett's fine Virginia troops, a part of Longstreet's corps, were chosen to lead the principal charge.[63]

At one o'clock the Confederate artillery opened up against the Union front. The Yankees returned the fire. When the guns went silent, General Pickett prepared his division for a desperate charge. Fifteen thousand Confederate troops in battle lines that stretched nearly a mile from flank to flank surged from the wooded crest of Seminary Ridge and headed toward a clump of trees marking the center of the Union line on Cemetery Ridge. Over the field, into the range of the Union artillery, and onward until they could hear the whine of rifle bullets, the Confederates moved. Soon they were stumbling and falling dead or crying out in anguish when they were hit. They pressed on until the line disappeared at the foot of Cemetery Ridge in dust and smoke. For a few minutes the rebel yell could be heard above the fire of thousands of rifles and scores of cannon. Then it died down; there were no more men to kill. Back toward the Confederate lines, the survivors of the charge streamed. The Union line had held. Lee had attempted the impossible and failed.[64]

Lee rode out to meet and rally the devastated troops as they fell back. "All will come right in the end," he told them; "we'll talk it over afterward; but in the meantime, all good men must rally." Soon he saw Pickett and rode over to him. "General Pickett," Lee said, "place your Division in rear of this hill, and be ready to repel the advance of the enemy should they follow up their advantage." Pickett was frantic. "General Lee," he cried, "I have no division now, Armistead is down, Garnett is down, and Kemper is mortally wounded." "Come General Pickett," Lee answered, "this has been my fight and upon my shoulders rests the blame." Lee tried to console General Cadmus Wilcox, whose brigade had been shattered. "Never mind, General," Lee replied, "all this has been my fault—it is I who have lost this fight, and you must help me out of it the best way you can."[65]

The loss to the Army of Northern Virginia at Gettysburg was devastating. Of the 75,000 engaged, 22,600 were killed or wounded. Union losses were high too; of the 83,300 troops, 17,700 were casualties. The loss of Confederate field grade officers would be felt for the duration of the war. Pickett's division was hit especially hard. Picket lost all three of his brigade commanders: Brigadier General Lewis Armistead, after being captured, died two days later in a Union hospital. Brigadier General Richard Garnett's body was never recovered. Brigadier General James Kemper was severely wounded and captured. When his wounds healed, he was exchanged in September.[66]

Late in the evening, Lee went wearily back to camp. "General," said one of his officers, "this has been a hard day on you." He paused, reflected, and then spoke out: "I never saw troops behave more magnificently than Pickett's Division of Virginia did today in that grand charge upon the enemy." Again he paused and added, "Too bad, too bad! Oh, too bad!"[67]

On July 4, Lee started his retreat toward the Potomac. Meade made no effort to engage Lee and allowed him to escape into Virginia. As the army retreated, Lee might have argued that he had been misled into battle, blaming Stuart who had not returned until the second day of the battle. Lee might have blamed Ewell and Longstreet for their hesitation at critical times during the battle. But, as the army's leader, he was to blame. He would not attempt to put the blame on others when he felt it was rightly his. To Longstreet he admitted, "It's all my fault. I thought my men were invincible."[68]

News of Lee's defeat sent a shock wave through Richmond; some were even critical of Lee. On August 8, Lee wrote a letter of resignation to President Davis, saying that he could not do what he himself wanted to accomplish. It had taken a dozen errors to lose Gettysburg, he said, and he had made most of them. Davis replied that he could not find a better man to command the Army of Northern Virginia than Lee, and he refused to accept his resignation.[69] As time passed, Lee was less inclined to blame himself for his defeat at Gettysburg. Officially he did not criticize his subordinates, but in private he intimated that Longstreet and Ewell had let him down. After the war, Lee told a friend, "If I had Stonewall Jackson with me . . . I should have won the Battle of Gettysburg."[70]

Lee had gambled for high stakes and lost. After Gettysburg he was never able to gain the offensive again. When Grant took over command of the

Army of the Potomac and crossed the Rapidan River in May 1864, Lee's army had to move back into entrenched positions to resist the heavily reinforced and experienced Union army. This proved to be the beginning of the end for the Confederacy.[71] Unlike other Union commanders that Lee had faced, Grant saw the war as a whole and developed a plan that involved simultaneous attacks on all Confederate fronts. In this way, Grant could take advantage of his numerical superiority.[72]

Lee's army fought brilliantly for nearly two years after Gettysburg, but they were faced with overpowering adversities. The Army of Northern Virginia had been thinned by heavy battle losses and desertions, with no opportunity for reinforcements. The soldiers that were left, "Lee's Miserables," as they called themselves in jest, had very little with which to fight. Thousands were barefoot, and all were without overcoats, blankets, or warm clothes for the biting winter. Food, too, was in short supply. Sometimes companies would go for several days at a time on nothing but hardtack and a bit of salt pork. Lee shared their privations, living in a tent in the open without heat or other comforts and eating dinners of potato and salt pork.[73]

When Lee had whipped McClellan, Pope, Burnside, and Hooker, they had accepted the verdict of the battle and retreated, but Grant did not wage war that way. He was, as Lee once said regretfully, "not a retreating man." Grant would smash at Lee and be hurled back; then he would pull his army together and, instead of retreating, file away to the south and attack again. Lee had never met an opponent like him. Lee's army fought a series of savage battles—Spotsylvania, the Bloody Angle, and Cold Harbor. Each time Grant struck, Lee's army was in position to repel his attacks, but Grant stayed in the field and kept right on going.[74]

Once, during a dire situation on the second day of the Wilderness campaign, Lee was caught in the middle of the battle. He quickly ordered the nearby Texas Brigade into action, telling its commander that the only way the enemy could be dislodged was by a charge. Caught up in the moment, Lee rode through the ranks and prepared to lead the charge himself. Concerned for his safety, the Texans shouted, "General Lee to the rear!" With a soldier holding Traveller's bridle, Lee was escorted to the rear. The inspired Texans continued the battle and moved back the enemy in an important phase of the battle.[75]

Even with the war going against him, Lee showed his compassion, expressing sympathy to Confederate General Wade Hampton who had lost his son in battle: "I grieve with you at the death of your gallant son. So young, so brave, so true. I know how much you must suffer. . . . We must labor on in the course before us, but for him I trust is in rest and peace, for I believe our Merciful God takes us when it is best for us to go. He is now safe from all harm and evil. . . . May God support you under your great affliction and give you strength to bear the trials He may impose upon you." Sadly, Lee must have written many letters similar to this one.[76]

As the war entered its final stages, Grant's army settled down at Petersburg and prepared to wear down Lee by sheer weight of numbers. No campaign of the Civil War lasted as long as the siege of Petersburg, Virginia. For 292 days, "the last bulwark of the Confederacy" held on. Supplies were channeled to Richmond through Petersburg; without Petersburg, Richmond would fall. Lee's army was melting away through desertion, disease, and death. "The struggle is to keep the army fed and clothed," Lee wrote. "Only fifteen in one regiment has shoes, and bacon is issued only once in a few days." Although the courage of the Army of Northern Virginia continued, their strength did not. Lee's army was now reduced to 40,000 and stretched to the breaking point. In February 1865, a new danger appeared. Sherman had completed his March to the Sea, taking Savannah and then turning north. Within a few weeks, Sherman would be joining Grant, and then Lee would face an army three or four times the size of his.[77]

On February 1, 1865, the Confederate Congress approved the appointment of Lee as general-in-chief of all Confederate armies. Davis had convinced the Confederate Congress that the move would "inspire increased confidence in the final success of our armies." Lee, however, was appalled at the prospect. "If I had the ability, I would not have the time," he said when informed of the promotion. Lee's reply came three days later in a memo to Adjutant General Samuel Cooper: "I am indebted alone to the kindness of His Excellency the President for my nomination to this high and arduous office, and wish I had the ability to fill it to advantage." A Southern staff officer later commented on the appointment as a "mockery of a rank no longer of any value." The promotion came too late for the Confederacy, which was gasping its last breath.[78]

Lee made one last desperate attempt on March 25 to break Grant's lines at Fort Stedman, east of Petersburg, but failed. Lee would have to give up Richmond—a city he had defended so heroically for three bitter years. As time progressed, it became clear to Lee that Petersburg and Richmond would have to be evacuated. "I see no prospect of doing more than holding our position here till night," Lee telegraphed Secretary of War Breckinridge. "I am not certain that I can do that."[79]

April 2, the retreat began, with Grant close behind. Finally, two courses were open to Lee—he could disperse his army and try to rally a new one to fight a guerrilla war, or he could surrender. "I would rather die a thousand deaths," Lee said about surrender. But he chose the course he thought was best for his soldiers and the people of the South. It would be wrong to condemn his people to years of guerrilla warfare. With a heavy heart, he wrote to Grant that he would discuss terms of surrender.[80]

On the afternoon of April 9, 1865, Lee waited half an hour for Grant in the parlor of Wilmer McLean's house at Appomattox. His thoughts were on the Army of Northern Virginia, lying hungry and exhausted in the fields near Appomattox, and on his three sons that had been reported missing. Perhaps he looked back upon all that had taken place in the four previous years and asked himself how he came to be at Appomattox. Lee wanted to spare his army any useless bloodshed. He was a man who would have taken advantage of any military option available, but there were no more options.[81]

When Grant arrived, he was in the uniform of a private, trousers spattered with mud tucked inside his boots. He wore no sword or spurs, nothing to show that he was the general-in-chief except his shoulder straps with their golden stars. Despite his dress, the Union commander was a gentleman. He did not ask for Lee's sword; his terms were generous. He sent rations to the starving Confederates and ordered the soldiers to refrain from cheering or firing volleys to celebrate their victory. "The war is over," he said. "The rebels are again our countrymen, and the best way of showing our rejoicing will be to abstain from such demonstrations."[82]

The Army of Northern Virginia was no more. Lee had taken command when it was disorganized and shaped it into one of the greatest fighting forces in history. He had led it to victory and finally to defeat. As he sat astride Traveller, his men crowded around him, many with tears streaming down their cheeks. Lee took time to talk to some of his men: "I have done what I thought was best for you. My heart is too full to speak, but I wish you all health and happiness." Then he turned and rode off.[83]

That evening, Lee prepared his final order, the famous General Order No. 9, to be read to his troops the following day.

After four years of arduous service marked by unsurpassed courage and fortitude, the Army of Northern Virginia has been compelled to yield to overwhelming numbers and resources. I need not tell the brave survivors of so many hard fought battles, who remained steadfast to the last, that I have consented to the result from no distrust of them. But, feeling that valor and devotion could accomplish nothing that could compensate for the loss that must have attended the continuance of the contest, I determined to avoid the useless sacrifice of those whose past service have endeared them to their countrymen.

By the terms of the agreement, officers and men can return to their homes and remain there until exchanged. You will take with you the satisfaction that proceeds from the consciousness of duty faithfully performed; and I earnestly pray that a merciful God will extend to you His blessings and protection.

With an increasing admiration of your constancy and devotion to your country, and a grateful remembrance of your kind and generous consideration for myself, I bid you an affectionate farewell.

—R. E. Lee, General[84]

Lee did not attend the formal ceremony of surrender on the morning of April 12; he remained in camp until his men returned. Then, with a few of his officers, Lee rode home. All along the way people came to see him and bring him food. On April 14, he stopped to spend the night at his brother's farm. The house was crowded, and Lee did not want to inconvenience any of his brother's guests. He insisted on spending the night in his old tent, which he pitched on the lawn.[85]

The next morning, Lee rode through the rain into Richmond. The once proud capital of the Confederacy now looked like a cemetery of destroyed homes, factories, and shops. Above the Capitol waved the Stars and Stripes of the Union flag. Despite the rain, Southerners and Northerners alike turned out to see the general and to greet him with cheers and tears. At last Lee came to 707 East Franklin Street, the home his wife had set up during the war. He bowed to the crowd, then went inside and took off his sword for the last time.[86]

Lee was not allowed to relax for long. When he learned of President Lincoln's assassination, he was deeply shocked. He stared at the floor and then exclaimed, "This is the hardest blow the South has yet received."[87] After returning to Richmond, Lee had no other place to go. His home at Arlington was gone, confiscated by Federal authorities for nonpayment of taxes. Its lawns now held the graves of thousands of Northern soldiers. "I am looking for some quiet place in the woods," he wrote, "where I can procure shelter and my daily bread if permitted by the victor."[88]

Robert E. Lee was concerned about his future. The assassination of President Lincoln only increased the North's desire for vengeance and a hard peace. In June, when Lee was indicted for treason, he asked Grant to help him. The terms of his parole at Appomattox stated that he would not "be disturbed by the United States authority." Grant agreed to help and threatened to resign from the army if Federal authorities arrested Lee. President Johnson suspended Lee's prosecution, and he was never arrested or brought to trial. During his lifetime, his citizenship was never restored, however.[89]

Lee's personal example after the war would be the South's model of how to live in its defeat. Southerners regarded Lee's honor as their own, Colonel Charles Marshall would say in eulogizing him. If Lee agreed to terms of surrender, then Southerners felt bound by them as well. Lee understood that attention would be continually upon him. This regard imposed a special burden of self-control and leadership. Lee was a model of propriety not only for the South but for the nation as a whole. Americans continued to expect it of him, and he did not let them down.[90]

During a Sunday service at St. Paul's Episcopal Church in Richmond, a black man rose and approached the altar rail for communion. This was a great surprise and shock to the communicants and others present. Blacks were expected to wait until all whites had left the rail before they were to step forward. Dr. Minnegerode, the pastor, was openly embarrassed and appeared not to know what to do. Lee, rising in his usual dignified manner, walked to the rail and knelt down beside the black man to take communion. Others in the congregation followed him, and the service continued.[91]

On another occasion, Jubal Early wrote to Lee from his self-imposed exile in Mexico to say, "I hate Yankees this day worse than I have ever done and my hatred is increasing every day." Lee wrote back to him: "We shall have to be patient and suffer for a while at least; and all controversy, I think, will only serve to prolong angry and bitter feelings, and postpone the period when reason and charity may resume their way."[92]

Lee's actions greatly influenced other Southerners. Captain George Wise, a son of Confederate General Harry Wise, protested to Lee that he did not think the terms of the parole obliged him to take the oath of allegiance, and he would rather leave the country than do so. Lee quietly told him, "Do not leave Virginia. Our Country needs her young men now." After Captain Wise signed the oath, his father contended that he had disgraced the family. When his son told him that General Lee had advised him to do so, he said, "Oh, that alters the case. Whatever General Lee says is all right; I don't care what it is." Thousands of Southerners felt the same way.[93]

Wherever Lee went he was admired and treated with respect. On one occasion when he entered a large dining room at a Southern resort hotel, five hundred guests rose and stood in respectful silence. Although Lee was heartbroken by the South's defeat, he tried not to display his feelings openly. Sometimes, however, it showed through. "Why do you look so sad?" asked a girl who saw him not long after Appomattox. "Why shouldn't I?" Lee answered. "My cause is dead. I am homeless—I have nothing on earth." Yet he continued to live a life that inspired Southerners to forget their hatred and once more become Americans.[94]

A short time after the surrender at Appomattox, Lee was offered several homes in which to live. Lee's family was of English origin. Now relatives and other admirers offered him the opportunity to come to England and share the luxury of their homes with them. But he positively declined, thanking them and saying, "No, I will not forsake my people in their extremity; what they endure, I will endure, and I am ready to break my last crust with them." He refused to leave Virginia. He wanted to help his people overcome the disasters of the war.[95]

Lee received many attractive employment opportunities after his surrender. He was offered $50,000 per year to head a New York firm being organized to promote trade with the South. An insurance company offered him $25,000 per year to act as its president. Another company proposed to pay him $10,000 per year merely for the use of his name. Lee's sense of personal honor would not permit him to accept any of these efforts to capitalize on his fame. "My name is not for sale at any price," he said.[96]

By the fall of 1865, Lee was forced to make plans for earning a living. He hoped to buy land and try his hand at farming. At the same time, a small college in the Shenandoah Valley had other plans for the general. Washington College was founded before the American Revolution and had received an endowment from Washington himself. The college had educated some of the most prominent men of Virginia. The war had taken its toll on the institution. Its buildings were greatly in need of repair, its professors and students scattered, and its resources crippled by the war.[97] At a board meeting, a proposal was made to elect Robert E. Lee to serve as president of the college. The board liked the idea and voted to offer Lee the position. A representative from the college was sent to Lee to see if he would accept. They had little hope, however, that a man of his stature would come to their college.[98]

Lee considered the college's offer and eventually accepted it. Lee saw this as a good opportunity to work with young people, and the cause of Southern education had a strong appeal to him. "If I thought I could be of any benefit to our noble youth, I would not hesitate to give my service," he told a friend. The position paid a meager yearly salary of $1,500, provided a house for him, and offered a yearly bonus based on the amount of tuition collected. The trustees were elated at Lee's acceptance, and he was officially installed as president in mid-September 1865.[99]

Lee quickly established rapport and built a kind of devotion with his new associates in the same way he had with his wartime staff. Trustees, faculty, and townspeople supported General Lee in efforts that quickly gave the college a vigor it probably had never known before. Only fifty students registered on opening day, but others soon came. Young men continued to arrive all through the first session until the enrollment reached 146. Gifts were generous, allowing Lee to consider improvements.[100]

In fact, Lee immediately embarked on his duties as college president and helped to revise the curriculum to meet the South's need for men who could rebuild it. In doing so, Lee began the transformation of Washington College from a nineteenth-century classical academy to a twentieth-century university. He solicited financial assistance and encouraged students to resume their studies after spending years in the war. One veteran told him that he was impatient to make up for the time he had lost in the army. Lee quickly responded. "Mister Humphreys!" he snapped. "However long you live and whatever you accomplish, you will find that the time you spent in the Confederate army was the most profitably spent portion of your life. Never again speak of having wasted time in the army."[101]

Lee devoted his time to work. He was constantly in his office, always available to all callers—faculty, parents, and students alike. No letter was unanswered; no effort of courtesy was too insignificant. Students were amazed at the president's familiarity with their scholastic standing, outside behavior, home life, and athletic achievements. When a student requested an appearance with Lee, the student knew that he would be treated with justice, courtesy, and gentleness. "His sense of personal duty was also expanded into a warm solicitude for all who associated with him," one of Lee's faculty later stated. "To the faculty, he was an elder brother, beloved and revered, and full of tender sympathy. To the students he was a father, in reproof. Their welfare and their conduct and character as gentlemen were his chief concern." Lee thought it was the responsibility of the college not only to educate the intellect but to make Christian gentlemen. For Lee, the moral and religious character of the students was more important than their intellectual progress. He would not tolerate dishonesty or meanness.[102]

Lee continued to hear from ex-Confederates who consulted him for advice. When General Beauregard wrote to him, Lee responded about the need for reconciliation and peace. "I need not tell you," he wrote, "that true patriotism sometimes requires of men to act exactly contrary, at one period, to that which it does at another." As an example, Lee cited George Washington as one who had served the king of England and, at a later date, served the Continental Congress of America against him. "He [Washington] had not been branded by the world with reproach for this, but his course has been applauded."[103] To the widow of a Confederate soldier, Lee spoke frankly, "Madam, do not train up your children in hostility to the government of the United States. Remember, we are all one country now. Dismiss from your mind all sectional feelings and bring them up to be Americans."[104]

By the end of the second session, the enrollment at Washington College had grown to almost 400 students. Although the college had made great progress under Lee's leadership, he continued his hard work and adherence to an exact schedule. Lee always attended chapel in the morning, then went to his office or elsewhere on the campus until noon. In the afternoon, he usually took a ride on Traveller. He went to bed early because he believed that "one hour's sleep before midnight is worth two after that time."[105]

In November 1867, a Richmond grand jury ordered Lee to testify during the legal proceedings against Jefferson Davis. The prosecution attempted to get Lee to admit that he had conducted military operations that were ordered by Davis. Lee, however, refused to place blame on anyone except himself. "I am responsible for what I did," he declared frankly, "and cannot now recall any important movement I made which I would not have had I acted entirely on my own responsibility."[106]

When his son, "Rooney" Lee, was to be married for a second time, the general was invited to attend the wedding in Petersburg. Lee was reluctant to attend the ceremonies; some of his saddest memories of the war were associated with Petersburg. He was not certain if the residents would welcome him there, but he finally consented to attend after his son came in person to Lexington to see him.[107] On the afternoon of November 28, 1867, Lee went to Petersburg. Much to his surprise, Lee was welcomed by an enthusiastic crowd. Everywhere Lee found people smiling, his old soldiers working, and the children welcoming him with laughter. Upon his return to Lexington, he wrote his son of the delight he had found in Petersburg: "A load of sorrow which had been pressing upon me for years was lifted from my heart."[108]

In the fall of 1870, the new session at Washington College began, the sixth since Lee became its president. He attended the opening exercises and met with students and faculty in the usual manner, but those who knew him well could see that he was failing. To others, he seemed like an old man; his hair was white, and he was now slightly stooped.[109] On September 28, Lee traveled through the rain to a vestry meeting where he presided for more than three hours in the chilly auditorium. From the church, Lee walked home in the rain. He took off his cape and went into the dining room. "You look chilly," Mrs. Lee said, but Lee responded that he was warmly clothed. Lee took his usual place at the head of the table and started to say grace. He tried to speak but could make no sounds. Doctors examined him later that evening and diagnosed his problem as a blood clot in his brain. After a week of silence, Lee sank into delirium.[110]

During that last morning of his life, Lee's mind returned to the battlefield. "Tell Hill he must come," he said, and then lapsed into unconsciousness. In his dreams, he may have been bringing his last campaign to a close. Finally he said, "Strike the tent." After that, he sank down into a silence that was never broken. At 9:30 a.m. on October 12, he crossed over the river to rest where his companions in arms had preceded him.[111]

Word of Lee's death spread quickly. *The New York Tribune*, which had been hostile toward the South during the war, described Lexington in its mourning: ". . . find the town overwhelmed with grief. . . . At the hotels, by the headstone, in the schools, on the streets, everywhere, the only topic of conversation is the death of General Lee. All classes of the community seem to be affected, even the colored people, who walk along in silence with sorrowful countenance and mourn the loss of 'Good ole Marse Robert.' Every house in town seemed to be draped with the emblems of mourning. . . . The students of Washington College, of which Lee was president, held a meeting this morning. . . . Many of the students were affected to tears. They seemed to have had for General Lee the affection of children for a father."[112]

Funeral services were held in Lexington and were attended by thousands. He was buried in a vault under the chapel on campus. In 1871, the trustees of Washington College voted to change the college's name to Washington and Lee. The two men who had so much in common were thus forever linked together. In 1875, a larger-than-life figure of Lee, lying as if asleep on a draped couch, was completed. The recumbent statue was placed in the Lee Memorial Chapel on the campus of Washington and Lee College.

Many consider Robert E. Lee to be the most able commander of the Civil War. The men in the Army of Northern Virginia worshiped him. A

North Carolina soldier wrote in 1863, "I felt proud that the Southern Confederacy could boast such a man." Real greatness is never found on the battlefield. Looking back, Lee had said, "I did only what my duty demanded. I could have taken no other course without dishonor, and if it all were to be done over again, I should act in precisely the same manner."[113] The fact that Lee was a great general did not automatically make him a great man.

It was after the war that Lee demonstrated his greatness as a man. Lee was a model of gracious defeat. That attitude would win him admirers among friends and foes alike. He did not spend his last years in bitter regret. Rather, as president of Washington College, he taught young Southern men the skills they needed to build a new life and future. He appealed to the defeated South to put aside its hatred and bitterness and join him in becoming a model citizen. Lee's manners and code of ethics were models for others to emulate. His deep religious faith let him accept the disappointment and hardships of his life. Few public figures in any age have left such an enduring legacy. Despite the passage of time and ever-changing popular culture, Robert E. Lee remains the foremost Southern hero.[114]

7 *Thomas J. Jackson*

"Stonewall"

He was laid in state in a reception room of the Executive Mansion. Thomas Jonathan Jackson's widow, dressed in black, came for a final look at her husband, but his coffin had been sealed and only his face could be seen through a glass plate, a view she said was "disappointing and unsatisfactory."[1] As word of Jackson's death spread throughout Richmond, men and women of all ages "gazed at each other in dumb amazement. Women were seen in the streets . . . wringing their hands and weeping as bitter as if one near and dear to their hearts had been taken." A Richmond newspaper proclaimed: "The affections of every household in the nation were twined about this great and unselfish warrior. . . . He had fallen, and a nation weeps."[2]

Jefferson Davis was among the visitors who looked in on Jackson. Davis stood a long time at the coffin and then left the room in silence. Another visitor was Brigadier General Richard Garnett, who had come to pay his last respects. Jackson had recommended Garnett for court-martial for withdrawing the "Stonewall Brigade" from the Battle of Kernstown in 1862, but his case never came to trial. Garnett never forgave Jackson for the great injustice he perceived had been done him, but like other Southerners, Garnett could not forget Jackson's military achievements.[3]

After viewing Jackson's body, Garnett spoke to Major Kyd Douglas and Lieutenant Colonel A. S. Pendleton, two of Jackson's aides: "You know of the unfortunate breach between General Jackson and myself; I can never forget it, nor cease to regret it. But I wish to assure you that no one can lament his death more sincerely than I do. I believe he did me a great injustice, but I believe also he acted from the purest motives. He is dead. Who can fill his place?" After Garnett spoke, Pendleton asked him to be one of the pallbearers. Garnett graciously agreed.[4]

The next morning, an escort of generals moved Jackson's body to the Confederate House of Representatives where more than 20,000 mourners viewed his body. The bells of the city tolled, and cannon fired in salute. Government offices and businesses were closed in respect for their fallen hero. Three days later, Jackson was buried in Lexington, Virginia.[5]

At the time of Jackson's death, no soldier or statesman in either the North or the South enjoyed a greater reputation than he did. Few men have been so admired in their lifetimes, and fewer still have enjoyed such a durable reputation as Lieutenant General Thomas Jonathan Jackson, an orphan boy who through tenacity, willpower, military skill, and great luck became the most acclaimed general of his era. An aura of genius and invincibility surrounded his name. Americans North and South marveled, and still do, at his exploits. No matter what the situation or how large the enemy force, Jackson always seemed to find a way to win, or at least, so it seemed. When he died, the entire South mourned and went into a state of shock. When the war was over and the Confederacy itself had perished, the South kept his memory alive and grieved for what might have been had he not died when he did. A prominent ex-Confederate wrote in 1877: "The star of the Confederate destiny reached its zenith on the 2nd day of May, when Jackson fell wounded at the head of his victorious troops; it began to set on the 10th of May, when Jackson was no more."[6]

The praise for Jackson from Northerners, who were victimized by his daring thrusts, was just as laudatory. Major General Gouverneur Warren, who would soon become one of the heroes at Gettysburg, wrote upon hearing of Jackson's death that he rejoiced for the Union causes, "and yet in my soldier's heart I cannot but see him the best soldier of all this war, and grieve at his untimely end." A New York paper praised Jackson as a "military genius" and declared, "Nowhere else will the name of Jackson be more honored."[7] Interestingly, Thomas Jackson reached the eve of the Civil War without revealing any hint that he had within him the making of a legend.

Jackson was born in Clarksburg, Virginia (now West Virginia), on January 21, 1824, the third of four children born to Jonathan Jackson and Julia Neale Jackson. Jackson's father was an aspiring but penniless lawyer; his mother, a frail schoolteacher. Marriage did not help Jonathan's financial position. Court records show evidence of numerous times the young couple borrowed money secured by livestock and even by Julia's household furnishings. The marriage lasted less than ten years. Julia was twenty-eight when her eldest child, six-year-old Elizabeth, died of typhoid fever. Less than three weeks later, young Tom's father succumbed to the same disease. The day after his death, Julia gave birth to a daughter, Laura Ann. The young widow was left with three small children, the oldest Warren, only five. Thomas was two years old at the time.[8]

In November 1830, Thomas's mother married Blake Woodson, a lawyer fifteen years older than she and a widower with eight children, none of

The last picture of Stonewall Jackson taken two weeks before his fatal wounding at Chancellorsville. When he died, the Confederate cause died with him.

COURTESY OF THE LIBRARY OF CONGRESS

whom lived with him. A year later, the couple moved to a house in New Haven, Virginia. It is not certain whether the three Jackson children moved with their mother and stepfather, but at about this time, for some unknown reason (perhaps because of Julia's health or because Woodson was unwilling or unable to support them), the three Jackson children were sent to live with relatives. Six-year-old Thomas and his four-year-old sister, Laura, went to live with their paternal uncles, John and Cummins Jackson.[9]

Thomas was not happy about leaving his mother and stepfather. T. J. Arnold, a family biographer, wrote of Jackson's reluctance to make the move: "Thomas, now six years of age, slipped off to the near-by woods, where he concealed himself, only returning to his home at nightfall. The uncle, after a day or two of much coaxing and the offer of numerous bribes, finally with the mother's aid, induced the children to make the visit to Jackson's Mill, a journey of several days."[10]

The separation was devastating to both mother and son, and throughout his life, Jackson would never forget the experience. "Nor could he speak of it in after-years," his wife would write, "without the utmost tenderness." As a young man, he imagined heaven as a place "where care and sorrow are unknown," where one could live "with a mother, a brother, a sister . . . and I hope a father."[11] Shuttled from one relative to another, young Jackson did not enjoy a stable environment until he finally settled down at the home of Cummins Jackson.

On October 7, 1831, Tom's mother gave birth to another son, William Wirt Woodson. It was a difficult birth from which Julia never recovered. When she found she was near death, she sent for her children; they were brought to her bedside by "Uncle Robinson," a trusted slave of the Jacksons. Robinson's wife described young Jackson at the time as a "rosy-cheeked, blue-eyed boy, with wavy brown hair, to whom she [Julia] clung with all mother's devotion." Julia's children arrived in time to receive their mother's dying blessings and prayers. Julia Woodson died at the age of thirty-three.[12]

Laura and Tom were welcomed at Jackson's Mill by the entire family. The Jackson clan was headed by tall, muscular Cummins Jackson, and under his leadership the family prospered. Standing more than six feet tall and weighing over two hundred pounds, Cummins was noted for his strength. He enjoyed a good time and loved to race horses; he had no interest in religion and belonged to no church. He was able, ambitious, energetic, and generous; above all, he was good to his orphan nephew who he took in.[13]

Although an adult, Cummins continued with many of his childhood pleasures, including fighting. He was constantly engaged in litigation, suing and being sued. In 1844, he was indicted for passing counterfeit coins but was never tried.[14] One thing no one ever accused Cummins of doing, however, was breaking his word. On the frontier, a man's word was his bond. All honor was lost when a person broke his word. When a man shook another's hand and said, "You have my word," a sacred trust was in effect between the two.[15]

Thomas always looked back fondly on his foster home and his years at Jackson's Mill. His Uncle Cummins was a great influence on his boyhood. As an affectionate and indulgent father figure, Cummins won Jackson's lifelong loyalty, despite his numerous faults and his unscrupulous ways.[16]

Despite his Uncle Cummins's brushes with the law, young Jackson grew to respect the law and have integrity. Stories are told of his honesty; one involved his sale of a fish. While fishing, Jackson pulled in a three-foot pike. Throwing it over his shoulder, he started for the nearby town. At the time, he had an outstanding agreement with Conrad Kester, a local resident, to sell him all the fish he caught for a given price. On the way to town, he passed the house of Colonel John Talbott. The colonel asked him how much he would take for the fish. "This fish is not for sale," Jackson replied. "I'll give you a dollar for it," Talbott said. "I can't take it, Colonel Talbott; this fish is sold to Mr. Kester," he replied. "But Tom," the colonel protested, "I'll give you a dollar and a quarter; surely he will not give you more than that." But Tom continued to hold to his agreement. "Colonel Talbott, I have an agreement with Mr. Kester to furnish him fish of a certain length for fifty cents each. He has taken some from me a little shorter than that; and he is going to get this fish for fifty cents." Kester, according to the story, offered to give a dollar for the prize catch, but Jackson would not accept more than the agreed amount. To him, some things were a matter of honor.[17]

A contemporary of Jackson, William E. Arnold, later said that young Thomas "learned slowly, but what he got in his head, he never forgot. He was not quick to decide; when he made up his mind to do a thing, he did it on short notice and in quick time."[18] Young Tom learned to trap, hunt, fish, and ride well enough to serve as a jockey on Uncle Cummins's horses in local races. Throughout his life, Jackson enjoyed music. On one occasion, he obtained a violin. With the help of a friend, he set about to teach himself to play. Although he gave it his best effort, he failed miserably due to a handicap he could not overcome—he was almost completely tone deaf.[19]

Jackson had little formal education, attending school at Jackson's Mill, Weston, and Clarksburg; but in the mountain country of western Virginia, this deficiency was not a handicap. During his teen years, Jackson worked briefly as an engineering assistant and town constable; his success at these two positions encouraged him to take a competitive examination at the U.S. Military Academy at West Point in 1842. Although he did not do well enough to get the appointment, he later was admitted when the successful candidate quit West Point after only a few weeks; Jackson was sent to take his place.[20]

When Jackson entered West Point, his knowledge of the social graces was deficient, for he did not know even which fork or knife to use in a meal. He was also lacking in the academic area, starting out well behind all the incoming cadets. During his first year, he ranked solidly in what cadets called the "Immortals," those at the very bottom of their class. But Jackson was not content to remain there.[21]

Jackson's experience at West Point exemplifies his life generally—starting out behind, catching up, and then moving ahead. His academic progress was not so much due to his brilliance or intuitiveness but rather to his remarkable determination. At West Point, he began to keep a book of maxims in which he would record statements that impressed him. One of his favorite maxims illustrated the way he lived: "You may be whatever you resolve to be." One of the cadets recalled how Jackson used his time for study: "All lights were put out at taps. And just before the signal, he would pile up his grate with coal, and lying prone before it on the floor, he would work away at his lessons by the glare of the fire, which scorched his very brain until a late hour of the night." Jackson's determination to succeed helped his academic efforts and impressed his instructors in his favor. His grades improved year by year until he finished within the top third of his class, ranking seventeenth in a class of fifty-nine. A common story around the Point had it that, if Jackson had stayed one more year, he would have been number one in his class.[22]

Jackson graduated in 1846. This particular class was purported to be the most outstanding one in the Academy's history. Of the fifty-nine members, the class supplied the Union army with fifteen generals, including George McClellan, and the Confederate army with nine, including George Pickett, who graduated at the bottom of the class.[23]

One of Jackson's classes during his final year greatly influenced his thinking when war came. The great military tactician during that time was professor Dennis Hart Mahan. Although he had never been involved in battle, Mahan had studied the military experts of the past, particularly Napoleon. Mahan believed two elements were vital to military success—speed in maneuvering and boldness, coupled with reason. Jackson would later employ these tenets with unprecedented success on the battlefield.[24]

Shortly after graduation, Brevet Second Lieutenant Jackson went off to join the war in Mexico. At the Battles of Contreras and Cherubusco in August 1847, Jackson distinguished himself. His gallantry under fire won him the permanent rank of first lieutenant as well as a brevet promotion to captain. During the fighting around Chapultepec, his handling of an exposed section of the artillery won him the admiration of the entire army. When the Mexican cavalry charged, Jackson's guns tore their attack to pieces, earning him the personal acclaim of the commanding general, Winfield Scott. During a reception after the fall of Mexico, Scott was introduced to Jackson. "I don't know that I shall shake hands with Mr. Jackson," he said. "If you can forgive yourself for the way you slaughtered those poor Mexicans with your guns, I am not sure that I can." Embarrassed, Jackson blushed profusely until Scott changed his demeanor and warmly shook his hand.[25]

As a result of his performance at Chapultepec, Jackson was promoted to the brevet rank of major. During the following months, while he served in the occupation forces, he increased his interest in Christianity. His immediate superior, Captain Francis Taylor, who was a devout Episcopalian, convinced Jackson that every young man had an obligation to study religion. Jackson was so impressed by Taylor's fervor that he began a program of regular Bible study and prayer.[26]

While in Mexico, Jackson learned to speak and read Spanish; he read Chesterfield's letters in Spanish and Humboldt's *History of Mexico*. This study might be useful, he thought, if he decided to try his fortune in Mexico, and it would be a mark of cultivation at home. At the same time, he was beginning to take his religion seriously, too. The Mexican culture impressed him so much that he considered becoming a member of the Catholic Church, studying the church's tenets and practices. He committed the same serious energy to the study of Catholicism as he had to his studies at West Point. After living in a monastery for some weeks and discussing points of doctrine with the archbishop of Mexico, Jackson decided he did not believe as the Catholics did.[27]

Eventually, Jackson's faith increased, partially because of his concern for his health. Jackson believed his poor health was a sign from God. "My afflictions," he wrote his sister Laura, "I believe were decreed by Heaven's sovereign, as a punishment for my offenses against his Holy Laws and have probably been the instrument of eternal death, to that of everlasting life." Believing this to be true, Jackson was baptized at an Episcopal church near Fort Hamilton.[28] A few years later, he settled for Calvinism and embraced the Presbyterian religion with such great zeal that his pastor labeled him as the "best deacon I ever had."[29]

It was during his days as a cadet at West Point that Jackson's health problems began. Dabney Maury, a classmate, believed it was then that he became a hypochondriac. William E. Jones, who graduated two years after Jackson, later said that Jackson believed that "insidious diseases were at his vitals" so that he always sat upright without touching the back of his chair for fear a bending posture might further injure his health. He wrote that Jackson "was convinced that one of his legs was larger than the other and that one of his arms was likewise unduly heavy." As a result, he developed the habit of raising the heavier arm straight up so that the blood could run back into his body.[30]

By his mid-twenties, Jackson's health had become a personal concern that would trouble him for the rest of his life. Jackson worried chiefly about his digestion, believing he suffered from "dyspepsia," a medical term used during the nineteenth century to describe any stomach and intestinal problem. After consulting a number of doctors, he decided to change his diet to the plainest of foods possible—stale bread, unseasoned meat and vegetables, and fresh fruit. At times, his digestive ailments caused him considerable pain, and in later years, he would remark that if anything could drive a man to suicide, it was dyspepsia.[31]

After nine months in Mexico, Jackson was ordered home. The Mexican War was over, and Jackson had distinguished himself. As a soldier during peacetime, all he had to look forward to was the dull routine of an army post. First, he was assigned to Fort Hamilton on Long Island and then in 1850 to Fort Meade near Tampa, Florida. To remove the monotony, he devoted most of his spare time to self-improvement. He pledged himself to read forty to fifty pages daily—more than 15,000 pages annually. Jackson's library contained well-known books in five languages, many with marginal notes in his handwriting and covering a broad spectrum of subjects.[32]

While at Fort Hamilton, Jackson learned that his Uncle Cummins had died. Greatly saddened, he wrote to his sister Laura that "Uncle was a father to me." Not only was his uncle gone, but he had died in debt, and Jackson's Mill had to be sold.[33]

At Fort Meade, Jackson clashed with the post commander, Brevet Major William H. French. Disagreements over jurisdictional issues soon escalated when Jackson heard of, and investigated, sexual impropriety on the part of French. When French learned of the investigation, he had Jackson arrested, charging him with insubordination. Eventually, the order was reversed, and Jackson was vindicated, but he feared his career had been tarnished. When the opportunity came to leave the army, he took it.[34]

In March 1851, Jackson received a letter from the superintendent of the Virginia Military Institute (VMI) informing him of a teaching position at the institution—professor of Natural and Experimental Philosophy (Physics) and Artillery Tactics. The Virginia Military Institute was located in the Shenandoah Valley in the small town of Lexington and was modeled after West Point; it was only the second such governmentally funded military academy in the country. In the same town stood the halls of Washington College (later to become Washington and Lee). Here young Major Daniel Hill, who had served with Jackson in Mexico, was an instructor in Mathematics. When Hill heard that Jackson was being considered for the position at VMI, he lobbied for Jackson's appointment.[35]

Other men besides Jackson were being considered for the position— George McClellan, Jesse L. Reno, William Rosencrans, and George W. Smith, all of whom would attain the rank of general in the Union or Confederate armies. Jackson was appointed to the position primarily because of his impressive military record in Mexico and the fact that he was a Virginian. When asked if he was afraid of teaching such advanced subjects since he had been away from West Point for so long, he replied, "I can always keep a day or two ahead of the class. I can do whatever I will to do."[36]

Problems began for Jackson from the very beginning. Lexington was one of the country's most sophisticated towns. Margaret Junkin Preston, his future sister-in-law, described Jackson as "eccentric in our little professional society, because he did not walk in the conventional grooves of other men." Jackson's eccentricities in speech and habits soon caused difficulties with the students he had to teach.[37]

Jackson's first year at VMI was a difficult one; he was forced to teach Optics, Analytical Mechanics, and Astronomy, of which he knew very little. As a result, he was forced to spend long hours preparing for his classes. Organizing his lessons was a difficult chore for him. Not only did he have to keep a "chapter ahead of his class," but he had to do so with eyes that were badly weakened. Because of his difficulty reading at night, Jackson adopted a schedule of study that took advantage of the limited daylight. In the morning after early classes, Jackson read over the next day's lesson materials; after evening mess, he would stand for hours in an upright position, face to the wall, going over the lesson he had read that morning. The hours of study at West Point had helped him develop the ability to concentrate; in addition, he had an almost photographic memory. After having committed the text to memory in the morning, he would think it through at night.[38]

In the classroom, Jackson was a disaster as a teacher. He lectured in a high-pitched voice and never achieved a level of explanation that all students could understand. When a student asked a question or said he did not understand, Jackson merely repeated what he had said in the same words in the same way. He was never known to rephrase an explanation or to take another approach to a problem.[39] When a cadet listed the three simple machines of physics as the inclined plane, the lever, and the wheel, Jackson corrected him saying, "No, sir. The lever, the wheel, and the inclined plane," as they had been listed in the textbook.[40]

Not only was Jackson a poor teacher, but he was unable to maintain discipline in the classroom. While listening to one student respond, others would throw "paper pellets and create wanton disrespect in his section room," recalled Cadet Giles B. Cooke. "We used to annoy Jackson a great deal by cat-calls, dog barks, etc. One day I was imitating a puppy. He tried in vain to find the cause, much worried. Finally Jackson said, 'There seems to be a puppy in the room.'"[41]

Jackson acquired nicknames such as Hickory or Old Hickory, Old Jack, Tom Fool Jackson, or Square Box, a reference to the size of his feet. The cadets frequently drew enormous feet on the blackboard of his room. Jackson ignored the cadets' pranks, but demanded of them the kind of discipline required of a military man. While the students in his class struggled, Jackson prayed for them. "When I go to my classroom, . . . that is my time to intercede with God for them."[42]

As a professor of Natural and Experimental Philosophy, Jackson was not a success; the superintendent received numerous complaints about his teaching ability and his harshness as a taskmaster. Sometime after Jackson left VMI and joined the Confederate army, Superintendent France Smith wrote: "As professor of Natural and Experimental Philosophy, Major Jackson was not a success. He had not the qualifications for so important a chair. He was no teacher, and he lacked the tact required for getting along with his classes. Every officer and every cadet respected him for his many sterling qualities. He was a brave man, a conscientious man, and a good man, but he was no professor."[43]

Most cadets came to admire and respect Jackson for his efforts, however. More than one said that Jackson taught a mighty dull course but that he wanted to serve under his command. Many of them would have the opportunity.[44]

On August 4, 1853, Jackson married Eleanor Junkin, daughter of the president of Washington College. He had known Eleanor for quite a while but until recently had given her little thought. Then, suddenly, he realized he was in love. Nine months later, they were married. The newly wed couple moved in with the Junkin family; Jackson suddenly acquired the family life he had never known.[45]

Then, fourteen months later, Eleanor died along with the unborn child she was carrying; the loss devastated Jackson. Filled with grief, he wrote: "I can hardly yet realize that my dear Ellie is no more, that she will never again welcome my return—no more to soothe my troubled spirit by her ever kind, sympathizing heart, words, and love." As a result of his loss, Jackson turned to his religion for comfort and for an answer as to why the only love he had ever known had been taken away. He increased his religious service, becoming a church deacon and beginning a Sunday school for African Americans, despite violating the state law that prohibited mixed racial assemblies.[46]

Jackson's early exposure to slavery was limited. Cummins Jackson owned a few slaves, but nothing like the number owned by the plantation owners and the Cotton Kings of the Deep South. Jackson's views on slavery were similar to many others in the South; the ownership of African Americans was a God-given right. Although he himself preferred to see the black man free, his interpretation of the Scriptures indicated that slavery was ordained by God; therefore, it must be correct.[47]

In July 1857, Jackson married again. His wife was Mary Anna Morrison, his friend D. H. Hill's sister-in-law. Anna's father was a minister and president of Davidson College near Charlotte, North Carolina. Both Jackson and Anna had difficulty socially and were extremely religious. Anna respected her husband's daily routine and allowed no disruptions of that schedule. In 1858, they acquired a home in Lexington. When their first child lived only a few weeks, Jackson again relied on faith to support his sorrow.[48]

Jackson was a states' rights Democrat who believed in the right of a state to secede, but he viewed the prospects of disunion with alarm. He hoped God would not allow war to erupt. When Lincoln was elected president, tensions ran high in Lexington. Jackson, who had experienced war firsthand, feared it "as the sum of all evils." Jackson joined eleven Lexington citizens in calling for a county assembly to discuss alternatives to war.[49] His other answer to the growing tensions was prayer. He organized a public prayer meeting for peace and prayed privately for divine guidance.[50] Although Jackson hoped and prayed for peace, if Virginia was invaded, Jackson was prepared to defend it with all his might.

By 1861, when the war began, Jackson believed it was his duty to defend his home state. It was a fight of faith, he believed. God had ordained a civil war for reasons he had no right to question. The war was a scourge on the land; the side that displayed the most respect for the Almighty would ultimately triumph in the war.[51]

With the outset of the Civil War in mid-April 1861, Jackson promptly offered his sword to Virginia. In doing so, he suffered a personal loss. His sister Laura was a strong Union supporter who refused to talk or communicate with him; dying when he did, Jackson would never have the opportunity to make amends. For Jackson, his immediate family was gone.[52]

On April 21, 1861, Jackson received orders to lead a contingent of cadets to Richmond; he was never again to see his home in Lexington. Accepting a commission as colonel of infantry, he was assigned to command the Southern garrison at Harper's Ferry. Harper's Ferry was an important outpost in Virginia since it was the northernmost stronghold of the Confederacy and the site of the largest arsenal in the South. Few sites had greater strategic location for either side. Upon arrival, Jackson found 2,500 inexperienced and poorly equipped militia and volunteers. He quickly went to work to whip them into shape. He instituted seven hours of drill a day and issued a series of regulations and restrictions. As a result, the complaints were many and loud, but Jackson remained unmoved by grumbling in the ranks.[53]

Three weeks after Jackson's arrival at Harper's Ferry, the garrison had grown to 4,500 troops. On May 23, General Joseph E. Johnston arrived to assume command. Johnston organized the troops into three brigades, giving the First Brigade to Jackson. The First Brigade, which would later bear his name, was soon to make its mark. Jackson took pride in his brigade from the very beginning, writing to Anna, "I am very thankful to our Heavenly Father for having given me such a fine brigade."[54] On July 3, Jackson received the commission of brigadier general. Political connections helped. Jackson had urged his friends in Richmond to get him the promotion, and they had been successful.

By the summer of 1861, Johnston commanded more than 10,000 men, with more arriving all the time. After analyzing the situation, Johnston decided to abandon Harper's Ferry for a more defensible position near Bunker Hill, Virginia. On July 16, when Brigadier General Irvin McDowell moved from Washington to attack Confederate General P. G. T. Beauregard, Johnston came to his assistance. Beauregard positioned his troops behind Bull Run, a stream that flowed north and east of Manassas.[55]

On Sunday, July 21, the armies finally clashed. As the battle developed, Union troops threatened both Confederate flanks, forcing them to fall back toward a small rise in the area known as Henry Hill. Jackson ordered his men to the woods on the east side of Henry Hill. Amid the roar of artillery and splintering trees, Jackson rode back and forth in front of his line, rallying his men. Occasionally, he would raise his left hand toward the heavens as if in prayer. At one point, Brigadier General Barnard Bee's Brigade was on the verge of being annihilated. Inspired by Jackson's gallantry, Bee galloped back to his men. Hoping to rally them, he delivered his famous statement: "Look, men, there stands Jackson like a stonewall! Rally behind the Virginians." A short time later, a Federal bullet killed Bee, but his words lived on, and a legend was born. Jackson's decision to stand on Henry Hill probably saved the Confederates from defeat. Quickly, Beauregard and Johnston constructed a defensive line and were able to hold it until reinforcements arrived.[56]

In the late afternoon, the Confederates counterattacked, forcing the Federal line to crumble. The Union offense turned into a retreat and then into a rout; soon the whole Union army was reeling back toward Washington. At the battle's end, Jackson received medical attention for a minor wound on his left hand.[57]

President Jefferson Davis arrived shortly after the battle ended; he and Generals Johnston and Beauregard decided not to pursue Federal troops that night. It was an irretrievable error. By their timidity, the South lost the opportunity that might have ended the war right then and achieved Southern independence. Jackson appealed to Davis to be allowed to pursue the enemy: "We have whipped them! They ran like sheep! Give me 5,000 fresh men and I will be in Washington City tomorrow morning." Jackson's request was rejected.[58]

Manassas was more than just a Confederate victory; the South also had its first hero. The fame that followed this battle became a part of Jackson and his command. The men who stood with Jackson at Manassas were promptly called the Stonewall Brigade; it was the only unit in the Confederate army with a nickname. All others were only numbered.[59]

For Lincoln and the North, the Battle of Manassas was a disaster. Lincoln began his quest for a general who could bring victory to the North. The first man he chose was one of Jackson's former classmates, George B. McClellan.

After Manassas, the Confederate army spread out defensively across northern Virginia to wait for the Federals to renew their attack. In October, Jackson was promoted to major general and then made commander of Confederate forces in the Shenandoah Valley. The valley was one of the Confederacy's most valuable regions, lying between the Allegheny Mountains at its west and the Blue Ridge Mountains at its east and extending more than 150 miles southwestward from the Potomac to Lexington, Virginia. The valley provided a natural route for an invasion of the North.[60] Because it was a bountiful source of grain, fruit, and livestock, it was labeled the "Breadbasket of the Confederacy." Jackson clearly understood the importance of the Shenandoah Valley, noting that "if the Valley is lost, Virginia is lost." To defend the valley, Jackson gathered a force of 3,600 infantry, 600 cavalry, and 27 guns in six batteries. Most of the soldiers were native to the Shenandoah Valley.[61]

Jackson returned to Winchester in December 1861 to enjoy Christmas with his wife. Anna stayed with him for almost three months, during which time she became pregnant.

During the spring of 1862, Jackson electrified the Confederacy with his dazzling Shenandoah Valley campaign. His objectives were twofold—to preserve Confederate control of the Shenandoah Valley and to tie down Union troops that might otherwise help McClellan. To accomplish these objectives, Jackson struck with boldness at the Battle of Kernstown on March 23. Although he suffered a tactical defeat by Union Major General Nathaniel Banks, Jackson succeeded in forcing the Federals to maintain a strong presence in the valley. It would be the only battle he would lose during the campaign. For the next six weeks, Jackson retreated into the mountains, luring the Federals southward and isolating them from other duty.[62]

Then in May, with reinforcements, Jackson took the offensive. In a series of long, rapid marches and daring attacks, he won battles at Front Royal and Winchester on May 23 and 25. With boldness, Jackson then moved all the way to the Potomac. At the last possible moment, he hurried back between two Federal columns closing in on him. At the end of his campaign on June 8, he enjoyed a victory at Cross Keys and again on June 9 at Port Republic.[63]

On the day after his victory at Port Republic, Jackson wrote his wife about the valley campaign: "God has been our shield, and to His name be all glory." Jackson's victories in the valley were military masterpieces and are still studied today by tacticians. To be successful in battle, Jackson believed that you must

> always mystify, mislead, and surprise the enemy, if possible. When you strike and overcome him, never let up in the pursuit so long as your men have strength to follow; for an army routed, if hotly pursued, becomes panic-stricken, and can then be destroyed by half their number. The other rule is, never fight against heavy odds if by any possible maneuvering you can hurl your own force at only a part, and that the weakest part, of your enemy and crush it. Such tactics will win every time, and a small army may thus destroy a large one in detail, and repeated victory will make it invincible.[64]

Using these tactics, Jackson's valley campaign was an overwhelming success. With never more than 16,000 men, he completely frustrated the efforts of 64,000 Union troops. Jackson fought four battles, six large skirmishes, and many minor actions, and with the exception of Kernstown, was able to accomplish the tactical purpose in every movement he made. In all but two of the engagements Jackson was able to maneuver his troops in such a way that he outnumbered Union forces by numbers ranging from two to one to seventeen to one, in spite of the fact that his army was outnumbered four to one. That Jackson was successful in continually concentrating more men in battle than his adversaries is an indication of his genius. He was able to achieve this feat by the use of forced marches. In forty-eight days, Jackson's "foot cavalry" marched 676 miles. As a result, the Federals suffered 7,000 casualties, with 10,000 muskets, 9 cannon, and numerous supplies captured. Jackson was able to accomplish it all at a cost of less than 2,500 casualties.[65]

Jackson's actions in the valley so alarmed Washington that 38,000 Federal troops were prevented from joining McClellan in his efforts to capture Richmond. Moreover, the effect of the campaign on morale, both in the

North and South, was tremendous. The South had a hero; his name was "Stonewall" Jackson.[66]

After the valley campaign, Jackson moved east toward Richmond to join Robert E. Lee, newly in command of the Army of Northern Virginia. When Lee took command on June 1, 1862, McClellan's Army of the Potomac stood only nine miles from Richmond. The fall of the capital seemed imminent. Lee, who always met desperation with audacity, planned a two-pronged attack on McClellan's right flank. Lee would strike from the west, while Jackson drove from the northwest. Success depended upon deception and a tight timetable. Things went wrong from the very start, however. Jackson's advance was uncharacteristically slow.[67] When Jackson did not arrive on time, Major General A. P. Hill launched his attack after waiting twelve hours for Jackson. Hill was furious over Jackson's absence; his disappointment and anger were apparent in his battle report: "It was never contemplated that my division alone should have sustained the shock of the battle, but such was the case."[68] The bloody Battle of Seven Days had begun.

After Seven Days, the siege of Richmond ended, despite Jackson's actions rather than because of them. For the only time during the war, Jackson had failed. It would be the last time. Historians studying the battle attribute Jackson's behavior to physical exhaustion or "stress fatigue," an ailment that occurs when the body's reactions are strained beyond their capacity.[69] Of the 80,000 Confederates engaged, 20,000 were casualties. The Federals, with 105,000 men, lost 16,000. The cost had been heavy, but the threat to Richmond had been removed. It would be two years before Federal armies would come so close again.[70]

Jackson's reputation suffered as a result of his inaction during the Battle of Seven Days, and his relationship with A. P. Hill was strained. Lee's confidence in Jackson, however, did not waver. Jackson possessed Lee's audacity, a trait that would bind the two together. During the next ten months, Jackson and Lee collaborated to rout the Federals at every turn. "I would follow him [Lee] blindfolded," Jackson said.[71]

When McClellan failed to take Richmond and continued to ask for more troops while taking no action, Lincoln recalled his army from the peninsula. In the meantime, he sent Major General John Pope with a newly formed Army of Virginia to attack Lee's army.

On August 7, a portion of Pope's army under Nathaniel Banks moved south from Culpeper. Jackson moved quickly to intercept the invaders but was unable to get all his troops into position before engaging Banks at Cedar Mountain. When Federal troops threatened to destroy Jackson's army, he rushed to the front, shouting for his troops to regroup and waving a Confederate flag as a rallying standard. Jackson drew his sword and carried the fight to the enemy. As Southern columns re-formed, A P. Hill's "Light Division" rushed onto the field. The result was a Confederate victory. Success for Jackson at Cedar Mountain resulted more from luck and personal leadership than from strategic planning. One of the Confederate dead at Cedar Mountain was the commander of the Stonewall Brigade. In a letter to Anna, Jackson wrote, "I can hardly think of the fall of Brigadier General C. S. Winder without tearful eyes. Let us all unite more earnestly in imploring God's aid in fighting our battles for us."[72]

After Cedar Mountain, Jackson joined Lee in a daring initiative that outmaneuvered Pope at Second Manassas. Flying in the face of conventional military tactics that call for concentrating forces when facing an enemy of superior numbers, Lee divided his smaller army. While Major General James Longstreet gave the impression of a frontal attack at the Rappahannock River, Jackson began a circular flanking march to the north. The plan was hazardous; if Pope discovered what was happening, he could maneuver his army to keep the two Confederate forces divided and then destroy them separately. Jackson's march into the rear was a success because of the determination of his soldiers. Living off green apples and corn, Jackson's column marched sixty miles in a little over two days. Late on August 28, Jackson struck the Federal column at Groveton. Pope launched one attack after another against Jackson, hoping to destroy his outnumbered force. Just a year earlier, Jackson had made his legendary "Stonewall" stand, and now he was set to do it again. In the heat of battle, Pope failed to detect Longstreet's portion of the army. On August 30, Longstreet's 30,000 troops attacked the weak Union left flank. The Union reeled in confusion. It was a complete victory for the Army of Northern Virginia. Pope's army had been soundly thrashed.[73]

During the Second Battle of Manassas, Jackson redeemed himself for his disappointing performance during the Battle of Seven Days. The secrecy and rapidity of his flanking movement, and the strong defense against repeated assaults by a larger Union force, brought Jackson additional respect inside the Army of Northern Virginia and throughout the South.[74]

On September 2, 1862, Lincoln combined Pope's army with McClellan's Army of the Potomac. Lincoln was faced with little choice despite his earlier statement that "McClellan can be trusted to act on the defensive, but having the 'slows' he is good for nothing for an onward movement." When the Union army learned of McClellan's return, the men were elated. Despite his failure during the Peninsula Campaign, the Army of the Potomac retained their loyalty to McClellan.[75]

Shortly after his victory at Second Manassas, Lee decided to invade Maryland, believing that a bold raid into the North would force a Federal withdrawal from Virginia and might encourage the secessionist movement in Maryland to take action. He also hoped that a victory in the North would encourage the European nations to recognize the Confederate states.

After marching his army across the Potomac River near Leesburg, Lee hoped to move over South Mountain into the Cumberland Valley and to follow this route to Harrisburg, the capital of Pennsylvania. At Harper's

Ferry, however, there were 11,000 Federal troops, with 2,500 more at Martinsburg. If these Union troops were left in Lee's rear, they could interrupt his communication and supply lines. Lee decided to send six of his nine infantry divisions to eliminate this threat.[76]

Both Jackson and Longstreet were opposed to dividing the army to capture the Union garrison at Harper's Ferry. Lee split the army anyway, ordering Jackson to Harper's Ferry, while Longstreet remained near Sharpsburg, Maryland. Lee counted on moving rapidly to confuse his opponent.[77] Then, on September 13, McClellan was the beneficiary of one of the most extraordinary pieces of luck; two Union soldiers accidentally found a copy of a Confederate dispatch indicating that Lee had divided his army. "Here is a paper," McClellan said, "with which if I cannot whip Bobbie Lee I will be willing to go home."[78]

In quick fashion, Jackson was able to capture Harper's Ferry and, with it, 11,000 prisoners and numerous arms, wagons, and supplies. Leaving A. P. Hill's division behind to arrange the parole of the prisoners, Jackson hurried back to rejoin Lee. Lee deployed his troops behind the Antietam Creek on a series of hills and ridges that provided a good defensive position. The presence of the Potomac River to their rear, however, was a major disadvantage. If the Union army succeeded in breaking the Confederate line, it would be difficult for Lee, if not impossible, to extricate his army in time to prevent complete disaster.[79]

Lee, however, was counting on McClellan's slow movement to allow time for all of his army to return. The next day, when McClellan did mount an attack, it was done in a piecemeal fashion, allowing Lee to shift his outnumbered forces from place to place to meet the attacks. Despite this, the Confederate army was still much in danger for most of the day.

During the heat of the battle, Lee noticed a man near the Dunkard Church coming toward him dragging a dead pig. With disaster so near, and straggling contributing to the danger, Lee momentarily lost his cool; he ordered Jackson to shoot the man as an example. Instead, Jackson gave the man a musket and placed him where the action was the hottest for the rest of the day. He survived the day unharmed and was afterward known as the man who had "lost his pig, but saved his bacon."[80]

Although Longstreet's and Jackson's men fought valiantly, the battle would have been lost had not A. P. Hill arrived from Harper's Ferry late in the day with 2,000 troops. Longstreet and Jackson had been correct to question the splitting of the army; Lee was fortunate to have survived the day. Antietam was the single bloodiest day in American history. The casualties exceeded 24,000—11,500 Confederates and 12,800 Federals. Over 3,700 soldiers lost their lives that day.[81]

McClellan considered Antietam the highlight of his military career; he, however, had acted more like a spectator than like the army's commander. Because of his slowness to engage Lee and his uncoordinated attacks,

McClellan missed the opportunity to destroy the Army of Northern Virginia. Lee's retreat from Maryland was seen in the North as a major victory. President Lincoln seized the opportunity on September 2, 1862, to issue the preliminary Emancipation Proclamation.[82]

Lincoln was disappointed that Lee's army had not been destroyed. He urged McClellan to advance promptly into Virginia, but McClellan refused to move his troops until he felt they were ready; he needed more men and equipment, he said. Ten days after the battle, McClellan had still not moved his army. On October 1, Lincoln visited McClellan in the field, hoping to get him to move his army. McClellan still insisted the army was not ready for an offensive campaign. Later, while reviewing the army, Lincoln asked a friend what he saw. The man responded that it was the Army of the Potomac. "So it is called, but that is a mistake," Lincoln said. "It is only McClellan's bodyguard."[83] On November 7, Lincoln removed McClellan from command of the Army of the Potomac, replacing him with Major General Ambrose Burnside.

In the lull that followed, Jackson refilled his ranks and tried earnestly to awaken in his men a greater sense of God's presence. He distributed religious tracts and Bibles among the troops. He encouraged his men to attend religious services and attended as many as he could, leading prayer whenever asked. He wrote to Anna several times telling her that after the war he hoped to purchase a home in the lower valley and become a gentleman-farmer.[84]

Shortly after the Battle of Antietam, Lee reorganized his army into two corps. Jackson was promoted to lieutenant general and given command of the Second Corps. In his recommendation, Lee stated that Jackson "is true, honest, and brave; has a single eye to the good of the service and spares no exertion to accomplish his objective." A month after his promotion, Jackson received word that Anna had given birth to a daughter. "Oh! How thankful I am to our ever kind Heavenly Father," Jackson wrote to his wife when he heard the news. "How I wish I could be with you and see my two darlings." It would be five months before he could.[85]

Although Burnside was reluctant to assume command of the Army of the Potomac, he was determined not to make the same mistake McClellan had. He would move his army as quickly as possible, hoping to catch Lee off guard.

On November 15, Burnside began his march toward Fredericksburg from Washington. To counter his movement, Lee concentrated his army on the south bank of the Rappahannock. On December 13, the Union's major thrust began. Their frontal attack was marked by courage and tenacity, but by the end of the day, the ground was covered with dead and wounded Federal troops. After the one-sided victory, Lee stated: "It is well that war is so terrible. We should grow too fond of it." Federal losses were more than twice those of the Confederates.[86] By evening, Burnside's attack had failed completely. The Army of the Potomac drew back to the northern bank of the Rappahannock, while the Army of Northern Virginia moved into winter quarters.

Jackson was extremely concerned over the welfare of his men, ensuring they had the best uniforms possible and that campsites were near fresh clean water. He kept a close watch over his men; he was the first sight they saw in the morning and the last at night.[87] For those who deserted or were not willing to fight, Jackson had no compassion; they, of course, should be shot. On the other hand, he had difficulty getting along with his subordinates. Subordinate after subordinate came under arrest for violating minor infractions of the military code. The men who answered to him directly, or just one layer below, often were called to task and had an uncomfortable time.[88]

On April 23, 1863, Jackson's wife arrived at Guinea Station with their daughter. Soldiers cheered as Jackson escorted his family from the train. A few days later, his young daughter was baptized and christened "Julia" in honor of Jackson's mother. Jackson was the happiest he had been during the war. The birth of his daughter, the crushing defeat of the enemy at Fredericksburg, and the increased religious fervor rampant in the Confederacy convinced him that God was looking favorably upon their fight for Southern independence. Victory and peace, he believed, were very close at hand.[89]

When the Army of the Potomac, now under the command of Major General Joseph "Fighting Joe" Hooker, crossed the Rappahannock late in April, Jackson was eager for combat. Lee moved his army to Chancellorsville to meet the enemy. When Hooker retreated into the Wilderness and assumed a defensive position, Lee took the offensive. As soon as Lee learned that Hooker's western flank was exposed, he again took a dangerous risk by splitting his already outnumbered army. He was left to face Hooker's 70,000 troops with a little more than two divisions (14,000 men), while Jackson, with 30,000 men, marched around the right flank of the Union army and attacked at its most vulnerable spot.[90] It was a dangerous move for the Confederates; if Hooker struck Jackson's column while on the move, it could easily be broken and scattered and his supply wagons captured or destroyed. If Hooker attacked Lee, he could easily overrun the much smaller force. The fate of the Army of Northern Virginia hung in the balance; the outcome would be determined by Jackson's ability to execute his flanking movement swiftly.[91]

Union troops spotted Jackson's movement almost immediately, but Hooker failed to take any real action, thinking the Army of Northern Virginia was retreating. By four in the afternoon, Confederate Major General Robert Rodes's division and two other divisions were ready for deployment. An hour later, Jackson's corps had created an attacking column a mile and a half wide, aimed straight at the weak Union flank. Federal soldiers were busy preparing fires to cook their dinners when Jackson signaled the Confederate charge. The surprise was complete. Hooker's Eleventh Corps fled in a disorganized and panicked retreat. Jackson galloped back and forth urging his troops to "press on! Press on!" As darkness came, Jackson wanted to pursue the enemy. Deciding that he needed more information, Jackson made a personal reconnaissance to observe the situation firsthand.[92]

The dense woodland was a mass of confusion; no one knew precisely where the enemy was. As Jackson returned to his lines, his troops opened fire, mistaking him for enemy cavalry. Jackson reeled in his saddle with bullet wounds in his right hand and left forearm and shoulder. Four other members of Jackson's party were killed by the friendly fire. "All my wounds are by my own men," Jackson said, and, "I fear my arm is broken." Two of his aides lifted him from the saddle and placed him on the ground. As Jackson was being carried off the field, a federal shell exploded nearby, knocking him from the stretcher. In the midst of the confusion, Brigadier General Dorsey Pender arrived. "I will have to retire my troops to re-form them," he said. Despite his pain, Jackson was still able to give orders: "You must hold your ground, General Pender! You must hold your ground, sir!"[93]

Jackson was taken by ambulance to Dowdall's Tavern, where Dr. Hunter McGuire, Jackson's trusted doctor and confidant, tended his wounds. Despite his condition and pain, Jackson remained calm. When the general was informed that his arm had to be amputated, he replied, "Do for me whatever you think is right." As he lay on the table breathing in chloroform fumes, he muttered, "What an infinite blessing." His shattered left arm was amputated two inches below the left shoulder.[94]

Later in the morning, a dispatch from Lee arrived congratulating Jackson for his victory and expressing his sorrow about his wounds. "Could I have directed events, I would have chosen for the good of the country to be disabled in your stead," Lee wrote. "I congratulate you upon the victory which is due to your skill and energy." When Lee's message was read to Jackson, he said, "General Lee is very kind, but he should give the praise to God." Jackson was moved to Guiney's Station, out of danger of the fighting. Anna was sent for and was to meet him there.[95]

For the next few days, Jackson seemed to be improving. He discussed theological matters with his chaplain, telling him that he believed his wounds were "one of the blessings of his life" and that God had ordained the injury. Before Anna could arrive, however, Jackson's health took a turn for the worse; he had contracted pneumonia.[96]

On May 7, Anna arrived from Richmond. Just eight days earlier she had seen her husband in the peak of health. Had he lived a century later, his chances for survival would have been much greater, but now his broken body, pale skin, and weak breathing attested to his critical condition. When Jackson saw the anguish on his wife's face, he tried to allay her fear: "My darling, you must cheer up, and not wear a long face. I love cheerfulness and brightness in a sick-room." His doctors knew that Jackson's death was near; it was just a matter of time.[97]

As Jackson lay close to death, Lee's struggle with Hooker ended. The Confederacy had won a major victory, but the cost had been high. When General Lee learned that Jackson's health had taken a turn for the worse, he said: "Give him my affectionate regards, and tell him to make haste and get well, and come back to me as soon as he can. He has lost his left arm, but I have lost my right arm." On the evening of May 9, Jackson asked his wife and brother-in-law to sing to him his favorite hymns. "The singing," Anna later wrote, "had a quieting effect and he seemed to rest in perfect peace." On the following day, which was Sunday, Anna brought Julia to his bedside.[98]

At one o'clock in the afternoon, Jackson's personal aide, Sandie Pendleton, came to see him. The general was awake and asked him who had preached at headquarters today. Pendleton told him that Rev. B. T. Lacy had presided and that the army was praying for him. "Thank God," Jackson said. "They are very kind. . . . It is the Lord's day Pendleton. My wish is fulfilled. I wanted to die on Sunday."[99]

At 1:30, the doctors told him he had only two hours to live—Jackson seemed to understand. A short time later he shouted, "Tell A. P. Hill to prepare for action! . . . Pass the infantry to the front! . . . Tell Major Hawks . . ." He grew quiet, and there was a long silence. Then he said clearly: "Let us cross over the river, and rest under the shade of the trees." He was gone; it was 3:15 in the afternoon.[100]

Shock waves of sadness spread through the South. Jackson's death was the greatest loss the Confederacy had suffered. At the age of thirty-nine, the mighty Stonewall died, and with him went the hopes of the South. Jefferson Davis praised Jackson: "He fell like the eagle, his own feather on the shaft that was dripping with his own life blood. In his death, the Confederacy lost an eye and an arm. Our only consolation being that his summons could have reached no soldier more prepared to accept it joyfully."[101]

"I know not how to replace him," a grief-stricken Lee declared. No one with his ability emerged. At Gettysburg, Jackson would be greatly missed. Lee, who never made excuses for his actions, said: "If I had had Jackson at Gettysburg, I should have won the battle, and a complete victory there would have resulted in the establishment of Southern independence."[102]

8 Albert Sidney Johnston

Texan, Soldier, Gentleman

"The morning of the 6th of April [1862] was remarkably bright and beautiful. The country toward Shiloh was wooded, with small fields interspersed, and with bold undulations from the hills bounding the river." Thus wrote Confederate Colonel William Preston, volunteer aide on the staff of his brother-in-law, Albert Sidney Johnston. For Preston, the day promised hope and victory. By evening that promise had been shattered by the death of the Confederate commander.[1]

Just before sunrise on April 6, sharp skirmishing began between Major General William Hardee's corps and the advancing Confederate troops. Mounting his horse, Johnston told his staff, "Tonight we will water our horses in the Tennessee River." With him was the Confederate Army of the Mississippi, 40,000 strong. Before he could decide what action to take, however, Johnston needed to see what was happening firsthand; he spurred his horse to the sound of the musket fire.

During the heat of the battle, Johnston rallied some of his men who were panicking. After he regrouped them, he spoke: "Men of Arkansas! They say you boast of your prowess with the bowie knife. Today you wield a nobler weapon—the bayonet. Employ it well." Then turning to Colonel John Marmaduke, he said, "My son, we must this day conquer or perish!"[2]

Johnston's sole goal this day was to win a decisive victory over the Union army that threatened both Mississippi and Tennessee. Four Union armies had invaded the lower Mississippi Valley at Pittsburg Landing in western Tennessee; two of these armies were attempting to unite and cut off the vital railroad connecting the Western Confederacy with the East and the Gulf of Mexico. If Johnston could not stop this Union threat, the Confederates were in danger of losing the railroad connections and the Mississippi Valley. "I have put you in motion to offer battle to the invaders of your country!" Johnston had written in his battle orders to his army. The eyes and hopes of the young Confederate nation and its eight million people rested on Johnston and the valor and resolution of his men.[3]

This was nothing new for Albert Sidney Johnston; people had counted on him all his life. A few months earlier, Johnston had received a letter from a Texan mother of a young Confederate officer; he must have been pleased and touched by it. In the letter, the mother petitioned that her son be transferred from Virginia to Johnston's army in the West. "I wish him," she said, "to be near the moulding influence of such a Texan, such a soldier, and such a gentleman." In a single poignant statement she had given Johnston the three labels most befitting his career.[4]

Johnston was a Texan. Almost three decades before the Civil War, he moved to Texas from his native state of Kentucky to help the new republic in its fight for independence. He loved Texas more as each year passed. He led her army and defended the frontier against Indians. On one occasion, he refused to give up his Texan citizenship despite the fact that it would cost him financially. When Texas left the Union, he sorrowfully joined the Confederacy, but his heart was torn between conflicting allegiances. "Texas has made me a rebel twice," he later said; "When I die I want a handful of Texas earth on my breast." There was no more loyal Texan than Albert Sidney Johnston.[5]

Johnston was a soldier. As a leader of men he was outstanding. He considered the welfare of the men under him as a trust he would not violate, and he was willing to share their hardships and hazards. His last words to his troops were, "I will lead you." Johnston's men not only respected him but loved him.[6]

Johnston was a gentleman and a devoted family man, raised in the chivalric tradition of the Old South. He was courteous to those he commanded and quickly gained the affection of all with whom he came into contact. "He was the most unselfish man I ever knew," recalled a former comrade, "and one of the most just and considerate to those under his command." To loyalty and valor, Johnston added grace.[7]

Johnston, like Robert E. Lee, regarded duty as a man's noblest ambition. A Union friend felt he might have been wrong in selecting to defend the South but admitted that "he followed his mental and moral instincts and conclusions with unwavering fidelity." General Beauregard had high praise for Johnston's leadership qualities: "[General Johnston] was a great and good man . . . and was a brave soldier and an unselfish patriot. I am one of many . . . who believe that, if he had been at the head of our Confederate Government during the war, the latter might have ended differently, if not with success to us, certainly with less disastrous consequences."[8]

Albert Sidney Johnston was born on February 2, 1803, in Washington, Kentucky. He was a New Englander by ancestry and a Southerner by birth and association. Despite his ancestry in the North, he died defending the South against the land of his forefathers. Albert's family was respectable—

General Albert S. Johnston was an outstanding soldier who considered the welfare of his men and was willing to share their hardships and hazards. His last words to his troops before he was killed were "I will lead you."

COURTESY OF THE LIBRARY OF CONGRESS

his grandfather, Archibald Johnston, having served in the Revolution. Albert's father, John, was a physician who moved his family from New England to Washington in Mason County, Kentucky.[9]

Mason County was on the frontier, with a population of less than 3,000 inhabitants. Washington was a village of huts circling a rude stockade; hunting provided the chief supply of food, and there was constant danger from Indian attacks. Only strong men and women could survive in such a country.

John Johnston was a strong man of sound body and keen mind. He developed a large medical practice in Washington and was often consulted by other physicians on difficult cases. By 1793, he was a member of the Washington Board of Trustees. That year his first wife died; a year later, he married Abigail Harris, who was to become Albert's mother. She, too, had settled in Kentucky, the daughter of another New Englander. Abigail was attractive, having a quiet and gentle personality and a strong intellect.[10]

Albert Sidney Johnston was John and Abigail's fifth child. Albert's mother died when he was three years old, leaving him to the care of an older sister and, later, a stepmother. Despite the loss of his mother, Albert's childhood was a happy one. These early experiences helped him develop a resilient personality. Albert received a sound education, attending a variety of private and preparatory schools. His early schooling provided him with a solid background and gave him a lifelong respect for learning. He was a quick learner and excelled in mathematics. He loved horses, hunting, and athletic contests, earning a reputation for extraordinary strength and courage.[11]

Young Johnston was generally well behaved, though at times he gave way to severe outbursts of temper. On one occasion, he lied to his parents; years later he told his son that his first lie had required so many others to conceal it that he had seen the fallacy of lying and had never done it again.[12]

Johnston's physician father wanted him to enter medicine as well. With this career in mind, he entered Transylvania University in Lexington, Kentucky. There he met a fellow Kentuckian and student, Jefferson Davis, future president of the Confederacy, and formed a friendship that would be the most important one of his career. Aspirations to a career in medicine fell by the wayside when Johnston obtained an appointment to the U.S. Military Academy at West Point.[13]

Johnston was a cadet at West Point when Colonel Sylvanus Thayer was the superintendent. Thayer had brought order and discipline to the Academy, insisting on excellence in curriculum and instruction. Military organization and discipline were rigorously enforced, along with the same duties as an army in the field. Routines were exact; reveille sounded at dawn, and lights out at ten. Virtually every minute in between was filled with instruction, preparation, or drill. At first Johnston's standing in the class was average, but as he became accustomed to Academy life, it improved.[14]

Bonds of friendship that were never broken were formed at West Point. Johnston's closest friend was Bennett H. Henderson of North Carolina. Future Confederate Generals Robert E. Lee and Leonidas Polk would entered the Academy during Johnston's years there, as did his friend from Transylvania University, Jefferson Davis.

Johnston was a capable student though never outstanding, valuing the mastery of a subject rather than high class standing. His strongest areas of study were in tactics and his old favorite, mathematics. Johnston was a splendid cadet and adapted to Academy routines with ease. His striking figure, sound judgment, and fine military bearing quickly marked him as a leader respected by his peers. Many of his fellow cadets spoke highly of him. Leonidas Polk wrote his family of the good fortune of having Johnston as his friend: "Cadet Johnston was popular among the officers of the staff on account of his strict attention to duty and steadiness of character."[15] Another classmate later wrote that "Johnston was esteemed by all."[16]

At the beginning of his senior year, Johnston had the honor of serving as the adjutant, the most coveted position of the corps. This honor did not go to the cadet with the highest academic rank but to the one who exhibited leadership and general soldierly qualities. Johnston served well, and all who knew him predicted for him a distinguished career. Johnston graduated from West Point in 1826, ranking eighth in his class. He was greatly impressed by the ideals—respect for man, reverence for God, personal honor, and duty to country—he had acquired at West Point. He carried these ideals with him all through his career.[17]

Johnston's ranking at graduation entitled him to an assignment in the artillery, but he chose the infantry instead. He believed the infantry would provide the best opportunities for distinction and promotion, and he even turned down an invitation to become an aide-de-camp on Winfield Scott's staff, the army's most distinguished soldier and future general-in-chief.[18] Johnston was wrong, however. He was commissioned a second lieutenant and remained at that rank for nearly eight years, spending most of his time at Jefferson Barracks near St. Louis, Missouri.

Soon after arriving at Jefferson Barracks, Johnston met the young woman who was to become his first wife. At a ball in the Chouteau mansion in St. Louis, he was introduced to Henrietta Preston of Louisville, the daughter of Captain William Preston, a veteran of the Revolution and one of the most respected citizens in Louisville. The attraction that began at this meeting soon developed into a romance. The couple was married on January 20, 1829.[19]

In the spring of 1832, a call to arms broke the monotony of barracks' life. The interruption in routine resulted when Black Hawk and his Indian warriors invaded the northwestern frontier. Three days later, General Atkinson and his regiment were on the move up the Mississippi by steamboat, with Lieutenant Johnston as aide-de-camp and assistant adjutant general. The Black Hawk War was Johnston's first exposure to war. From General Atkinson, he learned the importance of careful planning for supplies and logistics; however, the closest he came to actual combat was watching militiamen massacre Indians trying to surrender along the Bad Axe River in the upper Mississippi Valley.[20]

In debt and still a lieutenant with little hope of promotion, Johnston resigned his commission on April 22, 1834. Henrietta's failing health contributed heavily to his decision to leave the army. His resignation proved to be a mistake, at least initially. First his wife, and then his daughter, died. By 1836, at the age of thirty-three, he was a widower with two small children, little money, and no viable prospects for improvement. Distraught with grief and his life in shambles, Johnston withdrew to a farm near St. Louis, leaving his son and daughter with their grandmother in Louisville. For a few months he prepared the land for plowing but found no satisfaction in the task. He longed for the army; he was a man without a family and a soldier without a uniform.[21]

Just when Johnston's life looked its bleakest, an opportunity for redemption appeared from an unexpected source. In 1836, the simmering animosity between American settlers and the Mexican government came to a head. On April 21, after his defeat at the Battle of San Jacinto, Mexican General Santa Anna signed a treaty recognizing Texas as an independent territory. The Mexican government, however, repudiated the agreement and intended to re-conquer the Lone Star Republic. Seeing this situation as an opportunity to resume his military career, Johnston traveled to Texas to offer his services.[22]

Sam Houston welcomed Johnston to the new republic, and promotion came quickly for him. He became a colonel, adjutant general, acting secretary of war, and "senior brigadier general" in command of the Texan Army. Johnston's promotion to senior general placed him at a higher rank than the army's former top officer, Felix Huston. Huston believed that Johnston's appointment was an insult intended to "ruin his reputation," and he angrily challenged Johnston to a duel. Johnston accepted the challenge, and despite Huston's reputation as an excellent marksman, he agreed to duel him with pistols.[23]

Johnston was not given to dueling as a way of defending his honor, and later in life he would have ignored such a challenge; but now he was a victim of circumstances. If he refused the challenge, the volunteers would believe that he was afraid to fight, and without some evidence of physical courage, it would be difficult, if not impossible, to command them. His personal career and the authority of the government were at stake. He later said he fought the duel as a public duty to defend the dignity of the republic. Thus was the gauntlet taken up.[24]

At dawn, Johnston and Huston faced each other at the traditional distance of ten paces. Four times the duelists exchanged shots with neither being hit. On the fifth shot Huston found the mark, the bullet passing through Johnston's right hip. Fortunately it broke no bones, and Johnston was able to return to duty after a month of bed rest.[25]

Despite the loss of the duel, Johnston had earned the respect of Huston and his troops. They were now ready to accept him as their commanding general. When President Sam Houston heard of the duel, he was thunderstruck. In all his career he had never accepted a challenge, although he had received many of them; after his victory at San Jacinto, Houston was secure enough in the hearts of his troops that he could ignore these invitations without losing face. After a mild reprimand, a mere slap on the wrist, from Houston, Johnston was ready to resume his command of the army. A week after the duel, Houston wrote to Johnston that he had learned with great pleasure of the splendid condition of the army.[26]

When the Mexicans concentrated 5,000 troops at Matamoros and Saltillo, Johnston prepared his army for an invasion, but to his dismay, the attack never came. As army commander, Johnston eagerly hoped for a renewal of war, but it was not to be. Internal problems in Mexico prevented that country from making good on its threats to invade Texas. Houston refused to allow Johnston to invade Mexico, because he realized that this action would damage his relationship with the United States and his hope of American recognition of Texan independence. On March 21, 1837, President Houston wrote joyfully to Johnston saying that the United States had recognized Texan independence. This news was good for Texas, but it reduced the chances of further war with Mexico. Houston's successor, Mirabeau Bonaparte Lemar, also refused to continue hostilities with Mexico. Frustrated, Johnston returned to private life in May 1840.[27]

Leaving the Texan army proved to be almost as disastrous for Johnston as resigning from the U.S. Army. Johnston set out to make a fortune in land speculation, only to find himself heavily in debt. He attempted to establish a cotton plantation in Texas with borrowed money; this endeavor, too, failed, because he did not have enough money to purchase slaves. Without slave labor it was impossible for an agricultural venture of this size to be successful.

The only bright spot for him during this time was his marriage to his second wife, Eliza Griffin, in October 1843. Eliza was the twenty-three-year-old cousin of his first wife. One of Johnston's close friends later described her as the most charming woman in Louisville: "[She] was a dazzling beauty of the Spanish type. . . . She was a brilliant brunette and sang and played with great taste and skill, and drew and painted admirably."[28]

As before, Johnston's chance to escape his desperate personal situation came with war. This time the conflict was between the United States and Mexico. When the United States annexed the Lone Star Republic, the spark of war was ignited again. Mexico still claimed Texas, and on April 1846, it attacked American troops north of the Rio Grande. Few men welcomed the coming of war with Mexico as much as did Albert Sidney Johnston. For years, he had disliked the Mexicans because of their brutality toward Texas. He looked forward to the prospect of marching against his long-sworn enemy. At the outbreak of the war, Johnston was without a commission in the Army of the Republic. His commission had expired when the United States had annexed Texas.[29]

Failing to obtain a commission in the regular U.S. Army, Johnston secured a colonelcy in the First Texas Volunteer Infantry. The First Texas marched into Mexico under the command of General Zachary Taylor, but unfortunately Johnston's troops had enlisted for only six months. After the six-month enlistment was over, his troops went home, leaving him without a command. Taylor, however, found another position for him as a staff officer in one of his divisions. Johnston served with conspicuous valor in the battle at Monterrey, his finest moment of the engagement occurring when an Ohio regiment was overrun by a column of Mexican lancers. Sweeping across the plain and killing stragglers as they came, the lancers spread panic among the retreating volunteers. Those that were able to escape fled through a nearby cornfield. Although separated from his command during the attack, Johnston calmly rallied the frightened troops to form a line against the pursuers. The volunteers took cover behind a chaparral fence and opened fire on the lancers, forcing them to retreat.[30]

Captain Joseph Hooker, who would later command the Army of the Potomac during the Civil War, was with Johnston throughout most of the day at Monterrey. He later described Johnston as the outstanding officer of the entire division. Regarding the episode with the lancers, Hooker wrote, "It was through [Johnston's] agency, mainly, that our division was saved from a cruel slaughter. . . . The coolness and magnificent presence [that he] displayed on this field . . . left an impression on my mind that I have never forgotten."[31]

On another occasion, Johnston's quick thinking saved Jefferson Davis's life as well as his own. This episode greatly influenced Johnston's future career, because it increased Davis's admiration for his leadership quality. He said, "[Johnston] exhibited that quick perception and decision which characterize the military genius." Davis would continue to have a high opinion of Johnston until his death.[32]

Johnston's term of service expired soon after the fall of Monterrey. He left Mexico and returned to his struggle with poverty. In the fall of 1849, he sold his holdings for $2,000. Now nearly fifty years old, Johnston's attempt to secure his future looked bleak. Zachary Taylor, who won the presidency in 1848, came to his aid, appointing Johnston as army paymaster for western Texas with the rank of major. It was a very demanding job, requiring him to travel through rugged and dangerous country to perform his duties. It did, however, provide him financial security and put him in a position to benefit from his longtime friendship with Jefferson Davis.[33]

In 1854, Davis, now secretary of war in Franklin Pierce's cabinet, appointed Johnston colonel in command of the newly formed Second Cavalry Regiment. This regiment was an elite outfit with Robert E. Lee as lieutenant colonel, with George Thomas and William Hardee as majors, and with numerous other officers who would make a name for themselves during the Civil War.[34]

Johnston served in Texas for the next four years as department commander. Then, in 1858, he was placed in charge of a 2,000-troop force organized to establish government authority over Mormon settlers in Utah. The Mormon Church had great power in the territory and had actually formed an army of its own; it appeared that nothing short of an all-out military action could bring the situation under control. Johnston, however, displayed such resourcefulness, tact, and good judgment that he was able to prevent needless bloodshed and, at the same time, accomplish his objective. Out of admiration for his conduct in Utah, many of his friends began to talk of nominating him on the Democratic ticket for president.[35]

Johnston was not influenced by this praise; to all requests, he declined. "If success were certain," he told his son, "I still have honesty and patriotism enough to say that there are others more capable and more fit for the station, who ought to have precedence."[36]

In 1860, Johnston returned from Utah, now a brevet brigadier general. His next assignment was command of the Department of the Pacific, comprising California and Oregon. Shadows of war were gathering when Johnston and his family left New York for his new assignment in California. Like many of his fellow Americans, Johnston had mixed feelings. As a military officer, he had spent most of his adult life in the service of the United States. He was, however, just as loyal to Kentucky, the state that gave him birth, and to Texas, the state he now called home. Johnston supported slavery and resented the efforts of "fanatics" in the Republican Party who interfered with the "peculiar institution," but he was opposed to secession and felt it would do little to solve the problem.[37]

Since California was a free state, before Johnston left for San Francisco he disposed of the two black slaves that he owned. He sold his young female slave to his son for $1,200, and when his young male slave said he wished to go to California, Johnston gave him his freedom but contracted him to five years of service.[38]

The three-week trip to California was rough, but the Johnstons were charmed by San Francisco and the surrounding countryside. Each day brought further news of the widening split between the North and South. Johnston followed these reports with sadness. In California the great majority of the population favored the Union, but there was a substantial pro-Southern minority in the state. During the early months of 1861, a small number of Confederate sympathizers formed secret societies; their purpose was to advance the Confederate cause in California. Knowing that Johnston was a Southerner, some of these Confederates hoped to enlist him on their side. Their plans were to capture key points on the West Coast, thus crippling the Union defenses in the West.[39]

A committee of these Southern sympathizers visited Johnston in the hope that he would give them information to assist them with their plot. The meeting had barely begun when Johnston quickly put a stop to it, saying, "I have prepared for emergencies, and will defend the property of the United States with every resource at my command, and with the last drop of blood in my body. Tell that to all our Southern friends."[40]

When California's Governor John Downey heard rumors of a Southern conspiracy, he called upon Johnston to ensure the safety of arms located in his state. Downey later remembered Johnston's reply: "Governor, I have spent the greater part of my life in the service of my country, and while I hold her commission I shall serve her honorably and faithfully. I shall protect her public property, and not a cartridge or percussion-cap shall pass to any enemy while I am here as her representative."[41]

Although Downey had no doubts about Johnston's loyalty, there were some in California that did. A whispering campaign soon spread that Johnston was in league with the Southern plotters. The whispers quickly spread across the country to Washington, where they reached the ears of important people, including General-in-Chief Winfield Scott. Scott knew Johnston well enough to know he would not do anything dishonorable, but he feared Johnston's enemies might use this rumor as an excuse to replace him with one of their own. To head off such a move, Scott sent Brigadier General Edwin Sumner to relieve Johnston and ordered him back to Washington. Johnston was willing to turn over his command but not to return to Washington. News of Texas's secession had reached Johnston, and he used the occasion to send his resignation to Washington. It was to take effect upon his replacement's arrival in California.[42]

At first, Johnston considered staying in California and farming, but when news reports from the East indicated that Lincoln had called for 75,000 volunteers, he decided to return to Texas. Johnston would cast his lot with Texas. "It looks like fate," he told his wife. "Twice Texans have made me a rebel."[43]

The press coverage about Johnston's early military career in California produced exaggerated expectations of his ability. As a result, the personal flaws that ended up marking his Civil War career were not apparent when the war began. His prewar record exceeded that of Joseph E. Johnston, P. G. T. Beauregard, and Braxton Bragg. Among his peers, only Robert E. Lee's earlier accomplishments were more impressive than his. Although Lee graduated from West Point three years after Johnston and was subordinate to him in the Second Cavalry, he was offered top command of the U.S. Army at the beginning of the war, second only to Winfield Scott. When Lee declined the position, it was offered to Johnston, but he also refused.[44]

Throughout the South, messages poured into Richmond urging Davis to assign Johnston to an important position—preferably somewhere in the Mississippi Valley where his extensive Western experience could be put to good use. Major General Leonidas Polk, ranking officer in the Mississippi Valley, wrote to Davis urging him to appoint his old roommate as Western commander. "The success of our campaign in the valley may depend upon such an arrangement, and I know of no man who has the capacity to fill the position, who could be had but General Johnston."[45] But Davis needed no urging. He immediately sent for Johnston.

When Johnston arrived in Richmond, Jefferson Davis was seriously ill and confined to his bed. The door to the president's room had been left open to allow for ventilation, allowing him to hear voices in the downstairs hall. When Davis heard the strong, energetic footsteps of a man below, he gathered his strength and said, "That's Sidney Johnston's step! Bring him up!"[46]

Davis had been anxiously awaiting his old friend's arrival. Only a week before, Davis had submitted to the Confederate Congress the five names and order of rank of those whom he wished to commission as full generals. At the top of the list stood Samuel Cooper, adjutant general of the Confederate army. He was followed by Albert Sidney Johnston, Lee, Joseph E. Johnston, and P. G. T. Beauregard.[47]

On September 10, Johnston was given command of Military Department Number 2, which included Kentucky, Tennessee, Missouri, Kansas, Arkansas, and western Mississippi, as well as the vast and undefined "Indian Country" west of Missouri and Arkansas. The Federal build-up in the Mississippi Valley and the weakness of the scattered Confederate units made this assignment difficult and an administrative nightmare. Without delay, Johnston left Richmond for his new headquarters in Tennessee. When he arrived in Nashville on September 14, he was greeted by a large, cheering crowd. In a brief speech, he told the crowd that this was a people's war and could be sustained only by the people. His words electrified the crowd, and they cheered even more, impressed by Johnston's words and his powerful appearance. He stood over six feet tall and weighed a well-proportioned 200 pounds, with dark hair and mustache. No one appeared more appropriate for his position as military leader than Johnston. It was now up to Johnston to demonstrate that there was more to him than his good looks.[48]

Johnston's task was awesome: he had to provide leadership for troops covering an area stretching from the Alleghenies westward to the Indian territory beyond the Mississippi. In addition, his movements were restricted; he could not take his army northward to the Ohio River, the natural boundary for a frontier defense, because of Kentucky's neutrality. The same problem faced troops in Tennessee. They were forced to develop a river defense south of the state line despite superior positions that existed on Kentucky soil. As a result, Forts Henry and Donelson were hastily built. Once these forts were constructed, both state and Confederate authorities were obligated to defend them. The two positions were roughly twelve miles apart and seventy-five miles downstream from Nashville and not easily defended.[49]

Johnston had only 40,000 poorly equipped and trained troops spread along a 500-mile front, with little hope of substantial reinforcement in the near future. An even more pressing problem was his shortage of arms. Almost half his men were without firearms of any sort; many of those with weapons carried shotguns or hunting rifles. Johnston protested to Jefferson Davis about the lack of supplies and equipment. Davis reluctantly responded, saying, "Tell my friend General Johnston that I can do nothing for him, that he must rely on his own resources."[50] Davis had given him high rank and great responsibility but not sufficient military strength to defend the territories he believed to be important to the Confederacy.[51]

Johnston did what he could with the troops he had. Being too weak to take the offensive, he established a defensive cordon. These armies and forts covered the anticipated invasion routes between the Appalachian Mountains and the Mississippi. Throughout the remainder of 1861, Johnston's line held because the Federals believed Johnston's troops outnumbered theirs.[52]

Early in 1862, the Confederate line broke. On January 19, Union Brigadier General George Thomas routed Confederates defending the Cumberland Gap at the Battle of Mill Springs, Kentucky. Next, on February 6, Union gunboats bombarded Fort Henry into submission. General Grant's army was able to occupy Fort Henry without firing a shot. Finally, less than two weeks later, Grant took Fort Donelson and 12,000 prisoners.[53]

Johnston had no choice but to salvage what was left of his army by withdrawing from Kentucky and middle Tennessee. The Federals now advanced south toward northern Mississippi and southeast to Nashville, which they occupied on February 25. It appeared that the Western part of the Confederacy would soon collapse.

As a result of the disasters at Forts Henry and Donelson, the press and many Southern political leaders criticized Johnston and demanded his removal from command. Even some of the officers and men in his own command denounced his leadership. Others, however, came to his defense. Colonel Josiah Gorgas, at the Ordnance Bureau, defended Johnston and believed Davis was to blame for the setbacks. "Ten thousand men would have converted Donelson from an overwhelming disaster to a victory—and 18,000 men were literally doing nothing under General Bragg at Pensacola and Mobile. Our President is unfortunately no military genius and could not see the relative value of position. Pensacola was nothing compared to Donelson."[54]

Davis's trust in Johnston's ability, however, remained strong and unshaken. "If he is not a general," Davis said, "we had better give up the war, for we have no generals." Johnston accepted full responsibility for his military reversals and wrote to Davis, "The test of merit in my profession with the people is success. It is a hard rule, but I think it is right."[55]

The criticism of Johnston was understandable but, on the whole, unjustified. Johnston lacked the means to maintain his defensive line once the Federals had the will and power to break it. To add to the difficult situation, he was ill-served by subordinates, but Johnston had made his own mistakes too. In dealing with his subordinates he often advised rather than ordered. Like Robert E. Lee, Johnston tended to place too much confidence in their judgments. Johnston often did not involve himself with details, but allowed his second in command, Beauregard, to draw up the detailed plans for the army's operation.[56]

In the aftermath of the disasters at Forts Henry and Donelson, Johnston hoped to unite all his scattered forces before the enemy could unite its own. By the beginning of April, Johnston had succeeded in carrying out his plan, and now was within striking distance of a sizable Federal encampment. Grant's troops had for some time been camped on the west bank of the Tennessee River at Pittsburg Landing. Grant had 40,000 men and was waiting for Buell, with 35,000 men, to join him before he went on the offense. Buell was expected to reach Grant in a few days. Johnston knew if he struck now, before Buell could join Grant, his numbers would be at least equal to his opponent's.[57]

On April 2, Johnston gave the orders to advance. The specific plans for the march were left to Beauregard, but they fell short of what Johnston had hoped to accomplish. The result was a monstrous 40,000-man traffic snarl. The time for the attack had been set for the fourth, but because of the delay of moving his troops, it was not until the evening of the fifth that the army finally drew up within a mile or two of the enemy, ready to attack the next morning.[58]

That night the Confederate generals met together to discuss the attack in the morning. Beauregard's opinion was that the attack should be called off; it had depended upon surprise, and now he believed that this was not possible. The approach had taken three days instead of one as planned. In addition, many of his soldiers were concerned about their weapons and whether they would fire after the damp weather; so they decided to find out. The resulting musket fire should have been enough to alert every Yankee for miles around. The soldiers' lack of discipline had caused problems in other ways too. It was now learned that the men had managed to dispose of their five days' rations in just three days. Grant's 40,000 troops would be "entrenched to their eyes," Beauregard told Johnston, "the men were without their rations." It was time to call the attack off and return to Corinth. Even the usually more resolute Bragg favored calling off the attack.[59]

No matter how unfavorable things seemed at this time, Johnston believed it was still the best chance his army would have for a long time to come, and unless they did something now, it might be their last chance. That day a telegram had arrived from Davis, expressing his hope that they would succeed in catching Grant's army and destroying it before Buell would be able to join him. The awesome weight of responsibility for his 40,000-man army, and perhaps the nation, rested squarely on his shoulders. Dismissing the arguments for turning back, he insisted they must attack. "I would fight them if they were a million," he declared."[60]

At daybreak on Sunday, April 6, the Confederates began advancing in three waves; Hardee's corps first, then Bragg's and finally Polk's and Breckinridge's corps. This type of deployment weakened the offensive power of the attack, narrowing the fronts and mixing the units, causing confusion. The Federals should have been prepared for Johnston's army, ready to fight, but they were not. Grant was so preoccupied with his plans to combine his army with Buell's and then attack Johnston at Corinth, that it never occurred to him that Johnston might, in the meantime, attack him.[61]

Johnston's attack managed to come as a surprise. Grant's troops were not dug in as Beauregard had predicted. Rather, they were in the open and susceptible to attack. Thousands fled in panic, and those that kept fighting found it necessary to continue to fall back. So strong was Johnston's initial attack that Grant thought the Confederate forces were much greater than they were.[62]

Johnston rode his magnificent horse named Fire-eater closely behind his battle line. Passing through what had been a Union camp, he came upon some stragglers searching the area for loot. He shamed them back into fighting by picking up a tin cup and remarking, "Let this be my share of the spoils today." Normally, the army commander would not be as near to the front line as he, but rather, he would direct his forces from the rear. But Johnston had Beauregard to maneuver units, and so he believed he could best contribute to the victory by being up front, encouraging his men.[63]

By midday, the Confederates had driven within a few hundred yards of Pittsburg Landing, and it looked as though they would take the day. To General Johnston, victory seemed within his grasp. The Federal left, that had slowed his advance, had finally yielded. But now the Confederate attack seemed to stall at what became known as the "Hornets' Nest." Assault after assault failed. Despite his earlier success, Johnston now saw hundreds of his troops, demoralized by the heavy fire from the "Hornets' Nest," retreating across the field. Johnston sent his aide with orders to get the men back in line and continue pressing the enemy. General Breckinridge approached Johnston to say he could not get one of his regiments to advance. "Then I will help you," Johnston said.[64]

Johnston went with Breckinridge to the front of the reluctant regiment. Riding along the line, Johnston calmly spoke to the men, trying to encourage them by touching their bayonets and saying, "These will do the work. . . . Men they are stubborn; we must use the bayonet." When reaching the center of the line, he turned and called out, "I will lead you." With new spirits, Breckinridge's men swept forward behind their general, forcing the enemy to fall back; the objective of Johnston's charge was taken. Throughout the charge, Johnston was under heavy fire. Suddenly, a musket ball hit him in the rear of his leg and tore his popliteal artery.[65]

One of Johnston's aides, Isham G. Harris, noticed that he was reeling in the saddle. He quickly realized that something was extremely wrong with Johnston, who appeared flushed and faint. Harris grasped the General's shoulder to keep him from falling. When asked if he was wounded, Johnston replied, "Yes, and I fear seriously." Assisted by another aide, Harris guided Johnston to a small ravine out of danger from enemy fire. Now unconscious, Johnston was placed on the ground. When Harris examined Johnston's body, he expected to find a serious body wound, but the only one he noticed was in his right leg. He then lifted his head and gave him a swallow of brandy as a stimulant. Colonel Preston and others from Johnston's staff now arrived. Preston dismounted and knelt beside his stricken brother-in-law. "Johnston, don't you know me?" Preston asked, but there was no response. Preston called for whiskey and Captain Dudley Haydon attempted to pour it down Johnston's throat, but he did not swallow it. Haydon felt Johnston's chest for a heart beat, but found none. "My God," cried Preston as he realized the truth. Albert Sidney Johnston was dead.[66]

Unfortunately Johnston's personal physician had been left behind to care for Confederate and Union wounded. Johnston's initial wound, although not critical, was serious enough if not quickly attended. The loss of blood had not been noticed at first because it either collected internally or in Johnston's high boots. He had apparently been wounded for several minutes before Harris saw him reel in the saddle.[67]

Johnston may not have been aware that he had been seriously wounded for several minutes after being hit. Earlier in his life, he had been shot in the same leg. Since that time he had lived with a sensory numbness to pain and heat and cold in that leg.[68] So he may have lost a lot of blood before he realized the seriousness of the wound. A tragic irony of the whole affair was that in Johnston's coat pocket was found a field tourniquet, which might have saved his life if used quickly and properly. The physican who could have used the tourniquet was, by Johnston's order, attending wounded Confederate soldiers and Union prisoners in a nearby ravine. Johnston's earlier act of humanity may have cost him his life.[69] As the second highest ranking officer in the Confederacy, Johnston was the highest ranking general officer of either army to be killed in action during the Civil War.

Johnston's death stunned the members of his staff. Preston was his kin; Haydon was an old personal friend; and others of brief acquaintance had already come to admire him, even to look upon him with reverence. But they could not yield to their feelings now—the battle was still raging about them. Johnston's body was wrapped in a blanket and taken back to General Beauregard's headquarters at the Shiloh church. The General's identity was concealed, and those asking who he was were told that it was the corpse of Colonel Jackson of Texas.[70]

Beauregard's staff surgeon, Dr. Samuel P. Choppin, and Johnston's personal physician conducted an autopsy and located the fatal bullet. Later, Choppin injected whiskey into Johnston's blood vessels as a means of preventing rapid decomposition. A sad William Preston requested of Beauregard that he and the rest of the General's staff be permitted to take the body to New Orleans for temporary burial until the family could select a permanent resting place. Beauregard consented.[71]

That evening, Beauregard sent a message to Richmond announcing total success for the day's operations: "We this morning attacked the enemy in strong position in front of Pittsburg [Landing], and after a severe battle of ten hours, thanks to the Almighty, gained a complete victory, driving the enemy from every position. Loss on both sides heavy, including our commander-in-chief, General A. S. Johnston, who fell gallantly leading his troops into the thickest of the fight."[72]

The Battle of Shiloh resumed the next day, and would be at that time the largest land battle on the North American continent, involving nearly 100,000 infantrymen from three armies and various naval units. April 6 proved to be the costliest day of the entire war in proportion of casualties to the number of men involved—more than 23,000 would fall before the last shot was fired. Despite the fact that Northern casualties were 2,000 greater than those of the South, the Confederates had failed to destroy the Army of the Tennessee and were unable to hold the land they had captured the first day.[73]

In 1866, the Texas Legislature approved a measure to bring Johnston's remains back home to the Lone Star State. In 1903, $10,000 was appropriated for a sculpture honoring Johnston to be placed on his final resting place in Austin State Cemetery.[74] No spot could have been more fitting for Johnston's grave. He had played a part in the founding of Austin and lived there when it was the frontier capital of the Republic of Texas. Later, he had lived happily in Austin with his family. It was only appropriate that Albert Sidney Johnston should come home.[75]

Johnston's death created a "lingering despair" throughout the Confederacy. Jefferson Davis was grief stricken: "Our loss is irreparable." Years later, he often remarked, "When Sidney Johnston fell, it was the turning point of our fate; for we had no other hand to take up his work in the West." Indeed, Johnston would be missed. Although the merits of his ability as a general would be debated after the war, Johnston's character, leadership, and valor under fire would not. Generals and staff officers testified to the effect Johnston had on his men in battle. A young Confederate later described Johnston's last day at Shiloh: "To those who saw [Johnston] that day in all the glorious fever of that delirious success, mounted upon a magnificent steed, his massive figure seeming to enlarge to gigantic size with the ardor of battle, his noble face aflame with his indomitable spirit of fight, he was the ideal embodiment of the fiery essence of war."[76]

9   *Braxton Bragg*

"Quick-Tempered Martinet"

During the first six months of 1863, the armies of Confederate General Braxton Bragg and Union General William Rosecrans were no more than thirty miles apart in central Tennessee, inactive except for occasional cavalry raids. After Rosecrans's victory at Murfreesboro (Stone's River), Bragg had withdrawn to the southeast and dug in along the Duck River. Bragg's failure to take the offensive at the battle at Perryville and then at Murfreesboro had so disgusted his subordinates that they were almost in a state of revolt. Even his strong supporter, President Jefferson Davis, was on the verge of removing him from command of his army.

The general feeling at the time was that Braxton Bragg was incompetent and unfit to lead the army. It was said that he retreated whether he won or lost. A Confederate joke circulated that he would never get to heaven because "the moment he was invited to enter, he would fall back."[1]

"Bragg is not fit to be a general," a Confederate soldier wrote in his diary. "If Jeff Davis will just let Bragg alone, I think he will do more damage than the enemy." One general swore he would never fight again under Bragg's command, while another threatened to resign from the army and challenged Bragg to a duel. Major General Henry Heth believed that Bragg "lost his head" in battle and did not seem to know what was happening. In 1863, Lieutenant General James Longstreet, D. H. Hill, and Simon Buckner signed a petition requesting his dismissal from the army.[2]

General Braxton Bragg's outward appearance may have influenced the way his troops felt about him. Lieutenant Colonel James A. L. Fremantle, a visiting British officer who had the opportunity to meet many of the Southern officers, described Bragg as very unattractive, tall, bright-eyed, with a "sickly, cadaverous, haggard appearance, rather plain figure, bushy black eye-brows which united in a tuff on the top of his nose, and a stubby iron-gray beard."[3] By 1863, Bragg's troops resented his harsh discipline and questioned his competence. Curiously enough, no one doubted his ability when the Civil War began. Yet, less than two years later, Bragg was the South's most discredited commander.

Braxton Bragg was born on March 22, 1817, in Warrenton, North Carolina. His mother was released from prison to give birth to him. She had been awaiting trial on charges of murdering a freed black man, who she claimed had disrespected her. She, however, was never formerly charged with a crime and was soon released after young Braxton was born.[4]

Braxton's father was an ambitious man who was successful in his business and would eventually own as many as twenty slaves. Although successful, he was never fully accepted by the aristocratic community in the class-conscious culture of Warrenton. Bragg's father decided that his son should pursue his education at the Military Academy at West Point, and with the help of an older son who was a member of the state legislature, he was able to obtain the necessary appointment.[5]

Braxton entered West Point in 1833. Despite occasional demerits for drinking and child-play in the mess hall, he graduated in 1837, ranking fifth in a class of fifty. As a young officer in the artillery, Bragg established a reputation for being efficient and intelligent but also for being difficult to get along with. As a general later in his career, he was fiercely protective of his status as a commander, although as a junior officer, he was known to be rude and occasionally insubordinate. In 1843, while stationed at Fort Moultrie, South Carolina, he was contemptuous and rude to his commanding officer, Lieutenant Colonel William Gates. When, in a friendly gesture, Gates asked Bragg to join him in a drink, he replied: "If you order me to drink a glass of wine, I shall have to do it." On another occasion, he was court-martialed for openly criticizing General Winfield Scott; still not fearful of the consequences, Bragg again questioned his commander's competence. As a result, he was severely reprimanded and admonished to correct his behavior.[6]

In the nine years between graduation and the Mexican War, Bragg saw action in the Seminole War in Florida and served on the Western frontier. By the time the war with Mexico began in 1846, Bragg had risen to the rank of captain.

In the Mexican War, Bragg commanded a battery of light artillery under Zachary Taylor and distinguished himself at Monterrey and Buena Vista. Fighting alongside Jefferson Davis and his Mississippi Rifles, Bragg's bravery brought him fame and three brevet promotions. In addition to gaining national fame as a warrior, Bragg made valuable connections that would affect later his life and career. Among those connections was Jefferson Davis; both men admired each other and would become friends.[7]

Upon his return home from Mexico, Bragg was welcomed as a war hero

Although admired for his courage during the Mexican War, General Braxton Bragg became a contentious man, constantly at odds with subordinate officers and disliked by the troops in the field. It was a welcome change when Johnston replaced Bragg as commander of the Army of Tennessee.

COURTESY OF THE LIBRARY OF CONGRESS

from one end of the country to the other. He was now accepted and toasted by the citizens of Warrenton who had formerly scorned his family's humble beginnings. In 1849, Bragg married the rich and beautiful heiress, Eliza Brooks, from Louisiana.[8]

Despite the danger and comradeship Bragg and Davis had shared in Mexico, their relationship soon became strained. Bragg, as an artillery officer, was opposed to the policies that Davis, as secretary of war, proposed for the artillery. Bragg objected to Davis's plan to station artillery on the frontier, considering it a waste of men and horses "to chase Indians with six-pounders." In December 1855, Bragg went to Davis to discuss the plan. When Davis failed to consider Bragg's point of view, he turned in his resignation; Davis promptly accepted it.[9]

Bragg's dispute with Davis provided him with the perfect excuse to resign. The routine of army life was losing its appeal for him. At the age of thirty-nine, he was still a captain in the regular army (brevet lieutenant colonel) and ready for a change in career. With the use of his wife's money, he was able to buy and develop a sugar plantation near Thibodaux, Louisiana. Later, he was appointed the state's commissioner of public works, a job he held until the outbreak of the Civil War.[10]

When the war began, Bragg returned to the army and was appointed Louisiana's general-in-chief. In March 1861, he received a commission as a brigadier general in the Confederate army and was assigned to the command of the Gulf Coast defenses between Mobile and Pensacola. He quickly realized the vulnerable nature of the ports he had been sent to protect. In a letter to President Davis, he wrote: "Our strength consists in the enemy's weakness." There was not much he could do, he believed, to withstand an attack on the ports once the Union army was organized and ready to attack.

It was just a matter of time before the Union captured the ports; nevertheless, Bragg set about training the volunteers assigned to him. His efficiency in organizing and training troops and his unselfish offer to send four of his best regiments to Virginia in exchange for newly recruited ones did not go unnoticed. In September, he was promoted to major general and given charge of all of Alabama and West Florida.[11]

When General Albert Sidney Johnston assumed command of the Confederate Army of the Mississippi, he concluded that the military situation in the Western theater was desperate. He immediately asked for help from Jefferson Davis, stating that he had less than half the troops he needed and, even worse, no rifles or muskets to give arriving recruits. To cover the whole area, he had less than 20,000 men, most of them untrained and ill equipped. As one of Johnston's aides put it, "He had no army."[12]

In February 1862, Bragg was ordered to reinforce the hard-pressed General Johnston in Kentucky and Tennessee. When Bragg arrived at General Beauregard's headquarters, he was warmly welcomed. At this time, everyone seemed to have a good opinion of him; in fact, President Davis was beginning to compare him to Albert Sidney Johnston, a reputation he had earned. Bragg was highly self-disciplined and expected the same of those he commanded; when a person fell short in his responsibility, Bragg was severe with his punishment. As a result, the troops he commanded were some of the best drilled and trained in the Confederate army. Although he was a strict disciplinarian, Bragg also exercised a fatherly care for his men, making certain that they were well treated and often visiting with the wounded in the hospital.[13]

At the same time, Bragg had a quick temper and could be belligerent. He pushed himself hard, often to the detriment of his health. Poor health may have been one of the reasons for Bragg's grouchy personality and his lack of tact in dealing with subordinates. Throughout the war, he suffered from dyspepsia, rheumatism, chronic boils, a liver ailment, extreme nervousness, and severe migraine headaches. Often he was too sick to command. Bragg made a real effort to overcome these deficiencies, but when under pressure, he often reverted to his former undesirable behavior.[14]

Once again, Bragg was asked to train and discipline Beauregard's recruits. The men, he said, displayed "more enthusiasm than discipline, more capacity than knowledge, and more valor than instructions." Bragg worked hard to bring a semblance of order to the army before Beauregard joined Johnston's army. In Bragg's official report, he said that the condition of the army was so poor that he doubted if they "had ever so much as made a full day's march."[15]

By the end of March, Johnston and Beauregard had collected an army of 50,000 men at Corinth, Mississippi. Camped nearby was Grant's army of 42,000; Grant was waiting for the arrival of Don Carlos Buell's army before he attacked Johnston. On April 3, Johnston began to move eastward from Corinth. His plan was to launch a surprise attack on Grant before Buell's Army of the Ohio could arrive. Late on April 5, Johnston's army arrived within two miles of Shiloh Church and Grant's army. The next morning, to Grant's surprise, Johnston attacked. Noon came and went and the Confederate attacks continued, driving the Union army back until it made a stand at what became known as the "Hornets' Nest." When Johnston learned what was holding up his army's advance, he ordered renewed attacks against the Union line. Riding to the front of the Confederate line amidst a hail of Federal fire, Johnston received a mortal wound and died shortly afterward. Beauregard now assumed command of the Confederate army.[16]

The gallant defense by the Union forces at the "Hornets' Nest" gave Grant the time he needed to prevent disaster. The Confederate army had fought well, and Bragg's Second Corps was especially effective. Bragg had been one of the few Confederate generals who recognized the importance of pressing the attack before nightfall, and he ordered two of his brigades to form and prepare for an assault. "Sweep everything forward. Drive the enemy into the river," he said. The brigades obeyed Bragg's command but were met with strong resistance. After thirty minutes of heavy fighting, General Beauregard decided to call off the assault and rest his exhausted troops, hoping to resume the offensive in the morning.[17]

That night, Buell's army arrived to bolster Grant's left wing. The next day, now with fresh troops, Grant attacked. The Confederate forces fought hard, but exhaustion and the enemy's numerical superiority proved too much for Beauregard. Grant organized a charge that drove the last Confederate from the field. The battle at Shiloh was by far the bloodiest battle yet fought in the Civil War, with both sides suffering heavy losses. Beauregard fell back to Corinth.[18]

Jefferson Davis considered Corinth a critically strategic point. Beauregard agreed, writing: "If defeated here we lose the whole Mississippi Valley and probably our cause." By the middle of May 1862, the Confederates had

70,000 men at Corinth, but many were recovering from wounds, and others were ill from typhoid and dysentery. Faced with an inadequate water supply and the prospect of being surrounded by a siege, Beauregard decided to abandon Corinth, leaving behind only a skeletal force to conceal his evacuation. He claimed his escape was "equivalent to a great victory." But Jefferson Davis was shocked and angered by the news.[19]

Although Beauregard talked of resuming the offensive, Davis had had enough of his promises. When Beauregard took an unauthorized leave on the advice of his doctor to attend a spa at Bladon Springs, Alabama, Davis took the opportunity to replace him with his old friend, Braxton Bragg.[20] Beauregard was angered by his removal and believed that Davis had "revealed himself as little more than a traitor." The change pleased Davis, however, who felt more comfortable with friends in positions of high command.[21]

After taking command of Beauregard's disorganized forces, Bragg set to work whipping the army into shape. "Bragg is beyond a doubt the best disciplinarian in the South," a soldier wrote. "When he took command . . . the army was little better than a mob. . . . Firearms could be heard at all hours of the day. Now a gun is never fired without orders from the Brigade Commanders. Bragg had one man shot for discharging his gun without orders. . . . Since that time the discipline of troops [has] improved very much. Men are not apt to disobey orders when they know death is the punishment." The Confederate army could have used more of Bragg's discipline.[22]

In early July, Bragg began to move east in response to General Buell's threat to Chattanooga. Bragg's army was over 200 miles away, and it seemed unlikely there would be enough time to reach Chattanooga before Buell. But Bragg came up with a brilliant solution; rather than taking the direct 200-mile route to his destination, he would transport his troops by rail via a 776-mile roundabout trip south to Mobile, northeast to Atlanta, and then north to Chattanooga. Two weeks later, his troops were all in Chattanooga ahead of Buell's army. It was the largest Confederate railroad movement of the war.[23]

Bragg now decided to take advantage of Buell's inaction by taking the offensive himself. By invading Kentucky, he hoped to relieve pressure on Mississippi by forcing the Union to move troops north to oppose him. Bragg also believed that Kentucky, a slave state that had remained in the Union, hoped to be "liberated." When he reached Kentucky, he was sure the citizens would rise up to support the Confederacy.[24]

On August 28, Bragg started north, planning to coordinate his movements with those of General Edmund Kirby Smith. His instructions to Smith, however, were unclear, and the two forces followed divergent routes into Kentucky. When Buell learned of Bragg's movement, he hurried northwest toward Nashville, reaching the Tennessee capital early in September. Meanwhile, Smith marched north into the heart of Kentucky and, on September 2, captured Lexington. The steady advance of Bragg and Smith caused great alarm in the West as well as in Washington. All available Union troops west of the Appalachians were rushed to Louisville and Cincinnati.[25]

As Bragg moved north, he captured Munfordville after a stubborn defense by an outnumbered Federal garrison. Bragg stayed at Munfordville for several days, hoping Buell would attack him. When the challenge went unanswered, Bragg moved northeast toward Frankfort.[26] Crossing the border into Kentucky, Bragg issued a proclamation: "Kentuckians I have entered your State . . . to restore to you the liberties of which you have been deprived by a cruel and relentless foe. . . . If you prefer Federal rule, show it by your frowns and we shall return whence we came. If you choose rather to come within the fold of our brotherhood, then cheer us with the smiles of your women and lend your willing hands to secure you in your heritage of liberty."[27]

Bragg did not get the support he expected from the people of Kentucky. Although he installed a pro-Southern governor in the capital, there was no great interest in joining the Confederacy as he had hoped. Most of those that were interested had done so earlier. Bragg wired the War Department in Richmond that, if the Kentuckians should decline his offer of "liberty," he would have to abandon his plans.

On October 1, Buell's Army of the Ohio, now grown to 77,000 men, marched out of Louisville, Kentucky. He sent two divisions to feign an attack on Frankfort, while he took the remainder of his army in pursuit of Bragg. On October 7, the stage was set for a clash of the two armies at Perryville. Buell's deployment of a diversionary column had confused Bragg, as Buell had hoped it would. Bragg did not know that the main part of Buell's army was at Perryville, and he had a muddled picture of the enemy's strength and location; Buell's intelligence about Bragg's position was not that much better, however.[28]

Early in the battle, the Confederates came close to driving the larger Union force from the field when they attacked Buell's left flank. But when Bragg attacked the Union center, his troops were repulsed, receiving heavy losses. Eventually the attack stalled, and by evening, Bragg finally realized he was attacking a force larger than his.

That night, the moon was bright, and Buell's generals urged him to attack the enemy; but Buell, convinced that he faced Bragg's entire army, decided to wait until morning. By then it was too late; during the evening, Bragg had ordered a hasty retreat. The Battle of Perryville ended in a draw with most of the honors going to the smaller Confederate army. The battle had been a costly one for both sides; Buell had suffered casualties of 4,200 men, while Confederate losses were just under 3,400. In the end, no one was the victor.[29]

Buell's failure to pursue Bragg, despite his numerical advantage, cost him his job. A disappointed President Lincoln removed him from command and replaced him with Major General William Rosecrans. Although Bragg's decision to retreat into Tennessee was approved by President Davis, it was not sanctioned by his troops. His army felt they had held their own at Perryville against a superior force and could not understand why they had been ordered to retreat. Some believed that Bragg had lost his nerve; others, that the strain of the campaign had become too much for him.[30]

On October 11, General Kirby Smith joined Bragg at Harrodsburg. With their combined commands now larger than the Federal army, he urged Bragg to attack the enemy: "For God's sake, General, let us fight Buell here." Bragg considered the possibility but again lost his resolve and did not fight. Many believed he lost a great opportunity. "Had battle been joined at Harrodsburg," said General Basil W. Duke, "it would have been the only great field of the war—east or west—on which the Confederate forces were numerically the stronger, and every other conceivable factor was in their favor. Never was the morale of an army better than that of General Bragg's on the eve of that anticipated conflict. . . . General Bragg ought to have fought then and there, and must have won."[31]

A similar view was expressed by General C. C. Gilbert, who commanded the Third Corps of Buell's army: "It was a piece of good fortune for the Union side that the Confederates did not return to renew the battle, for they would have had such an advantage in numbers and in the character of their troops that the Army of the Ohio would have been placed in great peril." Gilbert continued: "In not returning to Perryville and resuming the battle, he [Bragg] lost for the Confederacy perhaps the only opportunity it ever had of fighting a great battle with decisive preponderance in numbers and character of its troops."[32]

Bragg explained his reason for retreating in a letter to his wife, attributing it to the fact that the Kentuckians had shown little interest in enlisting in the Confederate army: "Why should I stay with my handful of brave Southern men to fight for cowards?"[33]

By November, Bragg was the subject of increasing criticism in the South for his lack of aggressiveness. Since Bragg's withdrawal from Kentucky, the president had been under pressure to relieve him of command. On November 24, in partial response to this pressure, Davis placed General Joseph E. Johnston in the West over Bragg. As a result there was considerable tension in both Johnston's and Bragg's headquarters. Both generals knew they had to fight if they wanted to retain their commands.[34]

At the end of December, Bragg had a chance to redeem himself when Union General Rosecrans came to Murfreesboro to force a battle. The armies met at Stone's River, north of the city. Although Bragg had the opportunity to choose the ground upon which he would take a stand, he settled on open country with few natural defenses.[35] On the night of December 30, the two armies were camped northwest of Murfreesboro and only a few hundred yards apart. They were so close that soldiers on both sides could hear the bands in the enemy's camp. At the end of the evening, Confederate and Union soldiers joined in singing "Home Sweet Home."[36]

The plan of both commanders was to attack the other's right, but Bragg struck first, pushing the enemy all the way back to the center of its line. The Federals rallied under Major General George Thomas and halted the Confederate assault. When Bragg tried to bring up his reserves, they arrived piecemeal and were repulsed, receiving heavy losses. At the day's end, however, Bragg believed that he had won the day and that Rosecrans was in full retreat. On January 1, 1863, he wired President Davis: "God has granted us a Happy New Year."[37]

On New Year's Day, both sides maintained their positions while bringing up reinforcements. On January 2, Rosecrans attacked Bragg, supported by heavy artillery fire. During a forty-five-minute period, over 1,700 Confederates fell. One witness recalled that they had "opened the door of Hell and the devil himself was there to greet them." By the end of the day, Bragg's forces had been driven back to their original position.[38]

When Bragg learned that Rosecrans's army was going to be reinforced, he began his withdrawal. Both sides claimed victory, but soon afterward, Rosecrans's army was able to push the Confederates out of central Tennessee. During the two days of battle, the losses had been appalling on both sides. Bragg had suffered 11,800 casualties, while Union losses were 12,900.[39]

The battle at Murfreesboro was tactically a draw, but Bragg's withdrawal turned it into a strategic victory for Rosecrans. Twice now, Bragg had come close to victory, but in both cases he had lost his nerve; perseverance could have won him a big victory.[40]

The retreat from Murfreesboro frustrated Bragg's army, just as the earlier one from Perryville had. By January, the grumbling among the ranks threatened Bragg's ability to lead. When he became aware of the undercurrent, Bragg sought a vote of confidence from his top officers. "I desire that you will consult your subordinate commanders and be candid with me," he wrote. "I shall retire without a regret if I find I have lost the good opinion of my generals, upon whom I have ever relied as upon a foundation of rock."[41] The request for a candid expression of their feelings provided an opportunity for his subordinates to criticize him without being guilty of insubordination. The responses were not what he had expected. Most of them assured him that, while they had the utmost regard for him personally, they felt the army had lost its confidence in him and that he should step down.[42]

President Davis was already aware of the difficult situation Bragg faced with his subordinates. He did not blame Bragg for retreating from Murfreesboro, since he had advised him earlier to "fight if you can and fall back." Bragg had done just that. But Davis was disturbed when he learned about the letter he had sent to his generals.[43]

Although Davis had not lost confidence in Bragg, he nevertheless asked General Johnston to investigate the situation and make recommendations.

When Johnston arrived at Bragg's camp, he found that some of the generals were hostile to their commander, even threatening that they would never go back into battle under him again. General John Breckinridge even considered resigning his commission and challenging Bragg to a duel. But Johnston found a different situation when he spoke to the troops. He found them in good shape and showing no signs of having lost confidence in their commander. The army was well clothed, healthy, well disciplined, and, in fact, numbered more than the number taken into battle at Murfreesboro. Johnston approved of the action taken by Bragg during the recent campaign and recommended that he be retained in command.[44]

Davis could have helped Bragg avoid some of the trouble he was having with his subordinate officers by removing the most vocal of them, Leonidas Polk and William Hardee. After the war, one of his generals analyzed the situation: "It struck me that Bragg did not know whom to trust. He was not popular with his generals, and hence feared that zealous cooperation on their part was wanting. If he had caused even one or two of us to be shot, I firmly believe the balance would have done better."[45]

Davis considered replacing Bragg with Johnston, but when Bragg's wife became critically ill (actually, she survived the war and her husband), the president believed it would be cruel to remove him at that time. Bragg would remain commander of the Army of Tennessee, at least for the time being.[46] The controversy over command and his wife's illness affected Bragg's health, making his temper more formidable and his tongue sharper. When Rosecrans attacked Bragg at Chattanooga, his health failed him completely. Placing himself in the hospital, he said, "I am utterly broken down."[47]

When Rosecrans hesitated before resuming his attack, Davis detached James Longstreet's corps from Lee's army and sent it to Bragg's assistance. When Rosecrans finally resumed his attack, he forced Bragg out of Chattanooga without firing a single shot. Occupying the city with a portion of his command, Rosecrans, now confident, went after Bragg. Because he was retreating, Rosecrans assumed Bragg was beaten and that all he had to do was pursue and force a battle. Rosecrans forgot to consider that he had not beaten Bragg in the field, and he did not realize that Bragg's army was being reinforced and would soon outnumber his Army of the Cumberland. Rashly he moved forward. Bragg had withdrawn to find a better place to fight; now Bragg was ready for Rosecrans.[48]

Bragg began his "game of wits," trying to fool General Rosecrans into thinking that he was on the run. He used fake deserters to convince Rosecrans that he had no intention of stopping. Because Bragg was known for his harsh treatment of deserters, Union interrogators accepted their stories.[49] On September 19, 1863, Bragg encountered Rosecrans west of Chickamauga Creek, Georgia. His plan was to turn the Union left flank and cut off the enemy's supply line from Chattanooga. On the first day, however, Bragg simply held his ground until Longstreet's entire corps could arrive.[50]

With his army strengthened by reinforcements, Bragg believed he had a chance to redeem his reputation with a smashing victory. In a general order to his troops in the field, he wrote: "The troops will be held ready for an immediate move against the enemy. . . . Heretofore, you have never failed to respond to your general when he has asked sacrifice at your hands. Relying on your gallantry and patriotism, he asks you to add the crowning glory to the wreath you wear. . . . Trusting God and the justice of our cause, and nerved by the love of the dear ones at home, failure is impossible and victory must be ours."[51]

The next day, Bragg attacked Rosecrans's left flank, held by Major General George Thomas's Fourteenth Corps. For two hours, Union troops held off Bragg's assault, but then a gap opened in their line. Longstreet quickly took advantage of the situation and charged through the void in the line. His assault cut Rosecrans's army in half, and by afternoon much of it was streaming back to Chattanooga. Only Thomas's resolute stand, earning him the name "Rock of Chickamauga," prevented a complete Union rout.[52]

The Battle of Chickamauga was the most sweeping victory of Bragg's career, but Confederate losses were high. He needed time to rest his troops and care for his wounded. There would be time enough, Bragg thought, to occupy the high ground around Chattanooga and starve the enemy into surrendering. The failure to follow up the victory immediately disgusted Bragg's chief subordinates. Generals Longstreet and Nathan Bedford Forrest could hardly contain themselves when Bragg failed to move. Forrest angrily denounced him: "What does he fight for?" and accused him of being a coward and of dereliction of duty. Soon afterward, still angry over Bragg's reluctance to exploit the victory at Chickamauga, Forrest refused to serve under Bragg, shouting: "You have played the part of a damn scoundrel. . . . If you ever again try to interfere with me or cross my path, it will be at the peril of your life."[53]

Longstreet later said that he was convinced "nothing but the hand of God can save us or help us as long as we have our present commander." President Davis again considered replacing Bragg with Johnston, but had lost confidence in Johnston after the loss of Vicksburg. Bragg would remain in command.[54]

Two days after the Battle of Chickamauga, Bragg's forces occupied the heights of Missionary Ridge and Lookout Mountain and placed infantry at the Tennessee River crossing, sealing off Chattanooga. Lincoln acted quickly to avert disaster, sending two corps from the Army of the Potomac under Major General Joseph Hooker to help break the Confederate siege. In addition, he ordered Major General William Sherman and the Army of the Tennessee to Chattanooga. In mid-October, Lincoln assigned Major General Ulysses Grant to command the newly created Department of the Mississippi. Grant immediately replaced Rosecrans with General Thomas.[55]

On November 24, Grant attacked. Despite a spirited defense by Bragg's line, the center caved. Union troops swarmed through, shouting "Chicka-mauga." Thus began the Confederate retreat to Atlanta. After the collapse of the Confederate army, Grant boasted: "An army never was whipped so badly as Bragg's was. So far as any opposition the enemy could make, I could have marched to Atlanta or any other place in the Confederacy." Even Bragg admitted, "The disaster . . . is justly disparaging to me as a commander."[56]

On November 28, Bragg asked to be relieved of command. On the 30th, the president acceded to his request. Davis's first thought was to replace Bragg with Robert E. Lee, but he finally placed Joseph Johnston in command on December 2.[57] Three months later, Bragg was appointed as Jefferson Davis's military advisor. The news of Bragg's removal as commander of the Army of Tennessee was met with general approval. Many believed he had survived as long as he had because of his friendship with Davis, but Davis insisted that he needed Bragg because of his organizational ability. The *Richmond Examiner* wrote: "This happy announcement should enliven the confidence and enthusiasm reviving among the people like a bucket of water poured on a newly kindled grate."[58]

There were, however, some individuals within and outside the army who supported Bragg throughout the war. After resigning from command of the Army of Tennessee, he received numerous letters from generals and privates, as well as from government officials, who expressed their sense of loss. "I express to you my sense of the loss which the Army of Tennessee has sustained in your retirement," Joseph Johnston wrote to Bragg. "Let me assure you too, of a fellow soldier's appreciation of your high military ability."[59]

In July 1864, Davis sent Bragg to Atlanta. His mission was to investigate the military situation and to determine what Johnston's plans were for countering Sherman. Six months earlier, Bragg had left Georgia in disgrace after resigning as commander of the Army of Tennessee. Now, his report to Davis would, in a large measure, determine whether Johnston would keep his post and, if he did not, who would take his place.[60] "There is but one remedy—offensive action," Bragg wrote Davis. Johnston was not the man to lead the army offensively. Davis named Lieutenant General John Bell Hood to replace Johnston.[61]

In November, Bragg returned to field command in Wilmington, North Carolina, the last Confederate port remaining open to blockade runners. Bragg's performance here was less than satisfactory, failing to prepare properly for the anticipated enemy's movement. When Fort Fisher was attacked in January 1865, he delayed sending troops until it was too late to help. One month later, Wilmington fell, cutting off the Confederacy's last sea link to the outside.

Bragg spent the last weeks of the war as a subordinate to General Johnston, once again commander of the Army of Tennessee, as Johnston unsuccessfully attempted to block General Sherman's advance through North Carolina. Bragg recognized the South's desperate situation accurately, for he wrote to the president from North Carolina two weeks before Appomattox: "The sad spectacle [is] hourly presented of disorganization, demoralization, and destruction. . . . [Deserters] are scattered over the State of North and South Carolina, Georgia, Alabama, and Mississippi. . . . The state of things cannot last and no one is so blind as not to see the inevitable result. . . . The people are disheartened and do not see what more can happen from the enemy."[62]

When Union forces were at the door of Richmond, Bragg joined Davis as he fled the city, using his influence in convincing the president that the Confederacy was defeated. In May, after the group separated, a Federal cavalry unit caught up with Bragg and his wife as they worked their way home. He was paroled on the spot, despite the fact that his wife scolded her captors for their insensitivity.[63]

When he returned home, Bragg found that his Louisiana plantation had been seized and sold at auction. As a result, he was forced to live with his brothers in Alabama. Having lost all his possessions and being besieged by debtors, he seemed to have been deserted by his former friends. To earn a living, he tried his hand as a civil engineer, insurance salesman, and superintendent of New Orleans waterworks. As during his military career, Bragg had difficulty with personal relationships among those with whom he worked, making it difficult for him to hold a job.[64]

Just before his death, Bragg moved to Galveston, Texas, where he worked as a chief railroad inspector for the state of Texas. On September 27, 1876, while walking with a friend, he fell dead from a massive stroke. He was buried in Mobile, Alabama.

Bragg's personality may have been his greatest shortcoming. This flaw in his character frequently led to and exacerbated quarrels with his subordinates. As a result, he failed to win the loyalty of his chief lieutenants, and those disagreements undermined his army's morale and efficiency. Ulysses Grant, who served with Bragg in Mexico, remembered him as "a remarkably intelligent and well informed man, professionally and otherwise," who had an "irascible temper, and was naturally disputatious."[65]

It is sometimes forgotten that Bragg was the Army of Tennessee's most successful commander. Under his leadership for eighteen months, Bragg organized the army into one of the best fighting forces during the war. Perhaps one of the most complimentary evaluations of his service came from General Joseph E. Johnston in March 1863, in a letter to Senator Louis T. Wigfall: "I think you under rate [Bragg]. . . . He has exhibited great energy and discretion in his operations. . . . Thinking that a great injustice has been done to him by the country—that is to say by the press and congress—I should regret very much to see him removed. Since the battle at Murfreesboro, he has brought up his army to its former strength—indeed to a greater [strength]. This could have been done by nobody else."[66]

10 *Patrick Cleburne*

Stonewall of the West

A contingent of Confederate officers rode to the top of Winstead Hill for a view of the road ahead. Leading the group was General John Bell Hood, a large, sad-eyed general with a full beard. He was strapped in his saddle because he had only one good leg. He wore a prosthesis on the other leg that stuck out to one side. Going on ahead, General Hood rode to the top of the hill and looked out over the open plains toward the town of Franklin. What he saw was encouraging: a Union army, one he had been pursuing all morning, in full retreat. They had eluded him once, but he had no intention of letting it happen again. Returning to the group of officers, he announced, "Gentlemen, we will make them fight." Turning away, he led his staff down the hill to a nearby farmhouse; there he issued orders for an attack.[1]

At the same time, several miles to the south, Confederate Major General Patrick Cleburne was pondering the situation as he rode in front of his division. Only hours before, his corps commander, Major General Frank Cheatham, had informed him that Hood was angry that the enemy had escaped during the night and that he was blaming the debacle on Cheatham's corps, specifically on two of his division commanders: Major General John C. Brown and Cleburne. Hood had accused these two officers of being disobedient and unwilling to fight.[2]

Accusations such as these were hard for Cleburne to take, especially when they were directed at his division. He had built a reputation as being the leader of the most dependable division in the army. Because of its past performance, it was the only division allowed to fly its own battle flag; veterans on both sides recognized that, wherever Cleburne's blue division flag was seen, there would be the thickest fighting. Now, Cleburne was greatly concerned that Hood believed his command was at least partly responsible for the Union escape the night before. He was both hurt and angry: hurt that Hood could think he was not capable of giving his best effort, and angry because he had to hear the accusation from a third party rather than from Hood himself. Now Cleburne was determined to clear the air and demonstrate to his commander how committed he was to the Confederate cause.[3]

Hood knew that Brown and Cleburne were proven combat leaders, and he did not doubt their personal courage, but he did feel that the spirit of his army had been weakened. The army had lost its heart, and he felt he must reinvigorate it. Later that morning, he called a meeting of his corps and division commanders. Although a third of his army had not yet arrived, Hood did not want to wait for them; he wanted to attack at once. It would take only a good hard push, Hood insisted, and Franklin would be theirs. Without stating it, Hood made it clear to everyone in the room that this push would provide an opportunity for the generals who he believed had let him down to redeem themselves. Hood ordered a direct assault, straight up the turnpike and across the open plain. He assigned to the divisions of Brown and Cleburne the most dangerous part of the attack.[4]

Brown and Cleburne listened in silence. Nathan Bedford Forrest, the cavalry commander, protested that there was no need for a frontal assault. The enemy's back was to the river and could easily be outflanked. "If you will give me a strong division of infantry with my cavalry, I will agree to flank the Federals from their works within two hours' time," he said. But Hood objected. Driving the Federals from Franklin was not his objective. He wanted a decisive victory, for he believed that a successful assault would restore the fighting spirit of the army.[5]

Cleburne did not protest and was not emotional. As he left the room, Hood repeated his instructions. Cleburne looked at Hood and said, "I will either take the enemy's works or fall in the attempt." Then Cleburne spurred his horse and led his division on the charge. It would be his last.[6]

Patrick Cleburne went to war in 1861 as a private and died on the bloody field of Franklin in 1864 as a major general. He was known throughout the Army of Tennessee as the "Stonewall of the West." A comrade-in-arms spoke admirably of him: "He knew the very rudiments of fighting and had the genius to use his knowledge. Always ready and watchful, never depressed, beloved by good men, feared by bad men, trusted by all, indomitable in courage, skillfully headlong in attack, coolly strategic in retreat, thorough master of detail, yet with large generalship, obedient to the letter, capable in any crisis, modest as a woman, a resolute disciplinarian, Cleburne was a gem of a warrior."[7] The men of his command cherished the memory of "Old Pat," as they affectionately called him.

Patrick Ronayne Cleburne was born at Bride Park Cottage in Ovens Township, Ireland, on March 16, 1828—the eve of St. Patrick's Day. He was

Major General Patrick Cleburne built a reputation as the leader of the most dependable division in the Confederate army. His division was the
only one allowed to fly its own battle flag and was
always seen in the thickest fighting.

COURTESY OF THE LIBRARY OF CONGRESS

the third child and second son of Joseph Cleburne, a doctor and a Protestant. The Cleburnes were not a wealthy family by the standards of English
gentry, but their standard of living was well above the Irish laboring masses.
In addition to the status he earned from his profession, Dr. Cleburne had
married into a prominent, wealthy family, which procured for him the status of gentry. Patrick's mother was Mary Ann Ronayne. In addition to a substantial dowry, she brought to the marriage her family name. The family felt
it important that their son bear that name, and he was baptized Patrick
Ronayne in honor of his grandfather.[8]

A year after Patrick was born, his mother became pregnant again; this
time her health was so precarious that she decided to have the child at her
parents' manor home. A third boy was delivered successfully, but her recovery
was slow. Through the summer she remained in her bed, dying quietly in the
fall at the age of thirty-seven. Patrick's father was left with four children,

the oldest of whom was only four. The doctor immediately employed a governess to look after the children. She was Isabella Jane Stuart, an eighteen-year-old woman. She became young Patrick's surrogate mother, a relationship that became official a year later when his father, then thirty-nine, married her. Isabella was the only mother Patrick ever knew, and throughout his life he referred to her as "Mama," relying on her advice even into adulthood. The new marriage was fruitful; by the time Patrick was thirteen, he had a half sister and three half brothers.[9]

His father hoped that Patrick would follow in his footsteps. In preparation, the twelve-year-old Patrick attended a Protestant school at Greenfield. He embarked on a program that emphasized English literature, mathematics, and composition. Unfortunately, Patrick never had a chance to complete the program. That summer Dr. Cleburne died at the age of fifty-one.[10]

The death of his father was a personal tragedy for young Patrick as well as a financial one for the family. With the loss of her husband's income, Patrick's stepmother could not expect to pay all of her expenses. As a result, Patrick's older brother, William, returned from college, and Patrick dropped out of Greenfield School. William became the master of the estate, determined to make it a self-sustaining enterprise. Not wanting to add to the expenses of the house, Patrick left home and accepted an apprenticeship with Dr. Thomas Justice, a colleague of his father. As an apprentice, he would earn no money to send home, but at least he could save his family the cost of his own keep. At the age of fifteen, then, he left his home, never to return except for brief visits.[11]

As an apprentice, Patrick worked hard and learned quickly. Before long, Dr. Justice entrusted the mixing of most medicines to Patrick, who now aspired to a career as a pharmacist. After only a year of service with Dr. Justice, Patrick applied for admission to the Apothecaries Hall in Dublin. He was rejected, so he remained with Dr. Justice.[12]

Life was precarious for the Irish in the middle of the nineteenth century, but even the poorest generally had enough food to supply their needs. They relied on the potato for their survival. Then in 1845, some of the harvested potatoes began to show signs of blight. There had been small outbreaks before, but never before had so much of the crop been destroyed. Widespread starvation was the result. Unlike thousands of the poor, seventeen-year-old Pat Cleburne did not go hungry. As a member of the gentry, he did not face the prospect of starvation, but the potato famine did affect him. Dr. Justice found that he could no longer afford the luxury of an apprentice. Financial conditions at home were no better, so Patrick knew he must find another alternative.[13]

With few options, Patrick traveled to Dublin in the hope of qualifying for the program to which he had earlier been denied admission. Although he had practical experience as an apprentice, it was not enough to compensate for his inability to read Latin. As a result, he failed the test and was again denied admission. Ashamed and not wanting to tell his friends or family of his failure, Patrick enlisted in Her Majesty's Forty-first Regiment. He lied about his age, place of birth, and profession, listing it as a "laborer." His family did not learn of his whereabouts for nearly eighteen months.[14]

On July 1, 1849, Patrick was promoted to corporal. Cleburne did not enjoy his corporal's rank very long, because on September 22, he purchased his discharge from the army. Two months later, Patrick, two of his brothers, and his sister sailed for America. Years later, he attributed his success in the Confederate army to the useful lessons he learned in the British army.[15]

Patrick reached New Orleans on Christmas Day. He soon moved upriver to Cincinnati, where he found employment in a drugstore. In April 1850, Cleburne moved to Helena, Arkansas, where he became associated with the drugstore of Dr. C. E. Nash.[16] Patrick liked his new home and was quickly accepted by the people of Helena. Although not handsome, he had a striking appearance. He always carried his six-foot frame erect, and his broad shoulders helped make him an impressive figure. His eyes were quick to sparkle in humor or to grow dark and stern when he was angry. Cleburne became interested in many things: he joined a debating society, became a vestryman in St. John's Episcopal Church, and entered the Masonic order. His first employer and eventual business partner, Dr. Nash, said that Cleburne was "one of the most fastidious young men I ever knew." He never used "a vulgar expression, nor could he bear to hear anyone else use bad language."[17]

Patrick flourished in Helena, studying to become an attorney and eventually passing the bar in 1856. Cleburne's intelligence and drive ensured him of success in the legal profession. During the same period, he became an ally of the feisty, diminutive politician Thomas Hindman, who would have an important influence on young Patrick Cleburne. Hindman was the same age as Cleburne, but that is where the similarity ended. At the age of twenty-three, Hindman had campaigned for Jefferson Davis when he ran for governor. Although Hindman was small in stature, he made up for his lack of size with his dynamic personality and oratorical skill. He was also confrontational, uncompromising, and unrelenting. Never were two men so different; yet that spring Hindman and Cleburne became not only friends but close political associates.[18]

In 1855, a cholera epidemic struck Helena. As many panicked and fled from the epidemic, Cleburne and his friend Hindman prepared meals, carried water, and provided moral support for the townspeople. Their courage and commitment were noted and appreciated by the survivors and helped to improve their growing reputation as community leaders. Cleburne's Christian concern for others would continue throughout his life.[19]

Hindman's rough political style often got him into trouble. Opponents were occasionally inclined to take the debate into the street. On May 24, 1856, Hindman asked Cleburne to arm himself and accompany him to a dinner at Fadley's Hotel, because he had heard that a man named Dorsey Rice was out to get him. Cleburne took a pair of pistols and went with Hindman. On their way to the hotel, they met Rice and two others on the street. Rice demanded an apology from Hindman. When Hindman refused, Rice drew a gun and fired, the bullet creasing Hindman's right arm and striking him in the chest. Hindman was able to fire several shots before falling to the ground. At the same time, one of Rice's associates fired at Cleburne, hitting him in the chest. Cleburne returned the fire, wounding one of Rice's friends. When the smoke cleared, all three lay in the street badly wounded. Hindman soon recovered, but the wound to Cleburne was more serious.[20]

The pistol ball had struck Cleburne near his spine and passed through his lung. Friends carried him into a room above a dry goods store and laid him on a bed. Cleburne lingered near death for ten days with Dr. Nash at his side. The bullet was eventually removed, and Cleburne did survive, but his lungs were never the same. He caught colds on the smallest provocation; even an hour's debate would sometimes fill his mouth with blood. Cleburne and Hindman were exonerated by a grand jury for their part in the gunfight.[21]

Despite his action in the gunfight, Cleburne was modest and shy; friends were aware of his awkwardness in society. Dr. Nash thought him "a very bashful young man," while one of his law partners recalled Cleburne's lack of grace and embarrassment in the presence of most people, except for his close friends. His quiet demeanor, however, did not prevent him from becoming a rising star among the Democrats of the region. Although he himself owned no slaves, he sympathized with the Southern position on slavery and states' rights.[22]

Several months before the 1860 presidential election, Patrick Cleburne helped organize a militia company in Helena. It was named in honor of Archibald Yell, a former governor of Arkansas who had been killed in the Battle of Buena Vista during the Mexican War. The "Yell Rifles" was one of many companies formed across the South during the summer of 1860. Enlisting as a private, Cleburne was soon elected captain of the Yell Rifles.[23]

After the surrender of Fort Sumter, Arkansas cast its lot with the Confederacy. In May 1861, the Yell Rifles joined the rebellion against the Union. When the company was combined with others to become the Fifteenth Arkansas Regiment, Cleburne was elected colonel. In July, the Fifteenth Arkansas joined the command of General William Hardee.[24]

As a colonel, Cleburne exhibited all the characteristics that would make him an outstanding general of the Confederacy's Western armies. Diligently training his men, he imparted to them not only knowledge but discipline and confidence as well. Cleburne took great interest in everything connected with military tactics and spent hours each day training his men. His relentless efforts turned his unit into one of the best-drilled regiments in the army.[25]

As a regimental commander, Cleburne was a strict disciplinarian, but he believed that he was not only responsible for his troops but responsible to them. He asked a great deal of his men and did not hesitate to order them to risk their lives on the battlefield, but he was not willing to risk his men to indulge a general he thought was incompetent. Cleburne would display greater loyalty to his men than he would to his superiors.[26]

General Hardee, who had written the standard text on infantry tactics in the old army, quickly recognized Cleburne's leadership, character, and military ability. He watched with approval Cleburne's devotion to detail, his painstaking emphasis on drill, and his interest in mastering the art of tactics. Hardee identified him early for promotion, and the two quickly became close friends.[27]

An incident occurred during the early days of the war that clouded Cleburne's spirit until the day he died. While in Greenville, Missouri, he was quartered in a building with a local citizen who suffered from somnambulism. One night the sleepwalker noisily entered Cleburne's room. Thinking the intruder was an enemy raider attempting to free some nearby prisoners, Cleburne grabbed his pistol and shot, mortally wounding the innocent sleepwalker. Cleburne was absolved of guilt, but he brooded for the rest of his life over the unfortunate killing.[28]

Early in the war, Hardee was ordered to Kentucky. Shortly afterward, Cleburne was sent on a scouting mission. To Cleburne's dismay, some stragglers drifted to the rear pretending they were ill and stole poultry and other items from civilians along the road. When Cleburne learned what had happened, he made the men return the stolen articles. What he could not recover, he paid for out of his own pocket. Throughout the war, he would never lose his sense of justice.[29]

On March 4, 1862, General Hardee recommended Cleburne for promotion to brigadier general. General Albert Sidney Johnston had withdrawn from Kentucky following the fall of Forts Henry and Donelson and was concentrating his forces at Corinth, Mississippi. The true test of the Irishman's ability to command was yet to come—at a place called Shiloh. Cleburne was soon to get his baptism by fire, as would the entire Confederate Army of the Mississippi, later known as the Army of Tennessee.[30]

On the afternoon of April 3, Generals A. S. Johnston and P. G. T. Beauregard moved their army of 40,000 men on a twenty-two-mile march from Corinth to Shiloh. On the way, Cleburne encountered enemy cavalry, which he repulsed, capturing prisoners. When his brigade arrived at Shiloh, it was posted at the extreme left of the Confederate line assigned, to Hardee's corps. At daylight on April 6, Cleburne's brigade moved against Sherman's division. Sherman's troops repelled Cleburne's first assault, but the resolute Irishman rallied his men and led them forward again. This time the fury of his attack pushed the Union troops past their camp to the shelter of the bluffs at Pittsburg Landing.[31]

During the first day of the Battle of Shiloh, the army suffered a devastating loss when General Albert Sidney Johnston was mortally wounded; P. G. T. Beauregard took temporary command. During the night, Grant was reinforced by General Buell's Army of the Ohio, and at daybreak the Federal army charged the disorganized Confederate line.

The second day of the battle brought Cleburne into renewed contact with Grant's army. Bragg ordered Cleburne to lead his badly decimated brigade against a superior Union force. Cleburne replied that he had no support and his men would be destroyed. Bragg persisted, and the enraged Cleburne led his men into a bloody, useless action. After advancing a mile, he found his brigade without support, outflanked on his left, and between two artillery batteries engaged in a duel. When the firing stopped, Union troops swept forward and struck Cleburne's thin line. The fury of the attack shattered Cleburne's regiment. He managed to stop the rout by rallying the Fifteenth Arkansas and leading them in a counterattack. After Beauregard ordered a general withdrawal, Cleburne remained behind until he had rallied his stragglers, salvaged materials, and destroyed supplies that could not be removed.[32] The bad feelings that were generated between Bragg and Cleburne during this confrontation, however, would continue after the battle.[33]

By the day's end, Cleburne's brigade had been reduced from 2,700 to about 800 men. It was the greatest loss suffered by any brigade during the battle.[34] Hardee praised Cleburne for his valor and "conspicuous" gallantry. Reflecting on the senseless frontal attacks on the Union line, Cleburne remarked that the Battle of Shiloh was "gallantly won and as stupidly lost."[35]

The amount of blood shed by Cleburne's men at Shiloh had a profound effect upon him. He had learned that on the battlefield intelligence and common sense were more important attributes than textbook concepts based on Napoleonic frontal assaults. Taking advantage of what he had learned at Shiloh, Cleburne made tactical refinements in his battle plans and carefully trained his line officers, realizing that excellence starts at the top and works its way down. He also organized a company of sharpshooters to accompany his brigade. These men, armed with Whitworth and Kerr rifles, would become a source of pride for him. Their deadly fire often forced the enemy to change its battle plans.[36]

Cleburne's fierce performance at Shiloh demonstrated the characteristics of his leadership in the battles to follow. The men who served under him had great respect for him. Their diary entries and letters home described their affection for him, which almost reached the point of hero worship.

At the Battle of Richmond, Kentucky, during the Confederate Kentucky campaign in the fall of 1862, Cleburne suffered a painful wound. A bullet entered his left cheek and shattered his teeth on that side, rendering him temporarily unable to speak. He turned his command over to Colonel

Preston Smith, who successfully carried out Cleburne's battle plan. In his official report, Kirby Smith praised his brigade commander: "General Cleburne was badly wounded in the face, and then at a critical moment I was deprived of the services of one of the most zealous and intelligent officers in my army." The Confederate Congress passed a vote acknowledging Cleburne's service "for gallant and meritorious service" in the battle at Richmond.[37]

By October, Cleburne was well enough to join his command at Perryville. Here, he led his brigade in a successful attack against the Federal left. Cleburne's horse was killed by a cannonball, which also struck him in the leg. Despite his painful wound, he got another mount and continued the attack.[38]

In December, after Jefferson Davis visited with the Army of Tennessee, he appointed Cleburne a major general at the insistence of Generals Hardee, Buckner, and Bragg.[39] With his promotion came the command of a division under Major General Kirby Smith. Cleburne was assigned to the division recently commanded by Simon Buckner, who was transferred to another theater of the war. Two weeks after his promotion, Cleburne's division was ordered to Murfreesboro where Bragg's Army of Tennessee was being concentrated to meet General Rosecrans's southward thrust from Nashville. Cleburne's division was assigned the extreme left of Bragg's front. Surprising the Federals early in the morning while they were preparing breakfast, Cleburne's troops assailed them, allowing them no time to regroup. His men captured 1,000 prisoners and numerous supplies and weapons. In the mid-afternoon, however, Cleburne's drive was stalled when the Union troops were heavily reinforced and supported by artillery.[40]

The next day, Cleburne wanted to renew the fight, but Bragg decided to retreat, inviting criticism and demands from his subordinates for his removal. During the retreat, the army was forced to march all night and most of the next day. Morale was low, and many in the ranks saw this retreat as similar to their withdrawal from Kentucky two months earlier. Once again, they had won a victory at great cost, only to have their efforts wasted by Bragg's decision to retreat. These sentiments were an indication of the army's lack of confidence in its commander. The feelings about Bragg were strong; some felt that he worked hard but that the job was simply beyond him. Most of his generals were greatly opposed to his remaining in command. General Frank Cheatham told Governor Isham Harris that he would never serve under Bragg again.[41]

Bragg attempted to defend his position and asked some of his officers, including Cleburne, for their candid opinions about his service. Cleburne responded in writing: "I have consulted with all my brigade commanders . . . and they unite with me in personal regard for yourself, in high appreciation of your patriotism and gallantry, and in a conviction for your great capacity for organization, but at the same time they see, with regret, and it has also met my observation, that you do not possess the confidence of the army in other respects in the degree necessary to insure success."[42] Politically, this letter was the beginning of the end for Cleburne's career; Bragg had a long memory and never forgot those who failed to support him.

During the next nine months, the Army of Tennessee saw no action, leaving Cleburne time to train his men. By mid-1863, he and his command had achieved such fame and recognition that they were allowed to keep their distinctive blue battle flag with the white full moon in the center; all other units of the Army of Tennessee were required to fly the red battle flag with the St. Andrew's cross.[43]

By the summer of 1863, things were not going well for the Confederacy. On July 4, the Confederates surrendered at Vicksburg; in Pennsylvania, Lee was in retreat from Gettysburg; and in Tennessee, Bragg was giving up the state without a struggle. Following the fall of Vicksburg, General Hardee was replaced by Lieutenant General Daniel Harvey Hill. Hill now commanded the corps that contained Cleburne's division. Bragg was encamped around Chattanooga, the vestige of Tennessee still under Confederate control, waiting for an attack from Rosecrans.

Rosecrans launched a move to get behind Bragg and trap him in Chattanooga. To prevent this, Bragg evacuated Chattanooga and concentrated. The two armies finally met at Chickamauga on September 19. Cleburne's leadership during the terrible fighting at Chickamauga was described as the most spirited of his career. "I never saw Cleburne before or afterward so demonstrative," wrote one of his staff officers. He rode from brigade to brigade, encouraging and inspiring his men.[44]

On the second day of the battle, against his better judgment, Cleburne was ordered to attack a firmly dug-in enemy. His division was eventually repulsed, but they hit the line so hard that Union reinforcements had to be moved to prevent the line from breaking. The resulting confusion created a gap that Lieutenant General Longstreet's men were able to penetrate. After splintering the Federal line, Longstreet wheeled toward the enemy's flank, enabling Cleburne and Breckinridge to renew their frontal attack. Moving his artillery forward, Cleburne fired rounds of double canister, shattering the breastworks and enabling his troops to storm the Union's first line of defense. Unsupported, the Federals retreated; Rosecrans ordered a withdrawal, which quickly turned into a rout.[45]

With victory within his grasp, Bragg again inexplicably failed to deliver the knockout blow to Rosecrans's demoralized army. Bragg's officers, outraged and discouraged by his incompetence, organized a campaign to have him removed from the command of the Army of Tennessee. Cleburne supported this movement; by now, he had lost all confidence in Bragg. President Davis visited the army to hear their complaints, but he decided to give Bragg one more chance. The ringleaders of the move to replace Bragg—Longstreet, Polk, and D. H. Hill—were transferred, and Hardee was returned to his command. Cleburne's position was not affected, but he never received another promotion.[46]

At Chickamauga, Cleburne played a major role in the Confederate victory, receiving high praise from corps commander D. H. Hill: "I have never seen troops behave more gallantly than did this noble division."[47]

Cleburne's passion for battle was never more evident than during the Chattanooga campaign in November 1863. Cleburne's division, now numbering 4,000, was assigned the defense of the northern end of Missionary Ridge against Sherman's 30,000 available troops. In the battle of Missionary Ridge, Cleburne's men beat back repeated Union attacks. He personally led several successful counterattacks down the side of the ridge, capturing hundreds of prisoners.[48]

Late in the afternoon, Union General George Thomas launched a massive attack against Bragg's center, which, together with the left wing, gave way. As the Confederates fled down the side of the ridge, Cleburne moved his front to slow the Union thrust and cover Bragg's withdrawal. To prevent the dissolution of his army, Bragg issued orders for a retreat into Georgia. There he hoped to regroup in relative peace. First, however, he had to slow the Union pursuit long enough for his vulnerable wagon trains and artillery to make their escape.

Bragg was in trouble: his army was in disarray, and his wagon trains and artillery were in danger of being captured. Bragg was left with only Cleburne's 4,000 men to hold off Hooker's 16,000.[49] Given the odds, Bragg was understandably concerned. Privately he told his staff that he considered his trains and artillery as good as lost; however, he felt it imperative to try to save them, even if it meant sacrificing Cleburne's division. At midnight, Cleburne received a message from Bragg informing him to hold the enemy in check at Ringgold Gap until the trains, artillery, and the rest of the army could make their escape. At first, Cleburne balked, considering what that order would mean to his division. Reconsidering, he told Bragg's staff officer that he was not in the habit of disobeying orders but that this action might spell the end of his division; therefore, he wanted the orders in writing.[50] When the orders came, they were short: "Tell General Cleburne to hold his position at all hazards, and to keep the enemy until the transportation of the army is secure, the salvation of which depends upon him."[51]

Cleburne met the enemy at Ringgold Gap, engaging Hooker's forces long enough to save the Confederate supply train and artillery and to secure Bragg's line of retreat. As a result of Cleburne's efforts and his division's courageous action, he received a flood of congratulations. Bragg specifically commended him in his report to Davis; Congress passed a resolution of thanks; even the Federals offered a tribute to his efforts. One Union commander explained their failure at Ringgold Gap by reporting that, after all, Cleburne's division "was reputed as the best in Bragg's army."[52]

During the battle, Cleburne again exhibited his concern for the welfare of his men. During a charge, a stand of colors was left lying on the ground within fifty yards of the Confederate line. Captain McGehee of the Second Arkansas volunteered to take a squad and recover it, but Cleburne refused to let them risk their lives for the sake of recovering the flag.[53]

Amid the gloom of the disasters of the Army of Tennessee, Patrick Cleburne's star shone brighter than ever. He repeatedly demonstrated himself to be the outstanding infantry general in the army. His steadfast performance was a bright spot for the Confederacy, prompting Jefferson Davis to christen him the "Stonewall of the West." Cleburne was thus elevated to a status equal to that of the martyred Stonewall Jackson, who had fallen at Chancellorsville in May.[54] "The troops are as much devoted to General Cleburne as Stonewall Jackson's men were to him," Captain Buck, Cleburne's adjutant, later wrote. Like Jackson, Cleburne was a strict disciplinarian who would not tolerate any breach of discipline, but unlike Jackson, he got closer to his men. Despite his rigid discipline, Cleburne insisted that the punishment given violators be humane and that it serve a purpose, such as cleaning weapons or walking extra guard duty. He would not allow cruel or corporal punishment, which he believed degraded a soldier and destroyed his self-confidence. This kind of firm and friendly leadership was an inspiration to his men.[55]

Although Cleburne's division had displayed valor and earned recognition, the Army of Tennessee had suffered an appalling defeat. On November 27, Bragg sent Davis his formal resignation. Davis accepted it and placed Hardee in temporary command of the army. Despite his resignation, Bragg found it difficult to take responsibility for the army's defeat, blaming it on his enemies within the army itself. Cleburne was pleased with the change in command, and in late December, General Joseph E. Johnston assumed command of the Army of Tennessee.[56]

In January 1864, the outlook for the Southern cause was bleak. Cleburne believed that, unless things changed, there was little hope of overcoming the North with its abundant resources. The available supply of white males in the South was nearly exhausted. The only practical solution, Cleburne believed, was to enlist male slaves; the Yankees were using black troops, adding to their numerical superiority—some twenty black regiments had been organized in the Western theater alone.[57]

Cleburne worked out a proposal to enlist blacks in the Confederate army, terming it "a concession to common sense." The effects of emancipation, Cleburne argued, could only be beneficial for the South. Freeing slaves and arming them would provide the Confederate armies with an untouched source of manpower, sufficient to continue a long war. Cleburne warned that the slaves could not be expected to fight unless they were guaranteed their freedom. Furthermore, emancipation would deprive the North of a moral and psychological weapon that had motivated Northerners as well as foreigners. "It may be imperfect," he said, "but in all probability it would give us our independence."[58]

Before Cleburne presented his proposal, he invited Captain Buck, his adjutant, to read it and give his comments. Buck was skeptical, remarking that those holding slaves might not be willing to give them up. The proposal was certain to be controversial and would probably jeopardize his possible future promotion to corps commander. Cleburne's response showed his character: a crisis existed in the South, he said, and it was his duty to do whatever he could to avert it, irrespective of any result to himself.[59]

Cleburne requested a meeting with General Johnston and his staff to present his proposal. He acted as the spokesman for the fourteen officers who had signed their names to the document. "The subject is grave," he declared, "and our views so new, we feel it a duty both to you and the cause that before going further we should submit them for your judgment and receive your suggestions in regard to them."[60]

The responses to Cleburne's proposal were mixed, viewed with alarm and indignation by most and favorably considered only by a few. If Cleburne was disappointed by the lack of enthusiastic support for his proposal, he soon was even more discouraged. Major General William Walker said angrily that such a plan would mire the Southern cause in "ruin and disgrace." General Bate declared that Cleburne's proposal was "hideous and objectionable," and he added it was nothing less than "the serpent of Abolitionism." He predicted that the army would revolt at the suggestion of such a proposition. General Anderson said the proposal was "revolting to Southern sentiment, Southern pride, and Southern honor." He believed that if black troops were enlisted, white troops would desert in disgust. Walker was the most offended; "the proposal was nothing less than treason," he stated.[61] Cleburne did not argue his case any further.

General Johnston declined to forward Cleburne's paper to Jefferson Davis on the grounds that it was a political and not a military matter. Although disappointed at missing a chance to get his proposal to the president, Cleburne was too good a soldier to think of going over Johnston's head. Eventually the proposal did reach Davis's ear, but he, too, rejected it. The paper was finally returned signed by Davis: "While recognizing the patriotic motives of the distinguished author, I deem it inexpedient at this time to give publicity to this paper and ask that it be suppressed."

Within eight months of Cleburne's presentation, three vacancies for lieutenant general occurred in the Army of Tennessee, yet Cleburne was not promoted.[62] In May 1864, when the Army of Tennessee needed a general to succeed Major General John Breckinridge who commanded the Second Corps, Davis overlooked Cleburne. Two months later, Davis passed over Cleburne for corps command after Lieutenant General Leonidas Polk was killed at Pine Mountain, appointing instead Major General A. P. Stewart. The most disappointing of the three, however, occurred when Hardee left the army and Hood assigned the hard-drinking Cheatham to take command of his corps. In eight months, three corps commands had become available, and the best general in the army at that rank had been ignored. Although disappointed, Cleburne continued to do his job well, proving that he was deserving of corps command. He remained the idol of his men.[63]

A few months after Cleburne's proposal, Governor Harry Allen of Louisiana wrote to Davis saying that it was time "to put into the army every able-bodied Negro man as a soldier. . . . I would free all able to bear arms and put them into the field at once." That November, Davis himself proposed that the government purchase 20,000 slaves for use in the army, although his proposal did not include arming them. Later even Robert E. Lee proposed using slaves in the army.[64] Barely a year after Cleburne's proposal was suppressed, the Confederate Congress passed a law on March 13, 1865, that authorized the enrollment of slaves into the Confederate army. By this time, however, it was too late.[65]

Just a few days after meeting with General Johnston to make his proposal, Pat Cleburne found himself involved in a love affair. When his good friend General Hardee decided to get married, he asked Cleburne to be his best man. Cleburne readily accepted, and the wedding took place on January 13, 1864, in Marengo County, Alabama. The maid of honor was Sue Tarleton of Mobile, a cotton factor's daughter, described as "a young maiden of rare accomplishments and intelligence." Cleburne fell in love with her at first sight, and before the night was over he had asked permission to call on her. She consented.[66]

The dashing young general and the cultured twenty-four-year-old Southern belle hit it off at once. After calling on Miss Tarleton in Mobile, Cleburne asked her to marry him. She hesitated at first, as she was somewhat overwhelmed by the intense young general. Sue did not give him an immediate answer, but she did give him permission to write to her and promised to write back.[67]

Cleburne returned to the army at Tunnel Hill, Georgia, and his staff immediately noticed a difference in their general's behavior. Captain Buck wrote to his sister that "General Cleburne says he had a wonderful time. Rumor says he lost his heart with a young lady in Mobile. He has been in a heavenly mood and talks about another leave already."[68] Cleburne's delight at the prospects of marriage to Sue Tarleton more than balanced his disappointment at the failure of his proposal to arm the South's black population.

Upon his return to his division, Cleburne continued his courtship via correspondence. Sue finally consented to marry him. Whether the two ever met again is not certain, although Cleburne may have visited Mobile before fighting broke out again, or Miss Tarleton may have visited him at his camp.[69]

With the passing of winter, the Army of Tennessee braced itself for General William Tecumseh Sherman's long-awaited campaign against Atlanta.

By the time the two armies were ready to face each other, Sherman had a numerical superiority over Johnston of 110,000 to 61,000. During the Atlanta campaign, Cleburne was frequently seen on his horse inspiring his men to fight—at New Hope Church late in May and later in June at Kennesaw Mountain. At Bald Hill on July 21, his division engaged in fighting that he termed "the bitterest of my life." Again on July 22, during the Battle of Atlanta, Cleburne's men fought valiantly. During the assault, Cleburne led the charge, sword drawn and shouting, "Follow me, boys!" Despite the unsuccessful efforts of the Confederates to halt Sherman, Cleburne's division distinguished itself. Even though it had suffered heavy losses, the division captured more than 1,600 Union prisoners.[70]

On July 17, 1864, Lieutenant General John Bell Hood replaced General Johnston as commander of the Army of Tennessee. Johnston's heavily outnumbered army had battled Sherman for seventy-four days, limiting him to an advance of barely a hundred miles. Although the Army of Tennessee was retreating, it had not been beaten. Joseph Johnston's removal was received with anger and sadness by the army. Hood's accession to command was the beginning of the end for the Army of Tennessee. Hardee, embittered by Hood's appointment, soon requested, and received, a transfer. Hood immediately disregarded Johnston's policy of defense and set out to do what Richmond wanted—to take the offensive against a vastly superior enemy.[71]

Following the loss of Atlanta, Hood met with Davis to discuss plans for a last offensive into Tennessee. As Sherman marched farther into the interior of Georgia, Cleburne moved northward into Tennessee in a desperate campaign to disrupt Sherman's lines of communication and crush the Union's stronghold near Nashville. By late November, Hood had moved his army into position to attack 22,000 Federal troops under Major General John Schofield. Schofield hoped to delay Hood's offensive long enough for Major General George Thomas to gather his army at Nashville. Hood met Schofield along the banks of the Duck River at Columbia, Tennessee. After a brilliantly successful flanking movement, Hood placed his army between the Federals and Nashville, hoping to destroy them before they could reach Franklin.[72]

Major General Frank Cheatham, Cleburne's corps commander, misunderstood Hood's instructions. Instead of cutting off the critical Columbia-to-Franklin Road, which Cleburne was in the process of doing, Cheatham halted his advance and ordered him to attack northward toward the village of Spring Hill. The attack failed due to darkness and miscommunication. During the night, Schofield's troops were able to slip by the Confederates and head for Franklin. When Hood learned of Schofield's escape, he severely criticized his generals. He seemed most upset about what he believed to be the cowardice of his men. His anger that day was focused on Cheatham and his subordinate commanders, Cleburne and Major General John

Brown.[73] Hood lashed out viciously at his subordinates, placing the blame everywhere but where it belonged—on a misunderstanding of orders.

Hood was determined to punish Cheatham, Cleburne, and Brown for what he perceived as their poor performance. He would teach them a lesson in the aggressive style of fighting that he demanded. Hood issued orders for a giant frontal attack on the entrenched Union position. Cleburne's and Brown's divisions would lead the assault. Hood and his generals gathered on Winstead Hill to survey the situation. All except Hood thought a frontal attack would be foolish, but Hood announced: "We will make the fight." "I do not like the looks of this fight," objected General Cheatham. "The enemy has an excellent position and is well fortified." But Hood, nevertheless, insisted on fighting there.[74]

When Cleburne arrived, he examined the Union fortifications from the hill and said, "They are very formidable." General Hood later wrote in his book, *Advance and Retreat*, that in their meeting just before the assault, Cleburne spoke with "an enthusiasm, which he had never before betrayed in our intercourse." "General, I am ready," he purported Cleburne to say, "and have more hope in the final success of our cause than I have had at any time since the first gun was fired." "God grant it!" Hood says he replied.[75]

Just a few days earlier, Cleburne may have had a premonition of his impending death. As he rode past the little Episcopal Church of St. John at Ashwood on the march to Spring Hill, he stopped to enjoy the peaceful churchyard. Turning to one of his staff officers, he said, "It is almost worth dying for, to be buried in such a beautiful spot."[76]

At the Battle of Franklin, after routing an enemy outpost, Cleburne rode toward the main defense only to have his horse shot from under him. He mounted a second horse, which met the same fate. Cleburne dismounted, drew his sword, and led the charge on foot until an enemy bullet felled him.[77] An ounce of lead, little more than half an inch in diameter, ripped through his chest just below his heart. He collapsed to the ground, still grasping his battle sword. As blood saturated his shirt and uniform, he took his last breath. The man who many believed to be the South's most brilliant major general had died leading a suicidal attack.[78]

For nearly five hours, the battle raged while repeated Confederate attempts to dislodge the defenders failed. Dead and wounded rebels covered the ground before the Federal works. Blood purportedly ran in streams. "I never saw men put in such a hellish position," wrote a Union veteran. Colonel Virgil Murray of the Seventeenth Alabama later wrote, "To remain in this . . . dangerous position was worse than death." It was "the most furious and desperate battle of the war in the West," General Stewart later wrote. When Schofield's troops retreated to Nashville during the night, Hood declared the Battle of Franklin a Confederate victory. Hood then followed the Federal army to Nashville, where his army was virtually destroyed in December.[79]

Cleburne's division bivouacked that night with the knowledge that "Old Pat" was missing. Many prayers were offered that he was captured or wounded—no one wanted to believe the worse. But the next morning they found his body, just fifty yards from the enemy's line. "He lay flat upon his back, as if asleep, his military cap partly over his eyes. He had on a new gray uniform . . . a white linen shirt . . . stained with blood. . . . This was the only sign of a wound. He had only socks on his feet, his boots having been stolen," reported one of the men who found Cleburne.[80]

Back in Mobile, Sue Tarleton waited anxiously for word from her fiancé. Union raiding parties had cut the telegraph lines into the city. Six days after the Battle of Franklin, Sue heard a passing newsboy shout: "Big battle near Franklin, Tennessee! General Cleburne killed! Read all about it." She fainted dead away.[81] Sue was prostrate with grief. When she gathered the strength to appear in public, she wore black and did so for a full year. Eventually she did marry in 1867. She died less than a year later.[82]

They buried Cleburne first in Rose Hill Cemetery at Columbia, Tennessee. Later he was offered a plot at St. John's Episcopal Church at Ashwood, the quiet churchyard he had admired. In 1869, Cleburne's remains were moved to Helena, Arkansas, the place where he had started his military career.[83]

When President Davis learned of Cleburne's death, he wrote: "Around Cleburne thickly lay the gallant men, who in his desperate assault followed him with implicate confidence that in another army was given Stonewall Jackson, and in the one case, as in the other, a vacancy was created which could never be filled."[84]

Many appropriate epitaphs were written about Cleburne. To Robert E. Lee he was "a meteor shining from a clouded sky." To a subordinate officer, he was "the perfect type of a perfect soldier." But the best epitaph for Patrick Ronayne Cleburne came from his old friend General William J. Hardee: "History will take up his fame, and hand it down to time for exampling, . . . a courage without stain, a manhood without blemish, an integrity that knew no compromise, and a patriotism that withheld no sacrifice, and [was] honored of mankind."[85]

11 *Nathan Bedford Forrest*

"That Devil Forrest"

Early in the spring of 1864, Major General Nathan Bedford Forrest led his troops from northern Mississippi into Tennessee. Two years of war and occupation had left the state barren. "The whole of West Tennessee," Forrest observed, "is overrun by bands and squads of robbers, horse thieves, and deserters, whose depredation and unlawful appropriations of private property are rapidly and effectually depleting the country."[1]

The land Forrest returned to was depleted and brown, its farmhouses and barns burned to the ground. He learned that a renegade regiment of Federal cavalry had been plundering southwestern Tennessee, destroying property and demanding tribute from residents to spare their town. Even worse, several of his subordinates, who had returned to Tennessee to recruit, had been murdered by these renegades. Residents also warned Forrest of another "nest of outlaws" that was currently garrisoned in an abandoned Confederate fortification, Fort Pillow, forty miles north of Memphis.[2]

In April, Forrest turned his attention to Fort Pillow. The fort, named after the Confederate General Gideon Pillow, had been built in 1861 on the eastern bank of the Mississippi River. The Confederates were forced to abandon Fort Pillow after the fall of Corinth, Mississippi, in May 1862. On the morning of April 12, the garrison was occupied by about 600 men: half of these men were escaped slaves; the other half were the troops who had allegedly been terrorizing Confederate sympathizers in the region.[3] Forrest's troops surrounded the fort and began firing at the Federals huddling behind the breastworks. Under a flag of truce, Forrest issued his usual demand to surrender: "The conduct of the officers and men garrisoning Fort Pillow has been such as to entitle them to be treated as prisoners of war. I demand the unconditional surrender of this garrison, promising you that you shall be treated as prisoners of war. . . . Should my demand be refused, I cannot be responsible for the fate of your command."[4]

Major W. F. Bradford replied: "General: I will not surrender." A Confederate colonel later recalled that the Federals "openly defied us from the breastworks to take the fort." Forrest wasted no time attacking; the outcome was never in doubt. Within a short time, the fort was breached, and hand-to-hand combat quickly turned in favor of the Confederates. Once they gained control, the killing did not stop. To the Confederate soldiers, the sight of former slaves defending the fort, the reports of atrocities committed against families, and the excitement of battle worked together to inspire a deadly exhibition of vengeance.[5]

Before Forrest could enter the fort to restore order, his men shot and bayoneted many of the helpless Union soldiers. One Confederate sergeant recalled, "The poor deluded Negroes would run up to our men, fall upon their knees, and with uplifted hands scream for mercy, but were ordered to their feet and then shot down. The white men faced little better." The slaughter at Fort Pillow, and Forrest's failure to control the actions of his troops, constitutes the blackest mark on his service record.[6]

In a postwar interview, Forrest defended his action: "When we got into the fort, the white flag was shown at once. The Negroes ran out down to the river; and although the [white] flag was flying, they kept on turning back and shooting at my men, who consequently continued to fire into the crowd on the brink of the river. . . . But there was no deliberate intention nor effort to massacre the garrison."[7]

Nathan Bedford Forrest was a controversial Civil War officer and an unschooled yet brilliant cavalryman in America's most celebrated war. In the course of rising from private to lieutenant general in the Confederate army, he revolutionized the way armies fought. He was a superb tactician, a ferocious fighter, and a courageous soldier. Because he was not trained in military science, he relied solely on intuition. His tactics made him the most feared man in the Confederate army. He was known as the "Wizard of the Saddle" and was reputed to have killed more than thirty Union soldiers in hand-to-hand combat and to have had twenty-nine horses shot out from under him. He was wounded on four separate occasions.[8]

Forrest was a hero to Southerners and a symbol of what the Confederacy was willing to do to win. He consistently outmaneuvered the enemy and exploited every opportunity to confuse and deceive it. He struck fast and hard, and it is said that in a battle "he was always first with the most." He often defeated forces twice the size of his own command, using tactical designs that combined shrewd simplicity with savage aggressiveness. General William T. Sherman labeled him "that devil Forrest." While Sherman defined war as hell, Forrest was more specific, saying, "War means fighting, and fighting means killing."[9]

Forrest was a large man with a colorful personality and a violent temper,

This photo of Nathan Bedford Forrest was taken just prior to the Civil War, when he was forty years old. By this time he had amassed a considerable fortune through trading slaves.

UNITED STATES MILITARY HISTORY INSTITUTE

with which he struggled for most of his life. He thought nothing of killing other men and was proud of it. He knifed to death a fellow Confederate who made the mistake of assaulting him. On another occasion, a courier interrupted him as he paced about, trying to solve a difficult military problem. Annoyed by the interruption, he knocked the man unconscious with a single blow and resumed his pacing.[10]

Although he had only six months of schooling, Forrest displayed an instinctive grasp of mathematics. His business contacts and his constant reading of newspapers gave him an excellent command of words and phrases. During the war, after dictating a dispatch, he would read it over for corrections. If he detected a grammatical error or an awkwardly constructed phrase, he would say, "That won't do it; it hasn't the right pitch."

He would then change the wording so it would express what he wanted to say. He felt deficient in education and regretted not having spent more time in school. He once remarked: "No one knows the embarrassment I labor under when thrown in the company of educated persons."[11]

Forrest never drank or smoked, but he was far from perfect. The only personal vices he was ashamed of were his fondness for gambling and his use of profanity. He showed respect for women and clergymen and loved children. He enjoyed horse racing and had a pointed sense of humor. At a dinner during the war, when someone inquired why his hair had turned gray while his beard remained dark, he replied it was probably because he tended to work his brains more than his jaws.[12]

Stories of Forrest's episodes have been told and retold until they have taken on mythological qualities. One such story is that of the horseman who came to the aid of two women and their black driver who were stranded at a creek ford. The driver was struggling to free the carriage from a mud hole, while two young men sat on horseback beside the stream, leaving the slave to free the vehicle's wheels alone. It was the Sabbath, and the men did not want to soil their Sunday best. When the third horseman arrived, he did not hesitate to get his clothing wet. After hitching his horse to a fence, he waded out to the carriage and carried the women to dry ground. He set his shoulder to the carriage wheel and helped the driver free the vehicle. Then he turned to the onlookers and castigated them for their inaction, threatening them with physical harm if they did not leave at once.[13]

The women the horseman had helped were the widow Elizabeth Montgomery and her eighteen-year-old daughter, Mary Ann. The young man introduced himself as Bedford Forrest, a twenty-four-year-old mercantile dealer. He asked for permission to call on Mary Ann at home. Mary Ann was greatly impressed by young Forrest's direct manner; although she had never seen him before, she had heard of him. He had recently received some notoriety when he was involved in a shootout in which he was wounded and his opponents were left in a "doubtful state." Forrest did not waste time. A few days after their meeting, he called on the Montgomerys. Mary Ann invited him inside, and Forrest proceeded to propose marriage. She hesitated—after all, it was only the second time in her life she had spoken to him. He had a business and could support her comfortably, he said. Determined to marry her, he said he would bring a marriage license on his next visit. On the third visit, she accepted his proposal, and in September they were married. This whirlwind courtship fit the pattern of Forrest's behavior throughout the Civil War.[14]

Nathan Bedford Forrest was born on July 13, 1821, in a backwoods cabin in Tennessee. Nathan was his paternal grandfather's name; Bedford was the county in which he was born. The Forrests had moved to the Western frontier from Virginia in the 1730s. His ancestors had survived by working hard on the land and were barely able to fend off poverty.[15] His father, William, eked out a tenuous living in the backwoods of southern Tennessee. During the course of their marriage, William's wife, Mariam, gave birth to eleven children. Bedford was the oldest. None of the three daughters lived to adulthood, but six of the eight boys did, and all became soldiers. The family eventually moved to Tippah County, Mississippi, hoping to improve their lot. Three years later, William died, leaving Bedford head of the household.[16]

Like many children on the Southern frontier, Forrest had almost no formal education. Although functionally literate, his inability to spell was a problem throughout his life. At times during the war, this problem made it difficult for others to decipher his directives. Aware of this shortcoming, he dictated his letters to his adjutants whenever possible. Major Charles Anderson, one of his adjutants, later recalled a moment when the general looked down at the pen in his hand and said, "I never see a pen, but what I think of a snake."[17]

By the time Forrest was twenty-one, he had gone into business with his uncle in the town of Hernando, Mississippi, just south of Memphis. Three years later, when his uncle was killed in a brawl, Nathan shot the two attackers. Thus, at the age of twenty-four, he had killed his first man. This was not unusual on the frontier. There was little regard for the law, and a person often had to protect himself from danger. Violence was the most basic solution to these problems, and Forrest took a commonsense approach to his problem by killing the person who had wronged him.[18]

During the same year, Forrest married Mary Ann Montgomery. In 1846, she gave birth to a son, William, and, in 1847, to a daughter, Frances, who died six years later. Forrest remembered his childhood days of poverty and wanted a better life for his family. So, in 1851, he decided to move them to Memphis to seek his fortune as a planter.

Memphis was a boomtown on its way to becoming the inland slave-trading capital of the Southwest. By the late 1840s, Forrest had expanded his business to include slaves. Slaves were fast becoming the single most valuable commodity in the South. The value of slaves had become greater than the value of plantations themselves and all the livestock and crops associated with them. Extremely high prices were paid for slaves in the markets of Louisiana and Memphis.

Slaves were bought and sold at the auction block. Frequently, when they were sold, no effort was made to keep families together, but Forrest claimed that he tried to maintain his slaves' family structures. There were also some people to whom he would not sell slaves because they had reputations for being cruel masters.[19]

Forrest steadily built up his business, incorporating a number of partners. By 1860, he owned 3,000 acres of land at a value of $190,000 and had forty-two slaves. His personal estate was valued at $90,000. At the age of thirty-nine, he had become one of the wealthiest men in the South.[20]

Although Forrest was deeply involved in slave trading, he treated his slaves kindly. Forrest felt that slaves were property to be protected, and whipping or mistreating them would only make them less attractive to prospective buyers. Acquiring wealth through trading in slaves was his ticket to social esteem. In 1855, he was elected city alderman in Memphis. Due to his lack of education, uncouth way of expressing himself, and inability to read and write well, however, he was viewed by some local politicians as "white trash."

To some of the aristocratic young men who would serve under him, Forrest was a man of dubious standing. "I must express my distaste at being commanded by a man with no pretension of gentility," wrote one Mississippi gentleman. "Forrest may be . . . the best cavalry officer in the West, but I object to a tyrannical, hot-headed vulgarian commanding me."[21] Despite these feelings, Forrest was able to transcend his background and lack of education to become a powerful member of the community. This kind of determination enabled him to achieve significant goals throughout his life and brought him victory after victory on the battlefield.

When Tennessee seceded from the Union in June 1861, Forrest was forty years old; though well connected, he had no prior military experience. Nevertheless, he and his fifteen-year-old son enlisted as privates in a company of "mounted rifles." He was not in the unit long before the governor appointed him lieutenant colonel and authorized him to raise a cavalry regiment. This method of raising troops was common during the war. State governments often turned to prominent local citizens who could attract willing men to serve under them. Most were able to enroll a single company (fifty to one hundred men), but Forrest enrolled ten companies.[22] Using his own money, he was able to equip a cavalry regiment of about 600 men and collect a detachment of new recruits. The *Memphis Avalanche* of June 24, 1861, observed: "No better man could have been selected for such a duty of known courage and indomitable perseverance. He is a man for the times."[23]

Forrest's first military action took place in Kentucky in late December 1861. When a Union force of 500 troops moved toward the village of Sacramento, Forrest ordered his 200 men to follow them at all possible speed. When he intercepted the Union troops, he split his unit into three sections. While dismounted skirmishers moved forward through the brush, one force on horseback moved around the Union's left flank; at the same time, another mounted section circled the right end. With a loud Rebel yell, Forrest led the charge as the Confederates attacked from all three sides, causing mass confusion among the Union ranks. Panic seized the Yankee line, and those that could reach their horses tried to get away. Forrest gathered his cavalrymen and pursued the fleeing enemy. Finally, the retreating Union forces were able to form a line and block the road. Forrest charged into their midst. In the action, he killed or wounded three Yankees in the hand-to-hand struggle that raged until all the Union troops had been killed or captured.[24]

During the skirmish at Sacramento, Forrest employed the guerrilla tactics that would contribute to his legend. In his battles, he fought side by side with his men, applying his standing rule of combat: "Forward men, and mix with them." Forrest was the first in modern warfare to use the dragoon, a rifleman on horseback who thus had the mobility of a cavalryman. In his report of the Sacramento engagement, General Albert Sidney Johnston said, "For the skill, energy, and courage displayed by Colonel Forrest, he is entitled to the highest praise, and I take great pleasure in calling the attention of the general commanding and of government to his service."[25]

Forrest was unorthodox in his approach to leadership, yet in some ways he was a model commander. He never asked his men to do anything he was not willing to do himself. Always considerate of the welfare of his troops, he tried to keep casualties as low as possible. Whenever feasible, Forrest used skill or trickery to win a victory, but when all else failed and a fight to the death was necessary, he did not hesitate to do so. In the battle at Sacramento, what Forrest lacked in troop strength he gained by shock effect, surprise, aggressiveness, and valor.[26]

In February 1862, Colonel Forrest was ordered to take his cavalrymen to Fort Donelson, a Confederate stronghold on the Cumberland River in northern Tennessee. Just prior to his attack on Fort Donelson, Union General Grant had captured Fort Henry, ten miles west of the fort. Grant then turned eastward to Fort Donelson to complete his campaign. Fort Donelson was commanded by General John Floyd and garrisoned by 15,000 troops under Generals Gideon Pillow and Simon Bolivar Buckner. If Fort Donelson fell, it would mean the loss of Nashville and probably all of western and middle Tennessee as well.

On February 14, in below freezing weather, Union gunboats joined the Union forces and began shelling the fort. General Floyd decided his position was untenable and tried to break through the Federal lines. Early the next morning, he attacked and pushed the Union forces back. Forrest's cavalry cleared the Union soldiers from three roads leading from the fort to Nashville and provided what he believed was an opportunity for the Confederates in the fort to escape. By the end of the day, Forrest had lost his horse, and his overcoat bore fifteen bullet holes from the heavy fighting. Despite earlier gains, however, General Pillow ordered his men to withdraw to their original position, and Grant quickly regained the ground lost earlier.[27]

That night General Floyd met with his officers and decided to surrender the fort. The lone dissenting voice was Forrest's. "I did not come here for the purpose of surrendering my command," he said, and stormed out of the meeting. Forrest had no intention of surrendering and had even offered to conduct a rearguard action so that the garrison might attempt to escape. When his offer was rejected, Forrest returned to his men. "Boys," he said, "these people are talking about surrendering, and I am going out of this place before they do or bust hell wide open." Finding an unguarded breach in the Union line, Forrest led his men to safety.[28]

Behind them, at Fort Donelson, 12,000 Confederate troops surrendered. In his report of the battle, Forrest insisted that two-thirds of the army could have made it safely out of Fort Donelson but later tempered his feelings about the decision to surrender at the fort. "The weather was intensely cold; a great many of the men were already frost-bitten; and it was the opinion of the generals that the infantry could not have passed through the water and have survived it," he wrote.[29]

Forrest joined the main body of the Confederate army at Corinth, Mississippi, and within two months, he was in the midst of the battle at Shiloh. In the process of screening the Confederate retreat from Shiloh, he battled with the pursuing Union column led by General William Sherman at a place called Fallen Timbers. With a small number of men, Forrest attacked Sherman, forcing him to deploy his troops and allowing the Confederate army enough time to escape. During this battle, he rode out in advance of his men and was quickly surrounded by the enemy. Forrest fought back, swinging wildly with his saber and firing his revolver. As he turned away, a soldier shot him at point-blank range, but he was able to remain in the saddle. The ball penetrated his side and lodged against his spine. Forrest reached down, grabbed his assailant by the collar, and pulled him up onto his horse. Using him as a shield, he galloped back to his own troops. Troops on both sides were awestruck at what they had witnessed.[30]

Forrest returned home to Memphis to recuperate. His wound required two operations, and he was unable to return to action for several weeks. While convalescing, he was able to recruit additional men; his advertisment in the *Memphis Appeal* read, "Come on, boys, if you want a heap of fun and to kill some Yankees."[31] As a result of his action at Shiloh, Forrest was promoted to brigadier general.

In the late summer, Forrest returned to duty, forcing the Union garrison at Murfreesboro to surrender after threatening to "put to the sword" all of the defenders. To his old pattern of shock and surprise, Forrest added a new tactic: he began to bluff the enemy. He ordered his men to shoot anything they saw in blue and to "do all you can to keep up the scare." He continued to use this technique time and time again, as would his subordinates. On several occasions, they forced the surrender of superior Union forces simply by demanding it in Forrest's name, even though he was miles away.[32]

During an interview with a reporter from the *New York Times* later in the war, Union General D. S. Stanley claimed that Forrest had been involved in the cold-blooded killing of a mulatto man. The man was a servant to one of the officers captured at Murfreesboro. When he was brought to Forrest, Stanley reported, the general asked him what he was doing with a Union officer. When the mulatto man answered that he was a freedman and was acting as his servant, Forrest drew his pistol and blew the man's brains out. Although Forrest was angered by the participation of blacks in the Union army and often resorted to violence to express his anger, there is no conclusive evidence to support this story.[33]

By April 1863, Forrest had become an annoyance to Grant. He sent Colonel Abel D. Streight, with his 1,500 cavalry brigade, on a raid against Confederate rail lines in north Alabama and west Georgia. The raid came as a complete surprise, but within six days, Forrest had caught up with Streight. With a force of only 600 men and two guns, Forrest attacked Streight's larger army. For the next several days, the two sides fought a running battle.[34]

Finally, on May 3, Streight could run no further and decided to make a stand at Cedar Bluff. Again Forrest used deception effectively against his enemy. Stretching his men out in a line that appeared to overlap the Federals, Forrest ordered his troops to make as much noise as possible to give the impression that he had a larger force than he actually did. Streight's men were so exhausted from the chase that it was almost impossible to keep them awake long enough to eat. At that point, Forrest sent in a flag of truce requesting Streight's surrender "to avoid useless effusion of blood."[35]

When the two men met under a flag of truce, Forrest made sure that Streight could see his troops and his two artillery pieces moving around a nearby hill. Streight inquired about the size of his command. Forrest's response was, "I've got enough to whip you out of your boots." When Streight did not surrender, Forrest gave the command, "Sound to mount!" to his men, giving the impression that there were 5,000 men ready to attack. Forrest was so convincing that Streight surrendered. When the deception was exposed after the surrender, Forrest was alleged to have said, "Ah, Colonel, all's fair in love and war, you know."[36]

Not only did Forrest intimidate and bluff his enemies, but he did the same to his Confederate comrades. His own troops and even his commanding officers feared his explosive temper; he was often perceived as an overbearing bully with a homicidal rage who was capable of anything. An example of Forrest's explosive temper occurred in June when he got into a vicious fight with a subordinate, Lieutenant A. W. Gould. When Forrest criticized Gould and ordered him transferred, Gould pulled a gun on Forrest and fired a single shot into the general's side. Forrest retaliated by thrusting a knife into Gould's side. When Gould tried to escape, Forrest chased him into the street and shot him. Gould died two days later.[37] Forrest's wound was not serious; the shot missed all his vital organs, and within two weeks, he was back in the saddle again. Years later, Forrest expressed his regret over the incident, saying that he "never wanted to kill anybody except an enemy, and then only when fighting for his country."[38]

Following the Battle of Chickamauga in September 1863, General Bragg failed to follow up his victory and allowed the Union forces to regroup at Chattanooga. Infuriated by Bragg's inaction, Forrest went to the general's headquarters and verbally attacked him, listing a series of grievances and telling him: "You have played the part of a damn scoundrel, and are a coward, and if you were any part of a man I would slap your jaw. . . . I say to you that if you ever again try to interfere with me or cross my path it will be at the peril of your life." He demanded a transfer, which Bragg passed on to Richmond. Forrest never again served under Bragg, nor was he ever charged with insubordination. Bragg knew that Forrest would have no compunction about killing him, so he let the matter drop. Two weeks later, Forrest met with Jefferson Davis and was transferred to the West. On December 4, 1863, he was promoted to major general.[39]

Forrest continued to conduct raids into Union-controlled territory. These raids had important strategic value, as Union defenders felt the constant threat from Forrest and were forced to commit extra troops at positions where he might attack. During the winter of 1863 to 1864, Sherman sent cavalry forces after Forrest only to have them return without success. In February 1864 at Okolona, Mississippi, Forrest defeated General Sooy Smith's cavalry, 7,000 strong, in a running battle. Again, Forrest led a frontal assault on the enemy's rear guard. "His presence seemed to inspire everyone," a subordinate remembered. The Union troops, disheartened and panic stricken, withdrew to Memphis, but the victory had been costly for Forrest. His twenty-six-year-old brother Jeffrey, whom he had raised as a son and who was serving as a colonel in his cavalry corps, was killed. An hour after his brother's death, Forrest avenged it by killing three enemy soldiers with his sword.[40]

Forrest's victory over Smith earned him the respect of General Grant. Grant later wrote, "Smith's command was nearly double that of Forrest, but not equal man to man." Perhaps Napoleon said it best: "In war, men are nothing, a man is everything." Nathan Bedford Forrest was such an extraordinary man in war.[41]

As stated before, Forrest's most controversial exploit was the capture of Fort Pillow on April 12, 1864. When the commander refused to surrender his command and "openly defied the Confederates to come and take the fort," Forrest's troops did just that. The result became known as the Fort Pillow Massacre, and it did much to diminish Forrest's otherwise outstanding military career. Fort Pillow remains a severe blemish on Forrest's reputation. Whether Forrest ordered the massacre is still debated, but many modern scholars believe that Forrest at least sanctioned the killing of the U.S. colored troops and white officers. By the time the slaughter was over, there were 230 Union dead, and one hundred more were seriously wounded. Confederate losses were only fourteen.

The massacre galvanized the North, leading to redoubled efforts to stop Forrest. General Sherman sent General Samuel Sturgis to hunt him down. Sherman said that Forrest had to be stopped even "if it cost 10,000 lives and bankrupts the Federal Treasury."[42] On May 2, Sturgis pursued Forrest as he withdrew back into Mississippi, but he failed to catch him. In June, a mixed column of 5,000 infantry, 3,000 cavalry, and 22 artillery pieces caught up with Forrest. Although Forrest had no more than 4,800 men, when he learned of Sturgis's advance, he made plans to meet him head-on. Realizing that Sturgis's men had been on the march for a week in heavy, humid weather and through roads that consisted of deep, boggy mud, Forrest hoped to use the natural elements against his enemy. As he predicted, the long march had exhausted the Union soldiers. By mid-day, the two sides were locked in fierce combat. Forrest's men fought dismounted, each man armed with two Colt navy revolvers rather than a saber. This weaponry proved to be more effective than one gun and a saber in hand-to-hand combat. Using the same strategy as in other battles, Forrest divided his outnumbered troops into two groups and attacked from both flanks. When the Union line collapsed, the battle turned into a rout. By the end of the day, Sturgis had lost half of his command, and his demoralized force retreated. Forrest continued to chase the retreating Federals far into the night. The Battle of Brice's Cross Roads proved to be one of Forrest's greatest victories. Union losses were over 2,600, while Confederate casualties were less than 500. Forrest was now being called the "Wizard of the Saddle."[43] With Forrest still causing problems in Mississippi, Sherman sent two divisions to the region, making a promise that, in the long run, neither he nor his subordinates would be able to keep: "I will order them to make up a force and go out to follow Forrest to the death. . . . There will be no peace in Tennessee until Forrest is dead!"[44]

In February, Forrest was promoted to lieutenant general. He continued to wreak havoc on Union forces, but time was running out for the Confederacy. No amount of daring cavalry raids could prevent the inevitable. By the beginning of 1865, it was clear to Forrest that the war was lost. He had his last encounter with Union troops in April at Selma, Alabama. Union General James Wilson intercepted Forrest's cavalry with 13,500 cavalry troops. At Ebenezer Church, Forrest was wounded by a saber blow while engaged in a fight with a Union captain. Although seriously wounded, Forrest was able to draw his revolver and shoot the man dead. "If that boy had known enough to give me the point of his saber instead of the edge," Forrest said, "I should not have been here to tell about it."[45]

On May 4, Forrest's department commander, General Richard Taylor, surrendered. Although technically Taylor's action was binding on every soldier under his command, there was nothing to prevent Forrest from continuing to fight. Forrest, however, had had enough of war. His response to a question about why he did not fight on was simple: "Any man who is in favor of a further prosecution of this war is a fit subject for a lunatic asylum, and ought to be sent there immediately."[46]

On May 9, Forrest issued his farewell address to his men: "That we are beaten is a self-evident fact, and any further resistance on our part would be justly regarded as the height of folly and rashness." Instead, he urged his men to accept the verdict of the war, submit to Federal authority, and be good citizens. He concluded, "Obey the laws, preserve your honor and the government to which you have surrendered." In many respects, Forrest's farewell address was similar to that of Robert E. Lee.[47]

After the war, Forrest returned to what was left of his plantations. His former slaves refused to leave him, and, with their help, he soon restored his land. Although not as prosperous as before the war, he was able to earn enough to support his family plus a number of Confederate veterans who had lost everything during the war.

Forrest hoped to see the South restored to its rightful place in the Union. He said, "I did all in my power to break up the government, but I found it a useless undertaking, and I now resolve to stand by the government as earnestly and honestly as I fought it. I'm also aware that I am at this moment regarded in large communities of the North with abhorrence as a detestable monster, ruthless and swift to take life."[48] Forrest worked diligently to clear himself of charges stemming from the alleged Fort Pillow Massacre. He was anxious for a presidential pardon, but the Fort Pillow episode continued to be an obstacle to this effort.[49]

Like Lee, Forrest became a symbol of the Southern cause. Lee was careful to be reconciled to the new political order as soon as possible and became the symbol for those in the South who desired a true reunion. Forrest, on the other hand, became the symbol of white supremacy. Forrest was able to accept the abolition of slavery, but he never believed in political equality for African Americans. Their proper role in society, Forrest believed, was to labor under the domination of benevolent white employers.[50]

With Forrest facing the threat of arrest at any time, his friends advised him to go to Europe until he could return safely. Forrest declined, saying, "This is my country. I am hard at work upon my plantation, and carefully observing the obligations of my parole."[51]

Then, in the spring of 1866, two events occurred that disturbed Forrest. The first was connected with his indictment for treason. He was required to post a $10,000 bond until his trial in September. Although he had to renew the bond in September, the trial for treason never took place.

At the same time, Forrest was accused of killing Thomas Edwards, a freedman on his plantation. Forrest told the authorities that he was trying to stop the man from beating his wife and that Edwards had attacked him first. Edwards was a disgruntled worker who frequently abused his wife and his animals. In April, Forrest was indicted for the murder of Thomas Edwards. Bail was set at $10,000, and the trial was scheduled for the next term of the Circuit Court. Throughout the summer months, the court subpoenaed witnesses and summoned prospective jurors. On October 8, 1866, the trial began. Three days later, the jury found Forrest not guilty.[52]

Soon, white supremacy organizations began forming in the South. The largest of these was the Ku Klux Klan, a secret, quasi-fraternal order. The Klan's purpose was to intimidate Republican voters and leaders and to control the black population that had been granted political rights in the South. The Klan became a night-riding organization that would abduct individual Republican leaders, black and white, beat them, and sometimes even kill them.[53]

In 1867, Forrest was initiated into the Klan. He soon became very active and played a very powerful role within the organization. He fought to return rule of the South to the "proper hands." An intimidating person, Forrest was willing to go to great lengths and to employ violence when he believed it was necessary. He publicly counseled peace and submission to federal authority while privately waging war against the new order in the South. His later claim that he had no connection with the Klan is difficult to believe. While he may or may not have been the "Grand Wizard," as is often claimed, he certainly wielded enormous influence over the organization.[54]

Forrest's tenure with the Klan is believed to have lasted only about a year. He began to feel that the organization was getting out of control and becoming too violent. "Bad men" have taken it over, he said, and he wanted no part of it.[55] In 1871 General Forrest was summoned before a committee of Congress appointed to look into the affairs of the Ku Klux Klan. The committee believed that he could give it valuable information about the Klan. Forrest testified that, although he did not take an active part in the Klan, he knew it was an association of citizens in his state organized for their own self-protection. Forrest stated that he had advised against their engagement in violence and had urged them to disband. Afterward, he admitted to "gentlemanly lies." He had severed his relationship with the Klan, he said, but felt honor bound to protect former associates.[56]

Some of Forrest's business ventures floundered after the war. In 1867, he became president of the Planters' Insurance Company; a year later, he filed for bankruptcy. In 1868, the request he had made to have his U.S. citizenship rights restored was approved, and he received a pardon from President Johnson. For six years following his pardon, Forrest served as president of the Selma, Marion, and Memphis Railroad. He devoted himself to the railroad with a strong business sense, running it as he had his slave trading and his military career—in his own headstrong, independent way. In 1874, Forrest resigned from the debt-ridden railroad.

Forrest seemed to mellow with age. He adhered to his wife's wishes and gave up his lifelong gambling habit. With his wife's encouragement, Forrest was baptized, and in 1875, he joined the Presbyterian Church. As his health began to decline, he relied more and more on his wife for help; "I know Mary is the best friend I have on earth," he said.[57]

In 1876, Forrest's health began a rapid deterioration. At one time, he admitted that he had "not been in good health since the war." On September 21, he attended a reunion of the Seventh Tennessee Cavalry. In a moving address to his old comrades-in-arms, he concluded by saying, "Soldiers, I was afraid that I could not be with you today, but I could not bear the thought of not meeting with you." Forrest had always kept his promises to his men, but he was unable to keep the promise he made that day to continue meeting with them. His failing health would not permit it.[58]

During the spring of 1877, Forrest's health declined even further. In an effort to improve it, he traveled to Hurricane Springs to "take the waters." By the end of August, reports of Forrest's health were extremely negative. He had for months been afflicted with chronic diarrhea and a malarial impregnation that had brought on a combination of diseases.

Just a few months before his death, Forrest attended an African American barbecue in Memphis. Having undergone a religious conversion, he used the remaining time he had left to right some of his past wrongs. His speech was meant to do just that: "I came to meet you as friends and to welcome you to the white people. I want you to come nearer to us. . . . We have but one flag, one country. Let us stand together. We may differ in color, but not in sentiment. Go to work, be industrious, live honestly, and act truly, and when you are oppressed, I'll come to your relief."[59]

As he approached death, Forrest sought to settle his affairs in the hope of leaving his son free of the legal problems that had plagued him since the war. Near the end, Forrest reflected on his life: "My life has been a battle from the start. It was a fight to achieve a livelihood for those dependent upon me in my younger days, and independence for myself when I grew up to manhood, as well as the terrible turmoil of the Civil War."[60]

The man who had a reputation for having a terrible temper and being a ferocious fighter would admit, "I have seen too much of violence, and I want to close my days at peace with all the world, and I am now at peace with my Maker." For many of his war comrades, this statement must have come as a surprise; for Forrest, it was due to the acceptance of religion in his life.[61]

One of the last men to call on Forrest was Jefferson Davis. Forrest was hardly able to recognize the former president of the Confederacy. On the evening of October 29, 1877, Forrest uttered his last words. Unlike Stonewall Jackson, Robert E. Lee, and other former Confederates, he did not refer to a distant battle. His last words were a command: "Call my wife!"[62]

Forrest's funeral procession stretched for three miles from his brother Jesse Forrest's home to the Elmwood Cemetery. Twenty thousand people lined the streets or followed the casket. Former comrades, subordinates, and superiors were in attendance. Jefferson Davis served as one of the pallbearers. At his request, Forrest was buried in his Confederate uniform. He was eulogized throughout the country by both friend and foe. Sherman called him "the most remarkable man" the war produced, with a "genius for strategy which was original and . . . to me incomprehensible. . . . He seemed to always know what I was doing or intended to do, while I . . .

could never . . . form any satisfactory idea of what he was trying to accomplish." Joseph Johnston, when asked the name of the greatest soldier of the war, replied without hesitation, "Forrest."[63]

Not everyone, however, admired him. The *New York Times* published an obituary that was less positive. It noted that, while Lee had been an example of the "gallant soldiers and dignified gentlemen" of refined Virginia, Forrest typified the "reckless ruffianism and cutthroat daring" of the Southwest. It reported that he was "notoriously blood-thirsty and revengeful." The *Times* chose not to mention his reconciliation address at Gainesville at the time of his surrender. It did, however, describe the "cold-blooded massacre" at Fort Pillow as an event to which his name would ever be associated. Since the war, the paper stated, his principal occupation seemed to have been to try to explain away the Fort Pillow affair.[64]

In 1905, the city of Memphis unveiled an equestrian statue of Forrest in a park named in his honor. Both Forrest and his wife, who died fifteen years after her husband, were re-interred at its base. Recently, several African American groups have insisted that the monument be dismantled and removed from the park. For them, Forrest remains the slave trader, the butcher of Fort Pillow, the Grand Wizard of the Ku Klux Klan, and a racist.[65]

12 James Longstreet

"Scapegoat General"

On the afternoon of July 1, 1863, Confederate Lieutenant General James Longstreet, commander of the First Corps of the Army of Northern Virginia, rode into Gettysburg. Upon his arrival, he saw Confederate troops advancing through the streets; they had just won a decisive victory, and there was a possibility of even greater gains before nightfall. Meeting with General Lee, the two observed the ground east and south of the town where the Union troops were rallying. To Longstreet, their position appeared to be strong, and he concluded that an assault on the enemy should be avoided. Turning to Lee, he expressed his opinion. Little did he realize that his actions during the next two days would begin one of the greatest debates of the war.[1]

Few figures from the Civil War have generated more controversy than James Longstreet. During the war and immediately afterward, he was praised as one of the Confederate's best generals. Loved by his men and his subordinate officers, "Old Pete" was also held in high esteem by his opponents. Once referred to by Robert E. Lee as "my old war-horse," after the war he stood arraigned (in his own words) "before the world as the person and the only one responsible for the loss of the cause." Although Longstreet's statement was exaggerated, there were those who believed it to be true. But after the war, Longstreet made two great mistakes: he became a Republican, and he dared to criticize Lee's performance as a general. He had fought many battles on the battlefield, but never before had he encountered an enemy as formidable as that of his own people. Many Southerners blamed him for the Confederate loss at Gettysburg and the loss of the war that resulted. Longstreet, cast as a scapegoat, would spend the rest of his life defending his reputation.[2]

James Longstreet, of Dutch descent, was born in his paternal grandparents' home in Edgefield District, South Carolina, on January 8, 1821. He was the third child of James and Mary Ann Dent Longstreet. The Longstreets were financially secure, owning a cotton plantation in the Piedmont section of northeastern Georgia. Both of his parents belonged to families whose ancestry in America dated from colonial times. Mary Ann Dent counted among her kin Supreme Court Chief Justice John Marshall.[3]

Young James, called Pete by his family, spoke often of a military career and dreamed of glory on the battlefield. He enjoyed reading books about Alexander the Great, Caesar, Napoleon, and George Washington. When he was nine years old, he went to live with his uncle in Augusta, Georgia, so he could attend the Richmond County Academy. He spent half his childhood with his Aunt Frances and Uncle Augustus.[4]

Augustus was a talented, well-educated man with a good sense of humor. He had served in the state legislature and as a judge on the Supreme Court of Georgia. Augustus's family welcomed Pete as one of their own, and much of the personality and character that he acquired came from his aunt and uncle.

The Richmond County Academy had a good reputation for its curriculum and strict disciplinary code. Students studied mathematics, grammar, composition, Latin, Greek, and oratory; breach of conduct brought stern punishment. Young James was not fond of school. Like other boys his age, he preferred the outdoors and physical activities. He never seemed to adapt to his studies, and his grades reflected this inattention.[5]

In 1833, when his father died during a cholera epidemic, James continued to live with his aunt and uncle. Young Longstreet hoped to enter West Point, but when he sought an appointment, he found that Georgia's allotment had already been exhausted. His mother, who had remarried and moved to Alabama, was able to secure an appointment to West Point for him. In June 1838, he left for the Academy, traveling to New York and toward the career he had sought since he was a young boy.[6]

Longstreet was challenged by the academics at West Point from the very beginning and struggled in the classroom for all his four years there. In his memoirs, he admitted that he "had more interest in the school of the soldier—horsemanship, sword exercise, and the game of football—than in academic courses." In most subjects, he ranked near the bottom of the class. Longstreet's highest ranking was in the course on infantry tactics. He was a poor student, and his disciplinary record was little better. When he graduated in 1842, he ranked fifty-fourth in a class of fifty-six.[7]

Longstreet, however, was popular with his fellow students. His leadership in pranks, his sense of humor, and his open disregard for the Academy's rules made him a popular companion for his classmates. The friendships he made at West Point endured for a long time. Among the cadets that he would later serve with and against were George Thomas, William Rosecrans,

Following the successful Battle of Seven Days, Longstreet emerged as Lee's most reliable subordinate commander.

COURTESY OF THE LIBRARY OF CONGRESS

John Pope, Harvey Hill, and Lafayette McLaws. In the class of 1843, Longstreet found his best friend—Ulysses S. Grant. Grant was also a reluctant cadet, admitting in his memoirs that a "military life had no charms for me." Longstreet described Grant as "of noble, generous heart, a lovable character, a valued friend." Although the two would fight on opposite sides during the Civil War, their friendship never wavered.[8]

Longstreet's first assignment was to Jefferson Barracks outside St. Louis. "I was fortunate in the assignment to Jefferson Barracks for in those days the young officers were usually sent off among the Indians, or as near the borders as they could find habitable places," he later wrote. While there, he met Louise Garland, the daughter of his post commander, Colonel John Garland, and cousin to his friend Ulysses Grant. She was slender, petite, and quite attractive. It did not take long for them to fall in love. On March 8, 1848, they were married. They would have ten children, only five of whom would survive childhood.[9]

Longstreet remained at Jefferson Barracks until the fall of 1844. Following tours of duty in Louisiana and Florida, he joined the Eighth Infantry in Texas. It was during this time that a border dispute sparked the Mexican War. In April 1846, Mexico declared war on the United States. Longstreet fought at Palo Alto, Resaca de la Palma, and Monterrey under General Zachary Taylor. Casualties at Resaca de la Palma were so high that four companies had to be disbanded and the survivors sent to other units. Longstreet joined General Winfield Scott's army in the campaign against Mexico City. He distinguished himself at the Battle of Cherubusco and again at Chapultepec. Chapultepec was another hard-fought engagement; Scott's troops had to scale a nearly vertical slope through heavy musket fire to storm the stronghold. When the Eighth Infantry stormed Chapultepec, Longstreet was the flag bearer. As they were going over the fortress wall, he was shot in the leg and knocked down. He handed the flag to George Pickett, who then carried it across the wall. As a result of his action, Longstreet was promoted to brevet major. On September 14, 1847, the Americans entered Mexico City, ending the war.[10]

Longstreet's wound was painful and slow to heal. By early December, he was fit enough to return to duty. The Mexican War would serve as a training ground for Longstreet and his fellow officers for the Civil War. Longstreet had learned a great deal about war, including the power of artillery, the declining effectiveness of smooth-bore muskets, and the costliness of a frontal assault. But, more important to Longstreet, the Mexican War tested his physical stamina, skill, and bravery under fire.[11]

Longstreet returned to Jefferson Barracks after the war. In May 1849, he, his wife, and their newborn son traveled to San Antonio, Texas, where he resumed duties as an adjutant of the Eighth Infantry. For the next dozen years, he served at various posts throughout the country, and his family would continue to increase. In 1858, Longstreet was appointed paymaster and promoted to major.

After the election of Abraham Lincoln in November of 1860, South Carolina seceded from the Union, followed by six other Southern states. In February 1861, delegates from the seceded states met in Montgomery, Alabama, and formed the Confederate States of America. Years later, James Longstreet remembered the fall and winter of 1860 to 1861 as a time of "painful suspense."[12]

Longstreet remained at his post until the firing upon Fort Sumter. His allegiance belonged to the South. Although he did not favor secession, he felt he had little choice. He was a Southerner; his family was Southern. It was a difficult choice, one shared by many Southerners in the army, but he did not hesitate; in fact, he acted with surprising haste.[13]

When Alabama seceded from the Union in January, Longstreet offered his services to Governor Andrew Moore. On May 9, he submitted his letter of resignation from the U.S. Army and accepted a lieutenant colonelcy in the Confederate army. For the first time since he had worn gray as a West Point cadet, he wore it in defense of his own homeland. Recalling the day that he left, he wrote:

> It was a sad day when we took leave of lifetime comrades and gave up a service of twenty years. Neither Union officers nor their families made efforts to conceal feelings of deepest regret. When we drove out from the post, a number of officers rode with us, which only made the last farewell more trying. At every station old men, women, and children assembled, clapping hands and waving handkerchiefs to cheer the passengers on to Richmond. . . . Laborers in the fields, white and black, stopped their plows to lift their hats and wave us on to a speedy travel.[14]

When Longstreet reached Richmond, he met with President Davis. Davis, anxious to find any leaders with military experience, made him a brigadier general in command of a brigade of Virginia troops stationed at Manassas Junction in northern Virginia. In July, Longstreet led his brigade in an engagement at Blackburn's Ford on Bull Run. When his brigade started to fall back, he rallied his troops, inspiring them to hold the line. Longstreet demonstrated that he had the qualities to lead. He stood his ground and led his men from the front, giving them the kind of confidence needed to put their fears aside and stand and fight. Moxley Sorrell, an aide-de-camp to Longstreet, elaborated on the general's demeanor under fire, stating, "[He] was then a most striking figure. About forty years of age, a soldier every inch, and very handsome, tall, and well proportioned. Strong and active, a superb horseman and with unsurpassed soldierly bearing." There were two important standards for an officer in the Civil War. The first dealt with how he took care of his men at camp and in battle. The second was personal courage; officers had to demonstrate courage or they could not lead. General Longstreet excelled at both.[15]

Longstreet was a prudent man, cautious by habit, always ready to speak his piece, and stubborn in manner. Although he often ignored the social graces, he was not unattractive. Captain Thomas J. Goree said that "those acquainted with him think him short and crabbed, and he does appear so except in three places; first, when in the presence of ladies; second, at the table; and third, on the field of battle. At any one of these places, he has a complacent smile on his countenance and seems to be one of the happiest men in the world."[16]

Fearless and robust, Longstreet exuded confidence. He possessed a hearty sense of humor and enjoyed exchanging stories around the campfire with his men. When he was amused, he did not hold in his laughter. Men of his type were strongly attracted to him, and it was easy for him to form friendships.[17] On October 7, 1861, Longstreet was promoted to major general and given command of a division. While the army was in winter encampment, he spent time with his old army friends, playing cards, drinking, and reminiscing about their days on the frontier and in Mexico.

In January 1862, when it appeared that his military career was on the rise, tragedy struck. When an epidemic of scarlet fever swept Richmond, Longstreet was summoned home where four of his children were suffering from the dreaded disease. Three of them died shortly afterward; their deaths had a great effect on his personality. Much of his easy-going manner and sense of humor disappeared. He gave up cards and drinking, joined the Episcopal Church, and devoted his full energies to being a soldier.[18]

In March of 1862, the Confederate army under General Joseph E. Johnston abandoned its winter quarters and moved south. A month later, the Union Army of the Potomac, under the command of General George McClellan, began a movement up the peninsula between the York and James rivers, just east of Richmond. In May, the long lull in fighting came to an end. Longstreet fought several well-executed delaying actions against the numerically superior Union forces, which allowed Johnston to withdraw and form a defensive line around Richmond.[19]

On May 31, the first major battle of the spring campaign occurred at Seven Pines. Johnston assigned the main Confederate attack to Longstreet. Although he had spent the previous afternoon with Johnston, when the plan of attack was mapped out, Longstreet misunderstood his orders. In an early morning attack, Longstreet led his division down the wrong road. As a result, the attack had to proceed without his division. Johnston generously attributed Longstreet's actions to a misunderstanding of his verbal orders. In his report, Longstreet never offered an explanation for his error, blaming others as if he had done nothing wrong.[20]

During the early phase of the campaign, neither Johnston nor Longstreet performed well. Johnston had difficulty exercising control over the battle, and Longstreet, who actually conducted it, did a poor job. His orders to subordinates were unclear and caused confusion, which kept the full force of his troops from being engaged at the same time. Longstreet demonstrated that he was not as skillful on the offensive as he had been on the defensive.[21]

Later in the day, Johnston was badly wounded, and on June 1, President Davis assigned General Robert E. Lee to command the Army of Northern Virginia. Longstreet took heart when command of the army was given to Lee. Thereafter, Lee and Longstreet would be forever linked in history.

During the next phase of the Peninsula Campaign, the Battle of Seven Days, Longstreet performed flawlessly. In doing so, he won praise for his conduct and gained Lee's confidence as one of his ablest subordinates.

Lee expressed his feelings about him in a memo to Jefferson Davis: "Longstreet is a capital soldier and I have confidence in him."[22] Lee quickly recognized the talents of Longstreet and Stonewall Jackson, and, by July, they had become his two senior officers. Longstreet was placed in charge of five divisions.[23]

Lee and Longstreet became close friends, pitching their headquarters tents near each other. They were frequently guests at each other's camp for dinner and for conversation and companionship. Lee never developed a close friendship with Jackson as he did with Longstreet. Outwardly, it seemed that Lee would have had more in common with Jackson because of their religious faith and the fact that neither drank. But Lee preferred the company of Longstreet because of his gregarious personality and the warm, relaxed atmosphere of his camp.[24]

As McClellan began to move his troops from the peninsula, Lee moved his army toward the battlefield of Manassas to engage the Army of Virginia under the command of Major General John Pope. It was here that Pope walked into a trap, and Longstreet's counterattack was decisive in producing a Confederate victory. Although Longstreet's actions ensured a victory for Lee, some historians believe that, by not attacking Pope sooner, he deprived Lee of an even greater victory. Longstreet's actions at Manassas showed for the first time his reluctance to move quickly when the battle plans were entirely those of his superiors. Later, he would be even slower when he did not approve the plans. Despite these shortcomings, Lee still had full confidence in his "old war horse."[25]

The second campaign and battle at Manassas had been planned by Lee and had nearly crushed Pope's army before it could combine with McClellan's troops. Longstreet described the campaign as "clever and brilliant," giving the entire credit to Lee. He regarded it as an ideal blend of the strategic offense and the tactical defense. As the Army of Northern Virginia turned northward, James Longstreet remembered the plan that had worked so well at Second Manassas.[26]

In September, Lee decided to invade Maryland, believing that a bold raid in the North would force a Federal withdrawal from Virginia and encourage the secessionist movement in Maryland. He also hoped that a victory in the North would convince the European nations to recognize the Confederate states. Both Longstreet and Jackson supported Lee's plan to strike north but were opposed to dividing the army to capture the Federal garrison at Harper's Ferry. Longstreet believed the plan to seize Harper's Ferry was "a venture not worth the game," while Jackson urged that the army "be kept together."[27]

Despite the difference in opinion, Lee did split the army, with Jackson moving to Harper's Ferry and Longstreet remaining near Sharpsburg, Maryland, seventeen miles north of Jackson's position. Lee was counting on rapid movements to confuse his opponent, but General McClellan received a copy of Lee's plans that a staff officer had accidentally lost. Fortunately for Lee, McClellan was slow in reacting and was not able to take full advantage of the fact that Lee's troops were dispersed. After capturing Harper's Ferry, Jackson returned to Sharpsburg with most of his troops in time to take part in the action. Lee's army of only 40,000 troops was able to repulse a series of uncoordinated Federal attacks. Had McClellan made a stronger effort to engage all of the troops available to him, he probably would have been able to crush Lee's smaller army.[28]

At Antietam, Longstreet was at his best. The battle proved to be one crisis after another, with the thin Confederate line under constant attack, threatening to break at a dozen different points. Confident and unperturbed at the danger, Longstreet committed his scant reserves until they were depleted. Then he used his own presence at the front to bolster his weakening line in a display of courage that Moxley Sorrel termed "magnificent." His efforts undoubtedly stimulated his men to greater action. A Virginia captain claimed that "Longstreet was one of the bravest men I ever saw on the field of battle."[29]

Despite the vigorous efforts of Lee's army, the battle would have been lost had not A. P. Hill arrived late in the day with 2,000 troops from Harper's Ferry. Longstreet and Jackson had been correct in questioning the notion of splitting the army; Lee was fortunate to have survived the day. Antietam was burned into the American consciousness as the bloodiest day in American history. The casualties exceeded 24,000: 11,500 Confederates and 12,800 Federals. More than 3,700 soldiers lost their lives that day.

At Antietam, Lee had jeopardized his army, confident that he could beat McClellan. Although McClellan considered Antietam the highlight of his career, he missed the opportunity to destroy the Army of Northern Virginia. His attack had been piecemeal, without taking advantage of his superior numbers. Lee's retreat from Maryland gave Lincoln an opportunity to declare a major victory, however. Five days later, on September 22, he issued the preliminary Emancipation Proclamation.[30]

At Antietam, Longstreet demonstrated his great strength as a tactical leader, greatly impressing Lee. Lee rewarded Longstreet and Jackson with promotions to lieutenant general and the command of recently authorized corps. Longstreet's promotion predated Jackson's by a day, making him the senior subordinate officer in the Army of Northern Virginia. Longstreet now commanded the First Corps; Jackson, the Second Corps.[31] Despite the fact that Stonewall Jackson drew headlines and public adoration, Longstreet was the man Lee chose as his second-in-command. In the months that followed, Lee came to trust him more every day. Ironically, at the same time, Longstreet began to doubt the wisdom of Lee's strategy and tactics.[32]

On November 9, 1862, Major General Ambrose Burnside took command of the Army of the Potomac. Burnside moved swiftly to form an offensive plan. Within a few days, he decided to march to Fredericksburg, cross the Rappahannock on pontoons, and advance toward Richmond.

At Fredericksburg, Longstreet had the opportunity to fight his kind of battle, taking advantage of the topography to exploit a strong defensive position against superior numbers. Burnside attacked on the cold, misty morning of December 13, his major thrust coming against Longstreet's corps. The Union frontal attack was marked by courage and tenacity, but, by the end of the day, the ground in front of Longstreet's position was covered with dead and wounded Union troops. After the one-sided victory, Lee stated: "It is well that war is so terrible. We should grow too fond of it." Federal losses were more than twice those of the Confederates. J. E. B. Stuart, Lee's famous cavalry commander, wrote shortly afterward: "The victory won by us here is one of the neatest and cheapest of the war."[33]

By December 1862, James Longstreet had participated in five major campaigns and had acquired the reputation of a tireless fighter. The men who served under him regarded his inexhaustible pool of energy with awe. Longstreet was also known for his concern over the well-being of his men. On one occasion, when asked why he was taking so much time to dig his gun emplacements so deeply, Longstreet replied, "If we only save a finger of a man, that's good enough."[34]

During the winter and early spring of 1863, Lee sent Longstreet with two of his divisions to southeastern Virginia to obtain supplies for the army. As a result, his troops were unable to join Lee in time for the Battle of Chancellorsville. In May of 1863, Longstreet and his corps rejoined the Army of Northern Virginia.

Although Longstreet was not present at Chancellorsville in May, the battle was Lee's greatest victory. It was also a costly one: in addition to the 13,000 casualties the Army of Northern Virginia suffered, Lee lost his "right arm," Stonewall Jackson. To replace him, Lee promoted Richard Ewell and A. P. Hill to the rank of lieutenant general and created the Third Corps, which brought more flexibility to his command structure.[35]

Longstreet believed the war would be won or lost in the West. He felt reinforcements should be sent to the Western front, but Lee opposed any concentration of forces that would weaken the Army of Northern Virginia. Instead, Lee favored an advance into Pennsylvania, where he could supply his troops at the enemy's expense. The move, he believed, would draw the Federals out of Virginia and perhaps North Carolina as well. Lee was able to win Longstreet's support for the plan, forcing him temporarily to forget about his interest in the West.

When Jackson died, Longstreet believed he would immediately take his place. He had believed, incorrectly, that Jackson and Lee had been equal collaborators. Lee had welcomed suggestions from Jackson, but only within the context of a strategy developed by Lee himself. Jackson and Lee had shared a special understanding of each of their roles and both were comfortable with them. In contrast, Longstreet's short-term, defensive thinking was contrary to Lee's concept of war. In addition, he was slow and preferred to have everything just so before committing himself. By promoting Longstreet to corps commander, Lee believed that Longstreet had reached his fullest potential.[36] Lee would not consider him his equal in developing the battle strategy.

The campaign that followed was the most controversial of the war. Longstreet believed that Lee had actually promised that he would fight as Longstreet suggested he should. Later, Longstreet contended that he had "consented" to the invasion only because Lee had promised to fight on the defensive. The use of the word "consented" by a corps commander shows the depth of Longstreet's delusion about the equality of his relationship with Lee.[37] The campaign was marked with a courage and valor that historians today find breathtaking. It also stretched the friendship between Longstreet and Lee and brought into sharp focus the difference between their leadership methods.[38]

Unfortunately for Lee and the Confederate army, they stumbled into an unwanted battle at Gettysburg on the morning of July 1. Lee's cavalry commander, J. E. B. Stuart, had lost contact with Lee's army. Because he had not heard from Stuart, Lee was denied crucial intelligence about the size and location of the Union army. In effect, Lee was going into battle without his "eyes"; thus, he did not want a major engagement with the enemy until Stuart returned. Lee had given orders to avoid "a general engagement," but to no avail.[39] Longstreet arrived at Gettysburg on July 1, too late to participate in the fighting on the first day. Together, he and Lee examined the ground south and east of Gettysburg and saw that it favored the Federals who were regrouping there. Longstreet suggested moving around the Federals' left flank and placing their army between the Union army and Washington, D.C. With Lee's army so deep into Union territory, Longstreet reasoned that General Meade would have no choice but to attack a well-entrenched Confederate army.[40]

When Longstreet reached Gettysburg, he believed he would play a major role in developing the strategy that would be employed during the battle. He was deeply shocked and angered when Lee ignored his suggestions during that first afternoon at Gettysburg. But he was stubborn. That night, while his troops were resting, Longstreet made no plans for the early morning movement that Lee had requested. Rather, he was pondering ways of convincing Lee to follow his plan of action.[41]

Lee was in no mood for a defensive campaign after his success on the first day. It had given him a taste of the prize he wanted—a great Confederate victory on Union soil. Lee reasoned, "The enemy is here, and if we do not whip him, he will whip us." Lee, believing he had the enemy on the run, became overconfident. He thought his men could do anything he asked. In every situation in the past they had done just that.[42] Lee also felt that his army could not sustain a prolonged entrenchment in enemy territory and was convinced that a series of unexpected and well-timed attacks could crush the Army of the Potomac once and for all. On both July 2 and 3, Longstreet continued to argue for a flanking movement. Each time, Lee rejected it.[43]

On the second day, Lee ordered coordinated assaults on both flanks of the Union army, with Longstreet commanding the attack on the left flank. Longstreet stalled, playing for time, still trying to persuade Lee to do something other than what he had already ordered. As the time to attack drew near, General John Bell Hood, one of Longstreet's division commanders, requested permission several times to circle around and attack the Federals from the rear. Longstreet denied these requests. If Lee wanted a frontal attack, such was what he would get. He could have used his prerogative as a corps commander to honor Hood's request, but he was going to do exactly as Lee had told him and no more. He rode out himself at the head of William Barksdale's brigade; Barksdale would die a few moments later in the battle for Little Round Top. Hood also was wounded in the fight. The attack was later than Lee had hoped, giving the Federals a chance to prepare for the assault. The assault failed, coming within yards of capturing its objective.[44]

After the war, when the Battle of Gettysburg was analyzed, Longstreet's action on the second day came under scrutiny. The question was whether Longstreet deliberately delayed the ordered attack for so long that he prevented any chance for its success. Supporters of Longstreet, while conceding that he did not support the attack, believed he got his men to the battle area as quickly as possible given the circumstances. Because the entire attack plan had been based on concealment and surprise, the original route had to be changed when Longstreet discovered that his corps came directly into the Federal line of vision. The new route, while concealing their movement, required significantly more time to get the men to the battle area.[45]

On the following day, Lee planned to attack the center of the Union line with a frontal assault. Longstreet was strongly opposed to this attack. "I do not want to make this attack. . . . I do not see how it can succeed," he told one of his subordinates.[46] Longstreet told General Lee: "I have been a soldier all my life. . . . There are no fifteen thousand men in the world that can go across that ground." "There is the enemy," Lee said, pointing toward Cemetery Ridge, "and there I mean to attack him." Later, Longstreet wrote: "Never was I so depressed as upon that day. I thought that my men were to be sacrificed and that I should have to order them to make a hopeless charge."[47]

Two hours before the attack, Confederate artillery opened up on the enemy position. While Union guns on the opposite ridge responded, Longstreet showed himself at his most fearless. With the shells exploding all about him, he was observed by Brigadier General James Kemper of Pickett's

Division: "Longstreet rode slowly and alone immediately in front of our entire line. I expected to see him fall every instant. Still he moved on, slowly and majestically, with an inspiring confidence, composure, self-possession, and repressed power in every movement and look, that fascinated me."[48]

Later, Longstreet would write: "Never was I so depressed as I was on that day after personally examining the terrain over which the charge would have to go."[49] Just before the attack, Pickett came to Longstreet: "Shall I lead my division forward, sir?" "The effort to speak the order failed," Longstreet said, "and I could only indicate it by an affirmative bow." Pickett accepted the order, confident of success, leaped on his horse, and rode to his command.[50]

Pickett's three brigades led the charge across a mile of open field toward the center of the Federal line on Cemetery Ridge. His division was decimated by Union artillery and musket fire. While Pickett's charge is considered one of the great examples of valor during the Civil War, it ensured the Union victory at Gettysburg. Following the withdrawal of what remained of Pickett's division, Lee accepted the failure of the attack. He ordered Pickett to re-form his division. A dejected Pickett could only look up to his commander and reply, "Sir, I have no division left."[51]

After the war, Southerners fashioned their own interpretation of the battle. Lee became enshrined as the Southern hero, above blame, whereas for many Longstreet became the scapegoat, a former Confederate who had joined the Republican Party and accepted federal jobs. He became known as the man who lost the war. They believed that, had Longstreet done his duty, had he not sulked and stalled at Gettysburg, Lee would have achieved victory on July 2. Longstreet's conduct on the morning of July 2 warranted criticism, but he was not the only one who failed at Gettysburg.[52]

Colonel Edward Porter Alexander, who wrote extensively after the war, believed that Longstreet had been correct in his judgment at Gettysburg because "the Union position could never have been successfully assaulted." As for Longstreet's objections to Lee's attack plan, Alexander explained, "It is true that he obeyed reluctantly at Gettysburg, on the 2nd and on the 3rd, but it must be admitted that his judgment in both matters was sound and he owed it to Lee to be reluctant, for failure was inevitable, do it soon, or do it late, either day."[53]

After the war, at a reunion of veterans, a former officer in Pickett's division had his own opinion of Longstreet's performance at Gettysburg: "Longstreet opposed Pickett's charge, and the failure shows he was right. . . . We soldiers on the firing line knew there was no greater fighter in the whole Confederate army than Longstreet. I am proud that I fought under him here. I know that Longstreet did not fail Lee at Gettysburg or anywhere else. I'll defend him as long as I live."[54]

In September, at his own request, Longstreet was sent with two divisions to the West under General Braxton Bragg in Tennessee. His generalship contributed to a Confederate victory at Chickamauga, Georgia, on September 19 and 20. After the battle, when Bragg did not follow up his victory by pursuing the Yankees, Longstreet became involved in a plot to have the unpopular Bragg removed from command. President Davis supported Bragg, and the effort failed. Longstreet was dispatched to Knoxville in an attempt to seize the city. When his effort failed, he blamed his subordinates for an abortive attack, preparing charges against them. He even went so far as to tender his resignation, but it was not accepted.[55]

In April of 1864, Longstreet and his men rejoined Lee in Virginia. On May 6, during the second day of the Battle of the Wilderness, Longstreet was wounded by an accidental exchange of gunfire between two Confederate units. Longstreet reeled in his saddle, his right arm hanging limp at his side. He had been struck in the throat by a bullet that passed through his shoulder and severed nerves in his arm. He was lifted from his saddle and laid against a tree. Bleeding profusely and nearly choking from his blood, Longstreet told his aide to report his wound to Lee. Within minutes, Dr. Dorsey Cullen arrived to attend to him. As he was carried to the rear, one of the officers covered his face with his hat. When the troops saw him, they feared he was dead. With his left hand, he lifted his hat, and "the burst of voices and the flying of hats in the air eased my pains somewhat," he later recalled. When Lee heard that Longstreet had been wounded, a staff officer who was present said that Lee seemed almost overcome with emotion.[56]

Longstreet lost the use of his right arm, and his once-clear voice became hoarse and raspy. Longstreet's recuperation would take five months, depriving Lee of his most trusted aide at this critical time. By the time Longstreet returned to command, the war was winding down. Lee's army was close to collapse, but he would not surrender until the following spring at Appomattox.[57]

Longstreet was with Lee to the very end. He made the trek from the defense of Petersburg and Richmond westward to Appomattox. When Lee left to meet with Grant, Longstreet said, "General, if he does not give us good terms, come back and let us fight it out." But the terms were generous, and Lee surrendered.[58]

At Appomattox, Longstreet was united with his old friend, Ulysses Grant. When they met for the first time since the beginning of the war, Grant offered his friend a cigar. Their meeting was warm; there was no bitterness, recrimination, or judgment. They were still friends. Longstreet's feelings toward Grant had not changed during the four years of the war. He expressed his high opinion of his friend: "General Grant was the truest as well as the bravest man who ever lived."[59]

After the surrender, Lee bid farewell to the officers of the Army of Northern Virginia. Lee warmly embraced Longstreet and turned to T. J. Goree, one of Longstreet's officers. Shaking his hand, he said, "Captain I am going to put my old war-horse under your charge. I want you to take good care of him."[60]

In April 1865, Longstreet left the Confederate army a hero. He was quickly paroled by Federal authorities and made his way to New Orleans, where he became a cotton factor and started an insurance business. Longstreet made a smooth transition from military to civilian life, accepting defeat without bitterness. The tragic death of his three children, who died during the war, seemed not to prey on his mind; if it did, his grief did not show. D. H. Hill, Longstreet's friend, described him as "a genial, whole-souled fellow, full of fun and frolic." No one would have guessed that within a short time all this would change.[61]

In late October 1865, Longstreet went to Washington to meet with his good friend General-in-Chief Ulysses S. Grant and Secretary of War Edwin Stanton to secure a pardon from the government. Grant wrote to President Johnson recommending a pardon for him. When Longstreet met with Johnson, Johnson refused, saying, "there are three persons of the South who can never receive amnesty: Mr. Davis, General Lee and yourself. You have given the Union cause too much trouble." Like Lee, who applied earlier, Longstreet received neither amnesty nor political rights.[62]

As a businessman and citizen, Longstreet watched the turmoil and controversy brought about by Reconstruction. Southerners reacted to Reconstruction in various ways, but always in a heated manner. Longstreet urged "moderation, forbearance, and submission." He was quoted in the newspaper on March 18, 1867: "We are a conquered people. Southerners must recognize the fact 'fairly and squarely,' with but one course left for wise men to pursue, and that is to accept the terms that are now offered by the conquerors." Longstreet concluded that the best solution for the South was to cooperate with the Republican Party in order to use the Reconstruction Acts to preserve the South and to control the black vote. "My politics is to save the little that is left of us, and to go to work to improve that little as best we can," he said.[63]

On June 8, the *New York Times* published a letter by Longstreet in which he gave his support and offered his willingness to cooperate with the black Republicans, as many Southerners referred to them. His friends had warned him against writing such a letter. John Bell Hood told him, "They will crucify you!" His uncle, Augustus Longstreet, also advised him against it, saying, "It will ruin you, son, if you publish it." Undeterred by their warnings, he sent it to the *Times* anyway.[64]

To most Southerners, Longstreet's actions were paramount to joining forces with the devil. Republicans were believed to be exploiting the South, looting its wealth, and placing newly freed slaves in positions of power.[65] His words were carried across the country in many newspapers. In the North, the papers generally praised the contents, while Southern papers vilified both him and his ideas. The criticism and death threats he received surprised him.

He wrote to Lee seeking his endorsement, but his former commander refused to involve himself in public political disputes. Years later, in his memoirs, he dated the personal attacks on him from the publication of the letter.[66]

In June 1868, Congress restored political rights to a number of Confederates, including Longstreet. During the election year of 1868, Longstreet supported Grant in his campaign for president. Six days after Grant was inaugurated president, he appointed Longstreet to the position of surveyor of customs for the port of New Orleans. Newspapers accused Longstreet of placing self-interest over principle, calling him a scalawag, a Southerner who sold out the South. Even his old friend and fellow general, Harvey Hill, disapproved of Longstreet's actions: "Our scalawag is the local leper of the community. Unlike the carpetbagger [a Northerner], [Longstreet] is a native, which is so much the worse."[67]

After Lee's death in 1870, former army officers began accusing Longstreet of failing him at Gettysburg. Longstreet responded in anger, in the process criticizing Lee and losing even more support. Lee, he said in an interview, characteristically became "too pugnacious" when on the offensive and had "outgeneraled himself" at Gettysburg.[68]

In 1872, Jubal Early and Reverend William Pendleton publicly criticized Longstreet and defended Lee. For anyone to attack Lee at that time was considered unchivalrous; it was resented even more when Longstreet did it. To criticize Lee was to ask to be ostracized and subjected to severe criticism. The former Confederate officers who attacked Longstreet in print concentrated on his failure at Gettysburg, making him the villain of the battle. Longstreet fought back, declaring that Lee had failed at Gettysburg because he had refused to listen to him. He even went so far as to imply that, had Lee followed his advice, his plans would have worked and Longstreet would have been the hero of Gettysburg.[69]

Much of Longstreet's time and energy during the 1870s was devoted to defending himself in a war of words. Many former Confederate officers came to Lee's defense, blaming Longstreet for the loss at Gettysburg and, thus, for the loss of the war. They tried to discredit everything Longstreet wrote in his defense as soon as it was published. Sometimes they even made statements that Lee's own battle report did not support. There was no evidence that Lee blamed Longstreet for anything. In fact, Lee always spoke well of his old war-horse.[70]

Longstreet's participation in Republican politics continued to yield personal gain for him. In May 1880, President Hayes appointed him U.S. minister to Turkey. In 1881, he was recalled by the government, and the new president, James Garfield, nominated him to a four-year term as U.S. marshal for Georgia. His term as marshal was marred by charges of incompetence, which the Democrats used as an issue in the presidential campaign of 1884.[71]

On December 29, 1889, Longstreet's wife of over forty years died. Together they had had ten children, five of whom had died. She had endured the months of separation from her husband and followed him wherever duty or desire led him. To soothe his personal grief, Longstreet immersed himself in writing his memoirs. He said that his goal in writing a book was "to illustrate the valor of the Confederate soldier." *From Manassas to Appomattox*, a 690-page work, was published in 1896. As expected, the book engendered both praise and censure. His detractors especially condemned him for his criticism of Lee. On balance, the work enjoyed a good reception and is still considered one of the classic memoirs of the war.[72]

Longstreet became increasingly involved in veterans' activities, visiting battlefields and helping to mark unit locations. He was a frequent speaker at national parks and attended the dedication ceremonies of Grant's Tomb. Even though Longstreet had offended and angered many Southerners after the war, Confederate veterans who had served under him continued to respect and admire him. When he made public appearances, they cheered him and offered the Rebel yell. Such responses deeply pleased and gratified Longstreet.[73]

"Old men get lonely and must have company," Longstreet once remarked to his children. When he was seventy-six years old, he married thirty-four-year-old Helen Dortch, on September 8, 1897. Although she and Longstreet's children never got along, Helen was a devoted wife to her husband. Outliving her husband by fifty-eight years, Helen became his most ardent defender after his death. During World War II, at the age of 79, she worked on an assembly line in one of the defense factories. She died in 1962.[74]

During the presidential campaign of 1896, Longstreet canvassed for Republican William McKinley. McKinley rewarded Longstreet by appointing him the U.S. commissioner of railroads. Longstreet's predecessor was Wade Hampton, the former Confederate cavalry general and a bitter political foe of Longstreet. Hampton was so incensed at being replaced by Longstreet that he refused to assist him during the transition.[75]

By 1903, Longstreet was afflicted with an illness that doctors were unable to identify. He also suffered from rheumatism and was so deaf that he had to use a hearing aid. During the fall of 1903, Longstreet traveled to Chicago for X-ray treatment of a cancerous right eye. His health continued to deteriorate, his weight dropping from 200 to 135 pounds. On the morning of January 2, 1904, he visited his daughter in Gainesville and became gravely ill with pneumonia. The end came quickly—at five o'clock in the evening he died. It was just six days short of his eighty-third birthday.[76]

When Longstreet died, he was still being vilified by former friends and comrades. Before his death, he told Union General Daniel Sickles that Gettysburg "was the sorest and saddest reflection of my life for many years." Today the controversy of who was responsible for the loss at Gettysburg continues.[77]

On January 6, 1904, Longstreet's body was laid to rest. State and local dignitaries, militia units, and Confederate veterans participated in the funeral service. As the pallbearers prepared to lower his casket, a Confederate veteran walked to the grave. Silently, he lay part of his uniform and his enlistment papers on the lid of the coffin, and then stepped back. His comrades understood.[78]

For four difficult years, Longstreet fought the Union army. For the remaining years of his life, he fought his former comrades and friends who were less merciful. After the war, he made the mistake of becoming a Republican and of criticizing General Lee. As a soldier, Longstreet's record rivaled Jackson's, but he never received the recognition he sought in the South. Immediately after the war, numerous monuments were erected to the heroic images of Robert E. Lee, Stonewall Jackson, and many lesser generals. It was not until 1998 that a statue of Longstreet, the South's scapegoat general, was finally placed among the Confederate lines at Gettysburg.

13 J. E. B. Stuart

Bold Warrior

On the morning of May 11, 1864, one of the largest cavalry engagements of the Civil War was about to unfold just beyond the outer defenses of the Confederate capital at a small junction known as Yellow Tavern. Confederate cavalry leader J. E. B. Stuart arrived there first with his 3,000 seasoned cavalrymen. His task was to prevent Major General Phil Sheridan's raiders from entering Richmond. The task was an enormous one. Sheridan had more than 12,000 veteran troops and was capable of not only defeating Stuart, but even of capturing Richmond. Stuart, however, did not realize that the capital was not the main objective of Sheridan's plans—he was after Stuart and the destruction of his cavalry.[1]

Just days earlier, in an argument with his commanding officer, Major General George Meade, Sheridan mentioned Stuart's name. "Never mind Stuart," Meade remarked, "He will do as he pleases anyhow." "Damn Stuart, I can trash hell out of him any day," was Sheridan's reply.[2]

Later, when Grant heard of Sheridan's remark, he replied: "Did Sheridan say that? Well, he generally knows what he's talking about. Let him start right out and do it." Sheridan had earned Grant's respect by his past performances. The two had served together in the West, where Sheridan had earned a reputation for being a tough fighter. Grant gave Sheridan a free hand to demonstrate that he was able to carry out his boast.[3]

The man so feared and respected by Union troops, and hunted by Sheridan, was James Ewell Brown Stuart, called "Jeb" by his friends. He was born into a prominent Virginia family on February 6, 1833, at Laurel Hill in Patrick County. James was the son of Elizabeth and Archibald Stuart and the seventh child and youngest son in a family that eventually included ten children. Archibald was a popular lawyer and well known politically. Elizabeth is said to have been very strict and had "no special patience with non-sense," even requiring her sons to take an oath never to drink liquor. James began his education at home with his mother, but beginning at the age of twelve, he attended a succession of schools in southwest Virginia.[4]

Laurel Hill was a large, rambling house in an oak grove with a view of the Blue Ridge. Slaves did most of the work on the plantation and James came to love its hills, trees, and flowers. It was here that he developed his interest in collecting flowers.[5]

At the age of fifteen, Jeb attended nearby Emory and Henry College. Early in his school days, he gained a reputation for being quick to fight in order to preserve his honor. So frequent were his fights that it was a matter of pride when he wrote home one year, "Contrary to the expectations of all I have been so fortunate as not to have a single fight since I have been going to school, . . . but not from cowardice." Even though there were times when James enjoyed peace, fighting was a habit it was difficult for him to break. James's father approved of his fighting. "I did not consider you as much to blame," he wrote his son. "An insult should be resented under all circumstances." While at college, he blamed his poor performance on a History examination on a bloody nose he received in a fight requiring him to spend the first half hour of the test period taking care of his injury.[6]

Although James liked to fight, there was also a sensitive side to him. He displayed it in his concern for the feelings of others, his interest in writing poetry, and his appreciation of the beauty of nature. There was a tenderness that he hid behind his manly facade, imitating his father's behavior. It was not considered manly for a boy or young man to exhibit signs of tenderness, characteristics attributed to women. In a rural, mountain environment, refinement was rare; toughness was required and rewarded. As a result, even as a boy, James placed great importance upon physical courage and looked for opportunities to display his own whenever possible.[7]

Religion also played an important part in James's life. His initial training came from his mother; it was simple, sincere, and pious. During his first year at Emory and Henry, James joined the Methodist Church, but he did not show religious fervor until later in his life. During the war, he would seldom write a personal letter or publish a general order without invoking "Divine Providence" or mentioning prayers to God.[8]

Emory and Henry College provided an excellent preparation for James's entrance to the U.S. Military Academy at West Point. His father had been a U.S. congressman, but when he failed to win reelection, it looked as though he had missed the opportunity to gain an appointment for his son. Fortunately, Archibald's opponent made the appointment his first official act as congressman, and James entered the Academy in June 1850.[9]

To his friends at West Point, James was "Beauty Stuart," named so because of his plain appearance. He was of average size, about five foot nine inches

J. E. B. Stuart's ride around the Army of the Potomac during its Peninsula Campaign made him an instant Confederate hero. The *Richmond Daily Dispatch* reported: "History cannot show another exploit as this of Stuart's. . . . Stuart and his troops are now forever in history."

COURTESY OF THE LIBRARY OF CONGRESS

tall, with broad shoulders and a strong frame. He learned to carry himself erect, and many believed he was actually taller than he was. Later, when James grew a beard, one of his friends said that he was "the only man he ever saw that a beard improved."[10]

At West Point, James excelled in his studies and gained confidence. "So far as I know, there is no profession more desirable than that of the soldier," he wrote. His class standing improved each year, and by 1854, when he graduated, he finished thirteenth in a class of forty-six. Stuart became a friend of Custis Lee, son of Robert E. Lee, the superintendent of the Academy during Stuart's last two years there. Stuart was a frequent guest at the superintendent's home, and as a result, he greatly improved his social skills.[11]

Although Stuart was viewed as a rough-and-tumble young man, he also wrote sensitive and delicate letters to young ladies. One such letter, written to his cousin, shows this side of his personality: "Myriads of flowers leaned forth, laughing with joy." Despite Stuart's love of beauty, he was uncomfortable when in the presence of attractive young women. He was much more at ease with older women. Among the two that he had charmed were Mrs. Robert E. Lee and Mrs. Winfield Scott, wife of the general-in-chief of the Army. Both women were like mothers to him.[12]

As graduation drew near, James realized that his high grades would work against him, placing him in the corps of engineers, a branch he considered dull. As a result, he deliberately let up on his work to make poorer grades. After graduation, he was overjoyed when he received his orders to join the Mounted Rifles in west Texas to put down a Comanche uprising.[13]

In the spring of 1855, Stuart moved to Fort Leavenworth, Kansas for service with the First Cavalry. There he met and fell in love with Flora Cooke, daughter of the fort's commander, Colonel Philip St. George Cooke. Flora was from an old Virginia family and had graduated from a private school in Detroit. Although not pretty, she had a charming personality. After a brief, intense courtship, they were married on November 14 at Fort Riley. Stuart took her to Leavenworth the next day, and they began their life together on the raw post. There was soon good news for Stuart: a promotion to first lieutenant.[14]

In July 1857, Stuart was seriously wounded during a battle with the Cheyenne. Despite his wound, he led his unit back through 200 miles of hostile country. This was the only time he was wounded until the fatal shot in the battle at Yellow Tavern.[15]

Army life on the Western frontier, even in the cavalry, was generally boring and uneventful. Stuart found other things to occupy his time. Since his time at West Point, when he would spend hours after "lights out" reading, he had enjoyed classical literature. His letters contained references to Shakespeare, Byron, Scott, and Irving, and they revealed his keen eye for detail, a skill he would put to good use during the war. They also disclosed his dual personality. He was disappointed by the lack of opportunity for combat and a chance to prove himself; at the same time, Stuart was deeply moved by the sight of "a beautiful flower on the roadside." "Fond as I am of flowers," he wrote, "I did not pull it, but left it as an ornament to solitude."[16]

In 1859, when John Brown, a fanatical abolitionist, raided Harper's Ferry, Colonel Robert E. Lee was sent with a force of U.S. Marines to put down the rebellion and restore order. Stuart was assigned as Lee's aide and accompanied him to Harper's Ferry. Brown opened his campaign by capturing the Harper's Ferry's leading citizens and seizing the brick building where the village's fire engine was kept.[17]

After surrounding the engine house, Lee wrote out a message for Stuart to deliver to Brown. It demanded immediate surrender, assuring Brown that escape was impossible and promising to protect him and his companions if they surrendered. If they did not surrender, Lee said, he could not be responsible for their safety. Stuart delivered the message under a white flag of truce and made it clear to Brown that they would not accept anything but immediate surrender. If Brown rejected the demand, Stuart was to give a signal by waving his hat, and Lee would launch an attack on the engine house.

At seven o'clock in the morning, Stuart delivered Lee's message to the door of the engine house. "I approached the door in the presence of perhaps two thousand spectators," Stuart wrote to his mother, "and told Mr. Smith [Brown] that I had a communication for him from Colonel Lee. He opened the door about four inches and placed his body against the crack with a cocked carbine in his hand; hence his remark after his capture that he could have wiped me out like a mosquito."[18] Stuart read the message, and Brown began to bargain. Following Lee's orders, Stuart refused Brown's proposals. From behind the door, Stuart could hear pleas from the hostages inside that he intercede for their safety. Amid the clamor, one of the prisoners shouted. "Never mind us, fire!" At that point, Stuart broke off the conversation, waved his hat, and jumped out of the line of fire.[19]

The marines advanced and made short work of their task, killing two of Brown's men and capturing two others. All thirteen of Brown's hostages survived unharmed. Lee acknowledged Stuart's skill and service in the capture of John Brown in his report to the War Department. "Everyone involved witnessed his courage before the door of the engine house," Lee reported.[20]

During the winter of 1860 to 1861, when the Southern states began to leave the Union, Stuart was at Fort Wise, in what is now Colorado. He followed the crisis as best he could. Stuart's solution to the prospect of disunion was simple: "I go with Virginia." Stuart was on leave when Virginia seceded on April 17, 1861. Although he had just been promoted to captain of the First U.S. Cavalry, he resigned his position and secured a commission as lieutenant colonel in the Provisional Army of Virginia.[21]

The decision to fight for the Confederacy was not made lightly. His father-in-law, General George Cooke, was also Virginia-born, but he chose to remain loyal to the Union, despite the fact that most of his family did not. Stuart called the family split "a misfortune," and in anger over what he believed to be betrayal, he demanded that Flora pick a new name for their third son, who bore his grandfather's name. About Cooke's decision, Stuart wrote: "He will regret it but once, and that will be continually."[22]

Although many of the young Virginians who answered the call to arms had been superb horsemen from early childhood, the Confederate War Department was slow in organizing cavalry units. Experienced generals such as Lee and Joseph Johnston were put into positions of high command and charged with building a conventional army that only included infantry and artillery. Even Stuart's initial commission was as colonel of infantry.[23]

Stuart was sent to Harper's Ferry as second-in-command to Colonel Thomas J. Jackson. They soon became friends, and Stuart received permission to organize a cavalry troop. Most of the men were volunteers, and this was their first experience with a West Point–trained officer. Stuart imposed strict discipline on his men, and they quickly learned that life in the First Virginia consisted of long hours of training.

Despite Stuart's methods, the men under his command soon began to respect and admire him. George Eggleston, a member of the First Cavalry, noted: "We learned to hold in high regard our colonel's master skill in getting into and out of perilous positions. He seemed to blunder into them in sheer recklessness, but in getting out he showed us the quality of his genius. And before we had reached Manassas, we had learned, among other things, to entertain a feeling close akin to worship for our brilliant and daring leader."[24]

Stuart was fond of military pageantry and demonstrated this by his dress. He was always mounted on a superb horse, projecting a swashbuckling appearance. His true ability as a cavalry leader, however, is often overlooked because of his dress—the scarlet-lined cape, the rose in his lapel, the upturned hat with the plumed feather flowing behind, and daring exploits. His appearance created one of the most striking physical impressions of any leader on either side. Everyone knew when Stuart was in the area. He was fun-loving, full of energy, and always optimistic. His confidence was contagious. Despite his flamboyant appearance, Stuart still emerges as an outstanding cavalry commander, one who was imaginative and daring. As a leader, he was quick to earn the total support and respect of all those who served with him.[25]

Stuart understood the mission of the cavalry. It was to control the ground between their army and the enemy's, to discover the enemy's location, strength, and intentions, and to prevent the enemy from doing the same to them. The cavalry was also used to guard the flanks when armies met in battle as well as for reconnaissance. In addition, Stuart saw another important function of the cavalry: to raid the enemy's rear and disrupt its movement of supplies and its communications. As a cavalry commander, Stuart led his troops in all of these functions.[26]

Stuart's first opportunity to prove himself came in July 1861. He and his First Cavalry screened the movement of Johnston's Army of the Shenandoah from Winchester south to the Manassas Gap Railroad as they joined Confederate forces at Bull Run. At the First Battle of Manassas on July 21, Stuart led his troops in a charge on the New York Zouaves. Saber drawn, he slashed through them, creating confusion and panic in their ranks. His action sparked the Confederate rout of the Union army in the first important battle of the war. Stuart's strict discipline and training had paid off. General Joseph E. Johnston reported, "He is a rare man, wonderfully endowed by nature with the qualities necessary for an officer of light cavalry.

Calm, firm, active, and enterprising." Stuart's reward for his role at First Manassas was promotion to brigadier general and the command of more troops.[27]

In the spring of 1862, Major General George B. McClellan began his Peninsula Campaign against General Johnston and Richmond. For months, Stuart screened the Confederate withdrawals and fought rear guard actions as Johnston retreated up the peninsula. On May 31, the armies engaged in combat on the very outskirts of the capital in the Battle of Seven Pines. During the battle, Johnston was severely wounded and was replaced by Robert E. Lee. When Lee assumed command of the army, Stuart emerged as his cavalry commander.[28]

In June 1862, Lee ordered Stuart to gather information about the disposition of McClellan's troops on the Union right flank. So began Stuart's famous "Ride Around McClellan." Over three days, he led 1,200 cavalrymen around the Union army, discerning a weakness on McClellan's right flank, and destroyed railroad bridges, supply trains, and wagons.[29]

General Cooke, Stuart's father-in-law, commanded the Union cavalry force charged with the responsibility of maintaining security in the rear of McClellan's army. When Cooke was slow to react to Stuart's raid, all his troops found were traces of smoking and looted supply wagons. It was a sweet revenge for Stuart, who still harbored ill feeling against his father-in-law because he had sided with the Union. Finally, after a hundred-mile circuit around McClellan's army, Stuart returned to Richmond.[30]

When Stuart reported to Robert E. Lee, he received his personal congratulations for his "brilliant exploit," and for the "courage and skill so conspicuously exhibited throughout by the general and the officers and men under his command." Lee put Stuart's information into immediate use to plan a counteroffensive against McClellan. Lee's offensive was successful, but the price was heavy—8,000 Confederates killed or wounded. Lee won the battle on sheer nerve and good intelligence from Stuart. McClellan commenced a full-scale withdrawal, which would not stop until he reached the James River.[31]

Stuart's ride around the Army of the Potomac made him an instant hero and did more to unsettle McClellan than any other event during the early stages of the Seven Days' battles. Lieutenant John Esten Cooke, a member of Stuart's staff, said: "It was the conception of a bold and brilliant mind, and the execution was as fearless." The *Richmond Daily Dispatch* reported: "History cannot show such another exploit as this of Stuart's! The whole country is astonished and applauds. McClellan is disgraced. Stuart and his troops are now forever in history."[32]

On July 25, Stuart was promoted to major general and commander of all cavalry in the Army of Northern Virginia. Stuart now commanded three brigades of seasoned troops, but was required to remain in close proximity to Lee to coordinate the operations of his detachments. Fortunately, he was blessed with excellent subordinate leaders—Wade Hampton, Beverly Robertson, and Fitzhugh Lee, General Lee's nephew.[33]

Stuart's experiences during the Seven Days' Campaign gave him a certain seasoning, but his frivolity would remain. He continued his harmless flirtations with pretty girls. Despite these light moments, Stuart still took his responsibilities to his command very seriously. However, it did not seem so one day late in July when he was seen in Richmond, surrounded by young women, his horse covered with flowers the girls had brought him. Stuart was reciting poetry to his admirers when a column of infantry marched by, the men laughing and mimicking the young ladies. "Excuse me, ladies," the embarrassed Stuart said, and hurried away.[34]

In August 1862, Federal horsemen slipped through Southern lines where Stuart was napping. In the process of making good his escape, Stuart lost his plumed hat and cloak. Few events of the war so humiliated Stuart. The rest of the day, Stuart rode with his head wrapped in a bandanna, and for days after, he had to face the teasing of his friends.[35]

On the rainy night of August 22, Stuart rode to get revenge. With 1,500 cavalry, he swept through the Union line and descended on the headquarters of Major General John Pope, commander of the Union Army of Virginia. After destroying what they could, the Confederates took trophies, including money, gold, Pope's dispatch book, and the general's personal baggage containing his best uniform. Stuart sent Pope's uniform to Governor Letcher in Richmond as a prize of war. Letcher had it hung in the state library for all to see, and for the next several weeks it was a great attraction. Before sending the coat away, Stuart sent a message through the lines to General Pope: "You have my hat and plume. I have your best coat. I have the honor to propose a cartel for the fair exchange of the prisoners." John Pope never responded, but Stuart had his revenge.[36]

Lee began the Second Manassas Campaign in the late summer of 1862. Stuart and his cavalry accompanied Stonewall Jackson's corps through northern Virginia during the early part of the campaign. During the battle, Stuart scouted a route for Major General Longstreet's corps so they could join Jackson. Pope's preoccupation with Jackson allowed Longstreet to attack his flank. The result was a Confederate victory, very similar to their earlier one at First Manassas.[37]

After his victory at Manassas, Lee advanced his Army of Northern Virginia northward into Maryland, behind Stuart's cavalry screen. At Frederick, Stuart received a hero's welcome, and was invited to dine at the home of one of the residents. The celebration was a gala one with dashing cavalry officers escorting local young ladies and music filling the air. Near midnight, when word came that Federal troops were approaching, Stuart and his men excused themselves and rode off to face the enemy. After a brief skirmish, they returned to the ball, and the party resumed as though nothing had happened.[38]

On September 17, 1862, General Robert E. Lee's army of 40,000 troops faced a superior force of 75,000 Federals commanded by General George B. McClellan near the town of Sharpsburg, Maryland. When the casualties were counted, the cost of the battle would be more than 24,000, the bloodiest single day of the war. Despite his heavy losses and being outnumbered, Lee elected to face the enemy again the next day. When dawn came on the 18th, the Army of Northern Virginia was in place to receive another Union attack. Mercifully, the Union Army of the Potomac was equally battered, and General McClellan chose to avoid further engagement. After sundown, Lee withdrew from the field. His attempt to invade the North had been repulsed, and his army severely damaged, but the Army of Northern Virginia had survived to fight another day.[39]

During the withdrawal, Stuart spent a night with a family in Frederick and enjoyed dancing with the host's lively daughters. Stuart reported the instance to his wife in a letter. "The ladies of Maryland," he said "make a great fuss over your husband—loading me with bouquets, begging for autographs, buttons, etc. What shall I do?" She knew very well what he would do.[40]

In early October, Lee ordered Stuart to destroy a railroad bridge near Chambersburg, Pennsylvania and gather information about Federal troops in the area. Lee also wanted him to capture civilian hostages who might be exchanged for Virginians the Yankees were holding. On a rainy evening, Stuart reached Chambersburg. Although the iron bridge could not be damaged, Stuart's force came away with badly needed supplies and weapons, and civic leaders were held hostage for the release of Confederate prisoners. Federal troops were alert to Stuart's presence and hoped to cut him off before he could reach safety. "Not a man should be permitted to return to Virginia," came the orders out of Washington.[41]

Stuart's column left Chambersburg in the morning, returning through Maryland. Again he had fooled his pursuers—just as he had in June. Stuart's entire trip covered 126 miles—the final eighty miles nonstop—in less than thirty-six hours. For the second time, he had ridden around McClellan's Army of the Potomac, destroying enemy property and raising havoc. In addition, his troops had captured 1,200 horses and embarrassed the Federal cavalry.[42]

The South was elated by Stuart's feat. Major Channing Price noted that "General Lee was excessively gratified at the result of the expedition and expressed warmly his thanks to the cavalry, and their gallant and noble leader." Stuart believed the credit belonged elsewhere, saying that "the hand of God was clearly manifested in the deliverance of my command from danger, and the crowning success attending it, I ascribe to Him the praise, the honor, and the glory."[43]

Abraham Lincoln was not at all pleased when he learned of Stuart's escapades. "When I was a boy, we used to play a game," he said. "Three times around and out. Stuart has been around him twice. If he goes around him once more, gentleman, McClellan will be out."[44]

Stuart's star continued to rise, gaining him international attention. The *London Times* of October 28, 1862, wrote, "Anything more daring, more gallant, and more successful than the foray of General Stuart . . . has never been recorded."[45]

On November 3, 1862, Stuart suffered a personal tragedy when his five-year-old daughter Flora died. When he first learned of her illness, he felt helpless and told his officers, "I shall have to leave my child in the hands of God; my duty requires me here." When Stuart learned of her death, he broke into tears. His grief was genuine, more so because he had been unable to be with his child during her suffering. He sent a telegram to his wife asking her to come to Culpeper, so they could share their grief together. When General Lee learned of Flora's death, he visited Stuart and his wife to express his sympathy.[46]

On November 7, Lincoln replaced McClellan with Major General Ambrose Burnside. Shortly after, the Army of the Potomac moved eastward toward Fredericksburg. On the basis of information gathered by Stuart, Lee moved to face the Union threat, placing Longstreet on the high ground overlooking the town. Later, Lee brought Jackson from the valley to occupy the low hills that extended southward from Marye's Heights. Fredericksburg was to be a defensive battle for Lee. On December 13, Burnside's army crossed the Rappahannock and moved against Longstreet on Marye's Heights. During the long day's battle, Stuart operated from the right flank, directing his artillery batteries. Lee's army absorbed 5,000 casualties, but Federal losses were much greater. On the following day, neither army renewed the fight, and on December 15, a truce permitted the two sides to bury their dead. During the night, Burnside recrossed the Rappahannock.[47]

After the battle at Fredericksburg, Lee sent Stuart on another raid into Union-held territory. The mission was conducted amid snow and icy winds. The day after Christmas, Stuart started up the south bank of the Rappahannock with three full brigades, 1,800 strong, and four light cannon. When Stuart discovered that the objective of the raid, Dumfries, was heavily protected, he decided to bypass it. After sundown on December 28, the raiders approached Burke's Station, less than twelve miles below the Washington defenses. Surrounding the depot, they captured dozens of pickets, hundreds of mules and horses, and a large number of supplies. They struck so swiftly that the telegraph operator was not able to give the alarm. As a result, Stuart was able to intercept dispatches from Union General Samuel Heintzelman's headquarters telling of their troop dispositions. Stuart's men had been so successful in panicking their enemy that one of the intercepted messages gave instructions to destroy everything in case they were attacked by Stuart's raiders.[48]

After sacking the depot and burning a nearby railroad bridge, the brigades resumed their homeward jaunt. Stuart returned to camp on New Year's Day, just in time to take part in the holiday celebrations they had missed a week before.

Stuart was a hero to his men and very approachable. Colonel John S. Mosby, one of his officers, described riding with Stuart as "a carnival of fun." "Nobody thought of danger or sleep . . . all had perfect confidence in their leader," he said. Even the serious "Stonewall" Jackson was won over by Stuart. "Jackson was more free and familiar with Stuart than with any other officer in the army," Henry Kyd Douglas, a member of Jackson's staff, wrote, "and Stuart loved Jackson more than he did any living man."[49]

In the spring of 1863, Lee began to move north again, with Stuart securing Jackson's route toward Chancellorsville. On May 1, at the Battle of Chancellorsville, Stuart's cavalry discovered that the right flank of Major General Joseph Hooker's Army of the Potomac was exposed. The next day, Stuart and his men led Jackson's corps as it marched to attack the weak spot. At six o'clock in the evening, Jackson's corps crashed down upon the Union camp. As the Federals fled in disorder, Jackson pressed his advantage, determined to make victory as complete as possible. But then darkness set in, and the advance was stopped for the moment.

That evening, as Jackson and members of his staff were returning from a reconnaissance of their front line, shots rang out. One of the men hit by the friendly fire was Jackson. Moments later, Jackson's senior commander, Major General A. P. Hill, was wounded by artillery fire. Although he remained on the field for a time, Hill was unable to continue in command. With Jackson and Hill down, it was important for Jackson to find a replacement to command the corps as soon as possible.

Jackson's corps was at the brink of either a glorious victory or a disastrous defeat. Lee had divided his smaller force in the face of the enemy, and Jackson's troops were separated from the rest of the army. All Hooker had to do was to realize this, and he would have the chance to destroy either part of Lee's army. Someone had to restore Jackson's assault and reunite the separate parts of Lee's army. Stuart was the senior officer and the only major general in the area. Although Brigadier General Robert Rodes was next in command under Hill, he yielded to Stuart for the sake of morale among the troops. "General Stuart's name was well and very favorably known to the army, and would tend, I hoped, to reestablish confidence," Rodes later said.[50]

Stuart was aware of Lee's strategy for attacking Hooker, but the battle was only half won, and he was now responsible for continuing the attack. It was a formidable task, even for someone as confident as Stuart. The next day he renewed the attack on Hooker's flank, pressing the assault and seizing control of a crucial ridge. There he placed his artillery to support the Confederate advance. Finally, the Union troops were forced to retreat across the Rappahannock River.

Stuart had done well in his temporary role of corps commander.

Chancellorsville had been a stunning Confederate victory, and Stuart had played a major role in it. In his report to Lee, Stuart did not hesitate to point out that he had been "called to command . . . without any knowledge of the ground, the position of our force, or the plans thus far pursued, and without an officer left in the corps above the rank of brigadier general. Under these disadvantages the attack was renewed the next morning and prosecuted to a successful issue." He believed he had proven his ability to lead an infantry corps.[51]

In the aftermath of the battle, Stuart drew praise from many sources, including artillerist Colonel E. Porter Alexander, who would write, "I do not think there was a more brilliant thing done in the war than Stuart's extricating that command from that extremely critical position." Alexander added, "I always thought it was an injustice to Stuart and a loss to the army that he was not from that moment continued in command of Jackson's corps. He had won the right to it." Chancellorsville was a great tribute to the military genius of Lee and Jackson, but without Stuart, the battle might have ended far less successfully.[52]

Stuart had hoped to keep command of Jackson's corps, but he was too valuable as a cavalry commander to be assigned to the infantry. Stuart had been told that on his deathbed, Jackson had recommended that he should assume the command of his corps. "I would rather know that Jackson had said that," Stuart said, "than to have had the appointment."[53] After Jackson's death, Lee reorganized his army into three corps, commanded by Longstreet, A. P. Hill, and Richard S. Ewell. By June, Stuart's command had grown to almost 10,000 men. Although Stuart was an excellent leader, there were those who felt his reputation was exaggerated, owing to the fact that his enemy was inept; however, this would soon change.

In early June, Stuart held several reviews, which provided an opportunity for him to display his cavalry and to bring attention to himself. On the evening of June 8, there was a ball. Early the next morning, Major General Alfred Pleasonton, with 11,000 cavalry, crossed the Rappahannock near Brandy Station and converged on Fleetwood Hill, site of Stuart's headquarters. Stuart was taken by surprise and was hard pressed by Pleasonton from the very beginning. Only after he had assembled enough troops on Fleetwood Hill was Stuart able to stem the Yankee attack and organize his defense. A timely charge by Wade Hampton's men saved the situation.[54]

The battle at Brandy Station lasted for ten hours in fierce combat; it was the largest cavalry action ever fought in North America. Although Stuart gained control of the battlefield, there was still some question about who the victor had been. Stuart claimed a great victory in his report on the action. Although he had been genuinely surprised by the Union cavalry, Stuart had countered quickly, concentrating his forces where the danger was the greatest and leading his men in battle. "Here, there, and everywhere . . . ringing out the words of command," recalled a cavalryman.[55]

Despite Stuart's claim of victory, the Battle of Brandy Station had a profound psychological effect on him. He was surprised by the bold Union advance and the strong determined fight Pleasonton's troops had given him. The Union cavalry had finally found parity with the Confederates, and Stuart now faced an ever-growing, better-equipped enemy. The South still had great and inspired leadership, but it lacked supplies, good mounts, and experienced cavalrymen. All of these severely weakened the Confederate cavalry. Some scholars see Brandy Station as the point at which the tide turned in favor of the Union cavalry in the east.[56]

For the first time, the newspapers were critical of Stuart, some of which charged "negligence and bad management." The *Richmond Inquirer* wrote: "If he is to be the eyes and ears of the army, we should advise him to see more and be seen less."[57] A woman from the Culpeper area even wrote to Jefferson Davis to complain that Stuart's behavior had been "perfectly ridiculous, having repeated reviews for the benefit of his lady friends, he riding up and down the line thronged with those ladies . . . devoting his whole time to his friends' company."[58]

Stuart did pay a lot of attention to women, and his wife began to ask questions. Stuart was indignant, insisting that his friendships were innocent and would not damage their relationship. Furthermore, he believed he should be receiving her encouragement rather than her condemnation.[59]

During June, Stuart screened Lee's movement as he made his way into Maryland. Once Lee's army was safely in Maryland and on its way into Pennsylvania, Lee ordered Stuart to raid the Union rear. His orders to Stuart stated: "General, you will be able to judge whether you can pass around their army without hindrance, doing them all the damage you can. After crossing the river, you must move on and feel the right of Ewell's troops, collecting information, provisions, etc. Be watchful and circumspect in all your movements." Lee ordered Stuart to take only three of his five brigades on the raid, leaving two under capable leadership, which Lee could still use. As usual, Lee had given Stuart a great deal of leeway in carrying out his assignment.[60]

Stuart moved east of the Yankee army, tearing up railroad tracks and frightening the residents of Washington and Baltimore. These activities, however, were of little help to Lee, because Stuart did not keep the lines of communication open, and Lee had no idea where he or the Union army was. The only news that Lee received was brought by a scout, who informed him that Major General George G. Meade had replaced Hooker as Commander of the Army of the Potomac and that Meade was rapidly moving his army northward. Lee quickly began to consolidate his army a few miles west of Gettysburg.[61]

In the meantime, Stuart was delayed in crossing the Potomac when he encountered some of Hooker's troops. He tried to avoid contact with the enemy, but in the process he lost contact with Lee's army. En route, he captured a long wagon train and numerous Union prisoners, which he brought with him, greatly slowing down his progress. When Stuart finally learned that

Ewell had left York, he rode westward to Carlisle. But now it was too late to be of any help to Lee in the important battle that would follow.[62]

On July 1, Lee engaged Meade's army at Gettysburg, but it was not until the afternoon of July 2 that Stuart arrived. "General Stuart," Lee said, "where have you been? I have not heard a word from you in days, and you are the eyes and ears of my army." Stuart's reply was that he had brought 125 wagons and many prisoners. "Yes, General," Lee responded coldly, "but they are only an impediment to me now." Then Lee's anger subsided, "We will not discuss this matter any longer," he said. "Help me fight these people." The battle had already developed without the information that Lee had relied upon Stuart to provide. It was clear that Lee felt Stuart had let him down.[63]

Early on the morning of July 3, Lee sent eleven infantry brigades, with Major General George Pickett's division, in a frontal assault on the Union center. At the same time, Stuart was engaged in a skirmish behind the Federal line, where he attacked the northern flank of Meade's army. A melee followed as the clashing of sabers and the firing of pistols filled the air. Finally, Stuart's men withdrew from the field. The Battle of Gettysburg would be decided elsewhere.[64]

After the Battle of Gettysburg, questions and recriminations began. Disappointed Southerners refused to believe that Robert E. Lee could lose a battle. Someone else must be to blame. Although Lee had accepted full responsibility for the loss when he said, "It is all my fault," supporters inside and outside the army began to look for a scapegoat; they quickly found one in Stuart. Criticism of him soon appeared on the front pages of Southern newspapers. Stuart's failure to provide Lee with crucial information about Union troop movements and the lack of accurate intelligence, it was said, had caused Lee to engage in a battle he did not seek and on ground he did not choose. It was Stuart's fault for going off on a raid around the Union army when Lee needed him close at hand. Stuart, however, had followed Lee's orders and was innocent of the accusations made against him.[65]

Stuart did not help his own cause when he submitted his report of the Gettysburg Campaign. In his report, Stuart attempted to justify the virtues of the raid, and its strategic soundness. His self-righteous attitude and tendency to blame others for the failure of the campaign caused the report to be questioned and considered unreliable. By questioning the soundness of Lee's strategy, he incurred the wrath of Lee's defenders.[66]

Lee's confidence in Stuart had led him to give his cavalry leader considerable latitude in carrying out his orders. His instructions were more like suggestions than orders and provided no definite timetable or location on where to meet Ewell. They gave Stuart permission to raid the Union rear for an unspecified period of time. The ultimate responsibility for authorizing Stuart's raid lay with Lee.[67]

While Lee's army retreated from Gettysburg in the rain on July 5, Stuart's cavalry provided a screen until they were out of danger. In the months that followed, Stuart again performed up to the standards for which he had become famous.

After Gettysburg, the tide turned against the Confederacy. While Stuart continued to fight well, he faced serious problems. He was losing dependable men in battle and was unable to find capable replacements. Supplies were low, horses and weapons scarce, and Union forces continued to grow in strength. Stuart was also distracted by occasional criticisms, against which he always felt compelled to defend himself.[68]

The Battle of the Wilderness, which ended in early May 1864, left Lee the victor, but only marginally. The first confrontation with the new commander of the Union army proved to be very different from his victory on the same ground a year earlier. Then the Army of the Potomac, under Major General Hooker, had retreated in disorder. Now General Grant ignored his tactical defeat and ordered the army, under George Meade, to advance toward Richmond. His action served notice to the Confederacy that the Union had a leader who was not intimidated by Lee's legendary reputation.[69]

Throughout the fall and winter of 1863, Stuart remained vigilant. But in 1864, Stuart had to face a new threat. Grant's new cavalry leader, Major General Philip Sheridan, came to challenge Stuart and the Army of Northern Virginia.

In early May, Sheridan convinced Grant to allow him to conduct a raid behind Confederate lines and to go after Stuart. "We are going to fight Stuart's cavalry," Sheridan told his division commanders. "I shall expect nothing but success." With a line of 12,000 mounted troopers thirteen miles in length, Sheridan outnumbered Stuart's forces. "We're going through. There isn't cavalry enough in all the Southern Confederacy to stop us," bragged Sheridan.[70]

With General Grant's blessings, Sheridan headed for Richmond. Stuart, with 4,500 cavalrymen, tried to block his path. On May 11, Stuart took up a defensive position at Yellow Tavern, a crossroads just north of Richmond. Stuart sent a brigade to harass Sheridan's rear, leaving him only 3,000 men to meet Sheridan's full force.[71]

Sheridan never entered Richmond; Stuart prevented that. During the battle, Stuart led his men as he had in most battles, but this time he came too close to the action. A dismounted Michigan cavalryman shot him, the bullet plunging into Stuart's right side, below his ribs. As he watched his men, disorganized and retreating, he sat up and said: "Go back! Go Back! And do your duty, as I have done mine, and our country will be safe. Go Back! Go Back! I had rather die than be whipped."[72]

As the men went back to fight, Stuart turned to an officer and asked, "How do I look in the face?" When he was told he would be all right, Stuart replied, "Well, I don't know how this will turn out, but if it is God's will that I shall die, I am ready."[73]

Stuart was taken to the Richmond home of his brother-in-law, Dr.

Charles Brewer. Doctors applied ice to the wound and sent a telegram to Stuart's wife to come at once. Flora was not far away, but because of the battle nearby and condition of the roads, she arrived too late to see her husband before he died.[74]

Meanwhile, Stuart was making arrangements with Major Henry McClellan, his adjutant, for the disposal of his belongings. When he heard artillery outside the city, McClellan told Stuart that it was Fitzhugh Lee's troops attempting to trap Sheridan. "God grant that they may be successful," said Stuart, "but I must be prepared for another world." When President Davis arrived, he asked how Stuart was doing. "Easy," replied Stuart, "but willing to die, if God and my country think I have fulfilled my destiny and done my duty."[75]

As the afternoon passed, Stuart's condition worsened. His intestines, as well as numerous blood vessels, had been severed, and he was suffering from internal hemorrhaging and peritonitis. When Stuart was told that he would not survive the night, he said: "I am resigned if it be God's will, but I would like to see my wife. . . . But God's will be done." At seven p.m., the Episcopal Reverend Joshua Peterkin gathered all in the house around Stuart's bed and led them in prayer. They then sang Stuart's favorite hymn, "Rock of Ages." Stuart tried to sing along, but was too weak. When it was over, Stuart told Brewer, "I am resigned; God's will be done." He died at 7:38 p.m. on May 12, 1864.[76]

When Robert E. Lee was notified of Stuart's death, he could barely bring himself to speak. Finally, he said to his staff, "Gentlemen, we have very bad news. General Stuart has been mortally wounded." He stood silent a few minutes, then added, "He never brought me a piece of false information." Later that night, Lee remarked, "I can scarcely think about him without weeping."[77]

On May 13, Stuart was laid to rest in Hollywood Cemetery in Richmond. Later, Lee addressed the army, saying: "The commanding general announces to the army with heartfelt sorrow the death of Major General J. E. B. Stuart. The mysterious hand of an all-wise God has removed him from the scene of his usefulness and fame. To his comrades in arms, he has left the proud recollection of his deeds and the inspiring influence of his example."[78]

Before Stuart died, he said he was resigned to the will of God. He once said that all he ever wanted from life was to be killed at the head of a cavalry charge. Ironically, he died in bed after hours of pain and agony. Stuart lived by the saber; he hoped to die in the same way.[79]

Stuart remains one of the great romantic figures of the Civil War. But he was more than just a dashing figure with a plume in his hat. He was an outstanding cavalry commander and a gifted professional soldier who possessed an unconquerable resolution. He deserves to be remembered for these qualities.

14 John Bell Hood

The Fighting Texan

Early in the Civil War, John Bell Hood gained a reputation as a fierce, aggressive fighter who preferred to attack and meet the enemy head-on. He had served under both Lee and Jackson, subscribing to the "get 'em on open ground and hit 'em with all you've got" school of military thought. Although not a man of genius or a great general, Hood's eagerness to do battle with superior forces was exactly what President Jefferson Davis admired in him. In the West, the president had had enough of General Joseph Johnston's giving up ground without a fight. On July 17, 1864, he replaced him and appointed Hood as commander of the Army of Tennessee with the expectation that he would go on the offensive. And so the fate of the Army of Tennessee was sealed, for better or worse; it now had its leader, a "fighting general," to contend with Sherman.

Six months later, General Hood was relieved of his command. Under his leadership, the second largest Confederate army had been devastated during a murderous fall campaign in Tennessee, eliminating any opportunity for a Confederate victory in the West. "Our army has been badly whipped, and it seems that they are not going to get over it soon, especially if General Hood remains in command," a Confederate soldier reported.[1]

John Bell Hood was born in Owingsville, Kentucky on June 29, 1831, to John and Theodosia Hood. His parents were considered part of the Kentucky aristocracy, and John acquired aristocratic values and customs. His father was a physician who owned more than 600 acres of farmland and several dozen slaves. Young Hood never knew poverty, developing a taste for good living that followed him all the days of his life. Even on the battlefield, he carried a silver cup given to him by the ladies of Richmond. When his tent was pitched, he used his own fine china and silver, which was laid out on the camp table.[2]

Even as an adolescent, John loved women, and he would continue to pursue them until his marriage after the war. Beautiful women were as necessary to him as food and drink—and they, in turn, found him fascinating. Indeed, everyone who met Hood liked him almost at once. Women were attracted to him because of his good looks and admirable physique; Hood was six feet two inches tall, with broad shoulders, narrow hips, and auburn hair. They liked his shy manner and his sad eyes. Most of all, women were attracted to him because they sensed his admiration of them and his enjoyment of their companionship.[3]

Hood's father hoped his son would follow in his footsteps and study medicine, but young John had other ideas: he wanted to be a soldier and seek adventure. In 1849, Hood's uncle, a U.S. Congressman, was able to secure an appointment for him to West Point. His father signed the acceptance, giving his son permission to attend the Academy.

Hood's performance at West Point was far from spectacular. His first year was a sobering experience. The Academy was not what young Hood had expected; he had come dreaming of becoming an army officer, a knightly profession in which he could experience adventure, earn honors, and gain entrée into better society. In actuality, Hood was often a target of ridicule; his provincial accent, slow thinking, and large frame accentuated his awkwardness.

Hood soon became aware of his relatively poor academic preparation and had to work hard to make up for his deficiencies. Despite his efforts, by the end of four years, he ranked only forty-fourth in a class of fifty-five. To add to his problems at the Academy, his conduct record was even worse. At one point, Hood had accumulated 196 demerits, four short of expulsion. It was presumed that boys who were conditioned by discipline and punishment would mature into cadets and then into officers who would conform to the army's standard of behavior. Often this was true, but some cadets schemed to beat the system by smuggling women and liquor onto the post or sneaking off post, making a mockery of the school's regulation. There is no indication, however, that Hood was guilty of either of these infractions.[4]

In September of his senior year, Hood was made a lieutenant in the Corps of Cadets. In December, when he was found absent from his quarters without authorization, he was reduced to the rank of cadet private. The experience demoralized Hood to the point that he considered leaving the Academy and going home to farm. Instead, he "buckled down" for the rest of the year and managed to pass his January examination, graduating in July 1853. He ranked last in his class in ethics.[5]

While at West Point, Hood's association with Colonel Robert E. Lee, superintendent of the Academy, greatly influenced him. Lee's brilliant service

Despite General John Bell Hood's reputation as a "fighting general," he did not have the confidence of his subordinates. His appointment as commander of the Army of Tennessee proved to be a mistake.

COURTESY OF THE LIBRARY OF CONGRESS

in the Mexican War and his soldierly manner won the enthusiastic admiration of the young cadets. One of the cadets wrote that Lee was "the personification of dignity, justice, and kindness and was respected and admired as the ideal of a commanding officer." Hood later wrote that he had "become very much attached" to Lee while he was at West Point.[6]

At first, Hood's relationship with Lee was a painful one. It was Lee, as superintendent, who determined the punishment for his absence from quarters in December. When reprimanding Hood for dereliction of duty, Lee was careful to handle the matter so tactfully that there was no lasting ill-feeling; during the war, he never held the transgression against him. Although the relationship between Hood and Lee was strained during his West Point days, it marked the beginning of an association that would profoundly influence the younger man.[7]

Included in the cadet corps at West Point were many men with and against whom Hood would serve during the Civil War. The class of 1853 was headed by James McPherson, who had helped him with his studies; McPherson, unfortunately, would die in combat against Hood's army at Atlanta. J. E. B. Stuart and William Pender were in the class of 1854 and would emerge, along with Hood, as outstanding young officers of the Army of Northern Virginia.[8]

Hood's initial assignment was to the Fourth Infantry Regiment located in California. After two years of boring service in a remote setting, he was transferred to the elite Second Cavalry Regiment at Fort Mason, Texas—a new unit Secretary of War Jefferson Davis had staffed with the most talented Southern officers. The commander of the Second Cavalry was Colonel Albert Sidney Johnston, later to be the first commanding general of the Army of Tennessee. The deputy commander was Colonel Robert E. Lee, and one of the majors was George H. Thomas. The staff also included William Hardee and twelve others who would later become generals during the Civil War. Hood was fortunate to have the opportunity to learn his trade under such capable soldiers. Although duty in Texas was tough and the country barren and dull, Hood loved the state, and the temper of its people. Even after his tour there, Hood would consider himself a Texan.[9]

During the summer of 1857, while on patrol in Comanche country, Hood ran into an ambush. After taking an arrow through his left hand, he pulled the shaft out and managed to fight off the attackers, killing two. It was his first combat experience, but a pattern of attacking against great odds was set.[10] For his action during the Comanche encounter, Hood received a commendation for gallantry from the department commander and shortly thereafter was promoted to first lieutenant, a rank he retained until the end of his service in the U.S. Army.

During Hood's service in Texas, he had the opportunity to become closer to Robert E. Lee. One day, while riding in the countryside with him, Hood received some fatherly advice. Noticing that his young protégé was forming attachments to some of the less-reputable young Texan ladies, Lee advised him to "never marry unless you can do so into a family which will enable your children to be proud of both sides of the house." This advice made such a deep impression on him that he repeated it in his memoirs and did not marry until eleven years later.[11]

In the spring of 1861, Hood returned to Kentucky to offer his services to his native state. After learning that Kentucky would not secede, Hood boarded a train for Montgomery, Alabama, the Confederate capital at the time. He was appointed first lieutenant in the Confederate army and sent to Richmond to report to his old mentor, Robert E. Lee. He was immediately sent to Yorktown, Virginia to join Colonel John Magruder, who was expecting an attack from Federal troops.[12] To the beleaguered Magruder, Hood was a godsend—a bona fide professional. Magruder put him in charge of all cavalry companies and promoted him to captain and then to major. This unusual rate of promotion was brought about to provide young Hood seniority over the other company commanders.

Hood was pleased with his new assignment, leading patrols into enemy lines in much the same way he had stalked Indians with the Second Cavalry in Texas. For Hood, the war was providing opportunities for promotion undreamed of in times of peace. Quickly, almost effortlessly, he had become a major. He returned to Richmond, hoping for another assignment where he could see action. There he learned that Texas was sending troops to Virginia.[13] The companies were organized into the Fourth Texas Cavalry Regiment, and Hood was promoted to colonel and placed in command. During the winter of 1861, Hood drilled and instructed his troops. In the spring of 1862, he was promoted again. Now a brigadier general, he was given command of a Texas brigade.[14]

In just eleven months, Hood had advanced from first lieutenant to brigadier general. He had been an undistinguished soldier, except for his brief encounter with Indians in Texas, until he arrived in Virginia. Now, he commanded a brigade of 2,000 officers and men that daily grew in strength. They would be known simply as the Texas Brigade and would become an outstanding fighting force in the Army of Northern Virginia.

Hood had little difficulty establishing rapport with his men and proved to be an inspirational leader. "As a number of officers and men had known him on the frontier of Texas as a good Indian fighter, he was accepted without much opposition," one man wrote. Hood made little effort to control the carefree behavior of his Texans. He was demanding of his troops in battle, but was permissive of their behavior in camp. As one private put it: "West Pointer that Hood was, he not only knew Texas and Arkansas tastes and temperaments," but on occasion would let his men indulge. On one such occasion, many of the Texans decided to go absent without leave while passing through Richmond. When one of his officers tried to prevent the disintegration of the command, Hood called to him: "Let 'em go. Let 'em go. They deserve a little indulgence, and you'll get them back in time for the next battle."[15]

On May 7, the Union army under General George McClellan advanced up the Yorktown peninsula toward Richmond. Hood was ordered to drive them back. In their first serious action, Hood's Texans routed the Federals near Eltham's Landing in what Hood called "a happy introduction to the enemy."[16]

Although Hood's actions at Eltham's Landing established his reputation for gallantry, they also disturbed Johnston, who had not wished to provoke a major engagement at that time. After listening to Hood's explanation of his actions, Johnston said: "General Hood, have you given an illustration of the Texan idea of feeling an enemy gently and falling back? What would your Texans have done, sir, if I had ordered them to charge and drive back the enemy?" "I suppose, General," Hood replied, "they would have driven them into the river, and tried to swim out and capture their gunboats." Johnston smiled and ended the conversation by saying, "Teach your Texans that the first duty of a soldier is literally to obey orders."[17]

At Gaines's Mill, during the Seven Days' Campaign on June 27, Hood's reputation again soared. When a Confederate counteroffensive came to a halt against a stiff Union defense, Lee asked Hood to break the line. Hood returned to his troops and told them to follow him.[18] Men from A. P. Hill's division had tried for hours to pierce the line, but each time had been repulsed. The attack seemed like almost certain death, but the Texans broke through the center of the Union line with a wild, howling charge. Hood did not hesitate to go into the thick of the fighting, personally leading the Texas Brigade in a bayonet charge. Hood exulted in the excitement of combat. Those who saw him remarked how his eyes had glowed, how the battle had visibly changed him into a terrifying warrior whose fighting spirit enraptured his entire brigade. Hood's charge was considered the single most brilliant achievement during the Seven Days' Campaign, and his brigade was now viewed as the best in the army. Stonewall Jackson proclaimed: "These men are soldiers indeed!" The Texans' action at Gaines's Mill helped to gain an important victory for Lee, and Hood's name was soon being spoken of with favor in Richmond.[19]

Hood's reputation preceded him to Richmond and opened the door to him for entry into the social circles of the capital. At first, he was seen mainly in the poker parlors, where he gained a reputation as a man who played recklessly and for high stakes. "I saw Hood bet $2,000 with nary a pair in his hand," one soldier said. Then he began mixing with the more genteel society in the capital, making contact with high society, as well as with the president himself. Hood was said to have had "very winning manners" and to have used these "advantages actively for his own advancement." The diarist and friend of Hood, Mrs. Mary Boykin Chesnut, wrote extensively of his actions throughout the war. She thought his social behavior was not very subtle: "General Hood's an awful flatterer—I mean an awkward flatterer and once I warned him if you stay here in Richmond much longer, you will grow to be a courtier. And you came a rough Texan." But Hood was very ambitious and did not like taking anyone's advice. Even a private in the ranks would note, "Hood was as ambitious as he was brave and daring."[20]

Hood emerged from the Seven Days' Battle with a reputation as a bold and able combat officer and was rewarded by being promoted to division commander. At this point, Hood and his Texans were detached to the command of General James Longstreet and would be involved in the Second Battle of Manassas. There, Stonewall Jackson's corps swiftly maneuvered around the army of General John Pope, while Longstreet, with Hood's division in a prominent position, destroyed the Yankees' left flank. Pope was thoroughly defeated, and his army went reeling back to Washington.

Hood called it "the most beautiful battle scene I have ever beheld." Again, Hood had performed well; he was becoming one of the Confederate's rising stars.[21]

In August, after Second Manassas, Hood's temper got him into trouble with General Longstreet. On the final day at Manassas, Hood's men captured several Union ambulances and put them into action. General N. G. Evans, who was senior to Hood, ordered him to turn the ambulances over to him. When Hood refused, Evans placed him under arrest for insubordination; Longstreet ordered Hood to remain in Virginia. Hood explained his actions: "I would cheerfully have obeyed directions to deliver them to General Lee's Quartermaster for use of the army, [but] I did not consider it just that I should be required to yield them to another brigade of the division, which was in no manner entitled to them." The power of arrest was sacrosanct to Lee, and he would neither intercede for Hood nor overrule Evans—thus allowing a petty feud to remove one of his best fighting generals.[22]

After his victory at Manassas, Lee went on the offensive, moving his army into Maryland. Lee knew that Hood would be needed soon and offered him a way out. Lee said that if Hood would apologize, he would drop the entire matter. Hood refused, saying that he was in the right. Hoping that Hood and Evans would later reconcile, Lee compromised and ordered Hood to bring up the rear of his division and accompany them into Maryland.

When the Texans saw Lee, they shouted, "Give us Hood!" Lee sent for Hood and advised him: "General, here I am just upon the eve of entering into battle with one of my best officers under arrest." Lee again offered Hood the chance to apologize, but he still refused, citing the justness of his position. Lee shook his head, and then told him he was "suspending" his arrest until after the impending battle.[23] After their conference, Lee raised his hand to the men and said, "You shall have him, gentlemen." Hood moved to the front of his division amid wild cheering.[24]

Hood's star soared again as a result of the Maryland Campaign at Antietam, in which he commanded a small division. During the opening battle, Hood's division was held in reserve behind Jackson to allow them time to prepare their first hot breakfast in weeks. When Jackson's position came under fire in the cornfield by Major General Hooker's infantry, it looked as though the Northerners would sweep over the Confederates. Just in time, however, Hood's men came to their aid, holding their ground under awesome pressure from Union troops and suffering heavy losses. As his ranks thinned, he could be seen pacing and crying aloud: "For God's sake, more troops!" Despite being in desperate need of reinforcements, Hood continued to advance. The bodies were piled so thickly that he would later write: "Never before was I so consciously troubled with fear that my horse would further injure some wounded fellow soldier lying helpless on the ground."[25]

Hood's division was shattered, leaving him forever bitter. The high command, he believed, had betrayed his men. Lee had gotten Hood's division into a dangerous position without providing the means for it to defend itself. As a result, it had suffered more than 2,000 casualties. His pleas for reinforcements had gone unanswered. When their ammunition was depleted, he withdrew his troops. Despite the overwhelming odds against him and the heavy losses, it had been his finest hour.[26]

When the fighting stopped, Hood rode off to report to Lee on the conditions in his area. He was visibly and uncharacteristically shaken by the ordeal. Lee asked him how his men were. Hood's emotional reply was, "They're all dead on the field where you sent them."[27]

The action on the Confederate left had saved the day for Lee and the Army of Northern Virginia. Fighting against odds of nearly five to one, Generals Hood, McLaws, and Lawton had repulsed 30,000 Union troops. On September 27, 1862, General Jackson recommended that Hood be promoted to the rank of major general, saying that he had fought with "such ability and zeal as to command my admiration. I regard him as one of the most promising officers of the army."[28]

Hood expected to be placed back under arrest for the controversy over the ambulances, but Lee released him from the charges. Instead of arrest, Hood was recommended for permanent division commander and promoted. At the age of thirty-one, he had become the youngest of nine major generals of infantry. "In lieu of being summoned to a court-martial," Hood said, "I was shortly afterwards promoted to the rank of major general."[29]

After the battle, McClellan was removed as Union commander of the Army of the Potomac and replaced by General Ambrose Burnside, who promptly began to march his army toward Fredericksburg. Despite being outnumbered, Lee decided to fight the Union from the heights of Fredericksburg. Longstreet's corps, with Hood's division at its center, was on the left; Jackson's corps defended the right flank. In a series of fruitless charges up the slopes, Burnside's troops were slaughtered. Observing the foolish Union assaults, Lee remarked to Longstreet: "It is well that war is so terrible. We should grow too fond of it."[30]

During the winter of 1862 to 1863, Hood was in great demand in Richmond, welcomed at dances and other social events. It was at this time that Hood fell in love. She was Sally "Buck" Preston, eighteen-year-old daughter of an aristocratic South Carolina family. Buck was staying in Richmond that winter at the home of family friends Colonel and Mrs. John C. Chesnut. Chesnut was an aide to Jefferson Davis; his wife, Mary Boykin Chesnut, was a member of the social elite in Richmond. Hood impressed Mrs. Chesnut to the point that she wrote frequently of him in her diary. In one of those entries she gave her impression of him: "When he came, with his sad, Quixote face, the face of an old crusader who believed in his cause, his cross, his crown. . . . Tall, thin, shy, blue eyes and light hair, tawny beard and a vast amount of it covering the lower part of his face—an appearance of awkward strength. Someone said that great reserve of manner he carried only into ladies' society."[31]

Throughout the spring, Hood pursued Buck Preston whenever he could get down to Richmond. She was a true beauty, smart, and a born flirt, and had many suitors. Added to that list was Major General John Bell Hood. The trouble was that Buck enjoyed being pursued by more than one suitor.[32]

Early in 1863, Lee sent Longstreet's corps to forage and to keep the supply routes open from North Carolina. Hood was unhappy about the assignment, which placed him away from his love in Richmond and the excitement of Lee's preparation for the Battle of Chancellorsville.[33]

Hood was away from the Army of Northern Virginia during the next important battle in the East. After Fredericksburg, "Fighting Joe" Hooker was selected to replace Burnside. Hooker quickly tried to engage Lee at Chancellorsville, but was routed when Jackson attacked him from the flank. That evening, the Confederates lost their most able field commander, Stonewall Jackson. Hood, who had tried to model himself in Jackson's style, was deeply distressed at the news of his death.

With the loss of Jackson, Lee was faced with the problem of reorganizing the Army of Northern Virginia. Hood talked with Lee about the reorganization, hoping to be considered for one of the positions as corps commander. The corps were too large, said Hood. Four divisions were too much for one general to control in the rugged countryside of Virginia. Lee agreed with him. As much as he would miss Jackson, the loss gave Lee the opportunity to reorganize his army into smaller corps. Realizing that Hood was angling for a corps command, Lee informed him that, although he was good, he was not ready yet for corps command. "I rely much upon you," wrote Lee. "You must so inspire and lead your brave division as it may accomplish the work of a corps."[34]

Gettysburg was to be Hood's last battle under Lee's command. Hood had protested bitterly to Longstreet against a frontal attack on the enemy on Little Round Top. His scouts reported that the way was clear to circle around the south end of Round Top and attack the enemy from the rear. Three times Hood sent staff officers to Longstreet, recommending that he be allowed to bypass Round Top. Each time his request was denied. Under protest, "the first and only one I ever made in my military career," he later wrote, Hood ordered his four brigades to advance. Longstreet rode up, and Hood pleaded again. "We must obey the orders of General Lee," was Longstreet's only reply.[35]

Having watched his division advance, Hood rode down the slopes toward the center of his line. Just as he entered the Peach Orchard, a shell exploded over his head, raining iron fragments, which pierced his left hand and arm. "I saw him sway to and fro in the saddle and then start to fall from his horse, when he was caught by one of his aides," observed an officer nearby.[36]

Almost unconscious, Hood was taken to the rear and his troops proceeded without him. They struggled up the boulder-covered hills and almost seized Little Round Top, but Joshua Chamberlain's troops repulsed their attack. The Confederate survivors withdrew; half of Hood's division had been lost in the senseless frontal attack.[37]

At first, it was feared that Hood would lose his arm, but amputation was not necessary. He did, however, lose all feeling in his arm, and it remained useless for the rest of his life. His wound was cared for at Staunton and then at Charlottesville, and finally, he was moved to Richmond. There he resumed his courtship of Buck Preston.

A little more than two months after Hood was wounded, Longstreet's corps was ordered to join General Braxton Bragg's Army of Tennessee, now being threatened by General William Rosecrans's army. Although only partly recovered from his wound when he learned of his division's transfer, Hood placed his horse on a train and joined his troops in Georgia. Arriving on the battlefield at Chickamauga, he mounted his horse in the boxcar, jumped from the train, and joined his division, which was already in action. Assuming command of Confederate forces in the center, Hood's command led the breakthrough in the Union line. At the height of the action, Hood was struck by a minie ball high in the leg. He dropped his reins and slid out of his saddle. As he lay on the ground, he gave his last orders to the Texans. "Go ahead," he shouted, "and keep ahead of everything." Then he was carried from the field on a stretcher.[38]

Hood's wound proved more serious than originally thought; he had been shot through the right thigh a few inches below the hip. An amputation was performed by Dr. T. G. Richardson, chief medical officer of the Army of Tennessee.

The joy in Richmond at the news of the victory at Chickamauga was made bittersweet by a false report that Hood had been killed. When Lee heard of Hood's death he commented, "I am gradually losing my best men, Jackson, Pender . . . Hood."

Just before Hood had left Richmond, his arm still in a sling, he had proposed to Buck. Although she did not give him an answer at the time, he was under the impression that she would accept. Now, Buck read in the Richmond paper that Hood was dead and being eulogized as a "noble leader of gallant soldiers." According to Mary Chesnut, every officer who was smitten with Buck had been killed or seriously wounded.[39]

Soon the news was corrected. Hood was still alive and "in fine spirits" despite the loss of his leg. The Texas brigade passed a hat and collected nearly $5,000 to buy him an artificial limb. General Longstreet recommended Hood for promotion to the rank of lieutenant general for distinguished conduct and ability in the battlefield.[40] With good food, nursing, and encouragement, Hood was soon sitting up and asking when he could return to duty. He was offered a civil post but declined: "No bombproof place for me. I propose to see this fought out in the field."

Hood returned to Richmond, where he had the opportunity to see Buck Preston again, but he made a poor impression on her. He was not the same man she had known just two months earlier. At the age of thirty-two, Hood now moved about painfully on crutches, one pants leg hanging empty and a face that seemed to have aged years in just a matter of weeks. In fact, his attitude may have hurt his chances of capturing her heart. In one situation, when he chastised his black servant in a fit of temper, she became very annoyed. "I hate a man who speaks roughly to those who dare not resent it," she said. Later, on another occasion, she confided to Mrs. Chesnut that she would not marry him "if he had a thousand legs, instead of having just one." Hood's hopes of marrying Preston were slipping rapidly. "I was routed," he said, "She told me there was no hope."[41]

But still Hood continued to pursue her. In love, as in war, he knew only one method of combat—full-scale attack. Despite being turned down at least twice by Preston when he proposed marriage, Hood kept after her. Colonel Charles Venable, related by marriage to the Preston family, observed: "Buck can't help it. She must flirt. . . . She does not care for the man. It is sympathy with the wounded soldier. Helpless Hood."[42]

Hood was not as helpless as Venable thought. By continued persistence, he managed to get a contingent acceptance of marriage from Preston. "I am so proud, so grateful. The sun never shone on a happier man," he told Mrs. Chesnut. She was still not convinced. "So the tragedy has been played out," she wrote in her diary, "for I do not think even now that she is in earnest."[43]

Hood's love affair seemed to be prospering and so was his reputation. President Davis's association with him provided the most visible recognition of his favored status. Davis's carriage was at Hood's disposal, and Hood shared the president's pew at church. It was in both their interests to be seen together. Davis, who often battled with his senior officers, for once was in agreement with a popular hero. Hood, in return, was ambitious for promotion, and Davis could make that happen.[44]

Hood and Davis often discussed the course of the war and tactical matters. Davis considered himself a military expert, and Hood played up to this, going so far as to suggest that he might personally take command of the army. "I would follow you to the death!" Hood told the president. The two agreed that the South must take the initiative and attack the Union armies before they could consolidate their strength. These discussions enhanced Davis's opinion of Hood's military ability and raised the question of whether Hood's praise of Davis was to win promotion or whether he really was sincere.[45]

In February, Hood's promotion to lieutenant general came through. Although public sentiment favored his promotion, there was still some question about his ability for such a high command. Lieutenant generals commanded corps. The only corps position available at the time was one in the Army of Tennessee. To free up a corps position for Hood, Davis withdrew an earlier nomination of D. H. Hill. Although Hill had commanded a corps at Chickamauga, he had lost favor with Davis. Hood was now to command the corps intended for Hill.[46] At the end of February, Hood reported to Joseph Johnston, who had replaced Braxton Bragg. The Army of Tennessee was attempting to recover from its humiliating defeat at Missionary Ridge in the fall. Hood energetically organized his corps for battle and attempted to build the self-esteem of his men. He had them march in reviews and maneuver in mock battles, hoping to improve both their readiness and morale.

The pain in Hood's shattered left arm and the stump of his right leg was steady, sometimes dulled by drugs, but still always there. The pain was something he had learned to live with, just as he had adjusted to the artificial leg. For him, the leg was a badge of honor; the pain was the price of that honor.[47]

At midnight on May 11, 1864, in the hills of Georgia, Hood was baptized. Leonidas Polk, an Episcopal bishop who also served as an infantry corps commander in the Army of Tennessee, performed the ceremony. Using a horse bucket and a tin washbasin, Bishop-General Polk administered the solemn rites to his fellow general. Within three months, General Polk would be dead, and Hood would be poised to march the Army of Tennessee into the battles of Atlanta and Nashville and into oblivion.[48]

After joining Johnston in Georgia, Hood was disappointed. Until now, he had served under generals who had used defense as part of an overall plan that ultimately relied on going on the attack. But with Johnston, Hood was serving under the master of defense, a military strategy of which he did not approve.[49] On the other hand, Johnston was happy to have Hood on his staff; such a fighter would be helpful in the struggle ahead. His enthusiasm, however, would have been tempered had he known that Hood was sending secret reports to Davis.

Before Hood had left Richmond, he had agreed to send Davis confidential reports on the condition of the Army of Tennessee. The ambitious Hood took the opportunity to further his career by sending secret letters to Richmond, overstating the army's perilous condition, downplaying Johnston's requests for cavalry, and openly expressing his belief that Johnston should have taken the initiative and advanced into Tennessee and Kentucky. This was exactly what Davis and the Confederate high command had repeatedly urged Johnston to do. Later, Hood would justify his actions by stating that he wanted to encourage Davis to send reinforcements to Johnston. Unprofessional as it was for Hood to send these letters, it was equally unprofessional for Davis and his staff to spy on Johnston in this way.[50]

Members of the Confederate high command grew increasingly impatient with Johnston. They concluded that his reluctance to go on the offensive prevented the recovery of Tennessee. Hood's frustration increased too; he had come to Georgia expecting to advance against the enemy. On July

14, he told General Braxton Bragg, now an adviser to Jefferson Davis, that Atlanta was in danger of falling into enemy hands. Georgia Senator Benjamin Hill also believed that Atlanta was in extreme danger and reported the situation to Davis. Loss of Atlanta's railroads, hospitals, and industries would be a staggering blow to the Confederacy and have a negative impact on morale.[51]

As Johnston retreated to the outskirts of Atlanta, Davis continued to receive pressure from his cabinet, particularly Secretary of War Judah Benjamin, to replace him. When Bragg recommended that Johnston be removed from command, it was the last straw. Davis decided that Johnston must go.[52] Some of the president's advisers suggested that longtime corps commander Lieutenant General Hardee would be a good choice, but Davis cared little for Hardee, either personally or politically. Davis preferred his young friend and protégé, John Bell Hood.[53]

When Davis informed Lee that he was going to replace Johnston, Lee responded: "I regret the fact stated. It is a bad time to release the commander of an army situated as that of Tennessee. We may lose Atlanta and the army too."[54]

Davis knew that his choice was a risky one, and he again turned to Lee for advice. He telegraphed Lee wanting to know if Hood was capable of succeeding Johnston. Lee could only offer lukewarm commendation: "Hood is a bold fighter. I am doubtful as to other qualities necessary." In a tactful way, Lee let Davis know that Hood was gallant, zealous, and earnest, but that he had never been tested with that much responsibility. If Johnston had to be replaced, Lee suggested Hardee, but Davis and Bragg ignored his advice. On July 17, Johnston was removed from command of the Army of Tennessee.[55]

When he learned that Johnston had been replaced, Hood panicked. He immediately telegraphed Davis, requesting him to postpone the change: "The enemy being now in our common front and making as we suppose a general advance, we deem it dangerous to change commanders. . . ." Davis declined to suspend the order. Hood must command.[56]

When the news of Johnston's removal and his replacement by Hood was received by the Army of Tennessee, they were stunned. Johnston's cautious style of fighting, strategically retreating in the face of overwhelming Union odds, had kept morale high among his troops. According to one Tennessee private, Johnston was "loved, respected, admired: yea, almost worshipped by his troops."[57]

Grant and Sherman were pleased about Hood's leading the Army of Tennessee. In his postwar memoirs, Grant recalled: "Sherman and I rejoiced. Hood was unquestionably a brave, gallant soldier and not destitute of ability. But unfortunately, his policy was to fight the enemy wherever he saw him without thinking much of the consequences of defeat."[58]

Sherman's army and corps commanders were happy with the change too. They believed Hood would "hit like hell, now, before you know it." Although this would mean an increase in Union casualties, it was still a welcome change. Hood would take the Confederates into the open, where Sherman hoped to destroy their army. With an advantage of more than two to one in troop strength, Sherman had every reason to believe he would have the upper hand.[59]

On July 20, just two days after taking command, Hood attacked the enemy at Peach Tree Creek. The attack failed, and Hood had gained nothing at a cost of 5,000 men. This was the first of four attacks, none of which was successful. In his frustration, Hood began to blame his subordinates, particularly Hardee, for the failure of his plans. Hood fought Sherman the only way he knew—by aggressively attacking. The losses were heavy, and nothing was gained. Around Atlanta and again at Franklin, Hood flung his army at the enemy in hopeless assaults against strong positions, always thinking his demoralized army was made up of spirited, confident troops like his old Texas Brigade. On September 2, Sherman's army entered Atlanta. Hood's army retreated into Tennessee, leaving no one to stop Sherman from destroying Atlanta.

Hood blamed the loss of Atlanta on Johnston. "It seems the troops had been so long confined to trenches and had been taught to believe that entrenchment cannot be taken, so they attacked without spirit and retired without proper effort."[60]

Sherman did not pursue Hood into Tennessee; he was in no mood to go back the way he had come. He believed a "retrograde movement" to Tennessee would hurt morale. Instead, he sent Major General George Thomas's corps north to deal with Hood, while he continued his devastating March to the Sea across the heart of Georgia.[61]

By mid-October, Hood was ready to fight again. His objective was to retake Tennessee and Kentucky. As Hood came north, General George Thomas shifted his forces to meet him. Hood hoped to attack the Union troops under Major General John Schofield before he could join Thomas's army. Hood believed he had Schofield trapped just below Spring Hill. Instead of going to the front to personally direct his generals, he set up headquarters two miles from town and went to bed.[62]

After dark, Hood's army set up camp, but failed to physically block the Nashville Pike. In one of the most bizarre episodes of the war, Schofield moved his entire army through the midst of Hood's sleeping troops during the night. By morning, Schofield and his troops were well on their way to Franklin, the next town down the road. Hood's plan to trap Schofield had evaporated during the night.[63] An enraged Hood accused his generals of incompetence for allowing Schofield to escape. Schofield reached Franklin ahead of Hood and in time to have his army dig in. Hood pursued his enemy, reaching them only after they had fortified their position. Despite the strong position Schofield now enjoyed, Hood was determined to attack and ordered a frontal assault, which would take place across nearly two miles of open ground, against an entrenched army backed by massed artillery.[64]

Despite Confederate General Patrick Cleburne and others' strong argument for a flanking movement, Hood stuck to his suicidal, head-on assault. Again, he failed. This time, he lost 6,300 men, nearly a quarter of the attacking force. Among those who paid with their lives for Hood's reckless assault was General Cleburne. The Army of Tennessee was shattered and destroyed as an effective fighting force.[65]

The defeat at Nashville two weeks later ended Hood's military career. Despite a spirited Confederate fight, the army suffered its most crushing defeat of the war, followed by a vigorous Union pursuit. The Army of Tennessee's retreat was a brutal nightmare, conducted in the foulest weather imaginable. Between Nashville and the Tennessee River, the remnants of Hood's defeated army lay strewn along the line of retreat—broken caissons, overturned wagons, bloated horses, and frozen human corpses.[66]

A Tennessee private who had seen Hood prior to Nashville described him as "feeble and decrepit, with an arm in a sling and a crutch in the other hand, trying to guide and control his horse," and felt sorry for him. Now after the battle, when he went to secure "a wounded furlough," he felt even sorrier for him. Hood was alone in his tent "much agitated and affected" by the events of the past six hours "and crying like his heart would break." The private received his furlough paper, then went back into the darkness, leaving Hood to his pain. "I pitied him, poor fellow," the soldier wrote later, remembering the event. "I always loved and honored him, and will ever revere and cherish his memory. . . . As a soldier, he was brave, good, noble and gallant, and fought with the ferociousness of a wounded tiger; but as a general he was a failure in every particular."[67]

Hood asked to be relieved. President Davis reinstated General Joseph Johnston, whose campaign against Sherman was now viewed more favorably in light of Hood's failure. Johnston, now with an even weaker army than before, faced the task of stopping Sherman's advance through the Carolinas.[68]

When Hood returned to Richmond, he found that the city that once had acclaimed him as a hero now ignored him. Senator Wigfall later commented on Hood's career: "That young man had a fine career before him until Davis undertook to make him what the good Lord had not done—to make a great general of him. He had thus ruined Hood and destroyed the last hope of the Southern Confederacy."[69]

Mrs. Chesnut remained a friend but noticed how the war had affected Hood's appearance. "His face speaks of wakeful nights and nerves strung to their utmost tension by anxiety," Chesnut wrote in her diary. He spoke plainly of his defeat and said he had nobody to blame but himself.[70]

On February 7, the *Constitutionalist* published an article that placed the blame for the destruction of the Army of Tennessee on General William

Hardee for his failure during Hood's assaults in July 1864. Hood did nothing to correct that supposition. When Hardee learned of the article, he immediately wrote to Hood saying that he believed it had been written with his approval and asked if his impression was correct. Hood replied that if he wanted to know who had written the article and the rationale for its content, he should contact the paper that had published it. The two generals corresponded but did not reach a conclusion. Each believed he had had the last word.[71]

Hood also had trouble with another Confederate general. On April 1, Johnston notified President Davis's office that he had read Hood's report on the Atlanta Campaign and was going to prefer charges against him as soon as he could find time. In his report to Davis, Hood had blamed Johnston for the catastrophes that befell the army when he took it over. Johnston's actions, Hood said, had demoralized the army to such an extent that it had never regained completely its old fight and spirit.[72]

On the way to Richmond, Hood stopped in South Carolina to see Buck. Although depressed by his defeat in Tennessee, he still hoped to marry her. When Hood arrived, he encountered a wall of opposition from her family. His visit convinced him that their romance was finished.

On May 31, accompanied by two members of his staff, Hood surrendered to federal officials in Natchez and was paroled. For him, at last, the war was over. The cause he loved was lost, and he was overwhelmed with humiliation at the failure of his leadership.

When Hood returned to Texas, his outlook brightened. He was welcomed by people who knew him from before the war and those who knew him as the commander of the Texas Brigade. His arrival was hailed by a San Antonio paper that stated, "[I]t does our heart good to welcome him back . . . this truly great, good and gallant officer, soldier, and gentleman." Hood's old friends helped ease the pain of failure and defeat.[73]

In the winter of 1865 to 1866, Hood moved to New Orleans. He borrowed $250 from each of forty friends in Kentucky, planning to go into business in Crescent City. Hood lived in New Orleans for the rest of his life but was frequently absent from the city, traveling either for business or pleasure. Hood became a cotton factor and commission merchant, buying and selling cotton and other goods for a profit. After an unsuccessful venture, Hood went into the insurance business, selling policies and managing the Louisiana investments of the Life Association of America.[74]

On April 13, 1868, Hood married Anna Marie Hennen, the only daughter of a prominent Louisiana Catholic family. An eyewitness to the wedding noted that "it was a touching sight to see the tall slender form of the maimed soldier move slowly up, by help of crutches, to the altar rail, where he knelt with the poorest and humblest to partake of the most solemn rite of his faith, the Communion."[75]

Some time after their marriage, Hood, his wife, and his mother-in-law moved to a larger house that would be their home until 1879. In the eleven years of their marriage, the Hoods had eleven children—eight girls and three boys, including three sets of twins. Their last child, Anna Gertrude, was born just a few weeks before the deaths of Hood and his wife. When the family traveled, tradition has it that they were known as "Hood's Brigade," and it was sometimes necessary to telegraph ahead for milk.[76]

Hood was active in veterans' organizations, serving as president of the Southern Hospital Association of New Orleans, an organization established to care for "diseased and maimed soldiers." He was vice president of the Louisiana Branch of the Southern Historical Society and was also active in both the Association of the Army of Northern Virginia and the Louisiana Division of the Army of Tennessee. From time to time, he was invited to speak to various veterans' groups.[77]

In 1874, Johnston's book, *Narrative of Military Operations Directed During the Late War Between the States*, depicted Hood as an incompetent officer whose errors were largely responsible for the loss of northern Georgia. Johnston stated that Hood had often proposed impractical plans, took unnecessary chances in battle, lied, and had been a handicap to the effort to stop Sherman. As Hood read these comments, he was determined to write a "Reply to General Johnston" to present his side of the dispute.[78]

In 1875, Hood's ego received another setback when William Sherman published his memoirs. Although not as harsh as Johnston's book, it did not paint a favorable impression of Hood's actions at Atlanta. Sherman said that Hood was "rash" and had "played into our hands perfectly" by marching into Tennessee and leaving the main Union force free to march across Georgia.[79]

Sherman's memoirs encouraged Hood to broaden the scope of his own work. He decided to write an account of the siege of Atlanta and his battles in Tennessee to add to the "Reply to General Johnston." The major theme of the second part of his memoirs was an effort to shift the blame for failure in the campaign onto others—Johnston, Hardee, and Cheatham.

In 1878, Hood suffered a series of financial reversals, many of which were connected with an outbreak of yellow fever that brought his business activity to a halt. To offset his business losses, Hood tried to sell the federal government the letters and other historic papers that he had collected while working on his memoirs. For the documents, he was hoping to receive $12,500, but the sale had to wait for the appropriation of funds by Congress. Unfortunately, Hood never lived to receive the money.

Yellow fever attacked New Orleans again during the summer of 1879. Hood's wife died first, the eldest child next, and then Hood himself. His death left his children destitute. The maimed hero of the Confederacy, who had survived the shot and shell of war, had at last succumbed to a mosquito.[80]

Hood's friends decided on a quick and quiet funeral. Only a few former comrades-in-arms followed his casket from Trinity Episcopal Church to

Lafayette Cemetery the afternoon after his death. The presence of a detachment of a local company added a military touch to his last rites.[81]

Hood's memory would live on, thanks largely to his friend and comrade in arms, General P. G. T. Beauregard. Seeing the plight of Hood's children, Beauregard organized the Hood Orphan Memorial Publication Fund and took subscriptions for the publication of Hood's memoirs with profits to go to the children's support. Titled *Advance and Retreat*, it was an angry and bitter book that made no friends of former enemies.[82]

John Bell Hood had a reputation for being a fierce and dependable leader, proving to be a fine combat leader whose bravery inspired his men. Hood's Texas Brigade became renowned as one of the Confederate's toughest fighting units. As Hood was promoted up the chain of command, where combat leadership and courage were not as important, his deficiencies as an army commander became more apparent. These deficiencies were compounded by the injuries he had received earlier in combat. A writer for the *Clark County Democrat*, a Kentucky paper, summed it up best: Hood was a man "born and bred to be a soldier" who "had no aptitude for any other pursuit." It was Hood's tragedy that he was such "an excellent soldier but such a poor general."[83]

15 John C. Breckinridge

Statesman and Soldier of the Confederacy

On September 18, 1861, after months of debate over secession, the Kentucky legislature ended neutrality and took the side of the Union. Immediately, without the benefit of warrants or writ of habeas corpus, the arrests began; among the first arrested was the former governor of Kentucky, Charles Morehead. At the same time, freedom of speech was suppressed when the pro-Southern Louisville *Courier* was shut down. On the same day as these events occurred, Senator John Breckinridge received information that he was to be arrested. He quickly made preparation to leave Lexington. It was either escape to freedom or suffer arrest and indefinite imprisonment. After embracing his mother and whispering a few words of regrets to her, Breckinridge bid her farewell. She sensed that this parting might be the last time she would ever see her only son.[1]

Despite what federal authorities thought of Breckinridge's political views, he had been a strong Unionist until he was forced to flee his native state; he never supported secession. Breckinridge had fought for compromise, seeking peace and moderation, but he had failed in both. His closest friends would later testify that Breckinridge never intended to go South. He did so only because the government had ordered his arrest.[2]

Breckinridge's pride was deeply wounded; he had done what he considered to be his duty—he was not a traitor. He had served his country well as a soldier, a senator, and, at the age of thirty-five, the youngest vice president in American history. For now, it appeared all he could do was to commit his allegiance to the Confederacy. Breckinridge had never been able to play a passive role in any conflict, and he would not in this situation. Later, he claimed that the decision he made that day would be one he would regret for the rest of his life.[3]

John Cabell Breckinridge was born at "Cabell's Dale," near Lexington, Kentucky, on January 15, 1821, to Mary Clay and Cabell Breckinridge. He was the fourth of five children, and the only boy born to the Breckinridges. John's parents were devout Presbyterians whose ancestors had played an important role in the formation and development of the United States. This legacy of service was passed on to John and his sisters. Cabell remained active in politics even after he left the state legislature and until his health began to deteriorate in 1823. By the fall, his constitution was so weakened that he fell victim to a raging fever that swept Lexington. By September, after a violent illness of little more than a week, John's father died.[4]

Cabell's death left his family with a debt of $15,000. To ease her burden, Mary sent John to live with his aunt for a short time. Soon afterward, John and his family moved in with relatives at Cabell's Dale. It was here that young John developed a respect for authority and his passion for history. The religious Breckinridges tutored John in the Bible and church dogma, while his mother taught him to read and write. When John was ten, he attended Kentucky Academy, a church boarding school, where he received a standard classical education.[5]

By the fall of 1834, John was ready to enter the freshman class at Danville's Centre College, where the curriculum was also based on the classics. During his four years at Centre, John made a lasting impression on the faculty and his fellow students. One classmate later wrote that he was highly advanced for his "brilliancy of parts, readiness of wit, a happy force, and luxuriance of imagination, acuteness of argument, and felicity of expression, as a gentleman, scholar, statesman or companion," and no one could be compared to him. Four years later, Breckinridge received his bachelor of arts degree in a graduating class of fourteen. Afterward, he spent six months at Princeton as a resident graduate student preparing to study law; however, he did not receive a degree.[6]

Later, Breckinridge read law under Judge William Owsley. He applied himself to the study, spending seven hours a day reading the law, then an additional three hours reading history and literature. After completing his studies with Owsley, Breckinridge augmented his training by spending a year in the law department at Transylvania University in Lexington. Finally in February 1841, he graduated, receiving his LLB degree, and was admitted to the Kentucky bar. He then hung out his shingle in Frankfort, Kentucky, and began his practice.[7]

By 1845, he had moved to Lexington, which enabled him to build up a good practice and to live comfortably. Like his father, he soon became involved in politics and, similarly, became a giant in the field.

Breckinridge was also a big man physically. Standing over six feet in height, his jet-black hair and long mustache gave him a commanding presence. His crisp voice marked him as one destined to lead. His forceful,

The strain of defeat, disunion, and insult and accusation wrought a grimness to the face of John C.
Breckinridge. Before the end of 1861, he donned
the gray of the Confederacy.

magnetic personality quickly drew people to him, while his natural gift for
oratory enhanced his chances for success in politics.[8]

Breckinridge's appearance and personal qualities not only increased his
chances for political success but also made him appealing to members of
the opposite sex. During the spring of 1843, he met and fell in love with
pretty, seventeen-year-old Mary Cyrene Burch. The courtship was a fast
one, and, by September, they were married, taking up residence in nearby
Georgetown, Kentucky. The couple enjoyed a happy marriage and had
four children.

Even though Breckinridge had a brisk law practice, he still took time to
stay involved in politics. In the 1844 presidential election, he supported
the successful candidacy of James K. Polk of Tennessee. From the start,
Breckinridge plunged into the campaign, traveling about the state, making
speeches, and engaging in debates. He supported Polk's position on the

annexation of Texas and the expansion of U.S. borders. The exposure he gained and the political contacts he made while on the stump provided him with a base of support that he could later call on when he ran for office.[9]

On May 13, 1846, the United States went to war with Mexico. The war was popular in the West because it provided the promise of territorial expansion and greater power for the proslavery Democrats in Washington. Although in favor of Polk's policy toward Mexico, Breckinridge did not feel compelled to join the army; however, he did not remain a civilian for long.

In July 1847, Kentucky soldiers killed in Mexico were returned to Frankfort for a military funeral. Because of his reputation as an eloquent speaker, Breckinridge was selected to deliver the funeral oration. In the presence of a crowd of 20,000, he gave such an inspirational speech that the citizens demanded that he be made an officer in the army. The demand was met, and Breckinridge was commissioned as a major in the Third Kentucky Volunteers. Under his leadership, the regiment was sent to Mexico, but it saw no military action. Breckinridge's only notable action in Mexico was his legal defense of Major General Gideon Pillow, who had been charged with making false accusations against General Winfield Scott. Pillow was acquitted.[10]

After the war, Breckinridge returned to Lexington to continue his practice of law. Early in 1849, he ran for the state legislature and was elected to represent Fayette County.

In the fall of 1850, Henry Clay, now seventy-three, returned home to Lexington. A committee was selected to make preparations to honor him, and Breckinridge was elected to deliver the welcoming speech. Clay was so visibly moved by Breckinridge's testimonial that, in his impromptu thank-you speech, Clay praised Breckinridge. For many, this praise was construed to be Clay's endorsement of Breckinridge.[11]

The Democrats of Fayette moved quickly on Clay's endorsement. In the 1851 election, Breckinridge ran for Congress on the Democratic ticket. Despite Henry Clay's endorsement, Breckinridge was a clear underdog in the race. The Whig Party enjoyed a safe 1,500 majority out of a voting population of 11,000, and, to many, their advantage seemed insurmountable. During the last forty years, only two Democrats had won a seat.[12]

Breckinridge approached his campaign with enthusiasm, speaking daily for five and six weeks at a time without a break. His hard work paid off. He accomplished what had seemed impossible, luring over 1,000 Whig voters from his opponent and winning the race by 537 votes.[13]

During Breckinridge's first term in Congress, he increased his proslavery and states' rights leanings, opposing measures that would strengthen the federal government. In 1853, the Whigs ran the popular ex-governor, Robert Letcher, against Breckinridge. Just before the campaign, however,

Breckinridge delivered an inspiring elegy at the funeral for Henry Clay. As a result, Breckinridge suddenly became the most popular man in Kentucky. In November, Breckinridge was re-elected to Congress where he continued to take a strong position against the abolition of slavery and for states' rights.[14]

In 1856, Breckinridge's excellent record in Congress earned him the vice-presidential nomination on the James Buchanan ticket. Breckinridge was the perfect candidate to balance the Democratic ticket. He was a Southerner with great public appeal, and he had served two terms in Congress. "Buck" and "Breck," as the two candidates were labeled, were different in almost every respect. Although both were tall and dignified, Buchanan was stouter and nearly twice as old as Breckinridge. Breckinridge was vibrant; his presence, stimulating. Buchanan, on the other hand, was mediocre both in personality and character and gave the impression that he was older than his sixty-five years.[15]

Their differences reached beyond manner and appearance. Buchanan was often petty and standoffish; Breckinridge made friends easily. Buchanan held grudges against those that opposed him politically; Breckinridge had actually opposed Buchanan during the proceedings at the convention. Now they were running on the same ticket. It was unlikely that the two would become friends.[16]

Breckinridge dived into the rigors of the campaign with his usual energy. The Democratic platform stood for "cessation of further agitation over slavery, upholding the Compromise of 1850, and Popular Sovereignty." In November, the "Buck" and "Breck" ticket gained a victory over the Republican candidate, John Frémont. Breckinridge carried his home state for the Democrats by 6,000 votes. At the age of thirty-five, he was the youngest man ever to hold the vice presidency.[17]

As vice president of the United States, Breckinridge carried out his duties with honor and diligence. Even his political enemies had to admit that he had displayed great poise and fairness as president of the Senate, in spite of his sectional feelings. Breckinridge's popularity in Kentucky had reached such a level that in September 1859, more than a year before his term as vice president was to expire, the state elected him to the Senate for the term beginning March 4, 1861.[18]

As 1860 began, the issue facing the nation was union or disunion, war or peace. One hope still remained for the South—the election of a Democratic president. If a candidate who appealed to all factions of the party could be found, there was a chance he could defeat the Republicans. If a Republican candidate were to be elected, it was likely that the Southern states would secede.[19]

On April 23, the Democratic Convention met in Charleston, South Carolina. When the voting for the presidential nomination began, it became clear that neither the frontrunner, Stephen Douglas, nor anyone else would gain the two-thirds necessary for nomination. After fifty-seven ballots and no agreement on a candidate, the convention was adjourned until June 18, when they would try again in Baltimore. Breckinridge was acutely aware of the problem facing the South, writing: "The proceedings at Charleston threaten great calamities, unless there is wisdom and forbearance enough to redeem errors, at Baltimore."[20]

When the convention met in Baltimore, the party could not agree on the platform. As a result, Southerners walked out, and the 110 delegates that remained set up their own rump convention. With so many of the opposition delegates gone, Stephen Douglas easily received the two-thirds necessary of those present for the nomination. The Southern Democrats' choice for their candidate was Breckinridge, but he refused to allow his name to be put forth at the convention. Nevertheless, he was nominated on a platform that called for the federal government to "protect the rights of persons and property in the territories and wherever else the Constitution authority extended." Breckinridge declined the honor.[21]

The problem of who would oppose the Republican candidate was further complicated when a faction of Whigs chose John Bell of Tennessee as their standard-bearer. Realizing that a split in the Democratic Party would guarantee a Republican victory, Mississippi Senator Jefferson Davis suggested a last attempt at compromise. He proposed that Breckinridge accept the nomination, hoping Douglas would realize that, with a split in the party, his chance for election was near impossible. With this tactic, all three candidates would step down and allow a compromise candidate to be selected, one that the entire party could support. The plan was reasonable; both Bell and Breckinridge agreed, but Douglas did not. Douglas's refusal to participate in Davis's compromise left three candidates in the field to oppose the Republicans.[22]

By accepting the nomination, Breckinridge became the candidate of the Democratic splinter faction most closely associated with secession, although he himself did not support secession. Favoring compromise over disunion, he proposed a plan that would permit slavery in the territories south of latitude 36° 30', noninterference by Congress with slavery where it existed, and compensation to owners of fugitive slaves. To the very end, Breckinridge hoped for a compromise between the sections of the country: "I am an American citizen, a Kentuckian, who never did an act or cherished a thought that was not full of devotion to the Constitution and the Union." Breckinridge insisted that the Democratic Party was a Constitutional party; however, throughout the campaign, his opponents accused him of favoring secession and of being anti-Union.[23]

As predicted, the split in the Democratic Party resulted in a victory for the Republican Abraham Lincoln. Although Breckinridge lost his home state to the Constitutional Unionist John Bell, he carried eleven of the fifteen slave states and won 72 electoral votes to 39 for Bell and 12 for

Stephen Douglas. Abraham Lincoln, however, received sufficient electoral votes for a clear majority.[24]

As vice president, Breckinridge was responsible for counting the electoral votes before the Senate. Some believed he might try to juggle or lose some of the votes for Lincoln, but Breckinridge conducted himself with "scrupulous fidelity." When the votes were counted, he announced that "Abraham Lincoln, of Illinois, . . . is elected President of the United States."[25]

After Lincoln's inauguration, Breckinridge returned to Kentucky and continued his campaign for compromise right up to the attack on Fort Sumter. With the outbreak of the war, Kentucky declared itself neutral and demanded that both armies not cross her borders. Although Breckinridge disapproved of Kentucky's course of action, he went along with the will of the legislature.

In July 1861, Breckinridge returned to Washington to take his seat in the Senate for a special session of Congress called by Lincoln. He spoke against Lincoln's calling out of 75,000 troops, stating that it was this call to arms that had precipitated the war and the firing on Fort Sumter. He denounced Lincoln's forceful acts on the eve of the war as illegal: raising troops without congressional consent, blockading the South, suspending habeas corpus, and ordering unlawful searches and seizures.[26]

Throughout his brief stay in the Senate, Breckinridge continued to attack Lincoln and to identify himself more closely with the Southern cause. He was thought by many in Washington to be subverting the Union and aiding the Confederacy. Senator Baker of Oregon even went so far as to accuse Breckinridge of treason. Because of Breckinridge's opposition to Lincoln and his administration and what appeared to be his aiding of the Confederacy, the Kentucky legislature passed a resolution asking him to resign his seat in the Senate. By then, Breckinridge had fled to the South and joined the Confederacy in its fight. In December, Breckinridge was officially expelled from the Senate and declared a traitor.[27]

On October 8, 1861, Breckinridge gave his last address as a Senator representing Kentucky and the first as a Confederate. It was in the form of an open letter, which was widely published throughout the North and South. In it, he defended the position he had taken against Lincoln's administration stating that "I would have blushed to meet you with the confession that I had purchased for you exemption from the perils of the battlefield and the shame of waging war against your Southern brethren by hiring others to do the work you shrank from performing." "I resign," he said, "because there is no place left where a Southern Senator may sit in council with the Senators of the North. In truth there is no longer a Senate of the United States within the meaning and spirit of the Constitution."[28]

On November 2, Breckinridge was commissioned a brigadier general in the Confederate army. His goal was to bring Kentucky into the Confederacy.

To do this, he formed the Confederate Provisional Government of Kentucky. By the middle of November, he was assigned command of the First Kentucky Brigade, a part of General Simon B. Buckner's division in the Central Army of Kentucky.

Breckinridge's brigade was composed entirely of volunteers from a state still in the Union. The men had enlisted entirely on their own, under no duress, simply because they believed in the Southern cause. Most of the men had volunteered for the full duration of the war rather than the standard twelve months common for most organizations in 1861. Breckinridge quickly gained the respect and admiration of his brigade; the connection between Breckinridge and his men was one of the closest of any during the war. For the next two years, they would share the ordeals of war with him.[29]

By February 1862, Breckinridge was assigned command of the reserve corps of General Albert S. Johnston's army. There may have been some concern about giving this assignment to him. Of the high command of the Western army—Johnston, Beauregard, Bragg, Hardee, and Polk—Breckinridge was the only one with no formal military training and the only one who had not been tested in combat. Despite Breckinridge's lack of experience, Johnston had a high respect for his talents, and, more importantly, he wanted Kentucky on the Confederate's side; Breckinridge could play a key part in that effort.[30]

In April, Breckinridge's reserve corps saw action at Shiloh. On the first day he personally led his men in an all-out charge that drove back the Federals' left flank. On the second day, Grant was able to rally his forces and turn what seemed to be a defeat into a victory. After the battle, Breckinridge's corps covered the withdrawal of Johnston's army. The losses in Breckinridge's corps indicated the brutal fighting in which he was engaged. Approximately 35 percent of his corps engaged on April 6 were listed as casualties. Breckinridge had proven himself to be an able and courageous leader, willing to take part in the battle from the front of the line in the hottest part of the field. During the battle, Breckinridge was hit twice by spent bullets, and the holes in his uniform attested to the number of near misses.[31]

Breckinridge's efforts did not go unnoticed. General Beauregard, who now commanded the army after Johnston's death at Shiloh, expressed his satisfaction with Breckinridge's service. "There is not a nobler soul," he said. "The Kentuckian displayed great aptitude and sagacity, and handled his brigade with skill and judgment." Breckinridge had clearly made a name for himself at Shiloh, showing that in battle, as on the stump, he was a born leader. On April 18, Breckinridge was nominated by President Jefferson Davis for promotion to major general.[32]

After Shiloh, Breckinridge was assigned to central Mississippi. During the summer of 1862, he was ordered to capture Baton Rouge. This proved to be the worst time of the year for campaigning. Illness due to the heat, malaria, and "camp fever" claimed hundreds on the march. For the campaign, Breckinridge's division was reduced to barely 4,000 men. Although Breckinridge was opposed to the move, he followed orders. The fifty-mile march became a nightmare as hundreds of his troops fell along the way. "Almost every farm house on the roadside was converted into a hospital," wrote a reporter from the Chattanooga *Rebel*. Against a superior Union force at Baton Rouge numbering 5,000, and three gunboats to back them up, Breckinridge's attack was doomed to failure from the start.[33]

With his force now reduced to 3,000 men, Breckinridge personally led the attack. "His presence had a magical effect upon the men. There was no danger he did not share with them," wrote a witness to the battle. Although Breckinridge's troops fought valiantly, they were forced to withdraw. Both sides claimed victory. The next day, Breckinridge issued a congratulatory statement to his troops, ascribing their failure to the lack of naval support he had requested. Although the attack on Baton Rouge had not been successful, Breckinridge's troops were able to occupy Port Hudson. By taking this strategic point, the Confederacy now had control over a 130-mile stretch from Port Hudson to Vicksburg.[34]

Breckinridge returned to the Vicksburg area and participated in General Joseph E. Johnston's efforts to relieve the city. He joined General Braxton Bragg and the Army of Tennessee in time to take part in the Battle of Murfreesboro (Stone's River) in January 1863, commanding a division that included his old Kentucky brigade. In an attack ordered by Bragg, which Breckinridge disapproved of, his division suffered heavy losses. When Breckinridge looked at the remnant of his Kentucky brigade, he cried, "My poor orphans! My poor orphans!" From then on, the Kentuckians became known as the "Orphan Brigade." The destruction of Breckinridge's division was the price that had to be paid to prove to Bragg that the attack was a mistake. Behind him on the field lay over 1,500 casualties, 35 percent of the attacking force. The battle had lasted less than an hour, with the major part of the division's casualties occurring in just fifteen minutes.[35]

The Southern press was also critical of Bragg's battle decision. One, the Chattanooga *Daily Rebel*, charged that Bragg ordered the retreat from Murfreesboro against the advice of his generals. On January 11, hoping to clear up the matter, Bragg drafted a letter to his corps and division commanders asking their opinion on whether or not the army had lost confidence in him. In one letter, he invited them to be "candid" in their response; Breckinridge's response, however, was more candid than Bragg had anticipated. He noted that he had consulted his brigadiers, and "they requested me to say that while they entertain the highest respect for your patriotism, it is their opinion that you do not possess the confidence of the army to the extent which will enable you to be useful as its commander. In this opinion, I feel bound to concur."[36]

Breckinridge's division had performed magnificently at Stone's River despite their heavy losses. When Bragg later made unwarranted criticism of the division's performance in his report to Richmond, Breckinridge was tempted to challenge him to a duel. He held back, however, enduring the insult for the good of the cause and, at the same time, consoling his men that, after the war, there might be an accounting with Bragg.[37]

It was clear that Bragg and Breckinridge were at war with each other. In his response to Bragg's report, Breckinridge charged that Bragg was guilty of omitting pertinent facts and distorting others. He told General Samuel Cooper, adjutant general, "that failure of my troops to hold the position which they carried on that occasion was due to no fault of theirs or mine, but to the fact we were commanded to do an impossible thing." In view of all that had happened, Breckinridge requested that General Cooper convene a court of inquiry to investigate Bragg's charges. For a time, reports from both sides were published in newspapers, but, by late May, Breckinridge discontinued his part in the dispute, content to await a court hearing that never came. In time, Breckinridge would be vindicated. After Bragg's failure at Perryville, the tide of public opinion turned drastically against him.[38]

In August 1863, Breckinridge was ordered north to Chattanooga where he took part in the Battle of Chickamauga. On the morning of the second day of the battle, Breckinridge's division was able to get behind Union General Rosecrans's line; however, Bragg was unable to exploit the advantage, and Breckinridge was forced to retire. Afterward, when the Confederates were overrun, Bragg blamed Breckinridge, accusing him of having been drunk during the battle. Although Breckinridge did have a reputation of being able to outride and outdrink any man in Kentucky, there was no substance to Bragg's accusation, and Confederate leaders had learned to discount Bragg's frequent complaints and accusations.[39]

At the Battle of Chattanooga, Breckinridge was assigned command of Lieutenant General D. H. Hill's corps on Missionary Ridge. When Union forces under Major General George Thomas attacked Breckinridge's line, his troops fled. Although Breckinridge was blamed for the loss of Chattanooga, he made no excuses for the rout. Breckinridge was troubled by what happened at Missionary Ridge: "I have asked myself more than once tonight, 'are you the same man who stood gazing down on the faces of the dead on that awful battlefield? The soldiers lying there, they stare at you with their eyes wide open. Is this the same world?'"[40]

The feud between Bragg and Breckinridge continued. On December 15, Bragg relieved Breckinridge from duty, charging him with "unfitness throughout the army's retreat." He was replaced with Major General Thomas Hindman. Being relieved of duty was, although not entirely his fault, an embarrassing situation for Breckinridge. Guilty or not, such a disaster required a change in command.

On December 7, 1863, Breckinridge was surprised to read in the *New York Times* that he had been killed in action at Chattanooga. It became clear to Breckinridge that some in the North were happy about his demise, despite the service he had rendered to the nation earlier. "If it be true," said the *Times*, "that a loyal bullet has sent this traitor to eternity, every loyal heart feels satisfaction and will not scruple to express it." Usually the death of an enemy during the war brought sympathy from his adversary. Not so for Breckinridge. "God grant the country a speedy delivery of all such parricides," continued the article.[41]

In February 1864, Breckinridge was reassigned as commander of the Department of Southwestern Virginia. Breckinridge had to build his command from scratch, and on May 15, 1864, he had his first battle. He engaged Union Major General Franz Sigel, who was advancing up the Shenandoah Valley near New Market. With the aid of the cadets from the Virginia Military Institute, he defeated Sigel's larger force at New Market. It was perhaps Breckinridge's finest performance of the war.

Breckinridge quickly gained the admiration and respect of his troops as well as those of Robert E. Lee. Lee was overjoyed at Breckinridge's success in the valley; in just one stroke, he had eliminated the dangerous threat to Lee's flank. The wheat crop, so important to Lee's army, had been saved. The South was anxious to find another "Stonewall" to replace Jackson who had died a year earlier. For a time, Breckinridge filled that role in the valley.[42]

Breckinridge did not stay in the valley long. When Lee ordered him to join his forces at Cold Harbor, rumors spread that Breckinridge was soon to be a corps commander. Two of Lee's three corps were being temporarily led by Generals Richard Anderson and Richard Ewell. Breckinridge was senior to both generals, and had he been attached to the Army of Northern Virginia, it is likely he would have been given one of those commands. Since his division was still a separate organization, he was not in line for the promotion.[43]

At Cold Harbor, Breckinridge helped to check General Ulysses S. Grant's attacks. Lee sent his compliments to Breckinridge on the "gallant manner" in which he repelled the repeated Union assaults. During the battle, Breckinridge's horse was shot from under him; the horse fell on top of him, pinning him to the ground. As a result, his leg was badly bruised, and he was not able to ride for several weeks.

While recuperating from his injury, Breckinridge was ordered back to the Shenandoah Valley to check a new threat by Major General David Hunter. Serving under General Jubal Early in Maryland, Breckinridge distinguished himself at the Battle of Monocacy.

During the Maryland campaign, Breckinridge stopped long enough to perform an act of kindness. His friend and cousin, Montgomery Blair, now federal postmaster general, lived near Silver Spring. Although General Early had sent out orders forbidding plunder or destruction of private property, some of the unruly troops had not followed his instructions. To prevent damage to Blair's house, Breckinridge ordered a guard placed around it and forbade anyone to enter or in any way disturb the property.[44]

After pushing aside Union troops at Monocacy, Early's corps moved toward Washington. It soon became clear that Washington had been reinforced, and "Old Jube" had no choice but to call off the attack. Curious about the battle, Abraham Lincoln had come to the front to observe the scene. It was the only occasion in the history of the United States that two former presidential opponents faced each other across battle lines.[45]

By September, Breckinridge's division was back in the valley again, helping to turn the tide of battle in favor of the Confederates at the Second Battle of Kernstown.

Breckinridge fought his last battle in the valley at Winchester and ended his service with Early. His courage was not enough to stem the tide for the Confederates and the rout of the army. During the battle, Breckinridge appeared to be "desperately reckless." "He literally seemed to court death," said Confederate General John Gordon. When Gordon protested his unnecessary exposure by riding at his side, Breckinridge responded: "Well, general, there is little left for me if our cause is to fail."[46]

After Winchester, Breckinridge resumed command of the Department of East Tennessee. During the winter of 1864 and 1865, Breckinridge spent his time trying to drive Union forces from the area while rebuilding his department. Throughout the Confederacy, though, the breakdown in morale was paramount. Soldiers and civilians were simply tired of the war.

In Richmond, those tired of the war included Secretary of War Seddon, who was also weary of the criticism heaped upon him for the Confederate failures. In January 1865, the Confederate Congress placed pressure on Jefferson Davis to replace Seddon. On January 19, faced with humiliation, Seddon resigned. By February, it was generally accepted that the days of the Confederacy were numbered, but on February 4, Breckinridge was appointed secretary of war. Breckinridge had stayed out of politics while in the army and had gained the respect of virtually every faction in the government and the military, except for Bragg.[47]

Breckinridge took firm control of the War Department, effecting immediate improvement in its organization and in the movement of food and supplies to the Army of Northern Virginia. He ordered all department commanders to forward to him an honest evaluation of their military situation. In 1861, Breckinridge had doubted that the Confederacy could win the war, and now, from his new position, he soon concluded that the cause was hopeless. As a member of President Davis's cabinet, he worked to bring the struggle to an honorable ending, which, in his opinion, rejected guerrilla warfare. "This has been a magnificent epic," he said. "In God's name let it not terminate in a farce."[48]

In early April, when it became apparent that the end of the Confederacy was near, Breckinridge organized the evacuation of President Davis and his cabinet from Richmond. After seeing to the safe removal of the treasury and the government's vital records, he ordered all bridges on the James

River destroyed, as well as any other vital materials that might fall into the hands of the advancing Federal troops.[49]

After Davis left Richmond, Breckinridge, alone of the high officials, remained to oversee the rest of the evacuation. Finally, after meeting with Lee, Breckinridge headed south to join Johnston's army and the rest of the Confederate cabinet. On April 12, he arrived in Greensboro, bringing more details of Lee's surrender. After meeting with Generals Johnston and Beauregard during the night, Breckinridge agreed with them that further resistance would be aimless; however, there was still the matter of convincing Jefferson Davis that the time had come to end the war.

In late April, Breckinridge took part in the negotiations involved in Johnston's surrender to Major General William Sherman. Sherman was anxious to end the war and avoid the danger of continued guerrilla warfare with what he called "one single stroke of the pen." Davis was being difficult about ending the war, but Breckinridge was a realist and helped to persuade Davis to sign the agreement of surrender worked out by the generals. Immediately after Johnston's surrender, Breckinridge left for Washington, Georgia, to attend the last cabinet meeting.[50]

After meeting with the cabinet, Breckinridge led a party of forty-five men in a diversion to help with President Davis's escape. With Davis's departure, Breckinridge was now the commander-in-chief of all Confederate forces in the field and the only remaining officer of the Confederate government.

Breckinridge was now a wanted man. In January, the General Assembly in Federal-occupied Tennessee issued a resolution that Breckinridge, Davis, and others should be executed when caught. Lincoln considered Breckinridge to be an even bigger traitor than Robert E. Lee. As he traveled south, Breckinridge was denounced as a traitor in the Northern press, and a trial date was set for him and Davis. "The Davises, the Benjamins, and the Breckinridges," said the *New York Times*, "should die the most disgraceful death known to our civilization—death on the Gallows."[51]

Traveling as "Colonel Cabell," Breckinridge made his way on horseback until he was able to obtain a boat and escape to Cuba. His last official act was to tell his remaining detachment to surrender immediately and not to jeopardize their own safety for his sake.[52]

In July, Breckinridge sailed from Havana to England. From there he went to Canada to join his family. While in Canada, a movement was already under way in the United States to have him pardoned, or at least to allow him to return to Kentucky. When the pardon did not come, he and his family were forced to bide their time in Canada. In the spring of 1866, Breckinridge and his family moved to Niagara, Ontario, just across the Niagara River from New York. It was Breckinridge's love of his country that brought him there. "I could see it [Stars and Stripes] over the river which I might not cross," he said, "and there the first thing in the morning and last thing at night I watched it, and longed for it with a hunger few men may comprehend."[53]

On Christmas Day 1868, President Andrew Johnson issued his Universal Amnesty Proclamation, which removed all charges against the exiled Confederates. In the spring of 1869, Breckinridge returned to his beloved Lexington.

Once back in Kentucky, there was speculation that Breckinridge would again assume an important part in the nation's politics. Strange as it may seem, Breckinridge was now the most popular man in the state and could have had any elective office he wanted. He, however, declined to reenter politics, even at the urging of the now President Ulysses Grant for him to seek the governorship. Rather, Breckinridge accepted a position as vice president of the Lexington & Big Sandy Railroad.[54]

Life for Breckinridge settled down to a normal pace. He had only hope for the future; his position on Reconstruction was one of reconciliation. He would not dwell on the past and old hatreds. They must be forgotten.

In October 1870, when Robert E. Lee died, Breckinridge was asked to address citizens in Louisville. From the beginning to the end, his speech on Lee had but one theme—reunion. His eulogy was hardly conventional. He did not speak of Lee's glorious war record; rather, he used the occasion to express his hope and faith in the reconciliation of the nation, a hope that he and Lee had shared. Later, Breckinridge was appointed president of the Lee Memorial Association.[55]

In the fall of 1873, Breckinridge became ill, his friends noticing a decided change in his health. He was never well again. In March 1874, Breckinridge went to Arkansas, hoping a change in climate might do him some good. It did not. A month later in Lexington, his health took a sudden change for the worse. Again he rallied, but only slightly so. By the end of 1874, his lungs, which had hemorrhaged earlier, gave him no peace. Finally, on May 17, 1875, after a serious liver operation, Breckinridge died. He was only fifty-four years old.[56]

All of Kentucky went into mourning. Despite his wishes for a quiet funeral, the demonstrations on his behalf were enormous. A massive mile-long procession followed his remains to the cemetery in Lexington.

Breckinridge excelled in every field he entered. He was not only a leading statesman and soldier but also a man of honor, who became a symbol of peaceful reconciliation after the war. Just as he had hoped for the nation to unite, it did so to grieve his death. Only ten years earlier, Northern papers had sought his capture and immediate death. Now, one wrote: "Our country mourns from St. Paul to New Orleans, and from New York to San Francisco. There is no North and no South."[57]

16 Leonidas Polk

"The Fighting Bishop"

When Leonidas Polk put on the uniform of a Confederate major general, he outraged the secular and religious press in the North. How could the Episcopal Bishop of Louisiana, a priest of God, contribute to the death of innocent youth? It was the first time an American bishop had entered the military service, although the practice did exist during the Middle Ages. The event should not have been as surprising as it first appeared. After all, Polk had come from a family with a heritage of political and military leadership. Both his grandfather and father had served in the army during the Revolutionary War. He himself had attended West Point, where his roommate was Albert Sidney Johnston and fellow cadets were Robert E. Lee and Jefferson Davis. Earlier, he had shattered his father's hopes by giving up a military career for the Christian ministry.[1]

At West Point, Polk was the first cadet to be baptized publicly. After his public acceptance of Christ, an awakening swept the corps, with Leonidas being the first to kneel in the chapel. He surprised his father and fellow cadets by becoming the leader of a "praying platoon." Three months after graduating from West Point in 1827, Leonidas resigned from the army to enter Virginia Theological Seminary.[2]

The Polks arrived in America from Ireland in the late 1600s and by the middle of the eighteenth century were well established in North Carolina. The Revolutionary careers of Thomas Polk and his son William were distinguished enough to mark them as men of prominence in the new state. By the early 1800s, William Polk had become a man of fortune and family, owning 100,000 acres and numerous slaves. In 1801, William married Sarah Hawkins. Together they would rear twelve children; the fourth, Leonidas, was born on April 10, 1806, in Raleigh. The Hawkinses were politically active and successful, too; Sarah's brother was governor of North Carolina. As a young man, Leonidas had many opportunities open to him for future success.[3]

At the age of fifteen, Leonidas entered the University of North Carolina at Chapel Hill. Because his father hoped that he too would have a military career, Leonidas's stay at the university was a period of preparation for West Point. In 1823, he entered the Academy. Leonidas moved into the barracks in September, where one of his roommates was Albert Sidney Johnston of Kentucky. Johnston was very popular and senior officer of the cadets. It was through him that Polk became friends with Jefferson Davis.[4]

Polk was described by his friends as being full of life, high spirited, and good natured. Although Leonidas took his studies seriously, life at West Point was not all work. Cadet Polk found summer camp life far from "wearisome," making frequent trips to New York and even attending dance school.

It was while at West Point that Polk found religion. At the same time, Dr. Charles McIlvaine was appointed to West Point as a chaplain. Years later, McIlvaine recalled his first meeting with Cadet Polk who came to him for advice. "How must he conduct himself with regard to his feelings about Christianity?" he asked. McIlvaine suggested that he take steps to separate himself from the crowd and take his stand. The next day, Polk was the first cadet ever to kneel during services in the Academy chapel.[5]

The young cadet was aware of the fact that religious devotion was still not popular among his fellow cadets, but Polk's popularity and persuasiveness helped to change their attitude. By the time he graduated, there were other cadets who openly professed their religious faith. Soon a number of cadets were meeting with Chaplain McIlvaine for regular prayer meetings. Forty days after his first meeting with Polk, the chaplain baptized Cadets Leonidas Polk and William Magruder.[6]

In a letter home to his family, Leonidas explained his recent conversion: "This step was my most trying one. To bring myself to renounce all of my former habits and association, to step forward from the whole corps, acknowledging my conviction of the truth of the Holy religion which I had before decried and was now anxious to embrace. . . . I am clearly convinced that the most happy man on earth is, he who practices most faithfully the duties of Christianity."[7]

Leonidas's father and family were not pleased with what they read in his letter. William Polk was a practical businessman who had no time for emotionalism. When Leonidas learned of his father's displeasure at his decision, he wrote back expressing his "deep regret" that he had been "the cause of uneasiness to the family," but he could not control his feelings.[8]

Although clearly considering the ministry, Polk remained at West Point to complete his four years. By the time he graduated, Polk was sure that he would make the church and not the military his career. This was not

In the spring of 1861, President Davis called
Bishop Leonidas Polk to Richmond to offer him a
commission as brigadier general. After a week of
prayer, he reached a decision: "I find my mind
unable to say no to the call, for it seems to be a
call of Providence."

COURTESY OF THE LIBRARY OF CONGRESS

quite the effect the army hoped the chaplain would have on the cadets.
McIlvaine was dismissed by West Point two years later.[9]

On July 4, 1827, Polk graduated eighth out of a class of thirty-eight.
Three months later, Leonidas resigned from the army to enter Virginia
Theological Seminary at Alexandria. In 1830, he was ordained a deacon.

A month later, Polk married his childhood sweetheart, the wealthy
Frances Devereux of Raleigh, North Carolina. Shortly after his marriage,
Polk took an extensive tour of Europe, consulting noted physicians in
hopes of improving his failing health. Polk's doctor, concerned about his
patient's lungs, advised him to seek a life outdoors. Taking his father's
offer of a portion of his 100,000 acres in middle Tennessee, the young
couple moved to Columbia with slaves from the Devereux family.[10]

Polk was troubled by slavery but could never bring himself to support abolition or to give up his own slaves. He believed, however, that it was his duty
to educate his slaves and to prepare them for a gradual emancipation.[11]

At Columbia, the Polks began building Ashwood Hall, a plantation house. Polk also built an Episcopal church for the region and served as its rector. Years later, General Patrick Cleburne described the church as being so beautiful that "it is almost worth dying to be buried in such a place." When Cleburne was killed in the battle near Franklin in 1864, his wish was granted, although his remains were later moved to his hometown.[12]

At Columbia, Polk came under the charge of Bishop James Otey. Together they began the first college for females in 1837. A year later, Bishop Otey nominated Polk to be Missionary Bishop of the Southwest, encompassing a population of a million and a half. This was a high honor for one with such limited experience. His ministry included a conglomeration of dubious candidates for Christianization—Indians, outlaws, and other characters. Polk responded to the call, even though he knew he could not take his family.[13]

Polk's parish included a large Catholic population, and his reception was not always friendly. He was overwhelmed by the magnitude of the job; it would take him two years just to visit all the areas in his parish. In the first tour of the region, according to his son's biography, he "traveled 5,000 miles, preached 44 sermons, baptized 14, confirmed 41, consecrated one church, and laid the cornerstone of another."[14]

In 1841, Polk was appointed permanent Bishop of Louisiana. He purchased a sugar plantation, Leighton, near the town of Thibodaux, hoping he could best serve his parishioners by being part of the economy. Bringing with him 400 slaves to work the plantation, Polk was eager to put into effect his ideas about educating slaves. He started a Sunday school for slaves, seeing himself as an enlightened master.[15]

For several years, life at Leighton moved on in much the same fashion as other sugar plantations. In spite of Polk's frequent absences and his inexperience in the farming of sugar cane, his plantation prospered. Then, disaster struck in 1849. An epidemic of Asiatic cholera struck Leighton, killing a hundred slaves. The bishop himself was stricken while visiting a friend in New Orleans. The death of so many of his slaves was not only a personal loss but a financial one. Weakened and disorganized, the remaining field hands were unable to give the cane crop the proper attention.[16]

Five years later, a tornado and yellow fever completed the task of wiping out Polk's fortune. With Leighton in the hands of creditors, the Polks, now a family of ten, were forced to move to New Orleans. Now that Polk did not have to face the demands of running a plantation, he was able to devote his full attention to his ministry.[17]

Bishop Polk was now in the prime of life, standing over six feet in height with broad shoulders. Physically he was attractive, carrying himself much like a soldier, one born to command. Nevertheless, he was kind and equally effective as counselor and comforter. He always thought of himself as a soldier, both for his country and for his God. "His air of command never left him, yet he was always aware that he himself was under command."[18]

To Polk, living a Christian life was a pleasure, not a task. He disliked the puritanical approach to religion that many Northerners ascribed to, believing a kind smile was more Christian-like than a stern demeanor. "Faith is a charger that carries a man into battle," he said, "but he must fight when he gets there, and then Faith will bear him through the fight."[19]

Polk's ministry in New Orleans was an outstanding success. Religious education had always been a concern of his. While living at Ashwood, he had helped to found the Columbia Institute for Women. Now, there was a great need for an Episcopal university for the South. He believed that such an institution of higher learning would educate the children of slaveholders to take steps that would end slavery. The institution would stand for basic Christian principles with the Bible as its focus. The university would stand above other institutions of higher learning and would provide postgraduate education. Polk's ideas were well ahead of the times.[20]

Polk traveled tirelessly throughout the South trying to raise funds for the university. Land was donated near the town of Sewanee, Tennessee, and he was able to raise more than $500,000 in cash. On October 9, 1860, the cornerstone was laid for the new University of the South.[21]

Before the university could be completed, secession interrupted Polk's plans. Polk was an ardent secessionist, greeting the state's announcement of its departure from the Union with enthusiasm. He even went so far as to add his own contribution to the split by having the Louisiana diocese secede from the Protestant Episcopal Church of the United States. Despite Polk's support of disunion, he did not want to see war. To a friend, he wrote, "I cannot but think and hope that the good sense and Christian feeling of the North will prevail over passion and pride, and that we shall be saved from such a disaster and be permitted to go in peace."[22]

In November 1860, when Abraham Lincoln was elected president and the country was on the verge of breaking apart, Polk still believed war could be averted. In December, he wrote to President James Buchanan, imploring him to do what he could to prevent war. Believing he sensed the feelings of the people of the South, he hoped to furnish this information to the president. "The people of the South wish to prevent the ruthless carnage that would no doubt occur if they were to resort to arms," he wrote. They had resolved to stand upon their rights, he said, and to resist all efforts to infringe upon their rights, regardless of the source. But Polk was talking to the wrong man. Buchanan's term of office was drawing to an end, and he was anxious to leave. He had no idea how to stop the movement toward war.[23]

In the end, neither the North nor the South used "good sense and Christian feeling" as Polk had hoped, and his efforts to secure peace did not materialize. His letter to Buchanan, however, did provide a clue as to how he would later behave during the war. Polk believed he had the right to exercise discretion, despite orders from a superior, and to do whatever seemed best in his opinion, regardless of what his superior might command.[24]

In the spring of 1861, President Davis called Bishop Polk to Richmond to offer him a commission as brigadier general in the Confederate army. Although military and civilian friends urged him to accept, he declined, giving an immediate answer: "What my duties may be, I have not yet determined."[25]

Because of the great importance of his decision, Polk would not act hastily, he told his wife. The following day, he visited with Bishop William Meade, president of the Virginia Theological Seminary, to discuss the situation. Meade explained that as a general rule he did not approve of a member of the clergy accepting a military commission, but since "all rules have exceptions and taking all things into consideration as they relate to the condition of the country," he would not condemn him should he accept a commission.[26]

For a week, Polk thought and prayed over the matter. Finally, he reached a decision. "I find my mind unable to say no to the call, for it seems to be a call of Providence," he said. Polk's reasoning was accompanied by emotion. Although not favoring slavery and predicting its gradual collapse, he loved the South. To him, it was his native land; its principles were his own.[27]

Polk received numerous letters from clergy and laity expressing their disapproval of his decision to enter the military service. Others believed he should wait until the emergency became greater. Most of the correspondence he received, however, approved of his course of action. Finally, in June 1861, Polk accepted the commission of major general, hoping that "God will allow me to get through without delay, that I may return to my chosen and usual work." The cheers he received in the South were met with jeers in the North. Some friends wrote understanding letters, but most of the public outcry in the North was critical.[28]

Although Polk had no military experience since leaving West Point, he did have tremendous persuasiveness and charisma. But by any standard, Polk's military credentials were not impressive; he was barely qualified to serve as a second lieutenant. Nevertheless, President Davis made his friend a major general.[29]

Although accepting the high rank of major general, Polk did not consider it a promotion. When a friend congratulated him, he responded, "I do not consider it a promotion. The highest office on earth is that of the bishop in the Church of God." When another friend showed his surprise, stating "What! You a bishop, throw off the gown for the sword!" Polk replied, "No, sir, I buckle the sword over the gown."[30]

Polk did not resign his position as bishop, considering his service in the Confederate army only temporary. He explained his feelings to a friend: "I felt like a man who had dropped his business when his house was on fire to put it out; for as soon as the war is over, I will return to my calling." To his wife, he added that he had asked "the Lord to have mercy upon me and help me to be wise, to be sagacious, to be firm, and to be merciful."[31]

Polk's initial assignment was to head Department No. 2 and the defenses of the Mississippi above the Red River. He quickly recognized the vulnerability of the Confederate position there. When Polk learned that Union forces under Ulysses S. Grant were poised to enter Kentucky, a neutral state, Polk, on his own initiative, entered the state. His move gave Kentucky's Union-controlled legislature the excuse it needed to invite Federal troops into their state.[32]

In November, President Davis replaced Polk with General Albert Sidney Johnston as commander of Department No. 2. Polk was reassigned as commander of the First Division in the same department. When Polk learned of the change, he sent a letter to Davis announcing his resignation. Under a feeling of duty, he said, he had accepted a commission in the Confederate army. It was understood that he might be relieved from duty when his services were no longer required. The arrival of Albert Sidney Johnston in the West, he said, had made his own service no longer needed.[33]

Before Davis could respond to Polk's letter, Grant engaged Polk at Belmont, Missouri; it was the first battle for both. The battle at Belmont was of little importance, except in making veterans out of raw recruits. "The enemy fled and were pursued by gunboats," Polk wired Davis. It was a complete rout, he said, giving God the credit for his victory. Grant also claimed victory but did not recognize the assistance from a higher power. Casualties on both sides were light.[34]

Two days after the battle at Belmont, Polk had second thoughts about his resignation. He sent a copy of his letter to General Johnston with an explanation. "I am on many accounts strongly tempted to remain and continue to support you," if his services were necessary, he said. Davis had already decided not to accept Polk's resignation. "You have just won a victory, which gives you fresh claim to the affection and confidence of your troops," Davis reminded Polk.[35]

On December 8, after a little coaxing, Polk notified Davis of his decision to remain in the army: "I have concluded to waive the pressing of my application for a release from further service, and have determined to retain my office as long as I may be of service to our cause."[36]

General Johnston, now commander of the Western forces, was faced with the almost impossible task of defending a line that stretched 500 miles, from Arkansas across to the Cumberland Gap. Polk was assigned the task of protecting the Mississippi River route from invasion. In February 1862, Grant broke the center of the Confederate line at Fort Donelson, Tennessee. This forced Johnston to concentrate his forces at Corinth, Mississippi. Polk was ordered to join with his troops.[37]

In late March, General Johnston organized his Army of the Mississippi into corps. Beauregard was to serve as second in command and Major General

Braxton Bragg as chief-of-staff. The First Corps was to be commanded by Polk; the Second Corps, by Bragg; the Third Corps, by Major General William Hardee; and a Reserve Corps by Brigadier General John Breckinridge.[38]

On April 2, Johnston made plans to attack Union troops at Pittsburg Landing, hoping to catch the enemy by surprise. On April 5, he ordered all his troops to move into battle line by 3:00 a.m. During the night, the rains came and continued into the morning, slowing the movement of his troops. It was not until 10:00 a.m. that a battle line could be formed a half mile east of Shiloh Church.[39]

At the ensuing Battle of Shiloh, Johnston's meticulous plans fell apart, resulting in a series of disorganized melees. During the battle, Polk commanded the Confederate right against William T. Sherman. On the first day of the battle, his troops drove Sherman back, and only the strength of the Hornets' Nest, a small pocket of resistance on the Union left, prevented a Confederate encirclement of the Union army. During the violent fighting at the Hornets' Nest, General Johnston was killed. General Beauregard took command and at dusk ordered the attack to cease.[40]

Polk recorded the first day of the battle in a letter to his wife: "The enemy was badly whipped the first day, and we ought, from the advantage gained, to have captured the whole force. We would have done so if we had had an hour more of daylight." He did not mention Johnston's death nor criticize Beauregard for his decision to cease the attack when he did.[41]

After months of thought, and with the help of hindsight, Polk viewed the events of the first day at Shiloh: "We had one hour or more of daylight still left; were within from 150 to 400 yards of the enemy's position, and nothing seemed wanting to complete the most brilliant victory of the war but to press forward and make a vigorous assault on the demoralized remnant of his forces."[42]

During the evening of the first day at Shiloh, Grant's troops were able to hang on until reinforcements arrived in force. On the afternoon of the second day, Grant's army moved forward and forced the Confederates to fall back. It was a worn and discouraged army that retreated through the mud to Corinth, where with so much hope it had left less than a week before. It had been a costly battle for the Confederates who suffered over 10,000 casualties. During the battle, Polk had shown great personal courage, acquitting himself well. He personally led several charges, exposing himself to enemy fire.[43]

When Johnston's successor, General Beauregard, retreated even further to Tupelo, Mississippi, President Davis replaced him with Braxton Bragg. Upon taking command of the army, Bragg attempted to give his troops a pep-talk, stating that "a few more days of needful preparation and organization, and I shall give your banners to the breeze—shall lead you to emulate the soldiers of the Confederacy in the East, and with the confident trust that you will gain additional honors to those you have already won on other fields.

But be prepared to undergo privation and labor with cheerfulness and alacrity."[44]

Bragg quickly moved his army to Chattanooga by rail to put it in a position to invade Kentucky. Polk's corps was selected to lead the advance. When Bragg split his command, Polk was left with only half of the army, 16,000 men to face Major General Don Carlos Buell's army of 60,000. Rather than attack an army that greatly outnumbered his, Polk moved his corps to Perryville to join Bragg there.

The battle at Perryville was another confused engagement, with men fighting in small, unorganized engagements. This was due, in part, to the fact that Bragg had a confusing picture of the enemy's location. Later he reported: "Having ordered the attack and that no time should be lost, I was concerned at not hearing the commencement of the engagement early in the morning." What Bragg did not know was that, instead of attacking right away as ordered, Polk met with Generals Hardee, Buckner, and Cheatham to discuss the situation. Polk was disturbed by Bragg's decision to attack early in the morning, especially as the evidence mounted as to the size of the enemy force. As a result, Polk changed Bragg's orders and adopted a "defensive–offensive" mode. Later, when Bragg charged Polk with disobedience at Perryville, Polk said he had not regarded Bragg's orders as "mandatory" but "simply as suggestive and advisory."[45]

In the late evening, the units on both sides became intermingled. In the midst of the confusion, Polk came under fire from what he believed to be Confederate troops. Polk spurred his horse over to the group and demanded to know why they were firing on friendly troops. "I don't think there can be any mistake about it," the colonel in charge replied. "I am sure they are enemy." "Enemy?" Polk inquired. "What is your name, sir?" When the colonel gave his name and brigade, Polk realized he was inside the Federal line. He decided that "there was no hope but to brazen it out," hoping they would not notice his allegiance. "Cease firing at once!" Polk ordered. He then rode across the Federal line repeating the order and expecting to be shot any minute. Reaching a grove of trees, he spurred his horse and galloped back to the friendly Confederate lines.[46]

Polk felt the army had fought well enough to continue the battle the next day, but that night Bragg ordered the withdrawal of his outnumbered troops from Perryville. Neither Bragg nor Buell had acquitted themselves with glory, but with his supplies running low, Bragg abandoned the campaign, much to the dismay of Polk and the other corps commanders.[47]

After the decision to withdraw, Polk began to question Bragg's suitability for command. Bragg, however, commended Polk for his part in the battle, and later that month, Polk was promoted to lieutenant general.[48]

Six months later, when Bragg wrote his official report of the Kentucky campaign, he blamed his failure on those generals he had complimented so highly immediately after the Battle of Perryville. Among those was Polk, who Bragg now accused of disobedience. At Perryville, he claimed Polk had failed to attack immediately as ordered. Polk denied the charge, stating that the order had not been clear; therefore, he had not disobeyed the order.[49]

Some historians have excused Polk's disobedience of Bragg's orders, arguing that he was justified considering the circumstances and pointing out that Bragg was wrong about the location of the Union's main force. The "Perryville Affair," as Polk labeled the matter, soon became a point of controversy between Bragg and his generals.[50]

In November, Polk was summoned to Richmond for a conference with President Davis to discuss Bragg's leadership. Polk stated that Bragg had "great ability in the direction of organization and discipline, but lacked the higher elements of generalship in conducting a campaign." The Kentucky campaign, Polk said, had been a failure, and he believed Generals Smith and Hardee shared his opinion. He further said that Bragg had lost the confidence of his generals, and if a change of commanders was to be made, the assignment should go to Joseph E. Johnston.[51]

During the Battle of Stones River on the last day of 1862, Polk's corps held the center of the Confederate line. He was unsuccessful in breaking a strong Union position, and when reinforcements were sent to him, he made the mistake of deploying them in a piecemeal manner, resulting in additional casualties.[52]

On January 2, the slaughter began again. Of the 78,000 men engaged on both sides, 23,000 became casualties. Although the Confederate army, now known as the Army of Tennessee, was not driven from the field, Bragg ordered another retreat.[53]

During the heat of battle on the first day at Stone's River a curious event occurred. One of Polk's division commanders, Major General Benjamin Cheatham, stood beside Polk. To rally his men, Cheatham shouted "Give 'em hell, boys." Although Polk supported Cheatham's method of encouraging his men, as a bishop, he could not bring himself to repeat it. "Give them what General Cheatham says, boys," he shouted. "Give them what General Cheatham says."[54]

A storm of criticism surrounded Bragg after his retreat from Kentucky. Although the failure to hold Kentucky was not all his fault, as usual the commanding general had to accept the responsibility. Politicians, the press, and some of Bragg's own generals were calling for his removal. Polk, Hardee, and Edmund Smith openly denounced Bragg. Smith wrote to Davis saying he would rather serve at a lower rank anywhere else in the Confederacy than to keep his current rank and have to continue to serve under Bragg. Both Hardee and Smith had been greatly influenced by Polk, who seemed to be mounting a behind-the-scene campaign to have Bragg removed, speaking ill of his commander to both members of Congress and his fellow generals.[55]

When Bragg learned of the discontent of his generals, he decided to seek a vote of confidence from his top officers. "I shall retire without a regret if I find I have lost the good opinion of my generals, upon whom I have ever relied as upon a foundation of rock." This proved to be a big mistake. The unanimous vote was for Bragg to be replaced.[56]

The controversy between Bragg and Polk put Davis in an awkward position. It was difficult to decide who should be replaced. He respected Bragg for his devotion to the cause. On the other hand, Polk was his longtime friend whose faults he tended to overlook. In the end, Bragg and Polk both stayed.[57]

In March, General Joseph Johnston replaced Bragg briefly while he returned to Winchester to be at the bedside of his wife who was ill. During Bragg's absence, his staff made efforts to get rid of him, but in April Johnston notified the president that he was too ill for field command; consequently, Bragg was restored to his position.

After months of inactivity, the Union army, now under Major General William Rosecrans, and Bragg's army met at Chickamauga. On September 20, 1863, the final morning of a three-day battle, Bragg planned to attack the Union line, with Polk attacking the left flank, and Longstreet, the Federal right. Although Polk was four hours late in his attack, the battle ended in a smashing Confederate victory. Only a strong stand by Union Major General Thomas prevented a complete Union rout.[58]

Late that evening, Polk went to see Bragg. Polk insisted that the enemy had been routed and was "flying precipitately from the field," presenting the opportunity for Bragg to capture or destroy Rosecrans's army before it had time to reorganize at Chattanooga. Polk's appeal failed, and Bragg did not order a pursuit. As a result, Bragg missed the chance to dislodge the Union troops from Chattanooga. Instead, he besieged the city but failed to prevent Rosecrans from being reinforced.[59]

As after Chickamauga, Perryville, and Stone's River, the South wanted to know why Bragg had failed to follow up his victory. Bragg's generals were asking the same question; discontent within the Army of Tennessee reached a new height. Again Bragg looked for a scapegoat. One of those singled out was Polk. In Bragg's opinion, it was Polk's delay on the morning of the third day that had prevented him from a complete victory. A staff officer had reported to him that Polk had been seen eating breakfast and reading a newspaper two hours after the attack was scheduled to begin. Polk later explained that he did not receive orders to attack at 6:00 a.m. and understood that he was to attack when "in position."[60]

Bragg was fed up with Polk's insubordination and disobedience and finally relieved Polk of his command. His action was based on previous acts as well as on the case at hand. Polk did not take his removal lying down. He wrote to the secretary of war protesting Bragg's "arbitrary and unlawful order" and requesting a court of inquiry to review the action.[61]

"The truth is General Bragg has made a failure, . . . and he wants a scapegoat," Polk wrote to Davis. Longstreet supported Polk's position: "I am convinced that nothing but the hand of God can save us or help us as long as we have our present commander." Despite these reports, Bragg stayed.[62]

Davis responded to Polk's request for a court of inquiry, saying, "After an examination into the causes and circumstances attending your being relieved from command . . . I have arrived at the conclusion that there is nothing attending them to justify a court-martial or a court of inquiry, and therefore dismiss the application. Your assignment to a field of duty . . . is the best evidence of my appreciation of your past service and expectations of your future career."[63]

Polk's new assignment was to Demopolis, Alabama. In May 1864, Bragg was replaced, and Joseph Johnston became the new commander of the Army of Tennessee. Polk was returned to Georgia, where he joined Johnston's army. One of Polk's first acts was to baptize Lieutenant General John Bell Hood. It was his final official duty as a clergyman.[64]

In early June, the two armies maneuvered through northern Georgia, Sherman hoping to turn Johnston's flank. Johnston skillfully defended his flanks, while falling back to Atlanta. On the morning of June 14, Polk rode with Generals Johnston and Hardee to the top of a wooded hill called Pine Mount to inspect the Confederate lines. The observation point was exposed and within easy range of the enemy.[65]

Suddenly, without notice, a shell exploded a short distance away. The generals ducked for cover, but Polk did not move quickly enough. A split second later, a second shell exploded, the shrapnel striking Polk in the chest, killing him instantly. He was carried down the hillside and his body taken to Augusta. General Polk's death came as a severe blow to the army. General Johnston, who had been baptized earlier by Polk, was brought to tears as he viewed the mangled body of his friend and corps commander. In a short address to his troops, Johnston said:

> Comrades, you are called to mourn your first captain, your oldest companion in arms. Lieutenant General Polk fell today at the outpost of the army, the army he raised and commanded, in all of whose trials he shared, to all of whose victories he contributed. In this distinguished leader we have lost the most courageous of gentlemen, the most gallant of soldiers. The Christian patriot soldier has neither lived nor died in vain. His example is before you; his mantle rests with you.[66]

Jefferson Davis called Polk's death "an irreparable loss" and said that the country had sustained no heavier blow since Stonewall Jackson was killed.[67]

Polk's body was buried in the churchyard of St. Paul and later moved to the Episcopal cathedral in New Orleans. He was beloved by his officers and men for his personal qualities and respected for his bravery and ability to inspire his troops to give their best effort. But he was not a student of military science, much preferring the life of a planter and service within the church. He accepted a commission in the Confederate army because of his sincere desire to serve the South. He never doubted its right to secede, and to him that right was a duty.[68]

In 1902, a memorial was erected on the spot where he was killed, adjacent to the Kennesaw Mountain Battlefield. The last line of the inscription on the monument seemed to be an appropriate epitaph for Polk's contribution to the South: "And surely the gates of heaven never opened wider to allow a more manly spirit to enter therein."[69]

17 *John Hunt Morgan*

"Thunderbolt of the Confederacy"

For the Confederacy, John Hunt Morgan was a symbol of the Southern code of honor and system of ethics. His daring cavalry raids wreaked havoc on a numerically superior Union army, interrupting Federal plans to invade Tennessee. A son of one of Kentucky's aristocratic families, Morgan sacrificed his livelihood to fight for the Confederacy. Although breaking with the traditional form of warfare, Morgan became a hero like Robert E. Lee and Stonewall Jackson—but more than a hero, he was the Southern ideal of a chivalrous knight.[1]

John Hunt Morgan used his handsome appearance to his advantage. An old photograph portrays him as a man with a dark beard, his hat set back at a rakish angle, and his legs crossed so as to display his riding boots to the best advantage. His boyish smile was one that few forgot. "It comes over his face like a laugh over a child's countenance—having in it an innocence of humor which is very beautiful to me," one of his lady friends remembered. All types of people admired him, but none more than the young Southern belles. Wherever he went, they flocked to see him, touch him, and to get his autograph or a button from his jacket. Even his horse, Black Bess, had to be guarded to keep his admirers from cutting souvenirs from her mane and tail. Young ladies who had the opportunity to be with him, even for just a short time, immediately fell in love with him.[2]

Morgan's pleasing personality drew people to him. His persona was one that few could emulate; yet, when people met him in person, the attraction grew even stronger. Emma Holmes wrote in her diary about an evening a friend had spent with him: "She said he was extremely different from what she imagined. [He was] so mild and gentle in his manner that she would not have taken him for a soldier but for his boots and spurs, so unwarrior-like did he seem."[3]

His admirers called him the "Thunderbolt of the Confederacy." In the North, where Morgan was a source of grief, he was referred to as "King of the Horse Thieves," a label resented by his men and those who knew him well. In Kentucky, especially, one was either for him or against him; there was no middle ground.[4]

Although Morgan had no formal military training, his understanding of the role of cavalry in warfare was well beyond the times. His cavalry destroyed supply and communication lines, delaying Northern efforts to control a vast territory in the West. In one daring raid, he rode through the states of Indiana and Ohio, penetrating the North farther than any other Confederate force.[5]

John Hunt Morgan's family ties were all in the South. His father, Calvin Morgan, left his home in Alabama to go to Lexington, Kentucky to marry Henrietta Hunt, one of the city's most beautiful women. Born on June 1, 1825, John was the first of eight children born to Calvin and Henrietta. Calvin was proud of his family's heritage, despite the fact that he himself was not a large landowner. As a youth, Morgan was inculcated with the South's system of honor and the standards of conduct valued by his family.[6]

John's grandfather was one of the wealthiest men in Kentucky and reputed to be one of the first millionaires in the state. Although Morgan and his brothers grew up on a farm outside of town, he was a frequent visitor to his grandfather's mansion. As a result, this assertive man played a major role in the formation of Morgan's personality.[7]

Young Morgan was easygoing, soft-spoken, and very courteous. In the eyes of many Southerners, he was the archetypical gentleman. Those who knew him best said he was exuberant when he enjoyed success, but that when things did not go well, he sank into depths of gloom and despair.[8]

At the age of sixteen, Morgan entered Transylvania College in Lexington. Described as a restless, undisciplined youth by his instructors, he was not destined to be an outstanding student. His parents and grandfather were disappointed in his performance. Feeling that it was impossible to live up to their expectations, John compensated by committing boyish pranks, even going so far as to engage other young men in duels. Although dueling was illegal in Kentucky, Southern society recognized it as a test of manliness. It was the way a young man demonstrated his status as a gentleman and established the right to lead. Although unable to gain recognition for his academic achievement, Morgan easily attained it when he challenged a fellow student at the university to a duel. Because he had violated the university's rule prohibiting dueling, Morgan was suspended for the remainder of the term; he was never to return.[9]

In 1846, when the United States went to war with Mexico, twenty-one-year-old Morgan joined the First Kentucky Cavalry and was commissioned

John Hunt Morgan used his handsome appearance to his advantage. His good looks and rogu-
ishness made him a man with a strong sexual
attraction. Young women who had the opportunity to be with him, even for just a short time,
immediately fell in love with him.

COURTESY OF THE LIBRARY OF CONGRESS

lieutenant. The Kentucky Cavalry reached Mexico in time to participate in
the Battle of Buena Vista, where they gave an excellent account of themselves.

On July 8, 1847, Morgan was mustered out of the army. Now forced to
earn a living in the business world, he acquired a hemp factory and a
woolen mill. Both enterprises prospered, to the surprise of those who had
known him as an immature youth at Transylvania. Later, he branched out
to the slave trade. He also began to take a prominent role in community
activities.[10]

During this time, Morgan married his partner's sister, eighteen-year-old
Rebecca Grantz Bruce. In addition to being attractive, Rebecca was mild-
mannered and was said to have had all the Christian virtues of "gentleness,
meekness, forbearance, and long-suffering." Five years later, Rebecca gave
birth to a stillborn son. Shortly thereafter, she developed pain and soreness

in one of her legs and was diagnosed with septic thrombophlebitis, an infection of a blood clot in a vein in the leg. The condition grew worse, and she soon became an invalid. The situation frustrated Morgan; there seemed little he could do help her or make her comfortable. By the 1850s, his wife was totally dependent on him, and with the death of both his father and father-in-law, Morgan became the man of both households.[11]

While Morgan's business was settling into a routine, there was unrest in the nation over slavery and secession. If the Southern states left the Union, the border states would have to decide which side they would be on. Kentucky, which controlled the water passage on both the Mississippi and Ohio Rivers, was essential to both sides. "I think to lose Kentucky is nearly the same as to lose the whole game," said Abraham Lincoln.[12] When the fight for Kentucky began, Morgan made preparations; he organized a militia unit with pro-Southern sympathies, with himself as captain. They were known as the Lexington Rifles, and soon became the pride of Lexington.[13]

When the war began, Kentucky hoped to remain neutral. Kentuckians had no desire to see force applied against the South, nor did they desire to secede from the Union. Although many Kentuckians had strong Southern sentiments, the state would remain pro-Union. In April 1861, when President Lincoln issued a call for volunteers, Kentucky Governor Beriah Magoffin refused, stating that "Kentucky will furnish no troops for the wicked purpose of subduing her sister Southern states." John J. Crittenden, one of Kentucky's representatives in Congress, spoke in favor of neutrality: "Let us not be forced into civil strife for the North, nor dragged into it for the South—take no part with either." For John Morgan, however, there was no dilemma; he would cast his lot with the South.[14]

In July 1861, mercifully, Rebecca died. With her death, there was nothing left to prevent him from joining the Confederacy. Feeling a sense of relief after the loss of his wife, Morgan moved out on his own, taking twenty-five members of his Lexington Rifles with him. He was soon joined by four of his brothers and was made a captain of the Kentucky volunteers, assigned to conduct scouting missions. His brother-in-law, Basil Duke, became first lieutenant.[15]

Despite the hopes of many Kentuckians that their state would remain neutral, Confederate troops under Major General Leonidas Polk moved into Kentucky to fortify the western end of their defensive line. Two days later, Federal troops under Brigadier General Ulysses S. Grant occupied two strategic points in Kentucky. There would be no peace in Kentucky.[16]

In November, General Albert S. Johnston ordered Morgan and his Lexington Rifles to Bowling Green. His cavalry had just settled down when the vanguards of Federal Brigadier General Don Carlos Buell's army began to threaten the area. In a quick strike behind Buell's line, Morgan took numerous prisoners, disrupted the Federal supply line, and destroyed a vital bridge south of Louisville, all without suffering a single casualty. Morgan quickly realized the effectiveness of this "hit-and-run" type of warfare and wanted to expand and extend its use.[17]

By February of 1862, General Johnston, fearing he would be trapped behind enemy lines after the fall of Fort Donelson, ordered his army to march to Nashville. When Johnston abandoned Nashville, Morgan served as a rear guard. While Johnston reorganized his army, Morgan headed for Nashville with a raiding party of fifteen. Under the cover of darkness, Morgan found his target, the steamboat *Minnetonka*, tied up at the wharf on the Cumberland River. After setting the boat on fire, they were discovered by Federal cavalry and forced to flee. Morgan's Raiders suffered their first casualty, one of many that would follow as the war continued.[18]

Between raids, Morgan made frequent trips to the home of the genial Colonel Charles Ready, for dinner and to visit with his attractive twenty-one-year-old daughter, Martha. In a short time, he had fallen in love and moved his base of operation from La Vergne to Murfreesboro to be closer to her. Martha had other suitors, and even a proposal of marriage from Illinois Representative Samuel Scott Marshall, but she wanted to marry for love and not for position or convenience. Like other young women of the period, Martha was caught up in the spirit of romance that was so much a part of upper-class Southern society. It is easy to see why Martha and the gallant John Hunt Morgan were attracted to each other.[19]

On one occasion, when Morgan was visiting Martha, a large crowd gathered outside her house just to see him. On another occasion, Morgan halted his command before the Ready house and asked to see Martha. He told her that he was on his way to Nashville to capture a Union general to exchange for General Simon Bolivar Buckner, who had been captured at Fort Donelson. After promising to return with the prisoner, he mounted his horse and rode away.[20]

Dressed with Union overcoats over their uniforms, Morgan's party stopped a wagon train; the commanding officer assumed that Morgan and his men were Union soldiers checking their passes. When the raiders drew their revolvers, the Federals surrendered without a fight, but there was no general. He continued his masquerade, capturing other officers, but again no general. When Morgan returned from his mission, he went to the Ready house and presented the prisoners to Martha and her sister.[21]

On another occasion, again disguised as Union officers, Morgan and his aide rode into Gallatin and went to the telegraph office. Morgan asked the operator what news he had. "Nothing sir, except it is reported that that damned rebel, Captain John Morgan, is this side of the Cumberland with some of his cavalry." The operator then drew his revolver and said, "I wish I could get sight of the damned rascal. I'd make a hole through him larger than he would find pleasant." Morgan asked him if he knew who he was, the operator replying that he did not. When Morgan told him who he was, the operator dropped his gun in fear and stepped back while Morgan gathered up the code books and secret dispatches and made good his escape. Morgan continued to use this practice to throw the enemy off guard.[22]

Just four days after his visit to Gallatin, Morgan and his raiders were ordered to join General Albert Sidney Johnston's army at Corinth in northern Mississippi. On April 4, Morgan was promoted to full colonel. Within two days he would be engaged in one of the major battles of the war, near a little church called Shiloh.[23]

By the time Morgan's Raiders reached the battle, it had been raging for several hours. The Raiders quickly learned that cavalry units could not fight effectively in a wooded area. Dismounting, they fought like infantry, a tactic they would later repeat on other occasions. Confederate casualties were high; Basil Duke, Morgan's second-in-command, was wounded, but he would later return to action. When victory appeared to be in sight for the Confederates, a stray bullet struck General Johnston in the leg. At first the wound was thought to be superficial, but the bullet had severed an artery, and General Johnston bled to death. General P. G. T. Beauregard replaced him. When Grant moved 30,000 fresh troops into the battle, the Confederates were forced to fall back to Corinth.[24]

In May 1862, Morgan conducted a series of quick raids through Tennessee and Kentucky. He continued to employ the tactics that had proven successful for him—rapid movement to inflict maximum damage, never engaging the enemy when outnumbered, dividing the command to confuse pursuit, and disappearing as quickly as possible after a raid. In Tennessee, he took 400 prisoners; in Kentucky, he destroyed the railroad at Cave City.[25]

During his raid of Lebanon, Tennessee, Morgan was welcomed with open arms. Many of the residents opened their homes to the raiders, offering to share their food and shelter. Their stay in Lebanon, however, was interrupted soon after dawn when Federal troops rushed into town. Guards were able to spread the alarm, alerting Morgan and his men in time for them to make their escape. The chase that followed was later described as the "Lebanon Races." In his haste to escape across the Cumberland River on a ferry boat, Morgan had to leave his horse, Black Bess, behind.[26]

During his raid of Cave City, Morgan captured a train and was surprised to find most of the passenger cars filled with Union soldiers and their wives. One of the officers, Major W. A. Coffey, was an old acquaintance of his. Major Coffey's wife pleaded with him not to kill her husband. Morgan, always gracious in the presence of women, explained to her that he was not planning to kill anyone. He decided not to burn the train because he did not want the women passengers to be uncomfortable while they waited for him to leave. While searching the train, Morgan's men found $8,000 in federal currency. Taking the money, Morgan invited Major Coffey and the women passengers to join him and his men for lunch at the hotel in town. After lunch, Morgan placed Major Coffey and the women back on the train and ordered the engineer to take everyone back to Louisville.[27]

After returning from his raid at Cave City, Morgan was treated as a hero. An editor in Atlanta wrote: "Hurrah for Morgan! . . . Our people would rather get a sight of him than Queen Victoria. Again we say, Hurrah for Morgan!" The $8,000 taken at Cave City was exaggerated until it became $350,000 by the time the news reached Richmond. What attracted the most attention, however, was the manner in which Morgan had treated the women on the captured train, confirming their belief that Southern men were both gentlemen and chivalrous. Morgan's reputation as a "Christian, Southern gentleman, and a humane warrior" was now well-established.[28]

By the end of May, it was apparent that Chattanooga would be the next Union target. Morgan was given the manpower to carry on the type of warfare he preferred. He was authorized to organize the Second Kentucky Cavalry regiment with a complement of 400 men, including two companies of Texas Rangers. By December 1862, the regiment would grow to 900 men, not quite brigade size.[29]

On July 4, 1862, Morgan and his Second Kentucky left Knoxville and headed for Kentucky. The Raiders' first engagement with Federal troops was at Tompkinsville, Kentucky. After a short encounter, Morgan's men routed the Federals, taking 300 prisoners, a number of good horses, and a generous supply of food. A detail was assigned to take the prisoners back to Tennessee, while Morgan moved on.[30]

Taken by surprise at the Confederate raid on Kentucky, the Union tried to bolster key towns and cities with additional troops. After leaving Tompkinsville, the Raiders rode to Glasgow. Here, Morgan issued a proclamation urging local citizens to join him: "Kentuckians! I have come to liberate you from the hands of your oppressors." Although the message received a lot of publicity, few responded.[31]

At Lebanon, the Raiders captured the town without a single casualty, taking over 200 prisoners and destroying supplies valued at $100,000. Again Morgan issued a proclamation calling for "the willing hands of fifty thousand of Kentucky's brave" to join him in destroying the Union invaders. Once again, the response was not good.[32]

As Morgan's Raiders moved further into Kentucky, destroying railroad bridges and lines of communication, Union commanders throughout the state panicked. From Lebanon, the Raiders moved through the Kentucky towns of Springfield, Herrodsburg, and Versailles. When Morgan learned that there were several thousand troops at Lexington, he changed his plans and headed for Georgetown. Once in Georgetown, Morgan sent a few of his men into Lexington with recruiting posters, which they placed at prominent spots around town. This attempt to recruit was more successful; enough men showed up to form a new company.[33]

With Union troops closing in, it became clear to Morgan that he had to leave Kentucky as soon as possible. Weary, but pleased, the Raiders crossed the Cumberland River, and within a few days they were safe at home in

Tennessee. In what is referred to as Morgan's First Kentucky Raid, Morgan started with 900 men and returned with over 1,200, traveled over 1,000 miles, captured 1,200 Union troops, destroyed bridges and military supplies, and disrupted communication lines. His casualties during the twenty-four days were fewer than a hundred. In addition to the havoc he had caused in Kentucky, Morgan's success on the raid helped to raise Southern morale and demonstrated that the North was vulnerable to attack by raiding parties.[34]

Although Morgan was popular with his men, he often had difficulty with his superiors when questioned about his disciplinary procedures. His methods, however, were consistent with his own personal values. He permitted his men to keep their independence in personal matters as long as this did not interfere with official duties. If a man was missing from camp for a few days between raids, Morgan would not question his absence, as long as he was available for the next raid. "I prefer fifty men who gladly obey me, to a division I have to watch and punish," he said. When on a raiding party, his troops often had to operate on their own; this, Morgan believed, required self motivation, unity of purpose, and loyalty. Morgan knew his men and showed interest in their welfare. He was courteous and treated his men fairly. Morgan acknowledged his subordinates' achievements and used promotion to encourage bravery. He did not rely on seniority as a criterion for promotion, basing it entirely on merit. "Seniority means deeds," he said. In battle, Morgan led by example. His disregard for danger, his energy, and his dedication to the cause were admired by his men.[35]

In July 1862, General Bragg received recommendations from General Nathan B. Forrest and Morgan, who convinced him to attack Union General Don Carlos Buell in Kentucky. They believed that there were 30,000 Kentuckians anxious to join the Confederate army and that only arms and support were preventing them from doing so. In Bragg's plan of attack, Morgan would move northwest across Tennessee and cut Buell's supply line. Brigadier General Edmund Kirby Smith would move north from Knoxville and cross into Kentucky. Bragg was led to believe that the people of Kentucky had been forced to remain in the Union, and if given the opportunity, would force the Yankees from their state. On August 10, Morgan received orders to raid the L & N Railroad at Gallatin and cut off all of Buell's supply lines from Louisville. This they hoped would draw Buell's army northward.[36]

Morgan was turned loose to harass the enemy. He had learned how to tap into telegraph lines, intercept Federal communications, and send false orders to confuse the enemy. On August 12, his men captured Federal troops at Gallatin, destroyed a train and a nearby bridge, blocked a tunnel, and destroyed large stretches of tracks. The raid got Buell's attention just as Bragg had hoped it would. With 30,000 men, General Bragg marched out of Chattanooga toward Murfreesboro, Tennessee. A few days later,

General Buell's army of 35,000 moved northward to take up a position at Murfreesboro. At Richmond, Kentucky, General Smith captured 4,000 Federal troops and then moved northward to threaten Cincinnati, Ohio. As Smith approached Cincinnati, a citizen's army of 50,000 was formed to protect the city from his invasion.[37]

In the meantime, Morgan found a printing press. With members of his command who had newspaper experience, he published the first issue of a newspaper, the *Vidette*. In one of the early issues, Morgan published his policy of retaliation and information about the Raiders' activities, military operations, and letters from friends in Kentucky. Although the paper did not survive beyond November, it was unique because it had been produced by a cavalry unit while in enemy territory.[38]

Morgan saw himself as a liberator, distributing posters throughout the state. "Kentuckians," he wrote, "I have come to liberate you from the hands of your oppressors." Calling for 50,000 recruits, he said, "[O]nly the bravest need apply." Then he closed with the exhortation: "Strike—for your altars and your fires. Strike for the green graves of your sires, God, and your native land.[39]

On September 4, Morgan joined General Smith in Lexington. Wearing his best full-dress uniform and followed by his entire command of 900 men, Morgan rode into town. It was a moment of triumph for him and his command. Friends and Confederate sympathizers crowded the streets, cheering and waving as Morgan made his way to his family home at Hopemount. Admirers presented him with gifts, including a thoroughbred gelding named Glencoe. It was his finest hour.[40]

On September 30, Buell attacked Bragg at Munfordville, pushing past the Confederates and making his way to Louisville, where he received reinforcements. Bragg's plan to liberate Kentucky had failed. The 30,000 recruits did not materialize, and Bragg and Smith were forced to return to Tennessee. Despite the failure of the plan, Morgan returned in glory. News of his victories and the presence of 1,400 prisoners reached Richmond. War clerk J. B. Jones wrote in his diary: "Glorious Colonel Morgan has dashed into Kentucky, whipped everything before him, and got off unharmed. He has but a little over a thousand men, and captured that number of prisoners."[41]

Bragg's army returned to Murfreesboro in November and began to prepare their winter camp. At the same time, Morgan was planning a raid on Hartsville, Tennessee, forty miles north of Murfreesboro. Although 2,500 Union troops were stationed there, Morgan was confident he could capture the garrison. On December 7, 1862, in a freezing rain, Morgan, with 1,250 troopers, rode toward Hartsville. They arrived at their destination, catching the Union troops off guard, and quickly scored another victory. In addition to wagonloads of much needed supplies, Morgan took 2,000 prisoners. General Bragg congratulated Morgan, writing: "The intelligence, zeal, and gallantry displayed by [you] will serve as example and an incentive to still more honorable deeds." Soon after, Morgan was promoted to brigadier general and Basil Duke to colonel.[42]

The day after being promoted, Morgan took time out to marry Martha Ready in the parlor of the Ready residence. General Leonidas Polk, wearing his Episcopal bishop's robe, performed the ceremony. Four other generals—Bragg, Hardee, Cheatham, and Breckinridge—attended the wedding. Morgan did not have time for a long honeymoon. Soon after the wedding, General Bragg received information that Major General William Rosecrans was stockpiling supplies at Nashville in preparation for a spring offensive. Morgan proposed a raid north into Kentucky to cut the supply line behind Rosecrans.[43]

On December 21, Morgan assembled his men. His command had now grown to two brigades. General Forrest would operate in west Tennessee to harass Grant's supply line, while Morgan swept north around Rosecrans's garrison at Nashville. Morgan left Murfreesboro with 4,000 horsemen, crossing into Kentucky. On Christmas eve, they entered Glasgow and overpowered the small contingent of Federal troops stationed there. On Christmas day, Morgan's Raiders were met with stiff resistance, but they were soon able to sweep past it. The raid continued with little opposition, allowing Morgan's men to move at their leisure and to destroy selected targets.[44]

The size of Morgan's command made it difficult to move without being seen or reported. Pursued by Federal cavalry and harassed along the way by home guards, Morgan found it much easier to get into Kentucky then it was to get out. On December 30, heavy snows fell in southern Kentucky, making Morgan's trip back to Tennessee even more difficult. On January 25, 1863, Morgan's troopers arrived in Smithville, Tennessee with 2,000 prisoners and a large quantity of supplies. In addition, Morgan had accomplished his objective of disrupting Rosecrans's supply lines.[45]

While Morgan was busy in Kentucky, Rosecrans had marched from Nashville toward Murfreesboro to challenge Bragg's army. The four-day battle ended inconclusively, with Bragg withdrawing to his new headquarters at Tullahoma. Although Morgan's Kentucky Christmas raid had been a success, his efforts came too late to hinder Rosecrans.[46]

During the winter of 1862 to 1863, Morgan set up his headquarters at McMinnville, forty miles east of Murfreesboro, where he was united with his wife again. Although the Raiders kept active during this time, Morgan was not with them on most of their raids, preferring to spend the time with his wife. When his absence became a problem, one of Morgan's uncles wrote to Martha: "I feel you are sticking too close to your husband." In Morgan's absence, his command had become careless and less disciplined. Morgan sensed that it was time for another raid, something spectacular, to lift Confederate morale. For Morgan, the opportunity would soon come.[47]

During the summer of 1863, General Bragg fell back to Chattanooga when his army was in danger of attack from both General Rosecrans at

Murfreesboro and Major General Ambrose Burnside near the Ohio River. As he withdrew, Bragg sent Morgan's Rangers to harass and delay any Federal forces moving south into Kentucky. But he also gave Morgan very specific orders to stay south of the Ohio River so that he could be recalled quickly if he were needed. Morgan was convinced that another of his daring raids would divert forces under Burnside from linking up with Rosecrans. Despite Bragg's orders, Morgan had no intention of restricting his raid to Kentucky.[48]

Confident because of his earlier successes, Morgan decided on a bold move. Despite Bragg's orders, he would cross the Ohio River into Indiana, hoping to draw Union forces away from Bragg. Then he would march into Ohio and return to Confederate territory by way of western Virginia. On July 2, Morgan's Raiders, now a division with 2,500 men, crossed the Cumberland River. Morgan had turned the war into a personal crusade that was heightened when his brother Tom was killed just days into the raid. Scouts were sent ahead to the Ohio River to find a safe place to cross. On July 4, he encountered Union troops at Tebb's Bend. After a three-hour battle, the Raiders moved on, but the effort had been costly and the Federals had been alerted. Newspapers spread the word, greatly exaggerating the size of Morgan's force, with figures ranging from 4,000 to 11,000 men.[49]

Morgan reached the Ohio River at Brandenburg on July 8. Using the steamships that had been captured earlier, he crossed the river. Then he had the boats burned behind him so that none of his men would think of returning to Kentucky. At Corydon, Indiana, the Raiders encountered armed civilians, but they were easily brushed aside. From then on, Morgan would be constantly attacked and harassed by small groups of civilians and militia, all of which would take their toll on his command.[50]

The Raiders found Indiana to be a land untouched by war. With the approach of the Raiders, many families fled, leaving food and supplies for the taking. At Indianapolis, the governor declared a state of emergency, asking for all male citizens to arm themselves and form militia companies. More than 60,000 men from all parts of Indiana responded to the call. On July 13, Morgan crossed over the Whitewater River into Ohio, passing just to the north of Cincinnati. As the Raiders passed through the Ohio towns, the pillaging and looting increased. Morgan's men stole horses, broke into stores, and helped themselves to whatever they wanted.[51]

Morgan soon realized that he had made a mistake by going as far as he had. Local militia and armed citizens contested his advance at nearly every town. Now the raid turned from an adventure into an ordeal. Morgan's force was reduced by almost 500 men, mostly due to weariness and loss of horses. They were in the saddle hour after hour, trying to gain sleep whenever they could. "It was a terrible, trying march," Duke wrote; "Strong men fell out of their saddles for want of sleep." At Buffington Ford, a strong Union column under Brigadier General Edward Hobson intercepted Morgan. A portion of Morgan's command under Colonel Duke surrendered, but

Duke was able to hold the enemy at bay until Morgan could escape with a contingent of 1,200 of his men.[52]

When Morgan reached Senecaville, he knocked at the door of a house to get directions. A woman whose husband was serving in the war opened the door and invited him in. They talked for a few minutes, and she gave him directions. As he was leaving, she confessed that she had almost shot him through the window as he approached, but had decided against it. Morgan replied that she had not pulled the trigger because "at that moment, my wife [wa]s on her knees praying for my safety."[53]

The only issue now for Morgan was to escape, but Hobson's pursuit was relentless. The sweltering temperature now began to take its toll on the Raiders. Horses fell from the heat; exhausted men dropped off to sleep and tumbled from their saddles. For a while, Morgan was able to evade his pursuers, but each day more men were lost. Finally on July 26, Morgan and the remainder of his command surrendered. When Brigadier General James Shackleford refused to accept his formal military surrender, Morgan asked to be returned to the field so he could die in battle rather than be taken as a criminal. His request was denied.[54]

Under heavy guard, Morgan was taken to Cincinnati, where vengeance was swift. Ohio's Governor David Tod insisted that he and his men should be treated as civilian prisoners and not paroled. Because of his marauding actions, Morgan was not treated as a soldier, but rather as a horse thief. On July 28, General-in-Chief Henry Halleck directed that Morgan and the officers captured with his command be sent to the Ohio State Penitentiary at Columbus.[55]

Morgan and his men were insulted and degraded; authorities at the prison shaved their heads and beards as if they were civilian criminals. Morgan's treatment was regarded in the South as a barbaric humiliation, and later the governor of Ohio apologized "for an outrageous and disgraceful act." Prison rules were strictly enforced. The Raiders were held in separate cells and not permitted to speak to each other except during mealtime. Violation of any of the prison rules meant confinement in the "dungeon." Gradually, the restrictions were lifted, and the men were allowed to talk with each other.[56]

Morgan and his men soon began to think about escaping when they realized that a tunnel could be dug. Two table knives were smuggled from the dining room and used to chip away the floor. Eventually, they worked their way through the floor to the air duct below and then began to dig the tunnel. On November 20, the tunnel was completed. Just after midnight on November 27, Morgan and six of his men made their way through the tunnel to the prison yard and over the wall. From there they went to a friend's house, where they were provided with horses. Although a reward of $5,000 was offered for Morgan's capture, the general made good his escape and was united with his wife on Christmas.[57]

In January 1864, Morgan and his wife were honored in Richmond. Although Morgan was hailed as a hero, privately the Confederate high command was furious with him because he failed to follow orders. To some Southerners, Morgan's raid had been the greatest adventure of the war, but to others, it was an exercise in futility with no real military goal. In reality, it ended Morgan's usefulness to the Army of Tennessee.[58]

Morgan blamed the cool reception he received from President Davis on General Bragg, who was now serving as his military advisor. Bragg, Morgan believed, was still angry with him for disobeying his orders with his recent raid. For Bragg, it was more than that. During the Battle of Stone's River, when he had needed Morgan's cavalry, they had been unavailable.[59]

For nearly three months, Morgan campaigned for authorization to organize a new command so that he could continue his raids on Kentucky. When this did not happen, he issued a proclamation himself in an effort to recruit his own command. Morgan's personal magnetism still worked, and men came from all parts of the South to serve under him. By the middle of May, his brigade had grown to 2,000 men. Morgan sent a message to the Confederate War Department, not to request permission, but rather to inform it that he was going to make another raid into Kentucky. By the time the message reached Richmond, the raid into Kentucky was already under way.[60]

After robbing the bank at Mount Sterling, Morgan headed for Lexington, where the Union army had numerous horses quartered. Within minutes after his arrival, warehouses and other buildings along the railroad were torched. As the fires raged, Morgan ordered his men to take the horses and head toward Paris. In the meantime, he took this opportunity to visit Hopemount, where he hoped to see his mother. It was the last time he would see Hopemount.[61]

As the Raiders made their way through Kentucky, they gathered 1,000 horses and nearly 1,000 prisoners. Before returning to Virginia, Morgan decided to spend the night at Cynthiana, allowing his men to sleep late and have a leisurely breakfast. Without warning, Federal troops swept down on Morgan and his men. Although outnumbered and surprised, Morgan and half of his command were able to escape. It was several weeks before his scattered troops found their way back to Virginia. In their haste to escape, they were not able to bring a single prisoner or horse back with them.[62]

In August, Martha came to see her husband, hoping to raise his spirits. Despite his adventurous spirit, Morgan was a sensitive man. His last raid had been a failure. Because of the pillaging and looting by his raiders in Mount Sterling, he had lost much of the support of his friends in Kentucky. There had been reports that when his men captured Mount Sterling, they had held up the local bank. At first, Morgan claimed that he knew nothing about the robbery.[63]

After an investigation, the Confederate War Department charged Morgan with allowing "excesses and irregularities" associated with the armed robbery of the bank in Mount Sterling. The $59,000 taken from the bank belonged to private citizens, and under the rules of war, the stealing of private funds was illegal. There is no evidence that Morgan ordered or approved of the taking of nongovernmental funds or the pillaging of private property, but as commanding general, he would have to answer for the actions of his command.[64]

In a letter to Secretary of War Seddon, Morgan admitted that members of his command had robbed the bank at Mount Sterling, but contended that the critical nature of the situation had prevented him from making an investigation at the scene. A court of inquiry to investigate the matter was scheduled for September 10, but Morgan would be dead before it had a chance to convene.

On September 3, Morgan arrived in Greeneville, Tennessee, where he deployed his cavalry division on the outskirts of town. When Union Brigadier General Alvan Gillem received information that Morgan was in Greeneville, he made plans to march his troops all night and attack Morgan's headquarters in the morning. At five a.m., Federal cavalry slipped by Morgan's line. Charging into Greeneville, they caught the few Confederate troops in town by surprise.[65]

Morgan was awakened by rifle fire in the streets below his bedroom. A staff officer rushed into the room to warn him of the immediate danger. Morgan quickly slipped on his pants and boots and ran down the steps. He attempted to reach the stable and his horse, but was spotted and had to turn back, taking shelter in the bushes near the house. A spectator pointed out his hiding place to the Union soldiers searching for him. Unarmed and defenseless, Morgan came out from his hiding place with his hands raised. "Don't shoot. I surrender," he said. "Surrender and be God damned—I know you," one of the Union soldiers replied. Raising his carbine, he fired at point-blank range. Morgan groaned and fell to the ground. "I've killed the damned horse thief!" the soldier told his comrades.[66]

The jubilant troopers threw Morgan's body across a horse and paraded their trophy around town before stripping him down to his drawers and throwing his body into a muddy roadside ditch. Two of Morgan's staff were allowed to retrieve his body and place it in the house where he had slept the night before. After the Union soldiers left Greeneville, Morgan's body was taken to Abingdon, Virginia. His wife, now pregnant with their daughter, had his body moved to a vault in Richmond. After the war, he was returned to Kentucky, the land he loved, for interment in a cemetery in Lexington.[67]

John Hunt Morgan's raids made him famous. Making his own rules rather than following those of his superiors, Morgan terrorized citizens in three states. For Southerners, he was a chivalrous knight, the gallant cavalier of romantic literature. To Northern citizens, he was a rogue. To his own army, he was a maverick. The real John Hunt Morgan was a little of each.

18 *Ambrose Powell Hill*

Always Ready for a Fight

Ambrose Powell Hill was regarded by Robert E. Lee as the best division commander in the Army of Northern Virginia, an opinion shared by Jefferson Davis. Hill distinguished himself in every engagement, and his death in Petersburg, Virginia, on April 12, 1865, was a serious loss to the Confederacy. General Lee relied heavily upon him, and on Lee's deathbed, his memory would revert to Hill. Among his last words were: "Tell A. P. Hill he must come up."[1]

Although Hill was of average height and neat build, there was something in his appearance that caused Jefferson Davis and others to refer to him as "Little Powell." Hill was said by some to be handsome, although it is difficult to tell from photographs because of his thick beard. Perhaps it was the projection of his attractive personality rather than his looks that gave this impression. He had the affection and respect of his officers and men, despite the fact that in battle he was relentless, riding down slackers and whacking them with the flat of his sword. In battle, he wore a red hunting shirt, swore oaths, and was always where the action was. Off duty, he looked after his wounded, conferred informally with his staff, and drank his bourbon straight. He never lost his dignity or demeaned his subordinates when talking to them. He was contemptuous of Stonewall Jackson's public piety, but was not impious himself. He was loyal to his subordinates, often risking arrest and trial to defend them against what he thought were injustice and humiliation from superiors, particularly Stonewall Jackson.[2]

When not fighting, Powell Hill was soft-spoken and wore a friendly smile. His quick temper and combativeness went with his reddish hair and beard. His personal courage was remarkable, as was his tactical ability. A natural leader, "Little Powell" possessed a "commanding resolution" that was "inspired by his voice, his example, and his personal appearance." A fellow officer admiringly noted that "his every posture and movement was full of grace, . . . his military bearing and martial step would betray the soldier by birth and training."[3] But he did have flaws; he was impetuous, which Lee forgave on more than one occasion, because Lee loved a general who would fight, and A. P. Hill was always ready for a fight.[4]

Ambrose Powell Hill was born on November 9, 1825 to Thomas and Fannie Russell Baptist Hill of Culpepper, Virginia. Thomas's father served in the Revolutionary War under Colonel "Light Horse Harry" Lee; Fannie was descended from the Earl of Gainsboro, who lived during the reign of Charles II. Thomas and his wife soon developed contrasting life styles. Thomas became a highly esteemed merchant, farmer, and politician. He was a "splendid-looking man," tall, noted for his courage, and respected for his character. On the other hand, Fannie was frail, introverted, and had difficulty controlling her emotions. She preferred keeping to herself, sitting by the window, knitting, or gazing out across the fields. She spent most of her life battling ills, real or imaginary. Their union produced seven children, of whom Ambrose was the youngest.[5]

Powell enjoyed a pleasant childhood, and because he was the youngest son, he was closer to his mother than were the other children and thus more tolerant of her hypochondria. But he also enjoyed being with his father, who put him on a horse at an early age. As a result, Powell learned to ride as quickly as he learned to walk. Later in life, a comrade would describe him as a "perfect picture in the saddle and the most graceful rider I ever saw."[6]

In the 1830s, his family moved to the town of Culpeper Court House, where Powell was enrolled in a one-room school. He was a receptive student, self-reliant, and bright. He enjoyed reading and found books on Napoleon Bonaparte fascinating. Soon he was organizing neighborhood boys into miniature armies and playing war. At the age of twelve, Powell was sent to Black Hills Seminary, where he joined other well-to-do boys. Young Hill still continued to enjoy school, and a fellow classmate later wrote that his "devotion to his studies" exceeded that of "all his fellow students."[7]

At the impressionable age of fifteen, Powell suddenly found his youthful activities seriously hampered by the new religious outlook of his parents. In 1840, an ardent evangelist proselytized many Virginia churchgoers, including the Hill family, into the Baptist "new light" movement. The tenets of the religion forbade the playing of cards, dancing, and going to the theater. His parents insisted on adhering to these guidelines. Powell revolted against such rigid restraints and felt unjustly confined to this cloistered life. In later years, he attended church services more from duty than from devotion, and he always looked with disapproval on anyone who, like Stonewall Jackson, practiced religion openly and intensely.[8]

High-spirited and independent, Powell looked for an opportunity to

Ambrose Powell Hill was regarded by Robert E. Lee as the best division commander in the Army of Northern Virginia. Lee relied heavily upon him, and his memory would revert to Hill on his deathbed. Among his last words were: "Tell A. P. Hill he must come up."
COURTESY OF THE LIBRARY OF CONGRESS

escape his oppressive, fanatical environment. Influenced by the exploits of his military ancestors, along with his hero-worship of Napoleon, he decided on a military career. Through a political friend of his father, he obtained and accepted, over his mother's strenuous objections, an appointment to West Point.[9]

In late June of 1842, Powell prepared to leave Culpeper Court House for West Point with the one attribute of a future officer that he possessed— confidence. At age sixteen and a half, he was of average height and noticeably thin. His father's going-away present was a Bible in which was written: "Ambrose Powell Hill: Peruse this every day." His mother gave him a small ham bone as a good luck charm, which he carried all his life. His former Latin teacher, Albert Simms, bid him farewell, shaking his hand and saying: "My boy, remember: *Dulce et decorum est pro patria mori!*" Powell often repeated the translation: "It is pleasant and fitting to die for one's country."[10]

Young Powell Hill entered West Point in 1842. His graduating class of 1846 was destined to become one of the most famous in the history of West Point. Among his classmates were Dabney Maury, George Pickett, George McClellan, Thomas "Stonewall" Jackson, Jesse Reno, George Stoneman, and Cadmus Wilcox, all of whom who would become future Civil War generals. Hill quickly made friends, and he became close to two fellow Virginians, Birkett D. Fry and Dabney Maury. Pennsylvanian George McClellan was his roommate. Throughout their lives, they remained close friends. The fifteen-year-old McClellan quickly went to the top of the class and remained there until graduation, enjoying the affection and respect of all. McClellan's ease with studies undoubtedly helped Hill over the rough academic road of the first year at the Academy.[11]

Hill and Jackson were never friends at West Point. One reason for their lack of friendship had to do with their social standing. Hill was of a higher social class in Virginia than Jackson, and both knew it. But there were other reasons. While Jackson had to study hard at West Point, education came easily to Hill. Jackson was serious about all that he did, while Hill was always looking for a good time. Jackson practiced religion with a fervor that Hill disliked. Hill made friends easily; Jackson did not.[12]

Discipline at West Point was strict, and marks were given for being unprepared for class and for not following regulations. Demerits added up quickly. A cadet who accumulated one hundred demerits in six months was subject to dismissal from the Academy. In conduct, young Powell got off to a bumpy start. He picked up the usual demerits during the first term, but two major infractions—"not walking post properly" and "being absent from reveille"—raised his total demerits dangerously close to the dismissal point. He then got serious and applied himself diligently the next term, ending his first year near the middle of his class.[13]

During Hill's second year at West Point, he applied himself more intensely. By the end of the year, his rank had risen to twenty-third out of a class of sixty-six. Having reached the status of a second-classman, he was entitled to a two-month furlough. He returned home during the summer of 1844 and enjoyed the envy of many of the youths of Culpeper Court House. While returning to West Point after his leave, Powell passed through New York City. The cadets had been warned of the dangers of the "dens of iniquity" that existed there. Yet, for an eighteen-year-old man full of youthful exuberance, New York was an attractive, exciting place to visit, especially just before a return to the strict rules of West Point. For young Powell, his visit would prove to be disastrous.[14]

On September 9, Hill was admitted to the Academy hospital "with gonorrhea contracted on furlough." In the weeks that followed, more serious physical problems surfaced: severe pelvic pain, fever, and difficulty in urinating. The gonorrhea had led to a painful case of prostatitis. In November, Hill was sent home on a convalescent furlough. The attacks of prostatitis would occur more frequently as he grew older, causing periods of excruciating pain and times when he was incapacitated. It would ultimately lead to another potentially fatal illness.[15]

In late spring, his condition improved enough for him to return to West Point. He was disappointed when a faculty board reviewed his record and found that his long absence from class had left him deficient in his studies. As a result, they directed that he repeat his third year. The decision was difficult for him to accept. It meant leaving his good friends, who would now graduate a year ahead of him.[16]

Powell reported to camp that summer and soon struck up friendships with Henry Heth, Ambrose Burnside, and Julian McAllister. The four became close friends and were inseparable during their last two years at the Academy. That fall, Hill was appointed sergeant of his class, a promotion based primarily on his leadership qualities. With considerable envy, he watched his former classmates of the famous class of 1846 receive their commissions and head for action in Mexico. He hoped the war would last long enough for him to join in the hostilities.[17]

Graduating fifteenth in a class of thirty-eight, Brevet Second Lieutenant Powell Hill received his coveted orders to join the Light Battery of the First Regiment U.S. Artillery in Mexico. In Mexico, he was assigned command of a cavalry detachment and ordered to join General Lane, who was marching on the Mexican Capital. As the only member of his West Point class to see action in Mexico, he was filled with exuberance over the prospect of battle. Hill adopted a flamboyant uniform, consisting of a flaming red flannel shirt and coarse blue pants stuffed into red-topped boots, to which he attached a large pair of Mexican spurs. On his head, he wore a huge sombrero. His weapons were just as conspicuous: he wore a long artillery saber, a pair of horse pistols in large leather holsters, plus a pair of revolvers and a butcher knife, all stuck in a wide belt. To many, Hill resembled a mobile arsenal.[18]

Unfortunately for Hill, the war was in its final stages and he saw limited action. He participated in several of the closing engagements at Huamantla and Atlixco. Hill was promoted to second lieutenant on August 20, 1847 and assigned to Captain John B. Magruder's battery.[19]

When the capital fell, the officers were permitted to take up residence in private homes. Again, Hill succumbed to beautiful women, this time in Mexico. Writing to his father, Hill confessed, "'Tis a fact that the ladies of Mexico are beautiful. . . but very few of them ever read Wayland's *Moral Science*. . . . You know my failing. 'Tis an inheritance of this family, this partiality for women." All of Powell's infatuations ended with the peace negotiations in the spring of 1848. Hill left Mexico full of romantic memories, but disappointed at the limited opportunities he had had to prove himself in combat.[20]

In the fall of 1849, Lieutenant Hill began a tour of duty in the South. The First Artillery Regiment was ordered to subdue the Seminole Indians.

Powell thought the effort was senseless, writing to his sister Lucy that an all-out expedition against the Indians "'twould be unwise . . . expensive . . . and only to drive a few poor, lazy, harmless devils from the country that no white man could, or would, live in."[21] The only hazard that he encountered was a bout with yellow fever, which provoked a severe attack of prostatitis. For a few months, Hill was unable to perform any duties because of the weakness and pain that shot up through his body when he tried to mount his horse.[22]

As early as 1850, Hill was aware of the pending conflict between the North and South. In August, he learned that a Culpeper Court House mob had lynched a young black man for murdering a white man. Hill was livid at what the people from his hometown had done. In a letter to one of his brothers, he asserted, "Shame, shame upon you all, good citizens. Virginia must crawl unless you vindicate good order or discipline and hang every son-of-a-bitch connected with the outrage." After the war, Hill's wife stated that he "never owned any slaves and never approved of the institution of slavery, but [he] thought the government should not take slaves from their masters without paying something for them."[23]

Despite Hill's feelings about slavery, he was a Southerner at heart. In the same letter to his brother, he expressed his feelings about where his loyalties lay: "If the Union is dissolved, I shall make tracks for home, and offer my service to the Governor, and intimate my modest desire for a brigade at least. I've been a sub long enough, and wish now to seek the bubble reputation at the cannon's mouth."[24]

In 1855, Powell had another bout with yellow fever, prostatitis, or both. The attack was so severe that he was ordered home to recuperate. During his time at home, his social life did not suffer. One friend characterized him as the "gay lieutenant, social and sportive." His physical disability, however, became the overriding issue; his health continued to be a problem. Hill found it impossible to return to field duty and requested a transfer to a desk job. Secretary of War Jefferson Davis honored his request, and Hill was detailed for special duty in the United States Coast Survey.[25]

On November 23, 1855, Hill began his new assignment. It was during this time that he began his celebrated love affair with Ellen "Nelly" Marcy, the daughter of Major Randolph B. Marcy. Ellen was twenty-one years old and blond, blue-eyed, and attractive. She lived with her mother at Willard's Hotel in Washington, and the two ladies were regulars at all the important social affairs, Ellen attracting one suitor after another.[26]

Powell quickly fell in love with Ellen and proposed; she accepted. Hill had already given her an engagement ring before the Marcys were aware of the seriousness of the affair. Both parents reacted with anything but joy. They urged their daughter to wait at least six months before marrying. The major painted a harsh picture of life on the frontier as the wife of an army officer; moreover, Hill's means were limited. The major also pointed out the difference in their backgrounds. While the Marcys were Northerners, Hill was a Southerner brought up in a slave environment. In short, the Marcys did not believe Hill was good enough for their daughter. They preferred a former suitor of Ellen's, George B. McClellan.[27]

Mrs. Marcy quickly took action. Through a check of his service records, she learned of Hill's medical problem while at West Point. Within a short time, the story was circulating around Washington. Hill was outraged at what he regarded as an invasion of his privacy and wrote to Major Marcy, asking him to control his wife's gossiping. Major Marcy assured him it would not happen again. At this point, Hill's old friend and competitor for Ellen's hand, George McClellan, was drawn into the affair. When he learned of the stories being spread about Powell, he immediately wrote Mrs. Marcy defending his friend's honor: "You have been unjust to him, and you have said unpleasant and bitter things to me in reference to one of my oldest and dearest friends."[28] By then, however, the damage had been done, and in July, Ellen told her parents that the affair was over. She returned the engagement ring to Powell, who gave it to his sister Lucy.

Hill's episode with the Marcys and McClellan revealed an interesting insight into his character. Angrily aroused by Mrs. Marcy's inappropriate actions, Hill had been blunt in demanding that a proper apology should be made. On the other hand, he wrote to McClellan, expressing his concern that people would be given a false impression of his affair with Ellen. At the expense of his own vanity, he admitted to McClellan that it was she, not he, who had broken the engagement. To set the record straight, Hill revealed what had actually happened. The two continued to be good friends despite the fact that they both loved the same woman.

McClellan's persistent efforts finally won Ellen's hand.[29] On May 22, 1860, McClellan and Ellen Marcy were married in New York City. Hill was a groomsman at the wedding. His best wishes were sincere and strong.[30]

Although Powell Hill would soon find another love, his proud, sensitive nature was affected by his broken romance. He did not brood, but he could not forget it. During the war, a mutual friend wrote to Ellen, "I have seen at different times many of your old army friends, General A. P. Hill, Edward Johnston and many others and I assure you 'Miss Nelly,' as they still call you, is often spoken of."[31]

During the war, McClellan's Army of the Potomac would be assailed repeatedly in the front and on the flank by Hill's Light Division. McClellan's soldiers believed that Hill's fierce assaults were an attempt to wreak vengeance on his rival. After one of those attacks, a Union veteran exclaimed in disgust, "My God Nelly, why didn't you marry him [Hill]!" Later, when this anecdote was related to McClellan at an 1885 reunion, he smiled and said: "Fiction no doubt, but surely no one could have married a more gallant soldier than A. P. Hill."[32]

Two years later, Powell Hill fell in love with and married Kitty Morgan, who was from a prominent Louisville family. Kitty was a wealthy young widow, and Powell quickly fell for her charms. Her doll-like features as a child had earned her the nickname of "Dolly." Unhampered by parental opposition, Hill and Kitty were married on July 18, 1859. The bride's older brother, John Hunt Morgan, soon to achieve fame as "The Rebel Raider," was the best man at the wedding. Little did Kitty realize that just a few years later her wedding dress would be fashioned into a colorful battle flag for her husband's first command, the Thirteenth Virginia Infantry Regiment.[33] Kitty complemented her husband so naturally that the two became inseparable. Not even war could keep them apart, and whenever possible, Kitty would accompany her husband in the field. Her habit of remaining with the general until a battle was imminent caused him some anxiety, and her departure was a signal to the troops of impending action.[34]

With the birth of two daughters, Hill became a doting father. When Lucy was born in 1863, his men built a cradle for her, and General Lee, her godfather, held her in his arms when she was baptized. On the battlefield, Hill was restless and fiery, but in his private life, he was "genial, approachable, and affectionate" as well as "tender and generous."[35]

The election of Abraham Lincoln sparked the secession of South Carolina. Soon after, six other Southern states followed. Hill believed that war was imminent and was convinced that Virginia would inevitably join the rest of the South. Defending slavery and secession were not important to him, but his family's honor and Virginia's traditions were. On February 26, he submitted his resignation from the U.S. Army and cast his lot with the new Confederate States of America.

On May 9, Hill received his commission as Colonel of the Virginia Volunteers, assigned to command the Thirteenth Virginia Infantry Regiment. He was ordered to report to Harper's Ferry. Hill drilled his regiment rigorously, and in short time, the regiment caught the eye of General Johnston, who commented on its "veteran-like appearance." Hill and his unit did not see action at First Manassas.

Early in 1862, Hill received his first star and was ordered to report to General Joseph Johnston's headquarters. McClellan's massive Army of the Potomac now numbered 150,000. To combat it, Johnston ordered his brigades to consolidate on line along the Rapidan and Rappahannock Rivers. Hill's division commander was Major General James Longstreet; Longstreet was to become one of Hill's principal nemeses for the duration of the war. Longstreet had been a reasonably good-natured officer at the start of the war, but in January 1862 his family fell victim to a scarlet fever epidemic. Three of his four children died within a few days. This tragedy so affected the general that he became uncommunicative. At first all went well between the two headstrong officers, but this soon changed.[36]

In the Peninsula Campaign of 1862, Hill's brigade spearheaded the repulse of McClellan's attack on the Confederate rearguard at Williamsburg. The exploits of Powell Hill and his brigade quickly became a rallying topic of the army. His bold and skillful handling of men under fire was singled out by Longstreet for commendation: "Hill ably led his brigade, whose organization was perfect throughout the battle, and it was marched off the field in as good order as it entered it."[37]

The engagement at Williamsburg had provided a long-awaited opportunity to demonstrate his capabilities as one of the most promising young officers in the Confederate army. On May 26, Hill learned that he had been promoted to the rank of major general. Now in his thirty-sixth year, Hill had served the Confederacy just slightly over a year. He had joined the army hoping for a quick appointment to high command. For nine months he had marked time as a colonel. Then in rapid succession came brigade command and his first taste of battle, and now he found himself head of a division. He had jumped from regimental colonel to division major general in exactly ninety days. Powell Hill was now the youngest major general in the Confederate army, assuming broad and unfamiliar responsibilities as the Confederacy faced its worst military crisis to date.[38]

Hill assumed division command as if he had been born to it. Few generals cared for or were as affectionate toward their men as Hill. He named his new command the "Light Division." His troops believed "the name was applicable, for we often marched without coats, blankets, knapsacks, or any other burdens except for our arms and haversacks, which were never heavy and sometimes empty." "We became very proud of the 'Light Division',," said Colonel William McComb of the Fourteenth Tennessee, "because General A. P. Hill was an ideal soldier." Hill concentrated on his brigades and batteries, consolidating his division and preparing them for the battle that was soon to come.[39] In the Battle of Seven Pines, Hill and his troops remained inactive in a manner similar to First Manassas. The most significant event of the battle was the wounding of General Joseph Johnston and his replacement with Robert E. Lee. Henceforth, the army would be known as the Army of Northern Virginia.

Hill's first engagement involving his Light Division was a bloody one. At the battle of Mechanicsville, he acted on his own, after waiting twelve hours for Stonewall Jackson to make his attack. Hill was furious over Jackson's absence; his disappointment and anger were apparent in his battle report: "It was never contemplated that my division alone should have sustained the shock of this battle, but such was the case."[40]

In Lee's report of the campaign, he attributed Jackson's lateness to an unrealistic timetable. Lee made no mention of Hill's having launched an attack without permission or support, nor did he criticize him in his report.[41] Hill's achievement, however, was acknowledged by a Richmond editor who wrote: "In the battle of yesterday, he displayed, in the highest degree, all the talents of a commander, with the exception of proper caution of his own life, which he exposed from the first shot to the last, with the recklessness of a trooper."[42]

Hill and his Light Division continued to distinguish themselves during the Seven Days' Campaign. They marched promptly, executed movements effectively, rushed into attack without caution, and always fought hard. Hill acquired a reputation as a fighter who would attack whatever was in his path. The price, however, of gaining such recognition was high. His casualties for the campaign were 5,500. Because Hill led by personal example, he expected his brigade and regimental commanders to do the same. As a result, the losses among officers were heavy.[43]

As soon as the Seven Days' Battle was over, problems within the ranks began. The worst and most damaging incident involved Hill and Longstreet. It shattered their friendship and the harmony of the Army of Northern Virginia. The dispute began when John Daniels, editor of the *Richmond Examiner*, wrote a series of articles inflating Hill's accomplishments. According to Daniels, it was Hill and his division who "stood successfully opposed to at least four times their number." A few days later, Daniels's account of the Battle of Frayser's Farm was even more flattering of Hill's accomplishments: "The battle was fought under the immediate and sole command of General A. P. Hill, in charge of both divisions. . . . One fact is very certain, and that is that the battle of Monday night was fought exclusively by General A. P. Hill and forces under his command."[44]

As soon as Longstreet read the article, he became enraged, believing his leadership had been ignored. His letter to a rival newspaper was a scathing rebuttal: "No one in the army has any objections to Major General A. P. Hill being supplied with all the notoriety . . . provided no great injustice is done to others." When Hill learned of the letter, he too became angry, so angry that he requested to be relieved from Longstreet's command. For Hill, the matter had become an affair of honor. The dispute continued and reached the point where Longstreet had Hill placed under arrest. Hill was not one to sit back and sulk. In an angry letter to Longstreet, Hill requested that arrangements be made for a "hostile meeting" between himself and Longstreet.[45]

When Lee learned of the pending duel between two of his best generals, he interceded and transferred Hill and his 10,000 troops to Jackson's command. In his most tactful way, Lee told Jackson that Hill was a team man, but sensitive to military protocol and etiquette and that Jackson should keep Hill and his generals regularly informed as to what he was doing.[46]

Jackson ignored the suggestion, and this led to one of the Civil War's most heated feuds. The contrast in personality between Hill and Jackson did not lend itself to a harmonious relationship. Jackson held himself aloof from his subordinates and was relentless in dealing with their shortcomings. He insisted that his officers first obey his orders and question them later if necessary. Hill also demanded strict adherence to duty, but he was cordial and considerate of his subordinates. A fellow officer described him as "affable and readily approachable by the humblest private; but the officer next in rank never forgot when on duty that he was in the presence of his superior. No commander was ever more considerate of the rights and feelings of others under him, or sustained the authority of his subordinate officers with more firmness and tact." While Stonewall Jackson would spend most of his leisure time in prayer, Hill would smoke his pipe and enjoy conversation with his associates. Almost immediately, Hill ran into difficulty with Jackson. When there was a misunderstanding over a communication about the movement of troops, the curtain was raised on a prolonged dispute between the two.[47]

At the Battle of Cedar Mountain on August 9, 1862, Union troops under Major General Nathaniel Banks faced Jackson's outnumbered army. When the outcome of the battle hung in the balance, Hill saved the day by his timely arrival on the field. This instance revealed a strange twist in the ongoing dispute between Hill and Jackson. Although they frequently argued and disagreed, when it came time for a battle, they put away their differences and focused on their common goal—the destruction of the enemy.[48]

On August 28, fierce fighting erupted all along the Confederate front, beginning the Second Battle of Manassas. Jackson assigned Hill's division the "post of greatest danger," leaving the disposition of his troops up to him. As Hill positioned his men along a railroad bed, he left a gap between two of his brigades unattended. During the heat of the battle, Union troops were able to break Hill's line at the gap and pose danger to Jackson's left. Hill, however, did not allow the Union breakthrough to cloud his judgment or to shake his confidence. With the help of Major General Jubal Early's division, Hill was able to coordinate the deployment of troops to halt the Federal thrust. At one point, Hill's men ran low on ammunition and were forced to use musket stocks, stones, and bayonets to repulse General Pope's desperate attacks.[49] Hill sent a courier with news of their victory to Jackson, who, with a rare smile, replied: "Tell him I knew he would do it."[50] For a brief time the two generals shared a moment of peace amid the roar of battle.

During the fighting at Manassas, Hill displayed a compassionate quality that was part of his nature. When he learned that a captured Union surgeon was voluntarily caring for wounded Confederate soldiers, he accorded him full privileges as a noncombatant. From then on, the Union surgeon was welcomed at Hill's headquarters as a guest and allowed the freedom of the camp until he was passed through the lines a few days later.[51]

Unfortunately, the good feelings between Jackson and Hill did not last long. On the day following Hill's tenacious defense, Lee launched a counterattack, which swept Pope's army from the field. Jackson pursued the retreating Federals. During the pursuit, some of Hill's men straggled from the ranks, causing his division to fall behind. When Hill was unable to get the men back in line, he again incurred Jackson's wrath.

After his victory at Manassas, Lee decided on a bold move—to invade the North through Maryland. A successful Confederate offensive in the

North might induce the federal government to sue for peace. A victory might even bring England and France to their aid. Jackson's wing was chosen to lead the way toward the Potomac. When he discovered a large number of stragglers from Hill's division, he became perturbed. Exasperated, he rode to Hill's camp where he found the brigades casually preparing to break camp. Without consulting Hill, Jackson took matters into his own hands, and put Hill's division in motion.[52]

Once in motion, Hill and his staff rode at the head of the leading brigade, allowing his column to drift apart. This further irritated Jackson, who had instructed his lieutenants to ride back and forth along the line of march to prevent straggling. For Jackson, this was a violation of his orders. Since Hill was aware of Jackson's insistence on a strict following of his orders, it is surprising that he made no effort to adhere to them. By his actions, Hill continued to provoke Jackson.[53]

The feud between the two finally reached a boiling point on the morning of September 4. Jackson had adopted a policy while on the march of allowing his men to rest ten minutes every hour and a half hour at noon. To Jackson's amazement, Hill had ignored these rest periods by keeping the men marching continuously. This violation of his orders was the last straw for Jackson. He halted Hill's leading brigade and ordered them to stop and observe the rest period. When Hill learned what Jackson had done, he was infuriated and angrily approached him: "General Jackson, you have assumed command of my division; here is my sword, I have no use for it." Jackson's reply was cold, "Keep your sword, General Hill, but consider yourself under arrest for neglect of duty." Hill was stripped of his command and ordered to follow the Light Division on foot.[54]

Hill was humiliated; in his rage it was hard for him to be objective about the situation. In Hill's mind, Jackson was entirely responsible for their series of altercations. Jackson had refused to divulge his plans, changed orders without letting his subordinates know, and violated military protocol by dealing with Hill's subordinates directly. Hill requested a list of the charges against him. First, Hill was accused of not moving his troops fast enough; now Jackson was upset because he had not paused for a rest and was pushing his troops to move faster. In this uncompromising mood, Hill concluded that Jackson was unfit for command and decided to press charges against him.[55] While Lee's army was moving into Maryland for the battle he hoped would end the war, his most brilliant division commander was under arrest for the second time in two months. Hill had been relegated to marching on foot at the rear of his division as the army embarked on its most dangerous campaign. The feud between Hill and Jackson would end only with Jackson's death.

Finally, Hill swallowed his pride and asked Jackson to be reinstated. Jackson acknowledged that no one could lead his division as well as Hill, and he agreed to allow him to resume his command with the understanding that after the battle he would report himself under arrest again.[56]

Once Hill returned to duty, one of his officers stated that his spirits soared: "Donning his coat and sword, he mounted his horse and dashed to the front of his troops, and, looking like a young eagle in search of his prey, he took command of his division, to the delight of his men."[57]

Once in Maryland, the audacious and unpredictable Lee divided his forces, despite facing numerically superior Union forces. Jackson, in command of three separate columns, was to proceed southwest to Harper's Ferry. Then he would rejoin Lee at Boonsboro. Jackson's three divisions, including Hill's, embarked on a fifty-one-mile march toward Harper's Ferry. In addition to sending Jackson to capture the 11,000-man Union garrison at Harper's Ferry, Lee had ordered some of Longstreet's command to guard passes through South Mountain while other units of his corps moved toward Hagerstown in search of supplies and information. Only Lee would dare split his army in such a way, particularly in enemy territory.

This time, however, Lee's Army of Northern Virginia found itself in trouble, trouble caused by an unlikely accident of fate. Several days before, a Confederate soldier had dropped a packet of cigars in the road near Frederick, Maryland, where Lee's army rested before crossing the Potomac. As impossible as it might seem, a copy of general order number 191 from General Lee was wrapped around the cigars. The order gave details of Lee's plan to split his army and later to regroup near Hagerstown. Once General McClellan, who was newly reunited with the Army of the Potomac, received the information, he moved against Lee.[58]

McClellan now had the opportunity to destroy the Army of Northern Virginia piece by piece. In the hours that followed, however, McClellan should have pushed hard to engage the divided segments of Lee's army. Instead he vacillated, allowing Lee enough time to gather his fragmented army together again. Once Lee realized what was happening, he took up a defensive position and called for every unit to concentrate near Sharpsburg, a small hamlet between the Antietam Creek and the Potomac.[59]

As Lee watched the gathering Union army spread along the hills, 80,000 strong, he disposed his small force of only 40,000 troops behind Antietam Creek. Finally, late in the morning of September 16, Jackson arrived. He had been victorious at Harper's Ferry, without A. P. Hill's Light Division. All through the night, Lee waited for reinforcements.[60]

With dawn, hoping to destroy Lee's army once and for all, the Yankees came in steady lines. They came closer to accomplishing their objective than they realized; one more attack on the Confederate flank against Jackson's weakened brigades, and they might have carried the day. Then the battle shifted to the Rebel center, but again the Union attack failed in what would forever be known as the Bloody Lane. The last part of Lee's line to be attacked was south of Sharpsburg. If the Yankees prevailed there they could cut off Lee from the Potomac. The Union assault at the stone bridge was almost sure to be a success. Lee had only 5,000 men to face Burnside's 13,000. Everything in that part of the battlefield hinged on when A. P. Hill would arrive from Harper's Ferry.[61]

Lee sent a courier to Harper's Ferry, urging Hill to hurry to Sharpsburg. Wearing his famous red battle shirt, Hill left Harper's Ferry at 7:30 a.m. and marched his men to Sharpsburg at a brutal pace, ignoring the rest period and leaving dozens of stragglers by the wayside. The men in front were urged to maintain a fast pace. Hill was inspiring that day; he was everywhere, encouraging his men to push on with all dispatch. After marching all day, he arrived at Sharpsburg about four p.m. with only three-fifths of his division.[62]

Hill arrived just in time to put his men in line and to attack Burnside's flank. Hill's assault beat Burnside back and saved the day for the Confederates. When McClellan surveyed the field and ascertained that he had lost at least 10,000 men, he decided not to continue the attack, ending the Battle of Antietam. That night, the sounds of the wounded and dying could be heard as doctors and litter bearers worked between the lines in an attempt to save as many of the wounded as possible. Finally, the survivors slept. With their sleep went the last chance for a quick Northern victory.[63]

Total casualties for the blue and gray combined exceeded 20,000 men. It was the most bloody single-day battle in American history. Who won the battle is still a matter of debate. Lee could claim victory because he had stopped McClellan and taken the best the North could give. McClellan could boast that he had stopped Lee's invasion, driven him from Northern soil, and ended his string of military victories. At the same time, however, he had missed an opportunity to destroy Lee's army and perhaps bring a speedy end to the war. Despite the heavy loss of Union lives, President Lincoln claimed the Battle of Antietam as a Union victory and took this opportunity to issue his Preliminary Emancipation Proclamation. For Lincoln and the North, the war had given a new meaning to life and liberty.[64]

After the battle, Hill was declared the hero of the hour. "Three thousand men, only 2,000 of whom had engaged in the final counterstroke, had saved Lee's army from almost certain destruction," one authority declared. In his report, Lee stated that "Hill drove the enemy immediately from the position they had taken." Hill's action of turning most certain defeat for the Confederacy into a stunning victory emphasized again that he was the best division commander in the Army of Northern Virginia.[65]

After the battle, Hill issued a congratulatory statement to his men: "Soldiers of the Light Division: You have done well and I am pleased with you. . . . You saved the day at Sharpsburg and Shepherdstown." Hill's remarks were true, but his praise for his men actually was a way of responding to Jackson's recent criticism. Because of Hill's recent performances in battle, Jackson seemed content to let the issue drop; Hill, however, was not. He requested official charges from Jackson. Hill had been arrested for neglect of duty, a serious charge. He maintained his innocence, demanding a court of inquiry to resolve the situation.[66]

To resolve the issue, General Lee called a conference with the two generals. Lee told both generals, "He who has been most aggrieved can be the most magnanimous and make the first overtures of peace," but neither was willing to take the first step. Lee continued to try to persuade the two that they must put aside their differences for the good of the country. Jackson was the first to concede, tearing up his charges against Hill.[67]

Hill's success in his recent victories had been costly. Dorsey Pender, one of Hill's brigade commanders, wrote: "You have no idea what a reputation our division has. It surpasses Jackson's division both for fighting and discipline. . . . But when I tell you that this division has lost 9,000 killed and wounded since we commenced the Richmond fight at Mechanicsville, you can see what reputation has cost us." The six brigades in the Light Division now numbered barely 4,700 men.[68]

After Antietam, the need for dividing the Army of Virginia into corps for better control became evident to Lee. President Davis approved the reorganization, naming Jackson and Longstreet as corps commanders. At the same time, Lee expressed his faith in Hill: "Next to these two officers, I consider General A. P. Hill the best commander with me. He fights his troops well, and takes good care of them." It was clear that despite Hill's problems with Longstreet and Jackson, he would be Lee's choice should a third corps be created.[69]

After McClellan allowed Lee to slip back into Virginia without a pursuit, Lincoln lost his patience and replaced him with Ambrose E. Burnside. Burnside was a simple, honest, loyal soldier who was said to be "a man of remarkable enthusiasm with which he was but too apt to be carried away."[70]

By December 1862, Hill's Light Division had grown in strength to 11,000 troops. Lieutenant J. Hampden Chamberlayne wrote to his mother of the respite from fighting: "The men are cheerful, almost to recklessness, used to hardship, veterans in action and in camp life and becoming regular soldiers. We reckon ourselves up here to holding in check 100,000 men, whipping 60,000 and devouring 40,000."[71]

On December 11, the quiet was broken. Federal artillery pounded Fredericksburg, and using pontoon boats, Burnside's men forced their way across the Rappahannock. Yankee soldiers proceeded to sack the town and then formed their lines for battle. Lee was ready, having positioned his men so that the odds favored him when the attack came. Again, Hill's mind was not on defense, and again there was a weak spot in his line. When Hill deployed his troops along the forward slope of the ridge, there was a gap of 600 yards, about one-fifth of his entire front. The gap was a heavily wooded area of swampy ground and tangled underbrush. Hill assumed this area was impassable and left it undefended, allowing the enemy a covered approach to the heart of Confederate position. Almost as dangerous, Hill had placed General Gregg's brigade a quarter of a mile behind the gap.[72]

The gap did not go unnoticed. One of Hill's brigade commanders, Brigadier General Lane, called it to his attention. Hill made no attempt to correct it, probably because he was reluctant to disturb his troops, who had settled in for the night, and because he considered the wooded area impassable.[73]

When the Federal attack came, it was directed at two points, Longstreet on the left and Hill on the right. Longstreet was able to repulse the enemy, inflicting heavy losses; the attack on the right, led by George Meade's division, was able to break through the unprotected gap. Across their path lay Gregg's brigade. Gregg brought his troops into line and bravely jumped into the thick of the fighting. Seconds later a bullet tore through his spine, and he tumbled from his horse, mortally wounded. General Early's division came to the rescue, counterattacking and driving the Federals back, restoring the line. After heavy fighting, the losses were high on both sides, but Meade was forced to withdraw. On the left, Burnside persisted in dashing wave after wave of his demoralized troops against Longstreet in what Lee described as "war so terrible." Hill's poor deployment of his troops resulted in the only tense moment Lee's army experienced all day. Hill's responsibility for the gap was noted in Jackson's battle report.

Casualties were high in Hill's division, and there was some feeling that the losses would have been lower had Hill closed the gap in his line before the attack. Lee refrained from passing judgment, but Jackson had no doubt that he considered Hill negligent.[74]

After the battle, Hill again tried to clear his name. He reminded Lee of Jackson's charges and requested an early trial. Lee wanted the feud to end, writing to Hill: "I hope that you will concur with me that further prosecution is unnecessary, so far as you are concerned, and will be no advantage to the service." Hill, however, continued to press Lee into convening a court to try him on Jackson's charges.[75]

At the Battle of Chancellorsville in May 1863, the conflict between Hill and Jackson ended. After crushing the Federals' right flank with a sunset attack, Jackson and members of his staff rode forward to reconnoiter the Union position. Hill was traveling close behind when tragedy struck. Suddenly a volley of friendly fire erupted, striking Jackson and other members of both staffs. Hill rushed to Jackson's side and knelt down beside him; he unbuckled Jackson's belt and sword and gently removed his gauntlets to relieve the painful pressure. Then, resting Jackson's head and shoulders against his chest, Hill offered him brandy to bolster his strength until he could be carried to the rear.[76]

The impact of Jackson's wounding, and his later death, had finally softened Hill's animosity. Before Jackson died, he relinquished command to Hill, who was himself wounded shortly thereafter. Command of Jackson's

Second Corps temporarily went to Major General J. E. B. Stuart. On Sunday May 10, Jackson died. In his delirium, Jackson had called on Hill: "Order A. P. Hill to prepare for action."[77]

Following the irreplaceable loss of Stonewall Jackson, General Lee reorganized the Army of Northern Virginia into three corps and promoted Richard Ewell to command the Second Corps and A. P. Hill the Third Corps. In recommending Hill to President Jefferson Davis for the promotion, Lee praised his ability, saying he was "the best soldier of his grade with me." Hill's appointment was received enthusiastically by both officers and men, who expressed confidence in his bold, skillful, and tenacious leadership.[78] But there were also some negative reactions. Many, Longstreet in particular, thought that Hill had been chosen primarily because he was a Virginian. The other rejected candidates, Major Generals John Bell Hood, D. H. Hill, Lafayette McLaws, and R. H. Anderson, were all from states other than Virginia. To the rest of the army, Hill had plenty to prove as the Army of Northern Virginia headed for the battle that would decide the outcome of the war—Gettysburg.[79]

Although Hill was gratified at receiving this long-coveted promotion, he was concerned about the selection of a successor to command the Light Division. His unqualified choice was twenty-nine-year-old William Dorsey Pender. Spirits soared high in the new corps. The men were in excellent health and were better equipped than at any other time during the war. One veteran predicted that the army "will fight better than they have ever done, if such a thing is possible."[80]

With the North dispirited by Hooker's defeat at Chancellorsville, Lee felt the time was ripe for his long-contemplated invasion of Pennsylvania. While Ewell and Longstreet started Northward, Hill was instructed to contest any advance by Hooker. By May 14, all of Hooker's troops had withdrawn and Hill was able to join Lee in Pennsylvania. Lee planned to push northward and take Harrisburg, but when he learned that the Union army, now under the command of Major General George Meade, was advancing toward South Mountain, he ordered his army to concentrate east of Chambersburg. One important piece of Lee's army was missing—the "eyes" of J. E. B. Stuart, leaving him without information about the size and movements of the Army of the Potomac. From Chambersburg, Lee planned to go to Gettysburg, telling his officers: "Tomorrow, gentlemen, we will . . . go over to Gettysburg to see what General Meade is after."[81]

Hill's Third Corps led the eastward movement. On July 1, as they neared Gettysburg, Hill learned that there was a small Union cavalry detachment in town. Despite Lee's orders to avoid a general engagement, Hill sent General Heth's division to Gettysburg without his supervision. Before Hill knew what had happened and could stop it, the Army of Northern Virginia had stumbled into a confrontation.[82]

General Lee, unfamiliar with the terrain and ignorant of Union strength in the area, insisted that no general engagement be started until his army was concentrated. Ewell was several hours away and Longstreet a day's march to the west. At the same time, General Meade was preparing to lay a line of defense twenty miles southeast of Gettysburg, telling his corps commanders to be prepared to fall back to it.[83]

On the first day of the battle, Hill was ailing from an unknown illness. When Heth's division engaged Union troops, Hill was not fully aware of it. When General Lee questioned him in Cashtown about the sounds of battling in the east, Hill claimed ignorance and mounted his horse to investigate.[84]

When Hill reached the front with Lee, Heth informed the generals of the status of his division. Although not knowing exactly what he was up against, Hill decided to renew the battle on a larger scale. In the afternoon, Richard Ewell's Second Corps arrived. It soon became obvious to Lee that a full engagement was already under way and that the Union line was crumbling. Lee ordered Hill to drive forward.[85]

Hill's corps drove the Federals through Gettysburg up Cemetery Hill. By this time, Ewell's corps was also involved, and it appeared that one final assault would carry the hill and rout the Yankees. By mid-afternoon, Hill and Ewell had gained a decided advantage over Union forces west and north of Gettysburg. Although Lee had not wanted to fight the enemy here, when he saw that his troops had gained an advantage, he ordered Hill to press the enemy. The usually combative Hill, still not feeling well, complained that his troops were exhausted and disorganized by six hours of fighting. As a result, Lee did not order a fresh attack by the Third Corps that day. When Ewell and his Second Corps did not attack either, the opportunity to gain the high ground was lost. Some believe that one more round of assaults would have carried the two hills, Cemetery Hill and Culp's Hill, and sealed a major victory. This failure set the stage for two more days of bloody battles. Hill and Ewell had both entered Pennsylvania burdened with Stonewall Jackson's legacy. Unfortunately, Hill's performance at Gettysburg is often evaluated in comparison to Jackson's heroic Valley Campaign and Chancellorsville, and, of course, fails in the comparison.[86]

Hill's movements on the second day at Gettysburg are largely a mystery. Due to his illness, he displayed little vigor in his leadership. He was present on July 3 when Lee and Longstreet discussed the plans for the third day's assault. Heth's and Pender's divisions from Hill's corps joined Longstreet's corps for the attack on the Union center. Hill spent the last day of the battle virtually without an independent command. Before Pickett's charge, Hill asked Lee for permission to lead his entire corps in the attack. Lee refused permission.[87]

At Gettysburg, Hill's corps took heavy losses totaling almost 8,000 men. In addition, he suffered a great personal loss; one of his division commanders, William Pender, was mortally wounded.[88] Pender's loss was irreparable. Hill regarded him as the best officer of his grade he had ever known. Promotion to corps command had separated Hill from his men. Now, he had to watch while others took part in the battle, denied the opportunity to inspire his men. Hill was never able to handle the change his new role brought and was often frustrated in the attempt.[89]

As Gettysburg and subsequent battles would prove, Hill had finally been promoted to a position in which he did not excel. To add to Hill's demise, his health continued to deteriorate. That fall, he led his Third Corps into a disastrous ambush at Bristoe Station. In the spring of 1864, he brought Grant's army to bay in the Wilderness, only to be routed the next day because he had not ordered his commanders to straighten their lines and dig in. Believing Longstreet would relieve his divisions during the night, and because his men were dead-tired from a long day's fighting, he had failed to take the necessary precautions to prevent a counterattack by Grant's army.[90]

From the beginning of the Wilderness Campaign, Hill had been so ill that he could scarcely ride. Although army surgeons and colleagues had urged him to step down from his command, he had insisted on directing his troops. Finally, on May 8, he found he was unable to sit up, let alone ride a horse, and asked to be relieved. Lee immediately placed General Jubal Early in temporary command of the Third Corps. As his men moved southward, Hill followed along in an ambulance. Although he was unable to witness the actions of his troops himself, Hill was very pleased by the reports of their success under Early's leadership.[91]

By the end of May, Hill was well enough to return to command. Lee continued to slip away from Grant in a series of moves that frustrated the Union commander. At Cold Harbor, Grant decided to hurl his full army against Lee in a desperate headlong attempt to clear his way to Richmond. Through the early morning mist came the dense columns of charging Union troops. Line after line fell under the short-range cross fire from Confederate batteries and musket fire. Within ten minutes, the main Union threat had been repulsed. The Army of the Potomac suffered 7,000 casualties, and when Grant had time to reflect on the assault he wrote: "Cold Harbor is, I think, the only battle I ever fought that I would not fight over again under the same circumstances."[92]

When Grant's overland campaign reached the Richmond-Petersburg defense in June, Hill's corps capably manned their share of the forts and trenches that guarded Petersburg. Throughout 1864 and the early months of 1865, the Third Corps valiantly repulsed repeated enemy attacks. One of Hill's final victories came at Ream's Station. It was hailed as "one of the most brilliant victories of the war." Hill's troops moved rapidly, attacking the enemy before they could be reinforced and following through until there was a clear-cut victory. Hill was operating at a level where he was at his best.[93]

Late in October, Hill was battling illness again. With his health slowly deteriorating, the General and his wife preferred to spend their evenings at the cottage with their children, rather than in the field. Lee was a regular visitor to Hill's cottage. Dolly wrote her mother on one occasion: "General Lee comes frequently to see me. He is the best and greatest man on earth, brought me the last time some delicious apples."[94]

The fact that Hill was seriously ill became more noticeable to the people around him. George Tucker, his chief courier, felt that Hill was "an invalid" for the last six months of his life. A young officer, meeting him for the first time, was disappointed by his appearance. "General Hill," he said, "gave the impression of being reticent, or at any rate, uncommunicative. Neither in aspect nor manner of speech did he appear to measure up to his great fighting record."[95]

Most of February 1865 and into March, Hill was unable to perform his duties. On March 31, spirits rose in the Third Corps. "General Hill will be back from sick furlough—which will please us all," a headquarters clerk wrote. By April 1, however, his illness had returned. Every part of his body ached; his head throbbed from fever and fatigue; and his kidneys were not functioning properly, but he managed to carry on.[96]

Late in March, Lee made an effort to break through the Federal trenches at Fort Stedman but failed, suffering heavy losses. Now Sheridan, with the Union cavalry, was joining Grant from the Shenandoah Valley. Although Sheridan was threatening the Army of Northern Virginia, Lee did not have sufficient cavalry to meet the stronger Union thrust. Before retiring that night, Lee received reports that Sheridan had smashed a Confederate force under Pickett at a rural settlement called Five Forks; disaster was facing his army.[97]

Before daylight on April 2, Hill arrived at Lee's headquarters. Soon after his arrival, Longstreet came. He had been summoned with part of his small corps to help Pickett at Five Forks. While Lee was explaining the disposition of Longstreet's men, a staff officer interrupted the meeting with the news that the Union troops had overrun the Confederate trenches. The officers jumped up, Longstreet and A. P. Hill hurrying off to their troops. It was the last time Lee would see Hill alive.

Heading southward with a courier on Boydton Plank Road, Hill spotted two Federal soldiers in the trees ahead. "We must take them," snapped Hill, drawing his revolver. The Union soldiers took cover and leveled their rifles. "If you fire, you'll be swept to hell," shouted Hill's courier. Then bluffing, he said, "Our men are here—Surrender!" Hill repeated the cry: "Surrender!" The answer came in the form of a bullet that pierced Hill's heart. He was dead before he hit the ground. Hill's courier, C. W. Tucker, rode back to headquarters and reported the tragedy to Lee. Lee's eyes filled with tears, and he said, "He is at rest now, and we who are left are the ones to suffer."[98] Hours later, the Army of Northern Virginia began its retreat to Appomattox.

19 Richard Taylor

"Soldier Prince of the Confederacy"

Son of a president, a plantation owner, and an outstanding soldier, Richard Taylor represented the best of the South and of the Confederacy. Coming from a long line of Southern-bred prominent families, Richard Taylor personified the antebellum plantation aristocracy. He was the only son of Zachary Taylor, war hero and president, and the brother-in-law of Jefferson Davis. Widely admired for his intelligence and military ability, he was one of only three non–West Point graduates to reach the rank of lieutenant general during the Civil War. During the 1862 Shenandoah Valley campaign, Taylor was Stonewall Jackson's most effective brigade commander.

Richard was born on January 27, 1826, to Colonel Zachary and Mary Smith Taylor at "Springfield," a family estate near Louisville, Kentucky. The happy parents named their long-awaited son after his grandfather; Richard would be their only son.

Two years after the birth of their son, Colonel Taylor was assigned to Fort Snelling, Minnesota; after about a year, he moved his family to Fort Crawford at Prairie du Chien, located on the banks of the Mississippi. Life at Fort Crawford was dull. Colonel Taylor described it as a "most miserable and uninteresting country." For young Richard's inquiring mind, life at Fort Crawford provided very little opportunity for intellectual stimulation.

By the time Richard was ten years old, his father realized that his son was in need of a more formal education than that provided by his tutor. In 1836, Richard was sent to live with relatives in Louisville so he could attend a private school there. Just before leaving Fort Crawford, one of Richard's sisters, Sarah Knox, became romantically involved with a young lieutenant from Mississippi, Jefferson Davis.[1]

In 1840, Richard attended a prep school near Boston in Lancaster,

Massachusetts, in preparation for entry into prestigious Harvard College. Although bright, Richard did not prove to be a model student; his lapses of attention and stubborn attitude proved to be a problem. At the age of seventeen, Richard informed his father that he preferred to attend Yale rather than Harvard; reluctantly his father agreed. Richard was admitted to Yale's junior class in 1843.[2]

Although Yale enjoyed the reputation of being one of the best institutions of higher learning in the country, the method of instruction did little to motivate undisciplined young men like Richard. The college continued to rely on regimented curricula designed for memorization and recitation. The program did little to inspire Richard's carefree attitude toward learning. One student later recalled his dilatory behavior at Yale: "He was a man of good abilities, but rather lazy, and won no special distinction in college. But he was very popular in his class, a genial companion, full of fun and frolic, and known as a kind-hearted, good fellow." Richard was a voracious reader, enjoying the Greek and Roman classics as well as works in military history.[3]

In August 1845, Richard graduated from Yale with a respectable average of 2.8 on a 4.0 scale. A fellow classmate remembered him as a handsome, refined Southern gentleman who was always well dressed, popular, generous, talented, and easygoing. None of Richard's family was able to attend the graduation. Once again, military responsibilities prevented his father from being a part of his son's accomplishments.[4]

When war with Mexico erupted in 1846, Richard joined his father in Mexico as his military secretary. It was about this time that Richard first experienced an attack of rheumatoid arthritis, a painful inflammation of the muscles and joints in his limbs. Periodic attacks of this nature would occur throughout his life, afflicting him so badly that he could not walk or even stand up. He seemed more vulnerable to these attacks when extremely anxious or disappointed. As a result of this attack, Taylor's actions in Mexico were limited.[5]

In 1848, Zachary Taylor sought the nomination as the presidential candidate for the Whig Party. While campaigning, General Taylor asked his son to manage his plantation, known as Cypress Grove, a property with nearly 2,000 acres on the Mississippi River; over eighty slaves worked the plantation. General Taylor hoped that taking on this responsibility would force Richard to do something meaningful with his life. Richard accepted the challenge, and with his normal air of stubbornness went to work to prove himself.[6]

By 1850, Taylor had established himself as a successful plantation manager. While visiting Cypress Grove, an English aristocrat observed how well the plantation was managed and the slaves treated. "Men, women, and children all appeared to adore Mr. Taylor, who seemed extremely kind to them, and affable with them," she said. On a daily basis, Taylor distributed

Richard Taylor was the only son of Zachary Taylor, war hero and president, and the brother-in-law of Jefferson Davis. He was one of only three non-West Point graduates to reach the rank of lieutenant general during the Civil War.

COURTESY OF THE LIBRARY OF CONGRESS

to each slave a pound of meat, a ration of milk, and as much bread and vegetables as he or she wanted. On Sundays, he gave them coffee, flour for pastries, butter, sugar, and salt for the week. The men and women were comfortably dressed. The visitor described one of the slave cabins as "a most tastefully decorated and an excellent furnished one, . . . scrupulously clean and neat." Zachary Taylor, like any rational businessman, made certain that all his property (including human property) was well cared for.[7]

In early February 1851, Taylor married the lovely seventeen-year-old Myrthe (Mimi) Bringier. Her vivacious personality complemented Richard's polished demeanor. The couple would enjoy a happy marriage and have four children, two girls and two boys.

In the same year, Richard bought "Fashion," a plantation comprising more than 1,200 acres with sixty-four slaves. He purchased the plantation with the inheritance from his father, who died in 1850. The plantation was situated in the St. Charles Parish, above New Orleans, on the west bank of the Mississippi River.

Taylor settled down to the life of a planter. Relying on his father's past guidance and financial legacy, Taylor gained enough confidence to manage Fashion by himself. Along with running the plantation, Taylor built up a large library, acquired an extensive knowledge of literature, and established a racing stable. He involved himself in politics, first as a Whig, then in the American Party, and, finally, as a Democrat. In 1855, he was elected to the Louisiana legislature and was still a member when the secession crisis developed in 1860.[8] Taylor was a delegate from Louisiana in the 1860 National Democratic Convention in Charleston, South Carolina. He spoke out for peace and harmony, but the Democratic party split when Southern states walked out of the convention. Taylor also participated in the conventions in Richmond and Baltimore, during which time John Breckinridge was selected as the South's Democratic presidential standard bearer.[9]

In January 1861, when Louisiana adopted the Ordinance of Secession, Taylor was convinced that war was inevitable and urged his state to make immediate preparation for it. In July, when his plea was finally heard, he joined the ranks of the military and was appointed colonel of the Ninth Louisiana Infantry Regiment.[10]

Richard Taylor did not look the part of a military leader. He was small in stature, only five-feet-eight-inches tall, dark-complexioned, and displayed his mother's sharp features. He wore his hair cut short, as was his full dark beard. His high forehead, piercing eyes, and penetrating glare enabled him quickly to get the attention of his subordinates. Normally quiet and unassuming, Taylor could be high strung, irritable, and profane when things did not go his way or when his health bothered him. Taylor was also self-reliant and brilliant; he had deep affection for those he admired and contempt for those he did not. Although Taylor's military experience had been limited to service as his father's secretary during the Mexican War, he was, nevertheless, a student of military history.[11]

On July 6, Taylor was mustered into the Confederate army and ordered immediately to Virginia. Two weeks later, he arrived in Richmond, but his troops were too late reaching Manassas to engage in the first major battle of the war. Other Louisiana troops, however, fought valiantly in the battle. Just four days after the rout of Union forces at Manassas, Taylor's Ninth Louisiana Regiment was united with the Sixth, Seventh, and Eighth Louisiana regiments and Wheat's battalion to form the Eighth Brigade of Beauregard's First Corps. Brigadier General William H. T. Walker was placed in command of the brigade.[12]

During the fall of 1861, disease swept through the camps, and Taylor's regiment was hit particularly hard. He spent many hours in the hospitals, helping and comforting the sick. His close association with the sick and dying sapped his strength and impaired his health to the point that he, too, was taken ill. He was ordered to Fairguir Springs to recuperate.[13]

When General Walker was transferred to command Georgian troops on October 21, 1861, Taylor was promoted to brigadier general and assigned to command the Louisiana brigade. After two months, he turned the Louisiana brigade into one of the finest in the Confederate army and established excellent rapport with his men. Walker was furious when he was ordered to move. He did not want to leave his men. "Fighting Billy," as his men called him, wrote a letter of resignation, complaining that others had been promoted over him whom he had outranked in the old army. Now, his transfer from the Louisiana brigade was the final stroke of "insults and indignities."[14]

Although Taylor was pleased with his promotion, he was embarrassed by how it had come about. Later Taylor wrote: "Of the four colonels whose regiments constituted the brigade, I was junior in commission, and the other three had been present and 'won their spurs' at the recent battle. . . . Besides my known friendship for President Davis, with whom I was connected by his first marriage with my older sister, would justify the opinion that my promotion was due to favoritism."[15]

Taylor went to Richmond to meet with President Davis to explain the embarrassing position he had been placed in by the removal of Walker and the passing over of the other colonels in the brigade. Davis listened patiently to Taylor's explanation but decided not to change the situation, explaining that promotions were made for "consideration of the public good, of which he alone was the judge." Davis further explained that his plan was to reorganize regiments from the same state into brigades commanded by brigadiers from the same state. Accordingly, Walker from Georgia had been assigned a Georgian brigade, creating an opening in the Louisiana brigade; therefore, Taylor from Louisiana was assigned to command the Louisiana brigade.[16]

Taylor was pleased to learn that Walker held no ill feelings toward him, and they remained friends throughout the war. Walker returned to the army and was killed in the Atlanta campaign of 1864. Later, Taylor described Walker in his memoirs as one to whom "no enterprise was too rash to awaken his ardor, if it necessitated daring courage and self-devotion."[17]

During the winter of 1861 to 1862, Taylor drilled his men and prepared them for the spring campaign. The Louisiana Tigers, a battalion in his brigade commanded by Major Roberdeau Wheat, contained wild and unruly men. When not involved in battle, they brawled among themselves. One Virginia soldier wrote in his diary that "they neither fear God, man or the Devil." Another South Carolinian called them "the worst men I ever saw, . . . mostly wharf rats from New Orleans." Taylor was so anxious to rid himself of Wheat's battalion that he appealed directly to General Joseph Johnston. Realizing that no other brigadier would willingly accept such an undisciplined and riotous unit, he denied Taylor's request. Johnston did, however, promise to back him on any measure he chose to use in enforcing discipline.[18]

Late in November, Taylor ordered several Tigers confined to the guard-house for creating a disturbance in camp. Afterward, a group of comrades raided the guardhouse in an effort to free their incarcerated friends. The raiders were arrested, and two of the ringleaders were tried by a court-martial and sentenced to death before a firing squad consisting of their fellow Tigers.[19]

When Major Wheat learned what had happened, he rushed to see Taylor, requesting that the two men be pardoned. Taylor stood his ground and not only refused to pardon the men but insisted that the execution be carried out by other Tigers in front of his battalion. A firing squad of twenty-four Tigers lined up fifteen paces from the condemned men, while the rest of the battalion watched the execution in silence. Taylor later remarked that the "punishment, so closely following the offense, produced a marked effect." The shooting of the two Tigers was the first execution in the army and established Taylor as a general who would not tolerate undisciplined behavior.[20]

The cold winter of 1861 to 1862 aggravated Taylor's rheumatism and caused him to suffer severe headaches. During that time, his brigade was shifted to the newly promoted Major General Richard Ewell's division.

In the spring of 1862, Major General George McClellan moved his 100,000 Union army down the Atlantic coast to the Virginia Peninsula for an attack on Richmond. To defend against this invasion, General Johnston had 60,000 men. Robert E. Lee, President Davis's military advisor, was concerned that the 40,000 troops under Major General Irvin McDowell might move down from Fredericksburg to join McClellan. Lincoln, however, was reluctant to send McDowell to join McClellan, believing that the capital would then be left open for a Confederate attack from the west. In mid-March, Lincoln tried to reinforce McDowell by ordering Major General Nathaniel Banks to send 25,000 men from the Shenandoah Valley. This plan was foiled when Stonewall Jackson's small command of 4,200 attacked Banks. Jackson fooled Lincoln into believing that he had a larger force operating in the valley than he actually did. Jackson's campaign was so successful that Lincoln detained McDowell's 40,000 men at Fredericksburg and forced Banks to remain in the valley.[21]

In May 1862, Ewell's division was ordered to join Jackson in the Shenandoah Valley. On May 18, the two generals met to formulate a course of action. To deceive the enemy, Taylor's brigade was detached from Ewell's division and ordered to march west to Harrisonburg. From there, Taylor headed north, and after marching twenty-six miles, his brigade arrived in New Market on the evening of May 20.[22]

When Taylor's Louisianans marched into camp, Jackson's division lined the road to catch a glimpse of the famed Tigers. Taylor's brigade made quite a sight, as one man remembered, "stepping jauntingly as if on parade, . . . not a straggler, but every man in his place, in open column with arms at right shoulder shift."[23]

After his brigade broke ranks, Taylor sought out Jackson. Jackson asked Taylor how far his brigade had marched that day. "Keezletown Road, six and twenty miles," Taylor replied. Jackson noted that there had been no stragglers. "I never allow straggling," Taylor said. "You must teach my people; they straggle badly," Jackson responded.[24]

At Winchester, Taylor's brigade showed its ability to fight. When the Louisianans were ordered to attack the Federals' right flank, Taylor led his men forward. Despite heavy Federal artillery fire, the men continued to advance. As they moved forward, one of Jackson's staff observed the charge, writing that the brigade presented an impressive sight, "with a line of glistening bayonets bright in the morning sun, its formation straight and compact, its tread quick and easy as it pushed on through the clover and up the hill." The Union troops fired into the brigade's ranks, but this did not slow their advance. A great cheer rang out from the Confederates watching the scene from below as Taylor's troops stormed the enemy's right. Panic struck the Union troops, and they beat a hasty retreat through Winchester and north to Martinsburg.[25]

Taylor's men also fought well at Front Royal, where they helped to protect Ewell's faltering left flank. At Port Republic, his brigade supported Brigadier General Charles Winder's Stonewall Brigade by assaulting the key position in the extreme right of the Union line. Finally, after several charges, his brigade carried the position, and the battle was won. Jackson was so pleased with the Louisiana brigade that he personally congratulated Taylor and his men.[26]

The Battle of Port Republic ended Jackson's remarkable valley campaign and established Richard Taylor as one of the Confederacy's best fighting generals, but he did not take all the glory for himself. He gave credit to his brigade, writing, "The Louisiana brigade . . . in twenty days . . . marched over two hundred miles, fought in five actions . . . and, though it had suffered heavy losses in officers and men, were yet strong, hard as nails, and full of confidence."[27]

Immediately after the Battle of Port Republic, Jackson sent a message to Adjutant General Samuel Cooper recommending that Taylor be promoted to major general. Taylor's performance in the Shenandoah Valley had silenced all his detractors and their charges that presidential favoritism had made him a general.[28]

After the valley campaign, Taylor was plagued with depression. Camped at Ashland, sixteen miles north of Richmond, the general was in great pain, both in his head and back, and had lost the power to move his limbs. When his brigade moved out to engage the enemy outside of Richmond, Taylor was unable to mount a horse. Remaining behind in a small ambulance, he sent his brigade forward under command of Colonel Isaac Seymour.

When fighting broke out, Taylor asked to be taken to the front where the bitter Battle of Gaines's Mill was taking place.[29]

After several hours on a rough road, Taylor arrived at the front only to find that Ewell's division had sustained heavy losses. Concerned about the fate of his men, he struggled to mount his horse so that he could join his brigade. All about him lay the dead and wounded, including Roberdeau Wheat and Colonel Seymour. "I had a wretched feeling of guilt, especially about Seymour, who had led the brigade and died in my place," said Taylor.[30]

Throughout the rest of the Battle of Seven Days, Taylor was confined to an ambulance. He was taken to Richmond for treatment, and while there he learned of his promotion to major general and reassignment to his home state as commander of the District of Western Louisiana. Although happy to be returning home and to his family, it was with a heavy heart that he left behind the officers and men of the Ninth Louisiana, his old regiment. Not to be outdone, they wrote, ". . . Our desire to still be a portion of your command has grown and ripened into an attachment which we can trust may never be interrupted. . . . We wish to remain with you. Wherever you go, we desire to go, and let your destiny be our destiny."[31]

When Taylor arrived in Louisiana, he found that half of the state's population and three-quarters of its resources were under Federal control. With the fall of New Orleans and Baton Rouge, the Confederacy had no troops, arms, or money to defend the District of Western Louisiana. When Taylor realized how small were the resources at his command, he asked for help from Governor J. L. Pettus of Mississippi. With only a handful of troops available, Taylor applied a rigid enforcement of the Conscription Act of April 16, 1862. Despite the criticism he received and the reluctance of the citizens to comply with the law, by October he had increased his forces to nearly 6,000 officers and men.[32]

By employing hit and run action against the enemy, Taylor was able to capture much-needed stores, guns, and ammunition. Since assuming command of the district, Taylor had recovered a large portion of Louisiana from Federal control and restored the land to its citizens.

Taylor's efforts were recognized by Governor Thomas O. Moore in a letter to President Davis:

> I confess I was not prepared for the exhibition of the high qualities of a Commander which his services here have developed. We owe it to him, that the State is not now entirely overrun and occupied by the enemy, and it is the greatest merit, in that no time have forces under his command been adequate to accomplishment of such results. . . . General Taylor did what few men have the moral courage to do under such circumstances. . . . The General has become the object of the people's admiration to the same extent that he had been the object of their execration.[33]

In March 1863, Lieutenant General Edmund Kirby Smith assumed command of the Trans-Mississippi Department, which placed Taylor under his command. Almost immediately after Smith's arrival, the two men were at each other's throats, disagreeing over military strategy and the treatment of deserters. As relations between Taylor and Smith worsened in February 1864, Taylor wrote to Adjutant General Cooper requesting to be removed from under Smith's command. For an unknown reason, the request was not acted upon.

In March, Taylor requested reinforcements from Smith but was refused, which renewed their feud. Rather than arguing with each other, both generals could have been spending their time more profitably by preparing to meet Union General Nathaniel Banks's advancing army.[34]

Banks launched his Red River campaign in April, forcing Taylor's heavily outnumbered forces to fall back to Mansfield, south of Shreveport. Banks's plan called for a large combined naval and military operation. As he moved up the Red River to Shreveport, Admiral David D. Porter would provide artillery support and serve as transport for additional troops under Brigadier General Andrew Smith and Major General Frederick Steele. Sensing the importance of stopping this Union threat, Kirby Smith wrote to Taylor: "The battle must be decisive, whether with Steele or Banks. . . . When we fight, it must be for victory."[35]

On April 8, Taylor's troops encountered Union forces at Sabine Crossroads, three miles south of Mansfield. Taylor posted his small army at the edge of the trees on both sides of the road. He told Brigadier General Polignac, one of the brigade commanders, "I am going to fight Banks here [even] if he has a million men," and fight he did. Although outnumbered two-to-one, he counted upon Banks making mistakes as he had against Jackson in the valley. Taylor's men were in high spirits and ready for the fight. "If I am to die for my Country, I hope it will be in a blaze of glory that will shine upon my wife and children," one officer said.[36]

Shortly before noon, Union forces stepped into the clearing and tried to push back Taylor's left flank but were unable to do so. Later in the afternoon, after the Federal attack had been repulsed, Taylor counterattacked. Emerging from the woods, the Confederates led by Brigadier General Alexander Mouton charged across the open ground against the Union line. As they came within range, they were met by a hail of musketry and cannon fire, tearing holes in their ranks. Mouton fell, as did many of his officers and men in the charge. In just thirty minutes, the division lost more than 700 men, one-third of its strength. Then, in the late afternoon, Taylor ordered Major General John Walker's Texas Division to attack the Federal left, while his cavalry struck the Union rear. Faced with being encircled, the Union forces became confused, threw down their arms, and retreated in disorder.[37]

Later that evening, Taylor notified Kirby Smith of his victory, adding, "I shall continue to push the enemy with the utmost vigor." Ironically, the battle at Mansfield had been without General Smith's approval. During the battle, a courier had delivered a message to Taylor from Smith, cautioning him against a general engagement. "Too late, sir." Taylor replied. "The battle is won."[38]

On April 9, Taylor pursued Banks's retreating army twenty-three miles to Pleasant Hill and attacked him again, but this time not with the same success. When Smith arrived at the scene, he found Taylor's army "completely paralyzed and disorganized," but, to his surprise, Union forces were retreating. Left without adequate water and food supplies, Banks had no choice but to withdraw. Thus, what had appeared to be a Union victory was converted into one for the Confederates.[39]

Taylor accepted full responsibility for the failure at Pleasant Hill, declaring that "instead of entrusting the important attack to my subordinates, I should have conducted it myself." Tactically, Taylor had lost the battle, but strategically it was a victory because Banks was forced to give up the Red River.[40]

As soon as the battle was over, Taylor and Smith began feuding again. It started when Smith issued a general order commending his entire army but not singling out Taylor's troops, who were primarily responsible for the victory. Taylor was angered because he believed that his troops had not received full recognition for their efforts at Mansfield and Pleasant Hill. Later, Smith praised Taylor's army and its commander but did not specifically mention Taylor's name: "No need of praise is too great for that gallant little army and its skillful and energetic chief."[41]

In May, Taylor charged Smith with removing Walker's division when Taylor had the opportunity to crush Banks's army. One week later, he criticized Smith for his "system of bureaucracy" in the Trans-Mississippi Department. General Smith replied to Taylor's letters, calling them "unjust" and attributing them to his ill health. Finally, Taylor was critical of Smith's operations during the Red River campaign, labeling them as "a hideous failure," which turned the success of Mansfield "to dust and ashes."[42]

This was the last straw. Whether Taylor's charges were merited or not, he was guilty of insubordination. On June 10, Smith placed Taylor under arrest and relieved him of command. Ironically, on that same day, the Confederate Congress passed a resolution thanking him and his army for their success in Louisiana during the past year, especially for their victories during the Red River campaign.[43]

Friends rallied to Taylor's aid. One wrote to General Braxton Bragg in Richmond, stating that "the people of this state cling to Taylor as the very sheet anchor of their salvation." Taylor also wrote to Bragg requesting him to come to Trans-Mississippi and replace Kirby Smith. Taylor also offered to resign if no other suitable assignment could be found for him.[44]

On June 14, General Leonidas Polk was killed at Pine Mountain near

Atlanta, creating a vacancy for lieutenant general. Despite his feud with Taylor, Smith recommended him for promotion: "He is for his past service and eminent qualifications, justly entitled to the promotion." On July 18, the problem between Taylor and Smith was solved. Taylor was assigned to command General Polk's Department of Alabama, Mississippi, and East Louisiana, with the rank of lieutenant general.[45] With his new position, Taylor made frequent trips around his department and often conferred with President Davis. It soon became clear to him that the Confederacy's days were numbered. As a result, he recommended that General Beauregard be put in command of all Confederate forces in the West. Davis agreed.

During an inspection tour of Mobile, Taylor encountered several hundred slaves working on the city's fortifications. Taylor visited their camp and spoke to one of their leaders, inquiring about the food and working conditions. "Thank you," the slave replied and explained that they were being treated fairly. "If you give us guns, we will fight for these works, too. We would rather fight for our own white folks than for strangers." Taylor never advocated such a policy, but several other officers, including Robert E. Lee, would.[46]

After General John Bell Hood's army was crushed at Franklin and Nashville during the winter of 1864 to 1865, Taylor was ordered to assume temporary command of Hood's scattered army. "This was my first view of a beaten army," he wrote, "and a painful sight it was."[47]

By April, the war was all but over for the Confederacy. On April 9, Lee surrendered to Grant at Appomattox. On April 26, Joseph Johnston surrendered to Sherman in North Carolina. The last of the major Confederate armies to lay down their arms was Taylor's. On May 4, 1865, Taylor met with Brigadier General Edward R. S. Canby at Citronelle, north of Mobile, to discuss terms of surrender. His troops were allowed to keep their personal property and horses, while officers retained their side arms.

Taylor returned to New Orleans penniless and had to sell his two horses to pay his bills and passage for his wife and children to the city. His plantation had been confiscated, and, like other returning Confederate veterans, Taylor had to rely on friends for food, shelter, and financial assistance.[48]

Shortly after the war's end, Taylor went to Washington to seek help from his father's former Whig supporters, now Republicans, many of whom now held high positions in the government. The purpose of his visit was to get Jefferson Davis released from prison. Taylor argued that Davis should have been protected by the terms of surrender issued by General Grant. "If Mr. Davis had sinned, we were all guilty, and I could not rest without an attempt for his relief," he wrote.[49] For more than a year afterward, Taylor continued to fight for Davis's release, pressuring government officials and reassuring his wife, Varina Howell Davis. Finally in May 1867, Davis was released on bail; a year and a half later, President Johnson granted amnesty to all remaining former Confederates, including Davis.[50]

Taylor returned to Louisiana, hoping to regain the personal fortune he had enjoyed before the war. Learning that the Louisiana legislature was about to award a private lease to operate the New Basin Canal, a waterway that connected New Orleans with Lake Pontchartrain, Taylor lobbied to get the lease. In March 1866, he secured a fifteen-year lease, but the profits he hoped to gain from the venture did not yield the expected income. Throughout the time of the lease, Taylor was unable to pay the state a single dollar of rent on the canal as promised.[51]

Taylor was frequently in Washington on behalf of Southern rights and actively campaigned for the Democratic presidential candidate, Samuel J. Tilden, in the election of 1876. He spent several years in England, conducting business for American capitalists and making friends with the Prince of Wales.

In 1874, Taylor's wife Mimi fell gravely ill with a fever. In March 1875, her strength rapidly declined, and, on March 16, she died. She was just forty-one years old. "My devoted wife was relieved from her suffering long and patiently endured, originating in grief for the loss of her [two young sons] and exposure during the war," Taylor recalled. At Taylor's side was Jefferson Davis, hoping to bring some comfort to his friend. Mimi was buried in Metairie Cemetery in New Orleans.[52]

In 1877, Taylor began to write his memoirs, *Destruction and Reconstruction*, considered one of the most accurate of the period. To ensure the accuracy of the information, Taylor went to New Orleans to consult records kept by his former artillery officer, Joseph Brent. By January 1878, he had written 165 pages of the manuscript, and the book was finally published in the spring of 1879, just days before his death in New York.[53]

On March 5, Taylor suffered an attack of rheumatoid arthritis. "I was stricken down severely and can hardly hold up my head," he said. After showing some improvement, Taylor suffered a relapse, slipping in and out of consciousness and continuing to grow weaker. On April 11, he received Holy Communion; early the next morning, Richard Taylor died. He was only fifty-three years old.[54] His body was taken to New Orleans for burial alongside his wife in a family crypt in Metairie Cemetery.

Richard Taylor was devoted to the Confederacy and served it at the risk of his health and the loss of his plantation. He served it well, rising to the rank of lieutenant general. Steadfast to the Confederate cause to the very end, he gave dignity to defeat. His reputation as a gentleman warrior remains intact.

20 *Richard S. Ewell*

"Old Bald Head"

On July 1, 1863, four Confederate divisions swept the field of Union troops west and north of a small town in Pennsylvania called Gettysburg. What was to follow would be the most decisive battle of the war. Major General Jubal Early's division of General Richard S. Ewell's corps had slammed into the Union right and had the enemy on the run. Union troops tried to rally on a hill south of Gettysburg where the town's cemetery was located.[1]

General Robert E. Lee, commander of the Army of Northern Virginia, quickly grasped the situation and changed his mind about waiting for Longstreet's corps, still miles away, before engaging the enemy. Although the Union army was on the run, Lee could see that as long as the enemy held the high ground south of town, the battle was not over. He suspected that the rest of the Army of the Potomac was hurrying toward Gettysburg, and he believed his best chance to ensure a victory was to seize the high ground before they arrived. Lee ordered Ewell to attack Cemetery Hill "if practicable." In Ewell's opinion, it was not practicable; thinking that the Union position was too strong, he did not attack—thus creating one of the most controversial "what-ifs" of the Battle of Gettysburg. By dark, Union General Winfield Scott Hancock arrived with his Second Corps, occupying Culp's and Cemetery Hills and extending a defensive line from Cemetery Ridge to Little Round Top. Later that night, General Meade arrived with three more corps.[2]

After the war, some former officers of the Army of Northern Virginia tried to blame their defeat at Gettysburg on Ewell. They believed that the opportunity to gain the high ground had been lost on the first day of the battle because of Ewell's timidity in not attacking before the Yankees had a chance to dig in and bring up reinforcements.[3]

The man at the center of the controversy was Richard Stoddert Ewell, born on February 7, 1817, the sixth of ten children born to Dr. Thomas and Elizabeth Stoddert Ewell. Both of Richard's parents descended from early settlers of Maryland and Virginia. Though Elizabeth brought a large dowry to her marriage, Thomas Ewell was not at first dependent upon her wealth. He had a good start in building his medical practice after graduating from Pennsylvania University. By the time Richard was born, however, the family had fallen on hard times. Thomas's caustic personality made it difficult for him to retain patients, and his practice eroded to the point where he was forced to sell his home in Georgetown and move to a farm located in Centreville, Virginia.[4]

Because of his failure, Richard's father became bitter, blaming others for his situation. When Thomas died in 1826, his wife was faced with raising her eight young children. After her inheritance ran out, she was forced to support her family by teaching school. Richard was nine years old when his father died. He had never been close to his father; Thomas's alcoholism had created a chasm between them that was never bridged. Richard did, however, love his mother, whom he spoke of as being courageous, highly principled, and devoted to her family.[5]

Elizabeth never let her children forget their distinguished heritage. She considered the family's financial condition to be temporary and had no intention of allowing her children to mix with any of their "rough, uncultivated neighbors." She would not accept outside help and, instead, put her children to work. Despite the family's effort to support themselves, poverty was always looming. Supper often consisted of nothing more than a piece of cornbread.[6] At the age of fourteen, upon the death of his brother Paul, Richard became the head of the household. By this time, he had developed some of the character traits that would follow him into later life. It became very apparent that he was similar to his deceased father. Richard had a violent temper, a caustic tongue, great intellect, and exuded nervous energy.[7]

Elizabeth wanted her children to have more than a basic education. In 1834, she began inquiring about enrolling Richard at the U.S. Military Academy at West Point. To increase her son's chances of being accepted, she enlisted the support of prominent relatives. With their help, Richard was admitted to West Point in 1836. The die was cast; Ewell would be a soldier.[8]

At West Point, Ewell became acquainted with fellow Virginian George Thomas and roommate William T. Sherman, both future Union generals. Ewell's record at West Point was good. Unlike many Southern boys who were not as well prepared as their better-educated Northern counterparts, Ewell was able to hold his own academically. Ewell developed into a fine soldier; he had a natural inclination for military life that was quickly recognized by his superiors.[9]

On July 1, 1840, Ewell graduated, finishing thirteenth in a class of forty-

During the first day of fighting at Gettysburg, General Lee ordered Lieutenant General Richard S. Ewell to attack Cemetery Hill, "if practicable." Ewell did not believe it was practicable, thinking that the Union position was too strong. He thus created one of the most controversial "what-ifs" of the Battle of Gettysburg.

COURTESY OF THE LIBRARY OF CONGRESS

three. Given a choice between the infantry, the artillery, or the dragoons, Ewell chose the dragoons. After being trained for dragoon duty, he was transferred to Fort Wayne in the Cherokee Territory.

Service on the frontier was lonely and boring. To relieve the boredom, Ewell drank heavily, but never to the detriment of his duties. Later, he served at Fort Scott, Kansas, until he was recalled in 1846 upon the outbreak of the war with Mexico. After spending a few months on the East Coast, Ewell was reassigned to Louisville, Kentucky, and put on recruiting duty. In August, he was ordered to report to Lieutenant Philip Kearny at Jefferson Barracks. After assisting Kearny with the training of his company, Ewell joined the U.S. Army in Mexico.[10]

Serving under Lieutenant General Winfield Scott, Ewell saw limited action. At the Battle of Churubusco in 1847, he and Kearny led their troops in an attack, coming under murderous fire. Later, Ewell would remember, "Only a miracle saved Captain Kearny and myself. He lost his arm by grape shot. . . . I had two horses shot; . . . the second was able to bring me back at a walk."[11]

As a result of his action at Churubusco, Ewell earned a brevet promotion to captain for "gallant and meritorious conduct." Later, Ewell said, "I wish I had known . . . there was to be such an overwhelming quantity of brevets made out. I should certainly have tried hard for another."[12]

After the Mexican War was over, Ewell was sent to Baltimore, Maryland, where he served for two years before being assigned to the New Mexico Territory. In 1855, Ewell took the only furlough of his career. On his way home, he stopped in Tennessee to visit Lizinka McKay Campbell, the daughter of his mother's sister. Lizinka had been his best friend when growing up, and he had hoped to marry her after completing college.[13] Lizinka was as talented as she was pretty. As the daughter of a former senator and foreign minister, she had received the benefit of a first-class education. In addition, she was endowed with musical ability and had mastered several foreign languages.[14]

Although Ewell had always assumed that he would marry Lizinka, she had not considered him a suitor. Ewell was not alone in his admiration of Lizinka. Many men came to see her, some drawn by her beauty and charm and others by her wealth. It seemed only a matter of time before a proper suitor would come along and ask for her hand. While Ewell was away at West Point, Lizinka married James Percy Brown, a wealthy plantation owner from outside Spring Hill, Tennessee. At the time, Ewell thought he had lost Lizinka forever, blaming it on his financial condition. Although it seemed too late to gain Lizinka's hand, he was resolved not to remain impoverished.[15]

Ewell's personal life had been nonexistent after graduating from West Point. He had, however, stayed in contact with Lizinka and knew that her husband had died four years after their marriage, leaving her one of the wealthiest women in America and the mother of three.[16] Lizinka asked Ewell to resign from the army to manage her plantation. Although tempted, he was concerned about the great difference in their financial status. He still loved her, but his pride would not let him match his fortunes with hers. As a result, he declined her offer.[17]

Ewell returned to New Mexico with Lizinka foremost on his mind and determined to make himself wealthy enough to ask for her hand. Although busy chasing renegade Indians, Ewell found time to work a silver mine. Unfortunately, the lode proved to be barren. In his frenzied effort to build a fortune, his health collapsed. Suffering from malaria and dyspepsia, he applied for a sick leave. In January 1861, Ewell returned to Virginia—and the war.

Ewell was personally against secession and hoped that the Union might be saved. "If there were anything I had to dread and regret in '61, it was this war," he later remarked. "I was too sick and too busy . . . to think much about it, and I clung to the last ray of hope like a drowning man to straws." His duty, however, he saw clearly: he was a Virginian. On April 24, he resigned his commission in the U.S. Army. He later explained his actions: "It is hard to account for my course except from a painful sense of duty; I say painful, because I believe few were more devoted to the old country than myself. . . . It was like death to me."[18]

Like most Virginians, Ewell's decision to support the South was a matter of simple loyalty. On April 25, 1861, he entered the Confederate army with the rank of lieutenant colonel of cavalry. Ewell did not look much like an officer. Tall for the times, at five feet, ten inches, Ewell weighed only 130 pounds. He had just a fringe of brown hair on an otherwise bald head and was often referred to by his troops as "Old Bald Head." His bright, bulging eyes protruded above a prominent nose, creating a birdlike effect. He had a habit of muttering odd remarks during a normal conversation and was so nervous and fidgety that he often had trouble sleeping. Ewell seldom combed his beard, and according to John Wise, son of a former Virginia governor, "his grizzled mustache stuck out like . . . the muzzle of a terrier." General John B. Gordon described him as a "compound of anomalies, the oddest, most eccentric genius in the Confederate Army."[19]

Although Ewell did not look much like an officer, his troops soon grew to respect him and to appreciate his fairness. An example of this fairness surfaced early in his career: assigned to train recruits camped at Ashland, Virginia, Ewell set pickets around the camp with instructions that no one should be allowed to enter the camp without proper authorization—even Ewell himself. When Ewell appeared at the gate one evening, he was dressed in civilian clothes, without side arms or insignia of rank. Private George Eggleston, the guard at the gate, ordered him to halt. When Ewell said he would drive over him if he did not move, Eggleston drew his pistol and threatened to shoot him. "Ewell was livid with rage," Eggleston remembered, "and ordered the officer [of the guard] to place me in irons at once, uttering maledictions upon me."[20] The officer of the guard refused to arrest him, saying that the sentinel had done his job. Ewell realized he was right, and after he had cooled down, he called Eggleston to his tent and apologized for his behavior.[21]

In 1864, Ewell, then in command of the Richmond defenses, came in contact with Eggleston again. Ewell eyed the young man closely and asked, "Aren't you the man who came so near shooting me at Ashland?" Eggleston said that he was. "I'm very glad you didn't do it," Ewell replied.[22]

In June, Ewell was promoted to brigadier general for his conspicuous performance at Fairfax Court House. On July 21, Ewell commanded an infantry brigade at the First Battle of Manassas, but saw limited action. His brigade took up a position near Washington during the winter of 1861 to 1862, giving Ewell the chance to drill his men and to continue his quest for Lizinka's hand.

By virtue of his rank of brigadier general, Ewell now felt he had gained the social status necessary to approach Lizinka. When she visited the camp to see her son, Campbell Brown, the general summoned the courage to propose marriage. She accepted, but they agreed to keep their engagement a secret except to members of the immediate family. Days later, Cavalry Chief J. E. B. Stuart stated that "poor General Ewell is desperately, but hopelessly, smitten."[23]

In January 1862, Ewell was promoted to major general and given command of a division under Stonewall Jackson. His new command had three brigades, commanded by Arnold Elsey, Isaac Trimble, and Richard Taylor. Unlike many of his fellow officers, Ewell had not campaigned for higher rank. He was not sure if he was ready for the increased responsibility and was heard to complain, "Why me?"

In the spring of 1862, when Major General George McClellan moved south against Richmond, Ewell was dispatched to the Shenandoah Valley to join Jackson. Jackson's job was to create a diversion and to keep a large number of Union troops busy in the valley and away from McClellan's force. In a letter to Jackson, Lee wrote, "If you can use General Ewell's division in an attack on General Banks and to drive him back, it will prove a great relief to the pressure on Fredericksburg."[24]

Ewell reached Jackson's camps during the night of April 30 and bivouacked nearby. Both Ewell and his troops were surprised to find that Jackson's army was gone in the morning. Stonewall had already moved to hit the Federals as Lee had suggested. Ewell was ordered to hold the gap and engage Banks if necessary.[25]

Because Jackson kept his plans a secret, Ewell's experience in the valley was frustrating. At first, he considered his commander insane. "I tell you, sir, he is as crazy as a March hare," Ewell complained to one of his regimental commanders. "I will just march my division away from here. I do not mean to have it cut to pieces at the behest of a crazy man." Even after Jackson had won several victories in the valley, Ewell was not completely convinced that he was wrong about Jackson's mental state, but he did concede there were "methods in his madness."[26]

Although Jackson was the overall commander of the troops in the Shenandoah Valley, Ewell's division did most of the fighting. His troops engaged and defeated Union forces in the opening battle at Front Royal on May 23, 1862. Two days later, he attacked Banks at Winchester, routing his troops. After Jackson retreated to avoid a trap set by Generals John Frémont and James Shields, Ewell defeated Frémont at Cross Keys on June 8, 1862.[27]

After one of the violent cavalry battles in the valley, Ewell revealed a previously unseen side. With darkness settling over the battlefield, the

Confederates hurriedly gathered their casualties and moved off. Ewell personally helped load the wounded into ambulances. After the men were safely secured, Ewell gave money to a farmer who volunteered to take care of the injured. Captain William Goldsborough of the First Maryland always remembered Ewell's kindness. He later said that "he hadn't cared more for Ewell before than for any other commander, tho' he knew him to be a good officer, but after that evening his Regiment would have gone anywhere in the world for him and he loved him."[28]

During the battle at Port Republic, the Confederacy lost one of its great cavalry leaders, Turner Ashby. As a former dragoon, Ewell appreciated Ashby's daring mode of operating and envied the freedom of movement he had been permitted.[29]

At the Battle of Port Republic, Ewell had noticed a Union officer on a white horse directing a retreat. As he did so, he was recklessly exposed to Confederate fire. Ewell was so impressed by the officer's courage that he told his troops to hold their fire. When Jackson heard of the episode, he told Ewell never to do that again. "This was no ordinary war," he said, "and the brave and gallant Federal officers were the very kind that must be killed. Shoot the brave officers, and the cowards will run away and take the men with them."[30] The valley campaign was a real test of Ewell's ability to command. By leading his men into battle, joining them on the front line, and sharing their danger, he won the respect of the men he commanded. Ewell had proven that he was both an excellent tactician and superior leader of men; he was ready for greater command responsibility.[31]

In June 1862, Ewell moved with Jackson to Richmond to join Lee in defending the Confederate capital under attack by Major General George McClellan's army. Ewell's division arrived in time to take part in the Battle of Seven Days.

On July 1, Ewell's division was assigned a role in the attack on Malvern Hill. Arriving too late to join in the assault against the entrenched Union forces, Ewell was devastated when he saw the Confederate dead strewn on the slopes. Ewell's division was spared a similar fate when the attack was called off due to nightfall. During the night, McClellan's forces withdrew from the hill.[32]

Strategically, the Battle of Seven Days had been a grand victory for the Confederates, despite the heavy price. Richmond had been saved and the Union army driven back to the James River. Of the nine division commanders in the Army of Northern Virginia, Ewell alone had emerged from the campaign with his professional status still intact. Ewell's star was clearly on the rise.[33]

After seeing the disaster at Malvern Hill, Ewell's attitude toward war changed. Where he once talked of the road to glory, he now understood the price that must be paid to obtain it. In one letter to Lizinka, he revealed his revulsion for war. "For my part, I would be satisfied to never see another field. What pleasure can there be in seeing thousands of dead dying in every agony?" he questioned. "So many times . . . the wounded are left without help for hours."[34]

After the Battle of Seven Days, Ewell's division was reduced from the 10,000 troops that he had had in the valley to 3,000. The division had suffered less than 1,000 casualties in the fighting; malaria from the swamps accounted for the rest. Ewell was among those suffering from the disease.[35]

More harmful to Ewell's division than the malaria epidemic was the dissension sweeping through its ranks. Despite their success in the valley and at Richmond, many of Ewell's officers did not want to serve under Jackson, believing his harsh discipline was due to his unstable mental condition. Although Ewell, too, believed Jackson to be "crazy" and an "enthusiastic fanatic," he, nevertheless, was amazed at how his enigmatic chief outmaneuvered his opponents in the Shenandoah Valley. As a result, Ewell became one of Jackson's most ardent admirers. The feeling was reciprocated by Jackson, who had gained a high opinion of Ewell during the campaigns of that spring.[36]

With Richmond no longer in danger from McClellan's army, the ever-aggressive Jackson proposed that an army be sent into Maryland to threaten Washington. He had no desire to lead the effort himself but suggested that either Lee or Ewell lead the invasion, either of whom he would be willing to follow. It was apparent that Ewell had gained the admiration and respect of one of the Confederate's greatest generals.[37]

By the end of July, Ewell's division had returned to fighting size; many of its veterans who had fallen ill during the Battle of Seven Days returned to duty. They were just in time to meet a new threat in northern Virginia, one led by Major General John Pope. In his address to his Army of Virginia, General Pope had said, "I have come to you from the West where we have always seen the backs of our enemy."[38] "He'll never see the backs of my troops," Ewell responded, after hearing Pope's remarks. "Their pantaloons are out at the rear and the sight would paralyze this Western bully."[39]

Lee was concerned about the new threat from Pope, not because of his boasting, but because of his statement regarding his plans for feeding his troops. The Union general had asserted his intention to live off the land, confiscating food he needed for his troops from civilians along the way. He also declared a policy of having all Southern men take an oath of allegiance to the federal government. Those that refused were to be banished from their homes. If they returned, they were to be shot. Lee, the perfect gentleman, was enraged by Pope's disregard for the rules of "civilized warfare" and, from then on, would refer to him as the "miscreant general." On July 13, Lee ordered Jackson to engage General Pope's army.[40]

Lee's plan to deal with Pope was a daring one. Dividing his army, he sent Jackson and Ewell north in a wide flanking movement that would put them in the rear of Pope's army. On August 9, Jackson and Ewell defeated the main Union force under General Banks at Cedar Run and then raced north as ordered. The battle that followed was to be called the Second Battle of Manassas.

On August 28, Ewell engaged the enemy led by Union Brigadier General John Gibbon's troops at Groveton, Virginia. At the height of the battle, the Federals attempted to flank Ewell's position. When Ewell discovered the situation, he grabbed a musket, rushed to the threatened point, and led his troops in a rout of the enemy. One of the Union soldiers recognized the general and called out, "Here is General Ewell, boys." A group of Union troops immediately opened fire on him. A bullet pierced his knee, shattering the patella and the head of the tibia before lodging in the muscle of his calf. Troops from the Fifteenth Alabama, who saw him hit, offered to carry him to the rear, but Ewell would not allow it. "Put me down, and give them hell!" he snarled. "I'm no better than any other wounded soldier to stay on the field."[41]

Campbell Brown, Lizinka's son and a member of Ewell's staff, was the first official to reach the general. He found him in a little opening among the brush pines, "quite conscious, but in considerable pain." He rode off at once to find a surgeon and to inform Major General Isaac Trimble of what had happened and that he was now in charge of the division. Finding a surgeon, Campbell hurried back to Ewell's side. When litter bearers arrived, Ewell insisted that they take the wounded soldiers away first. Later, Ewell confided in Campbell that he had been touched and pleased by the devotion of some of the men who lay near him. They refused to be carried off the field before him.[42]

Ewell was moved safely to the rear. Later that night, Dr. Hunter McGuire, the corps' medical director, arrived and found Ewell suffering from shock. The next day, he removed Ewell's left leg above the knee. Throughout the operation, Ewell muttered orders to troops and spoke of their movements. He appeared to be oblivious to any pain until Dr. McGuire sawed into the bone. Then he groaned, "Oh, my God!"[43]

Ewell was taken to Dunblane, the home of his cousin, Dr. Jesse Ewell. With his family and friends at his side, his health steadily improved. Although still weak and experiencing pain when he moved his leg, he did not complain. In fact, his patience and thoughtfulness toward others earned him the family's love and respect. When his attendants learned that Federal troops were in the area looking for him, they moved him to Millboro Springs, where Lizinka was able to join him.[44]

By November 1963, Ewell was well enough to move to the home of Dr. Francis Hancock in Richmond. There, Lizinka kept house for him and "watched over him with sleepless vigilance." In all, Ewell was out of action for nine months, missing the battles of Antietam, Fredericksburg, and Chancellorsville.[45]

Ewell's recuperation took longer than anticipated because he slipped on ice on Christmas Day while walking with crutches. Another inch of bone snapped off during the accident and caused his leg to hemorrhage profusely. Although frustrated with the slowness of his recovery, he displayed his selflessness. He never sought public recognition for himself but fought hard for the reputation of subordinates and superiors. Ewell believed that Brigadier General Jubal Early, who had taken over his division in his absence, had earned the right to be its permanent commander. In a letter to Early, he wrote: "When I am fit for duty, they may do what they please with me, but I think your claim to the Division, whether length of time or hard service be considered, are fully equal, if not superior to mine. I do not presume they will interfere with you. What is very certain is that I will not ask for any particular duty or station, but let them do as they see proper with me."[46]

During wartime, men who experience near-death experiences often turn to religion as a source of comfort. While convalescing in Richmond, Ewell did just that. Some believe his spiritual faith began in the valley during his association with Jackson. The Reverend Moses Drury Hodge, who visited him frequently while he was recovering, also played a major role in Ewell's spiritual revival. The most noticeable change was in his language. After accepting Christ, Ewell gave up swearing. Those who knew him earlier, during his Western tour of duty, said that "he could swear the scalp off an Apache." After Ewell's reformation, Campbell Brown claimed that he only heard Ewell swear twice, "once to a stupid courier and once to a man who was riding his horse cruelly."[47]

On April 30, 1863, the Army of the Potomac, now under the command of Major General "Fighting Joe" Hooker, crossed the Rappahannock River above Fredericksburg and engaged Lee at Chancellorsville. Although Lee defeated Hooker, he lost the services of Jackson, who died on May 10 after being hit by friendly fire. Jackson's body lay in state at Richmond before being transferred to Lexington, Virginia, for burial. Ewell acted as one of the honorary pallbearers.

With the death of Jackson, Lee reorganized the Army of Northern Virginia into three corps. Longstreet retained the First Corps; Ewell was assigned Jackson's Second Corps; and A. P. Hill, the newly created Third Corps. The soldiers of the Second Corps readily welcomed Ewell as their commander. Ewell's health, however, was still fragile, and he was reluctant to accept the position.

Ewell had not sought the job. When he heard a rumor about his promotion, he wrote to General P. G. T. Beauregard, suggesting that he apply for the position: "Your name . . . would be a tower of strength. . . . You can not know the warmth of feeling and confidence . . . concerning yourself." Ewell downplayed his own qualifications for the position due to what he described as his "shortcomings in the way of legs."[48]

While Ewell was reluctant about taking command of the Second Corps, Lizinka was determined that he should. Perhaps as an inducement, she

agreed to marry him immediately. On May 23, Ewell was promoted to lieutenant general; one day later, he and Lizinka were married.[49]

The victory at Chancellorsville cleared the way for another Southern
invasion of the North. Confusion within the Union army and previous
Union losses gave Lee the opportunity he had hoped for: a chance to destroy
the Army of Potomac once and for all. Within weeks of his victory at Chancellorsville, Lee was on the move again, this time advancing into Pennsylvania. On July 1, 1863, the fighting began north and west of Gettysburg. Lee
had not planned to fight there, but part of his advance troops strayed into
the town and encountered the enemy. After the initial skirmish, both sides
threw in reinforcements. The Battle of Gettysburg had begun.[50]

Ewell arrived on the field at noon on July 1, in time to see his troops
deliver a devastating blow to the Union right flank. When the Union troops
retreated to the heights below the town, Ewell broke off the engagement.
Ewell soon saw the importance of gaining the high ground and requested
additional men to assault the slopes. Lee denied the request for reinforcements but did order the attack if Ewell found it "practicable."[51]

By 5:00 p.m., the disorganized remnants of the Union First and Eleventh
Corps were regrouping on Cemetery and Culp's Hills southeast of town.
Ewell considered the strength of the Federal position and the fatigued con-
dition of his troops and concluded that he could not dislodge the enemy.
Although his division commanders, primarily General Early, argued for
him to attack, he decided against it. Ewell's decision not to mount an
assault in the fading hours of July 1 opened the door for future criticism.
Critics claimed that Ewell should have followed up his success and seized
Cemetery Hill as Jackson surely would have done had he been alive. Such
criticism, however, did not take into account the strength of the Federal
position and ignored the obstacles in Ewell's path.[52]

The next day, Lee attacked the Union left with Longstreet's corps. Later
in the day, when Major General George Meade drew men from his right
flank to hold off the threat from Longstreet, Ewell had a chance to drive a
wedge into the Northern line. His corps was not ready at the critical time,
however, and his delayed, piecemeal attack failed.[53]

Although Lee recognized that his corps commanders had failed to take
advantage of favorable battlefield situations on July 1 and 2, he still remained
confident of victory and was determined to push the fight to a conclusion.
Lee's plan for July 3 was a continuation of the second day's attack, with one
important modification: Longstreet would make a massive frontal assault
on the Union center, while Ewell would continue to attack Meade's right
flank.[54]

Ewell planned to attack at dawn, but the Federals attacked first, opening
up with their artillery on his position. For almost six hours, his troops shed
their blood on the rocky slope of Culp's Hill. Although it should have become
obvious that the assault was not going to succeed, Ewell continued to order

the attacks anyway, hoping to draw attention away from Longstreet, whose assault was to begin shortly. Longstreet's attack, however, was delayed, and Ewell had sacrificed his men in vain. Finally, near noon, Ewell fell back and held his position for the rest of the day. "No further assault was made," he reported. "All had been done that it was possible to do."[55]

Longstreet finally made his attack at 1:00 p.m., hours behind schedule. After a heavy artillery barrage, 12,000 troops from Longstreet's and Hill's corps attacked Cemetery Ridge. The assault, which became known as Pickett's Charge, failed to break the Union line. Confederate losses were heavy and to no avail. The attack had been repulsed.

"It's all my fault," said Lee after the battle, but he was not the only one to blame. Ewell was just as frank as Lee in acknowledging his own part in the Confederate defeat. In a conversation with a fellow general months later, Ewell said it took "a dozen blunders to lose at Gettysburg, and he had committed a good many of them."[56] Lee had no choice but to withdraw to Virginia.

An odd event occurred during the Battle of Gettysburg when Ewell was shot in his wooden leg by a Union sharpshooter as he rode with General Gordon. Ewell jokingly said to Gordon, "Suppose that the ball had struck you: we would have the trouble of carrying you off the field, sir. You see how much better fixed for a fight I am than you are? It don't hurt a bit to be shot in a wooden leg."[57]

Over the next few months, Ewell tried to put the tragic experience of Gettysburg behind him. Lizinka rejoined him in camp, and together they enjoyed nightly parties, dining, and dancing. Because the balls contrasted so badly with the daily existence of the troops, a group of chaplains demanded that Ewell stop taking part in the affairs. Ewell wisely followed their advice.[58]

When Ewell returned to the field, he was greatly troubled by his lack of stamina. During the winter, he was offered a less demanding position with the Army of Tennessee, but he declined, electing to remain with the Army of Northern Virginia. No doubt, his decision was influenced by his wife, who saw the move as a demotion.[59]

While Ewell rested as much as he could during the winter of 1863 to 1864 to regain his strength, Lizinka "pitched in" by carrying out many of his chores of running the corps. When Ewell had a bad spill while riding a horse, she put him to bed, then threw herself into the center of a controversy. She proposed that Sandie Pendleton be assigned as brigade commander, thus paving the way for her son, Campbell, to become Ewell's chief-of-staff. The intent to advance her son was too obvious, and Ewell's advisors rejected her plan.[60]

Ewell and his wife's joint leadership of the Second Corps came to an end when Lieutenant General Ulysses Grant moved against Lee. Lizinka returned to Richmond, and Ewell led his corps into the Wilderness, an area of trees and thick brush west of Fredericksburg. On May 5, 1864, Ewell made initial contact with Union forces, showing great skill as he directed his troops while fighting off repeated attacks. To break the stalemate, Grant took his army south around Lee's right where the two armies met at Spotsylvania. Lee had removed Ewell's artillery just before Grant renewed his attack. Without his guns, Ewell's forces were quickly overrun. In the attack, Ewell lost half his corps before he was able to restore his line.[61] Union Major General Winfield Scott Hancock reported that Ewell's corps "was almost destroyed." This was only a slight exaggeration.[62]

During the heat of battle, Ewell resorted to his old habit of swearing. A Georgian noted the contrast between Lee's and Ewell's conduct: "General Lee, in the calmest and kindest manner said: 'Boys, do not run away, go back, go back, your comrades need you in the trenches.' Ewell, forgetting himself in the excitement of the moment, said: 'Yes, God damn you, run, run, run; the Yankees will catch you; that's right; go as fast as you can.'" The soldier added that Lee was successful in halting the fleeing troops, whereas Ewell was not.[63]

In late May, Grant resumed his attack on Lee's army. For three days, the two armies fought inconclusively around the village of Cold Harbor. Finally, Grant lost his patience and ordered an attack on the entrenched Confederate troops. In the brief struggle that followed, the Army of the Potomac suffered more than 5,500 casualties. Ewell did not participate in the fighting, having fallen ill with diarrhea and a touch of scurvy. In his absence, Major General Jubal Early took command of the Second Corps.[64]

When Ewell was well enough to return to duty, Lee refused to restore him to the command of his corps, urging Ewell to take more time to recover from his illness. Anticipating that Lee might use this as an excuse to remove him from command, Ewell asked his doctor to sign a certificate attesting to his fitness to return to duty. Nevertheless, Lee still blocked his return to duty, stating, "Your troops are now in line of battle under General Early and I do not think any change at the present time would be beneficial." This was General Lee's tactful way of releasing Ewell from duty. Despite Ewell's protest, Lee stuck to his decision. It was clear that Lee had lost confidence in Ewell. On June 4, Lee formally announced Early's promotion to lieutenant general and his assignment as permanent commander of the Second Corps.[65]

Ewell found himself a general without an army. Though Lee wished to remove Ewell from command of the Second Corps, he did not want to disgrace him. He recommended to Adjutant General Samuel Cooper that Ewell be placed in charge of Richmond's defenses. On June 15, 1864, Ewell was ordered to take command of the Department of Richmond. Many soldiers expressed their displeasure and sorrow at Ewell's leaving. Perhaps their feelings were best expressed years later by General E. Porter Alexander, who wrote that "no man in the army, in our corps, but loved and still loves the name and memory of good old Ewell or that did not see him leave with regret."[66]

Ewell's duties in Richmond were to manage the military of the city and to defend the capital. On September 29, a Federal force of 8,000 troops attacked Fort Harrison, the keystone of Richmond's defense. With only 1,000 troops to defend the fort, it was overrun, opening a path to the Confederate capital. Ewell was furious; "As mad as he could be," reported an observer. "[He was] shouting . . . and seeming to be everywhere at once." Ewell gathered 200 stragglers and put them in line. He gave them a choice of staying and fighting or turning and running and being shot in the back. Ewell's tirade paid off; the Union troops were held off until Lee arrived with reinforcements.[67]

Ewell's heroic efforts in saving Richmond went largely unnoticed. When his name was mentioned in the newspapers, it was to criticize him for being caught by surprise, a charge that Ewell denied. Ewell thought that his efforts at Fort Harrison had earned him another chance at field command, but an unfortunate accident killed his opportunity for that. While escorting Lee on a mounted tour, Ewell was thrown from his horse and his head bloodied. "Go back to Richmond," Lee ordered, "and stay . . . until [you are] completely well."[68]

In mid-December, Lee made an organizational change that revived Ewell's hope for a field command. Because of a series of victories by Union Major General Sheridan over Early in the Shenandoah Valley, Lee relieved him from command of the Second Corps. Lee's choice to replace Early, however, was not Ewell, but Major General John Gordon. Even though Ewell was not surprised by Lee's decision, he was crushed.[69]

The snub was too much for Ewell's wife; Lizinka decided to take the oath of allegiance to regain her U.S. citizenship and to prevent the Federal government from confiscating her property when the war was over. This would allow Ewell and his wife to live out the years after the war in comfort. Forced to choose between supporting his wife and the South, Ewell tried to do both. He remained on duty, while helping his wife slip across the line into the North. There, she was able to complete the paperwork necessary to regain her citizenship and be allowed to return to Nashville.[70]

On April 2, the Confederate army abandoned Richmond and headed for Appomattox, Virginia. Ewell led the garrison troops behind the main body of Lee's army. At Saylor's Creek, he was cut off from the main body of the army and surrounded. After a desperate fight, he was forced to surrender. Three days later, on April 9, Lee surrendered his army to Ulysses Grant at Appomattox.

Union authorities sent Ewell to Fort Warren in Boston Harbor. Burdened with his wife's "treason" and the disgrace of his capture, Ewell's spirit broke, and he drifted into a state of depression. In the wake of President

Lincoln's assassination, the nation was in no mood to be generous to Confederate prisoners, especially to their leaders.

Ewell abhorred the assassination of Lincoln. When he reached Fort Warren, Ewell tried to induce the generals confined with him to sign a letter he had written to General Grant disclaiming any involvement with the assassination. The letter was strongly rejected by the other officers, who felt it was an insult to their honor: "Do you think it becoming for thirteen gentlemen, though worthy to wear the stars of a general officer of the Confederate Army, to declare to the world that they are not assassins?"[71]

Not only did the generals refuse to sign the letter, but they added insult to their rebuff. One general, Eppa Hunton, added, "Where is the leg you lost at Manassas buried?" Before Ewell could answer, Hunton snarled, "I wish to pay honor to that leg for I have none to pay to the rest of your body." Ewell sent the letter to Grant anyway, without deleting the names of those imprisoned with him.[72]

Ewell was released from prison on July 18, 1865. Although freed from prison, he was on parole and confined to Virginia. Later the parole was transferred to Tennessee so he could live with his wife. With her wealth, Ewell was able to live the life of a gentleman farmer. He soon forgot the war.

During the winter of 1872, Ewell fell ill with pneumonia. When Lizinka attempted to nurse him back to health, she became ill with pneumonia herself and died on January 22. When Ewell learned of his wife's death, he requested that her casket be brought to his side. After looking at his beloved wife, he requested that they delay her funeral so his could take place at the same time. Forty-eight hours later, Richard Ewell died.[73]

The day Ewell had become ill, he had been wearing a pair of surplus U.S. Army pantaloons. They were thinner than the pants he normally wore, which, in his opinion, led to his illness. Recalling all the dangers he had faced during the war, Ewell said, "It's strange that an old pair of infantry pantaloons should kill me at last."[74]

News of General Ewell's death spread quickly throughout the country. Northern and Southern newspapers alike praised Ewell for his valor and unimpeachable character. The *Memphis Daily Appeal* expressed it well: "His honesty of purpose was attested by heroic self-devotion; his valor, by his wounds; his genius for war, by brilliant achievements."[75]

On January 26, General Ewell was buried beside his wife in the Nashville City Cemetery. On his tomb, only the essential facts of his existence were inscribed. On the reverse side of the tomb was added a short inscription stating that he had been a lieutenant general in the Confederate army and just a single word: "Peace."[76]

21 Jubal A. Early

"Old Jube"

Jubal Early was a Virginian and a West Point–educated Southern officer, but "Old Jube," as his troops called him, was not made in the mold of Robert E. Lee. Early was irreverent, abrasive, temperamental, and sarcastic. Although Jubal Early was respected for his military ability, almost no one liked him. One soldier under his command was quoted as saying that there were many Confederates who would shoot him "just as quick as they would a damned Yankee." As a disciplinarian, he was strict and often vindictive. On one occasion, when a regiment failed to perform as he expected, he threatened to put them on the front line "where he hoped every one of them would be killed and burn through eternity." He did what he had threatened, and the unit suffered heavy losses. Even the few that did like him admitted that he almost never showed a tender emotion.[1]

Early's appearance befitted his personality. Balding, with black hair, he had an unkempt beard that he seldom trimmed. He chewed tobacco and had a habit of shifting his quid from one side of his mouth to the other when he was excited. Standing six feet tall, his rheumatism caused him to stoop when he walked, so he appeared much older than his forty-six years. Although well educated, those that held a conversation with him would not have known it by the poor grammar and profanity he used to express himself.[2]

Early was equally rude to all he encountered. He was just as likely to be abrasive and sarcastic to his subordinates as to his superiors. "I was never blessed with a popular or captivating manner," he wrote. He swore, drank, and criticized viciously; his only redeeming feature as a soldier was that he was a fighter. Only Robert E. Lee enjoyed exemption from "Old Jube's" caustic bombardments. Although he was often critical of Confederate leaders, civic and military, he never criticized Lee; Lee he respected and held in high esteem.[3]

Early's attitudes about religion and women were also in conflict with the views of most Southern gentlemen of the time. In an army where most commanding officers called upon God for help and thanked Him for every success, Jubal Early stood out as a nonbeliever. Men of the cloth suffered his stinging wit and abuse. At Fredericksburg, when he saw a chaplain running to the rear, Early ordered the man to halt and, with his typical sarcasm, said, "For the past thirty years . . . you have been trying to get to heaven, and now when the opportunity is offered, you are fleeing from it, sir. I am surprised."[4]

A lifelong bachelor, Early reserved some of the most obnoxious comments for men he considered happily married or in love. He often showed disrespect for the fairer sex, treating genteel ladies no better than he did prostitutes.

The man who became famous for his service as a corps commander in Lee's army and for his dramatic "raid" on Washington in 1864 during the siege of Petersburg was born into a prominent family in Franklin County, Virginia, on November 3, 1816. He was the third of ten children in the Joab and Ruth Early family. His father gained social acceptance as a member of the Virginia legislature and as a colonel in the Franklin County militia. At one time or another, Joab held close to 1,000 acres on which he raised tobacco and other crops.[5]

Jubal's father saw to it that all of his children, including the girls, obtained a good education. Jubal attended a local one-room schoolhouse and, later, schools in Lynchburg and Danville. He received the usual "instruction in the dead languages and elementary mathematics." Then, in 1832, the family's serenity was interrupted when Jubal's mother died. It was a deep loss for him; of all those in the family, Jubal felt closest to his mother, continually seeking her companionship. This loss may explain why he never married, remaining a confirmed bachelor for his entire life.[6] "She was a most estimable lady," he later wrote, "and her death was not only the source of the deepest grief for her immediate family, but caused universal regret."[7]

In 1833, Early entered the U.S. Military Academy at West Point. Jubal was somewhat less than enthusiastic about his studies. "I was never a very good student," he recalled, "and sometimes quite remiss, but I managed to attain a respectable stand in my studies." Jubal came close to leaving West Point in 1835 when the Texans' struggle for independence from Mexico erupted. Feeling that the United States was obligated by "every principle of humanity" to step in and aid the Texans, Early asked his father for permission to leave the Academy and join the revolution. His father refused to give his permission, and Jubal remained at West Point.[8]

Early's military progress was hampered by his slovenly dress and care for his bunk and quarters. He admitted that he "was not a very exemplary

Lieutenant General Jubal A. Early was not a Southern general in the mold of Robert E. Lee. He was irreverent, abrasive, temperamental, and sarcastic. Although respected for his military ability, almost no one liked him.

COURTESY OF THE LIBRARY OF CONGRESS

soldier. . . . I had little taste for scrubbing brass and cared little for advancement to be obtained by the exercise of that most useful art." He was frequently on report for being out of uniform, and his caustic tongue got him into more than his share of scrapes. Nevertheless, he managed to graduate eighteenth in a class of fifty that included future Confederate generals James Longstreet and Daniel Harvey Hill, and future Union generals Joseph Hooker and John Sedgwick.[9]

When Early graduated in the summer of 1837, the country was at war with the Seminoles of Florida. Early was commissioned a second lieutenant in the Third U.S. Artillery and assigned to Company E at Fortress Monroe, Virginia. There he began drilling and training recruits for the Florida campaign.[10]

In December 1837, Early arrived in Florida, took temporary command of Company E, and led it into the Everglades. On January 24, 1838, Early was involved in his first battle when his troops engaged the Seminoles on the Locha-Hatchie Ford. Later, he admitted that "though I heard some bullets whistling among the trees, none came near me, and I did not see an Indian."[11]

When hostilities in Florida ended, Early was assigned to the Western frontier in anticipation of trouble with the Cherokee Nation. Early found, as many others did, that duty on the frontier was dull and boring, and, on July 31, 1838, he tendered his resignation. Just after resigning, he learned that he had been promoted to first lieutenant. In his memoirs, Early writes that he might have stayed in the army had he known that this promotion was forthcoming.

In the fall of 1838, Early returned to Franklin County and began to study law under N. M. Taliafeno. By the spring of 1840, he had acquired enough skill to be admitted to the bar and to begin a practice. As a lawyer, Early handled mostly small cases involving such matters as wills and disputes over debts and soon became recognized as a capable and honest practitioner of the law. That the practice of law did not lead him to the royal road of wealth did not seem to bother him. His fees were anything but exorbitant; five dollars was a standard charge for defending a suit. Early was generous with his time, often helping those in trouble without concern about being paid. Later, he admitted that his "practice was never very lucrative."[12]

In 1841, Early won election to the state legislature, although three years later, he was unsuccessful in supporting Henry Clay against James Polk in the presidential contest. While building up a successful law practice and making a name for himself in politics, he was appointed the prosecuting attorney in Franklin and Floyd counties.[13] Though Early had not supported Polk in the election, he nevertheless supported Polk's position on war with Mexico in 1846. He immediately sought a position in the Virginia militia and was commissioned a major in the First Virginia Volunteers. Once again, Early went to Fortress Monroe to train and drill recruits.[14]

By March 1847, Early and his volunteers were ready for service in Mexico. They were assigned to General Zachary Taylor's army, where they performed occupational duty. In April, Early was appointed military governor at Monterrey. His outstanding leadership in the position was quickly recognized, and he received many compliments, including one from Colonel Jefferson Davis. Early was impressed by Davis's soldierly bearing, and he never forgot the kind compliment from the future president of the Confederacy.[15]

During the fall of 1847, Early developed a severe cold that developed into chronic "rheumatism" and would remain a problem the rest of his life. In October, he was sent home on sick leave, returning to Mexico early in 1848 after regaining his health. In April, he was mustered out of the army and returned home.

It was during this time that Early became involved with a woman named Julia McNealey. Julia was only seventeen when Early met her, and until she married Charles Pugh in 1871, she came as close to being his wife as any woman ever was. She bore four children, whom Jubal supported and apparently regarded his own. He was not ashamed of them, giving them his surname and naming one of them Jubal.[16]

Once home in Franklin County, Early took up his practice of law again and was moderately successful at his profession. He ran again for political office but was unsuccessful. Early attributed his political defeats to the fact he was not a good speaker and did not have an attractive personality. "I was never blessed with popular or captivating manners, and the consequence was that I was often misjudged and thought to be haughty and disdainful in my temperament. . . . I was never what was called a popular man."[17]

When secession threatened to split the country, Early spoke against it. Although Early believed the North was threatening the rights of the South, he felt that cooler heads would prevail in the North to avert calamity. Early opposed the extreme states' rights position of the Southern Democrats as well as the antislavery position of the Republicans. In fact, he supported slavery, claiming it a positive social and moral good and that the "Creator of the Universe" had deemed it so. The real issue was not slavery but rather the right of states to govern themselves, he believed.[18]

Early worked diligently to keep Virginia in the Union. In 1861, he was elected to the Virginia convention to consider secession. Early defended Lincoln's inaugural address and urged the delegates to allow the president time to fulfill his pledge to carry out the law in all states. Early said it should be "hailed as a guarantee that he would perform his duty and that we should have peace and protection for our property [slaves]." Even the fall of Fort Sumter did not change his opinion or shake his unionist convictions.[19]

In April 1861, Early voted against the ordinance of secession, hoping against hope that war might be prevented. "The adoption of the ordinance wrung from me bitter tears of grief," he wrote, "but I at once recognized my duty to abide the decision of my native State, and to defend the soil against invasion." Lincoln's war measures finally convinced Early to take up arms against the Union, and he became one of the most confirmed "rebels" of them all. Early would never look back.[20]

Early offered his services to Governor John Letcher and received an appointment as a colonel in the state's forces. He was ordered to Lynchburg to take charge of the training and organization of recruits. Soon afterward, he joined Beauregard's army at Manassas Junction, where he took command of the Sixth Brigade.[21]

On July 18, Early led his brigade in a minor skirmish at Blackburn's Ford as part of the First Battle of Manassas. For most of the morning, his brigade guarded the ford while the major part of the battle raged north of Henry House Hill. In the afternoon, his brigade joined the fight on the Confederate left and provided the decisive blow that turned the Federal right, starting a Yankee retreat that soon became a rout.[22]

Early was rewarded for his performance at Manassas by a promotion to brigadier general. His promotion, however, was not universally applauded by his troops. Referred to as "Old Jube," Early had a reputation for treating his subordinates harshly, and his men had learned to fear his biting sarcasm and tough discipline.[23]

In the months that followed, Early's brigade joined General Joseph E. Johnston's army on the Virginia peninsula, opposing the advance of McClellan's Army of the Potomac. In May 1862, during the Battle of Williamsburg, he was wounded. The bullet that hit him in the neck did little damage, but another minie ball struck his arm in front of one shoulder joint and passed through his back to the opposite shoulder. The bone deflected the ball from vital organs, saving his life. Seriously injured, Early continued to command his brigade until he was so weakened by the loss of blood that he had to be relieved. His wound was reported as mortal in the *Richmond Dispatch.*[24]

At the end of June, doctors at the hospital in Lynchburg reluctantly gave Early permission to return to duty. He rejoined General Lee on the peninsula. Lee assigned Early to the command of a brigade recently led by Brigadier General Arnold Elzey, who had been wounded earlier in the Battle of Seven Days. This assignment placed him under the command of Thomas J. "Stonewall" Jackson. Although the two men never became friends, during the time they were together a bond of respect grew between them. They both were fighters who had committed themselves fully to "the cause."[25]

Early took command of his new brigade just in time for the start of the Battle of Malvern Hill, the scene of the final battle of the Seven Days' Campaign. On the evening of July 1, he received orders to move his brigade to support D. H. Hill on the right of Lee's position. His brigade, however, never got into the fight; Early was separated from his command and was not able to assemble his regiments in time for an assault on the enemy. As a result, his brigade was spared heavy losses. As for their part in the battle, Early acknowledged that they "did not draw trigger at all."[26]

Although Lee was disappointed with the outcome and heavy losses at Malvern Hill, Richmond had been saved. McClellan was forced to withdraw his men from the peninsula, freeing Lee to engage in another Union threat—this time from Major General John Pope's newly formed Army of Virginia. Lee contemplated a bold move to defeat it.

Jackson took his command west to Gordonsville to halt General Pope's advance. During the ensuing campaign, Early distinguished himself at Cedar Mountain and while supporting Jackson along the Rappahannock. Jackson, who was always stingy with praise, gave Early his due. In his report, Jackson wrote that "Early's right had held with great firmness." Early also drew praise from his division commander, Richard Ewell, who lauded him for "gallant and effective service" and for "repulsing repeated attacks of the enemy." In his report, Ewell also recommended Early for promotion to major general.[27]

Early followed up his strong performance at Cedar Mountain with a similar one at Second Manassas, protecting Jackson's left flank at a critical time during the battle. His actions at Manassas displayed his coolness under fire and sound judgment, and it did not go unnoticed by his superiors. When there was talk that Early might be promoted to major general and sent West, Ewell was reluctant to let him go and wrote to a friend in Tennessee: "Early is very able and very brave and would be an acquisition to your part of the world."[28]

At the Battle of Antietam, Early was ordered to hold his position by the West Woods at all costs until he could be reinforced. With only 1,400 men, his brigade held out against parts of three Union corps until Lafayette McLaws came to support him.[29] When General Alexander Lawton was wounded, Early was given command of his division. At this point, Early believed that he should be promoted to the rank of major general, but when his name was presented in Richmond, it was passed over. Although deeply disappointed, Early wisely held his tongue.[30]

Early was not always so politic when dealing with his superiors. One particularly undiplomatic episode occurred as General Jackson's Second Corps was on the march from the Shenandoah Valley to Fredericksburg in late November 1862. During the march, Jackson sent a note to Early inquiring why there were so many stragglers in the rear of his division. Early responded that these stragglers were mostly from other divisions and that "the reason that he saw so many stragglers in the rear of my division today is probably because he rode in the rear of my division."[31] Early's response provoked only a smile from Jackson, which indicated the high regard he had for Early as a soldier. Very few in the Army of Northern Virginia would have dared send such an impertinent response to Jackson. Such was Jubal Early's unique position in the army.[32]

Early continued as a brigadier general leading a division. In December, Major General Ambrose Burnside mounted a Federal offensive that resulted in the bloody battle at Fredericksburg. Early's quick reaction and expert handling of his division during this battle enabled him to close a break in Jackson's line. The result was a crushing Federal defeat. Early's long overdue promotion finally came through in January 1863 at Fredericksburg.[33]

In April 1863, Early assumed command of Ewell's division while Ewell recuperated from wounds. Again, he did not immediately endear himself to his troops. Early, a lifelong bachelor, stirred up the resentment of his men when he asked Jackson to order all visiting wives, mothers, and sisters to stay away from their encampment because he believed they were interrupting the army's work. When Jackson read Early's letter, his reaction was prompt: "I will do no such thing. I wish my wife could come to see me!"[34]

During the 1963 spring and summer campaign, Early demonstrated his fitness for divisional command. At Chancellorsville, Lee ordered him to keep Union troops under Major General John Sedgwick occupied along the Rappahannock at Fredericksburg while the rest of the Army of Northern Virginia engaged "Fighting Joe" Hooker's main force. The assignment demonstrated that Lee trusted Early more than any other division commander with an independent command. Hindered by confusing orders, Early's division was overrun by Sedgwick's Sixth Corps, but he remained cool and formed a new line, holding it long enough for Lee to defeat Hooker and come to his rescue. Lee's report of Early's action stated that it "reflected credit upon himself and his command."[35]

On June 22, 1863, Early's division crossed the Potomac, heading into enemy country and bringing up the rear of Ewell's corps. Early was once again serving under the direction of Richard Ewell, since Jackson's death the commander of the Second Corps. As Lee moved his army into Pennsylvania, he hoped to take advantage of his victory at Chancellorsville and a demoralized Union army.

On the morning of July 1, Early moved his division west from York to Gettysburg. By noon, Ewell's corps had engaged Major General Oliver O. Howard's corps and chased them through the town. Early occupied the town, but Union forces had taken up a position on Cemetery and Culp's Hills. Lee observed the battle for a time and saw the critical importance of the hills. He sent Ewell a discretionary order to take the high ground of Cemetery and Culp's Hill "if practicable," a phrase with a wide range of interpretations. Ewell decided it was not practicable. Ewell's decision to halt the battle stunned many of his subordinates, who were used to Stonewall Jackson's aggressiveness. Ewell was able to convince the normally combative Early that this action was the right course. Later, Early indicated that he had wanted to make the attack but that he had not argued forcefully enough to convince Ewell to change his mind.[36]

Later that evening, Ewell and his subordinates met with Lee to discuss strategy for the next day. Early made a strong argument for an attack on the Union left, at Little and Big Round Tops, but was opposed to an attack by his division on the Union right on Cemetery Ridge. Eventually, Early did attack Cemetery Ridge to relieve the pressure on the opposite flank, but it was uncoordinated and failed.[37]

On July 2, both Confederate attacks on the Union left and right were unsuccessful. In a desperate effort to break the Union line the following day, Lee ordered a disastrous frontal attack. When what became known as Pickett's Charge failed, all hopes of a Confederate victory at Gettysburg ended. Early's division was not involved in the attack on the third day and remained in its original position. Later, Early participated in the controversy over who was to blame for the loss at Gettysburg. He sided with the defenders of Robert E. Lee, who blamed James Longstreet.

In January 1864, Ewell suffered a bad fall from his horse, disabling him for a short time. In his absence, Early assumed command of the Second Corps. When Ewell returned, Early's relationship with his old friend had become strained.[38] After his unimpressive performance at Gettysburg and Early's rising ambition, it became apparent to Ewell that his own position was in jeopardy. In some important matters, Early assumed more authority than his position entailed. On one occasion, when Early went too far, Ewell had him placed under arrest for "conduct subversive of good order and military discipline." Lee interceded and dismissed the charges. The incident was not repeated.[39]

In the spring of 1864, when Lieutenant General A. P. Hill fell ill, Lee selected Early to command the Third Corps. When Hill returned, Early returned briefly to divisional command. By the end of May, Lee removed Ewell from command of the Second Corps because of his failing health. Lee selected Early to replace him. On May 31, 1864, Early was promoted to lieutenant general.[40]

By May 1864, Lieutenant General Ulysses Grant, now general-in-chief of the Union army, set in motion what turned out to be the final campaign of the war in the East. His plan for winning the war was to coordinate attacks by all Union armies at the same time on the already thin Confederate resources. Grant ordered Major General George Meade to follow General Lee's Army of Northern Virginia wherever it went and to engage it as often as possible. Realizing that Lee was most dangerous when he could maneuver, Grant's plan was to hem in Lee's army by exerting constant pressure on it. By June 1864, Union forces had besieged Petersburg and had begun to squeeze the life out of the Confederate army.[41]

To reduce the pressure of Grant's siege, Lee sought to repeat the strategy he had employed two years earlier when he sent Jackson to the Shenandoah Valley to prevent McClellan from obtaining reinforcements. Lee hoped that Early could create enough of a diversion in the valley to force Grant to release some of his troops to deal with him, relieving the pressure on Richmond. This would allow Lee more room to maneuver.[42]

Sending Early to the valley would also address another problem facing the Confederacy. Union forces under Major General David Hunter were advancing up the Shenandoah Valley and threatening Lynchburg. If Hunter was successful in reaching Lynchburg and cutting off the supply line from the valley, a vital food supply for the Confederacy would be lost. To Early, Lee assigned a twofold mission: clear Hunter from the valley and then move north to threaten Baltimore and Washington in the hope that Grant would divert troops from the Richmond-Petersburg theater.[43]

On June 13, "Old Jube" led his corps of 12,000 men west toward Lynchburg. After forcing Hunter to retreat westward, Early moved steadily down the Shenandoah Valley. As Early advanced, panic spread through the North. Uncertain of Early's objective, governors in Ohio, Pennsylvania, and Maryland called out their militias. Chaos spread as Early moved farther north, exactly as Lee had hoped. Early encountered very little resistance as he advanced and quickly captured Harper's Ferry; on July 5, he crossed the Potomac River at Shepherdstown. Becoming increasingly bold, Early dispatched Brigadier General John McCausland's cavalry brigade to Hagerstown, Maryland.[44]

When Early arrived in Frederick, Maryland, he demanded a ransom of $200,000 from local officials to spare their town from being torched, while McCausland made a similar levy of $20,000 at Hagerstown. Both demands were met. By July, the road to Washington lay open.[45] Dispatches were urgently sent to Grant for troops to defend Washington. He quickly responded by sending parts of two Union corps to Washington. It was doubtful that these troops could reach Washington before Early, and it was possible that the capital would fall if they did not.[46]

Other than some militia and home guard, the only Union troops between Early and the capital were commanded by Major General Lew Wallace, head of the Middle Department of Maryland at Baltimore. Wallace had under his command only 2,500 inexperienced troops. Using what he had, Wallace decided to take up a position at Monocacy Junction, two miles south of Frederick, a location that provided a strong defensive position.[47]

By the morning of July 9, Early realized he had a fight on his hands. He could have moved around Wallace's troops but later explained that "I could not leave the force in my rear." He thus chose to engage it. Not until mid-afternoon were Early's troops organized such that they could attack. The battle lasted only an hour and resulted in a rout of the Union troops, but it had cost Early 700 of his best troops and delayed his march on Washington by one full day. By the time Early's army reached Washington on July 11, the city had been reinforced.[48]

Early stopped his advance in front of Fort Stevens on Georgia Avenue, where his troops were driven back. During the skirmish, President Lincoln had ridden out to the fort to observe. Lincoln recklessly exposed himself until he was told to get down by a young Massachusetts captain named Oliver Wendell Holmes.[49]

Despite the hysteria created by the threat on Washington, Early elected to retreat. Lee's orders had been to threaten Washington, not to capture it. He had to settle for burning the house of Postmaster General Montgomery Blair at Silver Springs, Maryland, and with the fact that "we scared the hell out of Abe Lincoln."[50]

Early retreated slowly back into the Shenandoah Valley, fighting a few minor skirmishes along the way. After reaching the valley, Early sent General McCausland to Chambersburg to collect $100,000 in gold or $500,000 in paper currency as reparation for when Hunter burned private property in the valley. When the townspeople refused to pay the ransom, Early ordered the town to be torched. Early's action at Chambersburg backfired badly. Lee had given strict orders that there should be no "unnecessary or wanton injury to private property." "We make war only on armed men," Lee said. "We can not take vengeance for the wrongs our people have suffered without lowering ourselves in the eyes of all." The sacking of Chambersburg solidified public opinion in the North and drew criticism in the Southern press. General Bradley Johnson said that his men were demoralized by the events at Chambersburg and that "the grand spectacle of a national retaliation was reduced to a miserable hucksters for greenbacks."[51]

Despite the criticism Early received from all sources, he accepted full responsibility, absolving his subordinates of all blame. He wrote, "For this act I, alone, am responsible, as the officers engaged in it were simply executing my orders, and had no discretion left them. . . . I am perfectly satisfied with my conduct on the occasion, and see no reason to regret it."[52]

Grant was angered by the sacking of Chambersburg and decided to rid the Shenandoah Valley of Confederate troops once and for all. He assembled an army of 40,000 men under the command of Major General Philip Sheridan and sent them to the valley. His orders were to "eat out Virginia clean and clear as far as they go, so that crows flying over it for the balance of this season will have to carry their provender with them."[53]

It was now total war. After defeats at Winchester and Fisher's Hill, Early retreated down the valley. Sheridan followed and burned everything in his path. Residents of the Shenandoah Valley still refer to this march as "The Burning."[54]

Lee sent reinforcements to the valley hoping to stem the tide. As a result, Early went on the offensive at Cedar Creek, catching the unsuspecting Union force completely by surprise. After routing the enemy, Early was content to hold the advantage gained that day until the rest of his troops arrived and all captured property was secured. In the meantime, Sheridan, who had spent the night at Winchester, arrived on the field. He was horrified to see that his army was stricken by panic and "thoroughly demoralized." Even his own headquarters had fallen into enemy hands.[55]

Sheridan began personally approaching his men and urging them to return to the fight, vowing that he himself would sleep in his camp that night "or in hell." He rode among his troops, waving his hat and ordering them back into the battle. Encouraged by Sheridan's action, his troops gave him a wild cheer.[56] To further inspire them for a counterattack, Sheridan rode along the two-mile front waving his hat and shouting, "We'll get a twist on these people yet. We'll raise them out of their boots before the day is over." The men cheered "from throats of brass," as one witness reported, "and caps were thrown to the tops of the scattering oaks." It was all the Yankees needed to turn their beaten rabble into a conquering army.[57]

Sheridan's magnificent ride became one of the most celebrated incidents of the war. He was able to unify his scattered command and drive the Confederate forces from the field, forcing them to leave behind equipment and artillery that they could scarcely afford to lose. In describing his defeat, Early could only bring himself to say, "The Yankees got whipped, and we got scared."[58]

The defeat ended Early's ability to campaign in the Shenandoah Valley, forcing him to retreat southward. Lee returned a portion of his army to the lines at Petersburg, leaving him with less than 2,000 troops. On March 2, 1865, Union cavalry under Brevet Major General George Armstrong Custer engaged Early's remnant command at Waynesboro. Custer's audacious attack resulted in a complete destruction of what was left of Early's army, and as one Richmond diarist recorded, "General Early's little army is scattered to the winds." Most of it was captured, including Dr. Hunter McGuire, the Second Corps medical director; Early himself barely managed to escape.[59]

The Battle at Waynesboro closed a chapter on the war in the valley. The rich Shenandoah could no longer be counted on to feed and protect the Confederate army. The battle also ended Jubal Early's career as a combat general. Shortly afterward, Lee reluctantly responded to public and official pressures to relieve him from command.[60] In his letter of dismissal on March 30, Lee made a point of thanking Early for his "fidelity and energy," but he could not oppose the current opinion that he should be replaced. "To this end, it is essential that we should have the cheerful and full confidence of the soldiers," he wrote.[61]

Ten days later, Lee surrendered at Appomattox. For Early, however, the war did not end. He eluded Federal troops and headed West, hoping to continue the fight by joining up with General Kirby Smith, commander of the Trans-Mississippi forces. When he learned of Smith's surrender, Early traveled to Mexico by ship, arriving in Vera Cruz in December 1865. Faced with the prospect of living under Union rule or, worse, in prison, Early joined thousands of other Southerners who chose exile rather than submission.[62]

In May 1866, Early left Mexico and sailed for Canada, where he took up residence in Toronto, Ontario, in a colony of Confederate exiles. While he managed to make friends in Canada, Early refused all social invitations. "I cannot take pleasure in amusements of any kind," he wrote, "while our people [in the South] are in the condition they are in." While in Canada, he received financial support from his family at home and began work on his controversial book about the campaign of 1864 to 1865, *A Memoir of the Last Year of the War of Independence.* Through his memoir, he hoped to be vindicated for his lack of success in the Shenandoah Valley. He also began the long-range compilation of his complete memoirs.[63]

In 1869, Early returned to the United States after President Andrew Johnson pardoned former Confederates; he then settled in Lynchburg to practice law. In 1877, he became a commissioner of the Louisiana State Lottery; he also continued to be an outspoken champion of Lee and Jefferson Davis. He wore only gray and never apologized for his actions during the war, including the burning of Chambersburg.[64]

Early was an officer in both the Association of the Army of Northern Virginia and the Southern Historical Society. As a result of his involvement in these two organizations, he greatly influenced the way Civil War history was written. He helped develop the cult of the "Lost Cause," arguing that the odds were against the South from the very beginning. "The North had superiority in numbers and in its ability to produce weapons and supplies," he said. Early became the chief defender of Lee's reputation, elevating him to saint-like status. He led the campaign to raise funds for Lee's memorial statue in Richmond. When he learned that Longstreet had joined the Republican Party and had dared to publish an article critical of Lee at Gettysburg, Early conducted an all-out attack on him. A skilled trial lawyer, Early was more than a match for Longstreet. He portrayed Longstreet as a traitor responsible for the Confederate's loss at Gettysburg.[65] Although caustic and sardonic, Early also had a soft spot for those in need. He contributed large amounts of money to charity, especially to widows and orphans of former Confederate soldiers.

On February 15, 1894, with his health failing and still bothered by his old wounds, Early had a bad fall down a flight of stairs. Although he refused to admit there was anything seriously wrong, his health slowly faded. On March 2, 1894, Jubal Early died. He was seventy-seven years old. Early was buried in Spring Hill Cemetery on a hilltop with a view of the Blue Ridge Mountains.[66]

Early never accepted defeat. He remained an unreconstructed Confederate to the end. The Southern press praised him as a Southern eagle, the defender of the Confederate cause. One obituary described him as "a rough diamond. Beneath an exclusive and repellent exterior, he had a warm, sympathetic heart, even as the eagle that soars with an unwinking eye nearest the sun wears beneath his wing the softest down."[67] For some, however, this depiction of "Old Jube" was arguable.

22 *John Brown Gordon*

"A Soldier's Soldier"

The morning of April 12, 1865, was chilly and gray. It was to be the last day of the Army of Northern Virginia. Earlier, Lee had designated Generals Longstreet, Gordon, and Pendleton to make arrangements for the formal surrender of his army. In a cordial spirit, the two sides had agreed to the surrender of arms, for the transfer of public property, and for the departure of the Confederates under their own commanders. Now, general officers were mounted, regimental commanders were at their stations, and each man was in his place. Confederate battle flags were with their regiments, but a few flagstaffs were conspicuously absent from their standards. Some men had torn their flags into pieces; others had hidden their banners. There were no bands. Without the beat of drums and in the silence of their depression, the once proud army moved down the hill. At the head of the column rode John B. Gordon, his chin on his chest, his eyes downcast. No career in the army had been more remarkable than his. He was Lee's choice to represent him in the surrender.[1]

Beginning the war as a twenty-nine-year-old captain of a company of mountain volunteers, Gordon had no military training or experience. Nevertheless, he was a general within two years and eventually rose to the rank of major general and corps commander. As commander of a wing of Lee's army, he led the last charge at Appomattox and was hailed as the "most famous and brilliant soldier" that Georgia sent to the war. More than any other Georgian, Gordon captured the imagination and respect of the people of his native state. After the war, they elected and reelected him to the state's highest office, where he worked toward reconciliation and healing the nation's wounds.[2]

John Brown Gordon was the fourth of twelve children born to Reverend

Zachariah and Malinda Cox Gordon of Upson County, Georgia. He was born on February 6, 1832. In 1840, the Reverend moved his family to Walker County in northwestern Georgia, settling on property containing springs with an abundance of mineral water. Taking advantage of the medicinal value of mineral water, Zachariah built a large hotel that served as a summer resort, naming it Gordon Springs. In the years before the Civil War, Gordon Springs became one of the "most fashionable watering places in Georgia." Ironically, the Gordon homestead, where John enjoyed a happy childhood, would provide the site for the Battle of Chickamauga.[3]

Though young John enjoyed the outdoors, he also showed a great interest in religion. By the age of seven, he had already professed his Christian faith. Although reared as a Baptist, John would eventually become a Presbyterian. John attended rural schools but later went to Pleasant Green Academy in Lafayette, Georgia. By 1850, he had enrolled at the University of Georgia. Despite his outstanding grade average, Gordon did not graduate. For some unknown reason, he left the University of Georgia during his senior year, never to return. Gordon had demonstrated his academic prowess to the point that the president of the university sent his father a letter stating that, if his son had remained at school, he would have taken senior honors.[4]

In 1854, Gordon moved to Atlanta, where he pursued a career in law. Reading law under the tutelage of two of Atlanta's most competent attorneys, Basil Overby and Logan Bleckley, Gordon passed the bar examination and immediately joined their firm.[5]

Soon after beginning the practice of law, Gordon met Mrs. Overby's younger sister, Fanny Haralson. It was love at first sight; he pursued her with great passion, and in less than a month, Fanny agreed to marry him. On September 18, 1854, Gordon married the seventeen year old. She was a charming, intelligent young lady and the love of Gordon's life. Through the years, they were blessed with four children. According to one of the children, their marriage was "a perfect union, unmarred by discord through all their years together."[6]

In 1856, Gordon left his law practice to join his father in a coal-mining enterprise. Later, he moved from Georgia to nearby Jackson County, Alabama, where he continued to mine. Despite the poverty in the mountains, Gordon prospered with his coal mines, and, by 1860, he had become financially secure, having acquired real estate, personal property, and several slaves.[7]

Also by 1860, Gordon had become involved in politics, campaigning for the Southern Democratic presidential candidate, John C. Breckinridge. Gordon passionately supported secession and believed that Lincoln's election threatened the expansion of slavery into the territories. When Lincoln called for 75,000 volunteers to put down the rebellion, Gordon offered his military service to the newly created Confederate states.

Shortly after the firing on Fort Sumter, Gordon helped raise a company of volunteers from the states of Georgia, Tennessee, and Alabama, calling

General John B. Gordon surrendered the Army of
Northern Virginia to General Joshua Chamberlain.

COURTESY OF THE LIBRARY OF CONGRESS

them the "Raccoon Roughs." Well known among the mountain people,
Gordon was elected captain. When he took the Raccoon Roughs to Atlanta
to offer their services as a cavalry unit, Gordon was informed that they were
out of guns and that his unit was not needed at that time. Told to go home
and wait to be contacted, Gordon led his Raccoon Roughs to Montgomery
where they were armed and incorporated into the Sixth Alabama Regiment. Gordon was unanimously elected major.[8]

Gordon arranged to leave his two children in his mother's care so that
his wife could accompany him with the army. She followed him so devot-
edly that it became a tradition in the army that, when Mrs. Gordon was
sent to the rear, it was a signal that the action was about to commence.
With no military experience whatsoever but with the natural instinct to
lead men and the persuasive ability of an orator, Gordon quickly won the

confidence of his men. He was "the prettiest thing you ever did see on a field of fight," one of his men claimed. "It 'ud put fight into a whipped chicken just to look at him."[9]

Near the end of May, the Sixth Alabama moved to Corinth, Mississippi, for military training, but by early June, they were ordered to proceed to Richmond as quickly as possible. On the trip from Mississippi to Virginia, Gordon encountered signs of the South's divided allegiances. Whenever the train stopped, his troops were greeted with both cheers and jeers. In many towns, both Confederate and American flags flew openly.[10]

When Gordon and his men reached Virginia, General P. G. T. Beauregard assigned the Alabama regiment to the Second Brigade under the command of Brigadier General Richard Ewell, a part of the First Corps. At Manassas on July 21, the Sixth Alabama occupied the extreme right of Beauregard's line. Whereas other regiments routed the Union army at the Battle of First Manassas, Gordon's regiment only waited. Gordon had seen the enemy, but he had not participated in the action. He would have to wait almost a year before his first test in battle.

In the following months, Gordon's regiment remained in the vicinity of Manassas Junction while he devoted his time to training and drilling his men. To do so, Gordon had first to teach himself the techniques of warfare, using whatever military manuals were available. Gordon understood the importance of drill and discipline, as was evident to a private in the Sixth Alabama who wrote home, "Drilling every day—very hot. . . . Our employment is the same as ever—a very dull routine it is." Despite its monotony, Gordon believed that constant drilling was the only way to achieve effective control of troops during a battle.[11]

During the winter of 1861 to 1862, Gordon's troops suffered great hardships. Food and clothing were in short supply. The men from the Deep South were unaccustomed to the severe weather, and sickness spread throughout the Confederate camp. Gordon himself suffered from a crippling attack of diarrhea, which forced him to stay in quarters for six weeks. Returning to duty by the end of March, he was ready for the fighting that would come in the spring.[12]

In April, the period of encampment ended when Major General George McClellan began his long-expected move on Richmond, landing his army at the base of the Virginia peninsula at Fortress Monroe. On April 6, Gordon's regiment, now a part of Brigadier General Robert Rodes's brigade, left northern Virginia for Yorktown on the peninsula. Upon reaching Yorktown, Gordon was promoted to lieutenant colonel. After their arrival, the decision was made to fall back. While a portion of D. H. Hill's division retreated up the peninsula, Gordon's regiment served as the rear guard. Finally on May 31, Rodes's brigade and Gordon's regiment saw action in the Battles of Fair Oaks and Seven Pines. Sensing the apprehension his troops might have before their first engagement, Gordon addressed his men just before their advance. He spoke of the disaster that would befall both them and their cause if they were defeated. Strengthened by Gordon's words, his regiment pressed forward under heavy fire. During the fighting, General Rodes was wounded, and Gordon assumed command of the brigade. Finally, after suffering heavy losses, the brigade was ordered to the rear.[13]

At Seven Pines, Gordon lived up to the challenge of brigade commander. Leading his men in a deadly charge through murderous fire, he was the only field officer to survive. During his near-death experience, Gordon had his horse shot from under him, and numerous bullet holes were discovered in his jacket. The entire brigade suffered heavy losses, but the Sixth Alabama bore the heaviest casualties, losing nearly 60 percent of the men engaged. Despite the large number of casualties, the regiment never wavered, a tribute to the discipline instilled earlier by their leader.[14]

After the Battle of Seven Pines, Gordon remained in command of Rodes's brigade until late June when Rodes returned to duty. On June 25, General Robert E. Lee, who had now replaced General Joseph Johnston, seized the initiative from McClellan, attacking him north of the Chickahominy River. This was the beginning of what became known as the Battle of Seven Days. Gordon, now back with his regiment, first saw action on the afternoon of June 27 at Gaines's Mills. On the following day, not fully recovered from his prior wounds, a nearly prostrated Rodes again turned his brigade over to him. On July 1, the brigade saw action again, this time at the heavily fortified Union position on Malvern Hill. Despite D. H. Hill's belief that the Union position was impregnable, Lee decided to assault the hill.[15]

Just before sundown, Hill's division moved forward. Gordon led his brigade uphill across an open field under heavy enemy fire. During the costly charge, Gordon was temporarily blinded when an exploding shell filled his eyes with sand and dirt. Enemy bullets shattered the handle of his pistol and tore away part of his coat, but, again, he was able to escape injury. Finally, under darkness, Gordon withdrew his scattered command from the field. The cost had been high for the brigade—almost half of the men engaged had become casualties. Gordon's conduct had been an inspiration to his men; nothing raised their spirits more than his action under fire.[16]

Following Malvern Hill, Gordon retained command of Rodes's brigade and remained with D. H. Hill's division. Left in southeastern Virginia with Hill, Gordon did not see action during the Second Battle of Manassas. On September 4, Rodes's brigade, with Gordon still at its head, joined the Army of Northern Virginia on Lee's first invasion of the North. Once across the Potomac, Lee divided his forces, sending Longstreet and D. H. Hill northward. Though he realized the danger of splitting his army in enemy territory, Lee hoped to capitalize on the disorganization of the Union army after their defeat at Second Manassas.

At South Mountain, Gordon exhorted his men "not to allow their courage to falter" if he were to fall, "but to acquit themselves nobly, that their names as heroes might live forever." Words were not enough, however, as Gordon's troops were outflanked and outnumbered. After a stubborn resistance, they were forced to fall back.[17]

On September 15 at Antietam, Gordon's men defended Bloody Lane in the center of the Confederate line. While repulsing numerous Federal assaults, Gordon suffered his first wound of the war when a ball passed through his right leg. Despite the wound, Gordon continued to move among his men, encouraging them even after a second shot struck him higher in the same leg. Later a third ball ripped through his left arm, "making a hideous and most painful wound." Seeing the seriousness of the wounds, his men pleaded with him to go to the rear, but he refused. A fourth Union ball pierced his shoulder. Although weak from loss of blood, Gordon remained on his feet and alert. Moments later, a fifth minie ball struck him in the face, passing through his jaw and just missing his jugular vein.[18] Falling forward, Gordon lay unconscious with his face in his cap, while the cap slowly filled with blood. Had it not been for a bullet hole in his hat, it is likely he would have drowned in his own blood. Gordon's fall went unnoticed for a time, but finally he was carried behind the lines and placed in a barn where he could be treated.[19]

Gordon's wounds were so severe that it was believed he would die. The immense loss of blood and the severe wounds left Gordon in critical condition for several months. The fact that his jaw had to be wired shut further complicated his condition. Only Gordon's great will to survive and the loving care of his wife pulled him through.[20] After Antietam, D. H. Hill labeled Gordon the "Christian hero" and asserted that he "had excelled his former deeds" at Seven Pines and Malvern Hill. "Our language," Hill concluded, "is not capable of expressing a higher compliment."[21]

Given the severity of his wounds, Gordon recovered quickly, returning to duty after less than seven months. Gordon was promoted to brigadier general, and in April 1863, he was assigned to command a brigade in Major General Jubal Early's division. He had less than three weeks with his new command before leading it into action during the Chancellorsville campaign.

Gordon's brigade was selected to retake Marye's Heights, just behind Fredericksburg, from the Union troops. Before beginning the assault, Gordon asked every man willing to follow him up the heights to raise his hat. According to reports, every man did so. "I don't want you to holler," Gordon said, "until you get up close to the top, then let every man raise a yell and take those heights." "Will you do it? I ask you to go no farther than I am willing to lead!" he proclaimed. Again, Gordon had found the right words to inspire his men. "We all stepped off at quick time," wrote Henry Walker of the Thirteenth Georgia. Marye's Heights were undefended, however, and by the next day, the Federals had retreated across the river.[22]

After the death of Stonewall Jackson at Chancellorsville, Lee reorganized the Army of Northern Virginia, creating three corps out of two and shuffling both officers and men. Gordon's brigade remained with Early's division as part of the Second Corps, now under Lieutenant General Ewell.

In June 1863, Gordon's brigade was engaged in a heated clash with Union troops near Winchester. His action elicited praise from General Early, a man who was sparing with compliments. He reported that Gordon's actions "reflected equal credit upon himself and his brigade." General Ewell likewise described Gordon's advance as "skillful" and "one of the finest he had witnessed during the war."[23]

After Winchester, Gordon's brigade entered Pennsylvania and marched toward York. When he camped outside the town, a delegation from the town, including the mayor and leading citizens, visited him to surrender the town. The next morning, when the Confederates entered the town, they struck terror into the hearts of the citizens. To allay their fears, Gordon assured them that his command would respect their person and property. The town breathed a collective sigh of relief.[24]

Moving on to Wrightville, the Confederates found the town on fire as a result of the state militia burning the Susquehanna River bridge. Although his men were tired from their long march, Gordon organized his troops into a fire brigade to help the townspeople put out the fire. To show appreciation for their efforts, Gordon and his staff were invited to breakfast at the home of Mrs. L. L. Rewalt.[25]

Rejoining the Confederate army at Gettysburg, Gordon took an active part in the first day's engagement north of town. An officer who spotted Gordon riding his black stallion that day called the sight "the most glorious and inspiring thing, . . . standing in his stirrups, bareheaded, hat in hand, arms extended, and, in a voice like a trumpet, extorting his men. It was superb, absolutely thrilling."[26]

On the outskirts of the town, Gordon's troops engaged Major General Oliver O. Howard's Eleventh Corps, holding the extreme right flank of the Union line. An officer commanding one of the Union divisions that day was Brigadier General Francis Channing Barlow, who, like Gordon, had been a lawyer before the war. In the hand-to-hand struggle that ensued, the Union line broke and began a disorderly retreat. In the midst of the confusion, Gordon saw one of the Union officers go down. Impressed by the officer's bravery, Gordon rode to his side, dismounted, and bent down to check on his condition. Gordon gave him water, and asking his name, he found that the man was Barlow.[27]

Gordon had Barlow moved to a shady place in the rear, and at the wounded general's request, took a packet of personal letters from his pocket and destroyed them. Believing that Barlow's wounds were fatal, Gordon made him comfortable, remounted his horse, and followed his command into Gettysburg. When Gordon learned that Mrs. Barlow was with the

Union army, he extended the wounded general another kindness: he sent a message through the lines offering Mrs. Barlow safe conduct to her husband's side. It was the last time Gordon thought of Barlow, assuming he had died as the result of his wounds. He would have been surprised to learn that Barlow recovered.[28]

During the following year, a relative of Gordon's, James Byron Gordon, was killed in action. When Barlow saw the death notice in the newspaper, he assumed that this was the same Gordon who had come to his aid at Gettysburg. Both men thought the other was dead.[29]

After the war, Gordon was introduced to Barlow by a friend. Neither recognized the other from their brief encounter on the battlefield. Gordon innocently asked Barlow if he was related to the Barlow killed at Gettysburg. "I am the man wounded at Gettysburg, but I didn't die," Barlow responded. "Are you related to the Gordon who helped me?" "I am that man, sir," Gordon replied.[30]

In his memoirs, Gordon recalled his surprise at the news that Barlow had survived his wounds. "No words of mine can convey any conception of the emotions awakened by the startling announcement," he wrote. Overcome by the emotion of the situation, the men embraced. They remained friends for the rest of their lives.[31]

After his action during the first day at Gettysburg, Gordon's participation ended. On the second day, his brigade was placed in the rear of Early's divisions and, with the exception of being exposed to artillery and sharpshooters' fire, was not engaged. As the army retreated from Gettysburg on July 5, Gordon's brigade acted as a rear guard. After Gettysburg, Gordon saw no action for the next few months.

As a civilian volunteer in an army staffed and led by professional soldiers, Gordon had impressed Lee with his ability as a military leader. In early 1864, Lee complimented him in a letter to President Davis. In January, he wrote, "Of the brigadiers, I think General Gordon, of Alabama, one of the best."[32]

In May 1864, General Grant began his campaign in Virginia. By moving rapidly, he hoped to maneuver around Lee's right flank and come to battle in conditions that favored the Union. Early on the morning of May 6, Gordon scouted the Union flank and discovered that it was unprotected. He recommended to Ewell that the Confederates attack this point, but Gordon's immediate superior, Jubal Early, thought that an assault was too risky. Finally, after consulting Lee, Ewell authorized Gordon to launch the attack he had urged earlier. The Union line crumpled, but darkness descended before Gordon could consolidate his gains. During the night, the Union forces had time to establish a new line. For years after the war, Gordon festered at what he viewed a lost opportunity. While his superiors waited, he claimed, "the greatest opportunity ever presented to Lee's army was permitted to pass."[33]

During the spring, when A. P. Hill became incapacitated, General Early was assigned as temporary Third Corps commander. As a result, Gordon was temporarily elevated to division commander. Gordon's star was clearly on the rise.

On the evening of May 7, Gordon began his march to Spotsylvania Court House, arriving there on the afternoon of May 8. At Spotsylvania, Gordon was again drawn into the thick of the action. As he was preparing to lead his division in a charge, he noticed General Lee at the front. Gordon explained his plan of action to him; Lee readily agreed and ordered him to proceed. As he made his final preparations, Gordon noticed that Lee was riding to the center of the line. With hat in hand, Lee intended to join the division's charge. Gordon dashed back to appeal to Lee to move to the rear. "General Lee, this is no place for you. These men behind you are Georgians and Virginians. They have never failed you and will not fail you here. Will you boys?" In unison, they cried, "No, no, no; we'll not fail him." "Lee to the rear," they chanted. Gordon ordered two men to escort Lee to the rear.[34]

Gordon led his men into the center of the fray, carrying the colors and advancing at the head of his troops. Despite heavy resistance from Union troops, Gordon's men drove them back. Some of the most brutal fighting of the war took place at the Bloody Angle on that day. On the following day, the exhausted Confederates withdrew to a new line.

Gordon's efforts and gallantry at the Bloody Angle did not go unnoticed. On May 14, Gordon was promoted to major general as a result of Lee's recommendation and placed in command of a division. He was one of only three nonprofessional generals to be promoted to this level by General Lee.[35]

In June 1864, Gordon's division was detached from the forces around Richmond to participate in Early's Shenandoah Valley campaign. There he helped Early drive Union Major General David Hunter from the valley and deliver a crushing blow to Major General Lew Wallace at Monocacy during Early's aborted raid on Washington.[36]

As summer turned to fall, Gordon and Early's corps continued to maneuver and fight throughout the Shenandoah Valley. The Federal troops in the valley, now under the command of Major General Philip Sheridan, posed a new problem for Early. Sheridan's Army of the Shenandoah, with 48,000 men, outnumbered Early's army more than two-to-one. For months, the opposing forces continued to maneuver, while Sheridan prepared his army for battle. In September, Gordon's division fought in the Battle of Winchester and Fisher's Hill. When the entire Confederate line collapsed, Early had to retreat.[37]

The next major battle for Gordon's men was at Cedar Creek. Gordon planned the battle. Early entrusted the entire Second Corps to him, which was to lead the assault on Sheridan's flank. After an all-night march, Gordon attacked, pushing the enemy back. At nightfall, Early ordered the advance to halt. Gordon tried to convince him to continue the attack while Gordon had the Federals on the run. Early refused, saying that they had won "glory enough for one day." It was a critical mistake: Sheridan, who had been at Winchester when the attack began, returned to the field to take command. In one of the war's greatest reversals of fortune, Sheridan led his troops in a crushing counterattack. Sheridan's victory at Cedar Creek effectively ended the Confederate campaign in the Shenandoah Valley.[38]

In December 1864, Gordon and the bulk of the Second Corps joined Lee's army in the trenches at Petersburg, while Early remained in the valley with a skeleton force. With Early still in the valley, Gordon assumed command of the Second Corps. He did not receive a promotion to lieutenant general because it was not known when or if Early would return and assume his old responsibility.[39]

At Petersburg, Gordon's corps occupied the extreme right of Lee's army. With Longstreet north of the James and A. P. Hill's frequent illness, Lee came to rely on Gordon more and more for his advice. Although he had had no formal military training before the war, Gordon had displayed boldness, vigilance, and sound military sense. During the bleak months of 1865, Lee turned to the youngest corps commander on his staff as his chief confidant.[40]

Lee asked Gordon to study the Union lines around Petersburg to determine which point offered the best opportunity for attack. Gordon concluded that the weakest point was at Fort Stedman. He believed it was not only possible to capture the fort but that that position could be used to break through the Union line.[41] Gordon's plan called for a surprise attack after dark. After questioning Gordon in detail about his plan, Lee gave his approval. In the early morning of March 25, Gordon launched one of the most desperate assaults of the war.

The initial stage of the attack proceeded smoothly; Gordon's men quickly overcame the Union sentinels. In the predawn darkness, the surprise was complete. The sudden thrust of Gordon's troops captured 500 prisoners, but problems developed as dawn approached. At the arrival of daylight, Union forces were able to halt the Confederate advance and bring up reinforcements. With the aid of artillery and heavy infantry fire, they counterattacked. Gordon soon saw the futility of further engagement; his effort to break Grant's hold on Petersburg had failed.[42]

In the days after Fort Stedman, the worsening situation of the Army of Northern Virginia afforded Gordon little chance for rest. His corps had been reduced to just 5,500 men, who were being asked to cover a six-mile front. On April 1, Union cavalry and infantry overwhelmed Lee's right flank at Five Forks, forcing Lee to begin his retreat. Petersburg had to be abandoned; Gordon was ordered to hold his position at all costs so that other commands might withdraw. Gordon's corps served as the rear guard of the retreating army.[43]

Gordon's men trudged on, alternately forming and fighting and then retreating. By April 7, the Army of Northern Virginia had been reduced to two skeleton corps of 12,000 armed men under Longstreet and Gordon. Gordon's troops continued to fight until word came from Lee that a truce existed between the two armies. On April 9, Lee surrendered his army to General Grant.

Although the army had surrendered, Gordon's soldierly responsibilities continued. As one of the three Confederate commissioners appointed by Lee to complete the final details of the surrender agreement, Gordon met with the three Federal counterparts to complete the final details of the surrender. Long after the surrender, Gordon remembered the "marked consideration and courtesy shown by the victorious Federals, from commanding generals to the privates in the ranks."[44]

The morning of April 12 was a depressing one for the defeated army. The Confederacy and the dreams of an independent nation had died with Lee's surrender. Nevertheless, Gordon gathered his men together for their march to the formal surrender. The Third Corps had been selected for the lead position in the surrender column, with Gordon riding at its head. Union Major General Joshua Chamberlain, hero of Gettysburg, was honored by being selected to preside over the ceremonies. He aligned his troops on both sides of the road leading through Appomattox. There were no bands and no drums, just the sound of tramping feet. "On they come," wrote Chamberlain, "with the old swinging route step and swaying battle flags." All the Confederate units had been greatly reduced in size so that their battle flags were "crowded so thick, by the thinning out of men," said Chamberlain, "that the whole column seemed crowned with red."[45]

As the column neared the double line of Union soldiers, Gordon heard a spoken order and the clatter of hundreds of muskets being raised in salute. Gordon responded by raising his sword to acknowledge the Union tribute. Then he shouted a command, and the Confederates shifted to shoulder arms, returning the salute. "It was," wrote Chamberlain, "honor answering honor." Many of the veterans wept. "On our part," Chamberlain added, "not a sound of trumpet nor a roll of drum; not a cheer, nor motion of men standing again at the order, but an awed stillness rather, and breath-holding, as if it were the passing of the dead."[46]

After the exchange of salutes, the Confederates fixed their bayonets and stacked their muskets. Then, Chamberlain wrote, "lastly—reluctantly, with agony of expression—they fold their flags, battle-worn and torn, blood stained, heart-holding colors, and lay them down." "This was the most painful part of the ordeal," said a Confederate veteran. "We did not even look into each other's eyes."[47]

After the war, Gordon returned to Atlanta to resume his law practice. In the months that followed, he worked toward building a strong, more united nation. Like Lee, Gordon was a champion of reconciliation. He attempted to ease racial tensions and contributed liberally to funds designed to improve living conditions and the education of African Americans. Although he was generous with his time and funds, Gordon did not believe in racial equality. In his opinion, it was God's will that the white man should rule the black man.[48]

Gordon had an excellent memory for names, faces, and characters. He reputedly knew the names of all his soldiers—an ability that was very helpful when he entered politics. In 1868, Gordon ran for governor on the Democratic ticket. Although he ran an effective campaign, he was defeated by the Republican candidate.[49]

Gordon threw himself into the thick of the fight to restore home rule to Georgia and end the Reconstruction policies of the Republicans. In 1873, he was elected to the U.S. Senate. Despite charges that he was in the pay of railroad interests, Gordon was reelected in 1879, only to resign a short time later to accept a high position with the Louisville and Nashville Railroad.[50]

From 1886 to 1890, Gordon served as governor of the state of Georgia, establishing himself as a staunch spokesman for the state and the South. After his term as governor, Gordon was once again elected to the Senate. He was the first Georgian to be elected to the Senate three times.

Although the *New York Times* was often critical of Gordon, it named him "the ablest man from the South in either House of Congress." After serving out his term in the Senate, Gordon embarked on a speaking tour in the North and began to write his memoirs.

During the last years of his life, Gordon remained active in his efforts to vindicate the South and establish a new spirit of nationalism. He used the lecture circuit as his means, choosing "Last Days of the Confederacy" as his title. Traveling around the country, he delivered this speech hundreds of times. Gordon was inspiring and captivating as a speaker, but it was his message that moved his audience. One presentation in Vermont illustrated the effect he had on the crowds that came to hear him speak.[51]

At the conclusion of Gordon's lecture, an old man, tears rolling down his cheeks, confronted him. "General Gordon, I have hated you for more than thirty years; I have hated everything South[ern]. . . . You killed the noblest boy in my home, and he lies buried now in an unknown grave. We have mourned his loss all these years. When I listened to you and heard you tell the history and hardship, how the soldier marched barefoot, how he lived without a bite some days, how he suffered, I can see that he was fighting for the cause he esteemed more dear than life." As he extended his hand to Gordon, the man said, "I will never hate you any more. . . . My hatred for the South is gone forever."[52]

In 1903, Gordon published his *Reminiscences of the Civil War,* which was praised for its fairness to both sides in the war. His purpose in writing the book, he said, was to preserve the story of the soldiers who had fought, both Confederate and Union. *Reminiscences of the Civil War* became an instant success.[53]

In the winter of 1903, Gordon vacationed in Biscayne Bay, hoping to relax in the tropical breezes of Florida and regain his former energy. Having just finished a lecture tour through New England, Gordon was tired; the speaking tour always wore heavily on the seventy-one-year-old general. After several weeks in the sun and warm ocean breezes, Gordon seemed to regain his strength and "was feeling unusually well." All seemed fine.[54]

Then, suddenly, his health changed for the worse. His temperature quickly rose to 105 degrees, and he suffered a severe attack of nausea. A doctor was summoned, but with his advanced age and previously impaired health, it was doubtful he would recover. Several days later, his kidneys began to fail, and his heart weakened. Finally, on January 9, 1904, Gordon died as "peacefully as a little child falls asleep."[55]

When the news of the death of their beloved general reached Georgia, plans were made to honor their native son. But first, Miamians requested the opportunity to pay their final respects before he was moved to Georgia. A black-draped funeral car was provided for his journey back to Georgia. All along the route, Floridians and Georgians turned out to pay homage to their fallen hero.[56]

In one heartwarming incident an old Confederate veteran requested permission to lay his faded gray jacket on top of the coffin. Permission was granted, and the man accomplished his purpose. As he slipped the jacket back on his shoulders, he sobbed, "Now thousands couldn't buy it from me."[57]

Gordon's casket lay in state at the Georgia state capitol, where thousands of mourners came to pay their final respects. For the Confederate veterans who came to see their general, it must have been a particularly moving experience. Just one week earlier, they had experienced the passing of General James Longstreet. Now they realized that their days too were coming to an end.[58]

Gordon's final march came on January 14, an official day of mourning throughout Georgia. Flags hung at half-mast, and a seventeen-gun salute was fired every half hour. Gordon would rest among his fallen comrades at Oakland Cemetery near the Confederate Memorial Monument.[59]

John Brown Gordon was a "soldier's soldier." He possessed a rare combination of talents that set him apart from other military men. Gordon's outstanding speaking ability and his physical and moral courage inspired his men to great heights of valor and feats of endurance. He had a way of getting the most out of his men, yet he never asked them to do anything he would not do himself. During the last year of the war, Gordon became the evening star of the Confederacy. The name John Gordon thrilled the South more than any other. Idolized by his men, Gordon emerged from the war second only to Robert E. Lee in the hearts of Southerners.[60] As one eulogist declared, "His name becomes the heritage of his people, and his fame, the glory of a nation."[61]

23 Daniel Harvey Hill

"Maverick General"

During the heat of battle at Chickamauga in September 1863, Lieutenant General Leonidas Polk approached his subordinate, Lieutenant General D. H. Hill, to give him instructions. Like the battle raging on the field, Polk's instructions immediately caused friction and were ultimately disregarded by the North Carolinian. Captain William Carnes of Polk's staff, who was in attendance during the heated conversation, recalled:

> I had been sent by General Polk, . . . and on returning I found him and General Hill dismounted and sitting on a fallen tree. . . . At its conclusion [conference], General Polk arose and said to General Hill that he regretted that General Hill did not agree with him, but that he was so well convinced of the correctness of his views that he had to insist on compliance with them. With that, he turned away from General Hill, and as he approached me, I heard him say "That is the most pig-headed general officer I have ever had to deal with."[1]

Hill's behavior with Polk was completely in character for him. Although a man of unusual personal courage and moral integrity, he was cursed with a bad temper and a very sharp tongue. He lavishly commended those whose actions and opinions agreed with his, but he was often insulting and sarcastic to those who disagreed with him. It was said that he "offended many and conciliated none." Although sharp and stiff while on duty, when not in command he was a different person: relaxed and unpretentious.[2]

Physically, Hill was inconspicuous: five feet, ten inches tall, thin, and slightly bent from an earlier spinal injury, he had the hard look of a combat infantryman. His clamped jaw and heavy dark beard gave strength to his face and seemed to say, "Fight me, if you dare." Despite the impression of his appearance and behavior, Hill was a very religious man. He observed the Sabbath as diligently as did his brother-in-law, Stonewall Jackson, and always gave God the credit for his victory. During his career as a Confederate general, he clashed sharply with Lee, Bragg, and Jefferson Davis; his passion for justice seemed to inflame his spirit.[3]

Daniel Harvey Hill's life struggles began at an early age. Born July 12, 1821, on his family's plantation in the York District of South Carolina, he was the youngest of eleven children born to Solomon and Nancy Cabeen Hill. At the age of four, Daniel's father died, leaving his mother with bills that reduced the Hill estate to a small piece of land. Young Daniel grew up in "genteel poverty," a child of "sorrow and anxiety." "I had no youth," Hill later admitted.[4]

Nancy Hill was a loving mother, treating Daniel with tenderness tempered with discipline. She provided him with an education and a solid religious background. The religious education he received from his mother would play a major role in his adult life. At the age of twenty-two, Hill joined the Presbyterian Church and later became a ruling elder. During the Civil War, no general went into battle with a stronger faith in God.[5]

Along with religion, education played an important part in the Hill family. College education had been provided for the older boys when the family was more prosperous, but now the only recourse for a free college education for Daniel was the U.S. Military Academy at West Point. With an appointment from his congressman, young Hill entered West Point on June 1, 1838.[6]

Hill's first year at West Point was difficult. Weakened by a back problem, he was frequently ill. As his health improved during the final three years, so did his grades, and he rose from the lower to the middle position in class ranking. On July 1, 1842, Hill graduated twenty-eighth in a class of fifty-six. Among those in the graduating class who would see action during the Civil War were James Longstreet, William Rosecrans, John Pope, Abner Doubleday, Richard Anderson, and Lafayette McLaws.[7]

At West Point, an effort was made to instill patriotic pride, but for Hill national respect was not enough to outweigh his love for the South. He believed Southern men to be the bravest and Southern civilization to be the finest. Despite his strong Southern allegiance, Hill entered the army with a genuine loyalty for the United States and the flag he served.[8] Like many other West Point graduates, Hill valued his professional honor. In battle, he would prize his honor above his life and would defend it at the least provocation.[9]

After graduation, Hill was assigned as a brevet second lieutenant in the First Artillery, serving along the East Coast from Maine to South Carolina. In 1845, he joined Major General Zachary Taylor's command in Corpus Christi, Texas.[10]

Lieutenant General David Harvey Hill was related to "Stonewall" Jackson through marriage.
The brothers-in-law shared two other things in
common—both were devout Christians and hard-
fighting leaders.

COURTESY OF CULVER PICTURES INC.

At the outset of the war with Mexico, Hill served with General Taylor's
army in northern Mexico. After participating in the Monterrey campaign,
he was transferred to Major General Winfield Scott's command at Vera
Cruz. In the long campaign to capture the Mexican capital, Hill fought at
the Battles of Cerro Gordo, Contreras, and Chapultepec, earning two brevet
promotions. During the campaign, he displayed his fierce, reckless combativeness. He so impressed his fellow officers that they considered him
"the bravest man in the army." After the war, Hill returned to the United
States in March 1848, with the official rank of only first lieutenant in the
regular army.[11]

While on leave, Hill traveled to North Carolina, where he met Isabella
Morrison, daughter of Reverend Robert Morrison, a well-known Presbyterian Church leader. Isabella was twenty-three years old, intelligent, well

educated, and a devout Christian. Hill quickly fell in love with her, and they were married on November 2, 1849. He had two best men, the brothers John and Lardner Gibbon. Ironically, John Gibbon became a future Union major general and would fight against him at South Mountain during the Antietam campaign.[12]

Just a few months after his marriage, Hill resigned from the army to begin a new career as a mathematics teacher at Washington College (later to become Washington and Lee University). After leaving Washington College in 1854, Hill served for the next five years as the mathematics chair at the Presbyterian Davidson College in North Carolina. During this ten-year period, he established a reputation as a strict disciplinarian and an excellent teacher, one who was capable of getting the best from his students. Finally, on October 1, 1859, Hill became the superintendent of the new North Carolina Military Academy.[13]

While at Washington College, Hill formed a close friendship with Thomas Jackson, the future Confederate general who was then a professor of mathematics and artillery at the neighboring Virginia Military Institute. Jackson owed his position at the institute to Hill, who had recommended him for the position. The friendship became even closer when Jackson married Mary Ann Morrison, Isabella's sister. The brothers-in-law shared two other commonalities: both were devout Christians and hard-fighting leaders.[14]

When the Civil War began, it was just a matter of time before Hill and the cadets of military age from the North Carolina Military Academy would be mustered into the Confederate service. Ten days after the fall of Fort Sumter, Governor John Ellis appointed Hill colonel of volunteers and assigned him to the training camp at Raleigh, North Carolina. By early June, his regiment was ordered to the Virginia peninsula, where it was placed under the command of Colonel John B. Magruder.

On June 10, Hill and his volunteers faced their first test at the Battle of Big Bethel. Later, this battle would be viewed as little more than a skirmish. Hill's regiment repulsed the Union assault, inflicting over seventy casualties while suffering only eight. A month later, Hill was promoted to brigadier general in the provisional army of the Confederate states.[15]

Early in the war, Hill's caustic nature came to the fore. The first individual to receive his criticism was Brigadier General J. E. B. Stuart. In Hill's opinion, Stuart's performance in an engagement at Dranesville was unsatisfactory. "From what I have been able to learn, the enemy knew your strength and destination before you started," he said. "I would therefore respectfully suggest that when you start again, you should disguise your strength and give out a different locality from that actually taken." The suggestion, although a constructive one, infuriated Stuart.[16] Unfortunately for Stuart, Hill continued to find fault with him. He later complained to President Davis about Stuart's conduct at Leesburg, criticizing him for "his lack of diligence and watchfulness." The charge caused a breach between the two that would never heal.[17]

During the winter of 1861 to 1862, Hill became discouraged by the progress of the war. "The Confederate Congress seems to be made of fools," he wrote to his wife. He urged her to convert some of their Confederate bonds into land: "The expenses of the Confederacy are a million a day, and I fear these Bonds will never be redeemed, even should we succeed, which is doubtful."[18]

Hill was also dissatisfied by the limited amount of action he had seen thus far in the war. A man of action, he informed Secretary of War George Randolph that it was his "hope to have been a soldier in this war, but I have only been a passport clerk." Four days after writing to Randolph, he was promoted to major general and assigned to command a division in Joseph Johnston's army, now fighting Major General George McClellan's Army of the Potomac on the Virginia peninsula.[19]

During the early phases of the Peninsula Campaign, Hill's division supported Longstreet's division at Williamsburg and the withdrawal up the Virginia peninsula. Despite mud and the Union pursuit, Hill made an orderly retreat. By early May, Johnston's army was concentrated within thirty miles of Richmond.

Hill's first real test as a division commander came at the Battle of Seven Pines on May 31. In Johnston's plan, Hill's division was selected to spearhead the attack supported by Longstreet's and Major General Benjamin Huger's divisions. The battle raged for several hours, with Hill's division facing two Union corps. In the midst of heavy enemy fire, Hill mounted his horse and, with a cigar in his mouth, rode slowly across an open field between the opposing troops. When asked why he exposed himself to such danger, he replied: "I saw our men were wavering, and I wanted to give them confidence."[20]

Early the next morning, the fighting resumed, with Hill directing the charge. During the battle, Hill noticed some Virginians hiding safely in a roadside ditch. "Get out of the ditch," Hill ordered the men, "and fight like soldiers of the Confederacy." When they ignored him, Hill ordered Colonel Scales to "come and occupy the position that these cowardly Virginians have fled from!" Scales marched his men forward as ordered. At that point, Brigadier General William Mahone came to his troops' defense. "You should not abuse my men," he protested, "for I ordered them out of the fight." "If you ordered them out," Hill said, "I beg the soldiers' pardon for what I have said to them and transpose it all to you." Mahone was furious and never forgave Hill for this insult.[21]

The bungled Confederate offensive did not achieve the results Johnston had hoped for. Fortunately for the Confederates, the Union troops were just as disorganized. The battle caused heavy casualties on both sides, although neither side had deployed all its available strength. Hill's leadership, however, had been brilliant, the best by a Confederate at that level. Johnston and Longstreet praised him for his "courage and skill."[22]

There was one important result of the battle. At its height, General Johnston was severely wounded. When it became apparent that he would be out of action for a long time, President Davis looked for a successor. On June 1, Robert E. Lee was appointed commander of the Army of Northern Virginia. Hill came to respect Lee as a commander but did not regard him with the same affection so many others did. In his view, Lee was not above criticism.

After his appointment, Lee began a major reorganization of the Army of Northern Virginia in compliance with President Davis's desire for army units organized by states and his request to weed out commanders of doubtful ability. As a result, Hill now had the brigade commanders he wanted. Three of them, Rodes, Anderson, and Garland, had demonstrated at Seven Pines that they were capable of handling a brigade in combat. The other two, Colquitt and Riley, were yet to be tested.[23]

After Seven Pines, McClellan shifted most of his army south of the Chickahominy River, leaving one corps of 30,000 men under Major General Fitz John Porter north of the river. Lee decided to concentrate the bulk of his army, 60,000 strong, against Porter, leaving only 25,000 to protect Richmond. When the attack on Porter began, Hill, Longstreet, and A. P. Hill would coordinate their movements with Jackson, who would attack Porter's right flank. The attack did not come off as planned because Jackson did not reach the field on time. What would have been an enveloping maneuver turned into a frontal assault known as the Battle of Mechanicsville. Porter's outnumbered troops fought well and finally fell back, but Lee did not achieve the victory he had hoped for.[24]

On June 27, Lee hit Porter again at Gaines's Mill. Again, Lee planned to attack Porter's right, and, again, Jackson failed. Porter's troops were able to escape across the river, burning bridges behind them. Lee, however, was able to get a respectable victory this time.[25] Lee tried one more time to crack the Union line. This time it was at Malvern Hill against a Federal army that was well dug in and heavily supported by their artillery. Lee opened his attack with a heavy artillery barrage. When he saw movement along the Union line, he mistakenly took it to be a retreat and ordered an infantry attack. Hill, Longstreet, and Jackson reluctantly sent their men against the enemy. The attack was repelled with heavy losses.[26]

During the Seven Days' Campaign, which included those battles at Mechanicsville, Gaines's Mill, and Malvern Hill, Hill's division continued to distinguish itself. In a week of combat, his division paid heavily for its efforts, sustaining a casualty rate of 40 percent. Most of these casualties were incurred in frontal assaults, a tactic Hill did not approve of.[27]

For Hill's troops, the battle on the slopes of Malvern Hill was the bloodiest of all. Just before the attack, Hill had advised Lee, "If General McClellan is there in force, we had better let him alone," but Lee did not heed his warning. In his official report of the assault on Malvern Hill, Hill attributed the bloody result to the "blundering management of the battle."[28]

When the Battle of Seven Days was over, McClellan withdrew to Harrison's Landing on the James River, where he remained inactive for two months. For all practical purposes, the Peninsula Campaign was over, and Richmond had been saved for the moment.

For Hill, the fallout from the campaign was not over. On the night following the battle at Malvern Hill, Hill had accused Brigadier General Robert Toombs of "taking the field and leaving it too soon." Toombs was seething over the rebuke, interpreting the insult as aimed at both himself and his brigade. As a result, he demanded the "satisfaction usual among gentlemen."[29] The two generals corresponded with each other. Hill reminded Toombs that they were prohibited from issuing or accepting challenges to duel "by the plainest principles of duty and laws which we have mutually sworn to serve." Toombs had to be satisfied with publicly calling Hill a "poltroon" (coward), which no one took seriously because of Hill's well-established record on the battlefield.[30]

In July 1862, Hill was rewarded for his exemplary service during the Battle of Seven Days by being sent to command the Department of North Carolina. Holding the position only three weeks, Hill was ordered back to Virginia to join Lee's army, then moving against Major General John Pope's Army of Virginia. He rushed his troops, who had been assigned to fortify Petersburg, back to northern Virginia in an effort to join Lee in time for the Second Battle of Manassas but did not arrive in time.[31]

Lee, having defeated Pope's army at Manassas and driven his forces back to the defenses of Washington, now decided to carry the war into Maryland. It was here that Hill rejoined Lee's army. During the Antietam campaign, Hill's performance at both South Mountain and three days later at Bloody Lane demonstrated his outstanding ability in directing a division in combat. Hill also displayed great personal courage, leading his troops even after having his horse shot from under him. During a meeting with Lee and Longstreet during Antietam, Hill had another close call. Exposed on high ground, Lee and Longstreet dismounted. Before Hill could dismount, a shell came hurling down, severing his horse's forelegs. As the horse went down, so did Hill. Although embarrassed, he was not hurt. It was the second horse shot from under Hill since the start of the battle.[32]

Although Hill displayed great individual leadership and courage at South Mountain and Antietam, one event overshadowed his accomplishments. The result would affect Lee's strategy throughout the campaign and could have meant the destruction of the Army of Northern Virginia. Along the Confederate march into Maryland, someone dropped a copy of Lee's Special Orders Number 191, issued on September 9. Lee's adjutant had written out copies and sent one to each of the commanders involved.

The orders outlined Confederate movements for the next few days; the recipients were expected to take great care to prevent their copy from falling into enemy hands. Longstreet made a mental note of the orders, then put it into his mouth and chewed it into a pulp.[33]

Jackson, noting that the order involved Hill's division, personally copied the order and sent it to Hill, who read it and put it away for safekeeping. Jackson was unaware that an official copy of Lee's orders had been prepared for Hill. As it happened, that copy never reached Hill, and it fell into the hands of the Union army. McClellan made great use of the orders, getting his army into the best position to attack Lee.[34]

Writers on the subject of the lost dispatch have looked upon Hill and his staff with suspicion. Bitter Confederate veterans of the Antietam campaign, searching for a scapegoat, blamed Hill. In true Hill style, he did not shrink from these attacks. After the war, Hill went to great lengths to clear his name, suggesting that the orders could have been lost by Lee's own staff officers or couriers. He continued to defend his innocence until his death.[35]

The climactic moment at Antietam came when A. P. Hill and his troops arrived from Harper's Ferry. They crashed into the Union's exposed left flank, sending it back to the banks of Antietam Creek. At nightfall, both sides were exhausted. It had been a day of tremendous slaughter, the bloodiest single day of the entire war. Confederate losses were nearly 14,000 men, a staggering 22 percent of Lee's army. Two days later, Lee withdrew to Virginia.[36]

In the weeks following Antietam, Hill once again became critical of a fellow officer. This time James Longstreet was the recipient of his rebuke. Longstreet, Hill claimed, had not responded quickly enough on South Mountain and had not used his artillery appropriately during the battle. His report did little to endear himself to the army. "People up here are very generally beginning to call D. H. Hill a numskull," wrote an artilleryman.[37]

Hill's relationship with his division, however, was decidedly different. His readiness to look after the welfare of his troops and his willingness to share their dangers ingratiated him to his men. Hill's extraordinary courage and fearlessness in battle distinguished him in a war where these characteristics were prized and admired. Hill's behavior in combat was similar to that associated with his deep faith, and like that faith, it was intense. As Major J. W. Ratchford expressed it, Hill was a man with an "unusual force of character." When speaking of him, it was difficult to take a neutral position.[38]

During the fall of 1862, the pain in Hill's spine increased to the point that it was unbearable. In a letter to his wife, he wrote: "I often shiver in bed like [I have the] ague. . . . I simply bear it the best I can." If his health did not improve and if he was not promoted to lieutenant general as he believed he deserved, he told his wife he would resign from the army.[39] Although Hill believed he was ready for promotion, Lee did not. "D. H. Hill had such a queer temperament, [you] could never tell what to expect from him," Lee said. As a result, Hill remained at his present rank, commanding a division in the Army of Northern Virginia.[40]

During the December battle at Fredericksburg, Hill's division was held in reserve, twenty miles in the rear. On January 1, 1863, Hill carried out his intention of resigning from the army, using as a reason his poor health. Jackson tried to dissuade him from resigning, forwarding his resignation with sympathetic remarks: "General Hill has served the country with great zeal, fidelity, and success, and I am satisfied has endured exposure beyond the measure of his health, which from my personal knowledge has been for years impaired." Lee also made an effort to keep Hill in the service, with the idea of using his prestige and abilities in North Carolina. As a result of Lee's and Jackson's persistence, Hill agreed to remain in the army and return home to recuperate.[41]

Jefferson Davis soon offered Hill command of the Department of North Carolina and Southern Virginia, which he accepted. During the spring of 1863, Lee requested troops from Hill's department. When he refused the request, Davis intervened, smoothing things over with a compromise.

In May, Hill learned of the death of his brother-in-law and friend, Stonewall Jackson. Nothing in the war had affected him as much. "The great and good Jackson is dead," Hill wrote. "We have lost our greatest leader. May God help us. There is none to take his place."[42]

In July, Hill was promoted to lieutenant general and assigned as corps commander in General Braxton Bragg's Army of Tennessee. Hill was a complete stranger to the troops he was now to command as well as the country in which he was to operate. But he was no stranger to Bragg; the two had served together in Mexico, and Hill looked forward to pleasant service under his old captain. When the two generals met, Hill was surprised at Bragg's appearance. He was nervous, distraught, despondent, and showed signs of depression. To Hill, Bragg seemed prematurely old. Little did Hill realize at their first meeting that within days a rift would develop between the two friends that would soon widen into a chasm of hostility. Hill assumed command of his corps, consisting of the divisions of Patrick Cleburne and A. P. Stewart. He took up a position a few miles east of Chattanooga.[43]

Hill's diagnosis that Bragg was suffering from depression was accurate. Discouraged by the loss of middle Tennessee and the hostility of his subordinates, Bragg had become quite pessimistic. When Davis proposed reinforcing Bragg's army so he could recover the territory lost earlier in the summer, he declined. His attitude about holding Chattanooga was just as negative. "It is said to be easy to defend a mountainous country," he said, "but mountains hide your foe from you, while they are full of gaps through which he can pounce upon you at any time." Believing he could not stop the enemy from crossing the Cumberland Plateau, Bragg made no effort to track its movements. Hill, who was used to the aggressive style of the Army of Northern Virginia, was horrified by Bragg's lack of vigilance. "The want of information at General Bragg's headquarters was in striking contrast with the minute knowledge General Lee always had of every operation in his front," Hill wrote. "I was most painfully impressed with the feeling that it was to be a haphazard campaign on our part."[44]

At Chickamauga on September 19 and 20, Hill fought brilliantly and deserves much of the credit for delivering a crushing blow against the Union forces under Major General William Rosecrans. During the second day of the battle, a mix-up involving Hill, General Polk, and General Bragg delayed the planned assault by several hours. In a bitter controversy following the battle, Hill publicly criticized Bragg's failure to pursue the defeated Union army and the confusing orders he issued during the battle.[45]

Bragg, like Hill, blamed others for failures. He responded to Hill's criticism by accusing him of delaying an attack scheduled for the morning. In a letter to President Davis, Bragg complained about Polk and described Hill as "despondent, dull, slow, and tho' gallant personally, is always in a state of apprehension, and upon the most flimsy pretexts makes such reports of the enemy about him as to keep up constant apprehension, and require constant reinforcements. His open and constant croaking would demoralize any command in the world. He does not hesitate at all times and in all places to declare our cause lost."[46]

The accusations against Polk and Hill were unfair to both. Bragg's letter failed to state that he had given Hill discretionary orders. His statements that Hill was "always in a state of apprehension" and making alarming reports of the enemy on "flimsy pretext" are not borne out by the *Official Records*.[47] After Bragg sent this letter, Generals Polk, Butler, Hill, and Longstreet (who was now serving temporarily in the West) agreed to write letters to the president requesting Bragg's replacement. Bragg, however, acted first, relieving Polk and Major General Hindman.

As the controversy deepened, Davis was forced to come to Tennessee to confer with General Bragg. At Bragg's request, Davis relieved Hill of command on October 15 and ordered him to report to the adjutant general in Richmond. Upon receiving the order, Hill went to see Bragg for an explanation. Bragg's reply was simple. As he later wrote, "General Hill had [been relieved on] the ground that his removal would contribute to the harmony and efficiency of the Service." Bragg added that he had made "no charge or imputation" against him. He did not mention Hill's efforts at Chickamauga but claimed that the incident that had displeased him had occurred earlier. He could not successfully conduct operations if he did not have the full cooperation of his subordinates; he felt that he could not expect full support from Hill. Not satisfied by Bragg's explanation, Hill asked why he had been singled out for removal given all those officers who had expressed their lack of confidence. To this, Bragg gave no response.[48]

Hill believed himself to be the "scapegoat of Chickamauga." It is interesting to note that, when Davis visited Bragg, he made no effort to obtain from Hill or his subordinates their account of Hill's performance in the Chickamauga campaign. Davis would stick by his friend, Bragg. Even when one of Hill's generals, John Breckinridge, went to see Davis and strongly endorsed Hill, he could not move the president to look into Hill's side of the controversy.[49]

After his interview with Bragg, Hill issued a brief farewell to his troops in which he declared that it was his "honest conviction that the corps had no equal in the service." Hill received letters of support from his division commanders, Breckinridge, Cleburne, and Stewart. All told him that they still had full confidence in him and regretted his leaving.[50]

Upon returning to Richmond, Hill asked for a court of inquiry to review his case, but Davis refused his request. In November, Adjutant General Cooper informed him that "until a suitable opportunity is offered for placing you on duty according to your rank, you will consider yourself authorized to dispose of your time in such a manner as may best suit your convenience, reporting your address monthly to this office."[51]

Hill returned to North Carolina but would not let the issue drop. When Davis submitted a list of lieutenant general promotions to the Senate for confirmation, Hill's name was conspicuously absent. Congressmen and senators from North Carolina tried to intercede on Hill's behalf, but to no avail. It was now evident that Davis intended to allow Hill to revert to his former rank of major general. No other Confederate officer had been so humiliated.[52]

When Beauregard needed an experienced subordinate for duty in Charleston, Davis proposed assigning Hill, but at the rank of major general. In the proposal, Davis emphasized the point that this was the only time and place Hill could expect such an assignment. After several proposals and counter-proposals, Hill concluded that he would accept the position at the rank of major general only if the assignment was accompanied by a statement from the government of its full confidence in him. President Davis was unwilling to put laudation into his orders, so Hill remained at home.[53]

Hill spent most of the final months of the war at home, making numerous requests of the president to serve in another capacity. For a time, Hill served as a volunteer aide to General Beauregard during the spring of 1864. With the Confederacy in a crisis, it would seem that Hill had earned forgiveness, but not so. Davis showed no desire to return him to active duty. Both Hill and Davis were men of enormous pride and strong wills, and neither was willing to concede to the other. Finally, in February 1865, Hill was given command of the District of Georgia under Beauregard. In April, Hill surrendered with Joseph Johnston's army in North Carolina.

After the war, Hill settled in Charlotte, North Carolina. He became a well-known opponent of Reconstruction in the South. Because Hill believed the fall of the Confederacy was God's will, he was able to accept the defeat, but he would not repudiate the cause for which he had fought. His greatest sin, Hill admitted, was his "hatred of the Yankees."[54]

From 1866 to 1867, Hill published *The Land We Love*, a magazine devoted primarily to Southern literature. Later, he published *The Southern Home*, another publication for former supporters of the Confederacy. The magazine received the personal endorsement of former Confederate generals such as Beauregard, Johnston, and Hood. One of the rules he observed in his publications was to be kind to those who had been killed in battle or had died before he could write about them. In his article about Braxton Bragg, Hill presented a full analysis of his weaknesses as a general but did not attempt a full exposure of his former enemy.[55]

In 1877, Hill left the publishing business to accept a position as president of the Arkansas Industrial University (later the University of Arkansas). In 1885, he assumed the presidency of the Middle Georgia and Agricultural College.

In Georgia, Hill's health was stable except for the spinal ailment that never left him. But by the spring of 1888, he had developed cancer of the stomach. His health rapidly declined, and he lost a lot of weight, yet he did not leave his position. Although able to live without his salary, he did not want to be a burden on his family. "Besides," he said, "I doubt whether I could be happy in idleness."[56]

Hill was able to complete the school year despite intense pain. When the cramps got too severe, his doctor would administer morphine. "Thanks be to a merciful God, I got through the Commencement exercise without a breakdown," he said. When Hill resigned, the board refused to accept his resignation but instead gave him an indefinite leave of absence. He returned to North Carolina, hoping his health would improve, but it did not. In August, Hill again submitted his resignation; this time it was accepted. In a formal resolution, the college proclaimed his achievements "as a Soldier and as a Teacher." Finally, a year later on September 24, 1889, the old warrior died. Isabella and five of his nine children survived him.[57]

Daniel Harvey Hill possessed courage that approached recklessness, a quality that earned him the respect and affection of his men. But he was abrasive and outspoken toward his fellow officers; as a result, his relations with them suffered. Without fearing retaliation, Hill criticized two full generals, first Robert E. Lee and then Braxton Bragg, two of Jefferson Davis's favorite generals. In the end, his matchless valor and tactical skill could not outshine the flaws in his personality. His integrity and sense of justice allowed little, if any, room for compromise. Unfortunately, they also did not permit him to reach his full potential as a Confederate general.

24 William J. Hardee

"Old Reliable"

In 1861, after twenty-five years of service in the U.S. Army, William Hardee linked his fate with the Confederacy. Like Stonewall Jackson and James Longstreet, he was to become one of the outstanding corps commanders of the Confederacy. During the war, Hardee served in the Army of Tennessee, earning a reputation as an energetic and imaginative officer. Loved by his men, he earned the label of "Old Reliable." His *Light Infantry Tactics* became the infantry officers' handbook and was used by both sides during the Civil War. Like the Army of Tennessee, he suffered both heartbreak and eventual defeat.

William Hardee was born in the Georgia–Florida frontier on October 12, 1815. He was the last of seven children born to John and Sarah Hardee. His father held the rank of major during the War of 1812, owned a cotton plantation, and later served as a state senator from Camden County. Most of John's sons pursued business and professional careers, but William was destined to follow the military tradition of his ancestors.[1]

Camden County, Georgia was a romantic and exciting place in which to grow up. There were numerous tales of fighting during the Revolution and the War of 1812, as well as the conflict with the Spanish and Indians. It is no wonder that young William would have an interest in becoming a soldier. There were no schools in the area for the plantation children, forcing the families to engage tutors. The education imparted was limited, but William did receive a firm foundation in grammar, literature, and reading. In 1830, a local attorney evaluated William's academic progress: "I have no hesitation in saying that I find him much farther advanced than could have been expected in any young man of his age."[2]

Influenced by his family's military heritage and his father's encouragement,

William applied for entrance to West Point. Despite the support of some of his father's political friends, his application was rejected. Young Hardee was disappointed but decided to join his older brother, Noble, in his cotton business; however, he did not give up his desire to be a soldier and continued his studies.

Finally, in 1834, after four years of applications and rejections, William was accepted as a cadet at West Point. Hardee's record at West Point was mediocre at best. While a cadet, however, he matured into a tall, lean individual and was appointed a lieutenant in the cadet corps during his senior year. Soon after his promotion, Hardee embarrassed himself by being placed under arrest for leaving his post while officer-of-the-day. Although the infraction was considered serious, the penalty was light, and he was able to retain his rank. Hardee graduated in 1838, ranking twenty-sixth out of a class of forty-five.[3]

In November 1838, Second Lieutenant Hardee joined the Second Dragoons, a cavalry regiment located in Florida. Under the command of Colonel David Twiggs, the dragoons were involved in clearing the area of Seminole Indians. During his tour of duty, Hardee took part in numerous reconnaissance missions and raids against the enemy. As a reward for his efforts, he was promoted to first lieutenant in 1840.[4]

In the fall of 1840, Hardee received orders to attend the Royal Cavalry School at Saumur, France. He had long hoped for the opportunity, but now he faced a dilemma—he had recently become engaged to Elizabeth Dummett and did not want to leave the love of his life until she became his wife. Hardee, however, solved the problem. After a hasty preparation, the two were married, and, a week later, Hardee was on his way to France. The year Hardee spent at Saumur broadened his military perspective and demonstrated to him the importance of rigorous discipline.[5]

In May 1842, Hardee rejoined the Second Dragoon Regiment, now transferred to Louisiana. Life on the frontier was boring and uneventful. Hardee spent most of his time drilling and training troops, and mainly because of his success as a regimental drillmaster, he was promoted to captain. When war with Mexico seemed imminent, the Second Dragoons were ordered to join General Zachary Taylor along the Rio Grande. On a reconnoitering mission, Hardee and some of his dragoons were captured. Later, as part of an exchange of captured troops, Hardee was returned to his regiment.[6]

Upon his return to duty, Hardee received a cold reception from members of his regiment, who questioned the events surrounding his surrender and capture. After two weeks of censure, he requested that an investigation be made into the conduct of the affair. During the trial, Hardee defended himself against the accusation that he had "surrendered too soon and before a sufficient number of men were killed or wounded." Witnesses testified that his party had been surrounded and greatly outnumbered and

During the Civil War, Lieutenant General William
Hardee served in the Army of Tennessee, earning
a reputation as an energetic and imaginative
officer. Loved by his men, he earned the label of
"Old Reliable."

COURTESY OF THE LIBRARY OF CONGRESS

that Hardee had "wanted to fight" but the men did not have sufficient
arms. Hardee, they said, had acted in the best military tradition.[7]

Although the court of inquiry found him blameless and his conduct "in
all respects that of an intelligent and gallant soldier," Hardee's reputation
had been tarnished. He was resolved to erase this damaging episode with
outstanding service during future campaigns.[8]

In August, the advance guard of Taylor's army moved toward Monterrey
with the dragoons in the lead. Hardee moved forward with his Company C,
only to become ill after going just a short distance. When Hardee returned
to duty in December, the Second Dragoons were under the command of
General Winfield Scott. During Scott's move on Vera Cruz, the dragoons,
under Colonel Harvey's command, engaged the enemy in some of the heaviest fighting of the war. For Hardee's "gallant and meritorious conduct," he
was promoted to brevet major.[9]

At San Augustin in August 1847, Hardee again distinguished himself and was rewarded by being promoted to brevet lieutenant colonel. Because of their heroic efforts during the war, the dragoons had gained General Scott's admiration. In September, they were selected to escort the victorious Americans into Mexico City. At the same time, the Georgia senate passed a resolution honoring and proposing that Brevet Lieutenant Colonel Hardee be awarded a ceremonial sword for "his brilliant achievements in Mexico."[10]

After the war Hardee was given a new command, consisting of four companies of dragoons and several companies of Texas Rangers. His mission was to rid Texas of the marauding Indian bands that posed a problem for the settlers in the area. Hardee combed valleys and riverbanks, scattering the Indians until they were no longer a threat. His expedition was so successful that the following year he was sent into Comanche country to negotiate and collect intelligence.[11]

In 1851, Hardee took an extended leave to care for his wife, who had contracted tuberculosis. After months of illness, the suffering ended; Hardee's beloved Elizabeth died on June 10, 1853. His children went to live with their aunt in St. Augustine, while Hardee was ordered to Washington to work with Secretary of War Jefferson Davis on the preparation of a new army tactics manual.[12]

Jefferson Davis recognized the recent developments in military tactics, especially those by the French, and wanted the U.S. Army to incorporate these into their tactical system. The term "tactics" as used in the 1850s was more comprehensive than its current use. Tactics included not only the maneuvering of troops but drill and the use of small arms. In selecting Hardee for this important responsibility, Davis was undoubtedly aware of Hardee's combat experience and his training at Saumur. In July 1854, the manual was completed and approved at once.[13]

In 1855, the War Department created four new regiments. Hardee requested a transfer to one of the new regiments, the Second Cavalry, commanded by Colonel Albert S. Johnston. His request was granted, and he was promoted to major. Each officer in this regiment was hand picked by Jefferson Davis, and it included more military talent than any other regiment in American history. With Colonel Johnston at its head, Lieutenant Colonel Robert E. Lee was second in command, with Majors Hardee and George Thomas next in command. Among the other officers were Captain Edmund Kirby Smith and Lieutenant John Bell Hood. The Second Cavalry was indeed a "crack regiment" and was equipped accordingly. Each trooper was armed with a carbine, navy revolver, and saber. The uniform selected included gray trousers, blue tunic, and a gray coat of wool, designed to set the Second Cavalry apart from the rest of the U.S. Cavalry.[14]

The regiment had to be quickly trained at Jefferson Barracks, Missouri, before moving to Texas; the responsibility for the training fell to Major Hardee. The undertaking was made more difficult by an epidemic of cholera that swept through the ranks, killing several and lowering morale.

Nevertheless, Hardee was up to the task and was successful in completing the job. "Hardee was thorough in his knowledge of the tactics and seemed to take great delight in teaching others," a soldier wrote.[15] The primary mission of the Second Cavalry was to guard the frontier against the Comanche Indians. Although Hardee did not remain in this assignment long, his association with the Second Cavalry provided him with additional field and organizational experience.

In June 1856, Hardee left the Second Cavalry and headed eastward to his new assignment as commandant of the Corps of Cadets at West Point. Secretary of War Davis had selected him for the position so that he could bring about changes in what Davis saw as antiquated procedures at the Academy. Hardee's attempt to implement Davis's plan for change brought him into conflict with the superintendent, Major John Barnard. As a result, Davis decided to remove Barnard, giving Hardee a free hand to carry out his plan. Although Hardee's administration was characterized by strict discipline, the cadets gained many benefits, and his influence can best be judged by the Civil War performance of his students. One of his colleagues at West Point wrote: "The Commandant of the Corps exercised a more important influence on the military character and opinions of the junior officers of the army than any other individual."[16]

While at West Point, Hardee cultivated his friendship with Jefferson Davis. He invited Davis and his wife to visit at the Academy and even named one of the annual summer camps after him. During the winter of 1858, Davis became ill and lost the sight in one of his eyes. When Hardee was in Washington, he would come to visit Davis and sit with him for hours, reading to him and writing some of his correspondence.[17]

Hardee enjoyed the social life of Washington and was often invited to important events, including dining with President Buchanan and his family. The handsome widower was also a great favorite with the ladies. Hardee often escorted a group of them to West Point parades and struck up a close friendship with Clara Paige, the daughter of a friend of his. He often corresponded with her, even going so far as to hint at the subject of marriage in his letters.[18]

In September 1860, Hardee's tour of duty at West Point came to an end. He was promoted to lieutenant colonel and assigned to the First Cavalry Regiment. The months following his departure from West Point were as tumultuous for Hardee as they were for the nation. As talk of secession spread across the country, he, like other Southerners in the army, had to make a choice regarding his allegiance. In February 1861, Hardee followed the dictates of his conscience and resigned his commission.[19]

In March, Hardee was appointed colonel in the Confederate army and given command of the First Infantry Regiment at Fort Morgan, Alabama. His command consisted of nine companies of volunteers, all greatly in need of training before going into combat. Even for Hardee, who had served twenty-five years with regular army troops, this task was daunting. "I should dislike to fight this command in its present condition; indeed I should not like to see the face of an enemy for three months," he said.[20]

While the Confederates were strengthening their forces in Alabama, conditions were deteriorating in other parts of the Confederacy. In June, Davis responded by appointing Hardee to an Arkansas command, with the rank of brigadier general. Hardee's first opportunity to engage the enemy came in October of 1861, when his brigade was ordered to Bowling Green, Kentucky to reinforce Brigadier General Simon Buckner. There, Hardee was pleased to renew an association with General Albert Sidney Johnston, commanding general. Johnston organized his army into two divisions, the first under Hardee and the second under Buckner.[21]

Despite lacking men and supplies, Johnston advanced into Kentucky, adopting an "arrogant display of power." Hardee disposed his troops so that the enemy would believe he was about to advance. The ploy worked, and the Federal forces stopped their advance and fell back to Muldraugh's Hill.[22]

On October 21, Hardee was promoted to major general and division commander. To capture the loyalty of his men, Hardee designed a flag for his division; it was a silver full moon with crossed canons within the moon, all on a blue background. Later, when Patrick Cleburne commanded the division, his command was allowed to carry the flag into battle. It was the only Confederate division allowed to carry its own flag.[23]

Hardee took great care to prepare his division to fight, using the systematic manner for which he was well known. The regiments drilled daily and held frequent reviews. In December, when Union commander Major General Don Carlos Buell stepped up his offensive in central Kentucky, Johnston gave Hardee command of the Central Army of Kentucky and ordered him to engage the Union army. In heavy fighting, Hardee was repulsed. Christmas brought a temporary halt to the Union advance. As 1862 began, the poor weather continued to hamper Buell's offensive, but, on January 19, when the winter storm ended suddenly, the Confederate right flank collapsed.[24]

On February 6, Fort Henry fell. With Fort Donelson also threatened, the Army of Central Kentucky was in danger of being cut off from other Confederate forces. Hardee began an immediate retreat. On February 14, Buell caught up with Hardee at Bowling Green, forcing him to abandon the city. On the road to Nashville, Hardee's men suffered terribly as the temperature dropped along with the army's morale. Frustrated, the men turned on their officers and demanded that they stop the retreat and be allowed to fight. Hardee, however, was able to avert the mutiny by personally speaking to the men.[25]

Hardee found matters no better when he arrived at Nashville. After the news arrived of the fall of Fort Donelson, a mob came to Hardee's headquarters. Rumors had spread that the army was not going to defend Nashville. Only after Hardee spoke to the crowd did it disperse; but the defense of Nashville was not Hardee's decision to make. Johnston decided to consolidate his forces, ordering Hardee to join him at Murfreesboro. In late February, Johnston moved his army farther south to connect with Beauregard's retreating forces.[26]

Corinth, Mississippi, located near the south bank of the Tennessee River, was selected as the point for amassing the Confederate army in the West. Corinth united the Eastern and Western sections of the Confederacy and was the center of railroad communications. Grant was aware of the geographic importance of Corinth and had hoped to occupy the town before the Confederates could reach it. After arriving at Pittsburg Landing on March 17, however, Grant halted his advance, allowing Johnston's troops to occupy Corinth. By the end of March, Johnston had concentrated all his troops and was ready to do battle with Grant.[27]

Johnston reorganized the troops gathered at Corinth into a new Army of Mississippi, dividing it into four corps under Major Generals Hardee, Bragg, Polk, and Breckinridge. On April 3, Johnston moved eastward from Corinth with 42,000 men. His plan was to launch a surprise attack on Grant before he could receive reinforcements from Buell's Army of the Ohio, but poor roads delayed the advance. It was not until late in the day that Hardee's advance corps arrived within two miles of Shiloh Church. By the time the rest of the Confederate army was in place, it was too late to carry out Johnston's plan for April 4. Johnston thus ordered an attack for early on April 5.[28]

Had the weather cooperated at this point, Johnston's plan would have gone off as scheduled. Unfortunately, heavy rain fell during the night of April 4 and into the next morning. Hardee's orders called for him to attack at 3:00 a.m., but rain-swollen roads and ravines suspended the advance until dawn. Hardee was not able to get his corps into position until 10:00 a.m. Because of the muddy terrain, portions of the Confederate right were not able to get into line until noon. Finally by 4:00 p.m. on April 5, Polk's corps began to advance, but it was nearly dark before it was in position to attack. His troops were exhausted because they had been up all night. An infuriated Johnston had to cancel the attack until the next day.[29]

Johnston believed he had lost the element of surprise; Hardee's troops had been within two miles of Sherman's line, and there had been frequent skirmishes between the pickets on both sides. Nevertheless, Johnston ordered an attack for the next day, April 6.

Sunday morning, April 6, began bright and cheery; the heavy rain had ceased, and it gave "every promise of a fine day." By 7:30 a.m., Hardee's corps was within a half mile of the enemy; three hours later, Hardee engaged the enemy. Soon Hardee's corps was joined by Bragg's corps and then by Polk's. By noon, the Confederate attack was being pursued with unabated fury, driving the Union defenders farther back.[30]

Finally, in the late afternoon, Federal forces solidified their position at what became known as the "Hornets' Nest." Confederate attack after attack was repulsed. When Johnston discovered the strength of the Union position, he ordered renewed attacks on the enemy's flanks, while he himself prepared to lead another assault on the "Hornets' Nest." During the attack, Johnston received a mortal wound and died shortly afterward. General Beauregard now assumed command of the Confederate army.[31] The death of General Johnston seemed to sap the energy from the Confederates. Hardee emphasized the importance of the event: "In my opinion, . . . but for this calamity, we would have achieved before sunset a triumph."[32]

Though General Johnston had died, the struggle to capture the "Hornets' Nest" was not over. Beauregard ordered Hardee to make one last effort to dislodge the enemy. This time, Hardee led the charge himself. A soldier from the First Missouri Regiment reported that "General Hardee took his place in front of the Regiment, ordered the charge and led it in person. He was the bravest man I ever saw in my four years experience in the war. . . . We followed him with a yell of charge bayonets and drove back the enemy." Late in the afternoon, the resistance ended when 2,000 Union troops under Brigadier General Benjamin Prentiss surrendered. Hardee was presented with a captured stand of colors.[33]

The battle seemed to be won; the Union army was dispersed and on the run, and the Confederate commanders were ready to continue the attack and pursue the enemy. General Beauregard, however, ordered the attack to be discontinued for the day. His decision, Beauregard later said, was based on the fact that the army was disorganized and his men were exhausted. Many of the commanders were surprised at the order, believing that the attack should have continued. General Polk thought halting the battle cost the Confederates a much-deserved victory. Although Hardee never criticized Beauregard's decision, he stated in his official report that "advance lines were within a few yards of Pittsburg Landing, where the enemy were huddled in confusion, when the order to withdraw was received."[34]

On the evening of April 6, Grant rallied his men. Despite more rain and a sleepless night for his troops, Grant launched an attack at dawn. The Confederates fought hard, but exhaustion and the numerical superiority of the enemy—almost half of whom were fresh troops—proved to be too much for Beauregard's army. By noon, what had seemed like a complete Confederate victory had turned into a complete rout. The Battle of Shiloh was a costly one for the Confederates, who suffered more than 10,000 casualties. Hardee's losses were staggering, losing the highest percentage of men of any corps.[35]

To concentrate his battered forces once more, Beauregard returned to Corinth, but Grant did not pursue. The period of inactivity ended when Major General Halleck, now in command of Union forces at Pittsburg Landing, began his march on Corinth. It took him a month to cover the distance, and by the time he reached Corinth, Beauregard had abandoned it.

In June 1862, General Braxton Bragg replaced Beauregard as commander of the Army of Tennessee. Bragg hoped to replace many of the officers who had served under Beauregard and reorganize the army. When he asked Davis to remove the "dead weight" from the army before his next campaign, he referred to Hardee as his only "suitable major general." In the reorganization, Bragg made Hardee second in command and made him responsible for training the troops.[36]

While Hardee trained the men, Bragg made plans to move the army to Chattanooga before Buell's Union army could occupy it. Leaving some troops behind to slow Buell's movement, Bragg ordered Hardee to move the rest of the army to Chattanooga as fast as possible. In late July, Hardee reached Chattanooga. Bragg divided his army into two wings, one commanded by Polk and the other by Hardee. Bragg's campaign against Buell involved a joint movement of his army and Major General Kirby Smith's forces. Smith would move from East Tennessee to threaten Buell's communication line and serve as a screen for Bragg. In the meantime, Bragg would strike Buell's flank and join up with Smith's army. As often happens, the strategy did not go according to plan.[37]

On October 7, Buell's advance units encountered Hardee's cavalry near Perryville, Kentucky. As was the case in many Civil War battles, neither side had come to Perryville looking for a fight; in this case, Hardee's men were looking for water, a scarce item during that dry summer.[38]

In a short while, Polk arrived with half his corps and orders from Bragg to "give the enemy battle immediately" and to "rout him and then move to our support at Versailles." In the meantime, Buell had concentrated his entire army in front of Perryville. When Hardee arrived he did not know the size of Buell's force but sensed it was larger than his command could handle. Believing that Bragg's orders were unreasonable and hazardous, Hardee sent a dispatch to Bragg:

Don't scatter your forces. There is a rule in our profession, . . . it is to throw the masses of your troops on the fraction of the enemy. The movement last proposed will divide the army and each may be defeated. . . . If it be your policy to strike the enemy at Versailles, take your whole force with you and make the blow effective. If, on the contrary, you should decide to strike the enemy in front of me first, let that be done with a force which will make the success certain. Stick with your whole strength.[39]

Bragg's orders called for Polk's and Hardee's troops to destroy whatever enemy forces they met the next morning. Polk and Hardee elected to ignore Bragg's order for an "immediate" attack on the grounds that it was not clear what was meant by the term "immediate." Bragg had to go to Perryville in person to get the battle started. Although he did not know it, Bragg was attacking a force superior in size to his own.[40]

Fighting broke out on October 8, and soon Hardee's and Polk's corps were hotly engaged. Hardee was responsible for designing the plan of attack and the deployment of Confederate troops. Early in the battle, Bragg's forces came close to driving the enemy from the field. As Union reinforcements moved up, however, the Confederate attack was brought to a halt. When darkness approached, the battle ceased. The Federals had employed only nine of their brigades, while another fifteen had not been deployed. The battle had been a tactical success for Bragg mainly because of Buell's failure to engage all his troops. Hardee's troops had performed well, but Confederate losses were heavy.[41]

Bragg's decision to retreat from Perryville was not popular with the troops. The army expected to continue the fight the next day. Hardee and many of the other officers had lost confidence in Bragg and were communicating their feelings to the president. Hardee wrote: "Unfortunately for Bragg, he has given his enemies just grounds for attacking him. Grave, unpardonable errors were committed; errors which any man of good practical sense without military education or experience ought not to have committed. . . . To relieve Bragg is easy enough, to provide a competent successor is a more difficult matter. Bragg has provided a failure, it is true, but . . . have we any body who will do better." President Davis did not elect to replace Bragg.[42]

On October 27, 1862, Major General William Rosecrans replaced Buell as commander of the principal Union army in Kentucky; he immediately moved his army toward Nashville. In response, Bragg moved his troops to Tennessee near Murfreesboro. Hardee was promoted to lieutenant general and given command of one of the two corps in the newly named Army of Tennessee. After two months of preparation, Rosecrans began his offensive, marching toward Murfreesboro. Bragg, who had been criticized for his indecisive Kentucky campaign, now took up a defensive position along Stone's River.[43]

The morning of December 31 was cold; Hardee had his commissary men distribute whiskey to his shivering troops. Then he ordered an attack on the Union right flank, surprising the Federal troops while they were cooking their breakfast. In a short time, the Union right was crushed and in retreat. When Hardee paused his assault to reorganize his corps, Rosecrans took the opportunity to form a new line of defense. By late afternoon, the Union line had re-formed and stabilized. Hardee had failed to take advantage of his earlier success, and further assaults were repulsed. As the day ended, Hardee realized that further attacks over open ground would be futile and reckless. Despite Hardee's setback, Bragg could claim a victory on the first day of the battle.[44]

On January 1, neither army attempted to change its position; Rosecrans decided to wait for Bragg to attack. The morning and afternoon of January 2 passed, and then Bragg ordered an attack on the enemy east of Stone's River. Without consulting anyone, Bragg sent Breckinridge's division, a part of Hardee's corps, to attack a hill to his front. The attack failed, and Breckinridge was forced to fall back, suffering heavy losses. Breckinridge's repulse destroyed Bragg's hope for a complete victory; Bragg ordered Hardee to fall back from his advanced position.[45]

When Bragg learned that reinforcements were being sent to Rosecrans, he considered leaving the field of battle, but he did not want to turn his hard-won victory into a defeat. After consulting with his officers, however, Bragg ordered a retreat. Rosecrans's army, equally devastated, chose not to pursue Bragg; rather, they elected to occupy Murfreesboro.[46]

Bragg's retreat, after his glowing report to Davis of his success on December 31, came as a shock to the South. The seeds of discontent that had been planted during the Kentucky campaign about Bragg's leadership now burst into full bloom. One article in the *Chattanooga Rebel* blamed Bragg for the defeat at Murfreesboro and claimed that he no longer held the confidence of his army. Bragg's response to the criticism was to send a circular to his corps commanders asking them to submit written proof that they had supported his decision to retreat from Murfreesboro.[47]

Polk and his division commanders replied the way Bragg had expected (although, later, Polk did write to Davis asking that Bragg be relieved and recommending that Joseph Johnston replace him). Hardee's response, however, came as a complete surprise to Bragg: "I feel that frankness compels me to say that the general officers, whose judgment you have evoked, are unanimous in the opinion that a change in command of this army is necessary. In this opinion I concur." Breckinridge and Cleburne reinforced Hardee's response.[48]

Bragg was hurt by Hardee's response. He had entrusted Hardee with great responsibilities and believed they had worked well together. Hardee, however, felt obligated to speak frankly about the situation; his great sense of duty compelled him to do so. Although the president did not see fit to remove Bragg at this time, Hardee and Polk had opened the gates of controversy, weakening the army's command structure.[49]

Although harmony among the leadership seemed to be deteriorating, the strength and training of the Army of Tennessee improved during the spring of 1863. The surrender of Vicksburg in July, however, had a drastic effect on the military situation in Mississippi. As a result, Hardee was transferred to Johnston's army in Mississippi, but the move proved to be only temporary. On August 19, Hardee received orders to take command of paroling prisoners from the Vicksburg campaign and others from the fighting in Arkansas, Texas, and Missouri. This assignment was difficult, requiring him to hold together the paroled prisoners until they could be exchanged. In

October, his problem was solved when Union authorities decided not to exchange them.[50] As a result, Hardee was transferred to Chattanooga to replace Leonidas Polk.

During Hardee's three-month interlude in Mississippi, the Army of Tennessee fought one of its greatest battles at Chickamauga in September without the services of one of its best corps commanders. The fact that Hardee returned voluntarily to serve under Bragg indicated his patriotism and love for his corps.[51]

Bragg failed to capitalize on his victory at Chickamauga while the Yankees were in full retreat to Chattanooga. Rather than pursue the enemy, Bragg elected to lay siege to the Union forces in Chattanooga. Although Bragg held the heights outside the city, there was no way the South could win a war of siege. After Rosecrans was replaced with Grant, a steady Union buildup began. Although the Army of the Cumberland had been momentarily damaged at Chickamauga, it soon recovered with the help of reinforcements under the command of Major General Joseph Hooker, dispatched from the Army of the Potomac.[52]

The Confederate siege proved easy for Union forces to break. In late October, a pontoon bridge was constructed across the Tennessee River to allow supplies to be brought into the besieged city. The battle for Chattanooga began on November 23 when Thomas took his army out of the city for the first time since Chickamauga, hoping to clear Bragg's army from the heights nearby.

To counter Thomas's move, Bragg ordered Hardee to strengthen the Confederate right. On November 24, the Yankees attacked. Despite the brilliant Confederate defense, their line broke against a heroic uphill Union assault. After nightfall, Hardee began pulling out his units; it was his corps that slowed the Union pursuit, allowing what remained of Bragg's army to escape.

A soldier of the Union's Eighth Kansas reported the Confederate rout: "Gray-clad men rushed wildly down the hill and into the woods," he said, "tossing away knapsacks, muskets, and blankets as they ran. . . . In ten minutes," he continued, "all that remained of the defiant rebel army that had so long besieged Chattanooga was captured guns, disarmed prisoners, moaning wounded, ghastly dead, and scattered, demoralized fugitives. Mission Ridge was ours."[53]

The retreating Army of Tennessee left behind almost 7,000 men. Bragg's debacle at Chattanooga fanned the flames of criticism, and demands for his removal came from all quarters. Bragg himself felt it was time to step down; four days after the battle, he requested to be relieved. This time Davis granted his request, and on December 2, Hardee took over command of the Army of Tennessee.[54]

In his report, General Bragg commended Hardee for his preservation of the Confederate right. He concluded his report by saying, "Lieutenant

General Hardee, as usual, is entitled to my warmest thanks and high commendation for his gallant and judicious conduct during the whole of the trying scenes through which he passed." This was a surprising tribute from Bragg, considering how Hardee had criticized him earlier.[55]

Hardee served as interim commander of the Army of Tennessee for three weeks. During that time, he did not take any aggressive steps; rather, he took the time to rest his battered army and to help rebuild its morale. The Army of Tennessee needed additional manpower and was in desperate need of supplies. To obtain clothing, Hardee sent many of his Georgia and Alabama troops home where local authorities helped provide for them. To help restore the army's morale, Hardee set up a lenient furlough policy and promised an additional forty-day leave for men who brought back a recruit for the army. Hardee tried hard to keep the men busy, emphasizing military pomp and ceremony in his drills and parades. Army morale slowly rose as a result of these procedures.[56]

Hardee had little opportunity to prove himself as commander of the Army of Tennessee. When he was initially placed in the position, Hardee had wired back to Davis a conditional acceptance: "I fully appreciate the compliment paid to me by the President in the expression of confidence, but feeling my inability to serve the country successfully in this new sphere of duty, I respectfully decline the command if designed to be permanent. In doing so, permit me to add that I am desirous to serve the cause and the country and will cooperate cordially with any officer the President may select." President Davis selected Joseph Johnston.[57]

In December, Johnston took command of the army. This allowed Hardee to take much-needed time off and to make arrangements for his wedding to Mary Lewis. Hardee had met Miss Lewis in September 1863 and continued to see her as often as he was able. Described by most as beautiful, Mary had a refined appearance; she possessed charm, a quick wit, and an excellent education. She also came from a prominent family. The couple was married on January 13, 1864.[58]

Under General Johnston's command and with Hardee's assistance, the Army of Tennessee grew in strength and morale. By the spring of 1864, Hardee commanded the largest and best trained corps in the Confederate army. In March, the complexion of the war changed abruptly in the West with the appointment of Union Major General William T. Sherman to the command of the Military Division of the Mississippi. Late in April, Sherman began his preparation for an attack on Johnston.[59]

Sherman opened the campaign against Johnston with 100,000 troops, dividing them into the Army of the Tennessee under Major General James McPherson, the Army of the Ohio under Major General John M. Schofield, and the Army of the Cumberland under Major General George Thomas. Sherman's objective was Atlanta. Johnston, outnumbered by Sherman, decided to fight defensively until the opportunity to counterattack presented itself. President Davis, however, expected Johnston to recapture Tennessee. The campaign turned into a chess match between two masters. "I can see no other mode of taking the offensive here than to beat the enemy when he advances and then move forward," Johnston informed Richmond.[60]

With only 60,000 men, Johnston knew he could not hope to take the initiative. He believed his army was too weak to go on the offensive and saw no reason to expose it to a senseless slaughter. In a series of battles at Resaca, Cassville, New Hope Church, and Kennesaw Mountain, Johnston skillfully retreated, preventing Sherman from delivering a death blow. During these battles, Hardee's corps performed well but did suffer heavy losses. Although discouraged by the successive withdrawals, the tone of the army had improved since Johnston had taken command. The men had absolute faith in their new commander and looked forward to the upcoming battle for Atlanta.[61]

Johnston's time was running out. The Union army was moving closer to Atlanta. Prominent Georgian delegates came to Richmond to plead the president to relieve Johnston before he allowed Atlanta to fall. Convinced that Johnston had no plans to keep Sherman from capturing Atlanta, Davis decided to remove him. Johnston's replacement would have to be someone already with the army; this narrowed the selection to two men: William Hardee and John Bell Hood.[62]

Hood's selection would mean aggressive and, in all probability, competent leadership; "Old Reliable" Hardee promised competent leadership, but not necessarily aggression. Hardee had damaged his reputation with Davis when he turned down the command of the Army of Tennessee in December 1863.[63] On July 17, Johnston was relieved of command; John Bell Hood was his successor. Sherman was the most relieved man in Georgia when he heard the news. "At this critical moment," he said, "the Confederate Government rendered us most valuable service."[64]

Johnston's replacement with Hood was not well received by the army. One Confederate soldier wrote after the war that "the most terrible and disastrous blow that the South ever received was when Honorable Jefferson Davis placed General Hood in Command of the Army of Tennessee. I saw thousands of men cry like babies. . . . The private soldiers of the Army of Tennessee looked upon Hood as an overrated general."[65]

General Hardee did not hesitate to express his feelings about the new commanding officer. To him, Hood was incompetent to command an army of that size. He was so incensed by the appointment that he immediately applied to be relieved of duty. Davis tried to ease the situation by reminding Hardee that, when he had been offered the command earlier, he had said he would not object to Hood's being given command. Hardee responded that nothing he had ever written was intended to convey the impression "that the appointment of a junior to command me would be satisfactory." Hardee insisted on being relieved from a situation "personally humiliating," but after appealing to his patriotism, Davis persuaded him to carry on. The relationship between Hood and Hardee, however, remained openly hostile.[66]

The late summer of 1864 was a hard time for the Confederates. The fighting was heavy, and the results less than promising. For Hardee it proved to be the most difficult time of his military career. Hood attacked Sherman at Peachtree Creek three days after taking over command and was repulsed. By the time Hardee and General Alexander Stewart made their attack, Thomas had crossed the creek and was well entrenched. The assault failed and resulted in 5,000 casualties. General Hood attributed the defeat directly to Hardee.[67]

On July 21, Union General McPherson moved toward Atlanta, capturing positions close enough to threaten the city with bombardment. In an attempt to halt McPherson, Hardee's corps executed a daring night march to attack his flank. In fierce fighting, McPherson was killed, and the Union line temporarily pierced, but Hardee was eventually repulsed, suffering heavy losses.[68]

For the next month, Atlanta was besieged and subjected to intense bombardment. On August 30, Hardee tried to dislodge Sherman; he attacked at Jonesboro but again was repulsed. Finally, on September 2, Atlanta fell. Sherman telegraphed Lincoln: "So Atlanta is ours, and fairly won."[69]

Jefferson Davis was troubled by the fall of Atlanta. Adding to his problems were complaints of morale problems in the Army of Tennessee and strife among the officers' corps. Meanwhile, Hardee complained that Georgia and Alabama were in danger of being seized by Union forces, and he was adamant about not serving under Hood.[70]

During the Atlanta campaign, the relationship between Hood and Hardee had grown from bad to worse; as a result, Hardee had again requested to be relieved. Davis had immediately replied: "Your telegram of yesterday was received with regret and disappointment. . . . I now ask is this a time to weigh professional or personal pride against the needs of the country. . . . Let your patriotic instinct answer, rejecting all other advices."[71]

Davis's response closed the matter temporarily, but after the battle at Jonesboro, the Hardee–Hood feud flared again. This time, Hood took the initiative and asked to have Hardee transferred. "In the battle of July 20, we failed on account of Hardee," Hood claimed in his letter to Davis. In late September, Davis visited the dysfunctional army and had a series of conferences with his generals. After the meetings, Davis decided to relieve Hardee, stating that "I can say with certainty that General Hardee was not relieved because of any depreciation of his capacity, his zeal, or fidelity."[72]

On September 28, Hardee was transferred to Charleston, assuming command of the Department of South Carolina, Georgia, and Florida. The evening before he left for his new assignment, Hardee's corps gathered to say goodbye. Showing their affection for him, officers and men were moved to tears. Amid the cheers for "Old Reliable," the men rushed toward him, grabbing his hand and biding him farewell.[73]

To defend his new department, Hardee had less than 13,000 troops and only a few generals with undistinguished or controversial careers. While Hardee worked on his personal problems, Hood and Sherman were maneuvering against each other in Georgia. Anticipating an attack on Savannah, Hardee set to work preparing the city's defenses. When Sherman did approach Savannah, Hardee fought a delaying action, hoping to slow Sherman's advance until he could receive reinforcements.[74]

On December 10, the two armies engaged each other on a peninsula about thirteen miles wide. Opposing Hardee's 10,000 troops were Sherman's 60,000 men. Taking advantage of the terrain, Hardee flooded the fields in front of his line with water three to six feet deep. The advantage of the terrain, however, was not enough to overcome the Union superiority in numbers between the two armies. After a stubborn effort, on December 20, Hardee was forced to begin his withdrawal from Savannah. He had to leave behind many of his sick and wounded because he could not provide transportation for them. On December 22, Hardee departed from Savannah for Charleston, South Carolina, leaving the remnant of his army under the command of General Lafayette McLaws.[75]

The defense of South Carolina depended upon a force of just 20,000 men. The War Department ordered Hood's shattered Army of Tennessee to join Hardee in South Carolina in an effort to save Charleston. Early in January 1865, Sherman began his advance on South Carolina; by the second week in February, his relentless advance and the continued deterioration of the Confederate army forced Hardee to abandon Charleston.[76]

As he had at Savannah, Hardee was able to conduct a successful withdrawal from Charleston, but, during the retreat, his army suffered greatly from exposure, disease, and shortness of rations. Their spirits were raised, however, when they learned that Joseph Johnston had again been appointed commander of the forces opposing Sherman. Johnston immediately tried to concentrate all available troops in an effort to halt Sherman's advance. By early March, Hardee reached Fayetteville, North Carolina, where he joined Johnston. When Sherman reached Fayetteville, Hardee was forced to abandon the town.[77]

On March 15, Hardee halted his weary troops just south of the village of Averasboro. There he hoped to take a stand against four divisions of General Slocum's corps, a part of Sherman's army. Although Hardee's men were inexperienced, when his line was attacked, it held. Finally, Hardee had to retire, but he was pleased with the showing his troops had made. Hardee's delaying action as he retreated was a classic example of how an inferior force can hold off a superior one. It provided more time for Johnston to prepare for Sherman.[78]

Hardee's last battle as a commander was at Bentonville; it was one of his best efforts. Early in the afternoon, Hardee personally led a strong counterattack. In his report, Johnston wrote: "The Federals were routed in a few minutes, our brave fellows dashing successively over two lines of temporary breastworks." The Battle of Bentonville was the last victory for a Confederate army, but the losses were heavy, a result the Confederates could ill afford.[79]

The victory at Bentonville came at a great personal loss to Hardee. His sixteen-year-old son Willie, who was serving in the army as his aide-de-camp, was a casualty of the battle. Succumbing to his pleas, Hardee had allowed Willie to join the army. Hours after Hardee kissed his son goodbye, Willie was killed in his first combat action.[80]

When Johnston learned of Lee's surrender at Appomattox, he realized the end was at hand. On April 14, he sent a courier with a flag of truce through the lines with a request to discuss terms for surrender. On April 17, a meeting between Johnston and Sherman was arranged at the Bennett Farm, a few miles west of Durham. Final arrangements for the surrender of the Army of Tennessee were agreed to on April 26.

The four years of the Civil War had a telling effect on Hardee. He had joined the Confederacy as a lighthearted, affable, professional soldier, ambitious enough to look forward to the glory war could bring. As his friend William Preston Johnston recalled, "His personal appearance was striking." He was tall, wiry, and possessed a military bearing. "His smile," Johnston said, "matched his tempered, friendly manner, enhancing his popularity with men as well as women."[81]

By 1865, the war had changed Hardee into a grim, disillusioned old man. Before the war, his life had been organized, following a set pattern. He had mastered the rules of military science and hoped to employ them on behalf of the Confederacy. As the war progressed, this pattern of fighting changed. Trained in Napoleonic warfare, Hardee became far less effective as a commander when trench warfare emerged.

After the war, Hardee returned to Mary's plantations: Ash Place and Hermitage. Unlike many other plantation owners, Hardee returned to lands that were in relatively good condition. For a while, he managed Mary's plantations. Later Hardee moved to Selma, Alabama, where he became president of the Selma and Meridian Railroad.[82]

Hardee made frequent trips to see his relatives in Savannah and St. Augustine. He also enjoyed visiting White Sulphur Springs, West Virginia, during the hot summers in Selma. It was during one of these trips that he became ill. The exact nature of Hardee's illness is not known, but he had been suffering with cancer of the stomach. He was taken to Wytheville, Virginia, where he died on November 6, 1873. When Hardee's body was returned home, he received "the greatest public demonstration known at a funeral in Alabama." Above his grave is a large cross, marked simply: William J. Hardee, Lieutenant General, C.S.A.[83]

25 *Epilogue*

Davis as Commander-in-Chief

It is ironic that President Davis, who, after his death, was the beloved embodiment of the Lost Cause, would have been vilified while in office. Southerners laid the blame for the lack of progress during the war and eventual failure of the war on Davis. Although many of these beliefs were unjustified, the Confederate defeat was in part due to Davis himself.[1] One of Davis's failings was his need to be recognized as always being right. He was rarely willing to admit a mistake. He took disagreements over policies personally. Winning his point in a discussion seemed to be more important to him than winning the war.[2]

Davis's interest in and familiarity with the military proved to be a handicap to his direction of the war. He wished to manage every aspect of the war, down to the smallest detail. Stephen Mallory, secretary of the navy, wrote: "It induced his desire to mingle in them all [generals and admirals] and to control them; and this desire is augmented by the fear that details may be wrongly managed without his constant supervision." In addition to his unwanted intervention, "Davis was jealous of any infringement on [his] prerogatives as president and commander-in-chief. . . . This earth holds not the human being more jealous of his constitutional rights than Mr. Davis, and among those rights to which he clings with death-like tenacity is well known to be the supreme and exclusive control of military operations."[3]

Davis's unswerving loyalty made him the truest friend a man could have, but it also made him susceptible to cronyism and manipulation. Davis's loyalty and personal quirks might have been tolerated had the South possessed more men like Robert E. Lee. Lee stood by Davis through every trial of the war and in peace. From the outset of the Confederacy, there were those opposed to the president—in and out of Congress and the army—

but such movements never received support from Lee. Even during the last hours of the Confederacy, when Davis's enemies tried to replace him with Lee, the general would have no part of it. Lee had not forgotten how Davis had supported him after Gettysburg. Devotion to the Southern cause and respect for each other had held the two together.[4]

Unfortunately, generals such as Joseph Johnston and P. G. T. Beauregard never enjoyed the same relationship with Davis as did Lee. Joseph Johnston was the first general with an important command in the East. When Union General George McClellan's army landed on the Virginia peninsula, Johnston moved to intercept him. For two and a half weeks, McClellan plowed ahead, encountering little resistance from Johnston. When Union troops were virtually at the gates of Richmond, Davis ordered Johnston to give battle or he would appoint someone who would. Johnston launched a series of attacks that resulted in battles at Fair Oaks and Seven Pines. During the battle at Seven Pines, Johnston was badly wounded and replaced by Robert E. Lee. By the time Johnston recovered from his wounds, he had no hope of reclaiming his command of the Army of Northern Virginia.[5]

Davis did not want to give Johnston another important command, but the general's political friends in Richmond campaigned for him to get another assignment. Davis could not resist the pressure to reinstate Johnston. From 1862 to late 1863, the Army of Tennessee had been commanded by Braxton Bragg. Unfortunately, Bragg did not have an officer corps he could work with. After the army's defeat at Chattanooga in November 1863, Davis finally felt compelled to remove Bragg from command. Against his better judgment, Davis replaced Bragg with Joseph Johnston.[6]

Davis watched with alarm as Johnston refused to attack Sherman when he moved closer to Atlanta. To conserve his smaller army, Johnston was waiting for the right time to attack Sherman. To Davis, however, it seemed that Johnston was making no serious effort to stop Sherman. By July, Davis had seen enough. Against Lee's advice, the president dismissed Johnston and replaced him with John Bell Hood. When Hood failed, Davis returned Johnston to command. Johnston was not pleased with the news, believing that Davis was returning him to command only so he would be remembered as the man who surrendered the Army of Tennessee.[7]

Davis's plan for fighting the war made him the polar opposite of the hero of Fort Sumter and Manassas, P. G. T. Beauregard. Given to highly imaginative but often unrealistic plans, Beauregard clashed with Davis over the strategy for conducting the war. This difference of opinion continued throughout the conflict and gave ammunition to Davis's political enemies.[8]

Beauregard was one of the strongest advocates of offensive warfare in the Confederate army. In 1862, he wrote: "Our only hope of success lies in throwing all our forces into large armies, with which to meet and successfully overthrow the adversary. The result of one such victory would be worth more to us than [would be] the occupation of all important cities to the enemy." Beauregard's plan was sound, but it was in direct opposition to that of Davis, who believed in dispersing the troops to protect all parts of the Confederacy.[9] Davis was able to work successfully with Beauregard, however. Although they had numerous misunderstandings, the Confederacy did not suffer greatly from their dislike of each other.[10]

In some cases, Davis was slow in taking action when it was needed. In the West, Braxton Bragg held independent command but was saddled with several inept corps commanders. When Bragg failed to achieve his objective, his subordinates revolted against him. Although Davis continued to support Bragg, he failed to take action to relieve the situation. By the time Davis realized his mistake, a potentially effective commander was harmed beyond help.[11]

Another important failure of the president was his inability to promote capable men to senior commands. Some, such as Albert S. Johnston and Stonewall Jackson, died early in the war. But others, such as Patrick Cleburne, Nathan Bedford Forrest, and Richard Taylor, could have served the Confederacy in more responsible positions. Instead, they were left as corps commanders or put in positions in which their talents were not fully utilized. This type of attitude on Davis's part was a luxury the South could not afford.[12]

Before the war began, Jefferson Davis hoped to become a general, but had to settle for the presidency. A graduate of West Point, a hero of the Mexican War, and a former secretary of war, Davis overestimated his role as commander-in-chief. Davis took his responsibility very seriously. Early in the war, he showed a desire to lead his armies in person when they went into action. He had frequently visited various generals' headquarters, hoping to be present for the crucial battles. In his desire to control all aspects of the war, he often made enemies of his generals.[13] Yet Davis was loyal to certain generals. When Davis found a good general, as with Lee, he stood by him in the face of criticism; unfortunately, he did the same for weaker generals, too.[14]

The Southern people never loved Davis to the extent that they did Robert E. Lee, nor did they venerate him as they did Stonewall Jackson; but they did respect him for his stubborn pride, unyielding resolve, and determination to fight to the end.

Notes

CHAPTER 1. The Making of a Rebel

1. S. Foote, *The Civil War: A Narrative: Fort Sumter to Perryville* (New York: Random House, 1958), 3–4.
2. M. Grimsley, "We Will Vindicate the Right: An Account of the Life of Jefferson Davis," *Civil War Times Illustrated* 30 (July/August 1991): 40.
3. Ibid.
4. Foote, *The Civil War*, 5.
5. Ibid.
6. H. Strode, *Jefferson Davis: American Patriot, 1808–1861* (New York: Harcourt, Brace & World, Inc., 1955), 392–393.
7. Foote, *The Civil War*, 5.
8. Ibid., 6.
9. Ibid.
10. Grimsley, "We Will Vindicate the Right," 33.
11. Ibid.
12. W. J. Cooper Jr., *Jefferson Davis, American* (New York: Alfred A. Knopf, 2000), 39.
13. C. Canfield, *The Iron Will of Jefferson Davis* (New York: Harcourt Brace Jovanovich, 1978), 9.
14. S. E. Woodworth, *Jefferson Davis and His Generals: The Failure of Confederate Command in the West* (Lawrence: University Press of Kansas, 1990), 6.
15. Ibid.
16. Grimsley, "We Will Vindicate the Right," 33.
17. Foote, *The Civil War*, 9.
18. Grimsley, "We Will Vindicate the Right," 34.
19. W. Davis et al., *Civil War Journal: The Leaders* (Nashville: Rutledge Hill Press, 1997), 53–54.
20. Grimsley, "We Will Vindicate the Right," 34–35.
21. Canfield, *The Iron Will*, 27–28.
22. W. Jones, *After the Thunder: Fourteen Men Who Shaped Post-Civil War America* (Dallas: Taylor Publishing Company, 2000), 95.
23. Cooper, *Jefferson Davis*, 98–99.
24. Davis et al., *The Leaders*, 56.
25. Foote, *The Civil War*, 12.
26. Ibid.
27. Cooper, *Jefferson Davis*, 164.

28. Woodworth, *Jefferson Davis and His Generals*, 10.
29. Davis et al., *The Leaders*, 57.
30. B. I. Wiley, "Jefferson Davis: An Appraisal," *Civil War Times Illustrated* 6 (April 1967): 8.
31. Jones, *After the Thunder*, 96.
32. Grimsley, "We Will Vindicate the Right," 39.
33. Ibid.
34. J. Winik, *April 1865: The Month that Saved America* (New York: Harper Collins Publishers, 2001), 329–330.
35. Grimsley, "We Will Vindicate the Right," 39.
36. Davis et al., *The Leaders*, 58.

CHAPTER 2.   Jefferson Davis: Confederate Chief

1. Woodworth, *Jefferson Davis and His Generals*, 13.
2. Ibid.
3. Winik, *April 1865*, 328.
4. Grimsley, "We Will Vindicate the Right," 41.
5. B. I. Wiley, *Embattled Confederates* (New York: Harper & Row Publishers, Inc., 1964), 13–14.
6. Ibid., 14.
7. Cooper, *Jefferson Davis*, 330–331.
8. Ibid., 237.
9. R. Potter, *Jefferson Davis: Confederate President* (Austin: Steck-Vaughn Company, 1994), 86–87.
10. Grimsley, "We Will Vindicate the Right," 41.
11. Ibid., 47–48.
12. Ibid., 48.
13. Ibid., 46.
14. Davis et al., *The Leaders*, 62.
15. Ibid., 61–62.
16. Ibid., 62.
17. Ibid., 62–63.
18. Ibid., 63.
19. Ibid., 64.
20. Ibid.
21. Cooper, *Jefferson Davis*, 426.
22. Ibid., 426–427.
23. Davis et al., *The Leaders*, 64.
24. Potter, *Jefferson Davis*, 90–91.
25. W. C. Davis et al., *Civil War Journal: The Battles* (Nashville: Rutledge Hill Press, 1998), 83.
26. Grimsley, "We Will Vindicate the Right," 49.
27. Ibid., 51.
28. Cooper, *Jefferson Davis*, 363.
29. Ibid.
30. Ibid., 376–377.
31. Ibid., 378–379.
32. Grimsley, "We Will Vindicate the Right," 32.
33. Davis et al., *The Leaders*, 146.
34. Cooper, *Jefferson Davis*, 384–385.
35. Grimsley, "We Will Vindicate the Right," 60.
36. Ibid.
37. Cooper, *Jefferson Davis*, 430–432.
38. Grimsley, "We Will Vindicate the Right," 57.
39. C. Eaton, *Jefferson Davis* (New York: The Free Press, 1977), 160.
40. Grimsley, "We Will Vindicate the Right," 57–58.
41. Cooper, *Jefferson Davis*, 402.
42. Ibid., 403.
43. Grimsley, "We Will Vindicate the Right," 60–61.
44. Ibid., 63.

45. Potter, *Jefferson Davis*, 98.
46. Grimsley, "We Will Vindicate the Right," 63.
47. B. Sell, *Leaders of the North and South* (New York: Michael Friedman Publishing Group, 1996), 73.
48. Davis et al., "The Leaders," 66.
49. Grimsley, "We Will Vindicate the Right," 63.
50. Eaton, *Jefferson Davis*, 176.
51. Grimsley, "We Will Vindicate the Right," 64.
52. P. King, *Jefferson Davis* (New York: Chelsea House Publishers, 1990), 90–91.
53. Potter, *Jefferson Davis*, 100.
54. Cooper, *Jefferson Davis*, 443.
55. Eaton, *Jefferson Davis*, 184.
56. Ibid., 185.
57. Cooper, *Jefferson Davis*, 458.
58. Eaton, *Jefferson Davis*, 185–186.
59. Ibid., 186.
60. Cooper, *Jefferson Davis*, 472.
61. King, *Jefferson Davis*, 93.
62. R. Suhr, "The Kilpatrick Dahlgren Raid on Richmond," *Military Heritage* 1 (June 2000): 50.
63. S. J. Martin, "Kill Cavalry," *Civil War Times Illustrated* 38 (February 2000): 30.
64. S. J. Martin, *Kill Cavalry: The Life of Union General Hugh Judson Kilpatrick* (Mechanicsburg, PA: Stackpole, 2000), 169–170.
65. Davis et al., *The Leaders*, 68–69.
66. Jones, *After the Thunder*, 101.
67. Grimsley, "We Will Vindicate the Right," 67.
68. Ibid.
69. Ibid.
70. Ibid.
71. Eaton, *Jefferson Davis*, 255.
72. Jones, *After the Thunder*, 101.
73. Grimsley, "We Will Vindicate the Right," 67.
74. Ibid.
75. Cooper, *Jefferson Davis*, 504.
76. Grimsley, "We Will Vindicate the Right," 68–69.
77. B. Davis, *The Long Surrender* (New York: Random House, 1985), 5.
78. Cooper, *Jefferson Davis*, 510.
79. Ibid.
80. Ibid., 511–512.
81. Ibid., 512.
82. W. C. Davis, *Jefferson Davis, The Man and His Hour* (New York: Harper Collins, 1991), 601–602.
83. Jones, *After the Thunder*, 101.
84. Grimsley, "We Will Vindicate the Right," 70.
85. Canfield, *The Iron Will*, 128.
86. Grimsley, "We Will Vindicate the Right," 70.
87. Ibid., 71.
88. Davis, *Jefferson Davis*, 616–617.
89. Canfield, *The Iron Will*, 122.
90. Davis, *Jefferson Davis*, 628–630.
91. R. Murphy and the Editors of Time-Life Books, *The Nation Reunited: War's Aftermath* (Alexandria: Time-Life Books, 1987), 21.
92. Davis, *Jefferson Davis*, 640.
93. Canfield, *The Iron Will*, ix.

CHAPTER 3.   Martyr of the Lost Cause

1. Davis, *The Long Surrender*, 146.
2. Ibid., 150.

3. Ibid.
4. Ibid., 153, 155.
5. Grimsley, "We Will Vindicate the Right," 71.
6. Strode, *Jefferson Davis*, 238.
7. Davis, *The Long Surrender*, 177.
8. Davis et al., *The Leaders*, 73.
9. Davis, *The Long Surrender*, 180–181.
10. Ibid., 181.
11. Ibid.
12. Ibid., 205.
13. Ibid., 182.
14. K. Largent, "The Presidential Years," *Battlefield Journal* (February/March 2002): 2.
15. Davis, *The Long Surrender*, 214–215.
16. Davis et al., *The Leaders*, 74.
17. A. A. Hoehling, *After the Guns Fell Silent* (New York: Madison Books, 1990), 241.
18. Ibid.
19. Davis, *The Long Surrender*, 221.
20. Jones, *After the Thunder*, 105.
21. Hoehling, *After the Guns Fell Silent*, 242.
22. Strode, *Jefferson Davis*, 301.
23. Canfield, *The Iron Will*, 129.
24. Davis, *The Long Surrender*, 232.
25. Ibid., 241–242.
26. Ibid., 242.
27. Grimsley, "We Will Vindicate the Right," 72.
28. Davis, *The Long Surrender*, 248.
29. Grimsley, "We Will Vindicate the Right," 72–73.
30. Potter, *Jefferson Davis*, 114–115.
31. M. Ballard, "Cheer for Jefferson Davis," *American History Illustrated* 16 (May 1981): 9.
32. Ibid., 10.
33. Ibid., 11.
34. Grimsley, "We Will Vindicate the Right," 74.
35. Ibid., 74–75.
36. Wiley, "Jefferson Davis," 9.
37. Jones, *After the Thunder*, 109.
38. Grimsley, "We Will Vindicate the Right," 73–74.
39. Davis et al., *The Leaders*, 77.

CHAPTER 4.   P. G. T. Beauregard: "Napoleon in Gray"

1. G. Patterson, "Gustave," *Civil War Times Illustrated* 32 (July/August 1992): 30–31.
2. T. H. Williams, *P. G. T. Beauregard: Napoleon in Gray* (New York: Collier Books, 1962), 15–16.
3. Ibid., 76.
4. Patterson, "Gustave," 31.
5. Ibid., 30–31.
6. Ibid., 31.
7. Williams, *P. G. T. Beauregard*, 85.
8. Ibid., 17.
9. Patterson, "Gustave," 29.
10. Williams, *P. G. T. Beauregard*, 20.
11. G. Cantor, *Confederate Generals: Life Portraits* (Dallas: Taylor Publishing Company, 2000), 162.
12. Williams, *P. G. T. Beauregard*, 22.
13. Ibid., 24.
14. Ibid., 25.
15. Ibid., 26–27.
16. Cantor, *Confederate Generals*, 163.
17. Patterson, "Gustave," 30.
18. Cantor, *Confederate Generals*, 163.

19. Ibid.
20. Ibid., 164.
21. Patterson, "Gustave," 30.
22. Williams, *P. G. T. Beauregard*, 67–68.
23. Patterson, "Gustave," 30.
24. Davis et al., *The Battles*, 30.
25. Cantor, *Confederate Generals*, 166.
26. Editors of Time-Life Books, *Voices of the Civil War: First Manassas* (Richmond: Time-Life Books, 1997), 13.
27. Cantor, *Confederate Generals*, 166–167.
28. Patterson, "Gustave," 32.
29. Ibid.
30. Cantor, *Confederate Generals*, 167–168.
31. Patterson, "Gustave," 33.
32. Cantor, *Confederate Generals*, 168.
33. Patterson, "Gustave," 34.
34. H. Hattaway, *Shades of Blue and Gray* (Columbia: University of Missouri Press, 1997), 69.
35. Ibid., 70.
36. Ibid.
37. Ibid., 71.
38. Cantor, *Confederate Generals*, 169.
39. Woodworth, *Jefferson Davis and His Generals*, 105.
40. Patterson, "Gustave," 34–35.
41. Woodworth, *Jefferson Davis and His Generals*, 106.
42. Patterson, "Gustave," 35.
43. Cantor, *Confederate Generals*, 170.
44. Williams, *P. G. T. Beauregard*, 204.
45. Patterson, "Gustave," 35.
46. Ibid.
47. Ibid.
48. Williams, *P. G. T. Beauregard*, 253–254.
49. Ibid., 255.
50. Patterson, "Gustave," 52.
51. Williams, *P. G. T. Beauregard*, 256.
52. Cantor, *Confederate Generals*, 170.
53. Ibid., 170–171.
54. Ibid., 171.
55. Williams, *P. G. T. Beauregard*, 295.
56. Patterson, "Gustave," 53.
57. Williams, *P. G. T. Beauregard*, 307.
58. Ibid., 309.
59. Ibid.
60. Ibid., 310.
61. Ibid., 311.
62. Patterson, "Gustave," 53.
63. Cantor, *Confederate Generals*, 172.
64. Patterson, "Gustave," 54.
65. Williams, *P. G. T. Beauregard*, 395–396.
66. Cantor, *Confederate Generals*, 172.

CHAPTER 5.   **Joseph E. Johnston: "Retreatin' Johnston"**

1. G. S. Boritt, ed., *Jefferson Davis's Generals* (New York: Oxford University Press, 1999), 8–9.
2. Ibid., 10.
3. Ibid.
4. Ibid.
5. C. L. Symonds, *Joseph Johnston: A Civil War Biography* (New York: W. W. Norton & Company, 1992), 3.

6. R. Welch, "Book Review—Joseph Johnston: A Civil War Biography," *America's Civil War* 6 (November 1993): 58.

7. G. Govan and J. Livingood, *A Different Valor* (New York: Bobbs-Merrill, 1956), 13.

8. Ibid.

9. Ibid., 13–14.

10. Ibid., 14.

11. Symonds, *Joseph Johnston*, 19.

12. Ibid., 23.

13. Ibid., 24.

14. A. Mapp, *Frock Coats and Epaulets* (Lanham, MD: Hamilton Press, 1987), 369.

15. Symonds, *Joseph Johnston*, 25–27.

16. Ibid.

17. Cantor, *Confederate Generals*, 31.

18. C. Anders, *Fighting Confederates* (New York: Dorset Press, 1980), 71.

19. Symonds, *Joseph Johnston*, 43.

20. Ibid., 45.

21. Cantor, *Confederate Generals*, 31.

22. Symonds, *Joseph Johnston*, 52.

23. Anders, *Fighting Confederates*, 71.

24. Ibid.

25. Ibid., 71–72.

26. Symonds, *Joseph Johnston*, 71.

27. Anders, *Fighting Confederates*, 72.

28. Ibid.

29. Symonds, *Joseph Johnston*, 94.

30. Anders, *Fighting Confederates*, 72–73.

31. Cantor, *Confederate Generals*, 32.

32. Anders, *Fighting Confederates*, 73.

33. Symonds, *Joseph Johnston*, 97.

34. Ibid.

35. J. T. Glatthaar, *Partners in Command* (New York: The Free Press, 1994), 98.

36. Ibid.

37. Anders, *Fighting Confederates*, 74.

38. Ibid.

39. Ibid., 75–76.

40. Glatthaar, *Partners in Command*, 103–104.

41. Ibid., 104.

42. R. H. Bailey and the Editors of Time-Life Books, *Forward to Richmond: McClellan's Peninsular Campaign* (Alexandria: Time-Life Books, 1983), 17.

43. Ibid., 79.

44. Ibid.

45. Cantor, *Confederate Generals*, 32.

46. Glatthaar, *Partners in Command*, 112–113.

47. Welch, "Book Review," 58.

48. Cantor, *Confederate Generals*, 33.

49. Ibid., 34.

50. Woodworth, *Jefferson Davis and His Generals*, 178.

51. Ibid.

52. Anders, *Fighting Confederates*, 67.

53. Ibid.

54. Govan and Livingood, *A Different Valor*, 156.

55. Anders, *Fighting Confederates*, 68.

56. Ibid., 84–85.

57. Symonds, *Joseph Johnston*, 178–179.

58. Cantor, *Confederate Generals*, 35.

59. Woodworth, *Jefferson Davis and His Generals*, 178.

60. Anders, *Fighting Confederates*, 86.

61. N. Boothe, *Great Generals of the Civil War* (New York: Gallery Books, 1986), 147–148.

62. Welch, "Book Review," 62.
63. Woodworth, *Jefferson Davis and His Generals*, 221.
64. A. Julian, "From Dalton to Atlanta," *Civil War Times Illustrated* 3 (July 1964): 4.
65. Anders, *Fighting Confederates*, 95.
66. Ibid.
67. Cantor, *Confederate Generals*, 38.
68. Glatthaar, *Partners in Command*, 129–130.
69. Woodworth, *Jefferson Davis and His Generals*, 303.
70. Glatthaar, *Partners in Command*, 130.
71. Cantor, *Confederate Generals*, 39.
72. Govan and Livingood, *A Different Valor*, 320.
73. Ibid., 320–321.
74. Welch, "Book Review," 63.
75. Symonds, *Joseph Johnston*, 354.
76. Ibid., 354–355.
77. Ibid., 355.
78. Ibid.
79. Ibid., 356.
80. Ibid.
81. Ibid.
82. Ibid., 357.
83. Ibid., 358.
84. Ibid., 359–360.
85. Ibid., 360.
86. Ibid., 361.
87. Ibid., 362–364.
88. Ibid., 370.
89. Govan and Livingood, *A Different Valor*, 388–389.
90. Ibid., 389–390.
91. Ibid., 390–391.
92. Symonds, *Joseph Johnston*, 378.
93. Ibid., 379.
94. Anders, *Fighting Confederates*, 68.
95. Ibid., 68–69.
96. Symonds, *Joseph Johnston*, 381.

CHAPTER 6.   Robert E. Lee: Man of Honor

1. Jones, *After the Thunder*, 59.
2. Davis et al., *The Leaders*, 134.
3. Cantor, *Confederate Generals*, 3.
4. D. S. Freeman, *Lee of Virginia* (New York: Charles Scribner's Sons, 1958), 5.
5. Davis et al., *The Leaders*, 134–136.
6. M. Grimsley, "Robert E. Lee: The Life and Career of the Master General," *Civil War Times Illustrated* 24 (November 1985): 14.
7. Ibid., 14–15.
8. Davis et al., *The Leaders*, 136–138.
9. Sell, *Leaders of the North and South*, 78.
10. E. H. Bonekemper III, *How Robert E. Lee Lost the Civil War* (Spotsylvania: Sergeant Kirkland's Press, 1997), 19.
11. Grimsley, "Robert E. Lee," 16.
12. Freeman, *Lee of Virginia*, 44.
13. Grimsley, "Robert E. Lee," 16–18.
14. E. M. Thomas, *Robert E. Lee* (New York: W. W. Norton & Company, 1995), 37.
15. Jones, *After the Thunder*, 58.
16. Grimsley, "Robert E. Lee," 19.
17. Ibid.

18. Cantor, *Confederate Generals*, 7.

19. Ibid., 9.

20. Ibid.

21. J. Taylor, *Duty Faithfully Performed: Robert E. Lee and His Critics* (Dulles, VA: Brassey's, 1999), 77.

22. Ibid., 78.

23. Ibid., 80.

24. Grimsley, "Robert E. Lee," 25.

25. Ibid., 26.

26. Taylor, *Duty Faithfully Performed*, 81.

27. Ibid., 82.

28. Grimsley, "Robert E. Lee," 27.

29. Taylor, *Duty Faithfully Performed*, 87.

30. Ibid., 88.

31. Grimsley, "Robert E. Lee," 28.

32. P. Batty and P. Parish, *The Divided Union* (Topsfield, MA: Salem House Publishers, 1987), 90.

33. Ibid., 90–91.

34. Grimsley, "Robert E. Lee," 28–29.

35. Ibid., 29.

36. A. Castel, "George B. McClellan: 'Little Mac'," *Civil War Times Illustrated* 13 (May 1974): 9–11.

37. Grimsley, "Robert E. Lee," 30.

38. Editors of Time-Life Books, *Illustrated Atlas of the Civil War* (Alexandria: Time-Life Books, 1998), 85.

39. Grimsley, "Robert E. Lee," 31.

40. Ibid.

41. Freeman, *Lee of Virginia*, 102.

42. Ibid., 103.

43. Grimsley, "Robert E. Lee," 31.

44. Taylor, *Duty Faithfully Performed*, 110.

45. Davis et al., *The Leaders*, 145.

46. Batty and Parish, *The Divided Union*, 127.

47. Editors of Time-Life Books, *1863: Turning Point of the Civil War* (Alexandria: Time-Life Books, 1998), 13.

48. T. H. Williams, *Lincoln and His Generals* (New York: Alfred A. Knopf, 1952), 229.

49. Editors of Time-Life Books, *Turning Point*, 23.

50. Warren Hassler, *Commanders of the Army of the Potomac* (Baton Rouge: Louisiana State University Press, 1962), 4.

51. S. W. Sears, *Controversies & Commanders: Dispatches from the Army of the Potomac* (Boston: Houghton Mifflin Company, 1999), 69.

52. Freeman, *Lee of Virginia*, 117–119.

53. Grimsley, "Robert E. Lee," 33.

54. Taylor, *Duty Faithfully Performed*, 129.

55. Grimsley, "Robert E. Lee," 35–36.

56. Bonekemper, *How Robert E. Lee Lost*, 104.

57. C. Dowdey, *Lee* (New York: Bonanza Books, 1965), 363.

58. Thomas, *Robert E. Lee*, 293.

59. Bonekemper, *How Robert E. Lee Lost*, 104.

60. Jones, *After the Thunder*, 60.

61. Grimsley, "Robert E. Lee," 39.

62. Ibid., 40.

63. Thomas, *Robert E. Lee*, 296.

64. Freeman, *Lee of Virginia*, 133–134.

65. Ibid., 134.

66. Jones, *After the Thunder*, 61.

67. Thomas, *Robert E. Lee*, 301.

68. Freeman, *Lee of Virginia*, 135.

69. G. Smith, *Lee and Grant* (New York: McGraw Hill Book Company, 1984), 171.

70. Grimsley, "Robert E. Lee," 41.

71. Jones, *After the Thunder*, 61–62.

72. Grimsley, "Robert E. Lee," 41.

73. H. S. Commager et al., *America's Robert E. Lee* (Boston: Houghton Mifflin, 1951), 98–99.

74. Ibid., 100–103.

75. Davis et al., *The Leaders*, 150.

76. J. Stanchak, "Behind the Lines," *Civil War Times Illustrated* 24 (November 1985): 52.

77. Commager et al., *America's Robert E. Lee*, 106–108.

78. N. A. Trudeau, *The Last Citadel: Petersburg, Virginia, June 1864–April 1865* (Boston: Little, Brown and Company, 1991), 307–308.

79. D. J. Eicher, *Robert E. Lee: A Life Portrait* (Dallas: Taylor Publishing Company, 1997), 140.

80. Jones, *After the Thunder*, 63.

81. Davis et al., *The Leaders*, 133–134.

82. W. S. McFeely, *Grant* (New York: W. W. Norton, 1981), 219–220.

83. Eicher, *Robert E. Lee*, 150.

84. Ibid., 150–151.

85. C. Dubowski, *Robert E. Lee and the Rise of the South* (Englewood Cliffs: Silver Burdett, 1991), 120–121.

86. Ibid., 121.

87. Hoehling, *After the Guns Fell Silent*, 5.

88. Grimsley, "Robert E. Lee," 47.

89. Ibid.

90. M. Marshall, "A Soldier No Longer," *Military History* 7 (December 1990): 12.

91. S. F. Horn, *The Robert E. Lee Reader* (New York: Bobbs-Merrill, 1949), 462.

92. Marshall, "A Soldier No Longer," 13–14.

93. Grimsley, "Robert E. Lee," 47.

94. Marshall, "A Soldier No Longer," 14.

95. M. Preston, "Robert E. Lee after the War," *Civil War Times Illustrated* 7 (January 1969): 5.

96. Horn, *The Robert E. Lee Reader*, 469.

97. Jones, *After the Thunder*, 67.

98. Grimsley, "Robert E. Lee," 47–48.

99. Ibid., 48.

100. Freeman, *Lee of Virginia*, 218.

101. Thomas, *Robert E. Lee*, 377.

102. Horn, *The Robert E. Lee Reader*, 476–477.

103. Grimsley, "Robert E. Lee," 48–49.

104. Ibid., 49.

105. Freeman, *Lee of Virginia*, 220–221.

106. Grimsley, "Robert E. Lee," 50.

107. Jones, *After the Thunder*, 70.

108. Freeman, *Lee of Virginia*, 224–227.

109. Jones, *After the Thunder*, 71.

110. Freeman, *Lee of Virginia*, 234–235.

111. P. V. D. Stern, *Robert E. Lee: The Man and the Soldier* (New York: McGraw-Hill, 1963), 244.

112. Ibid., 247.

113. Ibid.

114. R. Gragg, *The Illustrated Confederate Reader* (New York: Harper & Row, 1989), 224.

CHAPTER 7.   Thomas J. Jackson: "Stonewall"

1. M. Grimsley, "Stonewall Jackson: The Biography," *Civil War Times Illustrated* 27 (April 1988): 13.

2. J. I. Robertson, *Stonewall Jackson: The Man, the Soldier, the Legend* (New York: Macmillan Publishing USA, 1997), 755.

3. G. Skoch, "Stonewall Jackson's Last March," *Civil War Times Illustrated* 28 (May 1989): 24.

4. J. Pierce, "Jackson, Garnett, and the Unfortunate Breach," *Civil War Times Illustrated* 12 (October 1973): 40.

5. Grimsley, "Stonewall Jackson," 13.

6. Ibid.

7. R. Krick, "Stonewall Jackson's Deadly Calm," *American Heritage* 47 (December 1996): 56.

8. B. Farwell, *Stonewall: A Biography of General Thomas J. Jackson* (New York: W. W. Norton & Company, 1992), 3–5.

9. Ibid., 6.

10. P. D. Casdorph, *Lee and Jackson, Confederate Chieftains* (New York: Paragon House, 1992), 19.

11. K. M. Kostyal, *Stonewall Jackson: A Life Portrait* (Dallas: Taylor Publishing Company, 1999), 7.

12. Casdorph, *Lee and Jackson*, 19–20.

13. Farwell, *Stonewall: A Biography*, 8.

14. Ibid., 8–9.

15. J. Bowers, *Stonewall Jackson: Portrait of a Soldier* (New York: William Morrow and Company, Inc., 1989), 42.

16. Farwell, *Stonewall: A Biography*, 8.

17. F. E. Vandiver, *Mighty Stonewall* (New York: McGraw-Hill, 1957), 7–8.

18. Casdorph, *Lee and Jackson*, 21.

19. Farwell, *Stonewall: A Biography*, 10–11.

20. Grimsley, "Stonewall Jackson," 14.

21. Davis et al., *The Leaders*, 83.

22. Ibid., 83–84.

23. Farwell, *Stonewall: A Biography*, 38.

24. Kostyal, *Stonewall Jackson: A Life*, 25.

25. Grimsley, "Stonewall Jackson," 14–15.

26. Ibid., 15.

27. A. Tate, *Stonewall Jackson: The Good Soldier* (Nashville: J. S. Sanders & Company, 1991), 46.

28. Grimsley, "Stonewall Jackson," 15.

29. Krick, "Stonewall Jackson's Deadly Calm," 58.

30. Farwell, *Stonewall: A Biography*, 29–30.

31. Grimsley, "Stonewall Jackson," 15.

32. Krick, "Stonewall Jackson's Deadly Calm," 58.

33. Kostyal, *Stonewall Jackson: A Life*, 41.

34. Grimsley, "Stonewall Jackson," 15.

35. Tate, *Stonewall Jackson: The Good Soldier*, 49.

36. Ibid.

37. Casdorph, *Lee and Jackson*, 107.

38. Vandiver, *Mighty Stonewall*, 77.

39. Farwell, *Stonewall: A Biography*, 96.

40. Kostyal, *Stonewall Jackson: A Life*, 45.

41. Farwell, *Stonewall: A Biography*, 97.

42. Kostyal, *Stonewall Jackson: A Life*, 46.

43. Farwell, *Stonewall: A Biography*, 97.

44. J. I. Robertson, "Stonewall Jackson: Molding the Man and Making a General," *Blue & Gray* 9 (June 1992): 13.

45. Grimsley, "Stonewall Jackson," 16.

46. Ibid., 16–17.

47. Kostyal, *Stonewall Jackson: A Life*, 51.

48. Robertson, "Stonewall Jackson: Molding the Man," 14, 16.

49. M. Grimsley, "Jackson: The Wrath of God," *Civil War Times Illustrated* 23 (March 1984): 15.

50. Kostyal, *Stonewall Jackson: A Life*, 55.

51. Davis et al., *The Leaders*, 90–91.

52. Robertson, "Stonewall Jackson: Molding the Man," 17.

53. Ibid., 17, 19.

54. Grimsley, "Stonewall Jackson," 19.

55. Ibid.

56. Ibid., 20.

57. Ibid., 20–21.

58. B. Alexander, *Lost Victories: The Military Genius of Stonewall Jackson* (New York: Henry Holt and Company, 1992), 31.

59. Davis et al., *The Leaders*, 93.

60. R. G. Tanner, *Stonewall in the Valley* (Garden City, NY: Doubleday & Company, Inc., 1976), 7.

61. S. C. Harris, "Stonewall in the Valley," *America's Civil War* 5 (January 1993): 36.

62. Krick, "Stonewall Jackson's Deadly Calm," 62.

63. Ibid.

64. J. I. Robertson, "Stonewall in the Shenandoah: The Valley Campaign of 1862," *Civil War Times Illustrated* 11 (May 1972): 42–43.

65. Ibid., 43.

66. Ibid., 43–44.

67. Robertson, "Stonewall Jackson: Molding the Man," 26.

68. P. Bradley, "Bad Blood Between Confederate Commanders," *America's Civil War* 10 (November 1997): 47.

69. Grimsley, "Stonewall Jackson," 33.

70. Ibid.

71. Robertson, "Stonewall in the Shenandoah," 52.

72. Ibid.

73. Editors of Time-Life Books, *The Time-Life History of the Civil War* (New York: Barnes & Noble, 1990), 132–135.

74. Robertson, "Stonewall in the Shenandoah," 52.

75. S. W. Sears, "Lincoln and McClellan," *Lincoln's Generals*, ed. G. S. Boritt (New York: Oxford University Press, 1994), 40.

76. R. Hoffsommer, "Jackson's Capture of Harper's Ferry," *Civil War Times Illustrated* 1 (August 1962): 12.

77. Jones, *After the Thunder*, 131.

78. Ibid., 233.

79. Grimsley, "Stonewall Jackson," 39.

80. Casdorph, *Lee and Jackson*, 330.

81. Jones, *After the Thunder*, 132.

82. Ibid.

83. Davis et al., *The Leaders*, 126.

84. Robertson, "Stonewall in the Shenandoah," 54.

85. Ibid.

86. B. Catton, *Never Call Retreat* (Garden City, NY: Doubleday & Company, 1965), 23.

87. Bowers, *Stonewall Jackson: Portrait of a Soldier*, 305–306.

88. Davis et al., *The Leaders*, 99.

89. Robertson, "Stonewall in the Shenandoah," 54.

90. Ibid., 54–55.

91. R. Cheeks, "Fire and Fury at Catherine's Furnace," *America's Civil War* 3 (May 1995): 32.

92. Grimsley, "Stonewall Jackson," 44.

93. Kostyal, *Stonewall Jackson: A Life*, 190–192.

94. Ibid., 192–193.

95. Farwell, *Stonewall: A Biography*, 516.

96. Kostyol, *Stonewall Jackson: A Life*, 199.

97. Grimsley, "Stonewall Jackson," 46.

98. Kostyal, *Stonewall Jackson: A Life*, 199–200.

99. B. Davis, *They Called Him Stonewall* (New York: Holt, Rinehart and Winston, 1954), 445.

100. Ibid., 445–446.

101. Davis et al., *The Leaders*, 104.

102. Tate, *Stonewall Jackson: The Good Soldier*, 320.

CHAPTER 8.   Albert Sidney Johnston: Texan, Soldier, Gentleman

1. S. Allen, "Shiloh! The Campaign and First Day's Battle," *Blue & Gray* 14 (Winter 1997): 7.

2. Ibid.

3. Ibid.

4. C. P. Roland, *Albert Sidney Johnston: Soldier of Three Republics* (Austin: University of Texas Press, 1987), 3.

5. Ibid., 3–4.

6. Ibid., 4.

7. Ibid.

8. Ibid., 5.

9. Ibid., 6–7.

10. Ibid., 7–8.

11. Ibid., 9–10.

12. Ibid., 10.

13. A. Castel, "Dead on Arrival," *Civil War Times Illustrated* 36 (March 1997): 30.

14. Roland, *Albert Sidney Johnston*, 13–14.

15. J. H. Parks, *General Leonidas Polk, CSA: The Fighting Bishop* (Baton Rouge: Louisiana State University Press, 1990), 24.

16. Roland, *Albert Sidney Johnston*, 17.

17. Ibid., 18–19.

18. Castel, "Dead on Arrival," 30.

19. Roland, *Albert Sidney Johnston*, 27.

20. Castel, "Dead on Arrival," 30.

21. Roland, *Albert Sidney Johnston*, 51–52.

22. Castel, "Dead on Arrival," 30–32.

23. Ibid., 32.

24. Roland, *Albert Sidney Johnston*, 59–60.

25. Castel, "Dead on Arrival," 32.

26. Roland, *Albert Sidney Johnston*, 61–62.

27. Castel, "Dead on Arrival," 32.

28. Roland, *Albert Sidney Johnston*, 108–109.

29. Ibid., 124–126.

30. Ibid., 135–136.

31. Ibid., 136.

32. Ibid., 138.

33. Castel, "Dead on Arrival," 33.

34. Ibid.

35. Ibid.

36. Roland, *Albert Sidney Johnston*, 233.

37. B. McGinty, "I Will Call a Traitor a Traitor," *Civil War Times Illustrated* 20 (June 1981): 26.

38. Ibid.

39. Ibid., 27–28.

40. Ibid., 28–29.

41. Ibid., 29.

42. Ibid.

43. Ibid., 30.

44. L. J. Daniel, *Shiloh* (New York: Simon & Schuster, 1997), 17–18.

45. Parks, *General Leonidas Polk*, 180.

46. McGinty, "I Will Call a Traitor," 24.

47. Ibid.

48. Castel, "Dead on Arrival," 34.

49. F. B. Cooling, "Forts Henry and Donelson: Union Victory on the Twin Rivers," *Blue & Gray* 9 (February 1992): 11.

50. D. Nevin and the Editors of Time-Life Books, *The Road to Shiloh: Early Battles in the West* (Alexandria: Time-Life Books, 1983), 54.

51. Castel, "Dead on Arrival," 35.

52. Ibid.

53. Ibid.

54. Daniel, *Shiloh*, 49.

55. Allen, "Shiloh!" 9–10.

56. Woodworth, *Jefferson Davis and His Generals*, 96.

57. Ibid.

58. Ibid., 96–97.

59. Ibid., 97.
60. Ibid., 98.
61. Castel, "Dead on Arrival," 36.
62. Ibid.
63. Ibid.
64. Roland, *Albert Sidney Johnston*, 336.
65. Ibid.
66. Ibid., 338.
67. Allen, "Shiloh!" 52–53.
68. Ibid., 53.
69. Roland, *Albert Sidney Johnston*, 338.
70. Ibid., 338–339.
71. Allen, "Shiloh!" 64.
72. Ibid.
73. C. Allen, "Devil's Own Day," *America's Civil War* 3 (January 1991): 24.
74. M. McKenna, "The Final Resting Place of General Albert Sidney Johnston," *Blue & Gray* 12 (February 1995): 35–36.
75. Roland, *Albert Sidney Johnston*, 354.
76. Allen, "Shiloh!" 64.

CHAPTER 9.   Braxton Bragg: "Quick-Tempered Martinet"

1. J. Korn and the Editors of Time-Life Books, *The Fight for Chattanooga: Chickamauga to Missionary Ridge* (Alexandria: Time-Life Books, 1985), 22.
2. G. McWhiney, "Braxton Bragg," *Civil War Times Illustrated* 11 (April 1972): 4–5.
3. Korn et al., *The Fight for Chattanooga*, 22.
4. Cantor, *Confederate Generals*, 138.
5. Woodworth, *Jefferson Davis and His Generals*, 90.
6. Cantor, *Confederate Generals*, 138.
7. Ibid.
8. Woodworth, *Jefferson Davis and His Generals*, 92.
9. Ibid.
10. Cantor, *Confederate Generals*, 139.
11. Woodworth, *Jefferson Davis and His Generals*, 93.
12. Editors of Time-Life Books, *Voices of the Civil War: Shiloh* (Alexandria: Time-Life Books, 1996), 9.
13. Woodworth, *Jefferson Davis and His Generals*, 94.
14. McWhiney, "Braxton Bragg," 47.
15. Cantor, *Confederate Generals*, 139.
16. E. Dupuy and T. Dupuy, *The Compact History of the Civil War* (New York: MJF Books, 1993), 72–77.
17. Editors of Time-Life Books, *Voices of the Civil War: Shiloh*, 134.
18. Dupuy and Dupuy, *Compact History*, 79–80.
19. J. M. McPherson, *Battle Cry of Freedom* (New York: Oxford University Press, 1988), 416–417.
20. Ibid., 417.
21. Cantor, *Confederate Generals*, 140.
22. McWhiney, "Braxton Bragg," 45–46.
23. McPherson, *Battle Cry of Freedom*, 516.
24. Cantor, *Confederate Generals*, 140.
25. Dupuy and Dupuy, *Compact History*, 177.
26. Ibid., 178.
27. McPherson, *Battle Cry of Freedom*, 517.
28. J. L. McDonough, *War in Kentucky: From Shiloh to Perryville* (Knoxville: The University of Tennessee Press, 1994), 228.
29. J. Street Jr. and the Editors of Time-Life Books, *The Struggle for Tennessee: Tupelo to Stones River* (Alexandria: Time-Life Books, 1985), 67.
30. Cantor, *Confederate Generals*, 141.
31. S. F. Horn, *The Army of Tennessee* (Norman: University of Oklahoma Press, 1952), 186–187.

32. Ibid., 187.

33. Ibid., 188.

34. Dupuy and Dupuy, *Compact History*, 202.

35. Cantor, *Confederate Generals*, 141.

36. F. E. Vandiver, *Civil War Battlefields and Landmarks* (New York: Random House, 1996), 115.

37. Cantor, *Confederate Generals*, 141.

38. Vandiver, *Civil War Battlefields*, 116.

39. Ibid.

40. Dupuy and Dupuy, *Compact History*, 207.

41. Cantor, *Confederate Generals*, 142.

42. Woodworth, *Jefferson Davis and His Generals*, 195.

43. Ibid., 196.

44. Ibid., 196–197.

45. Ibid., 199.

46. Ibid., 198.

47. Cantor, *Confederate Generals*, 143.

48. Williams, *Lincoln and His Generals*, 277–278.

49. Cantor, *Confederate Generals*, 143.

50. Davis et al., *The Battles*, 405.

51. Editors of Time-Life Books, *Voices of the Civil War: Chickamauga* (Richmond: Time-Life Books, 1997), 59.

52. Davis et al., *The Battles*, 405–406.

53. Winik, *April 1865*, 279–280.

54. Cantor, *Confederate Generals*, 145.

55. Vandiver, *Civil War Battlefields*, 127.

56. McWhiney, "Braxton Bragg," 7.

57. Cantor, *Confederate Generals*, 145.

58. Ibid.

59. McWhiney, "Braxton Bragg," 42.

60. A. Castel, *Decision in the West: The Atlanta Campaign of 1864* (Lawrence: The University Press of Kansas, 1992), 353.

61. Cantor, *Confederate Generals*, 146.

62. Wiley, *Embattled Confederates*, 247.

63. Cantor, *Confederate Generals*, 147.

64. Ibid.

65. McWhiney, "Braxton Bragg," 46.

66. Ibid.

CHAPTER 10.   Patrick Cleburne: Stonewall of the West

1. C. L. Symonds, *Stonewall of the West: Patrick Cleburne and the Civil War* (Lawrence: University Press of Kansas, 1997), 2.

2. Ibid., 3–4.

3. Ibid., 4.

4. Ibid., 5.

5. Ibid.

6. Ibid., 5–6.

7. C. L. Dufour, *Nine Men in Gray* (Lincoln: University of Nebraska Press, 1993), 75.

8. Symonds, *Stonewall of the West*, 10–11.

9. Ibid., 13.

10. Ibid., 15–16.

11. Ibid., 16–17.

12. Ibid., 17–18.

13. Ibid., 19–20.

14. Ibid., 21.

15. Dufour, *Nine Men in Gray*, 76.

16. Ibid.

17. Ibid.

18. Symonds, *Stonewall of the West*, 35.
19. W. Hassler, "Stonewall of the West," *Civil War Times Illustrated* 10 (February 1972): 6.
20. Symonds, *Stonewall of the West*, 40–41.
21. Ibid., 41.
22. P. Stevens, "Personality: Patrick Cleburne," *Military History* 2 (October 1994): 20.
23. Hassler, "Stonewall of the West," 6.
24. Dufour, *Nine Men in Gray*, 77.
25. W. Sword, "The Other Stonewall," *Civil War Times Illustrated* 36 (February 1998): 38–39.
26. Symonds, *Stonewall of the West*, 51.
27. Dufour, *Nine Men in Gray*, 77.
28. Hassler, "Stonewall of the West," 6.
29. Dufour, *Nine Men in Gray*, 78.
30. Ibid.
31. Hassler, "Stonewall of the West," 7.
32. Ibid.
33. Stevens, "Personality," 22.
34. Hassler, "Stonewall of the West," 7.
35. Sword, "The Other Stonewall," 39.
36. Ibid.
37. Hassler, "Stonewall of the West," 7–8.
38. Ibid., 8.
39. Sword, "The Other Stonewall," 39.
40. Hassler, "Stonewall of the West," 8.
41. Symonds, *Stonewall of the West*, 115–116.
42. Ibid., 117.
43. Hassler, "Stonewall of the West," 9.
44. Sword, "The Other Stonewall," 40.
45. Hassler, "Stonewall of the West," 44.
46. Ibid.
47. Sword, "The Other Stonewall," 40.
48. D. Brooms, "Daring Rear–Guard Defense," *America's Civil War* 6 (November 1993): 34.
49. P. Cozzens, "To Save an Army," *Civil War Times Illustrated* 33 (September/October 1994): 42.
50. Ibid., 42–43.
51. Ibid., 43.
52. Symonds, *Stonewall of the West*, 176.
53. Hassler, "Stonewall of the West," 45.
54. Symonds, *Stonewall of the West*, 158–159.
55. Hassler, "Stonewall of the West," 9.
56. Symonds, *Stonewall of the West*, 176.
57. Ibid., 184.
58. S. Davis, "That Extraordinary Document," *Civil War Times Illustrated* 16 (December 1977): 15.
59. Symonds, *Stonewall of the West*, 184.
60. Ibid., 186.
61. Ibid., 189.
62. Dufour, *Nine Men in Gray*, 102–103.
63. Sword, "The Other Stonewall," 41.
64. S. Connor, "Cleburne and the Unthinkable," *Civil War Times Illustrated* 36 (February 1998): 45.
65. Dufour, *Nine Men in Gray*, 103.
66. Ibid., 104.
67. R. Morris, "Editorial," *America's Civil War* 12 (July 1999): 6.
68. Ibid.
69. Dufour, *Nine Men in Gray*, 104.
70. Sword, "The Other Stonewall," 41.
71. Dufour, *Nine Men in Gray*, 108–109.
72. Sword, "The Other Stonewall," 41.

73. Ibid., 42.

74. Dufour, *Nine Men in Gray*, 116.

75. J. Bell Hood, *Advance and Retreat: Personal Experiences in the United States and Confederate States Armies* (Lincoln: University of Nebraska Press, 1996), 293–294.

76. Dufour, *Nine Men in Gray*, 115.

77. Hassler, "Stonewall of the West," 47.

78. Sword, "The Other Stonewall," 43.

79. Ibid., 44.

80. Dufour, *Nine Men in Gray*, 117–118.

81. Morris, "Editorial," 6.

82. Symonds, *Stonewall of the West*, 262.

83. Dufour, *Nine Men in Gray*, 118.

84. Hassler, "Stonewall of the West," 47.

85. Dufour, *Nine Men in Gray*, 118.

CHAPTER 11.   Nathan Bedford Forrest: "That Devil Forrest"

1. R. Morris, "Fort Pillow: Massacre or Madness," *America's Civil War* 13 (November 2000): 26.

2. Ibid., 26–27.

3. Ibid., 29.

4. M. Grimsley, "The Great Deceiver," *Civil War Times Illustrated* 32 (November/December 1993): 37.

5. Morris, "Fort Pillow," 31–32.

6. Davis et al., *The Leaders*, 384–386.

7. Morris, "Fort Pillow," 32.

8. Davis et al., *The Leaders*, 373.

9. Ibid.

10. M. Grimsley, "Millionaire Rebel Raider," *Civil War Times Illustrated* 32 (September/October 1993): 60.

11. J. A. Wyeth, *That Devil Forrest* (Baton Rouge: Louisiana State University Press, 1989), 554–555.

12. J. Hurst, *Nathan Bedford Forrest* (New York: Alfred A. Knopf, 1993), 9.

13. Ibid., 15–16.

14. Ibid., 15–17.

15. Cantor, *Confederate Generals*, 70.

16. Grimsley, "Millionaire," 60.

17. Davis et al., *The Leaders*, 377.

18. Ibid., 378.

19. Ibid., 375–376.

20. Ibid., 379.

21. Cantor, *Confederate Generals*, 71.

22. Grimsley, "Millionaire," 63.

23. Ibid., 63–64.

24. J. Ward, "Forrest's First Fight," *America's Civil War* 6 (March 1993): 51–56.

25. Anders, *Fighting Confederates*, 111.

26. Ibid., 112–113.

27. Davis et al., *The Leaders*, 380–381.

28. Grimsley, "Millionaire," 68.

29. Ibid.

30. Nevin et al., *The Road to Shiloh*, 152.

31. Cantor, *Confederate Generals*, 72.

32. Ibid.

33. B. S. Wills, *A Battle from the Start: The Life of Nathan Bedford Forrest* (New York: Harper-Collins, 1992), 77.

34. Cantor, *Confederate Generals*, 73.

35. R. Domer, "Rebel Rout of Streight's Raiders," *America's Civil War* 9 (September 1996): 36.

36. Grimsley, "Deceiver," 73.
37. Cantor, *Confederate Generals*, 73.
38. Ibid.
39. Davis et al., *The Leaders*, 384–385.
40. R. Rogge, "Devil at the Crossroads," *America's Civil War* 3 (September 1990): 44.
41. R. Domer, "Sooy Smith and 'That Devil Forrest,'" *America's Civil War* 11 (May 1998): 40.
42. G. Tucker, "Forrest: Untutored Genius of War," *Civil War Times Illustrated* 3 (June 1964): 36.
43. M. Grimsley, "Leader of the Klan," *Civil War Times Illustrated* 32 (January/February 1994): 41, 63.
44. Rogge, "Devil," 49.
45. Cantor, *Confederate Generals*, 76.
46. Grimsley, "Leader," 66.
47. Ibid., 68.
48. Davis et al., *The Leaders*, 389–390.
49. Ibid., 391.
50. Grimsley, "Leader," 68.
51. Wills, *Battle from the Start*, 323–324.
52. Ibid., 330.
53. Davis et al. *The Leaders*, 390.
54. Wills, *Battle from the Start*, 336.
55. Cantor, *Confederate Generals*, 78.
56. Ibid.
57. Grimsley, "Leader," 72.
58. Wyeth, *That Devil Forrest*, 551.
59. Cantor, *Confederate Generals*, 78.
60. Wills, *Battle from the Start*, 377–378.
61. Ibid., 378.
62. Davis et al., *The Leaders*, 391.
63. Ibid., 392.
64. Hurst, *Nathan Bedford Forrest*, 381–382.
65. Wills, *Battle from the Start*, 380.

CHAPTER 12.   James Longstreet: "Scapegoat General"

1. J. D. Wert, "No Fifteen Thousand Men Can Take That Position," *James Longstreet: The Man, the Soldier, the Controversy*, ed. R. L. Di Nardo and A. A. Nofi (Conshohocken, PA: Combined Publishing, 1998), 77–78.
2. J. D. Wert, "Lee's Old War-horse," *American History* 33 (March 1998): 17.
3. J. D. Wert, *General James Longstreet* (New York: Simon & Schuster, 1993), 19–20.
4. Wert, *Longstreet*, 22.
5. Ibid.
6. Cantor, *Confederate Generals*, 44–45.
7. Wert, *Longstreet*, 29–30.
8. Ibid., 31.
9. Davis et al., *The Leaders*, 212.
10. Ibid., 212–213.
11. Wert, *Longstreet*, 45–46.
12. Ibid., 51.
13. Ibid., 51–52.
14. Davis et al., *The Leaders*, 213–214.
15. Ibid., 214–217.
16. Cantor, *Confederate Generals*, 46.
17. C. Dowdey, *Death of a Nation* (New York: Alfred A. Knopf, 1958), 9.
18. Cantor, *Confederate Generals*, 46.
19. Ibid.
20. Wert, "War-horse," 18.
21. H. J. Eckenrode and B. Conrad, *James Longstreet: Lee's War Horse* (Chapel Hill: University of North Carolina Press, 1986), 49.

22. W. G. Piston, *Tarnished Lieutenant* (Athens: University of Georgia Press, 1987), 21.

23. Cantor, *Confederate Generals*, 47.

24. Piston, *Tarnished Lieutenant*, 22–23.

25. Cantor, *Confederate Generals*, 47–48.

26. J. D. Wert, "General James Longstreet," *Civil War Times Illustrated* 32 (November/December, 1993): 106.

27. R. V. Murfin, *The Gleam of Bayonets* (New York: Bonanza Books, 1965), 115–116.

28. Piston, *Tarnished Lieutenant*, 25.

29. Ibid.

30. Wert, *Longstreet*, 202.

31. Wert, "War-horse," 19.

32. Piston, *Tarnished Lieutenant*, 30.

33. Catton, *Never Call Retreat*, 23.

34. Cantor, *Confederate Generals*, 48.

35. Piston, *Tarnished Lieutenant*, 38.

36. Dowdey, *Death of a Nation*, 167.

37. Ibid., 170.

38. Piston, *Tarnished Lieutenant*, 45.

39. Wert, "War-horse," 22.

40. Ibid.

41. Dowdey, *Death of a Nation*, 167.

42. Davis et al., *The Leaders*, 221–222.

43. Sell, *Leaders of the North and South*, 96.

44. Davis et al., *The Leaders*, 222.

45. Cantor, *Confederate Generals*, 50.

46. Wert, "War-horse," 23.

47. Davis et al., *The Leaders*, 224–225.

48. Ibid., 225.

49. Cantor, *Confederate Generals*, 51.

50. Davis et al., *The Leaders*, 225.

51. Ibid., 220.

52. J. D. Wert, "Generals at Odds," *Military History* 11 (August 1994), 52.

53. Ibid.

54. Wert, *Longstreet*, 297.

55. Wert, "War-horse," 23.

56. Wert, *Longstreet*, 387–388.

57. Davis et al., *The Leaders*, 227–228.

58. Ibid., 228.

59. G. Faeder, "The Best of Friends and Enemies," *Civil War Times Illustrated* 26 (October 1987): 23.

60. Piston, *Tarnished Lieutenant*, 92.

61. Ibid., 95–96.

62. Wert, *Longstreet*, 408–409.

63. Ibid., 410–411.

64. Ibid., 412.

65. Cantor, *Confederate Generals*, 53.

66. Wert, *Longstreet*, 412.

67. Ibid., 413.

68. Wert, "War-horse," 24.

69. Dowdey, *Death of a Nation*, 168–169.

70. Piston, *Tarnished Lieutenant*, 129–130.

71. Wert, *Longstreet*, 419.

72. Ibid., 420.

73. Davis et al., *The Leaders*, 229.

74. Wert, *Longstreet*, 425.

75. Ibid., 426.

76. Ibid.

77. Wert, "Generals," 52.

78. Wert, *Longstreet*, 426–427.

CHAPTER 13.   J. E. B. Stuart: Bold Warrior

1. J. Trammell, "Little-Known Battle Where 'Jeb' Stuart Died," *Washington Times*, October 27, 2001.
2. J. Guttman, "Jeb Stuart's Last Ride," *America's Civil War* 7 (May 1994): 35.
3. Ibid.
4. E. M. Thomas, "The Real J. E. B. Stuart," *Civil War Times Illustrated* 28 (December 1989): 35.
5. B. Davis, *Jeb Stuart: The Last Cavalier* (New York: Holt, Rinehart and Winston, 1957), 18.
6. Thomas, "The Real Stuart," 35.
7. E. M. Thomas, *Bold Dragoon: The Life of J. E. B. Stuart* (New York: Harper & Row, 1986), 9.
8. Ibid., 13.
9. Thomas, "The Real Stuart," 35.
10. Thomas, *Bold Dragoon*, 18–19.
11. Thomas, "The Real Stuart," 35.
12. Mapp, *Frock Coats and Epaulets*, 440.
13. Davis, *Jeb Stuart*, 27.
14. Ibid.
15. Cantor, *Confederate Generals*, 58.
16. Mapp, *Frock Coats and Epaulets*, 441.
17. Anders, *Fighting Confederates*, 154.
18. Cantor, *Confederate Generals*, 59.
19. Thomas, *Bold Dragoon*, 56–57.
20. Ibid., 58.
21. Thomas, "The Real Stuart," 36–37.
22. Cantor, *Confederate Generals*, 59.
23. Anders, *Fighting Confederates*, 156.
24. Davis et al., *The Leaders*, 279–280.
25. V. L. L. Naisewalt, "Stuart as Cavalryman's Cavalryman," *Civil War Times Illustrated* 1 (February 1963): 46.
26. Thomas, "The Real Stuart," 37.
27. Cantor, *Confederate Generals*, 59.
28. W. Jones, *Behind Enemy Lines: Spies, Raiders, and Guerrillas* (Dallas: Taylor Publishing Company, 2001), 135.
29. R. Morris, "Richmond's Fate in the Balance," *America's Civil War* 1 (May 1988): 38–39.
30. Anders, *Fighting Confederates*, 160.
31. Morris, "Richmond's Fate in the Balance," 41.
32. Davis, et al., *The Leaders*, 282.
33. Anders, *Fighting Confederates*, 164.
34. Ibid., 163.
35. J. Hennessy, "Stuart's Revenge," *Civil War Times Illustrated* 34 (June 1995): 42.
36. Ibid., 45–46.
37. Thomas, "The Real Stuart," 41.
38. Anders, *Fighting Confederates*, 166.
39. Jones, *Behind Enemy Lines*, 137.
40. Mapp, *Frock Coats and Epaulets*, 464–465.
41. Cantor, *Confederate Generals*, 43.
42. Thomas, "The Real Stuart," 75.
43. W. Brooksher and D. Snider, "Around McClellan Again," *Civil War Times Illustrated* 18 (August 1974): 47.
44. Cantor, *Confederate Generals*, 63.
45. Davis et al., *The Leaders*, 284–285.
46. Thomas, *Bold Dragoon*, 188–189.
47. Ibid., 191–194.
48. E. G. Longacre, "Stuart's Dumfries Raid," *Civil War Times Illustrated* 15 (July 1976): 18–25.
49. Cantor, *Confederate Generals*, 62.
50. Thomas, *Bold Dragoon*, 210.
51. Ibid., 212.

52. S. French, "The Infantry Commander at Chancellorsville," *Battlefield Journal* (December/January 2002): 11.

53. Anders, *Fighting Confederates*, 173.

54. Ibid., 174.

55. C. Hall, "The Battle of Brandy Station," *Civil War Times Illustrated* 29 (June 1990): 45.

56. S. Fleek, "Swirling Cavalry Fight," *America's Civil War* 2 (September 1989): 47.

57. Cantor, *Confederate Generals*, 65.

58. Thomas, "The Real Stuart," 76.

59. Ibid., 76.

60. Davis et al., *The Leaders*, 293–294.

61. Anders, *Fighting Confederates*, 175.

62. Ibid., 175–176.

63. Ibid., 176.

64. Thomas, "The Real Stuart," 76–77.

65. D. Zimmerman, "J. E. B. Stuart: Gettysburg Scapegoat?" *America's Civil War* 11 (May 1998): 50.

66. Thomas, *Bold Dragoon*, 256.

67. Zimmerman, 57.

68. Davis et al., *The Leaders*, 298.

69. Guttman, "Jeb Stuart's Last Ride," 35.

70. Cantor, *Confederate Generals*, 67–68.

71. Thomas, "The Real Stuart," 77.

72. Davis et al., *The Leaders*, 298.

73. Cantor, *Confederate Generals*, 68.

74. Thomas, "The Real Stuart," 77.

75. Guttman, "Jeb Stuart's Last Ride," 79.

76. Thomas, *Bold Dragoon*, 294–295.

77. L. De Grummond and L. De Grummond, *Jeb Stuart* (Philadelphia: J. B. Lippincott, 1962), 155.

78. Davis et al., *The Leaders*, 298.

79. Thomas, *Bold Dragoon*, 300.

CHAPTER 14.   John Bell Hood: The Fighting Texan

1. M. Bagby, "Advance and Retreat," *American History* 37 (October 2002): 38.

2. J. P. Dyer, *The Gallant Hood* (New York: Smithmark Publishers, 1995), 22.

3. Ibid., 23.

4. T. B. Buell, *The War Generals: Combat Leadership in the Civil War* (New York: Crown Publishers, Inc., 1997), 9.

5. R. McMurry, *John Bell Hood and the War for Southern Independence* (Lincoln: University of Nebraska Press, 1982), 8–9.

6. Ibid., 10.

7. Ibid.

8. Ibid., 10–11.

9. G. Patterson, "John Bell Hood," *Civil War Times Illustrated* 9 (February 1971): 12.

10. Cantor, *Confederate Generals*, 103.

11. W. Groom, *Shrouds of Glory* (New York: The Atlantic Monthly Press, 1995), 28–29.

12. Ibid., 28.

13. Buell, *The Warrior Generals*, 53.

14. Groom, *Shrouds of Glory*, 30.

15. Patterson, "John Bell Hood," 14–15.

16. Groom, *Shrouds of Glory*, 30.

17. Govan and Livingood, *A Different Valor*, 127.

18. Cantor, *Confederate Generals*, 104.

19. Buell, *The Warrior Generals*, 93.

20. Patterson, "John Bell Hood," 15.

21. Groom, *Shrouds of Glory*, 30–31.

22. Buell, *The Warrior Generals*, 113.

23. Groom, *Shrouds of Glory*, 31.

24. D. Davis, "Tumult in the Gaps," *America's Civil War* 1 (November 1988): 31.
25. Cantor, *Confederate Generals*, 105.
26. Buell, *The Warrior Generals*, 17.
27. Patterson, "John Bell Hood," 10.
28. McMurry, *John Bell Hood*, 60.
29. Groom, *Shrouds of Glory*, 34.
30. Wert, *Longstreet*, 223.
31. M. Chesnut, *Mary Chesnut's War* (New Haven: Yale University Press, 1981), 441.
32. Groom, *Shrouds of Glory*, 37.
33. Cantor, Confederate Generals, 105.
34. Buell, *The Warrior Generals*, 219.
35. Ibid., 231.
36. N. Trudeau, *Gettysburg: A Testing of Courage* (New York: Harper Collins Publishers, 2002), 337.
37. Buell, *The Warrior Generals*, 331.
38. Patterson, "John Bell Hood," 18.
39. Cantor, *Confederate Generals*, 107.
40. Patterson, "John Bell Hood," 18.
41. Ibid., 18–19.
42. R. Morris, "Editorial: John Bell Hood," *America's Civil War* 11 (September 1988): 6.
43. Ibid.
44. Buell, *The Warrior Generals*, 349.
45. McMurry, *John Bell Hood*, 87.
46. Buell, *The Warrior Generals*, 349.
47. J. Keenan, "The Gallant Hood of Texas," *America's Civil War* 7 (March 1994): 43–44.
48. Groom, *Shrouds of Glory*, 5.
49. Cantor, *Confederate Generals*, 108.
50. Symonds, *Joseph Johnston*, 264.
51. P. Nobbitt, "Confederate Breakout Attempt at Peachtree Creek," *America's Civil War* 11 (September 1998): 56–57.
52. Cantor, *Confederate Generals*, 108.
53. Nobbitt, "Confederate Breakout," 57.
54. Cantor, *Confederate Generals*, 109.
55. Nobbitt, Confederate Breakout," 57.
56. Patterson, "John Bell Hood," 20.
57. R. Neul, "Battle Most Desperate and Bloody," *America's Civil War* 7 (January 1995): 31.
58. Davis et al., *The Battles*, 433–434.
59. Neul, "Battle Most Desperate," 32.
60. Cantor, *Confederate Generals*, 111.
61. Ibid.
62. Bagby, "Advance and Retreat," 41.
63. Ibid., 42.
64. Ibid.
65. Sword, "The Other Stonewall," 38.
66. J. Keenan, "Fighting with Forrest in the Tennessee Winter," *America's Civil War* 7 (November 1995): 72.
67. S. Foote, *The Civil War: A Narrative: Red River to Appomattox* (New York: Random House, 1974), 706.
68. J. G. Randall and D. Donald, *The Civil War and Reconstruction* (Lexington: D. C. Heath & Company, 1969), 523.
69. Patterson, "John Bell Hood," 20.
70. Chestnut, *Mary Chesnut's War*, 708.
71. McMurry, *John Bell Hood*, 185–188.
72. Ibid., 188.
73. Ibid., 192.
74. Ibid., 193–195.
75. Ibid., 195.
76. Ibid., 195–196.
77. Ibid., 197.

78. Ibid., 198–200.
79. Ibid., 200.
80. Keenan, "The Gallant Hood of Texas," 48.
81. Ibid., 203.
82. Patterson, "John Bell Hood," 21.
83. McMurry, *John Bell Hood*, 190–191.

CHAPTER 15. John C. Breckinridge: Statesman and Soldier of the Confederacy

1. W. C. Davis, *Breckinridge: Statesman, Soldier, Symbol* (Baton Rouge: Louisiana University Press, 1992), 285–286.
2. Ibid., 287.
3. Ibid., 287–288.
4. Ibid., 8–11.
5. Ibid., 11–13.
6. Ibid., 15–16.
7. Ibid., 17–18.
8. W. C. Davis, "John C. Breckinridge," *Civil War Times Illustrated* 6 (June 1967): 11.
9. Davis, *Breckinridge: Statesman, Soldier, Symbol*, 30–31.
10. Davis, "Breckinridge," 11.
11. Ibid., 11–12.
12. Davis, *Breckinridge: Statesman, Soldier, Symbol*, 53.
13. Ibid., 55.
14. Davis, "Breckinridge," 12.
15. Davis, *Breckinridge: Statesman, Soldier, Symbol*, 157.
16. Ibid.
17. Davis, "Breckinridge," 12.
18. Ibid., 12–13.
19. W. C. Davis and the Editors of Time-Life Books, *Brother Against Brother: The War Begins* (Alexandria: Time-Life Books, 1983), 109–110.
20. Ibid., 110.
21. Ibid.
22. Ibid., 111.
23. Davis, "Breckinridge," 13–14.
24. R. Current, *The Confederacy* (New York: Simon Schuster, Inc., 1993), 75.
25. Davis, "Breckinridge," 14.
26. Davis, *The Long Surrender*, 69.
27. Davis, "Breckinridge," 15.
28. Davis, *Breckinridge: Statesman, Soldier, Symbol*, 289.
29. Ibid., 296–299.
30. Ibid., 302.
31. Ibid., 313.
32. Ibid., 314–315.
33. Ibid., 318–319.
34. Ibid., 322–324.
35. Davis, "Breckinridge," 15.
36. Symonds, *Stonewall of the West*, 116–117.
37. Davis, "Breckinridge," 15.
38. Davis, *Breckinridge: Statesman, Soldier, Symbol*, 359–361.
39. Current, *The Confederacy*, 76.
40. Davis, "Breckinridge," 16–17.
41. Davis, *Breckinridge: Statesman, Soldier, Symbol*, 400.
42. Ibid., 430.
43. Ibid., 436.
44. Ibid., 447.
45. Ibid., 448.
46. Ibid., 454.

47. W. C. Davis, *Look Away: A History of the Confederate States of America* (New York: The Free Press, 2002), 390.
48. Current, *The Confederacy*, 76.
49. Davis, "Breckinridge," 17.
50. J. Korn and the Editors of Time-Life Books, *Pursuit to Appomattox: The Last Battle* (Alexandria: Time-Life Books, 1987), 158.
51. Davis, *Breckinridge: Statesman, Soldier, Symbol*, 530.
52. Davis, "Breckinridge," 18.
53. W. C. Davis, "Confederate Exiles," *American History Illustrated* 5 (June 1970): 31.
54. Davis, "Breckinridge," 18.
55. Davis, *Breckinridge: Statesman, Soldier, Symbol*, 609.
56. Ibid., 636–638.
57. Ibid., 639.

CHAPTER 16.   Leonidas Polk: "The Fighting Bishop"

1. A. Chitty, "Leonidas Polk: A Profile," *Civil War Times Illustrated* 2 (October 1963): 17.
2. Ibid., 17.
3. Cantor, *Confederate Generals*, 173.
4. Ibid.
5. Parks, *General Leonidas Polk*, 36.
6. Woodworth, *Jefferson Davis and His Generals: The Failure of Confederate Command in the West*, 28.
7. Parks, *General Leonidas Polk*, 36–37.
8. Ibid., 37.
9. Cantor, *Confederate Generals*, 174.
10. Chitty, "Leonidas Polk: A Profile," 17.
11. Cantor, *Confederate Generals*, 174.
12. Ibid.
13. Chitty, "Leonidas Polk: A Profile," 17–18.
14. Cantor, *Confederate Generals*, 174–175.
15. Ibid., 175.
16. Parks, *General Leonidas Polk*, 109.
17. Chitty, "Leonidas Polk: A Profile," 18.
18. Parks, *General Leonidas Polk*, 115.
19. Ibid.
20. Chitty, "Leonidas Polk: A Profile," 18.
21. Cantor, *Confederate Generals*, 176.
22. Woodworth, *Jefferson Davis and His Generals*, 29.
23. Parks, *General Leonidas Polk*, 155.
24. Woodworth, *Jefferson Davis and His Generals*, 29.
25. Parks, *General Leonidas Polk*, 167.
26. Ibid., 167–168.
27. Chitty, "Leonidas Polk: A Profile," 19.
28. Ibid.
29. Woodworth, *Jefferson Davis and His Generals*, 30.
30. Parks, *General Leonidas Polk*, 170.
31. Cantor, *Confederate Generals*, 177.
32. Ibid.
33. Parks, *General Leonidas Polk*, 189.
34. Ibid., 191–192.
35. Ibid., 195–196.
36. Ibid., 197.
37. Cantor, *Confederate Generals*, 178.
38. Daniel, *Shiloh*, 96–97.
39. Parks, *General Leonidas Polk*, 228–229.
40. Cantor, *Confederate Generals*, 178.
41. Parks, *General Leonidas Polk*, 236.
42. Ibid., 237.

43. Cantor, *Confederate Generals*, 178.
44. Parks, *General Leonidas Polk*, 249.
45. McDonough, *War in Kentucky*, 228–229.
46. S. Sanders, "'Every Mother's Son of Them Are Yankees,'" *Civil War Times Illustrated* 38 (October 1999): 57–58.
47. Ibid., 59.
48. Cantor, *Confederate Generals*, 179.
49. Ibid.
50. McDonough, *War in Kentucky*, 230.
51. Parks, *General Leonidas Polk*, 280.
52. Cantor, *Confederate Generals*, 180.
53. Ibid.
54. Ibid.
55. Woodworth, *Jefferson Davis and His Generals*, 161–162.
56. Cantor, *Confederate Generals*, 142.
57. Woodworth, *Jefferson Davis and His Generals*, 167.
58. Cantor, *Confederate Generals*, 180–181.
59. Parks, *General Leonidas Polk*, 340.
60. Cantor, *Confederate Generals*, 181.
61. Woodworth, *Jefferson Davis and His Generals*, 239.
62. Cantor, *Confederate Generals*, 181.
63. Parks, *General Leonidas Polk*, 351–352.
64. Cantor, *Confederate Generals*, 181.
65. Chitty, "Leonidas Polk: A Profile," 20.
66. S. F. Horn, *The Army of Tennessee* (Norman: University of Oklahoma Press, 1952), 332.
67. Horn, *The Army of Tennessee*, 332.
68. Parks, *General Leonidas Polk*, 384.
69. Cantor, *Confederate Generals*, 182.

CHAPTER 17.   **John Hunt Morgan: "Thunderbolt of the Confederacy"**

1. J. Ramage, *Rebel Raider: The Life of John Hunt Morgan* (Lexington: University Press of Kentucky, 1986), 1–3.
2. Ibid., 5–7.
3. Ibid., 7.
4. E. Thomas, *John Hunt Morgan and His Raiders* (Lexington: University Press of Kentucky, 1975), xi.
5. Cantor, *Confederate Generals*, 79.
6. Ramage, *Rebel Raider*, 11–17.
7. Cantor, *Confederate Generals*, 80.
8. Thomas, *John Hunt Morgan*, 5.
9. Ramage, *Rebel Raider*, 19–20.
10. Thomas, *John Hunt Morgan*, 6–7.
11. Ibid., 7, 11.
12. Cantor, *Confederate Generals*, 80.
13. Ramage, *Rebel Raider*, 39.
14. Thomas, *John Hunt Morgan*, 9–12.
15. Cantor, *Confederate Generals*, 81.
16. Thomas, *John Hunt Morgan*, 5–16.
17. Cantor, *Confederate Generals*, 81.
18. Thomas, *John Hunt Morgan*, 27.
19. Ramage, *Rebel Raider*, 57–58.
20. Ibid., 58–59.
21. Ibid., 59–60.
22. Ibid., 61–62.
23. Thomas, *John Hunt Morgan*, 29.
24. Ibid., 30–32.
25. Cantor, *Confederate Generals*, 81.

26. Ibid., 34–36.
27. Ibid., 36–37.
28. Ramage, *Rebel Raider*, 87–88.
29. Ibid., 89–91.
30. Thomas, *John Hunt Morgan*, 39–40.
31. W. Brooksher and R. Vickery, "Morgan Rides Again: Kentucky, 1862," *Civil War Times Illustrated* 17 (June 1978): 8.
32. Ibid., 10, 43.
33. Thomas, *John Hunt Morgan*, 44.
34. Ibid., 44–45.
35. Ramage, *Rebel Raider*, 108.
36. Thomas, *John Hunt Morgan*, 46–47.
37. Ibid., 48–50.
38. Ibid., 51–52.
39. Cantor, *Confederate Generals*, 83.
40. Thomas, *John Hunt Morgan*, 53–54.
41. J. Jones, *A Rebel War Clerk's Diary* (New York: Sagamore Press, 1958), 88–89.
42. Thomas, *John Hunt Morgan*, 59–61.
43. Ibid., 61–64.
44. Ibid., 65–69.
45. Ibid., 69–71.
46. D. Brown, "Morgan's Christmas Raid," *Civil War Times Illustrated* 13 (January 1975): 12.
47. Thomas, *John Hunt Morgan*, 72–75.
48. W. Kingseed, "The Great Escape," *American History* 34 (February 2000): 25.
49. Thomas, *John Hunt Morgan*, 77.
50. D. Phillips, *Daring Raiders* (New York: Metro Books, 1998), 72–74.
51. Thomas, *John Hunt Morgan*, 78–82.
52. Kingseed, "The Great Escape," 26.
53. A. Keller, "Morgan's Raid Across the Ohio," *Civil War Times Illustrated* 3 (June 1963): 36.
54. R. Creeks, "John Hunt Morgan's Ill-fated Ohio Raid," *America's Civil War* 9 (May 1988): 48–49.
55. D. Roth, "John Hunt Morgan's Escape From the Ohio Penitentiary," *Blue & Gray* 12 (October 1994): 16–17.
56. Kingseed, "The Great Escape," 26–27.
57. Thomas, *John Hunt Morgan*, 87–90.
58. Cantor, *Confederate Generals*, 87.
59. Thomas, *John Hunt Morgan*, 91.
60. Ibid., 92–93.
61. Ibid., 96–98.
62. Ibid., 100–101.
63. Cantor, *Confederate Generals*, 88.
64. Ramage, *Rebel Raider*, 218.
65. W. Stier, "Morgan's Last Battle," *Civil War Times Illustrated* 35 (December 1996): 84.
66. Foote, *The Civil War*, 596.
67. Ibid., 596.

CHAPTER 18.   **Ambrose Powell Hill: Always Ready for a Fight**

1. W. Nye, "A. P. Hill: Always Ready to Fight," *Civil War Times* 2 (December 1960): 8.
2. Ibid., 8.
3. W. Hassler, *A. P. Hill: Lee's Forgotten General* (Chapel Hill: The University of North Carolina Press, 1957), 3.
4. Nye, "A. P. Hill," 8.
5. J. I. Robertson, *General A. P. Hill: The Story of a Confederate Warrior* (New York: Random House, 1987), 5.
6. Ibid.
7. Ibid., 6.
8. Ibid., 6–7.

9. Hassler, *Lee's Forgotten General,* 9.

10. Robertson, *General A. P. Hill,* 7–8.

11. Ibid., 8–9.

12. Ibid., 9.

13. Ibid., 10.

14. Ibid., 11.

15. Ibid., 12.

16. Ibid.

17. Hassler, *Lee's Forgotten General,* 12.

18. Robertson, *General A. P. Hill,* 15.

19. Hassler, *Lee's Forgotten General,* 14.

20. Ibid., 14–15.

21. Ibid., 15.

22. Robertson, *General A. P. Hill,* 22.

23. Ibid.

24. Ibid.

25. Ibid., 25–26.

26. Ibid., 26–27.

27. Ibid., 27–28.

28. Ibid., 28–29.

29. Hassler, *Lee's Forgotten General,* 22.

30. Robertson, *General A. P. Hill,* 33.

31. Hassler, *Lee's Forgotten General,* 22.

32. Ibid.

33. Ibid., 23–24.

34. Ibid., 24.

35. Hassler, *Lee's Forgotten General,* 24–25.

36. Robertson, *General A. P. Hill,* 50.

37. Hassler, *Lee's Forgotten General,* 40.

38. Robertson, *General A. P. Hill,* 58.

39. Ibid., 63.

40. Bradley, "Bad Blood Between Confederate Commanders," 47.

41. Robertson, *General A. P. Hill,* 75.

42. Ibid., 77.

43. Ibid., 94–95.

44. Ibid., 95–96.

45. Hassler, *Lee's Forgotten General,* 68–70.

46. Robertson, *General A. P. Hill,* 95–96.

47. Hassler, *Lee's Forgotten General,* 74–75.

48. Bradley, "Bad Blood between Confederate Commanders," 49.

49. Robertson, *General A. P. Hill,* 125.

50. Bradley, "Bad Blood between Confederate Commanders," 50.

51. Robertson, *General A. P. Hill,* 126.

52. W. Hassler, "The A. P. Hill–Stonewall Jackson Feud," *Civil War Times Illustrated* 4 (May 1965): 39.

53. Ibid., 39.

54. Ibid.

55. Ibid., 39–40.

56. Ibid., 40.

57. Robertson, *General A. P. Hill,* 135.

58. F. E. Vandiver, *Their Tattered Flags* (College Station: Texas A & M University Press, 1970), 154.

59. Robertson, *General A. P. Hill,* 140.

60. Vandiver, *Their Tattered Flags,* 154–155.

61. Ibid., 155.

62. Robertson, *General A. P. Hill,* 141–142.

63. Vandiver, *Their Tattered Flags,* 155–156.

64. Ibid., 156.

65. Robertson, *General A. P. Hill,* 147.

66. Bradley, "Bad Blood between Confederate Commanders," 52–53.

67. Ibid., 53.

68. Robertson, *General A. P. Hill,* 151.

69. Ibid., 154.

70. Ibid., 157.

71. Ibid., 158.

72. W. K. Goolrick and the Editors of Time-Life Books, *Rebels Resurgent: Fredericksburg to Chancellorsville* (Alexandria: Time-Life Books, 1985), 61–62.

73. Hassler, *Lee's Forgotten General,* 119.

74. Ibid., 123.

75. Hassler, "Feud," 41.

76. Ibid., 42.

77. Bradley, "Bad Blood between Confederate Commanders," 53.

78. W. Hassler, "A. P. Hill: Mystery Man of the Confederacy," *Civil War Times Illustrated* 16 (October 1977): 8.

79. L. Tagg, *The Generals of Gettysburg* (Mason City: Savas Publishing Company, 1998), 303.

80. Hassler, "Mystery Man," 145.

81. J. Longstreet, *From Manassas to Appomattox* (Philadelphia: Lippincott, 1896), 383.

82. G. W. Gallagher, ed., *The First Day at Gettysburg* (Kent: The Kent State University Press, 1992), 32.

83. C. Clark and the Editors of Time-Life Books, *Gettysburg: The Confederate High Tide* (Alexandria: Time-Life Books, 1985), 44.

84. Tagg, *The Generals of Gettysburg,* 304.

85. Ibid.

86. Ibid., 304–305.

87. Ibid., 305.

88. Hassler, *Lee's Forgotten General,* 162.

89. Robertson, *General A. P. Hill,* 225.

90. Hassler, "Mystery Man," 8.

91. Hassler, *Lee's Forgotten General,* 199.

92. Ibid., 210–211.

93. Robertson, *General A. P. Hill,* 301.

94. Ibid., 308.

95. Ibid., 310.

96. Ibid., 313.

97. Freeman, *Lee of Virginia,* 188.

98. Editors of Time-Life Books, *The Time-Life History of the Civil War* (New York: Barnes & Noble, 1990), 395–397.

CHAPTER 19.   Richard Taylor: "Soldier Prince of the Confederacy"

1. T. M. Parrish, *Richard Taylor: Soldier Prince of Dixie* (Chapel Hill: The University of North Carolina Press, 1992), 11–12.

2. Ibid., 14–15.

3. Ibid., 16.

4. Ibid., 17–18.

5. Ibid., 19.

6. Ibid., 24.

7. Ibid., 32–33.

8. Dufour, *Nine Men in Gray,* 4.

9. Ibid.

10. Ibid., 4–5.

11. W. Brooksher, *War along the Bayous: The 1864 Red River Campaign in Louisiana* (Dulles, VA: Brassey's, 1998), 16.

12. Dufour, *Nine Men in Gray,* 7.

13. Ibid.

14. Ibid.

15. Ibid.

16. Ibid., 8.

17. Ibid.

18. Parrish, *Soldier Prince of Dixie*, 139.

19. C. Clark and the Editors of Time-Life Books, *Decoying the Yankees: Jackson's Valley Campaign* (Alexandria: Time-Life Books, 1984), 117.

20. Ibid.

21. Parrish, *Soldier Prince of Dixie*, 149–150.

22. G. Schreckengost, "Front Royal: Key to the Valley," *America's Civil War* 12 (January 2000): 29.

23. Ibid.

24. Ibid., 30.

25. J. Hollandsworth, *Pretense of Glory: The Life of Nathaniel P. Banks* (Baton Rouge: Louisiana State University Press, 1998), 66.

26. D. G. Martin, *Jackson's Valley Campaign: November 1861–June 1862* (Bryn Mawr, PA: Combined Books, 1998), 146.

27. Dufour, *Nine Men in Gray*, 22.

28. Ibid.

29. Ibid., 23.

30. Ibid.

31. Ibid., 24.

32. Ibid., 25.

33. Ibid., 26.

34. J. H. Parks, *General Edmund Kirby Smith, CSA* (Baton Rouge: Louisiana State University Press, 1954), 382.

35. P. Faust, ed., *Historical Times Illustrated Encyclopedia of the Civil War* (New York: Harper Row Publishers, 1986), 619.

36. A. M. Josephy Jr. and the Editors of Time-Life Books, *War on the Frontier: The Trans-Mississippi West* (Alexandria: Time-Life Books, 1986), 56.

37. Ibid., 57, 59.

38. Dufour, *Nine Men in Gray*, 31.

39. Parks, *General Edmund Kirby Smith*, 391.

40. Dufour, *Nine Men in Gray*, 31.

41. Ibid., 31–32.

42. Ibid., 32–33.

43. Ibid., 33.

44. Ibid., 35.

45. Ibid.

46. Parrish, *Soldier Prince of Dixie*, 423.

47. Dufour, *Nine Men in Gray*, 36.

48. Ibid., 37.

49. Ibid.

50. Parrish, *Soldier Prince of Dixie*, 455.

51. Ibid., 457–458.

52. Ibid., 480–481.

53. Ibid., 490–492.

54. Ibid., 495–496.

CHAPTER 20.   Richard S. Ewell: "Old Bald Head"

1. G. Kross, "At the Time Impractical," *Blue & Gray* 12 (February 1995): 53.

2. McPherson, *Battle Cry of Freedom*, 654–655.

3. Kross, "At the Time Impracticable," 53.

4. S. Martin, *The Road to Glory: Confederate General Richard Ewell* (Guild Press of Indiana, Inc., 1991), 3–4.

5. D. C. Pfanz, *Richard S. Ewell: A Soldier's Life* (Chapel Hill: The University of North Carolina Press, 1998), 11.

6. Ibid.

7. Ibid., 13.

8. Ibid., 13–14.

9. Ibid., 26.

10. Martin, *The Road to Glory*, 6.

11. S. I. Martin, "The Complex Confederate," *Civil War Times Illustrated* 25 (April 1986): 27.

12. Martin, *The Road to Glory*, 7.

13. Ibid., 5.

14. Pfanz, *Richard S. Ewell*, 82.

15. Martin, *The Road to Glory*, 5.

16. Martin, "Complex Confederate," 27.

17. Ibid., 27–28.

18. Pfanz, *Richard S. Ewell*, 121.

19. Tagg, *The Generals of Gettysburg*, 251.

20. Pfanz, *Richard S. Ewell*, 123.

21. Ibid., 124.

22. Ibid.

23. Ibid., 146.

24. Editors of Time-Life Books, *Voices of the Civil War: Shenandoah, 1862* (Richmond: Time-Life Books, 1997), 60.

25. Ibid.

26. Ibid.

27. Current, *The Confederacy*, 201.

28. Pfanz, *Richard S. Ewell*, 206.

29. Ibid., 206–207.

30. Ibid., 220.

31. Martin, *The Road to Glory*, 92–93.

32. Pfanz, *Richard S. Ewell*, 237.

33. Ibid., 236.

34. P. Hamlin, *The Making of a Soldier* (Richmond: Whittet & Shepperson, 1935), 111.

35. Martin, "Complex Confederate," 29.

36. Pfanz, *Richard S. Ewell*, 237–238.

37. Ibid., 238.

38. Martin, *The Road to Glory*, 125.

39. P. Hamlin, *Old Bald Head* (Strasburg, VA: Shenandoah Publishing House, 1940), 117.

40. Martin, *The Road to Glory*, 125, 127.

41. Pfanz, *Richard S. Ewell*, 257.

42. Editors of Time-Life Books, *Voices of the Civil War: Second Manassas* (Alexandria: Time-Life Books, 1995), 102.

43. Pfanz, *Richard S. Ewell*, 258.

44. Ibid., 263–264.

45. Ibid., 265.

46. Tagg, *The Generals of Gettysburg*, 252.

47. Pfanz, *Richard S. Ewell*, 266, 268.

48. Martin, "Complex Confederate," 30.

49. Ibid.

50. Jones, *After the Thunder*, 59–60.

51. Martin, "Complex Confederate," 31.

52. Pfanz, *Richard S. Ewell*, 322.

53. Current, *The Confederacy*, 202.

54. E. J. Stackpole, "The Story of the Three Days at Gettysburg," *Civil War Times Illustrated* 2 (July 1963): 4.

55. Pfanz, *Richard S. Ewell*, 319.

56. C. C. Osborne, *Jubal: The Life and Times of General Jubal A. Early, CSA* (Chapel Hill: Algonquin Books of Chapel Hill, 1992), 200.

57. Tagg, *The Generals of Gettysburg*, 255.

58. Martin, "Complex Confederate," 31.

59. Ibid.

60. Martin, *The Road to Glory*, 268.

61. Current, *The Confederacy*, 202.

62. Pfanz, *Richard S. Ewell*, 394.

63. Ibid., 388–389.
64. Ibid., 396.
65. Ibid., 397–398.
66. Ibid., 399–403.
67. Martin, "Complex Confederate," 32.
68. Ibid.
69. Martin, *The Road to Glory*, 341.
70. Martin, "Complex Confederate," 32–33.
71. Martin, *The Road to Glory*, 383.
72. Ibid.
73. Ibid., 390.
74. Pfanz, *Richard S. Ewell*, 495.
75. Ibid., 497.
76. Ibid., 498–499.

CHAPTER 21.   Jubal A. Early: "Old Jube"

1. Tagg, *The Generals of Gettysburg*, 256.
2. Ibid.
3. J. A. Early, *Narrative of the War Between the States*, introduction by G. Gallagher (New York: Da Capo Press, Inc., 1989), ii–iii.
4. Ibid., iv.
5. C. Osborne, *Jubal: The Life and Times of General Jubal A. Early, CSA* (Chapel Hill: Algonquin Books of Chapel Hill, 1992), 6.
6. W. C. Davis, "'Jubilee': General Jubal A. Early," *Civil War Times Illustrated* 9 (December 1970): 5.
7. Osborne, *Jubal*, 7.
8. Davis, "'Jubilee,'" 6.
9. J. A. Early, *Jubal Early's Memoirs*, introduction by C. Symonds (Baltimore: The Nautical & Aviation Publishing Company of America, 1989), i–ii.
10. Davis, "'Jubilee,'" 7.
11. Ibid.
12. Osborne, *Jubal*, 22–23.
13. Davis, "'Jubilee,'" 7.
14. Ibid.
15. Ibid., 7–8.
16. Osborne, *Jubal*, 31.
17. Davis, "'Jubilee,'" 8.
18. Ibid.
19. Cantor, *Confederate Generals*, 127.
20. Davis, "'Jubilee,'" 9.
21. Ibid.
22. Early, *Jubal Early's Memoirs*, iii.
23. Cantor, *Confederate Generals*, 127.
24. Osborne, *Jubal*, 81.
25. Davis, "'Jubilee,'" 10.
26. Osborne, *Jubal*, 88.
27. Ibid., 100.
28. Cantor, *Confederate Generals*, 129.
29. Early, *Jubal Early's Memoirs*, iii–iv.
30. Cantor, *Confederate Generals*, 129.
31. Early, *Narrative of the War*, i.
32. Ibid.
33. Ibid., viii.
34. Tagg, *The Generals of Gettysburg*, 257.
35. Cantor, *Confederate Generals*, 130.
36. Ibid.
37. Ibid.

38. Osborne, *Jubal*, 228–229.
39. Cantor, *Confederate Generals*, 131.
40. Current, *The Confederacy*, 182.
41. E. Wittenburg, "Roadblock en route to Washington," *America's Civil War Illustrated* 6 (November 1993): 50.
42. Cantor, *Confederate Generals*, 131.
43. Current, *The Confederacy*, 182, 184.
44. Wittenburg, "Roadblock," 53.
45. Davis, "'Jubilee,'" 44.
46. Cantor, *Confederate Generals*, 132.
47. Wittenburg, "Roadblock," 53.
48. Cantor, *Confederate Generals*, 133.
49. Wittenburg, "Roadblock," 82.
50. Cantor, *Confederate Generals*, 133.
51. Ibid., 134.
52. Osborne, *Jubal*, 310–311.
53. Cantor, *Confederate Generals*, 134–135.
54. Ibid., 135.
55. Osborne, *Jubal*, 371.
56. Ibid., 372.
57. Ibid., 372–373.
58. Cantor, *Confederate Generals*, 135.
59. J. D. Wert, "Old Jubilee's Last Battle," *Civil War Times Illustrated* 36 (August 1997): 27.
60. Ibid.
61. Osborne, *Jubal*, 391.
62. Davis, "'Jubilee,'" 46.
63. Ibid., 46–47.
64. Current, *The Confederacy*, 184.
65. Cantor, *Confederate Generals*, 136.
66. Osborne, *Jubal*, 474, 478.
67. Ibid., 474–475.

CHAPTER 22.   John Brown Gordon: "A Soldier's Soldier"

1. D. S. Freeman, *Lee's Lieutenants: A Study in Command* (New York: Simon & Schuster, Inc., 1998), 811–812.
2. C. Moore, "Gordon: The Pride of All Georgia," *Civil War Times* 2 (February/March, 1961): 8.
3. R. Eckert, *John Brown Gordon: Soldier, Southerner, American* (Baton Rouge: Louisiana State University Press, 1989), 7.
4. Ibid., 8–9.
5. Ibid., 10.
6. Ibid., 10–11.
7. Ibid., 11–12.
8. Moore, "The Pride of All Georgia," 8.
9. Tagg, *The Generals of Gettysburg*, 262.
10. Eckert, *John Brown Gordon*, 18–19.
11. Ibid., 20.
12. Ibid., 21.
13. Ibid., 23–25.
14. Tagg, *The Generals of Gettysburg*, 262.
15. Eckert, *John Brown Gordon*, 28–29.
16. Ibid., 29.
17. Ibid., 31.
18. Ibid., 35–36.
19. E. Williams, "Personality," *America's Civil War* 6 (May 1993): 14.
20. Eckert, *John Brown Gordon*, 37.
21. Tagg, *The Generals of Gettysburg*, 262–263.

22. Ibid., 263.
23. Eckert, *John Brown Gordon*, 44.
24. Williams, "Personality," 14, 16.
25. Ibid., 16.
26. Current, *The Confederacy*, 245.
27. Williams, "Personality," 16.
28. Ibid., 16, 18.
29. Ibid., 18.
30. Ibid., 20.
31. Ibid.
32. Eckert, *John Brown Gordon*, 60.
33. G. C. Rea, *The Battles: Wilderness & Spotsylvania* (Conshohocken, PA: Eastern National, 1995), 17–18.
34. Eckert, *John Brown Gordon*, 77.
35. Tagg, *The Generals of Gettysburg*, 264.
36. Current, *The Confederacy*, 245.
37. Dupuy and Dupuy, *Compact History*, 380–382.
38. Williams, "Personality," 18.
39. Eckert, *John Brown Gordon*, 105.
40. Ibid., 107.
41. L. Reed, "Battle in Desperation," *Civil War Times Illustrated* 34 (April 1995): 34.
42. Eckert, *John Brown Gordon*, 111–112.
43. Ibid., 114–115.
44. Ibid., 121.
45. Korn et al., *Pursuit to Appomattox*, 153.
46. Ibid., 155.
47. Ibid.
48. Eckert, *John Brown Gordon*, 130–131.
49. Moore, "The Pride of All Georgia," 8.
50. Ibid.
51. Eckert, *John Brown Gordon*, 316–320.
52. Ibid., 320.
53. Ibid., 334–335.
54. Ibid., 338.
55. Ibid., 338–339.
56. Ibid., 339.
57. Ibid.
58. Ibid., 340.
59. Ibid., 340–341.
60. Ibid., 124.
61. Ibid., 341

CHAPTER 23.   **Daniel Harvey Hill: "Maverick General"**

1. P. Cozzens, *This Terrible Sound* (Urbana: University of Illinois Press, 1992), 351.
2. Freeman, *Lee's Lieutenants*, 60.
3. H. Bridges, *Lee's Maverick General: Daniel Harvey Hill* (Lincoln: University of Nebraska Press, 1961), 6.
4. Ibid., 16.
5. Ibid., 17.
6. J. D. Wert, "I Am So Unlike Other Folks," *Civil War Times Illustrated* 28 (April 1989): 14.
7. Bridges, *Lee's Maverick General*, 18.
8. Ibid., 18–19.
9. Ibid., 18.
10. Ibid., 19.
11. Wert, "I Am So Unlike Other Folks," 14.
12. Ibid.
13. Bridges, *Lee's Maverick General*, 23.

14. Wert, "I Am So Unlike Other Folks," 16.
15. Ibid.
16. Bridges, *Lee's Maverick General*, 30.
17. Wert, "I Am So Unlike Other Folks," 16.
18. Bridges, *Lee's Maverick General*, 31–32.
19. Wert, "I Am So Unlike Other Folks," 17.
20. Ibid., 17–18.
21. Bridges, *Lee's Maverick General*, 49–50.
22. Stokesbury, *A Short History*, 89.
23. Bridges, *Lee's Maverick General*, 59–60.
24. Stokesbury, *A Short History*, 91.
25. Ibid.
26. Ibid., 92.
27. Wert, "I Am So Unlike Other Folks," 18.
28. Ibid.
29. R. Selcer, "The South's Feuding Generals," *America's Civil War* 3 (July 1990): 40.
30. Ibid.
31. Wert, "I Am So Unlike Other Folks," 19.
32. K. Toney, "Horrors of the Bloody Lane," *America's Civil War* 10 (September 1997): 65.
33. R. H. Bailey and the Editors of Time-Life Books, *The Bloodiest Day: The Battle of Antietam* (Alexandria: Time-Life Books, 1984), 21.
34. Ibid.
35. Bridges, *Lee's Maverick General*, 97.
36. Stokesbury, *A Short History*, 117.
37. Wert, "I Am So Unlike Other Folks," 19.
38. Bridges, *Lee's Maverick General*, 153–154.
39. Wert, "I Am So Unlike Other Folks," 19.
40. Ibid.
41. Bridges, *Lee's Maverick General*, 193.
42. Ibid., 179.
43. Horn, *The Army of Tennessee*, 240–241.
44. J. E. Stevens, *1863: The Rebirth of a Nation* (New York: Bantam Books, 1999), 325.
45. Faust, *Historical Times Illustrated Encyclopedia of the Civil War*, 362.
46. Bridges, *Lee's Maverick General*, 227.
47. Ibid., 228.
48. Ibid., 242–243.
49. Ibid., 247.
50. Ibid., 248.
51. Freeman, *Lee's Lieutenants*, 651.
52. Ibid.
53. Ibid.
54. Bridges, *Lee's Maverick General*, 273.
55. Ibid., 273–275.
56. Ibid., 277–278.
57. Ibid., 279.

CHAPTER 24. William J. Hardee: "Old Reliable"

1. N. C. Hughes Jr., *General William Hardee: Old Reliable* (Baton Rouge: Louisiana State University Press, 1965), 6.
2. Ibid., 7.
3. Ibid., 10–12.
4. Ibid., 16–17.
5. Ibid., 19.
6. Ibid., 27.
7. Ibid., 28–29.
8. Ibid., 29–30.
9. Ibid., 32.

10. Ibid., 35.
11. Ibid., 38–39.
12. Ibid., 39–41.
13. Ibid., 41–44.
14. Roland, *Albert Sidney Johnston*, 170–171.
15. Hughes, *General William Hardee*, 53.
16. Ibid., 56–59.
17. Ibid., 60.
18. Ibid., 60–62.
19. Ibid., 67–69.
20. Ibid., 72.
21. Roland, *Albert Sidney Johnston*, 270.
22. Ibid., 271–272.
23. Hughes, *General William Hardee*, 83–84.
24. Ibid., 86–90.
25. Ibid., 91–92.
26. Ibid., 92–93.
27. Ibid., 93–98.
28. D. G. Martin, *The Shiloh Campaign* (New York: Fairfax Press, 1987), 60–62.
29. Ibid., 63.
30. Dupuy and Dupuy, *Compact History*, 76–77.
31. Ibid., 77.
32. Hughes, *General William Hardee*, 107.
33. Ibid., 108.
34. Ibid., 109.
35. Dupuy and Dupuy, *Compact History*, 79–80.
36. Woodworth, *Jefferson Davis and His Generals*, 165.
37. Hughes, *General William Hardee*, 119–121.
38. Woodworth, *Jefferson Davis and His Generals*, 158.
39. Horn, *The Army of Tennessee*, 180–181.
40. Woodworth, *Jefferson Davis and His Generals*, 158.
41. Dupuy and Dupuy, *Compact History*, 179.
42. Hughes, *General William Hardee*, 134–135.
43. Hattaway, *Shades of Blue and Gray*, 103–104.
44. Hughes, *General William Hardee*, 141–144.
45. Ibid., 145.
46. Woodworth, *Jefferson Davis and His Generals*, 194.
47. Hughes, *General William Hardee*, 147–148.
48. Ibid., 148–149.
49. Ibid., 149.
50. Ibid., 158–159.
51. Ibid., 165.
52. Cantor, *Confederate Generals*, 145.
53. Korn et al., *The Fight for Chattanooga*, 149.
54. Woodworth, *Jefferson Davis and His Generals*, 253.
55. Hughes, *General William Hardee*, 177.
56. Ibid., 180–182.
57. Ibid., 183–184.
58. Ibid., 186–188.
59. Ibid., 196–197.
60. Cantor, *Confederate Generals*, 38.
61. Hughes, *General William Hardee*, 214.
62. Woodworth, *Jefferson Davis and His Generals*, 283.
63. Hughes, *General William Hardee*, 215.
64. Cantor, *Confederate Generals*, 39.
65. Horn, *The Army of Tennessee*, 345.
66. Ibid., 345–346.
67. Hughes, *General William Hardee*, 219–233.
68. J. Mills, *Fields of Glory* (Nashville: Rutledge Hill Press, 1989), 181.

69. Ibid.
70. W. Sword, *The Confederacy's Last Hurrah* (Lawrence: University Press of Kansas, 1992), 37.
71. Hughes, *General William Hardee*, 243–245.
72. Ibid., 247–248.
73. Ibid., 248–249.
74. Ibid., 251–258.
75. Ibid., 259–267.
76. Ibid., 273–277.
77. Ibid., 278–280.
78. Ibid., 283–286.
79. Horn, *The Army of Tennessee*, 425.
80. Mills, *Fields of Glory*, 75.
81. Hughes, *General William Hardee*, 301.
82. Ibid., 305–309.
83. Ibid., 312–313.

CHAPTER 25.   Epilogue: Davis as Commander-in-Chief

1. J. L. Stokesbury, *A Short History of the Civil War* (New York: William, Morrow and Company, Inc., 1995), 210.
2. Ibid.
3. C. Eaton, *Jefferson Davis*, 243.
4. S. E. Miers, "Jefferson Davis," in *The Rise and Fall of the Confederate Government*, 13 (New York: Collier Books, 1961).
5. C. L. Symonds, "A Fatal Relationship: Davis and Johnston at War," in *Jefferson Davis's Generals*, ed. G. S. Boritt (New York: Oxford University Press, 1999), 19.
6. Ibid., 19–20.
7. Ibid., 21–23.
8. S. E. Woodworth. *No Band of Brothers: Problems of the Rebel High Command* (Columbia: University of Missouri Press, 1999), xiv.
9. Eaton, *Jefferson Davis*, 244.
10. G. Boritt, *Davis's Generals*, 9.
11. Ibid., xiii.
12. Stokesbury, *A Short History*, 210–211.
13. Woodworth, *No Band of Brothers*, 44.
14. W. Davis. *Jefferson Davis*, 601–602.

Bibliography

Alexander, Bevin. *Lost Victories: The Military Genius of Stonewall Jackson.* New York: Henry Holt and Company, 1992.

Allen, Christopher. "Devil's Own Day." *America's Civil War* 3, no. 5 (January 1991): 24.

Allen, Stacy. "Shiloh! The Campaign and First Day's Battle." *Blue & Gray* 14, no. 3 (Winter 1997): 7, 9–10, 52–53, 64.

Anders, Curt. *Fighting Confederates.* New York: Dorset Press, 1980.

Bagby, Milton. "Advance and Retreat." *American History* 37, no. 4 (October 2002): 38.

Bailey, Ronald H., and the Editors of Time-Life Books. *Forward to Richmond: McClellan's Peninsular Campaign.* Alexandria: Time-Life Books, 1983.

———. *The Bloodiest Day: The Battle of Antietam.* Alexandria: Time Life-Books, 1984.

Ballard, Michael. "Cheer for Jefferson Davis." *American History Illustrated* 16, no. 2 (May 1981): 9–11.

Batty, Peter, and Peter Parish. *The Divided Union.* Topsfield, MA: Salem House Publishers, 1987.

Bonekemper, Edward H., III, *How Robert E. Lee Lost the Civil War.* Spotsylvania: Sergeant Kirkland's Press, 1997.

Boothe, Norton. *Great Generals of the Civil War.* New York: Gallery Books, 1986.

Boritt, Gabor S., ed. *Jefferson Davis's Generals.* New York: Oxford University Press, 1999.

Bowers, John. *Stonewall Jackson: Portrait of a Soldier.* New York: William Morrow and Company, Inc., 1989.

Bradley, Paul. "Bad Blood Between Confederate Commanders." *America's Civil War* 10, no. 5 (November 1997): 47.

Bridges, Hal. *Lee's Maverick General: Daniel Harvey Hill.* Lincoln: University of Nebraska Press, 1961.

Brooksher, William. *War along the Bayous: The 1864 Red River Campaign in Louisiana.* Dulles, VA: Brassey's, 1998.

Brooksher, William, and David Snider. "Around McClellan Again." *Civil War Times Illustrated* 8, no. 5 (August 1974): 47.

Brooksher, William, and Richard Vickery. "Morgan Rides Again: Kentucky, 1862." *Civil War Times Illustrated* 17, no. 3 (June 1978): 8, 10, 43.

Brooms, Doyle. "Daring Rear-Guard Defense." *America's Civil War* 6, no. 5 (November 1993): 34.

Brown, Dee. "Morgan's Christmas Raid." *Civil War Times Illustrated* 13, no. 9 (January 1975): 12.

Buell, Thomas B. *The War Generals: Combat Leadership in the Civil War.* New York: Crown Publishers, Inc., 1997.

Canfield, Cass. *The Iron Will of Jefferson Davis.* New York: Harcourt Brace Jovanovich, 1978.

Cantor, George. *Confederate Generals: Life Portraits.* Dallas: Taylor Publishing Company, 2000.

Casdorph, Paul D. *Lee and Jackson: Confederate Chieftains.* New York: Paragon House, 1992.

Castel, Albert. "George B. McClellan: 'Little Mac.'" *Civil War Times Illustrated* 13, no. 2 (May 1974): 9–11.

———. *Decision in the West: The Atlanta Campaign of 1864.* Lawrence: The University Press of Kansas, 1992.

———. "Dead on Arrival." *Civil War Times Illustrated* 36, no. 1 (March 1997): 30–36.

Catton, Bruce. *Never Call Retreat.* Garden City: Doubleday & Company, Inc., 1965.

Cheeks, Robert. "Fire and Fury at Catherine's Furnace." *America's Civil War* 3, no. 2 (May 1995): 32.

Chesnut, Mary. *Mary Chesnut's Civil War.* New Haven: Yale University, 1981.

Chitty, Arthur. "Leonidas Polk: A Profile." *Civil War Times Illustrated* 2, no. 6 (October 1963): 17–20.

Clark, Champ, and the Editors of Time-Life Books. *Decoying the Yankees: Jackson's Valley Campaign.* Alexandria: Time-Life Books, 1984.

———. *Gettysburg: The Confederate High Tide.* Alexandria: Time-Life Books, 1985.

Commager, Harry S. et al. *America's Robert E. Lee.* Boston: Houghton Mifflin, 1951.

Connor, Sam. "Cleburne and the Unthinkable." *Civil War Times Illustrated* 36, no. 7 (February 1998): 45.

Cooling, Benjamin. "Forts Henry and Donelson: Union Victory on the Twin Rivers." *Blue & Gray* 9, no. 3 (February 1992): 11.

Cooper, William J., Jr. *Jefferson Davis, American.* New York: Alfred A. Knopf, 2000.

Cozzens, Peter. *This Terrible Sound.* Urbana: University of Illinois Press, 1992.

———. "To Save an Army." *Civil War Times Illustrated* 33, no. 4 (September/October 1994): 42–43.

Creeks, Robert. "John Hunt Morgan's Ill-fated Ohio Raid." *America's Civil War* 9, no. 2 (May 1988): 48–49.

Current, Richard. *The Confederacy.* New York: Simon & Schuster, Inc., 1993.

Daniel, Larry J. *Shiloh.* New York: Simon & Schuster, 1997.

Davis, Burke. *They Called Him Stonewall.* New York: Holt, Rinehart and Winston, 1954.

———. *Jeb Stuart: The Last Cavalier.* New York: Holt, Rinehart and Winston, 1957.

———. *The Long Surrender.* New York: Random House, 1985.

Davis, Danny. "Tumult in the Gaps." *America's Civil War* 1, no. 4 (November 1988): 31.

Davis, Steven. "That Extraordinary Document." *Civil War Times Illustrated* 16, no. 8 (December 1977): 15.

Davis, William C. "John C. Breckinridge." *Civil War Times Illustrated* 6, no. 3 (June 1967): 11–18.

———. "Confederate Exiles." *American History Illustrated* 5, no. 3 (June 1970): 31.

———. "'Jubilee': General Jubal A. Early." *Civil War Times Illustrated* 9, no. 8 (December 1970): 5–10, 44–47.

———. *Jefferson Davis: The Man and His Hour.* New York: Harper Collins, 1991.

———. *Breckinridge: Statesman, Soldier, Symbol.* Baton Rouge: Louisiana University Press, 1992.

———. *Look Away: A History of the Confederate States of America.* New York: The Free Press, 2002.

Davis, William C., et al. *Civil War Journal: The Leaders.* Nashville: Rutledge Hill Press, 1997.

———. *Civil War Journal: The Battles.* Nashville: Rutledge Hill Press, 1998.

Davis, William, C., and the Editors of Time-Life Books. *Brother Against Brother: The War Begins.* Alexandria: Time-Life Books, 1983.

De Grummond, Lena and Lynn De Grummond. *Jeb Stuart.* Philadelphia: J. B. Lippincott, 1962.

Domer, Ronald. "Rebel Rout of Streight's Raiders." *America's Civil War* 9, no. 4 (September 1996): 36.

———. "Sooy Smith and 'That Devil Forrest.'" *America's Civil War* 11, no. 2 (May 1998): 40.

Douglas, Henry Kyd. *I Rode With Stonewall.* Greenwich: Fawcett Publishing Company, 1965.

Dowdey, Clifford. *Death of a Nation.* Alfred A. Knopf, 1958.

———. *Lee.* New York: Bonanza Books, 1965.

Dubowski, Cathy. *Robert E. Lee and the Rise of the South.* Englewood Cliffs: Silver Burdett, 1991.

Dufour, Charles L. *Nine Men in Gray.* Lincoln: University of Nebraska Press, 1993.

Dupuy, Ernest, and Trevor Dupuy. *The Compact History of the Civil War.* New York: MJF Books, 1993.

Dyer, John P. *The Gallant Hood.* New York: Smithmark Publishers, 1995.

Early, Jubal A. *Jubal Early's Memoirs.* Baltimore: The Nautical & Aviation Publishing Company of America, 1989.

———. *Narrative of the War Between the States.* New York: Da Capo Press, Inc., 1989.

Eaton, Clement. *Jefferson Davis.* New York: The Free Press, 1977.

Eckenrode, H. J., and Bryan Conrad. *James Longstreet: Lee's War Horse.* Chapel Hill: University of North Carolina Press, 1986.

Eckert, Ralph. *John Brown Gordon: Soldier, Southerner, American.* Baton Rouge: Louisiana State University Press, 1989.

Editors of Time-Life Books. *The Time-Life History of the Civil War.* New York: Barnes & Noble, 1990.

———. *Voices of the Civil War: Second Manassas.* Alexandria: Time-Life Books, 1995.

———. *Voices of the Civil War: Shiloh.* Alexandria: Time-Life Books, 1996.

———. *Voices of the Civil War: Chickamauga.* Richmond: Time-Life Books, 1997.

————. *Voices of the Civil War: First Manassas.* Richmond: Time-Life Books, 1997.

————. *Voices of the Civil War: Shenandoah, 1862.* Richmond: Time-Life Books, 1997.

————. *1863: Turning Point of the Civil War.* Alexandria: Time-Life Books, 1998.

————. *Illustrated Atlas of the Civil War.* Alexandria: Time-Life Books, 1998.

Eicher, David J. *Robert E. Lee: A Life Portrait.* Dallas: Taylor Publishing Company, 1997.

Faeder, Gustav. "The Best of Friends and Enemies." *Civil War Times Illustrated* 26, no. 6 (October 1987): 23.

Farwell, Byron. *Stonewall: A Biography of General Thomas J. Jackson.* New York: W. W. Norton & Company, 1992.

Faust, Patricia, ed. *Historical Times Illustrated Encyclopedia of the Civil War.* New York: Harper Row Publishers, 1986.

Fleek, Sherman. "Swirling Cavalry Fight." *America's Civil War* 2, no. 3 (September 1989): 47.

Foote, Shelby. *The Civil War: A Narrative: Fort Sumter to Perryville.* New York: Random House, 1958.

————. *The Civil War: A Narrative: Red River to Appomattox.* New York: Random House, 1974.

Freeman, Douglas S. *Lee of Virginia.* New York: Charles Scribner's Sons, 1958.

————. *Lee's Lieutenants: A Study in Command.* New York: Simon & Schuster, Inc., 1998.

French, Steve. "The Infantry Commander at Chancellorsville." *Battlefield Journal* (December/January 2002).

Gallagher, Gary W., ed. *The First Day at Gettysburg.* Kent: The Kent State University Press, 1992.

————. *Lee and His Generals in War and Memory.* Baton Rouge: Louisiana State University Press, 1998.

Glatthaar, Joseph T. *Partners in Command.* New York: The Free Press, 1994.

Goolrick, William K., and the Editors of Time-Life Books. *Rebels Resurgent: Fredericksburg to Chancellorsville.* Alexandria: Time-Life Books, 1985.

Govan, Gilbert, and James Livingood. *A Different Valor.* New York: The Bobbs-Merrill Company, Inc., 1956.

Gragg, Rod. *The Illustrated Confederate Reader.* New York: Harper & Row, 1989.

Grimsley, Mark. "Jackson: The Wrath of God." *Civil War Times Illustrated* 23, no. 1 (March, 1984): 15–21.

————. "Robert E. Lee: The Life and Career of the Master General." *Civil War Times Illustrated* 24, no. 7 (November 1985): 14–19, 25–36, 39–41, 47.

————. "Stonewall Jackson: The Biography." *Civil War Times Illustrated* 27, no. 2 (April 1988): 13–21, 33, 39, 44–46.

————. "We Will Vindicate the Right: An Account of the Life of Jefferson Davis." *Civil War Times Illustrated* 30, no. 3 (July/August 1991): 32–35, 39–41, 46–75.

————. "Millionaire Rebel Raider." *Civil War Times Illustrated* 32, no. 4 (September/October 1993): 6, 63–68.

————. "The Great Deceiver." *Civil War Times Illustrated* 32, no. 5 (November/December 1993): 37.

————. "Leader of the Klan." *Civil War Times Illustrated* 32, no. 6 (January/February, 1994): 41, 63–72.

Groom, Winston. *Shrouds of Glory.* New York: The Atlantic Monthly Press, 1995.

Guttman, Jon. "Jeb Stuart's Last Ride." *America's Civil War* 7, no. 2 (May 1994): 35, 79.

Hall, Clark. "The Battle of Brandy Station." *Civil War Times Illustrated* 29, no. 2 (June 1990): 45.

Hamlin, Percy. *The Making of a Soldier.* Richmond: Whittet & Shepperson, 1935.

———. *Old Bald Head.* Stasburg, VA: Shenandoah Publishing House, 1940.

Harris, Shawn C. "Stonewall in the Valley." *America's Civil War* 5, no. 6 (January 1993): 36.

Hassler, Warren. *Commanders of the Army of the Potomac.* Baton Rouge: Louisiana State University Press, 1962.

Hassler, William. *A. P. Hill–Lee's Forgotten General.* Chapel Hill: The University of North Carolina Press, 1957.

———. "The A. P. Hill–Stonewall Jackson Feud." *Civil War Times Illustrated* 4, no. 2 (May 1965): 39–42.

———. "Stonewall of the West." *Civil War Times Illustrated* 10, no. 10 (February 1972): 6–9, 44–47.

———. "A. P. Hill: Mystery Man of the Confederacy." *Civil War Times Illustrated* 16, no. 6 (October 1977): 8.

Hattaway, Herman. *Shades of Blue and Gray.* Columbia: University of Missouri Press, 1997.

Hennessy, John. "Stuart's Revenge." *Civil War Times Illustrated* 34, no. 2 (June 1995): 42–46.

Hoehling, A. A. *After the Guns Fell Silent.* New York: Madison Books. 1990.

Hoffsommer, Robert. "Jackson's Capture of Harper's Ferry." *Civil War Times Illustrated* 1, no. 5 (August 1962): 12.

Hollandsworth, James. *Pretense of Glory: The Life of Nathaniel P. Banks.* Baton Rouge: Louisiana State University Press, 1998.

Hood, John Bell. *Advance and Retreat: Personal Experiences in the United States and Confederate States Armies.* Lincoln: University of Nebraska Press, 1996.

Horn, Stanley F. *The Robert E. Lee Reader.* New York: Bobbs-Merrill, 1949.

———. *The Army of Tennessee.* Norman: University of Oklahoma Press, 1952.

Hughes, Nathaniel C., Jr. *General William Hardee: Old Reliable.* Baton Rouge: Louisiana State University Press, 1965.

Hurst, Jack. *Nathan Bedford Forrest.* New York: Alfred A. Knopf, 1993.

Jones, John. *A Rebel War Clerk's Diary.* New York: Sagamore Press, 1958.

Jones, Wilmer. *After the Thunder: Fourteen Men Who Shaped Post-Civil War America.* Dallas: Taylor Publishing Company, 2000.

———. *Behind Enemy Lines: Spies, Raiders, and Guerrillas.* Dallas: Taylor Publishing Company, 2001.

Josephy, Alvin M., Jr., and the Editors of Time-Life Books. *War on the Frontier: The Trans-Mississippi West.* Alexandria: Time-Life Books, 1986.

Julian, Allen. "From Dalton to Atlanta." *Civil War Times Illustrated* 3, no. 4 (July 1964): 4.

Keenan, Jerry. "The Gallant Hood of Texas." *America's Civil War* 7, no. 1 (March 1994): 43–44.

———. "Fighting with Forrest in the Tennessee Winter." *America's Civil War* 7, no. 5 (November 1995): 72.

Keller, Allan. "Morgan's Raid Across the Ohio." *Civil War Times Illustrated* 3, no. 2 (June 1963): 36.

King, Perry. *Jefferson Davis*. New York: Chelsea House Publishers, 1990.

Kingseed, Wyatt. "The Great Escape." *American History* 34, no. 6 (February 2000): 25–27.

Korn, Jerry, and the Editors of Time-Life Books. *The Fight For Chattanooga: Chickamauga to Missionary Ridge*. Alexandria: Time-Life Books, 1985.

———. *Pursuit to Appomattox: The Last Battle*. Alexandria: Time-Life Books, 1987.

Kostyal, K. M. *Stonewall Jackson: A Life Portrait*. Dallas: Taylor Publishing Company, 1999.

Krick, Robert. "Stonewall Jackson's Deadly Calm." *American Heritage* 47, no. 8 (December 1996): 56–58, 62.

Kross, Gary. "At the Time Impractical." *Blue & Gray* 12, no. 3 (February 1995): 53.

Largent, Kimberly. "The Presidential Years." *Battlefield Journal* (February/March 2002): 2.

Longacre, Edward G. "Stuart's Dumfries Raid." *Civil War Times Illustrated* 15, no. 4 (July 1976): 18–25.

Longstreet, James. *From Manassas to Appomattox*. Philadelphia: Lippincott, 1896.

Mapp, Alf J., Jr. *Frock Coats and Epaulets*. Lanham, MD: Hamilton Press, 1987.

Marshall, Michael. "A Soldier No Longer." *Military History* 7, no. 3 (December 1990): 12–14.

Martin, David G. *The Shiloh Campaign*. New York: Fairfax Press, 1987.

———. *Jackson's Valley Campaign: November 1861–June 1862*. Bryn Mawr, PA: Combined Books, 1998.

Martin, Samuel J. "The Complex Confederate." *Civil War Times Illustrated* 25, no. 2 (April 1986): 27–33.

———. "Kill Cavalry." *Civil War Times Illustrated* 38, no. 7 (February 2000): 30.

———. *Kill Cavalry: The Life of Union General Hugh Judson Kilpatrick*. Mechanicsburg, PA: Stackpole, 2000.

McDonough, James L. *War in Kentucky: From Shiloh to Perryville*. Knoxville: The University of Tennessee Press, 1994.

McFeely, William S. *Grant*. New York: W. W. Norton, 1981.

McGinty, Brian. "I Will Call a Traitor a Traitor." *Civil War Times Illustrated* 20, no. 3 (June 1981): 24–30.

McKenna, Mark. "The Final Resting Place of General Albert Sidney Johnston." *Blue & Gray* 12, no. 3 (February 1995): 35–36.

McMurry, Richard. *John Bell Hood and the War for Southern Independence*. Lincoln: University of Nebraska Press, 1982.

McPherson, James M. *Battle Cry of Freedom*. New York: Oxford University Press, 1988.

McWhiney, Grady. "Braxton Bragg." *Civil War Times Illustrated* 11, no. 1 (April 1972): 4–7, 42, 45–46.

Miers, Schenk E. "Jefferson Davis." In *The Rise and Fall of the Confederate Government* 13. New York: Collier Books, 1961.

———. *The Road to Glory: Confederate General Richard Ewell*. Indianapolis: Guild Press of Indiana, Inc., 1991.

Mills, Jim. *Fields of Glory*. Nashville: Rutledge Hill Press, 1989.

Moore, Charles. "Gordon: The Pride of All Georgia." *Civil War Times* 2, no. 10 (February/March 1961): 8.

Morris, Roy. "Richmond's Fate in the Balance." *America's Civil War* 1, no. 1 (May 1988): 38–41.

———. "Editorial: John Bell Hood." *America's Civil War* 11, no. 4 (September 1998): 6.

———. "Editorial," *America's Civil War* 12, no. 3 (July 1999): 6.

———. "Fort Pillow: Massacre or Madness." *America's Civil War* 13, no. 5 (November 2000): 26–32.

Murfin, Richard V. *The Gleam of Bayonets.* New York: Bonanza Books, 1965.

Murphy, Richard, and the Editors of Time-Life Books. *The Nation Reunited: War's Aftermath.* Alexandria: Time-Life Books, 1987.

Naisewalt, Van Loan L. "Stuart as Cavalryman's Cavalryman." *Civil War Times Illustrated* 1, no. 10 (February 1963): 46.

Neul, Robert. "Battle Most Desperate and Bloody." *America's Civil War* 7, no. 6 (January 1995): 31–32.

Nevin, David, and the Editors of Time-Life Books. *The Road to Shiloh: Early Battles in the West.* Alexandria: Time-Life Books, 1983.

Nobbitt, Phil. "Confederate Breakout Attempt at Peachtree Creek." *America's Civil War* 11, no. 4 (September 1998): 56–57.

Nye, Wilbur. "A. P. Hill: Always Ready to Fight." *Civil War Times* 2, no. 8 (December 1960): 8.

Osborne, Charles C. *Jubal: The Life and Times of General Jubal A. Early, CSA.* Chapel Hill: Algonquin Books of Chapel Hill, 1992.

Parks, Joseph H. *General Edmund Kirby Smith, CSA.* Baton Rouge: Louisiana State University Press, 1954.

———. *General Leonidas Polk, CSA: The Fighting Bishop.* Baton Rouge: Louisiana State University Press, 1990.

Parrish, T. Michael. *Richard Taylor: Soldier Prince of Dixie.* Chapel Hill: The University of North Carolina Press, 1992.

Patterson, Gerard. "John Bell Hood." *Civil War Times Illustrated* 9, no. 10 (February 1971): 12, 14–21.

———. "Gustave." *Civil War Times Illustrated* 32, no. 3 (July/August 1992): 30–35, 53–54.

Pfanz, Donald C. *Richard S. Ewell: A Soldier's Life.* Chapel Hill: University of North Carolina Press, 1998.

Phillips, David. *Daring Raiders.* New York: Metro Books, 1998.

Pierce, John. "Jackson, Garnett, and the Unfortunate Breach." *Civil War Times Illustrated* 12, no. 6 (October 1973): 40.

Piston, William G. *Tarnished Lieutenant.* Athens: University of Georgia Press, 1987.

Potter, Robert. *Jefferson Davis: Confederate President.* Austin: Steck-Vaughn Company, 1994.

Preston, Margaret. "Robert E. Lee after the War." *Civil War Times Illustrated* 7, no. 9 (January 1969): 5.

Ramage, James. *Rebel Raider: The Life of John Hunt Morgan.* Lexington: University Press of Kentucky, 1986.

Randall, J. G., and David Donald. *The Civil War and Reconstruction.* Lexington: D. C. Heath & Company, 1969.

Rea, Gordon C. *The Battles: Wilderness & Spotsylvania.* Conshohocken, PA: Eastern National, 1995.

Reed, Liz. "Battle in Desperation." *Civil War Times Illustrated* 34, no. 1 (April 1995): 34.

Robertson, James I. "Stonewall in the Shenandoah: The Valley Campaign of 1862." *Civil War Times Illustrated* 11, no. 1 (May 1972): 42–44, 52–55.

———. *General A. P. Hill: The Story of a Confederate Warrior.* New York: Random House, 1987.

———. "Stonewall Jackson: Molding the Man and Making a General." *Blue & Gray* 9, no. 5 (June 1992): 13–19.

———. *Stonewall Jackson: The Man, the Soldier, the Legend.* New York: MacMillan Publishing USA, 1997.

Rogge, Robert. "Devil at the Crossroads." *America's Civil War* 3, no. 3 (September 1990): 44.

Roland, Charles P. *Albert Sidney Johnston: Soldier of Three Republics.* Austin: University of Texas Press, 1987.

Roth, Dave. "John Hunt Morgan's Escape From the Ohio Penitentiary." *Blue & Gray* 12, no. 1 (October 1994): 16–17.

Sanders, Stuart. "'Every Mother's Son of Them Are Yankees.'" *Civil War Times Illustrated* 38, no. 5 (October 1999): 57–59.

Schreckengost, Gary. "Front Royal: Key to the Valley." *America's Civil War* 12, no. 6 (January 2000): 29–30.

Sears, Stephen W. "Lincoln and McClellan." In *Lincoln's Generals.* Edited by Gabor S. Boritt. New York: Oxford University Press, 1994.

———. *Controversies & Commanders: Dispatches from the Army of the Potomac.* Boston: Houghton Mifflin Company, 1999.

Selcer, Richard. "The South's Feuding Generals." *America's Civil War* 3, no. 2 (July 1990): 40.

Sell, Bill. *Leaders of the North and South.* New York: Michael Friedman Publishing Group, 1996.

Skoch, George. "Stonewall Jackson's Last March." *Civil War Times Illustrated* 28, no. 3 (May 1989): 24.

Smith, Gene. *Lee and Grant.* New York: McGraw Hill Book Company, 1984.

Stackpole, Edward J. "The Story of the Three Days at Gettysburg." *Civil War Times Illustrated* 2, no. 4 (July 1963): 4.

Stanchak, John. "Behind the Lines." *Civil War Times Illustrated* 24, no. 7 (November 1985): 52.

Stern, Philip Van Doren. *Robert E. Lee: The Man and the Soldier.* New York: McGraw-Hill, 1963.

Stevens, Joseph E. *1863: The Rebirth of a Nation.* New York: Bantam Books, 1999.

Stevens, Peter. "Personality: Patrick Cleburne." *Military History* 2, no. 4 (October 1994): 20–22.

Stier, William. "Morgan's Last Battle." *Civil War Times Illustrated* 35, no. 6 (December 1996): 84.

Stokesbury, James L. *A Short History of the Civil War.* New York: William Morrow and Company, Inc., 1995.

Street, James, Jr., and the Editors of Time-Life Books. *The Struggle for Tennessee: Tupelo to Stones River.* Alexandria: Time-Life Books, 1985.

Strode, Hudson. *Jefferson Davis: American Patriot, 1808–1861.* New York: Harcourt, Brace & World, Inc., 1955.

———. *Jefferson Davis: Tragic Hero.* New York: Harcourt Brace & World, Inc., 1964.

Suhr, Robert. "The Kilpatrick Dahlgren Raid on Richmond." *Military Heritage* 1, no. 6 (June 2000): 50.

Sword, Wiley. *The Confederacy's Last Hurrah.* Lawrence: University Press of Kansas, 1992.

———. "The Other Stonewall." *Civil War Times Illustrated* 36, no. 7 (February 1998): 38–43.

Symonds, Craig L. *Joseph Johnston: A Civil War Biography.* New York: W. W. Norton & Company, 1992.

———. *Stonewall of the West: Patrick Cleburne and the Civil War.* Lawrence: University Press of Kansas, 1997.

———. "A Fatal Relationship: Davis and Johnston at War." In *Jefferson Davis's Generals.* Edited by Gabor S. Boritt, 8–9. New York: Oxford University Press, 1999.

Tagg, Larry. *The Generals of Gettysburg.* Mason City: Savas Publishing Company, 1998.

Tanner, Robert G. *Stonewall in the Valley.* Garden City, NY: Doubleday & Company, Inc., 1976.

Tate, Allen. *Stonewall Jackson: The Good Soldier.* Nashville: J. S. Sanders & Company, 1991.

Taylor, John. *Duty Faithfully Performed: Robert E. Lee and His Critics.* Dulles, VA: Brassey's, 1999.

Thomas, Edison. *John Hunt Morgan and His Raiders.* Lexington: University Press of Kentucky, 1975.

Thomas, Emory M. *Bold Dragoon: The Life of J. E. B. Stuart.* New York: Harper & Row, 1986.

———. "The Real J. E. B. Stuart." *Civil War Times Illustrated* 28, no. 6 (December 1989): 35–37, 75–77.

———. *Robert E. Lee.* New York: W. W. Norton & Company, 1995.

Toney, Keith. "Horrors of the Bloody Lane." *America's Civil War* 10, no. 4 (September 1997): 65.

Trammell, Jack. "Little Known Battle Where 'Jeb' Stuart Died." *The Washington Times.* October 27, 2001.

Trudeau, Noah A. *The Last Citadel: Petersburg, Virginia, June 1864–April 1865.* Boston: Little, Brown and Company, 1991.

———. *Gettysburg: A Testing of Courage.* New York: Harper Collins Publishers, 2002.

Tucker, Glenn. "Forrest: Untutored Genius of War." *Civil War Times Illustrated* 3, no. 3 (June 1964): 36.

Vandiver, Frank E. *Mighty Stonewall.* New York: McGraw Hill, 1957.

———. *Their Tattered Flags.* College Station: Texas A & M University Press, 1970.

———. *Civil War Battlefields and Landmarks.* New York: Random House, 1996.

Ward, John. "Forrest's First Fight." *America's Civil War* 6, no. 1 (March 1993): 51–56.

Welch, Richard. "Book Review—Joseph Johnston: A Civil War Biography." *America's Civil War* 6, no. 5 (November 1993): 58, 63.

Wert, Jeffry D. "I Am So Unlike Other Folks." *Civil War Times Illustrated* 28, no. 2 (April 1989): 14–19.

———. *General James Longstreet.* New York: Simon Schuster, 1993.

———. "General James Longstreet." *Civil War Times Illustrated* 32, no. 5 (November/December 1993): 106.

———. "Generals at Odds." *Military History* 11, no. 3 (August 1994): 52.

———. "Old Jubilee's Last Battle." *Civil War Times Illustrated* 36, no. 4 (August 1997): 27.

———. "Lee's Old War-horse." *American History* 33, no. 1 (March 1998): 17–19, 22–24.

———. "No Fifteen Thousand Men Can Take That Position." In *James Longstreet: The Man, the Soldier, the Controversy.* Edited by R. L. Di Nardo and Albert A. Nofi, 77–88. Conshohocken, PA: Combined Publishing, 1998.

Wiley, Bell I. *Embattled Confederates*. New York: Harper & Row Publishers, Inc., 1964.

———. "Jefferson Davis: An Appraisal." *Civil War Times Illustrated* 6, no. 1 (April 1967): 8–9.

Williams, Edward. "Personality." *America's Civil War* 6, no. 2 (May 1993): 14, 16–20.

Williams, T. Harry. *Lincoln and His Generals*. New York: Alfred A. Knopf, 1952.

———. *P. G. T. Beauregard: Napoleon in Gray*. New York: Collier Books, 1962.

Wills, Brian S. *A Battle from the Start: The Life of Nathan Bedford Forrest*. New York: Harper-Collins, 1992.

Winik, Jay. *April 1865: The Month that Saved America*. New York: Harper Collins Publishers, 2001.

Wittenburg, Eric. "Roadblock en route to Washington." *America's Civil War Illustrated* 6, no. 5 (November 1993): 50–53, 82.

Woodworth, Steven E. *Jefferson Davis and His Generals: The Failure of Confederate Command in the West*. Lawrence: The University Press of Kansas, 1990.

———. *No Band of Brothers: Problems of the Rebel High Command*. Columbia: University of Missouri Press, 1999.

Wyeth, John A. *That Devil Forrest*. Baton Rouge: Louisiana State University Press, 1989.

Zimmerman, Daniel. "J. E. B. Stuart: Gettysburg Scapegoat?" *America's Civil War* 11, no. 2 (May 1998): 50, 57.

Index

of Perrysville, 153; at Battle of Richmond, 152–153; at Battle of Ringgold Gap, 155–156; at Battle of Shiloh, 151–152; biographical data of, 146–149; Bragg and, 153–155; in British army, 149; in Confederacy, 150–151; Davis's interactions with, 157–158, 161; death of, 160–161; description of, 22, 145; early life of, 146–149; education of, 148; eulogies for, 161; Grant's battles with, 152; gunfight wounding of, 150; Hardee's friendship with, 150–151; Hindman's friendship with, 149–150; Hood's criticisms of, 145–146, 159–160; illustration of, 147; immigration to United States, 149; legacy of, 161; marriage of, 158; military career of, 145–146, 151–161; personality of, 150; proposal to enlist blacks in Confederacy army, 156–158; "Yell Rifles" organized by, 150

Cleveland, Grover, 69
Cobb, Howard, 10
Coffey, W.A., 264
Confederacy: capital of, 12; centralization of, 18; civilian morale, 19; Davis's presidency of, 10–11; division of, 23; goals of, 12; Great Britain's lack of support for, 20; territory of, 12; White House of, 17, 22
Confederate army: enlistments in, 16–17; slaves in, 22, 24; volunteers for, 16–17
Confederate Congress: Davis's dealings with, 14; description of, 14
Cooke, George, 201, 203
Cooke, Giles B., 103
Cooke, John Esten, 203
Cooper, Samuel, 87, 125, 317
Corinth, 44–45, 135–136, 367
Craven, John B., 30–31
Crittenden, John J., 262
Cross Keys, 107
Custer, George Randolph, 332
Custis, Mary Anna Randolph, 73, 75

Dahlgren, Ulric, 21–22
Daniels, John, 282
Davis, Jefferson: admonitions by, 26–27; Beauregard's interactions with, 13, 43, 45, 48, 59, 380–381; Benjamin's interactions with, 14; biographical data of, 2–5; in Black Hawk War, 3; Blair's visit with, 24–25; bond for, 32; Bragg's interactions with, 13, 18, 133–134, 381; "Brierfield" plantation, 4–5, 20; cabinet of, 13–14; capture of, 27, 29–30; citizenship revocation, 33; commander-in-chief role of, 379–381; as Confederacy president, 10–12; Confederate Congress' dealings with, 14; Corinth's importance to, 135–136; Dahlgren's plans for, 22; death of, 34–35; demeanor of, 9–10; description of, 381; early life of, 2–4; education of, 2–3; escape by, 25–26, 242–243; failings by, 379; at Fort Monroe, 30, 35; Fort Sumter battle, 12; headquarters for, 17; Hill and, 289; Hood's interactions with, 223, 228; illnesses experienced by, 3–4; illustration of, 11; imprisonment of, 30–32; Johnston's (Albert) interactions with, 122, 124–126; Johnston's (Joseph) interactions with, 52, 59, 62, 64–68; Lee's interactions with, 13, 16, 33, 80, 379–380; legacy of, 35; loyalty of, 379–380; marriage to Varina Howell, 5, 9, 17, 24, 26–27, 31; martyrdom of, 31; memoirs of, 33–34; in Mexican War, 6; military career of, 3–7; military draft prepared by, 12; mocking of, 30; personal beliefs of, 10; personality of, 9–10; personal losses experienced by, 22, 35; personal qualities of, 35; physical appearance of, 1, 32; plantation owned by, 4–5, 8; political career of, 5–6, 62; political opponents of, 62; Polk's interactions with, 13, 256; postwar life of, 33–35; prison release of, 32–33; ranking of generals by, 15, 51–52, 60; respect for, 9–10; reward for, 26; schoolmates of, 3; secession speech by, 1–3; slavery views of, 4, 7–8; slaves owned by, 4, 35; Southerners' disillusionment with, 29; speeches by, 1–3, 34; support for, 32; Taylor's interactions with, 297, 303; trial of, 92; as U.S. senator, 1–2, 6–7; in Washington, 5–6; at West Point, 3

About the Author

WILMER L. JONES is an independent researcher who has spent the past 45 years studying the Civil War. He is the author of *After the Thunder: Fourteen Men Who Shaped Post–Civil War America* and *Behind Enemy Lines: Civil War Spies, Raiders, and Guerrillas.*